The Logic of Force

The Logic of Force

The Dilemma of Limited War in American Foreign Policy

Christopher M. Gacek

Columbia University Press   •   New York

Columbia University Press
New York   Chichester, West Sussex

Copyright © 1994   Columbia University Press
All Rights Reserved

Library of Congress Cataloging-in-Publication Data

Gacek, Christopher.
    The logic of force : the dilemma of limited war in American
foreign policy / Christopher Gacek.
        p.   cm.
    Includes bibliographical references and index.
    ISBN 0–231–09656–9. — ISBN 0–231–09657–7 (pbk.)
    1. United States—Foreign relations—1945–1989.   2. United States-
-Foreign relations—1989–   3. Limited war.   4. United States-
-Military policy.   I. Title.
    E840.G27   1994
    327.73'009'045—dc20   93–44798
                                                                                      CIP

Casebound editions of Columbia University Press books
are printed on durable and acid free paper.

c 10 9 8 7 6 5 4 3 2 1
p 10 9 8 7 6 5 4 3 2 1

For my mother,
Mary Shade Gacek

Contents

Acknowledgments

In 1989 my doctoral thesis, the first version of this study, was accepted at Stanford University. There were many there whose help was significant. I need to thank the following graduate student friends for their efforts on my behalf: Emily Goldman, Harry Papasitiriou, David Lumsdaine, Bob Griffin, Bill Lowry, and Leslie Eliason. Dorothy Blake, Jean Lee, and Arlee Ellis were particularly important for their administrative guidance over the years. I also must express my gratitude to Stephen D. Krasner, Condoleezza Rice, and Robert North who served on my dissertation committee and spent many hours reading and commenting with mercy and forbearance on the various drafts of my dissertation.

Alexander L. George, now professor emeritus, was my thesis adviser, and the debt I owe him is beyond estimation. Those who study international relations know of his numerous achievements as a scholar, but most readers of his books and articles are not aware of the great success he has had in directing the completion of doctorates. Alex George's participation in this process made my experience at Stanford about the best any graduate student could have. (The idyllic climate of Palo Alto didn't hurt, either.) He was always available to read and comment on his students' work on what now seems like a moment's notice: his efficiency was and remains legendary. There is little more to say because no expression of gratitude would be sufficient: clearly, without his efforts this book would not exist.

I must thank Dr. Gordon McCormick, then of the RAND Corporation, now at the Naval Postgraduate School in Monterey, California, for the many conversations we had discussing the great questions of diplomatic and military history. Donald Abenhheim of the Naval Postgraduate School and the Hoover Institution provided great insight into German military thought as he directed a small group called the "Clausewitz Society" at Stanford. Ambassador James Malone of Monterey, California, and I discussed many issues relating to international law and the use of force. Also, Professor John Norton Moore of the University Virginia School of Law provided sound advice in a pinch.

Professor Robert Kaufman of the University of Vermont's political science department strongly urged me to keep working on the revisions when I lived in Washington from 1990 to 1992 and was working. Without his encouragement and support, especially that derived from his experience as an author with Columbia University Press, this project might have been abandoned. At Columbia University Press, Kate Wittenberg, editor-in-chief, has been wonderful from our first discussions about the manuscript in the fall of 1989. Finally, it has been a joy to work with Leslie Bialler, my manuscript editor at Columbia Press. It helps so much to be able to like the person with whom you are working. His philosophy of editing struck an excellent balance in that it was not heavy-handed nor was it completely laissez-faire.

In 1989–90 I split the academic year between the Center for International Studies at the University of Southern California and the Center for International and Strategic Affairs (CISA) at the University of California at Los Angeles. It was my good fortune to win a postdoctoral fellowship referred to as the "USC/UCLA Visiting Scholar in Security Affairs." I would like to thank the following members of the staff at USC for their assistance: Cecilia Cicchinelli, Gregory Lintner, and Christopher Evans. John Odell, the director of the center at USC, is one of the true gentleman in political science; his encouragement of my efforts and praise of my work helped to keep me going. I would also like to express my appreciation to the other research fellows who were at USC that year: Professor Richard Smoke, Ian Bell, and Cynthia Weber. CISA, at UCLA, later changed its name to the Center for International Relations. At CISA I would like to thank its director, Professor Michael D. Intriligator, Ann Florini (senior researcher), Gerri Harrington (program coordinator), and CISA's wonderful office manager, Karl Arnold.

I had the good luck to live in Washington, D.C. from 1990 to 1992 before beginning my current studies at the University of Virginia School of Law. My experiences in Washington changed my understanding of international politics. I had the opportunity to work as the United Nations policy analyst for the Heritage Foundation. Holding that position required that I examine the place of the U.N. in the international system. This was a propitious assignment because modern political science has little interest in the United Nations and international law. Therefore, my ability to assess recent events like the Gulf War, the crisis in Somalia, and the war in Bosnia was expanded in a way that my academic training had not made possible. In particular, I need to thank Burton Yale Pines and Dr. Kim Holmes who made my tenure at the Heritage Foundation possible.

Following that, it was my great fortune to have the opportunity to move to the American Enterprise Institute and assist Ambassador Jeane J. Kirkpatrick in her various projects. She has had one of the most interesting careers in politics of which I am aware: all of that is reflected in her ability to analyze policy with an underlying wisdom and soundness of judgment that rests, even above intellectual ability, on great moral integrity. Working for her afforded me the opportunity to obtain a more intuitive feeling for the underlying premises that motivated the Reagan Administration's foreign policy. A.E.I. is a wonderful place to conduct research primarily because its president, Christopher DeMuth, and its top administrator, David Gerson, oversee their responsibilities recognizing that the highest quality writing will be produced in an environment that permits talented people to follow their intellectual interests without excessive management. A.E.I. resembles nothing so much as a first-rate university filled with dedicated scholars who are not required to teach classes and don't have to leave the building to get the best lunch in Washington.

I have been the recipient of much financial assistance in writing this book. First, as a graduate student at Stanford University, I received a university fellowship from 1983–1987. Later I received fellowship grants as a MacArthur Fellow at Stanford's Center for International Security and Arms Control, Fall 1987-June 1989. The source of these funds was the John D. and Catherine T. MacArthur Foundation. Travel grants were received from the Harry S. Truman Library Institute, Independence, Missouri; the John F. Kennedy Library Foundation, Boston, Massachusetts; from the Lyndon Baines Johnson Foundation, Austin, Texas; and from the Dwight D. Eisenhower Library Foundation, Abilene, Kansas. The United States Military History Institute at Carlisle Barracks, Pennsylvania, provided me with the funds to visit General Ridgway's papers. (David Haight, research librarian at the Eisenhower library, will always stand out in my mind as a great servant of the scholars who needed his help.)

During the summer of 1993 I was grateful to receive a grant from the Smith Richardson Foundation of Westport, Connecticut. These funds permitted me to undertake and complete another full revision of the manuscript between my first and second years of law school. Having this assistance from Smith Richardson provided an opportunity to make substantial improvements to the book. Ms. Devon G. Cross, Director of Foreign Policy Studies, and her assistant, Mark Steinmeyer, were of invaluable assistance. I also need to thank Audrey Mullen for her excellent guidance in the preparation of grant applications.

I must now thank my parents, Leonard and Mary Gacek, for the enormous contributions they have made over the years this book was being written. It would be difficult to conceive of parents who contributed more to their child's education and devotion to learning than mine have. No financial or personal sacrifice was ever too great to be made. I have dedicated this book to my mother in recognition of her extraordinary efforts in helping to prepare it for publication. For a number of years she was a proofreader at the *Miami News* and the *Miami Herald.* Over the last year she has read every page of the manuscript several times—the corrections made have been innumerable. There is simply no way that I could have performed the task that she has because proofreading requires a specific training and concentration that is not universally possessed. Once again, I would like to express my love and gratitude to my parents for all of their help and encouragement.

The reader should also note that Rick Atkinson's important contribution to the literature on the war with Iraq, *Crusade: The Untold Story of the Persian Gulf War,* was published too late in 1993 to be used as a source for this book. It has not been possible to keep the book up to date with events in Bosnia as there comes a time when every book must go to press. With that being said it is possible that war may escalate in the Balkans, involving the United States, but if that should happen it will take place within the strategic framework examined in the pages that follow. Nothing in the recent events of March 1994 indicates a weakening of the conceptual tension between the "all or nothing" and "limited war" approaches to using force. This point has been ably illustrated in a recent article on Bosnia: see Michael R. Gordon, "Pentagon Is Wary of Role in Bosnia," *New York Times*, March 15, 1994, sec. A, p. 6.

Charlottesville, Virginia
March 15, 1994

The Logic of Force

1

The Logic of Force, the Dilemma of Policy

"But once war is forced upon us, there is no other alternative than to apply every available means to bring it to a swift end. War's very objective is victory, not prolonged indecision.

"In war there is no substitute for victory."

—General Douglas A. MacArthur
Address to a Joint Session of Congress, April 19, 1951[1]

Delivered eight days after President Truman relieved the General of command in the Far East in the midst of the Korean War, the speech containing these remarks electrified its Congressional audience. MacArthur had returned to the United States for the first time since his departure in 1935 to direct the Philippine defense force. In 1941, he was reinstated in the U.S. Army, subsequently commanding a number of successful campaigns against Japan from 1942 to 1945. As commander of all U.S. Army forces in the Pacific, MacArthur had supervised the Japanese surrender on the battleship *U.S.S. Missouri* on September 2, 1945, in Tokyo Bay. His had been a great, public life, but on that day before the Congress, he told his audience that "Old soldiers never die, they just fade away." Although memorable for the drama and its oratory, in retrospect, MacArthur's speech marked America's entry into a new era: one in which there would be tremendous disputes within government, and the political community, as to the proper manner in which to wage war. Should limitations on the use of military power be allowed as policy may require? Or, should force be used only when the United States is prepared to decisively defeat its enemy? MacArthur's remarks were the first volley in the fierce political and intellectual struggle that has gripped the U.S. government since the Chinese overwhelmed American forces in North Korea. It was and remains a struggle of ideas, of conflicting concepts as to the nature of military power and, consequently, of the proper manner in which to wage war.

President Truman had dismissed MacArthur because the General publicly opposed the limitations on the use of force ordered by his Commander-in-Chief. Yet, by the fall of 1990 a different perspective on using military power was predominant in Washington, D.C. Whereas MacArthur was not permitted to expand the war against China, General H. Norman Schwarzkopf, the American theater commander in the Persian Gulf, told an interviewer in November 1990 as he was devising the military campaign to free Kuwait: "I think we have vastly superior fire power and technology, . . . and I can assure you that if we have to go to war, I am going to use every single thing that is available to me to bring as much destruction to the Iraqi forces as rapidly as I possibly can in the hopes of winning victory as quickly as possible."[2] Maoist China, with its ties to Stalin's Soviet Union, was a decidedly more dangerous foe than Iraq without Soviet protection. However, the difference in warfighting philosophy evinced by American leaders during the two crises reflected more than an awareness that Iraq could be beaten resoundingly whereas decisively defeating China might lead to war with the Soviet Union. Iraq's strategic weaknesses were no secret, but Schwarzkopf's confidence rested on the certainty that a dramatic shift had taken place in the thinking of America's foreign policy elites as to the proper manner in which force should be used. He knew there was no reason to fear his civilian leadership invoking Limited War theory to restrict his operations, for such theories had been moribund for at least a decade.

By that time those who argued that "victory" is the proper goal for the use of force had become predominant within the circles of power. Yet, this new preeminence of the All-or-Nothing perspective has been severely criticized. In August 1992, the *Washington Post* published an article containing the political analysis of one of its more respected writers on U.S. foreign policy, Jim Hoagland. He examined the Bush Administration's unwillingness to enter the fray to save Bosnia when it had been so eager to fight in the Gulf War. On August 5, 1992, presidential challenger, Governor Bill Clinton of Arkansas, called for the U.N. to authorize the use of air power in Bosnia against Serbian aggression. The Bush White House scrambled to make a similar request of the United Nations. The President soon restated a familiar theme on

Bosnia but applicable elsewhere: "We are not going to get bogged down in some guerrilla warfare."[3]

Hoagland contended that the action taken by the Bush Administration was "intended to quiet public opinion, not to change the situation on the ground in ex-Yugoslavia."[4] He correctly observed that the White House was "vulnerable" to the political criticism that President Bush "failed to develop intermediate policies to deal with an unsettled world of foreign crises that fall between the extremes of the need for Invincible Force and the possibility of doing nothing."[5] "Invincible Force" was a term Hoagland used to describe the modern American military's approach to the use of military power: "The Pentagon's all-or-nothing Invincible Force doctrine, formulated to counteract the disasters the American military suffered in Vietnam and Beirut, was a brilliant success in Iraq." Noting that President Bush's "tactical and political rather than strategic" response to the Balkan Crisis would only "reinforce the determination of the Joint Chiefs of Staff not to involve American forces in a situation where changing political goals instead of military criteria would determine the rules of engagement." His criticism of the Pentagon and Bush Administration's use of military power continued: "Invincible Force was conceived precisely to prevent that from ever happening again. The Pentagon leadership is determined to resist taking the first step onto a path of graduated force that does not have a clearly marked exit. Freed from the constraints of the Cold War, American commanders must be assured of political commitments and force levels sufficient to blow an enemy away quickly before they will initiate hostile action."[6]

Five days later, on August 14, an article appeared in the *Washington Times* written by Harry G. Summers, Jr., a retired U.S. Army colonel and distinguished fellow at the Army War College. Summers is the most noted author writing from an All-or-Nothing perspective. His book, *On Strategy*, caused quite a sensation within military intellectual circles by rejecting the Limited War framework upon which the strategy of the Vietnam War had been based.[7] Whether Summers was directly responding to Hoagland or whether he was writing in response to a general political mood in Washington is not clear. Whatever the cause, Summers' distress at a possible limited intervention in the Balkans, particularly through the initial use of air power, is palpable:

[Advocates of the limited use of force] believe that military force, almost literally in the case of air-strikes, can be used as a kind of God-from-a-machine to be inserted into a crisis situation and, by that act alone, put and end to the conflict. That's a dangerous illusion. As Sen. John McCain, Arizona Republican, has warned, it was precisely that kind of thinking that got us involved in Vietnam.

[Paragraph deleted]

While politicians can, and usually do, talk in platitudes, the military must deal in specifics. The most difficult task of a military strategist is to take the more often than not amorphous aims laid out by political leaders and translate them into concrete and attainable military objectives.[8]

He doubted, probably correctly, that air power would seriously affect the Serbs. In a later article written after Bill Clinton's inauguration in January 1993, Summers continued his defense of the Joint Chiefs who he felt were being criticized by "armchair strategists for reluctance to use limited military power to send 'signals' to Iraq or to Serbia and for their insistence that if we use military power, we do it decisively. *This has deep roots, not only in Vietnam but in the fundamental nature of warfare.*"[9] Summers continued by describing the "fundamental" element of war he had in mind:

As Mark Watson wrote in his official history of World War II: "The facts of war are often in total opposition to the facts of peace. . . . The efficient commander does not seek to use just enough means, but an excess of means. A military force that is strong enough to take a position will suffer heavy casualties doing so; a force vastly superior to the enemy's will do the job without serious loss of men.

JCS Chairman Gen. Colin Powell and the service chiefs know that from bitter battlefield experience. When it comes to military operations, Mr. Clinton pledged that he would listen to their advice. Let's hope that is one campaign promise he keeps.[10]

Clearly, within days of each other, two daily Washington newspapers contained articles expressing radically different philosophies for using force as an instrument of state policy. The tension, exemplified in the analyses by Hoagland and Summers, has existed throughout the Cold War and can be expected to persist in the future. Each presents a set of analytical and prescriptive propositions as to the nature of war, correct strategy, and the proper balance between civilian and military control over the use of force.

The causes of this debate and its continuous effect on American foreign policy is the primary focus of this book.

Who Are They? And What Are They Doing Here?

The emergence of a powerful Limited War perspective in the postwar period dramatically changed existing strategic debates. The Limited War School, as I refer to it, argues that various constraints on the use of force may be desirable or necessary depending on one's political objectives. This approach to using military power emphasizes altering the will and preferences of the opponent by using a wide range of options from small demonstrations of force to the employment of major levels of military power. As it developed after the Second World War, the Limited War School was most concerned that the United States have the capabilities and strategic sensibilities to resist local or regional Communist bloc aggression without permitting such conflicts to escalate into global wars between the superpowers.[11]

Even at the zenith of the Limited War School's influence, a traditional approach to the use of force always remained waiting for its turn to again take center stage. Proponents of this position argue that if force is employed, it should be used at whatever level may be necessary to efficiently and *decisively* achieve the military and political objectives of the state; in the period following the Korean War this All-or-Nothing approach has, on occasion, been associated with the term "Never Again School."[12] This book describes how the two perspectives have, through the actions of each's adherents, influenced decisions concerning military intervention in some regional crises since the Korean War.

A conceptual tension lies embedded in the nature of war and is reflected in this disagreement among policymakers. Theories of postwar U.S. foreign policy that are not cognizant of this politico-military friction do not adequately comprehend the causes of America's postwar policies regarding the use of force. Unfortunately, the most influential approaches, the orthodox arguments within the international relations discipline, fail in this regard. Thus, modern balance of power theory (or structural realism) argues that decisionmakers' actions are generally strongly influenced and constrained by the imperatives of the international system. Bureaucratic politics approaches argue that policy advice is influenced by the "interests" of the specific organization the actor represents. National military culture arguments claim that there is a uniquely American way to fight wars. Another model, found in the "Cult of the Offensive" literature, considers the "motivated" biases of military organizations. This book posits the existence of an unending, conceptual struggle within the nature of war itself: the two poles of this tension represent on one side the requirements of the ends of war, the policy goals or objectives; poised on the other is the logic of the instrument of war, which we call force. Force is directed, controlled violence aimed at the attainment of political goals. The logic of the instrument of war, then, is the logic of force. In short, the requirements of policy may clash with the requirements of force.[13]

The Military and Political Elements of War

Carl von Clausewitz (1780–1831)

The conceptual tension between the Limited War School and the Never Again School reflects an inner logic embedded in the very concept and phenomena of war that tends to pull its political and military elements apart from each other. This observation is most relevant when the political objectives of the war are limited. When the political objective is the total subjugation of the enemy, the military and political objectives will be closely aligned with less room for friction between them.[14] The greatest insights into this problem were presented by the Prussian general Carl von Clausewitz, in his lengthy unfinished study, *On War*, published posthumously by his wife, Maria. *On War* uses a dialectical analysis which Peter Paret, the foremost scholar of Clausewitz, perceives to incorporate the "thesis of the dual nature of war."[15] This dualism revolves around the tension between the logical possibility of "absolute" or "ideal" war and war as it is found in reality, that is, limited by numerous factors, the most important of which being the subordination of war to political considerations. Clausewitz, who used the dialectical relationship of first principles to great effect, presents his readers with the tools needed to understand the essence of the subject, but he does so by brilliantly revealing the opposing forces whose interaction and tension make up an essential element of war.[16] Michael Howard, the distinguished military historian, describes *On War*'s use of the dialectic in this way: "The dialectic was not Hegelian; it led to no synthesis which itself conjured up its antithesis. Rather, it was a continuous interaction between opposite poles, each fully comprehensible only in terms of the other."[17]

This dualism consists of two parts: the logical tendency of war to reach toward its violent "ideal" balanced against war as it is found in reality. The first part, which is described at the outset of *On War* notes that war's purpose is to compel submission and focuses on the decisive destruction of the enemy's capability to resist. Such exertion knows no logical limits and may require escalation to greater levels of violence.[18] This seemingly inexorable drive, which lies at the heart of physical compulsion, represents the logic of the instrument of war. We call that instrument "force."[19] "Ideal" or "absolute" war is "an act of force to compel our enemy to do our will (p. 75)." And, Clausewitz tells us, "To secure that object we must render the enemy powerless; and that, in theory, is the true aim of warfare (p. 77)." Extending his reasoning further, the Prussian general states, "Consequently, if you are to force the enemy, by making war on him, to do your bidding, you must either make him literally defenseless or at least put him in a position that makes this danger probable (p. 77)."

Peter Paret summarizes this aspect of Clausewitz's definition of war as "absolute war, that is, absolute violence ending in the total destruction of one side by the other."[20] This "ideal type of war," according to Michael Handel, "represented the way war ought to be from a purely logical point of view. Aspiring to the extreme, this type of war is a zero-sum game in which the fighting continues uninterruptedly until one side has won."[21] As Garry Wills has observed of Clausewitz's writing: "The process is reciprocal . . . which works each side up, ratchet by ratchet, toward the absolute in violence (*zum Äussersten*)."[22]

This aspect of war has been noticed by many students of conflict.[23] William G. Eckhardt of the U.S. Army War College has observed that in the nineteenth century "attempts then were made to reimpose limitations [on the use of force], primarily through international agreements defining military objectives and requiring respect for non-combatants." He then notes that the "primary hurdle to the attempt to restore limits to war was the German theory of *Kriegsraison*, whose main tenet was that any means necessary was permitted regardless of any law or rule."[24] This was the Clausewitzian ideal concept of war borne out in reality. Eckhardt reproduces a portion of "a German military manu-

al published by the German General Staff in 1902" to demonstrate that
it was expected that wars would be fought to their utmost extreme: "A
war conducted with energy cannot be directed merely against the combatants of the Enemy State and the positions they occupy, but it will
and must in like manner seek to destroy the total intellectual and material resources of the latter. Humanitarian claims such as the protection
of men and their goods can only be taken into consideration insofar as
the nature of war permits [sic]."[25]

In war, no sanctuary could be provided in the quest to dominate the
opponent. The realization of these ideas came during the horrors of the
First World War. In one of the most perceptive recent pieces on the
problem of controlling war, Michael Geyer of the University of Michigan's history department writes that the German high command of
Hindenburg and Ludendorf took war to a level of exertion never
attempted previously: their "first casualty" was "strategy as the principled analysis of war."[26] It was a war in which the relationship of means
and ends was reversed. It was a conflict in which the war's goal was driven by the logic of force. Geyer observes that the behavior of the German Command was fundamentally irrational for a nation on the verge
of defeat: "These war aims [for total defeat of the enemy] stood in sharp
contrast to a deteriorating military situation. In fact, the more precari-
ous the military situation, the more radical and encompassing the war
aims." Geyer then points out that this aspect of war did not conform to
the model of the rational actor calculating expected payoffs from various courses of action: "This paradox was unthinkable to the idealistic
strategy, with its marginal-utility calculus of violence. Idealistic strategy
would have counseled the limitation and scaling down of goals in an
increasingly desperate military situation. Escalatory strategy, however,
discarded this central calculus of limited and professional war. 'Strategy' thus thrived on the escalatory mobilization and use of force and, in
this process, lost its instrumental significance."[27]

This bears out a point made recently by Martin van Creveld in *The
Transformation of War*, where he discusses wars that are fought to preserve the community's existence. He writes that in the "life-and-death
struggle" our strategic vocabulary loses its value: " to say that war is an
'instrument' serving the 'policy' of the community that 'wages' it is to
stretch all three terms to the point of meaninglessness."[28] Total war
itself "merges with policy, becomes policy, *is* policy."

It bears repeating that just as Clausewitz acknowledged war's tendency to reach its absolute extreme, in his most developed thoughts on the subject he never lost sight of policy. Azar Gat, an Israeli military historian, observes of Clausewitz's view of war that while "all the characteristics of war are decisively influenced by politics, this influence is by no means part of the nature of war; on the contrary, the influence of politics is an *external* force which works *against* the true essence of war, harnesses it to its needs, and in the process modifies the imperatives which it imposes."[29] Clausewitz himself observes of this antinomy of the logic of force and the requirements of policy: "We will then find that war does not advance relentlessly toward the absolute, as theory would demand. Being incomplete and self-contradictory, it cannot follow its own laws, but has to be treated as a part of some other whole; the name of which is policy. . . . So policy converts the overwhelmingly destructive element of war into a mere instrument."[30]

Thus, the self-generating impulsion to absolute violence that is so much a part of the nature of war is modified in practice.[31] Real war is limited by numerous factors. Michael Handel describes the factors that could limit the expression of war: ". . . . (1) the political guidance which rationally relates ends to means in war; (2) the asymmetry of the superiority of the defense over the offense; (3) the lack of information as well as the uncertainty and friction; (4) the tendency of human nature to make worst case assumptions about the enemy, and play it safe in the absence of clarity and sufficient information; (5) the fact that all military forces cannot be concentrated in space and time simultaneously; and (6) the fact that results in war are rarely final."[32]

For our purposes the most important of these is the subordination of the violence in war to political considerations. This line of reasoning culminates in that most famous of declarations: "war is merely the continuation of policy by other means."[33] One section later Clausewitz clearly recognizes the problematic nature of *limited war*: "the less intense the motives, the less will the military element's natural tendency to violence coincide with political directives. As a result, war will be driven further from its natural course, the political object will be more and more at variance with the aim of ideal war, and the conflict will seem increasingly *political* in character."[34]

In this passage Clausewitz uses the term "natural course" to indicate the inner dynamic of war that drives it to greater levels of violence. He expected that the rational, political aspect of war would dominate the compelling logic of force—in this assessment his appreciation of rationality led him to overestimate the power of ends over means. On the famous statement that "war is the mere continuation of politics," Peter Paret explains: "In his view, the political nature of war affected both the actions of the armed forces and the relationship between the political and military leadership. Because wars were fought to achieve a political purpose, every action in war should, if possible, accord with this purpose. A purely military act did not exist."[35]

Because Clausewitz believed that the political element would dominate in wars of limited objectives, the reader should not mistakenly draw the conclusion that he saw no difficulty matching ends and means in such circumstances. In the passage just quoted, Clausewitz recognizes the tension between that component of war which logically dictates the performance of actions to physically compel the enemy to submit to one's will and those political considerations which limit this tendency in order to meet the higher objectives of policy. That does not imply, however, that he foresaw the tremendous difficulties that would arise in bringing the requirements of force into alignment with the ends of policy that one witnessed, for example, during the First World War.[36] In fact, Clausewitz may not have anticipated the extreme resistance the military element of war would provide to policy's claim of supremacy.

Henri Jomini (1779–1869)

In the nineteenth and early twentieth centuries the writings of Clausewitz were rivaled and possibly surpassed in popularity by the writings of Henri Jomini, a Swiss contemporary of Clausewitz's who served at the highest levels of the French armies under Napoleon. He wrote voluminously on military history, in particular, on the campaigns of Frederick the Great and Napoleon. Jomini is now most famous for his contribution to creating a set of "principles of war" which advocated that war be conducted in a manner that maximized the use of offensive and decisive military actions. Jomini's argument was influenced to a greater degree by the Enlightenment and its exaltation of science than was Clausewitz's. The Swiss general was attempting to fashion a set of quasi-Newtonian laws pertaining to military operations in the post-Napoleonic era. Azar Gat has observed that Jomini "synthesized the ideal of the Enlightenment with Napoleonic warfare, producing a penetrating and fertile rationale of the new type of operations. Hence both the enormous success and influence of his work in the nineteenth century and its decline in the twentieth."[37]

In keeping with the spirit of the Enlightenment Jomini sought to find a set of immutable principles that would serve to describe war across all times and places. Clausewitz was too much influenced by Romanticism, then on its intellectual ascent, to accept the universalism of which Jomini was enamored. It was not that Clausewitz rejected all of Jomini's insights but that he rejected Jomini's ideas "as a general science of war which he regarded as absurd."[38] Clausewitz, for example, shared an appreciation with Jomini of the centrality of concentrating one's forces on the decisive point that will bring the enemy's certain defeat. Unfortunately, Jomini focused excessively on providing geometrical tenets for fighting war that revolved around maintaining "central position" and "interior lines."[39] Clausewitz rightly noticed that such an approach was clearly too rigid to serve as the basis for a general science of war—an activity dominated at its core by political considerations and moral factors. The University of Michigan historian John Shy notes that Jomini first set down the essence of his approach to war in 1803, and it did not change to any great extent in the many years that followed:

That strategy is the key to warfare;

That all strategy is controlled by invariable scientific principles; and

That these principles prescribe *offensive action* to *mass forces* against weaker enemy forces at some *decisive point* if strategy is to lead to victory.[40]

Four years later Jomini listed a primitive set of what he sometimes referred to as maxims and sometimes as principles. John Alger writes, "the fact that they were presented as a list of general truths whose application contributes to success in war qualifies them as the prototype of the modern 'principles of war.'" These maxims or principles focused on such concepts as mass, initiative, and maneuver; their conceptual progeny continue to exist in more clearly defined form as central features of modern military field manuals.[41]

This Swiss strategic thinker had a tremendous impact on the development of modern military thought. His principles and other aspects of his work represented an attempt to demonstrate that there were laws regulating the conduct of war just as there were physical laws regulating the movement of bodies in space.[42] Subsequently, the faith by which these principles were followed reached a level of dogmatism that only rare individuals like Clausewitz dared challenge. Whereas for Clausewitz "ideal war" was a concept to be balanced against the reality and political purposes of war, for Jomini the "military element" became the essence of war in the mechanistic manner of analysis. Shy writes of Jomini's influence on military thought:

> Simplifying, reducing, prescribing—these had become inescapably dominant qualities of Western military thought at the turn of [20th] century. And, almost invariably, these qualities combined to extol the Napoleonic model of massing, attacking, and quickly winning decisive victories. Anything less or different was reckoned as failure. Defensive, attritional, protracted, and limited warfare were among those non-Napoleonic, non-Jominian forms of military action that were condemned in principle, doomed in practice.[43]

As one might expect, Jomini's influence was great in the young republic of the United States. Dennis Hart Mahan, the famous instructor at West Point for a generation before the Civil War, imparted his Jominian beliefs to his students. He also passed on the Jominian approach to his son, Alfred Thayer Mahan, the future naval officer and historian whose writings would redirect the naval strategies of the United States. It was Alfred Mahan who advocated in Jominian fashion that the United States acquire a battle fleet that could attain command of the seas through the use of offensive attacks on the fleets of America's opponents.[44]

Jomini's insight, and his error, was to separate the military component of war from the political purpose of conflict. This left him with a narrowed conception of war that excessively embodied its "military element." To be sure, Jomini's "principles," and those of his followers, do yield insight into the *logic of force*, but they are unbalanced because they ignore the political context and purpose of specific wars. As John Shy notes above this logic requires mass, surprise, and offensive action designed to achieve decisive victory regardless of the needs of the political circumstances at hand. Despite their excision of politics from war, Jomini's ideas are powerful because they provide insight into the tendencies of the force itself. Despite their significant differences, Clausewitz and Jomini appreciated that war is about conquest, domination, and compulsion—something that many modern scholars, in their efforts to recast him in our era's perspective, forget about Clausewitz.

One other point should be considered. Although Clausewitz and Jomini have had a profound impact on the intellectual training of generations of American soldiers, the tension between the military and political elements of war does not rest on the indoctrination of soldiers in their writings. Such education may reinforce these conceptions, and learning from wars like the Civil War, World War I, and World War II is a powerful factor in policy struggles. Yet, these factors are not sufficient to explain the persistent rivalry between the two concepts of the use of force.[45] The conflict between the Never Again and Limited War Schools has occurred because there is a dialectical tension within war that confronts all political and military leaders. Clausewitz and Jomini are still closely studied today not because of any widespread interest in ancient thought. Rather, their writings are pored over because each writer discerned some essential aspect of war's nature. Certainly, Clausewitz comprehended war as a totality, but the Jominian elements of strategic thought can be found easily in modern military descriptions of the "principles of war."

The "Never Again" and "Limited War" Schools

The phrase *never again* comes from the memoirs of General Mark Clark, who wrote after the Korean War that the United States should "never again" be "mousetrapped" into a limited war on the Asian mainland.[46] The term "Never Again Club" has been used more extensively than "Never Again School," but "school" conveys the sense of a community with shared beliefs better than "club" does. Consequently, "school" is used throughout this book. "Never Again" was also used within the government to describe a group of high-ranking Army officers and civilian leaders in the immediate post-Korean period who vowed to not become involved in a limited land war in Asia.[47] These officials believed that the United States should not become involved in a conflict unless it were willing to employ its full military power to achieve its wartime objectives. Consequently, the limitations on the use of force and of objectives in Korea were seen to be the source of American difficulties during that war. As mentioned above, I chose the term Limited War School for lack of an existing name to describe the set of ideas held by strategic thinkers and policymakers who favored a more flexible and "political" approach to the use of force.

These two approaches have been described by a number of prominent authors over the past twenty-five years. The first major book to discuss the subject was *The Professional Soldier* by Morris Janowitz.[48] Janowitz did not use the labels "Never Again School" or "Limited War School" to describe these strategic groups; instead, he referred to the groups, the origins of which he traces to the period before the Korean War, as "absolutists" and "pragmatists," For the absolutists "there is no substitute for total victory (p. 264)" To members of the pragmatic school "warfare is but one instrument of international relations, along with ideological and economic struggle. The political objectives of warfare are gained by adapting the use or threat of violence to the objectives to be achieved. To use too much or too little force is self-defeating (p. 264)". This characterization of the two approaches mirrors the theme developed in this study of a rivalry in post-war U.S. foreign policy between a more "military" and a more "political" approach to the use of force. Janowitz would have argued against the Allison-like point that a high correlation should exist between an actor's institutional location and his position with respect to the absolutist-pragmatist" split. "Such an explanation," is not appropriate, Janowitz argues, because it "does not account for the evolution of military doctrine, nor for substantial minority positions within particular services (p. 277)"

Another early reference to the Never Again School occurs in *Profiles in Power* by Joseph Kraft.[49] The author discusses the importance of the Never Again Club in the decision-making process during the Dienbienphu crisis and the decisions to insert ground troops into Vietnam in 1965. Kraft traces the origin of the Never Again School to the Korean War. Others have also noticed the existence of this approach to warfighting: Richard Betts refers to the "Never Again 'Club' " in his book *Soldiers, Statesmen, and Cold War Crises.*[50]

The Limited War School became prominent in the mid-1950s when a group of writers that included Robert E. Osgood, Henry Kissinger, and William W. Kaufmann urged the United States to abandon its reliance on massive retaliation and develop a credible capability for fighting limited conventional wars against the Soviet Union or its allies.[51] The Limited War theorists argued that a middle ground existed between being "red" or "dead." Communist aggression would be thwarted without causing general warfare between the superpowers. A successful American foreign policy in the Cold War, these writers believed, would entail resisting Soviet and Chinese probes with the lowest possible level of violence, thereby matching the opponent's level of commitment while taking all necessary steps to preclude unwanted escalation of conflict. Osgood noted this approach to war-fighting would require subordinating force to the dictates of policy: "The justification of limited war arises, in the most fundamental sense, from the principle that military power should be subordinate to national policy, that the only legitimate purpose of military force is to serve the nation's political objectives."[52] This statement clearly resembles the Clausewitzian maxim that "war is the mere continuation of policy by other means." General Maxwell Taylor supported this approach to war-fighting in his book, *The Uncertain Trumpet*, when he advocated the broad concept of "flexible response."[53] Soon, flexible response became a foreign policy shibboleth in the Kennedy-Johnson Administrations.

The war in Vietnam reinvigorated the debate over the proper manner in which to use force. In the post-Vietnam period, this Limited War approach has been sharply criticized by a number of writers such as Harry Summers and Stephen Peter Rosen for its ineffective use of military power.[54] In the 1970s and 1980s the Never Again concept of fighting wars became resurgent. And within the Reagan administration the policy debate between Secretaries Shultz and Weinberger corresponded to the cleavage between the Limited War and Never Again approaches to the use of force.

In the previous pages frequent use has been made of the term Limited War. As one might guess limited war exists conceptually in relation to total war, but neither term can be easily defined because of the many variations that characterize every war. One must remember that war is a purposeful act (or a series of actions) in which certain ends are achieved through means that one either chooses freely or must use because of a lack of options. Relating means to desired ends through planning and the execution of plans is the essence of strategy. It can be confusing, therefore, that wars are labeled limited or total by evaluating either the *ends* to which they are fought or the *means* by which they are fought.

What does Limited War mean? It can mean that either the ends or means, or both, are limited in the conflict. Often, as in the Korean War, both were limited: in that war, after the Chinese invasion, the United States limited its objectives to reinstating the *status quo*—preserving the Republic of Korea—but the United States also limited the means it used against China itself. Atomic weapons were not used and military, economic, and transport targets in China and Manchuria were not bombed; also the United States did not attempt to decisively defeat the ground forces it faced on the Korean peninsula when it had the opportunity to do so in May and June of 1951.

In the Falklands War of 1982, the United Kingdom fought Argentina, but it did not have the "total" objective of overthrowing the Argentine government; the British objective was to reassert sovereignty over the Falklands, a limited end. However, the British did not really limit the means they employed within the war zone of the islands. That is, they sought the total defeat of the Argentine forces on the islands themselves, so one might argue that this was a war in which the ends were limited but the necessary resources and blood would be spent to completely vanquish Argentine control over those islands.[55]

Finally, even though the Second World War was total, in the sense that the unconditional surrender of the enemy was sought and achieved, not all available weapons were employed: for example, chemical weapons were not used. In this study, it is the limitation on the use of force, the means, that concerns us primarily. Most critical to the proponents of Never Again thinking is their concern that limitations on force should not be permitted to interfere with the accomplishment of operational and strategic goals even if one's political goals/ends are limited. Thus, in limited wars ends may become divorced from means in two ways: excessive force can be used to achieve the limited, political objective, or insufficient force may be used in attempting to gain a still-limited, but more ambitious, objective.

Comparing Explanations

I use case studies to identify and explain several interrelated aspects of policy-making when U.S. leaders considered military intervention. The subjects to be explained (i.e., dependent variables) are: first, the policy preferences of leading decisionmakers in specific historical cases and, second, the policy decisions that flow from the interaction of these individual policy preferences and the impact of other causal factors. Four "orthodox" alternative approaches to explaining foreign policy decisions will also be briefly contrasted with the conceptual argument presented here: 1) balance of power theory (also called structural realism); 2) the bureaucratic politics model which argues that the policymakers' preference will depend on the interest of the relevant organization that person represents; 3) a "national attribute" argument which perceives a historical American proclivity for fighting wars with few limitations, and, 4) an approach examining the biases of military organizations arguing that they have "motivated biases," or prejudices that color their assessment of strategic reality. In sum, the pressures for funding and successes that offer legitimacy to the state cause military organizations to adopt offensive strategies for war. This literature examined pre-First World War staff planning noting that prior to the Great War a "cult of the offensive" existed. This bias is said to exist in military organizations in general.

A fifth argument, the approach favored by this book, establishes that a conceptual tension between the logic of the ends and the logic of the means of war is at the heart of the Never Again–Limited War rivalry. The relative strength of these perspectives has, at different times, influenced the policy decisions of American leaders. The more "orthodox" analyses to be described later in this chapter present inadequate analyses of these events. These five prospective explanations vary in theoretical sophistication; for example, structural realism is the most theoretically complex, whereas bureaucratic politics and American military culture models cannot be properly called "theories."

The most widely recognized formulation of structural realism, a rigorous, predictive reworking of classical balance of power thinking, was written by Kenneth Waltz, professor of political science at the University of California at Berkeley.[56] Although structural theory is the most formal approach to the study of international relations currently available, it is difficult to derive reasonably precise predictions from structural premises.[57] I posit that realism would predict the possession of large arsenals of deliverable nuclear weapons by both the United States and the former Soviet Union would have greatly altered the perception of the costs of nuclear war, making it an unusable policy option. Survivable nuclear forces would still be needed to deter the enemy from launching a surprise attack, but policymakers would soon focus on conventional warfare. Massive conventional wars, although preferable to nuclear wars, would be excessively destructive in their own right. Consequently, there would be pressure from the structure of the international system to attempt to limit even conventional warfare. One should expect a movement toward a Limited War strategy by the United States to reduce the likelihood that a major war would erupt in the future. Wars of limited aggression should become the new playing field for great power rivalries, if my interpretation of realist theory is correct.[58] Although it may be true that wars have been limited as structural realism predicts, it is also true that the frequent occasional and effective opposition to the use of limited force by adherents of the Never Again perspective cannot be deduced from balance of power axioms.

In their simplest form, bureaucratic politics models tell us that outcome of the decision-making process of large organizations results from the unavoidable bargaining between bureaucracies during that process. Characteristic of this analysis is the notion that the policy positions advocated by decisionmakers are determined by the interests of the organization in which that person works. Therefore, policy decisions are not the product of some omniscient, rational, and unified entity but emerge instead from a tug-of-war between influential individuals and groups who perceive themselves to be advancing what they believe to be the organization's "interests." Often, this political grappling leads to a mix of policies that none of the actors prefer.[59] Our interest in the bureaucratic politics model rests on whether the more "military" approach to using force correlates only with the positions advocated by the military and whether the more "political" approach is held by civilian policymakers.[60]

Next, a national attribute argument will be considered. It is widely believed that there is an "American Way of War" that is consonant with the most essential elements of our political culture and history. The All-or-Nothing approach to the use of force has become the American way to conduct wars. One of the more prominent arguments of this kind has been made by Russell Weigley who posits that the United States acquired the material wealth to fight wars of great duration and destructive power at about the time the Civil War erupted. That conflict made a lasting impression on the collective consciousness of Americans. Its effect on our military strategy thereafter is not surprising: "The Civil War tended to fix the American image of war from the 1860s into America's rise to world power at the turn of the century, and it also suggested that the complete overthrow of the enemy, the destruction of his military power, is the object of war."[61]

It is this manner of using force that the United States has carried forward to the present day. Caleb Carr, a military historian, wrote in a similar, if much less approving vein, that the Civil War made the advocates of decisive force the rulers of the American strategic debate:

> To the everlasting misfortune of the United States, America's military tradition—its characteristic styles of command, strategy, and tactics—crystallized not during the great gamble of the Revolution but during the butchery of the Civil War. The years 1861–65 produced a set of commanders whose cults of personality have had remarkable staying power, despite the very questionable military, racial, and social attitudes of almost all of them. . . . Thus American wars have continued and probably will continue to be fought with the same abysmally heavy emphasis on attrition and materiel, rather than creative thought, that marked both sides during the Civil War.[62]

Another historian, John Shy, makes a similar yet more nuanced argument to the effect that there are "deeply imbedded modes of thinking about war" that prompt Americans to naturally think of the fighting in totalistic terms.[63] Finally, Samuel Huntington has attributed the American penchant for All-or-Nothing fighting to this nation's immersion in liberal political philosophy.[64] This set of arguments will be considered as another explanatory approach whose contentions need to be addressed.

The "Cult of the Offensive" thesis makes a social science-based argument about the nature of military organizations and military strategy.[65] Jack Snyder and Stephen Van Evera, its two most widely known proponents, have opened war planning, particularly of the First World War, to heightened theoretical scrutiny. The arguments vary, but the "cult of the offensive" literature posits that the military staffs planning for World War I were affected by "motivated biases" that revolve around the institutional interests of the military in offensive strategies. For example, Snyder writes, "Offense is difficult and demands large budgets. It is also productive—productive in that decisive campaigns produce demonstrable returns on the state's investment in military capability."[66] There is a cognitive need to simplify the complexities of the real world so that an army can function: consequently, army doctrines stress the offensive.

This book rejects the various "orthodox" explanations listed above as being insufficient to adequately describe critical areas of postwar American foreign policy. The capacity of ideas or concepts in tension with each other to affect decision-making will be demonstrated. The *political* and *military* poles of war present conceptually salient ways to analyze the use of force and to evaluate experiences. This rivalry is enduring in that the struggle between the logic of the ends and the logic of the means will not disappear. However, the lessons we take from our experiences (like the Vietnam War) or our facility with certain concepts (military rather than political, for example) will influence the way we perceive this tension. We may perceive the struggle between the two elements or we may greatly exaggerate the weight of one in relation to the other. Therefore, it should be of little surprise that we observe the Never Again and Limited War philosophies persisting over time. These two perspectives have power not just as agents of cognitive simplification, but, as Clausewitz's dialectic reveals, because they each have significant explanatory power: each describes a significant element of truth. Additionally, this argument does not contend that policy choices are determined by the actor's environment whether international, organizational, or political-cultural. Instead, pure concepts pulling against each other affect the choices of policymakers.

Existing theory will be refined through the demonstration that structural, organizational, and domestic politics perspectives do not account for this strategic dichotomy and tension in American foreign policy. Only with the addition of this idea-based argument does our understanding of the problems to be explained become satisfactory. This study does not intend to exclude the possible operation of other cognitive variables. For example, Yuen Foon Khong persuasively argues that the use of historical analogies played an important role in the formation of policy preferences with respect to intervention in Vietnam.[67] It should be mentioned that other types of strategic concepts influence policy choices; for example, John Lewis Gaddis's *Strategies of Containment* describes, among other things, the influence of economic concepts on the formulation of grand strategy.

The Transmission of Ideas

The reader may wonder: "How are these ideas about the use of force transmitted and learned? Is there any formal mechanism by which these ideas are disseminated?" There is no simple response, yet it is fair to say that these contending approaches to the use of force have achieved prominence through different routes. First, one must realize that the two sets of ideas being considered are relatively simple; they are not complex in the sense Keynesian economics is. These concepts relate to the broadest notion of political strategy defined as the relationship between ends and means. The ends being the political objective of the state. The means or instrument being force which has a particular inner logic of its own. Consequently, the two concepts that form the "dual nature of war" are comprehensible to those who think lucidly about the fundamental nature of war. The existence of this tension between the military and political elements of war may be perceived by those like Clausewitz who are grappling for a deeper understanding of conflict.

The discovery of hidden truths by deep reflection is not the only manner in which these two ideas are perceived or appreciated. There are two other avenues by which the influence of this tension is much more likely to be felt. The first is the learning from the environment which takes place as society collectively remembers events. Consequently, the manner in which phenomena like the Korean and Vietnam Wars are recalled both personally and as history affects decisionmakers' beliefs about the proper relationship between the use of force and the attainment of political objectives. Books like Osgood's *Limited War* and Summers' *On Strategy* have influenced policymakers across bureaucratic-institutional perspective. The "lessons" learned from historical writings have focused on the problems central to the Never Again-Limited War debate because the nature of the political objectives being sought and the efficacy of the military means used to achieve those objectives are natural subjects for historical inquiry.

The second lies in the influence institutions have on our understanding of events. There is also an institutional reason for this convergence around these two concepts for the use of force. Institutions have great importance because they pass on traditions of thought concerning specific problems. With respect to the Limited War and Never

Again ideas the "political" and "military" components of governments tend to influence policy preferences in a number of ways. Military institutions as a rule are extremely self-conscious about the need to systematically indoctrinate soldiers with a set of coherent propositions that guide behavior during the confusion and friction of war. Historically, the American military have been impressed with the principles of war as concise vehicles for transmitting the essential nature of war to soldiers.[68] These principles, included in every Army field manual since World War I, focus on that essential element which is at the heart of the Never Again concept arguing for the overwhelming use of military power to decisively defeat the enemy. Discovering a mechanism that imparts the Limited War concept into the policy process is more complex because this idea is less well defined. According to this concept the political actor is placed under a general proscription to pursue the most highly prized political objectives. In matters relating to the use of force and the maintenance of the physical survival of the nation, the decision-making institutions are constricted and most closely approximate what is now, in many bodies of political literature, referred to as "the state." The "state" being that centralized, sovereign, and unified entity which exercises legitimate political authority over the conduct of the war.

In such circumstances, the most critical problem that central decisionmakers face is that of the purest manifestation of the problem of "strategy." That is, relating the ends of desired policy to the means. In the American system of governance, it is the president, who, in times when force is used, sets the objectives for state action and must balance the requirements of the means against those of the political objectives.[69] Even though there is no self-conscious inculcation of "principles," as there was in the case of the military, the more amorphous set of ideas that make up the Limited War position arises as a matter of course for the president because of his institutional position: objectives and means should be brought into alignment, and the means must be made subservient to policy.

It is not uncommon for historians to remark that one of the more important developments in the area of civil-military relations has been the gradual separation of the political authority of the state from the operational conduct of wars.[70] Leaders of states and legions such as

Napoleon, Frederick, and Alexander were quite familiar with the problems of balancing political objectives with the military instrument. This is not to say that they always balanced them wisely, but the central strategic problem had to be addressed by that single person. In a similar manner, the duties of the presidency predispose the occupant of that office to directly face this ambiguous problem and to be inherently more aware of the primacy of the political objective in the conduct of war. For that reason, an institutional counterbalance to the simple, direct ideas of the military does exist.

A Guide to the Historical Aspects of the Study

The Limited War versus All-or-Nothing tension is presented in the following chapters with the use of case studies and historical analysis. In chapter 2 a background discussion of America's use of force prior to the Korean War demonstrates that concerns were being voiced in and outside of government before 1950 regarding the way wars would be fought in the future. Nuclear bipolarity seemed bound to make direct conflict between the Americans and Soviets too dangerous to serve as a tool of policy, so analysts like George Kennan and Paul Nitze saw the necessity of limited war capabilities in a time when strategic airpower was considered a cure for American strategic weaknesses. Chapter 3 discusses the Korean War, a limited war that made the difficulties with fighting in such conflicts all too apparent. Lessons taken from that conflict by the Limited War and Never Again adherents is presented as well. The fourth chapter examines the 1954 Dienbienphu Crisis in French Indochina with regard to the Eisenhower Administration's refusal to become involved in the fighting: Never Again objections appear to have been an important influence in the policy deliberations. Chapter 5 discusses the full development of Limited War thinking in the 1950s and early 1960s demonstrating that the term Limited War meant different things to different people—leaving significant room for misunderstanding. The Laotian Crisis of 1960–62, described in chapter 6, presented another opportunity for military intervention in a limited war, but the U.S. did not take the bait. Why? In chapter 7 President Johnson's July 1965 decision to intervene in that conflict is considered in the context of the limitations placed on the use of military power against the North Vietnamese and American policy objectives. In the next chapter, the lessons from Vietnam greatly undermined the credibility of the Limited War position. Developments in military doctrine are also described: the Army's AirLand Battle of the 1980s is considered in greatest detail. Finally, the Reagan and Bush administrations are analyzed as being glimpses of the future within the post-Vietnam, post-Cold War context. An epilogue has been added, which deals with the problems confronted by President Clinton upon his assumption of office.

2 | Patterns in America's Use of Force Before the Korean War

Following the Second World War the United States sought an international strategy that would best preserve the political and economic institutions of America while avoiding an annihilatory conflict with the Soviet Union.[1] The devastation of Hiroshima and Nagasaki illustrated most vividly the potential destructiveness that could characterize future wars. Analyses of conventional warfare provided little comfort. The Second World War had inflicted such devastation and carnage with conventional weaponry that even though the United States could have prevailed in such a war—if given time to mobilize its vast resources against Moscow—a general war would be undertaken only under the gravest circumstances. The rapid postwar decline of the United Kingdom forced the United States to quickly assume the role of sole political leader in the West. The U.S. was gradually feeling its way into these added responsibilities when North Korea's invasion of the Republic of Korea provided the political consensus to support vast increases in military spending.

As the U.S. laid claim to its position of preeminence in world affairs, it was reasonable for states to wonder how it would use its power and armed forces. Most of its nineteenth- and twentieth-century experiences had left the United States with a tendency, when fighting wars, to use massive firepower to cause devastating attrition and the total defeat of its enemies. The policies of the Civil War and the two world wars were largely responsible for the entrenchment of this mentality.[2] It would be incorrect, however, to conclude that this all-out approach had been the sole method by which the United States had used force. On the contrary, in the years prior to 1950 there were occasions in which less than total objectives were used to guide war policies.

Reginald Stuart argues persuasively that the period in American politics up to the proclamation of the Monroe Doctrine (1823) was marked by a great affinity with those philosophies of international relations, whether based on natural law or principles of *realpolitik*, that argued for the limitation of means and ends in the conduct of warfare.[3] The validity of this conclusion is supported by the manifest realism of the *Federalist Papers* which were of a piece with the rational and measured political philosophies of the Enlightenment. Stuart also takes note of the "Quasi-War" between France and the United States which stemmed in part from the "XYZ Affair." This undeclared war with France was restricted to naval combat of a decidedly limited nature between 1798 and 1801. During the course of the conflict the small American navy inflicted significant casualties on French merchant shipping in the West Indies.[4] Alexander DeConde, the author of the definitive history on the Quasi-War, describes President John Adams's perspective on relations with France:

> Adams's own policies had not led to the Quasi-War. He had inherited the crisis from President Washington and had tried to immediately resolve it through negotiation. When this effort failed Adams aligned himself with the extremists of his own party and went along with their war program. Yet Adams did not, as many party leaders wanted him to do, ask for a declaration of war. He hesitated not because he believed in peace at all costs, but because a part of him recoiled at the thought of leading a disunited country into unlimited hostilities.[5]

The "measures Congress had passed permitted American commanders to capture French privateers and warships. These captures were, in effect, warlike actions without a formal declaration of war. The laws were half measures . . . because they did not call for the defeat of the French. These laws, then, were basically defensive, and were to expire when the commanders of French ships stopped their depredations against American commerce." DeConde adds that from the American perspective the clash with France was a "quasi-war" because it was a "limited war that Americans fought only at sea under self-imposed restrictions."[6]

The War of 1812 was also conducted in manner that did not offend limited war concepts.[7] It is true that attempts in the U.S. Senate to explicitly limit the war to the high seas failed narrowly. In fact, as Professor Donald Hickey, a historian at Wayne State College points out, the Madison Administration's foremost purpose in going to war "was to win concessions from the British on the maritime issues, particularly the Orders in Council and impressment." Hickey adds that Americans in the West "hoped to put an end to British influence over American Indians by conquering Canada or at least breaking the power of the British there."[8] This objective, however, was widely supported only in the West. The perspectives on the scope of the war are described by Hickey in the following passage:

> A limited maritime war in the tradition of '98 appealed to many people because it offered a cheap and direct means of vindicating American rights. The nation would avoid the costs of an extended land war, and the president could end the conflict by executive action without resorting to the sort of time-consuming negotiations that drew out so many years. The only problem with this strategy was the British were far more vulnerable in sparsely populated Canada than on the high seas. A maritime war might win some concessions, but it could hardly end in decisive victory.[9]

Even though stipulations narrowing American activities to the high seas were not included in the declaration of war, it is clear that there was no aversion to the sort of political realism that often supports limited wars. In the end, the war was fought on land and sea. The Americans and British negotiated the peace terms while fighting was underway and with no decisive end in sight. In fact, Andrew Jackson's famous victory at New Orleans on January 8, 1815, occurred two weeks after the Treaty of Ghent was signed (December 24, 1814,).[10] The British wanted the war to end and did not press their advantages as strongly as they might have.[11] The treaty pronounced moderate terms for both sides calling for a cessation of hostilities and a return essentially to the status quo. Matters of disagreement like Indian attacks, search and seizure of American vessels, Orders in Council, impressments, and confiscations were not settled on American terms.[12] The British were also permitted

to keep several islands in Passamaquoddy Bay (between Maine and
Nova Scotia) "until their ownership was determined." The War of 1812
was fought for limited objectives in which political considerations were
the foremost guide of state policy.

The next major war to involve the United States was fought against
Mexico from 1846–1848 primarily for the purpose of fulfilling the
nation's "Manifest Destiny" by taking Mexican land. Russell Weigley
has described General Winfield Scott's war-winning and "life-saving
strategy of limited objectives" in his campaign from the Gulf of Mexico to the capture of Mexico City in 1847.[13] Scott's strategy did not
envisage that an annihilatory blow be struck at the Mexican Army:

> Winfield Scott's greatest campaign, from Veracruz to the halls of Mon-
> tezuma in the Mexican War, permitted him to wage limited war in the
> pre-Napoleonic, eighteenth-century style most congenial to him. He
> conducted the campaign with strict regard for the rights of the citizens
> of the invaded territories, with every effort to confine bloodshed and
> suffering to the enemy's armed forces and to avoid inflicting them upon
> civilians.[14]

Rather, he used battles of maneuver to capture the political center of the
opposing country, believing that Mexico City's fall would force the
enemy to sue for peace. In essence, Scott waged a war against the Mexican state, not the Mexican nation, which he knew his small force
could not subdue if aroused. This is not to deny that Scott's strategy
was also affected by his army's being outnumbered and poorly maintained.[15] However, Scott did not wish to bring the Mexican nation to
war; he merely wished to gain acceptance of U.S. takings of Mexican
territories. In his pursuit of higher political objectives he refrained from
crushing the Mexican army, and on August 22, 1847, Scott accepted a
truce which the Mexican's used to rally themselves. This might be called
a great error on Scott's part, but it fit within his overall strategy of
achieving a settlement on American terms without escalating the war's
violence. When the fighting ended, this policy, Weigley observes "gave
Scott what he wanted."[16]

Weigley also offers an interesting analysis of the American Civil War,
which he acknowledges became the first total war of the industrial age.
Lincoln, he argues, wanted to quickly bring the Southern states back
into the Union before a "violent and remorseless revolutionary strug-

gle" had to be waged. Consequently, Lincoln began the war using a general, George McClellan, whose philosophy of war was consonant with Lincoln's desire for fighting a war of limited means. As the war dragged on, however, it became clear to Lincoln that only the total subjugation of the South could bring the desired end to the conflict. For that reason, his choice of generals finally ended with the selection of Ulysses Grant, the soldier who embodied more than any other the philosophy of modern war.[17] Therefore, even the Civil War, which grew to approximate a "total" war in the effort expended and the devastation wrought, was initially a war Lincoln hoped could be controlled and ended quickly.

Other noteworthy instances in which the United States limited the use of force should be recognized. First, when the Boxer Rebellion erupted in China in 1900 President McKinley dispatched a multinational force to relieve the besieged Legation Quarter in Beijing; this force included 2,500 Americans. Secretary of State John Hay combined the use of diplomatic initiatives and limited military force to "localize the uprising so that there would be no excuse for invading and perhaps dismembering the rest of China."[18] Second, in 1916, after border towns in New Mexico were raided by Pancho Villa on March 9, 1916, Woodrow Wilson sent a 12,000 man expeditionary force into Mexico under the direction of General Pershing. This expedition eventually went 300 miles into Mexico before being recalled in February 1917 as the military crisis with Germany worsened. Third, the years following the pronouncement of the December 1904 "Roosevelt Corollary" to the Monroe Doctrine saw the occasional use of "gunboat diplomacy" by the United States.[19] A particularly important example of this took place during the Cuban Revolution in 1933. Franklin Roosevelt did not intervene militarily in the affairs of Cuba but did have "about thirty warships surrounding the island, mostly small vessels" that moved out of actual sight from Cuba. "Their purpose seems to have been to make the Cubans think that they might intervene if disorder became too great,"[20] and this presence evidently did moderate Cuban behavior.

The pattern of America's use of force prior to the Korean War was mixed but heavily weighted toward involvements that made use of overpowering force to crush and overwhelm the opponent. To be sure, America had experienced important situations in which the use of force was more "political," necessitating restrictions on the use of violence: the Quasi-War, the War of 1812, the geographical limitations observed vis-à-vis Spain in 1898, Pershing's expedition, and the use of gunboat diplomacy provided instances of a different approach to the use of force, but these wars do not possess the precedential weight of the Civil War, World War I, and World War II. Consequently, they are less well remembered if not forgotten altogether.

The Emergence of Atomic Weapons

The years between the surrender of Japan and war in Korea marked the first phase in the development of American politico-military strategy in the atomic era. In that period a relatively small number of atomic weapons became a critical component of the structure of U.S. forces. However, this newfound predominance of weapons of mass destruction was soon challenged by strategic analysts, both in and out of government, who recognized the suicidal nature of atomic war with a similarly armed opponent. By the time NSC 68, the top-secret national security memorandum, was completed in the spring of 1950 the outline of a strategic debate that would continue through the Eisenhower Administration and end with John Kennedy's adoption of "flexible response" could clearly be seen. This debate focused on the extent to which the United States would rely on nuclear or conventional forces for its protection from Soviet threats or attacks against its vital interests in Europe and the Far East.

World War II unleashed a level of violence previously unknown to humanity. Even the horrors of the Great War twenty-five years earlier paled in comparison. A major source of this devastation was the massive strategic bombing of industrial and population centers, which had never before occurred. Consequently, there was great curiosity as to the effectiveness of strategic bombing. Michael Howard has discussed "the doctrines which were generally held in the mid-1940s as a result of the experiences of World War II." Such doctrines, Howard continues, often emerge not from the pen of a theorist like Clausewitz or Liddell Hart but from the lessons a group of soldiers learns from a particular "formative common experience." He believes that one set of lessons of this kind were those taken from World War II concerning the importance of strategic bombing:

it was agreed that strategic air power could do much–though *how* much remained a matter of controversy–to weaken the capacity of the adversary to resist. The general concept of war remained as it had been since the days of Napoleon: the contest of armed forces to obtain a position of such superiority that the victorious power would be in a position to impose its political will. And it was generally assumed that in the future, as in the immediate past, this would still be a very long-drawn-out process indeed.[21]

Immediately after the war, it appeared relatively certain that strategic bombing would be an integral part of any proper military effort.[22] To be sure a heated debate followed the war and the release of the Strategic Bombing Surveys conducted by the United States government. Proponents of air power argued that strategic bombing had been the decisive element in the defeat of the Japanese and the Germans; those who conducted the land operations in Europe and the naval operations in the Pacific disagreed vehemently with such conclusions. To the professional analysts, in general, the atomic bomb was obviously a much more destructive weapon, but it was not certain whether it would be a decisive one. The limitations on their supply and yield, the vulnerability of bombers to interception, and the lack of secure, forward air bases tended to diminish the stature of the new weapon in the eyes of many trained military and scientific specialists.[23]

However, the advent of atomic weapons and the image of the mushroom cloud surely strengthened the vague perception that strategic bombing would remain a deadly aspect of war. Even if one accepted the judgment that these weapons would not prove decisive, such arms could certainly contribute to any future war effort. These conclusions were probably drawn more commonly in popular thinking of the time because it was less encumbered by knowledge of the technical limitations evident to the military planners. The strategic thinker on the street could ponder the use of the weapons without reference to limitations in yield, deliverability, and basing. For the government, obtaining accurate assessments of the capabilities of atomic weapons was a matter of the highest priority. This was a particularly urgent task, for as declassified government documents now reveal, "American military planners believed as early as December 1945 that rapid demobilization of its armed forces had left the United States able to defend only the Western Hemisphere," while the Soviets had the capacity to capture

Western Europe (except for the United Kingdom), Turkey, Iran, the Persian Gulf, Manchuria, and Korea within a matter of weeks or months.[24]

In June 1946 the Joint War Plans Committee of the Joint Chiefs of Staff completed an interim plan, called "Pincher," that attempted to devise a strategy for meeting the Soviet military superiority. "Pincher" considered atomic weapons to be a "distinct advantage" for the United States in the event an air offensive had to be launched against the Soviet Union. A year later, on June 29, 1947, the JCS Evaluation Board released, in secret, its detailed analysis of the Bikini atoll tests of 1946 to the "assembled leadership" of the nation's armed services.[25] The report considerably increased the stature of atomic weapons within the mix of military options by firmly establishing their tremendous destructive potential against military, social, and economic targets. Starting in mid-1947 the armed services began to develop joint war plans, and by May 19, 1948, the emergency war plan, code-named "Halfmoon" had been approved by the JCS.[26] Under "Halfmoon" the air force's "Harrow" plan would be made operational in the event of war with the Soviet Union. "Harrow" called for "dropping 50 atomic bombs—apparently all that were available in the late spring of 1948—on target systems in 20 Soviet cities."[27] President Truman did not approve "Halfmoon" but asked instead that an alternative plan, relying solely on conventional weapons, be drawn up in case an international agreement on the control of atomic weapons had been reached. As the Berlin crisis worsened in the summer of 1948, the conventional war plan was dropped, and on September 13 Truman told Secretary of Defense James Forrestal that he would use atomic weapons "if it became necessary."[28]

Three days later he affirmed this position by signing NSC-30. This plan was devised to "determine the advisability of formulating, at this time, policies regarding the use of atomic weapons."[29] The document usefully reflects the strategic thought of government officials at the time but does not necessarily indicate whether decisionmakers would have followed its prescriptions in the case of a crisis. It went on to say that it would be imprudent to forswear the use of atomic weapons in the absence of agreement on their control internationally. The conclusions of NSC-30 (section 12) expressed the recognition "that, in the event of hostilities, the National Military Establishment must be ready to utilize promptly and effectively all appropriate means available, including atomic weapons" to attain the objectives set forth by the President.[30]

Facilitating the acceptance of war plans that envisaged the use of atomic weapons were the technological advances in bomb manufacture and the increase in the air force's bomber fleet. By January 1949 actual and foreseen shortages of bombers and bombs had begun to be alleviated. The Strategic Air Command (SAC) had acquired a total of 120 bombers and a sufficient number of crews to operate them. Additionally, the results of "Operation Sandstone" were available by late 1948. "Sandstone" was a series of atomic tests conducted at the South Pacific island of Eniwetok in the spring of 1948 to examine the viability of a new implosion-style atom bomb that would require much less fuel. The results were so positive that the Atomic Energy Commission (AEC) was able to guarantee the JCS that its request for a total of 400 bombs would be met two years ahead of schedule (on January 1, 1951,).[31]

Thus, the reliance of the United States on atomic weaponry was increasing rapidly and, for three reasons, no abatement seemed likely: First, the idea of strategic bombing with atomic weapons was consistent at first examination with the "lessons" that were learned from the strategic surveys of World War II; many military professionals believed that war would continue to develop and be conducted as it had since Napoleon and, thus, strategic bombing would have its place in such conflicts. Certainly, some proponents of strategic bombing saw a much greater role for this form of war-fighting. Second, contrary to earlier expectations the weapons became plentiful as a consequence of the technical improvements produced by "Sandstone." Also, the United States was acquiring a large number of forward bases. And, third, this increasing reliance on weapons of mass destruction was made necessary by the penurious defense budgeting mandated by the Truman Administration. For FY 1950 only $14.4 billion was allotted to national defense with Congressional reductions likely.[32] Consequently, Secretary of Defense Forrestal believed that there would be insufficient funding for conventional weapons, so he decided to support air power to obtain considerable brute force with fewer dollars.[33] This was an acute problem, for the United States had made, as the bulwark of its defenses, an extremely nondiscriminating weapon system. John Lewis Gaddis writes:

There was little doubt that if a full-scale war with the Soviet Union did occur, atomic weapons would be used: all war plans formulated after the summer of 1948 assumed this, and indeed given the cuts in conventional military forces there would have been no other choice.[34]

So it was that by 1949 the United States found itself, through the powerful combination of doctrinal premises, technological advances, and budgetary scarcity, embracing atomic weapons as the central element of its defense against the Soviet Union.

The Criticisms of Atomic Weapons

Although the march toward the acceptance of atomic weapons may seem to have been without dissent, such was not the case. In fact, within months of the first use of these weapons the seeds of arguments were being sown that would later present a severe challenge to the strategic thinking that was being incorporated into American war plans. The mere existence of these early counter-arguments did not prevent the absorption of atomic weapons into the American military plans and forces, but they did foreshadow the reevaluation of policy planning that would begin with the writing of NSC 68. The Korean War served as a catalyst for a debate concerning the proper way the U.S. should use force in the future.

The immeasurable damage caused by the Second World War greatly concerned theorists of international relations before the atomic bombs were exploded in August 1945. Basil Liddell Hart, the student of World War I and exponent of the "indirect approach," wrote most of *The Revolution in Warfare*, during 1944, but the book was not published until 1946 when it appeared with an epilogue that discussed the impact atomic weapons would probably have on warfare.[35] Lawrence Freedman calls Liddell Hart "the father of contemporary theories of limited war."[36] And his writings in this volume bear out Brian Bond's estimation that "Liddell Hart's contribution to the understanding of contemporary problems of war and peace did not abruptly end in 1940 or 1945."[37] To this British strategic thinker, the need to limit war was not driven by a reaction to the atomic or hydrogen bombs. He saw the developments in warfare from 1940 to 1945, and possibly those from 1914 to 1918, as threats to civilization's continued existence. Although he originally believed that air power would act as a devastating psychological weapon that could undermine the morale of the enemy's population, thereby freeing soldiers from the death of "direct" attacks in the trenches, he came to realize that, as Freedman points out, air power was a blunt instrument that might prove more horrific than the methods of World War I. Freedman goes on to tell us: "By the start of World War II he had come round to a view, that became quite prevalent after the war, namely that air power did not constitute a means of delivering a decisive, paralysing blow but was merely another means of attrition."[38]

By the end of the war, Liddell Hart's position that war would have to be limited in the future was well known. He was to criticize idealists (my term) for placing *all* their efforts behind the abolition of war. Instead, they should have, as Liddell Hart saw it, recognized the high probability that conflict would occur in the future and also directed their energies at institutionalizing limits on the use of force: "If experience has taught us anything, we should now be capable of realizing the danger of concentrating exclusively on the perfectionist policy of preventing war, while neglecting the practical necessity, if that policy fails, of limiting war–so that it does not destroy the prospects of a subsequent peace."[39] His writing was prescient in that it foresaw many of the strategic dilemmas of the period. Liddell Hart posited that there would be a "sub-atomic" role for the army because only it could halt subversion and infiltration (pp 88–89).

He was most accurate in recognizing that if one's opponent has atomic weapons that can survive and be delivered in retaliation for an attack, there may be very little utility in the use of these weapons of mass destruction: "When both sides possess atomic power, '*total* warfare' makes nonsense. Total warfare implies that the aim, the effort, and the degree of violence are unlimited. . . . An unlimited war waged with atomic power would make worse than nonsense, it would be mutually suicidal" (p. 85).

"That conclusion," he predicts, "does not necessarily mean that warfare will completely disappear." Instead new manifestations of this ancient human activity will emerge such that "any future warfare will be less unrestrained and more subject to mutually agreed upon rules. Within such limits it may develop new forms" (p. 85). Liddell Hart, as we see from this quote, perceived that a sword of Damocles would hang over war in the future. He was not alone in recognizing the tension between modern warfare as a policy instrument and its capacity for tremendous destruction. Liddell Hart's great distinction in this regard came because he recognized this fact well before the use of the atom bomb; in fact he considered the introduction of the V-1 on June 15, 1944, as the beginning of a new era in warfare (p. 32). Others would wait until Hiroshima and Nagasaki had underscored the point.

On November 16, 1945, Jacob Viner, professor of economics at the University of Chicago, delivered an address to the *Symposium on Atomic Energy and its Implications* of the American Philosophical Society. In that address Viner directly challenged the military useful-ness of atomic weapons: "There seems to be universal agreement that under atomic-bomb warfare there would be a new and tremendous advantage in being first to attack and that the atomic bomb therefore gives a greater advantage than ever to the aggressor. I nevertheless remain unconvinced."[40]

Viner continued the argument, "What difference will it then make whether it was country A which had its cities destroyed at 9 A.M. and country B which had its cities destroyed at 12 A.M., or the other way round?"[41] He brilliantly anticipated the logic in holding back the use of atomic weapons once war had begun:

> A much more plausible hypothesis is that in a war between two-fairly-equally-matched states possessed of atomic bombs each side would refrain from using the bombs at the start; each side would decide that it had nothing to gain and a great deal to lose from reciprocal use of the bombs, and that unilateral use was not attainable. The bombs *would then either never be used* or would be used only when one of the coun-tries, in the fear of imminent defeat, falls back upon their use in a last desperate effort to escape a dictated peace. In such a war the first stages *at least* would be fought with all the standard apparatus of war.[42]

Viner's analysis was consistent with an essay written by Bernard Brodie for the Yale University Institute of International Affairs dated Novem-ber 1, 1945, in which he argued, "it seems hardly likely, at least as among great powers at some distance from each other, that an attack can be so completely a surprise, and so overwhelming as to obviate the opponent's striking back with atomic bombs on a large scale."[43] Even if one side were clearly better prepared to withstand the attack, it would still be confronted with the prospect of massive destruction and loss of life; Brodie then observed that "the atomic bomb may prove in the net a powerful inhibition to aggression." In his edited volume, *The Absolute Weapon* (1946), Brodie, in a passage which has become classic, expressed his belief that the deterrence of war through the possession of a retaliatory capability was now the paramount role of armed forces:

> Thus, the first and most vital step in any American security program for the age of atomic bombs is to take measures to guarantee to ourselves in case of attack the possibility of retaliation in kind. . . . Thus far the chief purpose of our military establishment has been to win wars. From now on its chief purpose must be to avert them. It can have almost no other useful purpose.[44]

Although Brodie may have engaged in hyperbole to make his point, it was a powerful argument. Liddell Hart and Viner had realized that wars might be fought without atomic weapons being used. Brodie later wrote that his remarks cited above were primarily concerned with deterrence and that these thoughts contained no ideas about fighting limited war: "Missing from them altogether is the notion of limited war, which was not to develop until the early 1950s–stimulated both by the advent of thermonuclear weapons and by the Korean War."[45]

It is true that a school of detailed writings about limited war did not appear until the 1950s (and is a major focal point of this study), but it is unfair to Liddell Hart and Viner not to recognize the far-sightedness of their work. Within the government some individuals were beginning to call attention to the problems attendant with the use of atomic weapons. Among them was George Kennan who would become Director of the Department of State's Policy Planning Staff in 1947.

In his memoirs Kennan discusses his stay at the National War College (in Washington, D.C.) from September 1946 to May 1947. It was a period in which Kennan presented papers to his fellow students at the War College and to important government officials, like Secretary of Defense Forrestal, who frequented those talks. While on leave at the War College he wrote prolifically and was able to think about "the interrelationship of military and nonmilitary means in the promulgation of national policy." He describes how this was the first time that he had seriously studied the topic of strategic-political doctrines.[46] It was, in fact, the first time in which the U.S. government had brought members of the three branches of the armed services together with Department of State officials to study these questions in a formal environment. The dearth of relevant reading materials on the subject surprised Kennan:

> Not only were we all new to this subject, personally and institutionally, but we had, as we turned to it, virtually nothing in the way of an established or traditional American doctrine which we could take as a point of departure for our thinking and teaching. It was a mark of weakness of all previous American thinking about international affairs that there was almost nothing in American political literature of the past one hundred years on the subject of the relationship of war to politics. (p. 308)

To obtain a more balanced perspective on the relationship of politics to war the students at the War College were " thrown back, perforce, on the European thinkers of other ages and generations: on Machiavelli, Clausewitz, Gallieni–even Lawrence of Arabia" (p. 308). The *Makers of Modern Strategy*, edited by Edward Mead Earle (1943), was invaluable in tracing the intellectual origins of the military doctrines which prevailed before World War II. But as helpful as these sources were in providing the background of current politico-military issues, Kennan believed that a fundamental reassessment of these topics had to be done out of consideration for the changes wrought by atomic weapons.

Kennan thought considerably about the purpose of warfare and credits his stay at the War College with a tremendous maturation of his understanding of the subject:

> The precedents of our Civil War, of the war with Spain,[47] and of our participation in the two world wars of this century, had created not only in the minds of our soldiers and sailors but in the minds of many of our people an unspoken assumption that the normal objective of warfare was the total destruction of the enemy's ability and will to resist and his unconditional capitulation. . . . This sort of victory placed you in a position to command total obedience on the part of the defeated adversary; it thus opened the way to the unhindered realization of your political objectives, whatever they might be.(p. 309)

The "American Way" in war, as Kennan saw it, had outlived its usefulness. It was probably an unwise and politically costly strategy in the preatomic era, but with the advent of these weapons of mass destruction such notions of "total" war were suicidal. Additionally, he felt that the Soviet Union was too immense to be physically occupied; Kennan's experience with German occupation did not imbue great faith in America's ability to deal efficiently with such problems. The strategic concepts by which our nation had guided its action in the past would have to be modified to resemble more ancient strategies:

> The doctrine of total war had been a doctrine of the nineteenth and twentieth centuries. We would now have to revert to the concepts of limited warfare prevalent in the eighteenth century. The aims of warfare, accordingly, would have to become limited. If weapons were to be used at all, they would have to be employed to temper the ambitions of the adversary, or to make good limited objections against his will–not to destroy his power, or his government, or to disarm him entirely.(p. 310)

Kennan does not cite Liddell Hart as a contributor to his intellectual development, so he was probably unfamiliar with Liddell Hart's work. It is clear, however, that their ideas were tending in the same direction. Kennan expressed it in a slightly different manner, "Man would have to recognize, in short, that the device of military coercion could have, in the future, only a relative—never an absolute—value in the pursuit of political objectives"(p. 310). Although the point may be a bit overstated, one sees a clear recognition by a senior government official of the constraints that needed to be imposed on the use of atomic weapons and on the force, more generally.

Later during his stay at the War College, Kennan came to the conclusion that the U.S. should use atomic weapons only as a retaliatory measure for atomic attack. His conception of an adequate military was very different from that being offered up as the conventional wisdom. Kennan's force requirements stressed "the maintenance of small, compact, alert forces, capable of delivering at short notice effective blows on limited theaters of operation far from our own shores" (p. 311). We would also need to be able to "mobilize our strength rapidly if a clear threat of major war developed." Kennan probably underestimated the amount of time mobilization would take, and his recommendations don't seem capable of addressing the massive conventional imbalance that would have allowed the Soviets to quickly conquer Eurasia. However, his thinking does reflect an awareness that conflicts might arise in areas that would not precipitate global war. He placed great emphasis on the deterrent value of these mobile forces vis-à-vis our adversaries. In a talk he delivered to the National Defense Committee of the United States Chamber of Commerce on January 23, 1947, he said, among

other things, that a failure to maintain adequate forces such as these
would provide: "an incentive to unruly people elsewhere to seize isolated and limited objectives on the theory that we would be able to do
nothing about it at the moment and that they could count on making
the seizures with impunity and talking about it afterward" (p. 312).
Because of their emphasis on atomic weapons, military forces prior to
Korea did not come to resemble Kennan's ideal. Kennan took this as a
sign of the gulf that had developed between his thinking and that of the
leaders on Capitol Hill and in the Pentagon who were responsible for
creating the structure of U.S. forces.[48]

The Harmon Report

Worried about the adequacy of the plans for a strategic air offensive,
Secretary of Defense Forrestal asked for a "detailed analysis of the ability of the air force to deliver the bombs to their assigned targets and an
estimate of what the impact would be if all the bombs were delivered."[49] Skepticism within the government over its dependence on
nuclear weapons was supported by the Harmon Report, completed
May 12, 1949. Air Force Lt. General H. R. Harmon chaired the committee that issued the report to the Joint Chiefs of Staff.

Harmon cast considerable doubt on the ability of a single atomic
blow to drastically diminish the Soviet Union's capacity to wage war.
The study lowered the estimated amount of Soviet industrial capacity
that would be knocked out by this strategic attack to 30–40
percent–from the 50 percent estimate of "Harrow." It stated, "This loss
would not be permanent and could either be alleviated by Soviet recu-
perative action or augmented depending on the weight and effectiveness of follow-up attacks." To be sure, millions would be killed and
wounded in the attacks, but this "would not, per se, bring about capitulation, destroy the roots of Communism or critically weaken the
power of the Soviet leadership to dominate the people."[50]

Worse yet, the bombings themselves would validate Soviet propaganda causing the Soviet people to fight with greater commitment and
passion. "The capability of Soviet armed forces to advance rapidly into
selected areas of Western Europe, the Middle East and Far East, would
not be seriously impaired, but capabilities thereafter would progressive-
ly diminish," due to a combination of factors like petroleum shortages,

loss of industrial capacity to replace aircraft, and logistical and transportation problems.[53] Finally, all limitations would have been removed, making maximally destructive actions by the Soviets highly probable.

As a result of the study, the United States began to greatly increase the size of its nuclear program so that it could inflict even greater atomic devastation on the Soviets. Cognizant of its commitment to the new alliance in Europe, the United States took note of the fact that NATO possessed little capability to stop "Soviet advances in Western Europe" and ordered the Strategic Air Command to assume partial responsibility for halting any Soviet invasion.[52]

Interestingly, neither Kennan nor his successor as director of the Department of State's Policy Planning Staff in January 1950, Paul Nitze, were convinced by these calls for greater atomic power. Kennan was vociferous in his criticism of arguments emphasizing the Soviet military threat to Europe relative to the dangers of an atomic arms race. Nitze, having been a member of the U.S. Strategic Bombing Survey in 1945, was able to envision the use of weapons of mass destruction with greater ease than was Kennan. He knew of the limited effect of the bombing of Hiroshima and Nagasaki and of the great problems associated with strategic bombing using conventional weapons during the war. He also doubted the utility of tactical nuclear weapons as early as 1949. Nitze was not convinced by arguments that atomic weapons should be used against a conventional attack in Europe: he wanted the allies to have sufficient conventional forces to repel such an attack. However, "he found the air force's arguments for increasing America's ability to launch an atomic blitz on the Soviet Union itself very persuasive"[53]

While writing NSC 68 Nitze became increasingly alarmed about the possibility of a Soviet first strike. This was more of a theoretical concern based on an analysis of the grave instabilities that existed due to the capacity for a Soviet counterforce attack on American bombers and bases. The incentive for a first strike could only be nullified if the U.S. possessed "overwhelming atomic superiority and obtained command of the air."[54] Thus, Nitze's NSC 68 would include a call for greater atomic capabilities but not for the reasons given by strategic air power advocates who wanted the weapons for their war-fighting potential. Nitze desired that the United States have overall military superiority so that no area of weakness would tempt Soviet attack.

A Re-examination Begins: The Formulation of NSC 68

Following the Second World War the United States had come to rely on atomic weapons as the underpinning of its defenses. The planning for war focused on "total" war with Russia in which there would be few restraints placed on the use of force. Two events prompted American officials to reconsider its national security plans for waging war against the Soviet Union. The first was the Soviet atomic test of August 1949, discovered soon thereafter from radioactive fallout and made public by the White House on September 23, and the second was President Truman's January 31, 1950, decision to proceed with the construction of a thermonuclear bomb.[55] In a letter from the President to the Secretary of State of the same date, Truman directed "the Secretary of State and the Secretary of Defense to undertake a re-examination of our objectives in peace and war and of the effect of these objectives on our strategic plans, in light of the probable fission bomb capability and possible thermonuclear bomb capability of the Soviet Union."[56]

The explosion of the Soviet atomic bomb exposed the shortsightedness of the American reliance on its atomic arsenal as a retaliatory countermeasure to Soviet conventional strength in Europe.[57] The test also demonstrated that the Soviets might be able to produce an H-bomb within a reasonable amount of time. The U.S. H-bomb project was troubling to a number of government officials like David E. Lilienthal, Chairman of the Atomic Energy Commission. Lilienthal had grave moral reservations about constructing such a destructive weapon; he was also unsure of the strategic implications from greater American reliance on weapons of mass destruction. Steven Rearden informs us, "Nitze concurred that there were legitimate grounds, including the moral ones, for concern, but he disagreed with Lilienthal's contention that the H-bomb should be shelved until its full implications could be ascertained."[58]

The National Security Council (NSC) decided these considerations warranted that a new strategic appraisal of America's security position be undertaken (January 5, 1950); on January 18, the Department of State established a group to write its section of the study.[59] The presidential letter of January 31 took the study out of the NSC and placed responsibility for its composition under the auspices of the Secretaries of State and Defense. An ad hoc committee was formed combining individuals from both departments. Acheson delegated his responsibil-

ity to Paul Nitze, chairman of the Policy Planning Staff. Secretary of
Defense Johnson appointed the Assistant for Foreign Military Affairs,
Maj. Gen. James H. Burns (ret.), to head the Department of Defense
contingent.[60] Work began in mid-February and ended in late March
1950. The final draft was read by Truman who decided to have it
referred to the NSC for further study (this was done on April 12, 1950);
the study was then placed in NSC files under "NSC 68."[61]

NSC 68, which reflected the new realities imposed by the explosion
of a Soviet atomic bomb, greatly redirected official American strategic
thinking. The content of NSC 68 is usefully foreshadowed by the minutes of the Department of State's Policy Planning Staff of October 11,
1949. The meeting focused on "major issues facing the U.S." during
which Kennan was critical of the U.S. government for not having a
clear set of war aims in the event war with the Soviets should erupt.
Kennan stated that "neither total annihilation nor complete surrender
of the enemy is possible and, therefore, that limited rather than total
warfare should be our objective." The potential for Soviet retaliation
elicited insightful comments from Kennan and Nitze:

> Mr. Kennan also mentioned the concept of retaliation by atomic bomb-
> ing in the light of the knowledge that the Russians now have the atom-
> ic bomb and suggested that it may now be impossible for us to retaliate
> with the atomic bomb against a Russian attack with orthodox weapons.
> Mr. Nitze pointed out that this fact might make conventional arma-
> ments and their possession by the Western European nations, as well as
> by ourselves, all the more important.[62]

The seriousness with which Nitze considered this issue, is revealed by
his continuing of this thought with a description of how it might be
necessary to reduce the production of European and American con-
sumer goods in order to build the needed armaments. However, Secretary of State Dean Acheson did not favor this idea, saying "we must
examine these problems from the point of view of what peoples *will* do
rather than what they *can* do."[63] Although he may have thought such
European and American behavior unlikely, Acheson did not contradict
the analytical point concerning the increasing importance of conventional arms.

NSC 68, itself, stated that the U.S. had two broad policy thrusts:
"One is a policy that we would probably pursue even if there were no

Soviet threat. It is a policy of attempting to develop a healthy international community. The other is the policy of "containing" the Soviet system."[64] The key here lies in how "containment" is defined. What sort of concept of "containment"—aggressive, reactive, counter-attacking—did the memo provide? The essential elements of that policy are described as follows:

> As for the policy of "containment," it is one which seeks by all means short of war to (1) block further expansion of Soviet power, (2) expose the falsities of Soviet pretensions, (3) induce a retraction of the Kremlin's control and influence and (4) in general, so foster the seeds of destruction within the Soviet system that the Kremlin is brought at least to the point of modifying its behavior to conform to generally accepted international standards.[65]

The establishment of a "strong military posture" would be critical to the "ultimate guarantee of our national security," so "superior" force "in being and readily mobilizable" would have to be available to the Commander-in-Chief.[66] NSC 68 refers to Kennan's official statement of containment in NSC 20/4 of 24 November 1948 and notes that "the threat is of the same character . . . as had been previously estimated."[67] However, the U.S. faced a new contingency in that:

> within the next four or five years the Soviet Union will possess the military capability of delivering a surprise atomic attack of such weight that the United States must have substantially increased general air, ground, and sea strength, atomic capabilities, and air and civilian defenses to deter war and to provide reasonable assurance, in the event of war, that it could survive the initial blow and go on to the eventual attainment of its objectives.[68]

As NSC 68 presented it, four courses of action were available to the U.S.: 1) follow present policies; 2) isolationism; 3) war; and 4) a "more rapid building up of the political, economic, and military strength of the free world than provided under [a continuation of current policy], with the purpose of reaching, if possible, a tolerable state of order among nations without war and of preparing to defend ourselves in the event that the free world is attacked."[69] Not surprisingly, the final option was chosen. Isolationism and preventive war were rejected quickly.[70] NSC 68 predicted that the continuation of current policies would in the long run lead to a loss of American power relative to that of the Soviet Union. This trend was due not to any errors in objectives but from "the inadequacy of current programs and plans." The bottom line was the following: "It is imperative that this trend be reversed by a much more rapid and concerted build-up of the actual strength of both the United States and the other nations of the free world. The analysis shows this will be costly and will involve significant domestic financial and economic adjustments."[71]

It was the awareness of the need for greatly increased conventional military forces, understood primarily by Nitze but also to some extent by Kennan, that distinguished NSC 68 from preceding government statements. Yet, one must recall that NSC 68 did not propose a conventional increase at the expense of atomic weapons. Rather, the size of the pie would increase for all areas in the military budget, but it would grow most rapidly in the conventional area. Atomic weapons would be built more rapidly so that the survivability of the United States forces in being could be ensured in the event of a surprise attack. NSC 68 reads, "A further increase in the number of and power of our atomic weapons is necessary in order to assure the effectiveness of any U.S. retaliatory blow."[72]

NSC 68, crafted under the direction of Paul Nitze, did not reject Kennan's conception of containing the Soviet Union which appeared in NSC 20/4's vague call for a "level of military readiness which can be maintained as long as necessary as a deterrent to Soviet aggression."[73] Melvyn Leffler describes NSC 68's more ambitious agenda as follows:

> U.S. aims, however, were not limited to deterring war, containing Soviet expansion, and thwarting internal subversion. Nitze stressed that U.S. goals were designed to reduce Soviet power on its periphery, establish independent countries in Eastern Europe, revive nationalist aspirations among subject peoples within the Soviet Union, and "foster a fundamental change in the nature of the Soviet system, a change toward which the frustration of the design is the first and perhaps the most important [step]."[74]

Although both men recognized the importance of military preparedness, Kennan clearly did not attach the same importance to military power as Nitze did. Nitze writes of NSC 68:

The major change recommended in NSC 68 was a stepped-up level of effort to counter recent developments, with the emphasis on strengthening our military capabilities in the face of significantly increased Soviet capabilities. Heretofore, our foreign policy had stressed economic assistance, as under the Marshall Plan, and collective security through the North Atlantic Treaty, backed by a very modest program of military aid to our allies. These measures while obviously important, did not appear to me to be sufficient.[75]

Kennan argued that the threat of general war with the Soviet Union was not great and that the United States should be able to fight limited probes in far off places by Soviet proxies.[76] He advocated the "development of a small, mobile task force, approximately the size of two divisions, to meet and to deter military challenges on the Soviet perimeter."[77]

The study group agreed with Kennan about the importance of being prepared for limited wars. "The group had reasoned that the atomic stalemate would neutralize the American nuclear deterrent," Hammond informs us.[78] They were also focused on defending the United Kingdom and Western Europe from Soviet pressure, and, of course, deterring those attacks was also of the highest priority. This would require a large increase in spending on *conventional* forces as Richard Smoke, professor of political science at Brown University, points out. He observes, "Although the report [NSC 68] did not point it out explicitly, defense against the enormous Red Army formations in Eastern Europe would mean a large commitment of American ground troops to Europe."[79] Thus, while Nitze may have retained the broad notion of "containment" at the core of his memo, the manner of its effectuation was to be clearly more aggressive. All that being said it does not seem that the Nitze-Acheson concept of being on the strategic offensive necessarily implied any concept of "rollback" of the Soviet empire.

John Lewis Gaddis enumerates three conclusions of NSC 68.[80] First, the Soviet threat was world-wide and required a sharp increase in military expenditures by the United States to thwart it. Second, the national economy could sustain the increased spending without damaging the foundations of prosperity; this point is also made by Hammond who says, "NSC 68 was preoccupied with the task of breaking out of a mode of thinking in which means had seemed to dictate ends."[81] And, third,

NSC 68 called for a dramatic public relations campaign to jolt the nation into greater awareness of its formidable security problems.

"What is often not realized about NSC 68," according to Gaddis, " is the conviction that pervaded it that nuclear weapons were not likely to be of very much use in the kinds of wars the United States was most likely to confront."[82] Gaddis probably overstates the point, for it was clearly thought that an inadequate retaliatory capability would jeopardize American safety. His point is essentially correct. Lawrence Freedman writes NSC 68 recognized that the American lead in hydrogen bomb capabilities would be eroded as had its lead in fission weaponry, but that lead time could be used as a "shield, providing cover while a process of conventional rearmament was set in motion."[83] Smoke argues persuasively that a new logic was implicit in NSC 68: "In effect the two nuclear forces would balance and *mutually deter each other*. A nuclear stalemate would develop, in which neither side would dare launch an atomic attack on the other."[84] For that reason, the U.S. needed to greatly expand its conventional forces while maintaining sufficient nuclear forces.

The report's willingness to consider fighting limited wars comes early on in a paragraph beginning: "But if war comes, what is the role of force?"[85] A general recognition of the problem of matching the means used in war to the objectives being sought is underscored by the inclusion of a sentence from *The Federalist* (#28: Hamilton) which reads, "The means to be employed must be proportioned to the extent of the mischief." The document then endorses the Clausewitzian notion that political considerations should inform America's grand strategy and its specific uses of military power:

> The mischief may be a global war or it may be a Soviet campaign for limited objectives. In either case we should take no avoidable initiative which would cause it to become a global war. Our aim in applying force must be to compel the acceptance of terms consistent with our objectives, and our capabilities for the application of force should, therefore, within the limits of what we can sustain over the long pull, be congruent to the range of tasks which we may encounter.[86]

A great problem will face the free world if its armed forces are inadequate to fight local expansion: "The United States will therefore be confronted more frequently with the dilemma of reacting totally to a limited extension of Soviet control or of not reacting at all (except with ineffectual protests and half-measures)."[87] Atomic bipolarity it was argued would place a "premium on piecemeal aggression against others, counting on our unwillingness to engage in atomic war unless we were directly attacked. We run all these risks and the added risk of being confused and immobilized by our inability to weigh and choose, and pursue a firm course based on a rational assessment of each."[88] In sum, the United States had to acquire the military strength that would provide it with the option of military response when the occasion so demanded.

Recently a well-researched, revisionist interpretation of NSC 68 has been offered. Marc Trachtenberg, a historian at the University of Pennsylvania, argues that it was widely recognized that America's nuclear "monopoly" was in fact a "wasting asset."[89] Trachtenberg argues that NSC 68 was neither defense-minded nor focused on building limited war capabilities:

> The most important government officials at the time were quite hostile to the "preventive war" thesis. But this is not to say that they were not concerned with the problems that would result from the ending of America's nuclear monopoly. . . . Contrary to what is commonly believed, the strategy called for in NSC 68 was *not* essentially defensive in nature, and the aggressive˚ thrust of the document was probably linked to concerns about long-term trends in the strategic balance. (p. 11)

Trachtenberg does not believe that either Acheson or Nitze wanted war. Instead, "what they wanted was to create such overwhelming power that the United States could achieve its goals without actually having to fight." He continues, "War itself was never desired, but it does seem clear that Nitze was willing to risk a nuclear conflict, but only *after* the trends had been reversed and American power had been rebuilt (p. 15)."

It may "seem clear" to Trachtenberg, but this assertion about Nitze appears unsupported, and in fact Trachtenberg later backs away from this suggestion: "This is not to argue that NSC 68 had a hidden agenda and that the real goal of the aggressive strategy was to generate situations that might lead to war before America's nuclear advantage was lost forever (p. 15)." When taken in totality his analysis of NSC 68 offers a valuable reappraisal, but statements like the one above are a bit extreme (and unfair to Nitze).

In his memoirs Nitze attempts to counter the claim that NSC 68 "urged a buildup of our forces because we anticipated a war with the Soviet Union sometime in 1954."[90] He states that NSC 68 merely claimed that in 1954 without an American response "the Soviets would have atomic weapons and delivery aircraft in sufficient number to threaten extensive (even unacceptable) damage to the United States." The writers of NSC 68 were not predicting that such an attack would come but that Soviet military capabilities would be overwhelming by that time if left uncontested. They were most certainly not "willing to risk" a nuclear war even after "trends had been reversed." Trachtenberg's recognition that Nitze, in early 1950, "leaned toward the line that nuclear forces tend to neutralize each other" is exactly correct.[91] NSC 68's oft cited statement that "two large atomic capabilities . . . might well act, therefore, not as a deterrent, but as an incitement to war" is a hypothetical consideration that is not consistent with the basic argument of the document.[92] It resembles what lawyers call "obiter dictum": a remark not essential to the holding that nevertheless makes a related point or observation.

As Trachtenberg correctly writes, NSC 68 was not a defensive document. Grand strategically, it called on the U.S. to assume the initiative. This could occur only if the U.S. and its allies had sufficient military forces to credibly defend itself in the face of powerful Soviet efforts to undermine Western power. Leffler observes that NSC 68's innovation lay in Nitze's request "for more, more, and more money to implement the programs and to achieve the goals already set out."[93] This call for a shift to the offensive and for greater funding of national security programs does not substantiate Trachtenberg's attack on the traditional interpretations of NSC 68. His implication, given above, that there was something untoward in the U.S. hopes of reaping political benefits from military power without having to actually fight a war is odd. Who wouldn't want the benefit free—without paying in blood, as Clausewitz might have put it? The American planners were concerned about a possible Soviet preemptive strike against the U.S., they wanted to increase U.S. readiness, civil defenses, and retaliatory power to minimize any advantage an attacker might have after a strike on America. This being said, the thrust of American policy was still political. NSC 68 echoed

Kennan's advice that pressure placed on the Soviet Union would over time win the day: "The only sure victory lies in the frustration of the Kremlin design by the steady development of the moral and material strength of the free world and its projection into the Soviet world in such a way as to bring about an internal change in the Soviet system."[94]

The phrase "only sure victory" is critical here, for it imparts the truth that the use of force is always risky. Even if the U.S. had overwhelming military strength there would be no "sure victory," and the stakes here were too great to risk when a "sure victory" was possible via the comprehensive strategy of containment outlined in NSC 68. Trachtenberg reminds us of the strategic nuclear balance's importance as background to the discussions taking place in the Truman Administration. This study's interpretation argues that NSC 68 set forth a broad outline urging that the U.S. regain the grand strategic initiative vis-à-vis the Soviets by building up conventional and atomic military strength as a necessary condition for launching the long-term political offensive that would protect the West's security. The American atomic preeminence is regarded as a "wasting asset" in the sense that the fast-approaching bipolar world would eliminate it. Finally, although the atomic balance and concerns about atomic war between the Soviet Union and the United States were extremely important, NSC 68 placed great emphasis on the need to counter conventional military threats because the "wasting asset" would no longer be able to bully the Soviets into good behavior. When that time arrived, it was suggested, limited war in the "peripheral" regions of the world would be the battleground of the future.

Leffler notes correctly that NSC 68 did not boldly confront the limited war problem with a specific calculus for assessing American interests with respect to possible limited wars. As he writes, after NSC 68 "much ambiguity remained, generated by the knowledge that the United States did not have the forces to wage a limited war in these areas and be prepared to fight a global war at the same time."[95] In some sense this critique may be asking too much of those who were formulating U.S. policy, almost 50 years of living with atomic weapons has provided us with sufficient time to analyze the problems posed by these weapons. In 1950 Nitze and his staff had a much tougher task, and it may be that it would take American involvement in a limited war before some of these issues would be clarified.

Acheson, NSC 68, and the Impact of Korea

In the late 1940s many top-level officials in the American government came to the conclusion that a heavy reliance on strategic air power could no longer be the nation's primary basis of defense. The nuclear approach left the President with too few options in a crisis: he could either capitulate or enter into "total" war; more limited options were needed to counter "piecemeal aggression." Consequently, just as weapons of mass destruction were becoming the primary weapon in the arsenal of the United States, a new school of thought arose which challenged their utility. Although NSC 68 was a long, multifaceted document, one aspect of it is clear. Acheson said of this policy paper that "the purpose of NSC 68 was to so bludgeon the mass mind of 'top government' that not only could the President make a decision but that the decision could be carried out."[96] However, one should *not* draw the conclusion that its analysis and recommendations, however starkly and histrionically presented, were mere bureaucratic propaganda.

The thinking in the document represented a continuation of the debate that took place both in and out of the government after World War II concerning the role force should play in future conflicts and the structure American standing forces should take. Acheson's defense of NSC 68 against "some liberals and Kremlinologists" supports this view. They claimed that the fundamental weaknesses of the Western European nations were social, economic, and political *not* military. Acheson rejected this argument with dispatch:

> This I did not believe. The threat to Western Europe seemed to me singularly like that which Islam had posed centuries before, with its combination of ideological zeal and fighting power. Then it had taken the same combination to meet it: Germanic power in the East and Frankish power in Spain, both energized by a great outburst of military power and social organization in Europe. This time it would need the added power and energy of America for the drama was now played on a world stage.[97]

Opposing this ideological-military threat would be expensive because there could be no reliance on atomic weapons alone. Conventional forces would have to be built and maintained. Lawrence Freedman explains the strategic conclusions to which the Truman Administration was drawn: "The U.S. nuclear superiority was destined to be lost, and so provided no basis for a long-term strategy. Increasingly, nuclear forces would be expected to do little more than neutralize those of the other side. The struggle for advantage would be with conventional arms."[98]

Acheson tells us that while NSC 68 did not contain budget figures, officials in the government had estimated that the rearmament would cost $50 billion per annum.[99] Thus, as the Secretary of State was to testify before a congressional hearing in February 1951: "The best use we can make of our present advantage in retaliatory air power is to move ahead under this protective shield to build the balanced collective forces in Western Europe that will continue to deter aggression after our atomic advantage has been diminished."[100]

The recommendations of NSC 68 would remain a "dead letter" until the outbreak of the Korean War; in fact, Truman had sent it back to the NSC for further study, particularly with regard to the budgeting agenda it recommended. The tripling or quadrupling of defense spending was politically unthinkable. Only a surprise attack, reminiscent of Pearl Harbor, could have evoked the popular support necessary to fund these increased military budgets. The Korean War, taken up in the next chapter, would be America's crash course in limited war. Ironically, while the war created a political consensus for increased military spending, which even Eisenhower could not remove, Korea left much disagreement over the manner in which force should be used.

3

Korea: The Struggle to Wage Limited War

On June 25, 1950, the armed forces of North Korea attacked South Korean troops below their common border, the 38th parallel. Within days the United States had committed air, sea, and ground forces to the defense of the Republic of Korea. Following American leadership, when the Soviet Union was boycotting the Security Council, the United Nations called on its members to assist in repelling the North Korean attack. The Security Council established a unified command under the direction of the United States on July 7, 1950. After the invasion of the Republic of Korea the Truman administration, deciding that its credibility and prestige would be severely damaged if South Korea were conquered, made the restoration of the territorial and political integrity of the Republic of Korea its major objective.[1]

Fortunately for the Republic of Korea, American occupation troops in Japan were available for immediate use by the commander of U.N.-U.S. forces, General Douglas MacArthur. Throughout July 1950 the U.N. forces retreated steadily, finally withdrawing into a heavily defended perimeter around the southeastern city of Pusan.[2] At this time, nevertheless, General MacArthur was planning an offensive that would push the North Koreans beyond the 38th parallel. On July 17, 1950, President Truman instructed the NSC to consider the issues that would be posed if U.N. forces were to cross the 38th parallel. The final version of the report that followed, NSC 81/1, was signed by President Truman on September 11, 1950.[3] Its policies represented a change from the June 1950 intention of restoring the status quo. The new goal was for the United Nations Commander to pursue and destroy all enemy forces even if that entailed crossing the 38th parallel.[4] The approval given to MacArthur was *not* a blank check, however. He was to proceed as would be prudent depending on the military situation facing him.[5] MacArthur struck back on September 15, 1950, as U.N. forces effected a devastating amphibious invasion of Korea behind the North Korean lines at Inchon. Within days the U.S. Eighth Army had broken out of Pusan and the North Koreans were retreating steadily up the peninsula.

The subject of the possible use of atomic weapons during the initial phases of the Korean War must be considered momentarily. Roger Dingman has conducted one of the most thorough investigations of this topic, and he argues: "Forced repeatedly by battlefield circumstance to consider their tactical use in and around Korea, the Truman administration time and again turned away from such action."[6] Dingman's research demonstrates that the Truman administration *did* use the movement of nuclear-capable bombers as a signal intended to deter more direct intervention on the part of the Soviets. For example, President Truman acted in concert with British prime minister Clement Atlee to send a number of B-29 bombers to the United Kingdom. The B-29s were configured to carry atomic weapons as were the B-29s used during the Berlin Crisis two years earlier. However, as was the case during that crisis, the planes did not carry atomic bombs; similarly, on this mission they did not carry the fissionable cores of the bombs. Atlee and his cabinet agreed to this demonstration, designed to impress the Soviets, on the condition that the movement of the bombers be declared a routine rotation of these military aircraft, and President Truman agreed to this proviso on July 11, 1950.[7] Within three weeks ten more similarly equipped B-29s were sent to Guam. The world found out about the bomber movement to Guam from a story leaked to the *New York Times*.[8]

Dingman presents a series of plausible hypotheses concerning the motivations for the decision, but he is unable to decipher from these records a definitive reason for the second bomber deployment. Instead, he reasonably concludes that "the decisions of late July 1950 demonstrated the strength of Washington's belief that such weapons, even if deployed without explicit statements of intent, could serve as deterrents." "They also intensified the Truman administration's determination," he continues, "to be ready in the event that atomic arms might be needed."[9]

Allied forces entered North Korea even though the Chinese stated they would counter the movement of American forces. On September 25, 1950, the acting chief of the People's Liberation Army (of Communist China) warned that the Chinese would not "sit back with folded hands and let the Americans come up to the border."[10] Five days later Premier Zhou Enlai remarked to the People's Political Consultative Conference that "the Chinese people absolutely will not tolerate foreign aggression nor will they supinely tolerate seeing their neighbours being savagely invaded by imperialists."[11] And, finally, on October 3, Zhou Enlai formally summoned K. M. Panikkar, India's ambassador to China, to a midnight meeting at the Ministry of Foreign Affairs in Beijing. Zhou told Panikkar that should American troops cross the 38th parallel, China would enter the war. The South Koreans could cross the line but not the Americans.[12] Nevertheless, on September 29 the JCS approved MacArthur's plan, which was "cleared on the highest governmental level," to conduct significant operations north of the 38th parallel.[13] MacArthur and ROK President Syngman Rhee entered Seoul together that same day, and the next day South Korean forces crossed the 38th parallel. A week later, after a great deal of hedging, the U.N. General Assembly voted 47 to 5 to adopt Resolution 376, which recommended that "all appropriate steps be taken to ensure conditions of stability throughout Korea."[14] American ground forces crossed the parallel on October 7, shortly after the resolution was passed.[15]

As United Nations forces continued to move north, unbeknownst to them Chinese "volunteers" had begun to cross the Yalu on October 14. The U.N. advance continued and MacArthur ordered American units into the Northern Korea-China border areas despite an order that had prohibited such deployments. On October 25, eleven days after they began their infiltration, Chinese forces attacked and halted the advance of some South Korean forces less than 40 miles below the Yalu River; this action continued for approximately ten days. The U.N. advance stopped to regroup.

On November 6, following a meeting with Secretary of State Acheson, Secretary of Defense Marshall, and Deputy Secretary of Defense Robert A. Lovett, the Joint Chiefs of Staff sent MacArthur a telegram issuing orders that allowed him to bomb the Korean ends of the Yalu River bridges (which were being used by Chinese forces advancing from Manchuria) and the Korean frontier areas. According to the *JCS History*, later on that evening a consensus was reached by those in attendance at the JCS conference that U.N. forces should withdraw to the waist of Korea, after which, a diplomatic conclusion to the war should be sought. No written recommendation to this effect was given to the President.[16] Another opportunity was lost when, three days later, MacArthur's orders were not changed after an NSC meeting. Meanwhile, MacArthur continued his northward advance to the Yalu, as the intense combat with communist Chinese forces wound down. The enemy withdrew from the battlefield between November 6 and 8.[17]

On November 21, top-level State and Defense Department officials met in the Pentagon to discuss the military situation in Korea. There was again concern that war with China might erupt: Acheson did not object to MacArthur's planned offensive, but he wanted military action confined to the Korean peninsula.[18] Secretary Acheson and Dean Rusk (from State) reported that there was "anxiety" on the part of friendly nations that a war with the Sino-Soviet bloc might begin. The discussion drifted along with the cautious expectation and hope settling in that MacArthur's drive to the Yalu would end the war.

"An Entirely New War": Limitations on Force Put in Place

On November 24, 1950, General MacArthur finally launched the drive to the Yalu after an additional ten day delay. Two days later the Chinese attacked in mass, and within another two days the gravity of the situation hit fully in Washington after a cable was received from MacArthur which stated flatly: "We face an entirely new war."[19] On that day an emergency meeting of the NSC was held at the White House. The striking feature of this meeting was the swiftness with which the Joint Chiefs and Secretary Marshall had come to the conclusion that the war must be kept limited. General Bradley noted that the Chinese had "300 aircraft back in Manchuria" that could strike a severe blow against crowded and vulnerable U.N. airfields in Korea and Japan.[20] Consequently, Bradley informed President Truman that the "JCS do not think we should violate the border [with China] pending developments." General Marshall continued on the same theme summarizing the conclusions of an earlier discussion with the department secretaries:

> Our purposes are to fulfill our UN obligations but not to become individually or as a member of the UN involved in general war in China with the Chinese Communists. To do so would be to fall into a carefully laid Russian trap. We should use all available political, economic and psychological action to limit the war. Strong military support is needed for the localized action. We should not go into Chinese territory and we should not use Chinese Nationalist forces.[21]

Within three days of the Chinese offensive a Limited War policy was being haltingly pieced together by members of the Administration. Later in the discussion the point was made that the prospects were gloomy unless more U.N. troops could be brought into the fighting. Secretary Marshall replied "that this was a gloomy possibility and that he did not know the answer. We want to avoid getting sewed up in Korea and how could we get out with honor." Marshall was clearly worried that unless the military effort in Korea were constrained the United States would bring itself into this war too deeply—thus, exposing Western Europe, the crown jewel of containment, to encroachment from the Soviets.

This feeling was more clearly articulated during a high-level meeting in the JCS Conference Room at the Pentagon on December 1. This point was stated succinctly by Deputy Secretary of Defense Lovett who "said he understood there was a consensus on two points: first, that Korea is not a decisive area for us; and second, that, while the loss of Korea might jeopardize Japan and perhaps bring about its eventual loss, Western Europe was our prime concern and we would rather see that result than lose in Western Europe. It was best to hold Korea for political motives."[22] Much of the conversation concerned possible American responses to an escalation of the war by the Chinese or by direct Soviet involvement. General Nathan Twining (USAF) and Admiral Forrest Sherman expressed willingness to attack China if they ceased allowing U.N. air superiority over Korea. As long as the Chinese allowed this limitation on the use of their own air forces Sherman recognized that "the advantage of keeping our air on our side of the frontier outweigh the disadvantages."[23]

So it was that even though a course of retaining limitations on the use of force was preferred in Washington, responsible officials had to consider American responses in the event that either the Chinese or Soviets expanded the war. In those cases, a number of high-ranking officials were willing to escalate in retaliation. Officials in the navy and the air force (like General Vandenberg) advocated retaliatory actions like a naval blockade and bombardment of China if the U.N. forces were compelled to evacuate the peninsula; these actions would serve as a form of payback to the Chinese Communists for their actions.[24]

By December 4 MacArthur began to cable Washington with vague statements about the need for "some positive and immediate action" to save the situation. Soon thereafter he publicly criticized the restrictions placed on his command. During December the military situation stabilized for a short time as the U.N. forces settled on a line roughly north of the 38th parallel. However, "by the end of December a new communist offensive was clearly in the offing."[25] MacArthur recommended the use of the atomic bomb on December 24, 1951, when he sent Washington "a list of retardation targets which he considered would require 26 bombs" and asked that "4 bombs be used on invasion forces and 4 bombs be used on critical concentrations of enemy air power, both targets of opportunity."[26] Michael Schaller notes that these latter four bombs were to be used "presumably in Manchuria."[27] On December 30, 1950, General MacArthur cabled his plans for widening the war to the Joint Chiefs of Staff. Its four primary features were that the U.N. forces should, first, blockade China's coast; second, destroy China's industrial war-making capacity through heavy air and naval bombardments; third, reinforce the U.N. command with Chinese Nationalist forces; and, fourth, allow the Chinese Nationalists to undertake diversionary actions against vulnerable areas of the Chinese mainland.[28]

Rosemary Foot also notes that even though there was general agreement at the highest levels of the administration that the war had to be contained in order to protect greater national security interests there were still differences of opinion as to how stringent the limitations on force should be. "Philip Jessup," she writes, "confirmed in late December that the Truman administration was struggling to establish a governmental military position on a limited war against China. The Pentagon was not united on this, he reported, and there were doubts that bombings and a blockade could 'actually defeat Mao's regime' "[29] Most notably, Admiral Forrest P. Sherman, the Chief of Naval Operations, suggested a course of action in a memo of January 3, 1951, that echoed MacArthur's proposal and those of the Joint Strategic Plans Committee. Admiral Sherman's argument and the perception that the situation in Korea was grave influenced the Joint Chiefs of Staff which forwarded a memo to the NSC on January 12, 1951,—it was numbered NSC 101. The memo gave qualified support for some of General MacArthur's ideas for expanding the war.[30]

On December 31, 1950, the Chinese began their third major attack. Soon thereafter it became apparent to Lieutenant General Matthew B. Ridgway, who had assumed command of the U.S. Eighth Army on December 23, after Lieutenant General Walton H. Walker was killed when his jeep was struck by a truck, that the lines of the U.N. forces could not hold. He ordered a retreat. Seoul was abandoned on January 4, 1951, and the Eighth Army, using its superior mobility, fell back to a prepared line that was 35 miles below the South Korean capitol.[31] These events appeared to be a disaster in the making, yet by January 10 the Chinese advance was being checked in bloody fighting. General Ridgway was encouraged that his forces had not been routed, were fighting cohesively, and were launching limited counterattacks.[32] However, the situation was not perceived as being so well in hand from Washington. Messages from MacArthur contradicted Ridgway's more optimistic cables causing confusion for decisionmakers.[33] On January 12 the NSC met and agreed to send Army Chief of Staff General J. Lawton Collins and Air Force Chief of Staff General Hoyt Vandenberg to assess the situation firsthand. In the following days the JCS and the President sent conciliatory messages to General MacArthur, but American policy did not change.

It would be incorrect to conclude that *only* MacArthur, various members of the military, and some elements of the Republican party were willing to widen the war. An important civilian member of the administration made a series of recommendations to the President that advocated escalatory options that went beyond MacArthur's. Stuart Symington, chairman of the National Security Resources Board and former Secretary of the Air Force, who would later serve as a Democratic Senator from Missouri, advocated the evacuation of ground forces in Korea and the commencement of "an open and sustained attack upon lines of communication in China and Korea; and also upon aggression-support-industries in Manchuria as considered militarily advisable;" such actions should be accompanied by a U.S. announcement that other aggressive Soviet actions "would result in the atomic bombardment of Soviet Russia itself."[34] Symington thought that the United States had now found itself "in a war of survival" which it was losing.[35] He believed that the United States needed a much more vigorous military policy that was not hampered by political limitations. Later in life Symington would state his belief that: "the military should be wary of diplomacy until war is declared; then the State Department should keep its nose out and let the military do whatever is necessary to win. Then we wouldn't get into these "no-win" wars. Try to stay out of wars, but, once in, do what is necessary to win."[36]

In essence, Symington advocated an "all-or-nothing" approach to the use of force. (His thinking contains that Jominian insight that crushing the opponent is the proper manner in which to fight a war: once hostilities begin, the military component, force, must have its needs met until the contest is concluded. In fact, these statements echo aspects of General MacArthur's testimony before the United States Senate in May 1951.) As one could imagine Secretaries Acheson and Marshall were shocked by these proposals, which they believed would lead to a world war with the Soviets.[37] President Truman wrote a stinging condemnation of Symington's recommendation on his copy of the memo.[38]

In Korea, the military situation took a dramatic turn for the better. On January 15, 1951, General Ridgway launched a successful limited counterattack. General Collins, greatly encouraged by this development, sent a cable to Washington from Tokyo on January 17 that read: "Eighth Army in good shape and improving daily under Ridgway's leadership. Morale very satisfactory considering conditions."[39] As one might have expected, this message and the reports of Collins and Vandenberg upon their return to the United States produced great relief in the nation's capitol. James Schnabel observes, "For the first time since late November, authorities in Washington saw reasonable hope that catastrophe might be forestalled in Korea and that all was not as black as had been painted."[40] In fact, Secretary Acheson reported to a meeting of State Department officials that Generals Collins and Vandenberg had agreed, in a report to the Cabinet, that the restriction which denied the U.N. forces the permission to attack outside Korea "was not a limitation of any importance."[41] Vandenberg then observed that if one wanted to destroy the supplies being used by the Chinese it would not be sufficient to attack Manchuria; Vladivostok and other Russian areas would have to be hit. The Air Force Chief of Staff made it clear that he was not advocating that course of action. In fact, the Limited War policy that had been in effect took firm root after the return of Collins and Vandenberg. NSC 101, the JCS paper that was forwarded on January 12, 1951, "went into virtual discard."[42] The desperate situation that might have pulled the United States away from its restrained attitude toward the use of force had ebbed away as the Chinese offensive was mauled by Ridgway's forces.

This new stabilization in the fighting also signalled a change in MacArthur's standing within the government, for after Collins and Vandenberg returned from Korea the General's influence declined dramatically.[43] The distance between Washington and MacArthur only widened as time went on. As MacArthur's sense of frustration grew, his criticisms of the administration became more frequent and more public. A consensus on the various aspects of Korean War policy was slowly reached over the next months during meetings between representatives of the Departments of Defense and State. It was felt that the U.N. forces should fight up to a line approximating the old border between the two Koreas while inflicting massive attrition on the Chinese; during that period a diplomatic settlement would be sought by the State Department. The *JCS History* concludes, "Most important, all of them–the military no less than the civilians–were united in rejecting any major expansion of hostilities."[44]

The policy of limited war received formal reaffirmation in NSC 48/5, which as Rosemary Foot observes, "has rightly been regarded as a major statement of America's Limited War policy at a time when a truce appeared attainable."[45] This policy paper was approved by President Truman on May 17, 1951. The goals of the fighting were greatly altered in this new policy paper from what they had been in NSC 81/1. There was now no hope of destroying all enemy forces above the 38th parallel. Instead, the United States would "seek a political settlement in Korea" that protected its interests in the region including maintaining the independence of the Republic of Korea at roughly its pre-invasion boundaries.

James Schnabel considered this paper to be a statement that "implied no hope of military victory in Korea; but it did bespeak a certain confidence that Communist designs could be thwarted even though United States aims could not be fully accomplished."[46] The portions of the document that consider expanding the war to China by naval blockade or direct military action were included to cover the *contingency* of escalatory actions by China on U.N. or American forces *outside* Korea.[47]

Pursuant to NSC 48/5 the command authorities in Washington specified tighter restrictions on military action in orders sent to Ridgway on May 31, 1951, and July 10, 1951.[48] The Allied commander in Tokyo operated under these directives, derived from NSC 48/5, until the armistice was signed more than two years later. John Lewis Gaddis observes, and Rosemary Foot quotes him, NSC 48/5 "brought the administration surprisingly close to MacArthur's recommendations just at the time it was seeking publicly to refute them."[49] Such an interpretation focuses excessively on the documents contingency plans in the event the enemy expanded the war. Essentially, the policy adopted on May 17 recognized the outcome desired by the United States could be achieved only by *political* not military means. It is true that NSC 48/5 "instructed the Joint Chiefs . . . to prepare detailed plans for punitive action against China itself should China take aggressive action outside Korea or if United Nations forces were compelled by military action to evacuate Korea."[50] It is also true that those plans resembled the recommendations made by MacArthur. However, the General wanted to attack China when the fighting was occurring inside Korea alone, this was not true of Truman's policy paper. NSC 48/5 expressed an American willingness to embrace MacArthur's proposal for a wider war, as a logical retaliatory possibility.[51] In point of fact, the war was kept limited as Richard Smoke observes:

> What was so interesting about Korea . . . was the fact that the war had remained so very limited compared to what it might have been. The two sides had fought for years inside a narrow area, with large forces and huge potential for destruction poised and ready for use—but never used. The U.S.—U.N. side had not only refrained from using nuclear weapons but had also prohibited its aircraft from flying north of the Yalu River, even though Chinese air bases, army staging bases, and supply routes on the other side, crucial to the Chinese war effort, could have been bombed easily. The Chinese had observed a similar hands off policy regarding Japan,

which the West had used as its main staging area and supply area for the war. . . . Thus each side had respected the other's "sanctuary" and had confined its operations to the arena of the Korean peninsula itself, although neither side was constrained by military or technical reasons. This had happened, furthermore, in spite of the fact that both sides found the war, limited in this way, very costly, and the outcome unsatisfactory.[52]

1950: The Chinese Puzzle

Some of China's caution was the result of Soviet unwillingness to directly enter the war with air support. After the successful Inchon landing and MacArthur's drive up the peninsula, Mao moved rapidly toward a clear military commitment to save North Korea. The U.N. forces crossing the 38th parallel convinced Mao that military intervention against the United States was necessary. Mao cabled this decision to Stalin on October 2, 1950, informing him that Chinese troops would enter Korea on October 15 and "there assume a defensive posture, letting the enemy forces know that they faced a new situation." Mao wanted Stalin to provide equipment for his ground forces so they would have an offensive capability, if necessary; he also asked for Stalin's help "in fending off possible American naval and air attacks on Chinese cities and industry." Stalin denied the request for air support in a meeting with Zhou Enlai on the evening of October 9–10. He told the Chinese that the "Soviet air force . . . needed more time for preparation before engaging even in the defense of Chinese airspace."[53]

However, Stalin did promise that military supplies for twenty divisions would immediately begin being shipped to the Chinese. Nevertheless, the Chinese Politburo came to unanimous agreement on October 13 "to send troops to Korea despite the lack of Soviet air support."[54] In fact, Thomas Christensen argues that had MacArthur not gone to the Yalu, stopping instead at the Pyongyang-Wonsan Line (the "Neck"), Mao would still have attacked but after waiting six months to strengthen his forces.[55]

MacArthur's Dismissal and the Senate Hearings

The events which led President Truman to relieve General MacArthur are well documented and need not be described in detail.[56] MacArthur criticized the policy of limited war which the Truman Administration pursued in Korea. In violation of Truman's prohibition against issuing policy pronouncements without State Department approval, MacArthur let his displeasure with U.N. policy become public through a series of actions. On April 11, 1951, President Truman relieved the General of the post of Commander-in-Chief, Far East, replacing him with Ridgway.

Later that evening the President addressed the nation. Truman's message began bluntly: "My fellow Americans: I want to talk to you plainly about what we are doing in Korea and about our policy in the Far East. In the simplest terms, what we are doing is this: We are trying to prevent a third world war."[57] The President then explained, "A number of events have made it evident that General MacArthur did not agree with that policy. I have therefore considered it essential to relieve General MacArthur so that there would be no doubt or confusion as to the real purpose and aim of our policy."[58] American public opinion decidedly favored General MacArthur who returned to the United States, was met by enormous crowds, and in a famous address overwhelmed a joint session of the Congress on April 19, 1951. The Senate investigation of the causes of General MacArthur's dismissal began on May 3, 1951. A wide range of issues was discussed during the hearings; however, this study will consider only those parts of the testimony related to the matter of the proper role of force in U.S. foreign policy in general and Korea in particular.

General MacArthur was the first witness to come before this special committee of the United States Senate. In his testimony he repeatedly expressed dissatisfaction with limitations on force that would deny the field commander the capability to produce decisive military results. Of the policy of limited war the General observed:

> That policy. . . seems to me to introduce a new concept into military operations–the concept of appeasement, the concept that when you use force, you can limit that force. . . . To me that would have a continued and indefinite extension of bloodshed, which would have limitless–a limitless end.[59]

In his statement MacArthur touched on a problem of Limited War policy (which is not unknown to those attempting to deter an opponent), namely, how does one bring an opponent to terms if military force does not threaten the defeat of the opponent. He again expressed the problem in Korea as follows: "You would not have the potentialities of destroying the enemy's military power and bringing the conflict to a decisive close in the minimum of time and with a minimum of loss."[60]

Later, the General offered this analysis: "War, in itself, is the application of superior force, and as we chose that path, and have entered upon that path, it seems to me that we must end it some way."[61] MacArthur did not seem to see war as *part* of "political intercourse," as Clausewitz had, but he mangled Clausewitz's dictum so as to make them separate entities. He expressed this understanding of the relationship of politics to war as follows:

> The general definition which for many decades has been accepted was that war was the ultimate process of politics; that when all other political means failed, you then go to force; and when you do that, the balance of control, the balance of concept, the main interest involved, the minute you reach the killing stage, is the control of the military.[62]

MacArthur believed that when *political* means fail, one then goes to war. This is not the same as saying that war *is* a political interaction between states. To MacArthur, war and politics stood discretely beside each other–each with its own particular logic and mode of behavior.

After General MacArthur testified, he was followed by the Secretary of Defense, George C. Marshall. Marshall had been the Chief of Staff of the United States Army during World War II and served as Secretary of State in the late 1940s. Marshall, in defense of the administration's position with regard to MacArthur's dismissal and the general conduct of the Korean War, summarized the goal of administration policy in Korea as continuing "to be the defeat of the aggression and the restoration of peace. We have persistently sought to confine the conflict to Korea and to prevent its spreading into a third world war."[63]

Force would not be used to effect a *decisive* blow upon the enemy, rather it would be used to erode the enemy's will to continue the struggle while a political settlement was being sought: "That method was to *inflict the greatest number of casualties* we could in order to break down not only the morale but the trained fabric of the Chinese Armies."[64] In effect Marshall was describing a war of attrition. He provided these details as to how the administration's plan might work:

[We would] inflict terrible casualties on the Chinese Communist forces. If we break the morale of their armies, but, more particularly, if we destroy their best trained armies as we have been in the process of doing, there it seems to me, you develop the best probability of reaching a satisfactory negotiatory basis with those Chinese Communist forces, without getting ourselves into what we think would be a great hazard toward developing a much enlarged struggle with consequently large casualties or a complete world war.[65]

Marshall did not delude himself that such a course of action would be easy or painless, but he felt the burden would have to be born if the post-Korean world were to be a favorable environment for the United States.

In response to a question from Senator Harry P. Cain of Washington as to how the Secretary would characterize the fighting in Korea (i.e., police action or war), Secretary Marshall responded, "I would characterize it as a limited war which I hope will remain limited."[66] This reply and those that preceded it shed much light on Marshall's thinking about the use of force and its relationship to policy. The Secretary clearly was able to subordinate military activities in one theater to a larger geostrategic conceptual framework. Politics and war did not stand side by side, as they did for MacArthur; rather, the use of force was subsumed under political objectives. Consequently, Marshall did not feel that military power had to be set loose so that it could apply the *decisive* logic of force to a political situation; military efforts could be used as part of a larger process of political bargaining.

After Secretary Marshall completed his testimony before the committee, the Chairman of the Joint Chiefs of Staff, General Omar Bradley, appeared as the next witness on May 15, 1951. In short, his position closely resembled Marshall's. General Bradley's opinion concerning the relationship of the political and military elements of war may be seen not only in his testimony but also in documents taken from the *Foreign Relations* volumes. At a Department of State-Joint Chiefs of Staff meeting of February 13, 1951, dealing with the issue of the 38th parallel in future operations, the memorandum states, "General Bradley expressed the opinion that the situation in Korea requires a determination of our political objectives. Then the military requirements to achieve these objectives can be determined."[67] Bradley's grand strategic outlook emphasized the importance of preserving European independence from Communist domination and did not favor being sucked into a large Asian war that might undermine that objective. As he said a general war with China "would involve us in the wrong war, at the wrong place, at the wrong time, and with the wrong enemy."[68] Because he did not want to let Korea fall to the Communists in North Korea and China, Bradley was willing to continue the fight in Korea–but at a level that did not threaten larger objectives. As he told the committee in his opening remarks:

> The fundamental military issue that has arisen is whether to increase the risk of a global war by taking additional measures that are open to the United States and its allies. We now have localized conflict in Korea. Some of the military measures under discussion might well place the United States in the position of responsibility for broadening the war and at the same time losing most if not all of our allies.[69]

To Bradley the purely military requirements of the conflict had to be subordinated to political necessity. Consequently, operations and tactics would need to be adjusted accordingly. Marc Trachtenberg objects to this remark being taken as a "symbol" or endorsement of " 'limited war' policy." He takes Bradley to mean "that if the United States were forced to fight the communists, the *right war* was a war against Russia herself, and the *right place* to fight was not at the periphery, but at the heart of Soviet power. Most important, it implied that if it had to be fought at all (Bradley of course hoped that it could be avoided), there was a *right time* for fighting it, namely, after American power had been built up."[70] To paraphrase a great line from Shakespeare: this interpretation of Bradley out-MacArthurs MacArthur.[71] It is clear that Marshall and Bradley thought that the true contest was with the Soviets and that America needed time to build up its own strength. They also felt, according to Foot, that MacArthur's proposed extension of the war "not only could not guarantee an end to the conflict but would very likely bring the Soviet Union directly into the hostilities, at the same time estranging America from its allies."[72] These facts, however, do not refute the belief that a limited war policy existed. In his Senate testimony, Secretary Marshall gave a credible defense of limited war not just in the periphery like Korea but for the entire U.S.—Soviet struggle:

> There can be, I think, no quick and decisive solution to this global struggle short of resorting to another world war. The cost of such a conflict

is beyond calculation. It is, therefore, our policy to contain Communist aggression in different areas without resorting to total war, if that be possible to avoid.

This policy may seem costly, if maintained over a period of years, but those costs would not be comparable at all to what happens if we get involved in what you might call an atomic war. Korea is only the latest challenger in this long, hard, continuing, world-wide struggle.[73]

Thus, Marshall was in no sense looking to atomic weapons as some way to end this long-run struggle with the Soviets in a quick and decisive manner. Rather, the thinking was that it was far better to fight these limited engagements than a total war, but if it had to be total war this was neither the time nor the place on which to embark on such an adventure, as Bradley stated.

Bradley indicated, as had Marshall, that a strategy of attrition was to be pursued. This point became clear as his testimony continued; he told the committee:

> From the military point of view we hope that by inflicting severe casualties on the enemy and proving to them that they are not invincible . . . that it is too costly a matter . . . that they will be willing to negotiate a peace with the United Nations.[74]

However, one should *not* overstate General Bradley's commitment to maintaining an endless war of attrition. In his testimony, he was asked by Senator Wayne Morse of Oregon (then a Republican he would later become an Independent and end his Senatorial career as a Democrat) if he had ever completely ruled out General MacArthur's recommendations. The Chairman of the Joint Chiefs of Staff replied:

> No, I have never taken the view that we would not—might not—take these very courses of action but we do not think that we ought to take them now. We ought to try every way we can to solve it without taking and thereby increasing the risks of war. Now if war comes anyway, or you cannot solve it without taking some of these steps, in a few months we may say, "Yes, we cannot do it any other way, and now we will do these things," and we are better prepared to risk the war, and there is no other solution, so we go ahead and take that risk; but I have never said we might not take that risk later on.[75]

Later General Bradley told Senator Bourke B. Hickenlooper (R-Iowa), "the Chiefs of Staff are unanimous in believing that we should fight this war as we are now fighting it, and try to run it this way, and if we can-not, we may try something else."[76]

In conclusion, General Bradley's attitude concerning the relation-ship between war and politics was presented clearly in an exchange he had with Senator Morse. The Senator asked, "Is it not true, General, that we no longer in the world can fight a war on a strictly military basis, but that we have to fight it also after giving consideration to diplomatic problems as well as military problems?" Bradley replied: "That is correct, and certainly your objectives in a war are not entirely military. In other words, the end results of a war are a combination of military and political considerations, and you use the military to obtain your political objectives."[77]

The Senate committee issued no final report, but a clear message emerged from the hearings. The administration had made it clear to the public that the war would remain limited and that attrition would be the method used to bring the enemy to terms. The decisive use of force entailed too many dangers and would, therefore, not be the means by which the U.S. achieved its objectives in Korea. Additionally, the hear-ings carried another message to the American people. The *JCS History* tells us, "It was made clear that this policy, contrary to General MacArthur's allegations, commanded the firm support of the nation's highest military advisors, the Joint Chiefs of Staff."[78]

The War Continues

Ridgway's military style was blunt and powerful. He intended to bleed the Chinese of their offensive strength. The fourth Chinese offensive was cut to pieces in February by American firepower after which U.N forces went on the offensive.[79] Seoul was liberated on March 14, 1951. In the months of April and May two Chinese offensives were absorbed and then repulsed. The number of casualties suffered by the Chinese during this period was horrific. In the month of April alone, the Chi-nese sustained 70,000 casualties.[80]

Once again Roger Dingman has brought our attention to the move-ment of atomic weapons by the United States in April 1951. By the end of March the U.N. command knew that a massive Chinese attack was in the offing. General Bradley was considering the possibility that this ground offensive might be accompanied by decisive military blows originating outside the Korean peninsula in China or the Soviet Union. In a meeting with the chairman of the Atomic Energy Commission, Gordon A. Dean, on April 6, 1951, President Truman painted a bleak picture of the military build-up that was facing the U.N. forces: bombers were concentrated in enormous numbers in Manchuria; Soviet submarines had become concentrated in the port at Vladivostok; and a large force of submarines had moved south of Sakhalin.[81]

As Dingman tells it, Truman's description of this concentration of forces was more alarming than the situation warranted. Chairman Dean was convinced of the seriousness of the situation, returned to his office, and made arrangements with General Vandenberg so that nine atomic bombs could be placed in air force custody. On April 7, 1951, the 99th Medium Bomb Wing "was ordered to pick up atomic bombs for transshipment to Guam." The wing flew to Guam and was ordered to remain there; as the sense of military urgency eased, the military task force never received orders to proceed to Okinawa.[82] Late in April after the Chinese resumed their offensive President Truman sent a second group of "nuclear-configured" aircraft across the Pacific.[83] Washington also issued General Ridgway new orders on April 28, 1951, that would allow him to "launch atomic strikes in retaliation for a major air attack originating from beyond the Korean peninsula."[84]

The B-29s and the atomic bombs returned to the United States in June 1951, and Truman did not send nuclear-armed bombers overseas again. Even though the effect of these deployments on Chinese and Soviet behavior was unclear, Dingman believes that the Truman administration had taken from these actions the lesson that these atomic weapons "could be used to convince enemies to respect and allies to support an armistice in Korea." He argues that it was this belief that supported Dean Acheson's efforts during an optimistic phase of the truce talks to gain prior allied approval of the "Greater Sanctions Statement." The statement, which was to be publicly issued after fighting stopped, would state the willingness of the allied nations to expand the war beyond its current limitations as to geographical boundaries. Given the atmosphere of the times it seems fair to say that the Greater Sanctions Statement, at least for the United States, also carried that vague aura of escalation to more destructive types of weaponry. It was intended to act as a deterrent against future communist aggression and indicated that the Truman administration "believed that nuclear superiority, when used with subtlety and restraint, could help manage the Korean War to an acceptable conclusion."[85]

As June began, the offensive power of the massive Chinese army had been completely drained from it; what remained was a mere shadow of the fighting force that had sent the U.N. troops reeling from the vicinity of the Yalu six months earlier.[86] Truce talks began on July 10, 1951, at Kaesong; later, on October 25, they were moved to Panmunjom, a location more suitable to the U.N. Command. By the end of 1951 the ground fighting in Korea had "tapered off to patrol clashes, raids, and small battles for possession of outposts in no-man's-land." On December 20, 1951, President Truman signed NSC 118/2 which stated that it would be in the overall interests of the U.S. to continue its Limited War policy even if the negotiations at Panmunjom did not bear fruit.[87] For the Chinese, the truce talks became the center of a war of propaganda waged to score points in international public opinion. With all of these obstacles to contend with, the negotiators were able to hammer out agreements on all but one of the agenda items by the spring of 1952, by which time Mark Clark had succeeded Ridgway as Far East Commander. The final diplomatic logjam occurred over the issue of the repatriation of prisoners of war.

With regard to the ground fighting in 1952 Maurice Matloff writes, "While argument over repatriation went on at Panmunjom, action at the front continued as a series of artillery duels, patrols, ambushes, raids, and bitter contests for outpost positions."[88] In late 1952 the lines of resistance remained substantially the same as they had been one year earlier despite the "furious and small-scale battles that took place." Even though American offensive action on the ground was limited, this was not the case with the bombing of North Korea. American and allied ground forces were never substantially threatened from the air, but the U.N. Air Force, despite increasingly difficult opposition from enemy fighters, was able to bomb the North.

During the course of the war restrictions on strategic bombing were gradually lifted. By the end of 1950 the city of Sinuiju had been razed by a mass fire raid using napalm. In one raid in July 1952 against Pyongyang, 2,300 gallons of napalm were used.[89] Fearing an enemy supply build-up in Rashin, a city located next to the Soviet Union, General Ridgway asked for and was granted permission to bomb that city; the raids were successfully carried out in August 1951. During the next sum-

mer (1952) the Yalu hydro-electric complexes on the Korean bank were
bombed as Washington tried to gain leverage which could break the
deadlock in the peace talks, and in April 1953 "air attacks were extended to the irrigation dams which supported rice production."[90]

Ending the War: Eisenhower and Atomic Weapons

Dwight D. Eisenhower was inaugurated President of the United States
on January 20, 1953. His campaign against Adlai Stevenson was highlighted by a speech in Detroit on October 24, 1952, in which he
pledged that immediately following the election he would "forego the
diversions of politics and concentrate on the job of ending the Korean
War. . . . That job requires a personal trip to Korea. I shall make that
trip. Only in that way could I learn how best to serve the American people in the cause of peace. I shall go to Korea."[91] Eisenhower did go to
Korea, on November 29, and began his return trip on December 5,
1952. Stephen Ambrose believes that the trip was valuable because it
convinced the president-elect that the military situation was intolerable
and that the war had to be ended.[92] Ambrose supports this point with
a quotation from Eisenhower's memoirs: "My conclusion as I left Korea
was that we could not stand forever on a static front and continue to
accept casualties without any visible results. Small attacks on small hills
would not end this war."

On March 5, 1953, Joseph Stalin died. It is not clear what impact
his death had on ending the war, but, at the very least, the Chinese
would have expected Moscow's reliability as suppliers and allies to
diminish as the struggle for internal power consumed the political energy of the Soviet Union. However, McGeorge Bundy argues that Stalin's
death was a turning point because it was he who had been pressuring
the Chinese to keep fighting.[93] At the end of March 1953 Zhou Enlai
proposed that negotiations should begin immediately on the exchange
of sick and wounded and then should proceed to an overall settlement
of the prisoner of war question.[94] He also indicated that the fate of the
POWs could be determined by a neutral country "so as to insure a just
solution to the question of their repatriation."[95] Indeed, this was a
major step toward solving the POW issue. Yet, upon the resumption of
talks on April 26, 1953, it was a matter of minutes before the negotiations were deadlocked over details of the POW exchange.[96]

While events outside the United States were changing the diplomatic environment, appropriate agencies within the U.S. government began to review American policy (as described in NSC 118/2 on December 20, 1951) and consider possible courses of action in Korea.[97] By April 2, 1953, the NSC Planning Board circulated the resulting report (numbered NSC 147). The underlying assumption of NSC 147 was a loss of faith in the bargaining process; consequently, its recommendations were based on an assumption of terminated or hopelessly stalled negotiations. The Planning Board recognized two broad categories of possible actions designed to bring an end to the fighting in Korea. The first alternative was to maintain the current restrictions on military operations; the second alternative removed those restrictions. "Under each major alternative there [were] analyzed three possible specific courses," which were labeled "courses" A to C and D to F.[98]

Courses A, B, and C appeared under the heading "Alternative I: Maintain Current Restrictions on Military Operations Against Manchuria and Communist China."[99] Course A called for a continuation of military activity at the then current level while building up ROK forces in order to redeploy U.S. forces from Korea. Course B proposed that military activity against the enemy be increased "with a view to making hostilities more costly to the enemy in the hope that he might agree to an armistice acceptable to the United States." Course C favored the continuation of aggressive air and naval actions while launching "a series of coordinated ground operations along the present line"; there would also be a major offensive whose goal would be to advance to the waist of Korea while inflicting maximum attrition on the opponents.

Courses D, E, and F appeared under the heading "Alternative II: Remove Current Restrictions on Military Operations Against Manchuria and Communist China." Course D suggested that pressure on the enemy be intensified "by stages" that would include air attacks and naval blockades against China and Manchuria; the goal under this proposal was to make the war "so costly to the enemy that a favorable settlement of the Korean war might be achieved." The next proposed course of action, E, called for a ground offensive to the waist of Korea, naval and air attacks against China and Manchuria, and a naval blockade, all intended "to inflict maximum possible destruction of enemy forces and materiel in Korea consistent with establishing a line at the waist, and to achieving a favorable settlement of the Korean War."

Course F, the last contending option, was the most aggressive: it envisaged a "coordinated, large scale offensive in Korea, and a naval blockade and air and naval attacks directly" against China and Manchuria with the goal of destroying "the bulk of the communist forces" in Korea and establishing a "unified, non-communist Korea."[100] The objectives of the second group of possible courses of action may be summarized as follows: for D, make the war of attrition much more costly; for E, move to the Korean "waist" while inflicting maximum casualties; for F, unify Korea under noncommunist rule.

The use of atomic weapons was also considered in the accompanying NSC staff study. Under the heading "Possible Alternatives" after which "Use of Atomic Weapons" is listed, the NSC study states, "Each of the suggested courses of action (except Course A) permits but does not require employment of atomic weapons."[101] The seriousness with which the use of atomic weapons was considered is revealed in appendices to a JCS memo "Future Courses of Action in Connection with the Situation in Korea."[102] The memo, written by the JCS, described the cause of the failure of American policy to end the war:

> It is believed that one of the basic reasons for failure to achieve an armistice is that sufficient military pressure has not been exerted to impose the requirement for an armistice on the enemy. As a result, the U.N. Command is confronted with enemy forces, with good morale numerically superior in strength with adequate logistical support, disposed in extremely well organized defensive positions in depth. A growing air potential, including jet light bombers, adds to these complications. Under these conditions the U.N. commander has stated that aggressive military action designed to achieve victory or an armistice on U.N. terms is not feasible with present forces operating under current restrictions. Furthermore, removal of restrictions cannot be exploited to the fullest without augmentation of forces.[103]

With respect to expanding military activities against China it is observed "that the most potentially effective weapon at our disposal is military air power."[104] A bit later it is argued that "Atomic attacks against enemy air bases and other targets would destroy or neutralize them quickly." The destruction of the Chinese air force was a necessity due to "its increasing offensive threat to U.N. security," and the military planners estimated that the requisite atomic attacks "would require temporary deployment of two medium bomb wings with atomic capability for the specific operations." The use of atomic weapons against China and Manchuria would in turn allow for the "reduction. . . for fighter-interceptors to possibly two wings" after the enemy air force had been destroyed.[105] As must be apparent, these are not the observations of officials who are lightly tossing about the idea of using atomic weapons. The study also made the point that the "efficacy of atomic weapons in achieving greater results at less cost of effort in furtherance of U.S. objectives in connection with Korea points to the desirability of re-evaluating the policy which now restricts the use of atomic weapons in the Far East."[106]

Discussions over possible courses of action in Korea continued throughout the month of April. In an NSC meeting of May 4, 1953, Eisenhower requested that the JCS prepare a briefing which "amounted in effect to a JCS review and comment on NSC 147."[107] At the next NSC meeting on May 13, 1953, the President brought up the cost-effectiveness of atomic weapons. The minutes read:

> The President . . . thought it might be cheaper, dollar-wise, to use atomic weapons in Korea than to continue to use conventional weapons against the dugouts which honeycombed the hills along which the enemy forces were presently deployed. This, the President felt, was particularly true if one took into account the logistic costs of getting conventional ammunition from this country to the front lines.[108]

It is clear that Eisenhower did not think of the atom bomb as being in a class of "unusable" weapons. On the other hand, he was also aware of the political difficulties connected with their use. In this meeting he argued that expanding the war to China was filled with political danger for the United States. In the NSC minutes Eisenhower comments that "the simple truth of the matter was that many people in the European countries believe that global war is much worse to contemplate than surrender to Communist imperialism."[109] He added that the Europeans were critical to our national defense and we could not afford their desertion. In this discussion one can discern two sides to President Eisenhower's thinking: one that was willing to use atomic weapons in order to apply force in the most powerful and cost-effective manner available and another that recognized the political pitfalls of using such horrific weapons.

During the next week the Joint Chiefs determined its recommendations and sent a memo to the Secretary of Defense on May 19, 1953. The next day, General Bradley and General Collins briefed the President and the NSC as to their conclusions. In the memo of May 19 the JCS adopted the majority position of the Joint Strategic Plans Committee.[110] The Joint Chiefs started their analysis by observing that Course A was "in accord with the national objectives outlined in NSC 118/2" and that this course had been followed by the U.N. since the commencement of the armistice negotiations.[111] In the "Comments on the Courses of Action" the Chiefs asserted that Course C, which did not call for attacks on China, "would very likely require extending the war into Manchuria in order to counter enemy air forces which would have our troops within striking range as they advance."[112] The Chiefs also made this important recommendation:

> Further, the Joint Chiefs of Staff feel that from the Military standpoint no Course of Action beyond "A" or "B" should be undertaken without a concurrent decision to employ atomic weapons on a sufficiently large scale to insure success. A piecemeal or limited employment, with the attendant risk of failure, or at best limited success, is not recommended.[113]

The memo also stated that these courses of action contained these substantial risks and costs. With these dangers well in mind, the Joint Chiefs recommended to the Secretary of Defense "that a combination of actions under Courses D, E, and F would be the most effective and the most economical in the long run for the United States to pursue in Korea." The Joint Chiefs summarized their recommendation as follows: "Extend and intensify military action against the enemy, to include air and naval operations directly against China and Manchuria, a coordinating offensive to seize position generally at the waist of Korea and be prepared for further operations."[114] They also stressed that "the necessary air, naval, and ground operations, including extensive strategical and tactical use of atomic bombs, be undertaken so as to obtain maximum surprise and maximum impact on the enemy, both militarily and psychologically."

The next day, the Joint Chiefs presented their conclusions to the President and the National Security Council. The President clearly understood the Chiefs; he summarized part of their position saying "if we went over to a more positive action against the enemy in Korea, it would be necessary to expand the war outside of Korea and that it would be necessary to use the atomic bomb."[115] Eisenhower expressed concern that Japanese population centers would be completely open to Soviet atomic reprisals, and General Collins replied "that there was no clear answer to the President's anxiety." Collins also repeated his concern that the U.S./U.N. positions at Inchon and Pusan were exposed to such attacks. The President then indicated that a reasonable estimate of the D-Day for this operation might be in May 1954; then a discussion of American readiness and mobilization followed. The time needed to prepare for the offensive would be considerable because more conventional forces would have to be redeployed to Korea from other areas and new forces would have to be mobilized. Eisenhower told the assembled group, "Everything . . . should be in readiness before the blow actually [falls]."[116] General Bradley supported the President on this point by observing that the Joint Chiefs "were themselves convinced of the necessity of carrying out the proposed operation with great speed if it were to be done successfully."

The unwillingness of the allies to go along was then considered. Eisenhower advocated beginning a gradual campaign to get the allies on board. He felt this would be much better than springing the decision on them. Under Secretary of State Walter Bedell Smith indicated that he had already begun to plant such ideas with the British and the Dominion Ambassadors. Smith added "that a quick victory would go far to sell our allies on even the most drastic course of action in Korea."[117] The minutes of the meeting's conclusion read:

> At the conclusion of the discussion, the President stated that if the members of the Council agreed, he wished the record to show that if circumstances arose which would force the United States to an expanded effort in Korea, the plan selected by the Joint Chiefs of Staff was most likely to achieve the object we sought. His only real worry . . . was over the possibility of intervention by the Soviets. He feared the Chinese much less, since the blow would fall so swiftly and with such force as to eliminate Chinese Communist intervention.[118]

Thus, the inhibitions with respect to widening the war had been greatly eroded by mid-May 1953 when the National Security Council met to consider its options. In fact, the brief memo summarizing the discussion and decisions of the meeting (numbered NSC Action 794) stated that the NSC "agreed that it was the sense of the National Security Council that, *if* conditions arise requiring more positive action in Korea, the course of action recommended by the Joint Chiefs of Staff should be adopted as a general guide."[119] The seriousness and importance of this meeting has been noted by other scholars. In the introduction to the *JCS History*, Terence Gough observed, "The successful conclusion of an armistice two months [after the May decision] apparently came none too soon to preserve the status of Korea as a limited war."[120] The statements of the President during the meeting and the content of the NSC action paper should not be interpreted as having given orders to put these ideas into effect: as Robert J. Watson observes, "The Council noted and discussed these recommendations but took no formal action."[121]

Richard Betts supports this conclusion, "NSC Action 794 was not a commitment, but it was as close to a final decision as a president can come, short of the moment of execution."[122] In this case "moment of decision" might be more appropriate than "moment of execution" because Eisenhower's decision to proceed with solving the logistical, manpower, and strategic problems of the operation would have preceded the actual order to execute by nine months to a year.[123] Betts notes that Eisenhower wanted a settlement with China and did not want the situation in the Far East to reach the point in which the Joint Chiefs' plans would be needed. Nevertheless, Betts regards the May 20 meeting as a "climactic" event in which the President "went to unusual lengths to formalize and confirm a plan for [the] use of nuclear weapons."[124]

During this period of governmental contingency planning, the negotiations at Panmunjom crept along. It was at this time that the atomic strategy, was in the words of Richard Betts "being translated in vague—*very* vague—diplomatic pressure."[125] Secretary of State Dulles began a trip to India on May 20 for three days of meetings with Prime Minister Nehru. The record of their first conversation is illuminating. Dulles wrote:

> Mr. Nehru urged the importance of concluding an armistice, stating that he feared otherwise the fighting would extend. I agreed with his estimate, stating that if the armistice negotiations collapsed, the United

States would probably make a stronger rather than a lesser military exertion, and that this might well extend the area of the conflict.[126]

Dulles wrote in the memo, "(Note: I assumed this would be relayed.).". Dulles indicated that the United States would not compromise on the POW issue. The next day in his meeting with Dulles, Nehru twice brought up the Secretary's remark of the previous day that a breakdown in the armistice negotiations would lead to more intense fighting. The second time Dulles "made no comment [and] allowed the topic to drop."[127] It is worth noticing that Dulles does not record having specifically made an atomic threat, although it might have been interpreted by Nehru to have been one.

Similarly obscure statements were delivered by the American Ambassador to the Soviet Union, Charles E. (Chip) Bohlen, who indicated to the Department of State on May 24, 1953, that in relaying the "importance and seriousness" of America's final bargaining position to Soviet Foreign Minister Vyacheslav Molotov he "would avoid all indication of threat." Bohlen also observed that it "might not be harmful to point out . . . that a rejection by North Koreans and Chinese of these proposals and consequent failure to reach agreement in armistice talks would create a situation which the US Government is seeking most earnestly to avoid."[128]

"Seeking most earnestly to avoid" is very subtle indeed, and it is not surprising that scholars like Roger Dingman do not see this message as part of a campaign of atomic diplomacy. He writes, "[Bohlen's] words in Moscow, like Dulles's in New Dehli, represented an appeal for cooperation more than a threat of atomic action in the absence of agreement." Earlier in his article, Dingman makes a similar point when he concludes that the 'decision' of May 20, 1953, was not "the prologue to an attempt at coercive atomic diplomacy. Instead, Washington engaged in milder, non-nuclear diplomacy."[129]

General Andrew Goodpaster, a member of the Eisenhower Administration, recalls explicitly that the nuclear threats were sent to the Chinese. In an oral history interview he discusses Eisenhower's account of these events in his memoirs, "I'm not sure he identifies how it was passed, but in fact I think it's known that it was passed through the Indians. The message was essentially that if the war continued, we would not be limited in our choice of weapons, and that included the nuclear weapon. So he was, in effect, sending word of the possibility of [the] use [of] the nuclear weapon if the war dragged on or if they increased its scale."[130]

Rosemary Foot, who is skeptical of the effect of this atomic diplomacy, admits that "[t]he threat had been made, the opponents in the conflict had supposedly been apprised of the position."[131] Foot is wary of the argument that this nuclear gambit ended the war because she does not believe that the Chinese received the signals.[132] Nevertheless, Foot, ex-Eisenhower Administration officials, and other scholars assert convincingly that the United States at the least *attempted* to play the atomic card and would have been willing to use it. Foot informs us with some dismay that in the May 20 NSC meeting no direct reference was made to an NSC subcommittee report of May 18, 1953, "Net Capabilities of the USSR to inflict Direct Injury on the United States." That paper estimated "that a Soviet attack would result in casualties of 9 million, would destroy 24% of U.S. bombers with an atomic delivery capability, and damage air bases so as to reduce the sortie rate per month by 50 percent."[133] Sherman Adams, presidential chief of staff, relates in his memoirs that "atomic missiles" were moved to Okinawa in the spring of 1953, and he supports the position that Dulles did send a message to China via Nehru.[134]

Foot also brings our attention to Dulles's statements at a conference in Bermuda with the British and French in December 1953, during which Dulles told the two allies that had the war not been ended the United States intended to use atomic weapons against the Chinese and to eliminate geographical restrictions on the use of force. She notes that the Secretary of State's remarks did not "even suggest that administration had been bluffing."[135] And the British perceived the talks in this way. In a December 4 meeting Churchill accepted Eisenhower's proposed use of atomic weapons if a deliberate breach of the armistice occurred; the Prime Minister also told Eisenhower that the President's briefing had "put him in a position to say to Parliament that he had been consulted in advance and had agreed."[136] They spoke about Korea again at dinner on the evening of the fifth of December, and President Eisenhower "reiterated what he had told Churchill on the previous day, that America was prepared to use the atomic bomb."[137]

The talks at Panmunjom seemed likely to become deadlocked. On May 22, 1953, while the negotiations were recessed a "final" negotiating proposal was sent to General Clark in Tokyo.[138] It was to be made clear to the Chinese and North Koreans that this would be the final American offer. If it was rejected General Clark "was authorized to *break off* the truce talks rather than recess them, and to carry on the war in new ways never yet tried in Korea."[139] This was to include even heavier bombing of sensitive targets in North Korea and the addition of many more dikes, vital to flood prevention in the North, to the target list. The United Nations delegation at Panmunjom made its final proposal on the POW issue on May 25, 1953.

Fortunately, the Chinese did not provoke these harsh actions by continuing their refusal to block an agreement. On June 4, 1953, at the next plenary session of the negotiations "the Communists accepted, with minor changes, the final UNC plan for prisoners."[140] The last details were rapidly settled, and an armistice was signed on July 27, 1953, despite obstructions by South Korean President Syngman Rhee. After the hostilities ended the "Greater Sanctions Statement" was released on August 7, 1953, in a statement from General Clark to the U.N. Security Council. The sixteen United Nations members with forces in Korea had signed the declaration in Washington on July 27, 1953. The statement, which is also referred to as the "Statement of Sixteen," pledged the support of these nations in maintaining the armistice and in bringing about a "united, independent and democratic Korea."[141] The penultimate paragraph of the Greater Sanctions Statement read:

> We affirm, in the interests of world peace, that if there is a renewal of the armed attack, challenging again the principles of the United Nations, we should again be united and prompt to resist. The consequences of such a breach of the armistice would be so grave that, in all probability, it would not be possible to confine hostilities within the frontiers of Korea.[142]

Nor would it be likely that the weapons employed would remain non-atomic. The last paragraph was brief but contained an explicit warning to the communist nations concerning aggression in Asia: "Finally, we are of the opinion that the armistice must not result in jeopardizing the restoration or the safe guarding of peace in any other part of Asia."[143]

The planned severity of the response did not decrease after the signing of the armistice; the understandings reached at the NSC meeting of

May 20, 1953, were reaffirmed in late 1953 and early 1954.[144] On
November 20, 1953, President Eisenhower signed NSC 170/1, which,
in the event of renewed hostilities in Korea, directed that military and
diplomatic measures approved at the critical NSC meeting of six
months earlier be implemented.[145] If war erupted in Korea again,
Eisenhower told Congressional leaders that the plan was "to hit them
with everything we['ve] got."[146] On January 8, 1954, another NSC
meeting discussed the contingency of the resumption of the war in
Korea. The President did not seem to be planning atomic retaliation
without reflection: late in the meeting he commented:

> we should get tough right away quick and get into the business with
> both feet. Let's have all our plans ready to go full out. It is easier to
> retreat from this kind of situation than to go ahead promptly without
> preparation. *When you finally decide to resort to force you should plan no
> limits to its use.*[147]

One could hardly ask for a more concise statement of the All-or-Nothing philosophy that force should be used decisively to quickly crush
one's opponent once war commences.

Ending the War: Considerations on the Scholarly Debate

A detailed presentation of the events leading up to the termination of the
Korean War has been given because this aspect of the conflict sheds light
on how the Truman and Eisenhower administrations viewed the limitations on the use of force that were in place. The Truman administration
after having approved NSC 48/5 and confirmed this policy with NSC
118/2 had settled on a course of limited war; had the talks broken down
it is hard to conceive of that administration going beyond "Course A" or
"Course B" as listed in NSC 147. The new administration was willing
to accept a settlement at the 38th parallel, if the settlement came within
a reasonable amount of time. However, President Eisenhower did not
view the use of force in the same way as his predecessor did. As he said,
"When you finally decide to resort to force you should plan no limits to
its use."[148] Later chapters will support the conclusion, as does this one,
that Eisenhower's approach to the use of force was Jominian.

Another issue bears notice: to what extent did the "atomic diplomacy" of Eisenhower and Dulles in late May 1953 cause the war to end?

The historical field is in some turmoil on this question at the present, and it will probably take some time for the issue to be resolved.[149] Lewis and Litai present convincing evidence when they argue that the Chinese did feel atomic pressure from the United States. But the outcome of that debate is not the crucial issue for our purposes here. What is of importance is whether Eisenhower's decision of May 20, 1953, signified his approval of greatly expanding the war. The documents and the opinions of Rosemary Foot, Richard Betts, JCS historians, and George and Smoke support the conclusion that the President was willing to expand the war to China and use atomic weapons if the Chinese did not come to terms.[150] By the spring of 1953, the Limited War policy of NSC 48/5 and NSC 118/2 was on the verge of bankruptcy, and had the Chinese not ended the war it is most likely that a devastating blow would have been visited upon them.

In an important reinterpretation of events in Korea Marc Trachtenberg, professor of history at the University of Pennsylvania, argues that a short period of American nuclear superiority at the beginning of 1953 was an important cause of the more aggressive American policy in Korea. "The resurgence of American military power in late 1952 and 1953," he writes, "led to a much greater willingness to escalate, if that was needed to bring the Korean conflict to a successful conclusion."[151] In effect, he makes a structural, balance-of-power argument. Accordingly Trachtenberg sees little philosophical difference between the Truman and Eisenhower administrations in terms of their perspectives on war-fighting. With this in mind the question becomes whether this strategic shift, if it occurred, brought a change in the American conduct of the war. Additionally, Trachtenberg must demonstrate that a strategic shift did occur.

According to a 1951 government estimate, the U.S. would still maintain a marked atomic superiority over the Soviets in mid-1953.[152] A briefing memorandum for that document stated that the Department of State's policy planning staff believed that "a surprise mid-day attack on our most heavily populated and industrialized centers, about 12–14 bombs might be delivered on target with casualties upwards of 4,000,000 persons."[153] NSC 140/1 of May 18, 1953, which Trachtenberg cites, estimated that the Soviets would be able to produce a maximum of 9 million casualties in 1953 and 12.5 million in 1955; half of these would be deaths. As for economic damage: "Initial paralysis of all industry, including war-supporting industry, located within the areas attacked. This paralysis would affect one-third of the total U.S. industrial production in 1953 and two-thirds in 1955."[154] Trachtenberg concludes from this and other estimates available at the time that "even as late as 1953 or 1954 fighting and, in some meaningful sense, winning an air-atomic war was still 'thinkable.' It would probably be a long war, and the devastation would be terrible, but the United States would survive as a functioning society."[155] This is an extreme judgment. It is hard to imagine that an American administration would see such a situation as a "window" for action unless its back were against the wall. This sense of exhaustion with the Korean War appears to have been the motivating force behind the shift in American policy. Reason and bargaining had produced no fruitful results: escalation was beginning to be the only way to end the fighting. Certainly, had the U.S. been in a position of inferiority compared to the Soviets these plans would not have been considered, but, having a short-term edge on the USSR could not have been all that reassuring.[156]

The great value of Trachtenberg's article is its demonstration, through massive documentation, that the Eisenhower administration was much more at ease with the thought of using nuclear weapons than was its predecessor. Eisenhower thought that if weapons were available, human nature being what it is, they would be used.[157] It therefore is quite possible that the President would not have been so impressed by a temporary favorable strategic balance. He seemed resigned to the existence of nuclear weapons and appeared to be ready to conduct his policy come what might. Trachtenberg correctly concludes that "the Eisenhower strategy has to be taken seriously, that it was not at bottom (as some people argue) simply a gigantic bluff."[158] However, the Eisenhower perspective was conceptual and not a mere reflection of structural power relationships in the world at large. Trachtenberg recognizes this truth as well when he notes that Eisenhower's thinking could have come from the first few pages of Clausewitz's *On War* in which "war has an innate tendency to become absolute."[159] As stated above, it is difficult to conceive of President Truman moving beyond options "A" or "B" in NSC 147. One can draw this inference from Truman's Korea policy. He simply was not predisposed to using atomic weapons.

Limited War Theory and Korea

As discussed in the previous chapter, by the time of the Korean War's outbreak a number of government officials were beginning to question the general strategic reliance of the United States on doctrines of total retaliation and all-out war. George Kennan and Paul Nitze were the most prominent of these strategic planners. The war in Korea provided powerful support to arguments of this kind. Korea, by its mere existence, demonstrated that the United States and the Soviet Union could clash in ways that did not demand total war. Bernard Brodie tells us, "Shortly, after the Korean War ended, the theory of limited war became increasingly a subject of discussion and development."[160] He dates the beginning of the *public* debate on limited war as "about 1954."[161] Brodie is not alone in this assessment. One of the most important writers in the 1950s on limited war, Robert Osgood, wrote of the Korean War's impact:

> One can hardly overestimate the importance of the United States achievement in containing the Communist attack on South Korea without precipitating total war. By this achievement the nation went a long way toward demonstrating that it could successfully resist direct military aggression locally by limited war in the secondary strategic areas, where a demonstrated capacity for local resistance was the only effective deterrent to Communist military expansion.[162]

It would be incorrect to assume that those attracted to Limited War thinking were solely civilian. Maxwell Taylor, the last commander of the Eighth Army in Korea, argued vehemently for Limited War capabilities as Chief of Staff of the Army in the late 1950s. He writes, however, that it was difficult to successfully advance the Limited War position within the Eisenhower Administration because that term "suggested Korea, a thought which was repulsive to officials and public alike."[163] Civilian officials did not adhere to just one view of how best to employ military force: if Taylor is correct there was a major divergence of opinion between the civilian members of the Truman and Eisenhower Administrations—the attitudes of Truman and Eisenhower themselves differed greatly with respect to keeping the limits on the use of force in place and considering the use of atomic weaponry.[164] And—as will be shown below—some military personnel did not share

Taylor's enthusiasm for this more political form of warfare. It should not surprise us then that one of the Senate's most distinguished leaders, Robert A. Taft (R-Ohio), criticized fighting a limited war in Korea. John Lewis Gaddis writes that in 1951, "Taft too warned strongly of the dangers of protracted, limited wars, and of the loss of strategic initiative they entailed." These complaints sound very much like those lodged by some military personnel and some high-level civilians in the Eisenhower Administration.[165]

With all that being said, William O'Brien provides an accurate summary of Korea's central importance to the development of Limited War thinking when he writes:

> The Korean War was a limited war that provided a basis for development of the limited war theories of the 1950s and 1960s. Not withstanding considerable dissatisfaction with the conduct and results of the Korean War, it was widely accepted as a preferable alternative to the contemporary alternatives of total war and acquiescence in aggression.[166]

It is safe to say then that the Korean War provided the tangible experience which was of tremendous assistance in the construction of theories of limited war. The extent to which it was "widely accepted as a preferable alternative" to traditional approaches to the use of force depended on the specific community one was considering. O'Brien's assertion is certainly true of the cadre of civilian, strategic analysts that was amassing in the 1950s. More detailed consideration of Korea's impact on Limited War thinking will be deferred until a later chapter focuses on the most important aspect of political-military thinking in the 1950s: the decline of "massive retaliation" and the rise of "flexible response."

One other point should be made. To the extent that threats of total war caused the Chinese to come to terms, it undermines Limited War theory as a viable policy guide. That is, if the policy of limited war succeeded only because the Chinese believed destruction was imminent, then the "lessons" taken from Korea in the 1950s and 1960s, were poorly grounded in historical fact. Even if one concludes that the Chinese did not perceive an atomic threat, the mere fact that President Eisenhower was willing to abandon the Limited War policy of NSC 48/5 and 118/2 in order to obtain an armistice points to the tremendous difficulties that inhere in using force nondecisively against an opponent possessing great resources and the will to fight.

Korea and the Never Again School

Another widespread reaction to the Korean War was that the United States should refrain from becoming involved in limited wars in the future, particularly in Asia. There was a number of reasons for this sentiment, not the least of which was the war's unpopularity. Robert Osgood states without equivocation, "The United States has never fought a war more unpopular than the Korean War."[167] The roots of that unpopularity lay in the very nature of the war itself: its indecisiveness. In his extremely important book on civil-military relations Richard Betts observes:

> The wounds and divisions that three years of indecisive war had wrought within the military and between the military and political leaders ran deep and led many [Betts is referring to members of the military with "many"] to resolve not to be caught in another war of attrition. In the long term this frustration led to more acrimony between military and civilians from 1964 to 1968, as the United States slid into a limited war in Vietnam. In the shorter term, it led the soldiers to resist any ground combat commitments in Asia.[168]

Roger Hilsman makes a similar point in his book, *To Move A Nation.* Hilsman, appointed Director of the State Department's Bureau of Intelligence in February 1961 and an expert in counterinsurgency, describes the thinking of many in the military when he writes "by 1961 it was a shibboleth among the Joint Chiefs of Staff that the United States ought never again to fight a limited war on the ground in Asia or perhaps never again to fight any kind of war on the ground in Asia."[169] While the military was unsettled by the domestic unpopularity of the war, it was the manner in which the war was conducted that was deemed most odious to those who had fought in Korea.

It was difficult for many in the military to adapt to the constraints of limited war. Callum MacDonald says, "Only Ridgway adapted comfortably to the demands of a limited war, regarding Korea as but one element in a global struggle with Soviet communism."[170] Generals Edward M. Almond, James A. Van Fleet, and Mark Clark each chafed under the restrictions placed on their commands. Even Ridgway took the lesson from Korea that limited wars of the Korean-type were disastrous and did his utmost to prevent American intervention at Dienbienphu, so it appears that Ridgway's tolerance of the policy may have been due to military respect of civilian authority especially in the wake of MacArthur's firing.[171] Van Fleet did not challenge his political superiors in public, as MacArthur had, but he quickly made his feelings known after leaving the armed forces in February 1953.

On the day of his departure from the command of the Eighth Army Van Fleet created a small controversy. The *New York Times* reported, "In answer to a question whether the United Nations forces could launch a successful ground offensive 'at this time,' General Van Fleet replied with one word—'certainly.' "[172] Van Fleet's comment stirred up a debate which had then been going on as to the amount of time that would be needed to prepare the U.N. forces for a general advance to the waist of Korea. Later in the week the *New York Times* reported that Van Fleet was expected to testify before Congress that the launching of a decisive attack on the Chinese would require an extension of Selective Service and greatly increased level of war materiel.[173] So, even though his initial statement was exaggerated the General made no retraction about the feasibility of a decisive attack on the communist positions.

Van Fleet saved his broadside against American policy in Korea for a two-part article he wrote in *Life* magazine for May 11 and 18, 1953. Early in the first piece he posed a question which set the tone for the article, "Why, when we are so thoroughly and completely superior to the Chinese Reds in North Korea, do we even consider anything less than genuine peace?" (p. 127) Van Fleet admitted his consternation and asserted, "Having never trusted the communist intentions in the long and futile peace talks that began in 1951, I always favored fighting the war to its conclusion (p. 128)." In the second article he told his readers that the only policy that made sense was to achieve military victory over the aggressor: "There is no easy way out. The only bright side to the picture is that victory in Korea is much easier to obtain than our government's weak policy in the past would have indicated (p. 172)." He assured *Life*'s readers that a continuation of the war of attrition being fought in Korea would be much more costly than an "all-out battle for victory." In the two articles Van Fleet listed at least two opportunities that the United States had to easily defeat the communist forces.[174]

Further Never Again sentiments of Van Fleet and Almond may be found in the record of the hearings of the Senate Subcommittee to Investigate the Administration of the Internal Security Act and Other Internal Security Laws. The committee was chaired by Senator William Ezra Jenner (R-Indiana). The testimony before the committee is not very diplomatic and some prominent figures of the Truman administration are harshly criticized. The following is an excerpt of Van Fleet's testimony which began on September 29, 1954:

> Counsel: Could we have won the war in Korea?
> Van Fleet: Certainly. Let me say that everybody in the Eighth Army, to include our United Nations allies and the Koreans, believed in victory and believed they could achieve victory. I still believe we could have achieved victory in Korea.

On the next page of the record, Van Fleet took the point even further:

> The Chairman: General, let me ask at this point: Would you want to fight another war with American boys under those conditions?
> Van Fleet: Of course, I have seen so much destruction and horror of war, Mr. Chairman, that I think to fight in any war is a terrible thought. But under justified reasons and to preserve our freedom, I believe I would be ready to go to war again and that in any future war . . . . *we would never do it again like we did in Korea.*[175]

The record of the subcommittee then moves on to the testimony of Lt.-General Edward Almond, commander of the X Corps (the Inchon invasion force).[176] After the General was introduced to the committee an interview with *U.S. News and World Report* published on February 13, 1953, was reproduced. The record of excerpts of Almond's interview reads as follows:

> I had no confidence in the armistice talks then, and I don't now. . . . to harangue and delay and allow your opponent to become stronger so that he can fight you harder later on is unpardonable, in my opinion as a soldier. . . . My philosophy is to engage the chosen enemy to defeat him in battle. . . . My belief is that when we engage an enemy, we ought to defeat that enemy.[177]

Almond also discussed his feelings concerning the restrictions that were placed on his command:

> Almond: I have a great resentment when I find . . . that I am not permitted or I am prevented from obtaining recompense for those losses when the mission of any battlefield commander is to win in the field and not be denied a victory for his forces.[178]

These words of Almond's carry a particularly strong endorsement of the idea that force should only be used when it can bring "victory" over the opponent in the field of battle.

Van Fleet and Almond were not the only military leaders from Korea to criticize the war. General Clark, the American Far East commander, was also reluctant to repeat the experience of limited war. The most quoted statement of the Never Again thinking was made by Clark in his memoirs:

> Never, never again should we be mousetrapped into fighting another defensive ground war on [the Korean] peninsula. Never should we commit numerically inferior American troops—the first team at that— against numerically superior forces of the enemy's second team unless we are prepared to win.[179]

Throughout these remarks one does not hear a criticism of going to war per se. Rather, it is focused on fighting in nondecisive engagements of attrition that have little prospect by themselves or as part of a larger operational level strategy of defeating the enemy. The reader should note that even though these are military men testifying, they are doing so before the Jenner Subcommittee which was extremely vocal in its denunciations of the Truman administration's handling of the war. The generals were clearly invited before a sympathetic body of civilian politicians who desired support for their public arguments against the way the Korean War was conducted.

Korea and the Morale of United Nations Forces

The Korean War and limited wars, in general, have been criticized for the negative effect they have had on the morale of fighting forces. Callum MacDonald describes the problem in Korea as follows:

If many professional soldiers found the constrictions of limited war frustrating and believed that there could be "no substitute for victory," it
also produced problems of morale and motivation. The war seemed to
lack any clear political aim and its purpose was sometimes questioned.[180]

Having clear objectives is very important to soldiers. Anthony Kellet
describes their importance, "The concept of goals or objectives is central
to the understanding of both motivation and morale; it has been shown
that a group's cohesion is very much dependent on its having a mission
or objective."[181] He adds that soldiers need to have some means by which
they can "measure the progress of the fighting and assess the importance
of their contribution." Such means were generally not available in Korea
after the war became static. There would be "no long movements, no
great concentrations for large operations, no deep penetrations of the
enemy's front, no 'victory.' "[182] General Van Fleet was completely frustrated by the static war of Korea. According to MacDonald he called it
"a canker slowly eating at the morale of his troops."[183]

The effects on the U.N. forces were not imagined. The official history of Canadian participation in the Korean War sheds much light on
the matter. The history says of Korea, "This was a business-like war, if
one can tolerate the term in this context, in which the aim was not the
total destruction of the enemy. Commanders at all levels bitterly resent-
ed every dead soldier as a loss which could never be made up merely by
killing Chinese."[184] Herbert Wood, a Canadian historian, quotes in his
book *Strange Battleground* a psychologist who had studied the war and
its destructive effect on morale and fighting spirit: "A desire for social
approval, for continued acceptance by peers, is a very important reason
why a soldier will face a danger despite fear. When social approval is
possible without all-out effort, it is little wonder that there was less than
a total commitment in . . . attitude."[185] The concluding sentence of
Strange Battleground reads, "This was a new situation, without precedent in Canadian military experience, and it is clearly imperative that
someone decide just what attitudes and techniques are necessary if the
traditional kind of Army is to endure it."

The same condition was observed in the American Army as General Van Fleet's remark indicates. In fact, it was reported that the morale

of U.S. forces collapsed in May 1953. General Maxwell Taylor, commander of the Eighth Army, described the situation as follows: "Political objectives hold little appeal and are not highly evaluated generally by soldiers in battle positions, whereas a clearly defined physical objective constitutes a goal, attainment of which tends to hold promise of a cessation of conflict."[186]

Thus, the practice of limited war is not as simple as it seems in theory. In fact, the article by James Thomas, just cited, was written to urge the U.S. Army to train its soldiers so they could deal with the psychological rigors of limited war.

The power of Limited War policy on the effectiveness of fighting forces has been examined here for two reasons. First, the destructive impact on morale has reinforced the Never Again argument within the nation and the armed services concerning possible intervention into limited wars. Second, this negative effect of limited war on morale is related to the very nature of force itself. As stated in the introductory chapter, a tension exists in limited war between the political objective and the instrument of the state, organized violence or force. The logic of force is the logic of compulsion, and it exerts pressure to expand one's military efforts until decisive results are achieved. Anything that inhibits the decisive use of force obstructs the fulfillment of the instrument's potential. The soldier, restricted by the constraints of limited war, feels this intuitively. The soldier senses, as many did in Korea, that he is not being allowed to fulfill his purpose or function as part of the military instrument. With these factors in mind and the empirical results described above, it is not surprising that the United States witnessed a pronounced decline in the morale of its fighting forces in Korea and later in Vietnam.

The Korean War was the first limited war the United States fought in the Twentieth Century. Prior to Korea, the United States believed itself to have a tradition extending back to the Civil War of fighting decisive, all-out wars. This changed after the Chinese invasion of November 1950. The United States government decided to seek a negotiated peace, and after two years of bargaining the war finally came to a conclusion. The conceptual tension within the nature of war was confirmed as the experience of limited war dramatically pointed to the opposing tendencies within war. Those who advanced the inchoate position of the Limited War School argued, true to the Clausewitzian dictum, that the means of war would have to be made the servant of the political objectives if catastrophic escalations of conflict were to be avoided. The first members of the incipient Never Again School advanced the proposition that future military interventions must be guided by the willingness to engage one's enemy with the goal of seeking decisive military "victory"; otherwise the employment of force would lead to ineffective wars of attrition. Thus, as a matter of intellectual history two distinguishable schools of thought were now more clearly defined whereas prior to Korea the ideas at the heart of this problem of properly using force were not formulated to this degree. This is not to say that the members of the two respective groups perceived themselves as belonging to recognizable "schools." Rather, the various actors knew that they opposed the policies and recommendations of other strategists and government officials. It would be a few more years before conceptions of "flexible response" and "massive retaliation" would bring the divisions into even sharper relief.

4 | The Dienbienphu Crisis

The May 1954 surrender of the French garrison at Dienbienphu provides an early opportunity to study post-Korean all-or-nothing conceptions of the use of force. The Eisenhower Administration's decisionmakers did not favor limited war policy for a number of reasons; among the most important of them was a deep distrust of fighting wars that way. While an account of the entire war between the French and the Vietminh, the communist, revolutionary forces of Ho Chi Minh, is not required here, a brief description of events leading to Dienbienphu is useful.[1]

From the End of World War II to Dienbienphu

Japan's defeat in the Second World War ended that nation's occupation of Indochina. The Vietnamese Emperor Bao Dai abdicated his throne, on August 25, 1945, just a week before the Japanese officially surrendered, ceding power to Ho Chi Minh. France, the colonizer of Indochina, did not recognize the new government and decided to reassert its imperial control of the region. In November 1946 war broke out between the Vietminh and the French. During what would become a prolonged struggle the United States allied itself with the French. Direct U.S. financial and military aid to France became available in ever-increasing quantities after the outbreak of the Korean War, but this did not stop the steady decline of France's military position in Indochina.

In the spring of 1953 Paris appointed a new commander for Indochina after the Eisenhower administration, which had been underwriting a large portion of French war costs, made known its displeasure with the quality of French military leadership there. Lt. General Henri Navarre, a veteran of both world wars, was given the assignment and soon presented a new plan for fighting the war—one designed to eventually take the French forces off the strategic defensive and restore maneuver and aggressiveness to their operations.[2] The United States approved the Navarre Plan in September 1953. Then, the French and Vietminh began to prepare for a test of strength in Laos which had increasingly fallen under the control of the communist forces. The strategic concept for a French strike at Dienbienphu had been germinating since the summer of 1953, and on November 11, 1953, operational instructions were sent to the air and ground elements that would participate in the recapture of the distant village in northwest Vietnam near the Laotian border. Dienbienphu lay in a valley near the intersection of several important roads in northwest Vietnam; Navarre hoped to hold the area and block an expected Vietminh invasion of Laos while inflicting unacceptable casualties on the enemy in a setpiece battle.

Situated in a valley surrounded by commanding heights some 10 to 12 kilometers distant, Dienbienphu clearly did not present a suitable site for a series of defensive outposts. The French believed these high points too distant for the effective deployment of artillery, but that judgment proved to be tragically incorrect. The French began to drop their paratroop forces at Dienbienphu on November 20, 1953, and they encountered stiff resistance which they were able to overcome. However, it soon became clear that Dienbienphu could not be reached by friendly forces on the ground; to those with military training it was apparent that the outpost was becoming increasingly isolated. In fact, on December 29, 1953, General Navarre ordered that a contingency plan for conducting a fighting withdrawal be prepared, although he had never seriously contemplated putting it into effect. Indeed, the plan was not submitted until January 21, 1954, by which time the garrison was surrounded by a major enemy force that made withdrawal impossible in any case.[3] By late February 1954 French and colonial forces of 12,000 in Dienbienphu were surrounded by Vietminh troops numbering approximately 35,000.[4] The crisis intensified on March 13, 1954, after the Vietminh infantry overran one of the defensive strong points established by the French. The siege of Dienbienphu rapidly became an international crisis when France attempted to secure direct American military support for its beleaguered forces.[5]

Eisenhower and Indochina: Background to the Crisis

With respect to Indochina the Eisenhower administration's general statement of national security policy, NSC 162/2, had made this assessment well before the crisis at Dienbienphu occurred: "Certain other countries, such as Indo-China or Formosa, are of such strategic importance to the United States that an attack on them probably would compel the United States to react with military force either locally at the point of attack or generally against the military power of the aggressor."[6]

The primary aggressor being considered was China, and Ronald Spector notes of NSC 162/2: "American leaders thus seemed determined to fight for Indochina if necessary, but the question of what form American defense of Indochina might take continued to trouble them."[7] Two and one-half months after NSC 162/2 was approved, but before the French garrison began to be overrun, President Eisenhower signed NSC 5405, which clarified the administration's assessment of America's interests regarding Indochina.[8] The document stated, "The loss of the struggle in Indochina, in addition to its impact in Southeast Asia and in South Asia, would therefore have the most serious repercussions on U.S. and free world interests in Europe and elsewhere."[9] The Eisenhower policy would be to have the French maintain their direct military involvement while the United States provided financial and material support. In the event of Chinese intervention, NSC 5405 indicated, the U.S. would provide air and naval forces for interdiction but the introduction of American ground forces was not mentioned; even direct military action against China was contemplated.[10] Yet, NSC 5405 was most concerned with political and military reform of the French war effort and with the growing concern of what to do to prevent France from capitulating in peace negotiations with the communists.[11]

The text reflected concerns of the political leadership in Washington. This may be discerned in the minutes of the NSC meeting held on

January 8, 1954, well before the crisis, which focused attention on Indochina.[12] Soon after the intelligence briefing Eisenhower commented that the French were confused about their need for allies in the United Nations and other public forums. The President then told his national security staff, as stated in the minutes:

> For himself, said the President with great force, he simply could not imagine the United States putting ground forces anywhere in Southeast Asia, except possibly in Malaya, which we would have to defend as a bulwark of our offshore island chain. . . . I can not tell you, said the President with vehemence, how bitterly opposed I am to such a course of action. This war would absorb our troops by divisions![13]

Later in the meeting, after Secretary of the Treasury George M. Humphrey told the group that he could not conceive of "sending people, as opposed to money, to bail out the French."[14] Admiral Radford, the Chairman of the Joint Chiefs, responded that the U.S. had large numbers of soldiers in Indochina already and that "we are really in this war today in a big way."[15]

The President then expressed some tolerance for the idea of sending U.S. planes and mechanics to Indochina (without the pilots) for use near Dienbienphu, but he later stated that "while no one was more anxious than himself to keep our men out of these jungles, we could nevertheless not forget our vital interests in Indochina."[16]

A bit later in the meeting, Radford pressed for air relief of Dienbienphu: "Admiral Radford went on to speculate that if we could put one squadron of U.S. planes over Dien Bien Phu for as little as one afternoon, it might save the situation. Weren't the stakes worth it? We were already in this thing in such a big way that it seemed foolish not to make the one small extra move which might be essential to success."[17]

No consensus on policy emerged from the meeting, and Eisenhower seemed torn between the responsibility he felt to protect the region and the undesirability of becoming involved in fighting a war there. The President's statements reflected his long-term doubts that the West could hold Indochina. In his diaries of 1951, Eisenhower was already gloomy about Indochina:

> If they [the French] quit and Indochina falls to the Commies, it is easily possible that the entire of Southeast Asia and Indonesia will go, soon

to be followed by India. That prospect makes the whole problem one of interest to all. I'd favor heavy reinforcements to get the thing over at once; but I'm convinced no military victory is possible in that kind of theater. Even if Indochina were completely cleared of Communists, right across the border is China with inexhaustible manpower.[18]

In 1954 the President "retained his conviction that no purely military victory was possible in the Indochina theater," but, according to Billings-Yun, "he felt just as strongly that a long-term political solution was attainable, if the democratic players acted together."[19] Consequently, in its final form, NSC 5405 "sidestepped the question, raised by the JCS, of what the United States would do if France gave up the struggle."[20]

The skepticism within the Administration over an Indochinese intervention was not limited to civilians: the Army Plans Division, G-3, viewed such a war with alarm. At the end of 1953 G-3 prepared two studies on Indochina, and Ronald Spector informs us, "Army leaders were convinced that with or without atomic weapons a successful U.S. defense of Indochina would be far more difficult than was generally realized." G-3 concluded that a French withdrawal would require seven U.S. Army divisions plus a Marine division to replace them. There would, Spector continues, be important effects on America's worldwide defense posture: 1) an Indochinese involvement "would preclude further assistance by the United States in the building up of NATO stockpiles, particularly ammunition," 2) the Army would be unable to fulfill "its NATO commitments in the event of general war." The Plans Division, Spector concludes, also estimated that destroying the political organization of the Vietminh would require "five to eight years of effective political and psychological measures like those being carried out by the British in Malaya." The G-3 documents then suggested that "the importance of Indochina and Southeast Asia in relation to the cost of saving it" be reconsidered.[21]

There were other positions bouncing around the Defense Department as well. On January 6, 1954, the Chief of Naval Operations, Admiral Robert Anderson, urged the Secretary of Defense to press the government for a commitment "to employ combat forces in Indochina on the 'reasonable assurance of strong indigenous support of our forces,' whether or not the French government approved."[22] A sharp response was delivered by the Director of the Office of Foreign Military Affairs in OSD, Vice Admiral A. C. Davis, who wrote: "Involve-ment of U.S. forces in the Indochina War should be avoided at all practical costs. If, then, national policy determines no other alterna-tive, the U.S. should not be self-duped into believing the possibility of partial involvement—such as 'Naval and Air units only.' One can-not go over Niagara Falls in a barrel only slightly." Davis went on to say, "It must be understood that there is no cheap way to fight a war, once committed."[23]

The International Stage

From January 25 to February 18, 1954, the foreign ministers of the United States, the United Kingdom, France, and the Soviet Union came together in Berlin to discuss a series of international problems. The armistice in Korea had created a potent political issue in France. Namely, if the United States could end its war with communism by negotiations, why, then, could France not do the same? The logic of the argument was powerful, but the United States opposed negotiations fearing that France would give up the fight. The six months prior to the Berlin Conference had shown the Vietminh at their strongest, so the weary French could not be dissuaded from placing Indochina on the agenda of a future conference scheduled to begin in Geneva in May 1954. Consequently, after the Berlin Conference ended in mid-Febru-ary the Indochinese battlefield became the locus of an intense military struggle to obtain diplomatic leverage.

The Crisis Begins

On March 13, 1954, communist forces under the command of Gener-al Vo Nguyen Giap launched their first assault on the French positions at Dienbienphu.[24] Navarre later claimed that he went into Dienbien-phu to give political and military support to Laos. Prime Minister Laniel stated that although the protection of Laos was a high priority, his foremost concern, as expressed to General Navarre, was "above everything else, to insure the safety of the Expeditionary Corps."[25] Bernard Fall has written (p. 315) that no matter what his motivation, there is no disputing the fact that Navarre did not inform his superiors of his intention to stage a battle at Dienbienphu until the operation was under way. Because Dienbienphu was so remotely situated (over 200 miles without proper roads from Hanoi), troops were brought in and resupplied by airplanes which landed on newly built airstrips in the valley. These airstrips lay beneath two hills at the more northern end of the valley; they were held by the French and called Gabrielle and Beatrice. These hills were roughly 150 meters higher than the rest of the valley and were one to two miles from the airstrip; when the Vietminh attacked on March 13, 1954, they overwhelmed these two key outposts. Beatrice was captured on the night of March 13–14, and Gabrielle was overrun on March 15.

These losses had immediate tactical significance: As Fall notes, "Once hills Gabrielle and Beatrice were lost—and they were lost within twenty-four hours after the actual battle began—the Communist gunners had a continuous view of all the French positions, and the airfield (upon whose continuous use the success of the battle hinged) became useless within a few days (p. 317)." Fall adds on p. 321, "Giap now controlled the commanding heights. The battle of Dienbienphu was already lost ."

The Ély Visit

On March 20, 1954, as the noose began to tighten at Dienbienphu, General Paul Ély, the highest ranking French military officer, arrived in Washington at the invitation of Admiral Radford.[26] Ély, fresh from a tour of Indochina as part of a major policy review by the French government, was asked to repeat his findings, and hear the suggestions of his American counterparts. Ély's mission for a French government, "deeply concerned about the possibility of Chinese intervention," was to obtain " 'ironclad assurances of United States aerial intervention in the event of direct Chinese intervention,' while at the same time convincing the Americans to abandon 'the opinion that a military solution to the conflict was possible within a reasonable time.' "[27] The content of the meetings between Ély and the American officials has been steeped in controversy due primarily to Ély's claim the United States agreed to some form of direct intervention in Indochina.

The first meeting took place on the evening of March 20 at the quarters of Admiral Radford; Vice President Nixon, General Ridgway, CIA's Allen Dulles, and State's Douglas MacArthur II were in attendance.[28] Ély, answering candidly and seemingly realistic about the prospects for the war, told his hosts that the French nation was tired of the war and that the outcome of Dienbienphu would greatly affect France's morale and determination. The General recognized that "progress on the military front was definitely related to ability to achieve success on the political front in order to obtain the full support of the local populace against the Communists."[29] The focus of the conversation soon shifted to Dienbienphu. The French Chief of Staff pointed out that even though his forces had a strong position they were surrounded by the major portion of Vietminh forces. What the communists wanted at Dienbienphu was a "*political* victory" to undermine French morale. Militarily even if the stronghold succumbed to Giap's forces, the Vietminh would be dealt a far greater loss than the 5% of its forces in Indochina which the French would lose. So, the crisis after defeat would not be essentially military—it was the political consequence which had to be avoided.

According to the minutes, "In response to questions, General Ély indicated that the most serious deficiency of the French forces in connection with Dien Bien Phu was in the air. He indicated that there was urgent need for more combat type aircraft. He judged that the prospects for the French holding out at Dien Bien Phu were 50–50 at this time.[30]

Ély then made some detailed requests for equipment. At the end of the conversation, Secretary Dulles expressed concern that General Navarre seemed to be doing little to fight the insurgency. Dulles believed the Vietminh to be waging a "politico-military struggle" and Ély acknowledged that the French Union forces were losing because they "lacked the political support of the mass of the people."[31]

Matthew Ridgway also took notes of this conversation and his impressions shed light on the meeting.[32] The General was pessimistic after this conversation and observed:

> 2a. I detect no vigorous offensive intention on the part of the French Government or top French military authorities, so far as General Ély reveals that attitude. He stated early in the conversation the French saw little chance of military decision in either 1954 or 1955 with respect to Indo-China as a whole.

Ridgway then wrote that the establishment of a "stable political foundation" was the "key to military success." In this paragraph there seems to be the unstated assumption that the French were failing to build that foundation. He concluded, as Ély had, that Dienbienphu's impact would be political rather than military. Ridgway ended his summary with a sharp criticism of the idea that air interdiction would solve the French problems at Dienbienphu:

> At one point in the conversation, RADFORD, in seeking to sum up, asked Ély, "What you really need then for success is more air power?" At the end of this question and before Ély could reply, I said I wanted to challenge that statement right then. The experience of Korea, where we had complete domination of the air and a far more powerful air force, afforded no basis for thinking that some additional air power was going to bring *decisive* results on the ground.[33]

Henceforth, Ridgway would oppose direct American intervention in the Administration's policy debates that were to follow. In this memo one can get a sense of the intellectual basis for his resistance to intervention.

In the following days Ély met with many U.S. officials, but he proved disappointing to the Americans. It became clear that the French were willing to discuss only those topics that related to the material support of their war effort.[34] Radford expressed disapproval of the French Chief's unwillingness to consider increasing the U.S. training role in Indochina; Ély was also not interested in U.S. suggestions "in the fields of psychological, clandestine, and guerrilla warfare."[35] Radford's pessimism about the ability of the French to carry on the fight became greater after Ély's visit. He concluded his memo on Ély's stay in Washington with the following:

> I am gravely fearful that the measures being undertaken by the French will prove to be inadequate and initiated too late to prevent a progressive deterioration of the situation in Indo-China. If Dien Bien Phu is lost, this deterioration may occur very rapidly due to the loss of morale among the mass of the native population. In such a situation only prompt and forceful intervention by the United States could avert the loss of all of South East Asia to Communist domination. I am convinced that the United States must be prepared to take such action.[36]

The President seems to have come out of the Ély meeting with a settled view of the Indochina situation and direct military intervention. Dulles recorded the President as saying "that he agreed basically that we should not get involved in fighting in Indochina unless there were the political preconditions necessary for a successful outcome. He did not, however, wholly exclude the possibility of a single strike, if it were almost certain this would produce decisive results."[37] Dulles had also indicated that if the U.S. were to directly intervene in Indochina, and he expressed no support for such action, it must offer the prospect of success:

> I did . . . think it appropriate to remind our French friends that if the United States sent its flag and its own military establishment—land, sea, or air—into the Indochina war, then the prestige of the United States would be engaged to a point where we would want to have a success. We could not afford thus to engage the prestige of the United States and suffer a defeat which would have worldwide repercussions.[38]

General Ély left Washington on March 24, 1954, without having inspired any confidence in the ability of the French to conduct the war. The French general, a man facing a desperate military situation in Indochina, was looking for any sign of relief from the Americans. Apparently, Admiral Radford's sympathetic demeanor and Ély's misunderstanding of some crucial remarks led the French general to tell his political superiors "that he and Radford (and, by projection, the Eisenhower government) had reached 'complete accord on all matters.' "[39] In fact, Radford insisted that he had made no promises to the French with respect to airstrikes. Billings-Yun summarizes Radford's position: "He merely told Ély, he said, that were Paris formally to request United States military assistance, *and were Washington to authorize that assistance*, he could guarantee the availability for action within two days of 350 carrier-based aircraft and a smaller number of medium bombers."[40] Richard Immerman, a historian specializing on the Eisenhower Administration, finds Ély's claim to be on firmer footing. Of Radford's intentions, Immerman writes, "Yet in all probability, Ély received the impression that Radford intended. The JCS chairman personally favored an air strike, and he may well have feared that Ély's unsatisfactory talk with Dulles would adversely affect France's commitment to continue. His morale needed a boost."[41] However things may have actually transpired, the General returned to Paris believing he had considerable American support, when in fact he had little.

The Question of Intervention

The day after General Ély's departure, March 25, was also the day on which a critical NSC meeting took place.[42] At that meeting a wide range of issues on Indochina were considered, but military intervention was the theme that dominated the conversation. In response to a query by Secretary of Defense Wilson as to what the American response would be "in the event that the Chinese Communists sent MIG aircraft for operations over Indochina," Mr. Cutler, the Special Assistant to the President for National Security Affairs, responded that the U.S. would respond militarily to such "overt aggression" as prescribed in NSC 5405.[43] To this Secretary Dulles added that Congress would have to be notified and its approval obtained; the President had made the same point earlier in the conversation. Soon thereafter, Dulles astutely observed that "he thought it quite unlikely that the Chinese Communists would engage their MIGs in battle over Indochina prior to the Geneva Conference. The Communists were seeking a political rather than a military victory at this stage, and we could therefore safely discount overt Chinese intervention in Indochina."[44]

The conversation moved on to the need for allies if intervention were to take place. It was agreed that the Associated States would have to support the intervention.[45] The support of Britain and France would also be crucial, and the help of other Asian nations would be beneficial. At this point in the discussion Secretary Wilson, in what must have been despair at the difficulty of this task, asked "whether it would be sensible to forget about Indochina for a while and concentrate on the effort to get the remaining free nations of Southeast Asia in some sort of condition to resist Communist aggression against themselves."[46] The President responded by expressing "great doubt as to the feasibility of such a proposal, since he believed that the collapse of Indochina would produce a chain reaction which would result in the fall of all of Southeast Asia to the Communists."[47]

The *JCS History* refers to another set of minutes taken for the meeting.[48] According to this account the meeting was framed by Dulles's question: "what would the United States do if the French attempted to sacrifice the position of the Free World in Indochina?"[49] Dulles painted a stark picture of American options: the U.S. could either write off the region or assume responsibility for it. In response

Eisenhower revealed that he was not absolutely opposed to intervention but *four* hurdles would have to be cleared before U.S. troops
could be used in Indochina. These were his requirements: (1) the
Associated States would have to request assistance; (2) the United
Nations would have to sanction the response; (3) other nations,
including Vietnam, would have to join the United States in answering; and (4) Congressional authorization would have to be received.[50]
Also, not to be forgotten were the requirements that the French grant
independence to the Indochinese states.[51] As he had in the earlier
NSC meeting of January 8, 1954, Eisenhower conveyed deep reservations about sending troops to Indochina; these doubts were not
insurmountable but they would be difficult to overcome. By the end
of March he was willing to consider direct involvement to save
Indochina but only if his demanding preconditions could be satisfied.
Billings-Yun concludes that there was so little enthusiasm for intervention at this meeting that "no one on the NSC even raised the possibility of intervening to prevent the defeat of the French forces at
Dien Bien Phu."[52] The bureaucratic result of the meeting was a directive to have the NSC Planning Board present a study to the Council
before the Geneva Conference (the Indochina phase of which was to
begin on May 8, 1954) on the circumstances and extent to which the
U.S. should multilaterally or, even unilaterally, commit forces to the
defense of Indochina.[53]

The Call for United Action

On March 29, 1954, in an address to the Overseas Press Club, Secretary Dulles began the administration's international campaign for a unified response to communist aggression in Indochina. The speech was
entitled "The Threat of Red Asia" and began by describing the nonvi-
olent ways in which the Chinese were assisting the efforts of the Vietminh. Later in the speech he made this important policy pronouncement calling for "united action":

> Under the conditions of today, the imposition on Southeast Asia of the
> political system of Communist Russia and its Chinese Communist ally,
> by whatever means, would be a grave threat to the whole free commu-
> nity. The United States feels that the possibility should not be passively
> accepted but should be met by united action. This might involve seri-

ous risks. But these risks are far less than those that will face us a few years from now if we dare not be resolute today.[54]

Gibbons believes that Eisenhower and Dulles made the decision to pursue "united action" on March 21, 1954, the day after Ély's arrival in the capitol.[55] On March 22 meetings were held with Congressional leaders "for the purpose of getting their tentative approval for United Action." That meeting included only Republican congressional leaders, but other meetings held from the 22nd to the 29th of March discussed united action "with leaders of both parties in Congress, by members of both foreign policy committees of Congress, and by major U.S. allies."[56] On the morning of March 29 the President and Vice President met with Republican congressional leaders. From that meeting only Nixon's memoirs provide a first hand account of what transpired. According to the then-Vice President, Eisenhower told the assembled congressmen that direct action against China might be necessary as a diversion to relieve Dienbienphu. Then Eisenhower "very simply, but dramatically" said, " 'I am bringing this up at this time because at any time within the next forty-eight hours, it might be necessary to move into the battle of Dien Bien Phu in order to keep it from going against us, and in that case I will be calling in the Democrats as well as our Republican leaders to inform them of the actions we're taking.' "[57]

The President had been kept completely apprised of the contents of Dulles's speech as it was being drafted.[58] Nevertheless, the "United Action" Speech appears to have misrepresented the eagerness of the Administration for war. It was the immediate cause of great consternation in London where Foreign Minister Anthony Eden had no intention of becoming involved in the jungles of Southeast Asia. Across the English Channel the French viewed "united action" as an indication of American willingness to use military power against their Indochinese enemies.[59] Unfortunately, this interpretation of the Dulles speech appeared to confirm Ély's fictitious guarantees of American support at Dienbienphu. Now, the French would be less solicitous of American opinions thinking they had achieved U.S. support by succumbing to U.S. demands about the conduct of the war.

In short, now that the United States had publicly endorsed united action, that policy's debits and credits would be tallied by the members of Congress, by the American populace, and by the allies whose support

America was attempting to enlist. And, finally, as Billings-Yun observes, "The biggest question mark of all concerned the position of President Eisenhower. In the wake of the Overseas Press Club speech the world turned to him for an answer."[60] She believes that as of the end of March he had not decided exactly what he would do. Eisenhower thought the military situation was unwinnable, but, according to Billings-Yun, he had to consider the effect that his actions would have on the morale of the French, the anti-communist Vietnamese, the Associated States, and on the domestic politics of the United States, which was still experiencing the punishment of Senator Joseph McCarthy's attacks against the government.

The President's remarks to the press on March 31 subtly attempted to pull back from Dulles's speech of two days earlier with respect to military intervention, but his new line was drowned out by the reverberations of those earlier remarks that expressed interest in a multilateral response. The French, for example, were in no mood to reinterpret the Secretary of State's offer of deliverance and would attempt to involve the U.S. as quickly they could.[61]

Congress Considers the Question

We do not know with certitude how Congress would have acted on a vote in late March 1954 to enter the Indochina War. In general, the Congress did not support plans for the unilateral introduction of American troops in support of the French. However, just as Eisenhower had a list of preconditions for involvement the Congress seems to have had a list of its own. The requirements on this list became known to the administration in the week that followed Dulles's March 29 speech. The possibility of losing Southeast Asia aroused predictable support on Capitol Hill for the anti-communist forces in Indochina. Unilateral or unconditional intervention was not, however, a viable option as far as the Congress was concerned. The mood of the Congress supported "united action" because there would be others with whom to share the burden, but the members were "wary about becoming involved in an anti-colonialist struggle in Indochina" in which the U.S. would be propping up the colonial regime.[62] Gibbons describes the Congressional perspective as follows: "Most Members also seemed to be aware that implicit in Dulles's March 29 speech was the willingness of the U.S. to enter the Indochina war through the united action framework, and there was general support for going to war, if necessary to Southeast Asia, provided that other nations carried their share of the burden."[63]

Congressional opinion became very clear to the Administration after a meeting on April 3, 1954, at the State Department. Secretary Dulles and JCS Chairman Radford (and others) met Senators William Knowland (R-California), the Senate majority leader, Eugene Millikin (R-Colorado), Lyndon Johnson (D-Texas), then the minority leader, Richard Russell (D-Georgia), Earle Clements (D-Kentucky), House Speaker Joseph Martin, Jr. (R-Massachusetts), Congressman John McCormack (D-Massachusetts), the House minority whip, and J. Percy Priest (D-Tennessee). The meeting began with a thorough briefing by Radford on the perilous state of the forces at Dienbienphu and the critical importance of Southeast Asia.[64] Dulles told his guests that the President would need the support of the Congress for the use of air and sea power. As the discussion proceeded a unanimous consensus emerged that: "there should be no Congressional action until the Secretary had obtained commitments of a political and material nature from our allies. The feeling was unanimous that "we want no more Koreas with the United States furnishing 90% of the manpower."[65]

At this point Radford and Dulles told the Congressional leaders "that the Administration did not now contemplate the commitment of land forces." The congressmen were not satisfied, for they believed that "once the flag was committed the use of land forces would inevitably follow." The meeting continued with heavy criticism of French political and military policies in Indochina. It appeared that the Congress would *not* support an intervention to which the British were not deeply committed.[66]

Secretary Dulles did not miss the importance of these remarks. During a pivotal NSC meeting on April 6 he summarized the congressional sentiment; the full text bears repeating:

> [Dulles] deduced that it would be impossible to get Congressional authorization for U.S. unilateral action in Indochina. To secure the necessary Congressional support would be contingent on meeting three conditions. One, U.S. intervention must be part of a coalition to include other free nations of Southeast Asia, the Philippines, and the British Commonwealth nations. Secondly, the French must agree to accelerate their independence program for the Associated States so that there could be no

question of U.S. support of French colonialism. Thirdly, the French must agree not to pull their forces out of the war if we put our forces in.[67]

The Administration suffered no illusions as to the tough task which it would face in obtaining Congressional support for intervention. It should not come as a surprise that Congressional attitudes reflected America's popular opposition to involvement on behalf of the French. Gallup polls taken at the time indicate this. When Gallup asked whether the United States should send troops to Indochina to take part in the fighting the responses were: in May 1953, yes—12%, no—78%, no opinion—10%; in August 1953, approve—8%, disapprove—85%, no opinion—7%; in May 1954, approve—20%, disapprove—72%, no opinion—8%.[68] As the threat to Indochina increased there was a slight increase in the number of those willing to enter the war. That the Congress supported intervention to the extent that it did testifies to the weight of the balance-of-power worries that policymakers had stemming from the zero-sum Cold War competition and the effect that the loss of Indochina would have on America's future.

The Joint Chiefs and Intervention

The issue of direct intervention was soon brought before the JCS. On March 31, within days of General Ély's departure, Chairman Radford asked the Joint Chiefs of Staff for their opinions about Operation Vulture, which would provide air and naval units in defense of Dienbienphu. As Radford wrote to the Secretary of Defense, "The Individual Service Chiefs and the Commandant of the Marine Corps unanimously recommended against such an offer at this time."[69] Only Chairman Radford supported Vulture. General Ridgway also questioned Radford's authority to personally place this issue before the JCS: "Unless the question emanated from proper authority, any such recommended action—for or against—was clearly outside the proper scope of authority of the JCS. This body was not charged with formulating foreign policy, nor advocating it, unless its advice was specifically sought by the President, or the Secretary of Defense. To do otherwise would be to involve the JCS inevitably in politics."[70]

But Radford was not stopped by this setback. By April 2 he had arranged it so that the Secretary of Defense had asked for the opinions of the Joint Chiefs. In a meeting on that day each of the Service Chiefs and the Marine Corps Commandant presented a written response for the JCS Chairman. Their positions were pretty much the same as they had been previously except that General Twining gave a qualified "yes" the second time. General Ridgway restated his views on the "specific issue" of intervention:

> From the military viewpoint, the United States capability for effective intervention in the Dien Bien Phu operation was altogether disproportionate to the liability it would incur.
>
> From the military viewpoint, the outcome of the Dien Bien Phu operation, whichever way it might go, *would not in itself decisively affect the military situation there.*
>
> If recommended and executed, intervention by United States armed forces would greatly increase the risk of general war. If the United States, by its own act, were deliberately to risk provoking such possible reaction, it must first materially increase its readiness to accept the consequences.[71]

Billings-Yun summarizes Ridgway's stance as follows: "The Army chief of staff bitterly opposed Radford's efforts to commit US forces to the French-Indochina War, which he believed would result in a war of attrition more costly in American lives and dollars than the Korean War had been."[72] The Chief of Naval Operations, Robert Carney, also opposed intervention. He recognized the importance of Indochina and stated that its loss should be averted if possible; his main reason for arguing against Vulture was "that the foregoing contribution [of Vulture] would improve the French tactical situation, with particular reference to the battle of Dien Bien Phu, but [we] are not prepared to state that such contribution would be decisive."[73] General Lemuel Shepherd, Commandant of the Marine Corps, strongly opposed Vulture because any such "improvised air offensive" could not produce significant military results against guerrilla forces.[74] Again Billings-Yun's analysis of General Shepherd's "no" vote seems correct in the prominence it places on the memory of Korea:

> The weight of America's failure to decisively win the Korean War hung heavily on Shepherd's words. Like the chiefs of the Army and Navy, the Marine commandant did not want to risk having to pull the Air Force's irons out of the fire and take the blame for another military "failure,"

more humiliating than Korea, given Indochina's terrain and the French Union's poor morale. "For us to participate in a defeat cannot be accounted as a means either of combating Communism effectively, or of enhancing our position in the eyes of the Asiatics," he dryly concluded.[75]

Only General Twining of the Air Force was willing to give a *qualified* yes; his approval was dependent on actions the French were unlikely to undertake.[76]

Herring and Immerman interpret these negative answers in a manner consistent with the Never Again explanation offered in this thesis: "The Joint Chiefs of Staff (JCS) later endorsed military intervention in Indochina provided that it included authorization to attack China if necessary. What they apparently wanted to avoid was a limited war fought under tight restrictions as in Korea."[77]

General James M. Gavin, the officer in charge of plans for the Army under Ridgway, remembered in February 1966 the actions that he and General Ridgway took that Spring with these words:

> We had one or two old China hands on the staff at the time and the more we studied the situation the more we realized that we were, in fact, considering going to war with China, since she was supplying . . . Ho Chi Minh. If we would be, in fact, fighting China, then we were fighting her in the wrong place on terms entirely to her advantage. Manchuria, with its vast industrial complex, coal, and iron ore, is the Ruhr of China and the heart of its warmaking capacity. There, rather than in southeast Asia, is where China should be engaged, if at all.[78]

For all practical purposes, the Joint Chiefs with the exception of Radford opposed Vulture—air-strikes launched to save the garrison at Dienbienphu.[79] They were not convinced that it could provide the desired outcome, and its costs would have been too great relative to the benefits. Not even Radford was advocating a Limited War policy such as the U.S. had seen during the Korean War and would see again during the Johnson Administration. In fact, shortly before Dulles traveled to Europe on April 10, the most solid supporter of intervention, Admiral Radford, wrote a note to the Secretary of State informing him that if "united action" could be arranged "the fastest and most effective way of getting help to the French Union forces at Dien Bien Phu would be to drop three tactical atomic bombs on Indochina."[80]

The French Request Vulture

In early April the Vietminh launched a new offensive at Dienbienphu which pushed the French defenders to their breaking point. General Navarre had come to believe that a massive air strike, if launched by April 10 or 11, might save Dienbienphu. Consequently, the American ambassador to France, Douglas Dillon, was called to a restricted cabinet meeting on the night of April 4. French Prime Minister Laniel and Foreign Minister Bidault spoke with Ambassador Dillon. They told him that Radford had promised Ély "that if [the] situation at Dien Bien Phu required US naval air support he would do his best to obtain such help from [the] US Government."[81] Relying on that pledge they asked for carrier-based air support at Dien Bien Phu, and proceeded to stake out the claim that the Chinese were directly involved in the war by supplying huge amounts of materiel and equipment to Hanoi.[82] They made this set of assertions as part of an argument asking the United States to fulfill a pledge to provide air support to the French if China intervened. However, to the extent that any Ély-Radford understanding existed, it may have contemplated Chinese air strikes, not logistical intervention.[83] One might question whether supplying the Vietminh was the sort of "intervention" contemplated by the Americans at all. Using Korea as a pattern it would seem that Radford was probably most worried about direct Chinese military involvement as occurred in November 1950 in Korea.

Dulles spoke with Eisenhower the next morning, after Dillon's cable reached Washington.[84] Eisenhower expressed annoyance that Radford had pledged to "do his best" for the French, but Dulles was quick to tell the President that "Radford did not give any committal talk" when Ély was in Washington. Moving to the subject of Dillon's message Eisenhower told Dulles that air and naval support were out of the question. Congressional support could not be obtained unless the political groundwork were laid out first. Dulles told the President that in a conversation earlier that morning Radford was quite reconciled to the fact that this course of action was now politically infeasible—he had "no idea of recommending this action."

Dulles responded to Ambassador Dillon in Paris on the same day. He told Dillon he had explained to Ély that the United States could not commit itself to hostilities "without [a] full political understanding with France and other countries."[85] Congress would also have to give its assent. He added that "such action is impossible except on coalition basis with active British Commonwealth participation." The United States would help in any way short of involvement in the conflict, but direct military action would have to await these political developments. Thus, the French request for the implementation of Vulture was rejected.

The Diplomatic Pursuit of United Action

On the next day, April 6, 1954, the NSC met to consider the Indochina situation. Interpreting the minutes of this meeting is difficult because there was no clear sense of Administration policy. While the President clearly did not want Indochina to fall into communist hands, it was hard to determine how to prevent a French defeat. In his speech, Dulles had deliberately left the concept of "united action" vague, not only because of political reasons, but also because the administration had not decided on a course of action. At the April 6 NSC meeting the discussion turned to the related but tangential issue of the formation of a Southeast Asian coalition along with Great Powers like Great Britain, France, and the United States.[86] It was after this NSC meeting that Dulles began a frenetic international diplomatic campaign for "united action," and the diplomatic machinery of the State Department became focused toward this end. In a letter delivered to Prime Minister Churchill on April 5 the United States requested British assistance in forming a "coalition" that could bolster the French position at Geneva and "bring greater moral and material resources" to the struggle in Indochina. A little later in the letter Eisenhower told Churchill:

> The important thing is that the coalition must be strong and it must be willing to join the fight if necessary. I do not envisage the need of any appreciable ground forces on your part. If the members of the alliance are sufficiently resolute it should be able to make clear to the Chinese Communists that the continuation of their material support to the Viet Minh will inevitably lead to the growing power of the forces arrayed against them.[87]

The letter's statement that there would be no need for "appreciable ground forces" from Britain indicates that if the coalition had formed the United States would have been willing to put in at least a small number of troops on the ground.

On April 11 Dulles met with Eden, who, as Dulles remembered it, was willing to consider the formation of a defensive coalition for Southeast Asia but doubted whether Indochina could be held. The British Foreign Secretary felt that air and naval assistance would prove ineffective, and he could not see where they would get the soldiers to support a commitment.[88] The British also expressed their belief that the creation of a coalition prior to the Geneva Conference would only destroy any chance for a negotiated settlement.[89] In a meeting on April 12 between lower-ranking American and British officials the British expressed the view that as an alternative solution "the territorial division of Vietnam seemed the least bad."[90] The British felt that the French still had enough leverage vis-à-vis the Vietminh to obtain a beneficial settlement.

Despite these large differences, Dulles came away from the meetings encouraged about the progress he had made with the British,[91] although more than two weeks later Livingston Merchant, Assistant Secretary of State for European Affairs, would tell two of Eden's aides that the coalition being created was "intended as a deterrent, which by creating restraints on the other side would reduce the risk of our being forced to intervene." He would also comment that "the failure to create the coalition was actually increasing the risk of intervention."[92]

The American delegation flew from London to Paris on April 13, 1954, where they found the French government reluctant to grant the Associated States genuine independence. Bidault told Dulles that "French public and parliamentary opinion would not support the continuation of the war if the concept of the French Union were placed in any doubt whatsoever."[93] Dulles replied that one of the Congress's preconditions for American participation in united action was the clear intention on the part of France to grant and maintain the independence of the Associated States. The French were also wary of any coalition arrangement because that might lead to the "internationalization of the war" which would take the command and control away from France. They wanted to retain their oversight of the war, but they also must have foreseen the loss of prestige they would suffer were this "internationalization" to take place.

Dulles returned to Washington with little reason for hope on April 15, only to return to Paris six days later to discuss the upcoming Geneva Conference with French and British officials.[94] In a meeting on April 22, 1954, Bidault made a second request for a direct air strike at Dienbienphu, informing Dulles that France would end its opposition to the internationalization of the war if the U.S. would save Dienbienphu. This urgent appeal ushered in a flurry of diplomatic activity among France, Great Britain, and the United States. The French wanted a brief American strike to save Dienbienphu; the United States did not care so much about Dienbienphu as it did about a long-term involvement (with all Congressional preconditions met) that would save Southeast Asia; and the British wanted no part of any Southeast Asian war.[95] Ultimately, the possibility of united intervention was ended by the British on April 25 when Eden told Dulles that "the United Kingdom is strongly opposed to any intervention at Dienbienphu. . . ."[96]

Ridgway Continues the Fight

Ridgway's opposition to intervention at Dienbienphu never abated. This is borne out by a memorandum he wrote on April 6.[97] The memo was slightly modified by Chairman Radford and then forwarded to Secretary of Defense Wilson on April 22, 1954.[98] Ridgway begins his analysis by recognizing that the loss of Indochina to the communists would be a serious defeat for American interests, after which he presents an argument as to how the United States should keep Indochina out of communist hands: while the protection of Indochina is the goal of the policy, "it does not follow that the military measures required to attain that objective would find any decisive objectives in Indo-China itself."[99] Ridgway then gets to the heart of dealing with the Vietminh which we saw in a statement by Lieutenant-General Gavin above, quoting him: "The immediate and major source of Viet Minh military power is Communist China. With that source destroyed or neutralized, the Viet Minh would cease to present a major military problem to the French in Indo-China."[100]

Ridgway continues the argument by stating that American planning should think beyond intervention in Indochina. To place American troops on the ground "would commit our armed forces in a non-decisive theatre to the attainment of non-decisive local objectives." Rather than go down such a path, the United States, if it feels compelled to defend this region, should gather as many allies as possible and "inform

Communist China and the world of its intentions to employ its armed forces to destroy or to neutralize the sources of Viet Minh military power, unless Communist China halts military aid to the Viet Minh."[101]

Ridgway was not advocating war with China. Rather, as the Army Chief of Staff "later noted, he had no wish for a war with China or a preventive war with the Soviet Union but merely wished to point out, in the starkest terms, the magnitude of the decision confronting the country on the issue of intervention in Vietnam."[102] Ridgway's difference of opinion was not merely over who the correct enemy was. In essence, his philosophy of fighting wars which focused on attempting to defeat the enemy with the decisive application of military power was critical to his estimation that Indochina was not the place to fight a war.

The Debate Proceeds

As the situation on the ground worsened for the French at Dienbienphu a critical NSC meeting was held on April 29, in advance of the portion of the Geneva Conference devoted to Indochina, which would convene on May 8.[103] Early in the NSC meeting Chairman Radford discussed a conversation he had with General Ély on April 25: "he came to ask for American intervention, realizing that such intervention could have no direct bearing on Dien Bien Phu. The point he wanted to stress was that American aid should be given before Dien Bien Phu fell, for the psychological effect in France and in Indochina, and to prevent deterioration."[104]

Radford's briefing of the NSC continued. At its end a silence ensued. Harold Stassen, the Director of Foreign Operations, spoke vehemently in favor of taking a strong stand in Indochina, and Eisenhower parried his remarks with skeptical comments about intervention. Stassen remarked that the United States would be able to bring its forces in as the French withdrew theirs. Eisenhower offered his opinion that "if the United States were to intervene in Indochina alone, it would mean a general war with China and perhaps with the USSR, which the United States would have to prosecute separated from its allies."[105] Stassen expressed doubt that the Chinese would come into the war. The discussion continued, Stassen reiterated his view that the United States should intervene, and then Eisenhower made the following remarks which reflect an All-or-Nothing attitude:

The President answered that before he could bring himself to [decide for intervention], he would want to ask himself and all his wisest advisers whether the right decision was not to launch a world war. If our allies were going to fall away in any case, it might be better for the United States to leap over the smaller obstacles and hit the biggest one with all the power we had. Otherwise we seemed to be playing the enemy's game

The conversation moved on, and then Eisenhower added:

. . . . that perhaps Governor Stassen's diagnosis was correct, but went on to say that before he would be prepared to commit U.S. divisions to Indochina—six, eight, ten . . .—he would earnestly put before the leaders of the Congress and the Administration the greater question whether it would not be better to decide on general war and prepare for D-Day. The cause of the free world could never win, the United States could never survive if we frittered away our resources in local engagements. This process would go on indefinitely, with the Communists trying elsewhere to involve the United States in *indecisive engagements* which would ultimately sap its strength.[106]

In his memoirs, Eisenhower states that the meeting ended with agreement that even if no formal mechanism for united action existed the U.S. could still provide the French with aid.[107] Undersecretary of State Walter Bedell Smith was leaving for Geneva the next day and would make such an effort.[108] President Eisenhower also describes the part of the meeting in which he made his All-or-Nothing observation:

During the course of this meeting I remarked that if the United States were, unilaterally, to permit its forces to be drawn into conflict in Indochina and into a succession of Asian wars, the end result would be to drain off our resources and to weaken our over-all defensive position. If we, without allies, should ever find ourselves fighting at various places all over the region, and if Red Chinese aggressive participation were clearly identified, then we could scarcely avoid, I said, considering the necessity of striking directly at the head instead of the tail of the snake, Red China itself.[109]

The meeting ended without any argument to intervene on behalf of the French forces at Dienbienphu. It is fascinating that Ridgway's argument that China, not Indochina, be the object of American military action should also be voiced by the President. The similarity indicates a common core of beliefs shared by Eisenhower and Ridgway: that is, when force is used it should be used to defeat the opponent.[110] Eisenhower was not advocating an attack on China (neither was Ridgway) but, rather, he was expressing deep reservations about the consequences of nondecisive intervention. Had his rigorous preconditions been met and American forces introduced into Southeast Asia, it is very likely that Eisenhower would have pursued an outright victory over the Vietminh (and China had that nation entered the war), for neither he nor Dulles wanted another Korean-style stalemate. By the first week of May 1954 the United States was still unable to find a way to directly intervene in Indochina.

After Dienbienphu

On May 7, 1954, the French garrison at Dienbienphu fell to the Vietminh. That event, however, did not end all of the efforts that were pushing the United States toward direct military action in Southeast Asia. On May 11, 1954, at which point intervention was still viable, Secretary Dulles was given a memo covering points for discussion with the President. The memo stated that "all US estimates agree on at least a 50 per cent chance of Chinese Communist reaction to US intervention. A split among the US and its allies might well increase this risk materially."[111] The memo concluded with a section on "Method of Conducting Operation" which read:

> Major foreign ground forces will be required to hold areas while Viet Nam forces are being trained. Present French forces will provide greater part, but US should assume need for some US ground forces and for large forces under some contingencies. US should not intervene with the idea it can be done cheaply by air and naval forces.
>
> Any use of atomic weapons will raise very serious problems of Asian opinion and attitude of our allies.[112]

On May 11 the American ambassador to France was sent a list of six conditions that would have to be met before the "President would ask Congress for authority to use armed forces of US in area to support friendly and recognized governments."[113] They were much the same as the previous lists except that solid British support seemed to be downplayed in this cable. As important as the de-emphasis on direct British participation was, the clarity and forcefulness in the "demand that the

Associated States be accorded real independence" attained equal signif-icance and was made extremely explicit.[114]

The list touched on matters requiring military planning. According to Ronald Spector "the acting secretary of defense asked the Joint Chiefs of Staff to prepare contingency plans for submission to the National Security Council."[115] Within a week several important gov-ernment documents were produced that criticized intervention. The Joint Chiefs' position came closer to Ridgway's in terms of language and reasoning. Before the first JCS memo was sent, Secretary of the Army Robert T. Stevens wrote to the Secretary of Defense on May 19, 1954. Stevens's memo focused on the logistical difficulties of any interven-tion; his first and last paragraphs convey the essence of his concerns:

> 1. I am becoming increasingly concerned over the frequency of state-ments by individuals of influence within and without the government that United States air and sea forces alone could solve our problems in Indo-China, and equally so over the very evident lack of appreciation of the logistics factors affecting operations in that area.
>
> 8. The complex nature of these problems would require a major Unit-ed States logistical effort. It explodes the myth that air and sea forces could solve the Indo-China problems. If United States land-based forces are projected any appreciable distance inland, as would be essen-tial, they would require constant local security at every location, and for their every activity. The Army would have to provide these forces, their total would be very large, and the time to provide them would be extensive.[116]

The Army clearly did not believe that this would be a small war. On the next day, May 20, 1954, the JCS sent a memo to the Secretary of Defense that discussed "U.S. Military Participation in Indochina."[117] After pointing out "the limited availability of U.S. forces for military action in Indochina" and stressing the "undesirability of basing large numbers of U.S. forces in Indochina," the memo also states that the U.S. should do all that it can through the augmentation of its Military Assistance Advisory Group to assist the "development of effective native armed forces."[118]

The *Pentagon Papers* writes of this document that the "Chiefs were simply taking their traditional position that any major U.S. force commitment in the Far East should be reserved for a war against China in the event the President decided that such a conflict was necessary for the preservation of vital American interests."[119] The analysis notes the "New Look" defense posture had not placed the U.S. in a position to fight large-scale "brushfire" wars. These comments were certainly true, but the Chiefs were not merely making a knee-jerk argument asking that all their wishes be granted or they would oppose intervention. Their position made sense: it was and is a mark of military wisdom to be wary of nondecisive military involvements. At the level of grand strategy the Chiefs, as well as Eisenhower himself, felt that Indochina was not a decisive theater. At the theater level the JCS was worried that the U.S. would become involved in a geographically circumscribed war which they could win only with a lengthy effort and massive attrition.

In response to the Acting Secretary of Defense's request of May 18, 1954, (see Spector in note 115, cited above), the JCS prepared a memo that was sent to the Secretary of Defense on May 26, 1954. In this note, which contained some general contingency plans, the first major item included this summary analysis:

> 2.a. . . . . The Joint Chiefs of Staff desire to point out their belief that, from the point of view of the United States, with reference to the Far East as a whole, *Indochina is devoid of decisive military objectives and the allocation of more than token* U.S. armed forces *in Indochina would be a serious diversion* of limited U.S. capabilities. The principal sources of Viet Minh military supply lie outside Indochina. The destruction or neutralization of these sources in China proper would materially reduce the French military problems in Indochina.[120]

This, of course, is a slight rearrangement of sections 7 and 8 of the May 20 memorandum, but here we do have the significant addition of "in China proper" when the location of the Viet Minh sources of supply is being discussed. It is clear that the Joint Chiefs wanted to make their objections known.

Another revealing memorandum linking lessons taken from the Korean War with an undesirable style of war-fighting was sent to the Secretary of Defense on May 21 from the Joint Chiefs of Staff. Its subject was the "Defense of Southeast Asia in the Event of the Loss of Indochina to the Communists."[121] The memo states that "two basic military concepts for the defense of Southeast Asia" exist:

> a. Static type defense (Korea type).

b. An offensive to attack the source of military power being applied in Southeast Asia.

The document clearly considers the "static type defense" to be militarily unsound (sec. 7); the two most important reasons given are that:

6e. The dissipation of allied strength through the commitment of forces of this magnitude to a "static" defense of Southeast Asia would contribute to the realization of the politico-military objectives of the USSR vis-à-vis the free world.
f. Execution of static defense would result in maldeployment and seriously reduce the flexibility of employment of United States forces. This could seriously jeopardize the United States capability of supporting logistically our present war plans.

The memorandum makes the following recommendations in sections 9 and 10:

9. In view of the above, the United States should adopt the concept of offensive actions against the "military power of the aggressor," in this instance Communist China, rather than the concept of "reaction locally at the point of attack," which the thesis of the action [outlined above in points 5 and 6 of the source document].
10. . . . it is felt that adoption of this concept [attacking the source of enemy power], would provide a more acceptable return for the manpower and resources expended than would be the case in the concept of a static defense.[122]

In this document two important strands of thought come together. First, one sees the repudiation of the kind of war waged in Korea—limited, static, and reactive. According to the argument presented here, the aggressor, China, was allowed to dictate the tempo and style of the war—a mistake not to be repeated. Second, one discerns the related point that force should be used most effectively: that is, it should be directed with economy at those objectives that will defeat the opponent—"the United States should adopt the concept of offensive actions against the 'military power of the aggressor.' " Third, it was clear that a war in Indochina was regarded as one that would pull the U.S. off its world-wide strategy vis-à-vis the Soviet Union—into nondecisive theaters for non-decisive objectives.

We have other evidence that the JCS considered Indochina to be only a part of the problem in the Far East. In a memorandum by Dulles concerning a phone conversation with Eisenhower, Dulles expressed the view that the attitude of the Joint Chiefs with respect to the defense of Indochina could present a diplomatic problem at an upcoming five-power military meeting. Dulles's memo reads:

> I said that I was concerned lest the JCS viewpoint should be presented in a way which would have undesirable repercussions. Their judgment [the JCS] had been that there was little use discussing any "defense" of the Southeast Asia area or any substantial committal of U.S. force to this area; that United States power should be directed against the source of the peril which was, at least in the first instance, China, and that in this connection atomic weapons should be used.[123]

The British, Dulles believed, wanted to discuss the kind of defensive perimeter the West would form if all or part of Indochina were lost. Dulles believed that the JCS position would isolate the United States from the other nations. He added:

> it was not politically good judgment to take it for granted that any defensive coalition would be bound to become involved in a general war with China, and perhaps with Russia, and that this would be an atomic war.
>
> The President said he wholly agreed with me and that he was strongly opposed to any assumption that it was necessary to have a war with China.

The President, as Dulles recollected, added that the Joint Chiefs should not act in any way that interferes with the political purposes of the government and that he would talk to the military representatives of the other governments in case Radford did not relay the "political position" of the United States accurately.

Such stiff opposition might have been difficult for a military figure of even Eisenhower's stature to overcome. Events did not force the issue, *and Eisenhower was not in great disagreement with the JCS analysis or philosophy.* The American demands on the French to internationalize the war and to grant the Associated States real independence insulted the French. Likewise, the French wanted the United States to commit some ground forces and to give assurances that it would counteract Chinese air power. The United States was not willing to make such a pledge. By the middle of June there appeared little possibility that the French and Americans could come together, putting aside differences, and create the conditions for "united action."[124] Consequently, the French did their utmost to reach a negotiated settlement. Ronald Spector argues the fact that "intervention [did] not [take] place was in large measure attributable in part to General Ridgway and the Army staff, whose skeptical view of the prospects in Vietnam had prevailed, at least for the moment."[125] Herring and Immerman believe that the severe differences among the U.S., British, and French over the terms of "united action" destroyed any chances of American intervention.[126] Billings-Yun believes that Eisenhower did care deeply about not "losing" Indochina to the communist side, yet he did not want to fight in Indochina: "Eisenhower skillfully negotiated a path that kept American forces out of the French-Indochina War while maintaining America's commitment to the security of Southeast Asia."[127] So, "he put a high priority on inducing the French to win the war in Indochina or at least to negotiate from strength at Geneva."[128]

In light of these sentiments, Merchant's comment to the British diplomats that the effort on behalf of "united action" was an attempt to gain leverage at Geneva by deterring increased communist activity makes more sense.[129] With that said, it is doubtful that Eisenhower needed to be persuaded by Matthew Ridgway that entering an indecisive war in Southeast Asia was contrary to American national interests. Eisenhower and Ridgway had much more in common than they realized with respect to their thinking about the nature of war and the proper way to use force. None of the major actors in the Eisenhower Administration evinced sympathy during the debate over Dienbienphu for a "limited war" position as was seen in Korea under the Truman administration (i.e., Eisenhower, Dulles, Radford, Ridgway). At Dienbienphu one sees confirmation of the impression that a strong All-or-Nothing reaction to Korea had emerged and had become prevalent in the Eisenhower Administration. Clearly, the President and Ridgway were both influenced by their Korean War experiences.[130]

The Ascendance of Limited War Theory in the 1950s and 1960s

A retreat from Limited War thinking followed Dwight D. Eisenhower's inauguration in January 1953. The incoming administration's basic national security policy, the "New Look," resembled Jominian political-military thinking. The New Look was also intended to defend America for the economic long haul. The Truman defense costs troubled Eisenhower, a conservative on spending issues. Savings could be achieved, the President believed, by relying more on strategic and tactical nuclear weapons and by declining to respond to enemies on their terms. In sum, the United States would develop forces in which it had a comparative advantage and would defeat communist aggression by using the counterattack, not a purely reactive defense. Militarily, the New Look argued for the continuing validity of traditional military principles like initiative and surprise; its rejuvenation of the concept of the strategic offensive hearkened back to traditional military thought. Yet, for all the good intentions, the intellectual credibility of the New Look was undermined by the loss of American nuclear superiority. This became clear in the mid to late 1950s with the emergence of literature emphasizing the need for limited war capabilities in a bipolar nuclear world.

The new emphasis on nuclear weaponry was made possible by programs begun during the Truman administration that had produced technological breakthroughs that enabled nuclear weapons to be mass produced by 1954.[1] Consequently, these weapons of mass destruction were no longer a scarce resource for the United States, and the declaratory policy of the New Look stated that nuclear weapons would be used in any conflict in which their use would have military utility.[2] Such sentiments were expressed publicly by members of the administration:

> In December 1953 the Chairman of the Joint Chiefs of Staff observed that "Today atomic weapons have virtually achieved a conventional status within our armed forces." In a March 1955 press conference, President Eisenhower argued that "Where these things are used on strictly military targets and for strictly military purposes, I see no reason why they shouldn't be used just exactly as you would use a bullet or anything else.[3]

In its private and public statements the administration stressed the policy that nuclear weapons would be available for use. David Alan Rosenberg notes that in February 1956 President Eisenhower made it clear that "in the event of a conflict where Soviet forces attacked either the United States or U.S. forces, there was no doubt that the United States would use atomic weapons."[4] Whether they would have actually been used in particular crises can only be speculated upon.

The New Look attempted to balance the competing financial concerns of the government on the assumption that painful tradeoffs would have to be made. NSC 68, on the other hand, had finessed the problem of "guns or butter" by assuming that the economy could expand to meet the demand for more arms. Thus, in a memo to the NSC, Hamilton Q. Dearborn of the Council of Economic Advisers argued that concerns about NSC 68's call for increased defense "stem in large measure from an inadequate appreciation of our capacity for growth. They stem from a conviction that increased defense must mean equivalently lowered living standards, higher taxes and a proliferation of controls."[5]

The Eisenhower Administration disapproved of such an analysis and regarded the Truman budget deficits with alarm. The Administration's budgetary conservatism is seen clearly in a top secret report approved by the NSC on April 28, 1953. The report, entitled "Basic National Security Policies and Programs in Relation to Their Costs," begins as follows:

1. A vital factor in the long-term survival of the free world is the maintenance by the United States of a sound, strong economy. For the United States to continue a high rate of Federal spending in excess of Federal income, at a time of heavy taxation, will weaken and might eventually destroy that economy.[6]

To prevent the deterioration of the economy the United States, it was
argued, should return to a balanced budget as soon as possible. On
October 30, 1953, President Eisenhower signed NSC 162/2, his
administration's basic statement of national security policy. The theme
of economic concern was present in this document as well. NSC 162/2
said of the U.S. economy that "threats" to its "stability and growth"
endangered the coalition of noncommunist nations. The document
warned:

21. Excessive government spending leads to inflationary deficits or to
repressive taxation, or to both. Persistent inflation is a barrier to long-
term growth because it undermines confidence in the currency, reduces
savings, and makes restrictive economic controls necessary. Repressive
taxation weakens the incentives for efficiency, effort, and investment on
which economic growth depends.[7]

What was the solution to America's fiscal woes? The Eisenhower
Administration did not reject the Truman Administration's general
strategy of containment, nor did its assessment of the Soviet Union
threat differ markedly from its predecessor's. Eisenhower and Secretary
of State John Foster Dulles stressed more cost-effective means for
accomplishing the same objectives.

Dulles attempted to explain the policy in a speech to the Council
on Foreign Relations on January 12, 1954. It is best remembered as the
"massive retaliation" speech (even though he did not use the phrase
that evening) in which Dulles was perceived as saying the United
States would respond to even minor communist aggression with massive retaliation using nuclear weapons, if necessary. This interpretation
came from Dulles's statement that it would be the policy of the United States to "depend primarily upon a great capacity to retaliate,
instantly, by means and at places of our choosing." In an April 1954
article in *Foreign Affairs*, Dulles tried to allay many of the fears aroused
by his January speech. In this article a picture was painted of a flexible
strategy in which massive retaliation would lie in a range of options

that the administration would have at its disposal. Dulles told his readers that the fundamental military problem of the age was that of the deterrence of war. The cost of the conventional forces needed to block communist aggression in all regions could not be sustained. Therefore, the United States needed to devise a new strategy that would satisfy this description:

> To deter aggression, it is important to have flexibility and the facilities which make various responses available. In many cases, any open assault by Communist forces could only result in starting a general war. But the free world must have the means for responding effectively on a selective basis when it chooses. It must not put itself in the position where the only response open to it is general war.[8]

Dulles recognized the importance of "local defense." He argued that all free nations must possess "a sufficient military establishment to maintain order against subversion and to resist other forms of indirect and minor satellite aggressions."[9] But, he added, "in such areas the main reliance must be on the power of the free community to retaliate with great force by mobile means at places of its own choice."

There was no backing away from the administration's intention to rely more heavily on mobile strategic forces to achieve deterrence. The article also recognized that the possession of strategic forces alone might not be able to deter limited war in the future because the threat of nuclear retaliation for minor conventional aggression would not be credible. In NSC 162/2 of October 1953 the administration had recognized that the increasing nuclear equivalence between the superpowers could virtually eliminate the possible utility of total war; consider this passage from NSC 162/2:

> 6b. When both the USSR and the United States reach a stage of atomic plenty and ample means of delivery, each will have the probable capacity to inflict critical damage on the other, but is not likely to be able to prevent major atomic retaliations. This could create a stalemate, with both sides reluctant to initiate general warfare; although if the Soviets believed that initial surprise held the prospect of destroying the capacity for retaliation, they might be tempted into attacking.[10]

By the same reasoning, the threat of all-out, nuclear response as a deterrent to some low-level aggression in the world's periphery could lose its credibility as well. In fact, the often-drawn portrait of Eisenhower and Dulles as being excessively fond of nuclear weapons clearly misrepresents their opinions. As John Lewis Gaddis has noted of Dulles, the secretary of state told Eisenhower in April 1958 that there were "increasing possibilities of effective defense through tactical nuclear weapons and other means short of wholesale obliteration of the Soviet Union, and . . . these should be developed more rapidly."[11] Gaddis believes that Dulles "anticipated many of the criticisms advocates of 'flexible response' would later make [of the New Look]; and that he even contemplated, as a long-range goal and on both geopolitical and moral grounds, the abolition of nuclear weapons altogether."[12] Dulles was also particularly worried about the effects that Soviet nuclear capabilities would have on the resolve of America's European allies who were well within range of the Soviet arsenal. He believed that "talk of atomic attack tended to create 'peace at any price people' and might lead to an increase of appeasement sentiment in various countries."[13]

The Administration also noted that the Soviet Union's "capacity for political warfare against the United States as well as its allies will be enhanced by their increased atomic capability."[14] A strengthened Soviet Union would be likely to become more aggressive in peripheral areas in which the deterrent effect of American atomic power would be eroded.[15] As a response NSC 162/2 argued that the United States must "take all feasible diplomatic, political, economic, and covert measures" to counter Soviet expansion in the free world; of particular importance in the Eisenhower administration was the use of covert action to diminish the prestige of the Soviets and undermine communist movements throughout the world.[16]

Gaddis imparts the significance of Eisenhower's policy with the assessment that "covert actions did not really come into their own as an instrument of national strategy until the Eisenhower administration."[17] With regard to the newly acknowledged problem of limited war, the Eisenhower administration, as Samuel P. Huntington notes, adjusted its policies but there was no wholesale alteration of its programs.[18] The administration's major effort in this area focused on the development and incorporation of *tactical* nuclear weapons into the American force structure. These weapons had yields much smaller than the strategic weapons already in the American arsenal, and the administration intended that they would find a place on the battlefield of the future—

not only for deterrent purposes but also for reasons of war-fighting as well. Thus, the massive retaliation component of the New Look was softened by the addition of the concept related to these developments called "graduated deterrence."[19] The Eisenhower administration did not endorse enlarging conventional force budgets to counter the threat of limited war, but in its later years "allowed the services individually to take steps, within prescribed budget limits, to improve their limited war capabilities."[20]

What then was at the heart of the New Look? Gaddis has perceptively distilled the essence of this approach to national security policy:

> . . . . the central idea was that of asymmetrical response—of reacting to adversary challenges in ways calculated to apply one's own strengths against the other side's weaknesses, even if this meant shifting the nature and location of the confrontation. The effect, it was believed, would be to regain the initiative while reducing costs. Nuclear weapons were a major component of that strategy, to be sure, but so too were such other elements as alliances, psychological warfare, covert action, and negotiations.[21]

The New Look should be understood as a threat to escalate low-level conflicts to the advantage of the United States, but it *did not require* nuclear war as an immediate or eventual response to aggression.[22]

If the economic essence of the New Look was that federal expenditures and revenues would have to be balanced for the long-term economic health of the nation, the military soul of the doctrine was its restoration of the initiative as an option in American politico-military thinking. As Lawrence Freedman observes, "On one level it was a revival of the spirit of the offense in military strategy."[23] This revival of the offensive lived more in the abstract than in reality, for the growing Soviet nuclear capability dictated caution and prudence. With this in mind, Freedman makes an incisive observation relating the Korean War to the New Look:

> If anything, the strategy was more retrospective than prospective. It explained how the Korean War ought to have been fought. It explained how a new war might be fought during the remaining period of grace of patent nuclear superiority. Observing the influence of US airpower on Soviet conduct, it sought to exploit this to avoid meeting the cost of conventional rearmament. A nuclear strategy was far cheaper than a conventional strategy.[24]

Thus, the New Look clearly reflected two aspects of Eisenhower's thought. First, it emphasized his concern with fiscal responsibility. Second, it contained those Jominian elements in his thinking that emphasized the traditional principles of war—like initiative, surprise, and mass—which were absent from the Korean War after it bogged down into a static war of attrition in the summer to autumn of 1951.[25] This observation is supported by Marc Trachtenberg who, as discussed in chapter 3, writes of Eisenhower's philosophy of war-fighting, "His thinking was right out of the first few pages of Clausewitz: war has an innate tendency to become absolute. Winning was the only thing that mattered."[26]

As may be recalled from chapter 1, both Clausewitz and Jomini recognized the importance of decisive action in war. Clausewitz took that insight and placed it within the structure of an examination of war as a political phenomenon in which force is subordinated as the instrument of policy. Eisenhower read Clausewitz when he was stationed in Panama in the 1920s where he studied "under the tutelage of a remarkable senior officer, Fox Conner."[27] The question then arises as to how Eisenhower understood Clausewitz. Did he misunderstand him and apply a "Jominian" interpretation to his writings or did he grasp the political nature of Clausewitz's conception of war? Gaddis maintains Eisenhower learned from *On War* "that in politics as well as in war, means had to be subordinated to ends."[28]

It would be expecting too much of Eisenhower to demand the understanding of *On War* that we now have with the publication of the Howard/Paret translation and the voluminous English writings on Clausewitz that have been prompted by Peter Paret's *Clausewitz and the State*. In the nuclear era the *political* dimension of his thought has been given much greater attention than was the case before 1945. Thus, it is not surprising that Eisenhower, who graduated from West Point in 1915, might not describe these relationships with the greatest of clarity. Also, as Richard H. Immerman, a revisionist Eisenhower scholar, notes: Eisenhower was not "an intellectual or a Rand-type theorist."[29] Given those limitations, Eisenhower's actions bespeak an understanding of the need to place war-fighting within a political context. His thinking seemed to embody the conceptual struggle that lies at the heart of the tension discussed here between the political and military elements of war and of the tendency of force to reach for its absolute.

He told a press conference: "Remember this: when you resort to force as the arbiter of human difficulty, you don't know where you are going; . . . if you get deeper and deeper, there is just no limit except what is imposed by the limitations of force itself."[30]

Eisenhower understood the dangers of force and recognized why it had to be subordinated to policy. At the same time the President was fully aware of the horror of nuclear war; at a press conference on September 30, 1953, he remarked that the "only possible tragedy greater than winning a war would be losing it."[31] Immerman observes that Eisenhower had a sophisticated sense of balance between the various elements of geopolitics.[32] All that being said, the Eisenhower defense policy had conceptual weaknesses. In fact, the New Look's credibility was bound to be undermined by the advance of weapons technology and nuclear bipolarity. The inner conflict one sees in Eisenhower's philosophy of war between his comprehension of the inexorable realities of using force and the need to place the use of force within a political context is analogous to the tension that this study has said exists within the nature of war itself. In essence, Eisenhower personifies, in his actions and thoughts, the tension between the logic of force and the demands of policy.

The New Look's concern with the economic costs of military policy can hardly be contested, but its weakness lay in the declaratory policy's incompatibility with the emerging world of the 1950s. Possibly, intelligence gathered from U-2 flights indicating American strategic superiority over the Soviets assured top-level U.S. officials, but that condition would not remain indefinitely. Because most observers were not privy to such information, they perceived the strategic balance as shifting in the Soviets' favor during the late 1950s; this caused a sense of alarm in the national security community. A widespread feeling emerged that the military posture of the United States was insufficient to deter limited war in peripheral regions. Would the United States, the critics asked, really use nuclear weaponry in such areas? The deterrent, they concluded, lacked credibility.[33] Also, the New Look was problematic because it publicly assumed a monolithic communist threat to the free nations—if this were not the case, what good would it do to threaten retaliation in "places of our choosing" which were not the areas of provocation?[34]

In practice the administration was cautious when crises occurred, and the New Look's emphasis on diplomatic, psychological, and covert action was subtle. These truths, however, do not erase the fact that Eisenhower attempted to maintain worldwide commitments at less expense by relying on a declaratory policy which lacked credibility. President Eisenhower was very skeptical of arguments positing the possibility of limited war with the Soviets in which nuclear arms would not be used. George Kistiakowsky, the President's Special Assistant for Science and Technology, describes an NSC meeting of October 6, 1960, in which limited war scenarios were discussed. Eisenhower "thought the whole thing was very unrealistic and that we were unfortunately so committed to nuclear weapons that the only practical move would be to start using them from the beginning without any distinction between them and conventional weapons and also, assuming there was direct Russian involvement, mount an all-out strike on the Soviet Union."[35]

Trachtenberg writes that as the 1950s went by "the strategy of massive retaliation was viewed increasingly as bankrupt, even at the highest levels of the administration, although a certain effort was made to conceal this from the outside world."[36] In a December 22, 1954, memo from Dulles to Eisenhower, the Secretary of State queried whether the U.S. was "prepared to deal adequately with the possible 'little wars' which might call for punishment related to the degree and locality of the offense, but which would not justify a massive retaliation against the Soviet Union itself."[37] Even though Eisenhower disagreed with the fundamental premises of this strategic perspective, he "acquiesced in the drift away from massive retaliation, but in his heart remained skeptical: as terrible as it was, there was no getting away from the massive strike as the ultimate basis of policy; it was just self-deception to pretend otherwise."[38] When the Eisenhower Administration left office in January 1961 its limited war capabilities were substantial. In May 1961 the U.S. had the ability to sustain 250,000 to 300,000 combat personnel in one locality.[39]

The Development of a Limited War School

As stated in chapter 2 writers like Basil Liddell Hart, Jacob Viner, George Kennan, and the drafters of NSC 68 (primarily Paul Nitze) had recognized before the outbreak of the Korean War that conflicts of the future would have to be limited if civilization were to survive and war were to retain some rational purpose. After the Korean experience and the explosion of the first thermonuclear device in 1953 these arguments became even more convincing. But the policy debate found the Eisenhower administration and the air force "ranged against almost every other interested party" because of their support for the New Look's emphasis on massive retaliatory capability as a deterrent to aggression.[40] The army, navy, and a great majority of civilian military specialists argued against the administration's position.[41] The common theme of these works is that the raw power of nuclear weapons would make "total" wars suicidal. If states were to avoid self-destruction they would have to limit the objectives of war and the means used in war. Also, many of these writers questioned the deterrent effectiveness of nuclear weapons. Would a nuclear power really be able to deter peripheral aggression with weapons of mass destruction? If nuclear weapons could only deter the use of other nuclear weapons, how would large conventional wars be deterred?

Within a month of the outbreak of the Korean War the *Bulletin of Atomic Scientists* contained articles arguing that conflicts of the future would be "small wars" in which atomic weapons would be of limited value:

> If we concentrate on [the] fabrication of weapons of mass destruction, and do not balance this development by the creation of a sufficiently large, well supplied, and strategically distributed land force, we will run a double danger: We will be in danger of losing out in peripheral skirmishes with Soviet satellites, such as the Korean War; and we will have deprived ourselves of freedom of decision in the event of an open Soviet aggression against nations of the Atlantic Pact.[42]

After the Korean War this perspective became more thoroughly developed. In the mid-1950s an explosion of similar writings appeared, probably prompted by Dulles's statements about the New Look. Two of the earliest works in an explicit Limited War philosophy were written by William Kaufmann and appeared in his edited volume *National Policy and National Security* (1956).[43] The two most relevant chapters, "The Requirements of Deterrence" and "Limited War," when taken together called into doubt the credibility of massive retaliation as a deterrent, especially in instances of conventional or peripheral conflict. Credibility, Kaufmann argued, was the most important element in deterrence, and credibility would be obtainable if the United States had the capability to "fit the punishment to the crime."[44] Consequently, a wide range of options must be ready, not just the All-or-Nothing deterrent of massive retaliation.

"Limited War" argued that the defense of American interests in the future would require that the United States develop the willingness and the capabilities to engage in these kinds of wars. The American public reaction to Korea was extremely negative, but, Kaufmann observed, "the American people did put up with the Korean War for three long and painful years."[45] It was Kaufmann's desire that the American polity "give up the concept of victory in its traditional meaning" and replace it with a more realistic understanding of the need to use limited violence to seek limited ends in a nuclear world.[46]

In 1957 two major works were published. The first, Robert Osgood's *Limited War*, presented another plea for the United States to develop the capacity to limit its aims in war so that it could still remain a rational policy option for the United States.[47] Osgood may have been the first author in this school to invoke Clausewitz's dictum in the debate.[48] In short, Osgood wanted war, when regrettably necessary, to be available as a policy instrument. He feared, as did Kaufmann, that the American tradition of all-out war-fighting would make it very difficult for the country to limit its objectives during a conflict. Osgood hoped that these old patterns of behavior could be altered for the future.

Henry Kissinger's *Nuclear Weapons and Foreign Policy* was the first book written in the area of strategic studies to become a best seller in the United States.[49] Kissinger also discussed the American propensity to fight total wars with absolute victory as the objective. He voiced the criticism that the New Look fit into this tradition of all-out war and, thereby, constrained U.S. policy options. There needed to be room for policies between total war and stalemate.[50] That middle road lay in the area of limited war. Kissinger argued that a limited war strategy needed to be adopted: "A doctrine for limited war will have to discard any illusions about what can be achieved by means of it. Limited War is not a cheaper substitute for massive retaliation. On the contrary, it must be based on an awareness that with the end of our atomic monopoly it is no longer possible to impose unconditional surrender at an acceptable cost."[51]

He later gave three reasons for developing a limited war strategy: first, the use of limited means was the only way to check Soviet bloc expansion into peripheral regions at a bearable cost; second, the wide array of options necessary to fight limited wars might become a decisive factor in the outcome of a major war between the United States and the Soviet Union; third, "intermediate applications of our power offer the best chance to bring about strategic changes favorable to our side."[52]

It was at this point that Kissinger went on to cautiously argue that the United States develop the capability to use tactical nuclear weapons. These were munitions of very low yield with "limited" radioactive fallout. Kissinger recognized that the traditional tactics of our grand forces would have to be radically changed with an emphasis being placed on dispersion of forces to avoid nuclear blast. The capacity for rapid deployment to distant regions was also critical. It needs to be mentioned that the late 1950s saw the eruption of a debate over the use of tactical nuclear weapons. The term *escalation*, borrowed, of course, from the image of an escalator moving inexorably upward, was introduced by writers critical of the idea that wars using limited nuclear weapons could be controlled.[53] In general, the participants in the debate came to the conclusion that the great advantage of these weapons would be minimized when the Soviets acquired them and that it would be difficult to control these wars. It was also learned in military field exercises that the collateral damage and fallout created by the use of these weapons in a realistic setting would be horrific. So it was that by the early 1960s much of the enthusiasm for these weapons had dissipated. In fact, within a few years Kissinger reversed his position with regard to tactical nuclear weapons and now argued that conventional forces should be the central element in our limited war posture.[54]

Another significant policy-oriented book appeared three years later. It was General Maxwell Taylor's *The Uncertain Trumpet* (1959). Taylor, a two-term Chief of Staff of the U.S. Army, had retired in 1959 over policy disagreements with the Eisenhower administration. *The Uncertain Trumpet* argued that the United States had to acquire sufficient conventional forces to meet its defense needs without placing primary reliance on nuclear weapons. He stated his position as follows:

> The strategic doctrine which I propose to replace Massive Retaliation is herein called the Strategy of Flexible Response. This name suggests the need for a capability to react across the entire spectrum of possible chal-

lenge, for coping with anything from general atomic war to infiltrations and aggressions such as threaten Laos and Berlin in 1959. The new strategy would recognize that it is just as necessary to deter or win quickly a limited war as to deter general war. Otherwise, the limited war which we cannot win quickly may result in our piecemeal attrition or involvement in expanding conflict which may grow into the general conflict we all want to avoid.[55]

Later in the book, Taylor qualified the notion that limited wars could always be won quickly. He added, "Bearing in mind that limited wars are not necessarily either small or short wars, the modernization program [he was advocating] would take into account the needs of the first six months—both our own and those of our allies."[56] This remark is quite significant for it recognizes that these limited wars might be protracted conflicts for which a national mobilization of resources might be needed. Taylor's statement contradicted much of the current wisdom of the time which had assumed the existence of nuclear weapons would dictate that future wars would end quickly. For Taylor the inadequacy of our nuclear forces as a deterrent for conventional war was irrefutable; consequently, the United States would have to prepare for war "by accepting the fact that primary dependence must be placed on conventional weapons while retaining readiness to use tactical atomic weapons in the comparatively rare cases where their use would be to our national interest."[57]

A further development in the limited war school involved the inclusion of ideas conceived of by an economist, Thomas Schelling, and a physicist, Herman Kahn. These writers fleshed out the bargaining and escalation elements that could take place in limited wars. Schelling was among the earliest writers to pursue this theme. One of his most important contributions was the idea of tacit bargaining between opponents. He argued that bargaining of this type would take place in limited wars and that the limiting points in these wars, which he referred to as "saliencies," must be distinct and recognizable. Such limiting points might be geographical or weapons related. For example, the difference between the use of nuclear and non-nuclear weapons was distinct in a way that gradations of use within these two categories were not.[58] Richard Smoke supports this interpretation of Schelling's work in this area: "Schelling suggested that limited war should be seen as a kind of 'bargaining' process in which the bargaining was tacit.

That is, each side bargained with the other about what the ground rules should be by deliberately escalating the conflict a certain amount, but not more, or by ostentatiously holding itself to some particularly obvious self-limitation."[59]

Herman Kahn's earlier books had focused on central war between the two great powers (*On Thermonuclear War*, 1960), but even that work made the point that there were many different scenarios for nuclear war. Depending on the scenario followed, the level of death and destruction would vary. This idea, of the different levels of war-fighting, was taken to its utmost in Kahn's book *On Escalation*.[60] As Freedman tells us, ". . . . *On Escalation*, became notorious, mainly because of his description of an 'escalation ladder' of 44 rungs, in which nuclear weapons were first used at rung 15."[61] It is worth noting that the meaning of "escalation" had in only a short time come full circle since Wayland Young first used the term in 1959; "escalation" no longer implied an escalator relentlessly moving upward; now the term was being used to convey the idea of a possibly controlled increase in the use of force where intensification of the violence employed did not necessarily imply a loss of control by the political authorities engaged in the war.[62] According to Freedman, Kahn's argument was essentially that "it was possible that controlled, discriminating patterns of behavior would continue even in a conflict being resolved in the presence, and with the occasional use, of nuclear weapons."[63] Limited War had come a long way from those first days after Hiroshima.

First, a corpus of writing had accumulated that established to almost everyone's satisfaction that limited war capabilities were sorely needed. Then the writings became more abstract as game theorists began to consider the problem. Schelling offered important ways to think of tacit bargaining's focal points, and Kahn added a hypothetical degree of precision and discrimination in our understanding of the process of escalation. Kahn's use of the rungs of a ladder as a metaphor for the steps in the escalation process made the problem easier to understand but also trivialized the differences between the different positions on the ladder. Undoubtedly, Limited War theory had reached a degree of sophistication and refinement not present a decade earlier, but it was this element of cold rationality and detached intellectualism that led the to the Limited War School's defeat at the hands of the more worldly North Vietnamese.

The Army and Limited War

The army opposed the strategic orientation of the New Look. Its arguments bore some resemblance to those made by civilian defense experts. The army, which felt that the most likely future wars would be limited, localized conflicts like Korea, foresaw the decreasing credibility of the American deterrent unless it contained substantial conventional forces. It also argued that substantial ground forces would be needed to secure bases for the navy and air force and that ground forces would be needed to occupy enemy territory in the event of a major nuclear war with the Soviets. These criticisms of the New Look surfaced within the government late in 1953. During the process of approving NSC 162/2 in late October of that year, the NSC requested that the Planning Board of the NSC submit a revision of the paper "U.S. Objectives vis-a-vis the USSR in the Event of War." The army used this opportunity to voice some of its basic criticisms of the New Look.[64]

The preliminary draft of the new document was numbered NSC 5410. In it "the NSC Planning Board defined the primary US wartime objective as the 'destruction of both the military capability and military potential of the Soviet bloc.' "[65] This was, in essence, the statement of New Look war aims. The army's main points were that such a scenario for war-fighting would alienate the potentially friendly nations of Eastern Europe, it would make the rehabilitation of the defeated nations extremely difficult, and it would strain relations with allies and neutral nations after the war.[66] When the Planning Board's revised draft did not incorporate any of the army's points, another army paper was submitted. According to A. J. Bacevich this document argued for a limited role for atomic weapons. Specifically, it wanted the following war policy:

- The prohibition, or minimum use, of weapons of mass destruction.
- The restriction of attacks by weapons of mass destruction, if used, to selected targets which would cause minimum human loss and material loss and promote achievement of military objectives by conventional forces.[67]

This paper from the army prevented agreement on NSC 5410 within the Planning Board, so the issue was brought before the NSC and the President on March 25, 1954.[68] At the meeting, General Ridgway, the

Army Chief of Staff, did not present the counter-argument to NSC 5410. In an odd twist of bureaucratic maneuvering that task fell to the Chairman of the JCS, Admiral Radford, who supported the New Look. Radford summarized the army's major points as being: first, that the destructive effect of these weapons would be so great that it would be difficult to cope with the victory; second, that major war planning should take place in advance of war rather than in the course of a conflict. The President then responded with a series of informative comments. The minutes read as follows:

> [The President] said he was speaking very frankly to the Council in expressing his absolute conviction that in view of the development of the new weapons of mass destruction, with the terrible significance which these involved, everything in any future war with the Soviet bloc would have to be subordinated to winning that war. This was the one thing which must be constantly born in mind, and there was little else with respect to war objectives that needed to worry anyone very much.[69]

After that the President said he might have been more sympathetic to the Ridgway-Carney qualifications ten years ago but not now.[70] He emphasized his vehemence on this point by "turning to paragraph 1 of the report which read: 'To achieve a victory which will ensure the survival of the United States as a free nation and the continuation of its free institutions in the post-war period.' This, said the President, he would change by putting a period after 'victory' and deleting the rest of the paragraph, if not the paper."[71] Needless to say Ridgway's objections did not get very far and NSC 5410 was approved with slight modification of the New Look plans. Over the course of 1954 the debate continued within the government. At the end of the year on December 3, 1954, Ridgway presented his position orally to the NSC and the President. Bacevich provides the following summary of Ridgway's remarks:

> He challenged the thesis that "massive retaliatory power" could be "the major deterrent to aggression." He suggested that the use of nuclear weapons in future wars was not inevitable; that if used their effect might not prove decisive; that if used indiscriminately their effect would prove so destructive as to call into question the very contemplation of such a course. He called on the NSC to "reject emphatically any policy of *preventive* war" as "devoid of moral principle." In lieu of relying on nuclear weapons Ridgway advocated the creation of forces that were "properly

balanced and of adequate readiness," contending that their availability would be "the most effective deterrent to general war." Furthermore, he insisted such forces were entirely affordable.[72]

The President listened to the remarks of General Ridgway, and after Ridgway had left the room he said "he had a strong feeling that General Ridgway was sincere in his view of the need for balanced U.S. military forces rather than reliance upon atomic retaliatory capacity." Eisenhower did not believe that the General was expressing a "parochial" army point of view.[73] Nevertheless, he believed that the funds required for such a program would bankrupt the nation and jeopardize its free institutions. A bit later in the discussion President Eisenhower "stated that our only chance of victory in a third world war against the Soviet Union would be to paralyze the enemy at the outset of the war." In order to prevent the United States from becoming an "armed camp or a garrison state" the atom bomb would have to be used in a major war.[74]

Ridgway became an irritant to the administration. He even made his opposition to the New Look known on Capitol Hill.[75] As a result of this disenchantment with him, Ridgway was not asked to serve a second term as Army Chief of Staff in June 1955. He then retired from active service in the army, and his letter of resignation was leaked to the *New York Times*. The published letter gave the American people a sense of his unhappiness with the New Look. The letter contained a thorough attack on massive retaliation:

> In a situation of nuclear plenty, mutual cancellation of nuclear advantage can occur in terms of mutual devastation; or, depending on the degree of parity, in terms of mutually limited use; or, finally, in common refusal to use nuclear weapons at all. It seems doubtful that the USSR would initiate employment of nuclear weapons in the face of a preponderance of nuclear weapons possessed by the United States. On the other hand, should the Western nations initiate their use, the USSR would have no choice but to respond in kind, in the hope that the resultant destruction to the West would circumscribe the ability of the United States to continue effective prosecution of such a war. In the light of this major possibility for the future, it is at least debatable whether the United States really has the freedom to rely preponderantly on nuclear weapons to exert its military power.[76]

Ridgway later asserted in the letter that the military weakness of the United States was concentrated in its inability to fight non-nuclear war in a variety of terrains and climates.

Although they vehemently opposed each other on budgetary and force structure issues, Eisenhower and Ridgway shared a view of the way wars should be conducted. Neither Eisenhower nor Ridgway held the Korean War up as a model worthy of emulation. Both men believed that it was critical to the effective use of force that it be employed with power and concentration. Eisenhower also seemed to believe that the next great war would almost be impossible to keep below the nuclear threshold; consequently, this belief and his fiscal conservatism led him toward skepticism of Limited War arguments. Ridgway seemed confident that nuclear weapons had nullified themselves as effective weapons, so it was natural for him to consider a major conventional war as a genuine possibility. Neither Eisenhower nor Ridgway would have commented favorably on the antiseptic war-fighting that Schelling and Kahn envisaged in the 1960s.

Ridgway's replacement as Army Chief of Staff added no support for administration policies within the JCS. The new Chief of Staff, Maxwell Taylor, would, as mentioned above, later write one of the more important works in the Limited War tradition. Taylor was more politically astute than Ridgway and began to cloak army policies in terms of deterrence as early as October 1955.[77] Thus, as the civilian administration began to reduce the role of the army within the defense establishment, the army was concerning itself with the problems of fighting in various terrains and climates.

Let there be no doubt, the army under Ridgway and Taylor was preparing to fight nuclear war as well. This included the development of *tactical* nuclear weapons which the army saw as a kind of extremely powerful artillery. The army never gave much support to strategic nuclear weapons. A battlefield in which tactical nuclear weapons were used would require one's ground forces to be flexible, mobile, and dispersible. In fact an entirely new organizational plan was instituted. It reorganized the traditional division into the "Pentomic Division." The regiment was eliminated, and the new battalion was so radically altered that it was renamed the "battle group."[78] The term "pentomic" referred to the fact that each division would have five battle groups. The battle groups were supposed to resemble amorphous independent cells that could be detached from the main unit and exist by themselves in the nuclear field of combat. In the fall of 1956 the 101st Airborne Division was the first division to be reorganized along this pattern.

The pentomic division hearkened back to tactics of an earlier era—that of World War I:

> Its principal aspect mirrored the approach [the French and British officers of World War I] had unflinchingly pursued through years of deadlocked trench warfare in France: a stubborn faith in the ability of fires to shatter prepared defenses; a belief that preliminary bombardments reduced the attacker's role to securing by rapid, controlled advances the gain that fires had made possible; and a consequent attempt to improve responsiveness and control by simplifying tactics—attacking straight ahead, using stereotyped formations, and de-emphasizing factors such as deception or surprise that complicate an operation.[79]

The problem with the pentomic army was that it turned out to be an unworkable mess.[80] It proved so problematic that when John Kennedy took office in 1961 this entire military concept was tossed aside without much fanfare. Bacevich makes the point that it is ironic that the army which came to regard all but the most limited use of nuclear weapons as problematic should have spent so much time and effort building these munitions and restructuring the army to accommodate them as a contingency. The effort expended on the possibility of nuclear warfare unquestionably left the army in a weak position with respect to limited, conventional warfare. And, possibly of greater importance, the preoccupation with atomic war-fighting diverted attention from the growing problem of counterinsurgency and other more directly political forms of conflict.[81]

Limited War with a Dash of Decisive Military Action

The reader may have noticed a shift in the thinking of Matthew Ridgway from the last chapter to this one. At the time of Dienbienphu Ridgway was unwilling to commit the United States to any activity that would not produce decisive results in Southeast Asia. Yet in this chapter we have seen Ridgway become an outspoken advocate of American limited war capabilities. I believe that an important conceptual development underlies these seemingly inconsistent actions.

Ridgway's espousal of limited war capabilities does not appear to have been determined by the parochial budgetary needs of his service. Ridgway considered limited war to be *non-nuclear war*,[82] therefore, he could conceive of fighting a limited war while simultaneously complying with the self-imposed requirement that decisive results be attained from the use of force. Ridgway's (and the army's), conception of limited war differed from that of the civilian writers, but using the term allowed the army to play on the same intellectual field with the most influential critics of the New Look. The army, its officers, or military writers were not perpetrating a fraud but were most likely unaware of the different meanings that were being given to these terms. There were also differences within the army itself. While Ridgway and Taylor both alienated themselves from the Eisenhower administration by asserting the need for limited war capabilities and arguing against the New Look's budget constraints there was nevertheless a philosophical distance between Ridgway and Taylor. Ridgway, as we have seen, held to a more traditional conception of how force should be used—in the style of the Jominian principles of war. Taylor's approach was more flexible and pragmatic. He stressed the importance of the political object in war and was willing to enter wars like Korea if the national interest required it.

Taylor was not a closet dove—he believed that the achievement of political objectives required sustained military pressure. However, Taylor's frustrations with Korea did not lead him to condemn limited wars in which "victory" was not sought.[83] When he testified before the Senate in 1966, Taylor stated that the United States was not trying to "defeat" North Vietnam, but rather "to cause them to mend their ways." He described the concept of victory in war as resembling "Appomattox or something of that sort."[84] Taylor's belief that the United States needed to be able to fight wars like Korea and Vietnam may be seen in a question he posed at the end of a chapter in *Swords and Plowshares*: "Finally, both wars raised an unanswered question: Can a democracy such as the United States carry a prolonged limited war to a successful conclusion?"[85] The phrasing and placement of the question imply that Taylor believed the United States would not always be able to prosecute such wars. The passage also leaves the reader with the feeling that Taylor thought the United States ought to have that capability even after Vietnam.

A remark by General Ridgway concerning intervention at Dienbienphu sheds light on the degree of his affinity for truly limited war. He wrote these words after his retirement from the army in 1955: "If we did go into Indo-China, we would have to win. We would have to go in with a military force adequate in all its branches, and that meant a very strong ground force. . . . We could not again afford to accept anything short of decisive military victory." Less than fifty pages later in these memoirs, the reader can find a copy of his letter of resignation to Secretary of Defense Wilson; in that letter the former chief of staff argues that the United States government should enhance its limited war capabilities.[87]

In the minds of Ridgway and many others, these two shades of thought were fused in the following manner. Limited war came to refer to non-nuclear war or, more precisely, to nonstrategic nuclear war: some small-scale use of tactical nuclear weapons was considered consistent with the definition of limited war. Consequently, the term "limited war" was able to encompass wars of great violence like the old-fashioned conventional wars that pursued decisive military force to achieve one's objectives (e.g., World War II). The civilian writers, on the other hand, used "limited war" to argue in favor of wars like Korea in which the means used in war were kept below a specified level and decisive military victory was not necessarily achieved or sought.

It may be instructive to consider how the conceptions of warfare presented by Eisenhower, Ridgway, and Taylor compare to the model that Clausewitz has provided. Eisenhower embodied the Clausewitzian tension within his thinking about war and in his actions. Rather interestingly, his position was balanced on each side by Ridgway and Taylor—each of whose conceptions of using force appears to lack a sense of the whole nature of war. Ridgway's position lacked the balance provided by a greater comprehension of the *political* element of war. Taylor, on the other hand, was so committed to the precise use of military power, as his testimony about the Vietnam War demonstrates, that he came to underestimate the difficulty of applying military power effectively. Taylor was more aware of this problem, as will be shown in a later chapter, than were other high-level officials in the Johnson Administration, but by the beginning of the 1960s he seems to have made this intellectual error. President Eisenhower struggled with these problems. He was clearly inclined to use force decisively if it had to be used, but he, like Clausewitz, recognized that force was a dangerous tool that could sweep untaught practitioners into treacherous territory.

The Operational Field Manual and a Critic

A concept of war, consistent with the interpretation given above, appears in the army's operational field manual, FM 100–5, published in September 1954 and released while General Ridgway was still Chief of Staff.[88] The introductory chapter contained a section called "Army Forces"; it defined ground forces as follows:

> Army forces, as land forces, are the decisive component of the military structure by virtue of their unique ability to close with and destroy the organized and irregular forces of an enemy power or coalition of powers; to seize and control critical land areas and enemy lines of communications and bases of production and supply; and to defend those areas essential to the prosecution of a war by the United States and its allies.[89]

The statement continued by contentiously and incorrectly notifying the other services that ground forces do not support "the operations of any other component." A bit later the manual states, "The basic doctrine of army operations is *the defeat* of an enemy by application of military power directly or indirectly against the armed forces which support his political structure."[90] And in the next section the overall mission of the army was stated as bringing "to bear upon an enemy's military capacity sufficient power at decisive points and times to render it ineffective." These statements reflect the traditional military concept of the army's role. The repeated use of the word "decisive" does not lend itself to the description of political wars in which force might not be the determining element in the outcome—i.e., limited wars of Schelling-like bargaining. Until this point in the manual the army describes itself as existing solely for the purpose of defeating its enemy.

In section 8, entitled "Limitations," restrictions on the use of force are presented in terms similar to those of the civilian proponents of limited war capabilities:

Military forces are justifiable only as instruments of national policy in the attainment of national objectives. Since war is a political act, its broad and final objectives are political; therefore, its conduct must conform to policy and its outcome realize the objectives of policy. Victory alone as an aim of war cannot be justified, since in itself victory does not always assure the realization of national objectives. If the policy objectives are to be realized, policy and not interim expediency must govern the application of military power.[91]

The supremacy of the political objectives could not be stated more clearly, but this description of the relation of political ends to military means is soon contradicted. In the section on the "Principles of War" one sees a reversion to the more traditional approach to fighting wars. The FM 100–5 describes the principles of war as follows:

69. General
The principles of war are fundamental truths governing the prosecution of war. Their proper application is essential to the exercise of command and to successful conduct of military operations. The degree of application of any specific principle will vary with the situation.[92]

The most telling aspect of the section on the "Principles of War" is the definition of the "Objective" and the "Offensive":

Every military operation must be directed toward a decisive, obtainable objective. The destruction of the enemy's armed forces and his will to fight is the ultimate military object of war. The objective of each operation must contribute to this ultimate objective. . . . It must permit the application of the maximum means available.[93]
  Only offensive action achieves decisive results. Offensive action permits the commander to exploit the initiative and impose his will on the enemy. The defensive may be forced on the commander, but it should be deliberately adopted only as a temporary expedient while awaiting an opportunity for offensive action or for the purpose of economizing forces on a front where a decision is sought. Even on the defensive the commander seeks every opportunity to seize the initiative and achieve decisive results by offensive action.[94]

The point is carried further in the discussion of the principle of "Mass" which states, *"Maximum available combat power must be applied at the point of decision."*

Even though the army espoused the view that political objectives had to predominate in war, its "principles of war" were more consistent with the total war notions of the Civil War or World War II than with the limited war ideas of the nuclear age. It is clear that the army regarded the upper boundary of limited war as being roughly equivalent to large-scale conventional war which employed the tactical use of nuclear weapons. The 1962 FM 100–5 supports this point. The 1962 manual, written during the Kennedy administration's emphasis on flexible response, contained a section that discussed limited war.[95] The term *limited war* has an asterisk beside it; the corresponding footnote reads, "This term describes a wide range of armed conflicts among which are those commonly called local aggressions, conventional war, or limited nuclear war." The text of section nine also states:

> The term "limited" does not imply that a limited war is little or that it is ever unimportant. It may be armed conflict between small forces in a relatively restricted area, in which only conventional weapons are used. On the other hand, it may involve extremely large forces, engaged over a large area.[96]

Limited War by this definition might include any war up to the scale of World War II in which there were no strategic nuclear strikes by the opponents.[97]

A contemporary article, entitled "War Without Victory?" by Colonel Trevor N. Dupuy appeared in 1956. It argues that the inclusion of a section in the manual that undercuts the conceptual necessity of military victory erodes the morale and operational well-being of the army.[98] The pieces appeared at roughly the time that these debates about the role of the army and the appropriate manner of using force were taking place. "War without Victory?" begins by assessing the 1954 FM 100–5: "It is reassuring and comforting to read its sound, forward-looking exposition of current army doctrine. Thoughtful soldiers will appreciate the restatement of the principles of war as fundamental truths proved by lessons of history" (p. 28). Dupuy agrees with the manual's qualification of these principles as depending on the circumstances in which the soldier finds himself and also praises the categorical statement of the FM 100–5 that "the ultimate decision in war must be achieved . . . on the ground." But the author then launches his major criticism of the new manual:

Yet in this splendid manual one can perceive "a cloud no larger than a
man's hand." . . . there are indications that the text is catering to a wider
audience, apparently to those who might not understand or be sympathetic to the forthright statement of some fundamental truths which are
so well expressed in other parts of the book. In this respect one wonders
if the manual is trying to "sell" possible critics, to reassure them as to the
liberality and unregimented nature of the military mind." (p. 28)

The passage that he deems most offensive is the section in the new FM
100–5 discussing "Limitations": "More serious, however, is a startling
statement as to the relationship between victory and national objectives: 'Victory alone as an aim of war cannot be justified, since, in itself,
victory does not always assure the realization of national objectives' " (p.
28).

Dupuy then wonders why the army's basic manual on doctrine
should be telling soldiers that victory is an "outmoded concept." He
points out that the rest of this 1954 field manual presents the case for
the opposite position: "*Practically everything else in the manual* is anti-
thetical to this suggestion that our political and military policy can
envisage committing Americans to armed conflict for objectives which
do not warrant energetic and successful prosecution of the conflict.
Why, then, was it made?" (p. 28; my emphasis)

The author traces the problem back to the Korean War. He posits
that this passage on "limitations" may have been included to prepare
disillusioned soldiers for "future comparable frustrations" such as Korea
or it may be that the army wanted to impress civilian readers with the
fact that "Army doctrine recognizes the validity of Clausewitz's dicta on
the relationship between war and policy" (p. 29).

What Dupuy failed to recognize is that the writers of the FM 100–5
(1954) and the leadership of the army wanted future wars to be conducted in much the same way he does. In 1956, the year in which
Dupuy's article was published, General Ridgway had this to say about
the purpose of the army:

There is one phrase, I think, that should be engraved on the heart of
every civilian in a position of control over the military.
    That phrase is "Success in Battle."
    The sole role of any army, the sole criterion by which it will be judged
by history, is embodied in these words. An army is one thing only—a

fighting organization, from the front-line rifle platoon to the great rear-echelon components, must serve one purpose only—*the achievement of victory in war.*[99]

To its credit, the army recognized the need for some limitations because war at the nuclear level would be so devastating, but that does not mean that they were endorsing the inconclusive manner in which the Korean war was waged. If one looks at the FM 100–5 as a whole it is clear that it opposes military involvements of that kind. Consequently, Dupuy's article, even though he did not recognize it, reveals a great deal about the army's plans for conducting future conflicts. Its new doctrine was a complex amalgam of limited war doctrine with traditional Jominian principles emphasizing the necessity of achieving decisive military victory.

Further Comments on Interpreting Limited War

Many officers like General Ridgway were able to reconcile the need for limited war capabilities with the enduring desire for military victory. In a private meeting at the Council on Foreign Relations in February 1955, Ridgway told his audience, "The army exists for the single purpose of victory in battle and success in war, although it may have the subsidiary purpose of being a deterrent. . . . The basic function of the army, therefore, is to gain victory on the land and hold it."[100] Bacevich tells us, "Certain common principles, described by General [Lyman] Lemnitzer as 'by their very nature . . . immutable,' governed the conduct of war and would continue to do so in the future."[101] Soldiers like General Lemnitzer (Army Chief of Staff 1959–60; Chairman of the Joint Chiefs 1960–62), and General George Decker (Army Chief of Staff, 1960–62), did not change their attitudes because of the new emphasis on limited war.[102]

On the other hand, there were soldiers like Maxwell Taylor who were more receptive to the "civilian" concept of limited war. For example, Taylor's distance from the "hawkish" posture of the military in the Cuban Missile Crisis of 1962 has been noted by David Welch and James Blight who write of the discussions of the ExComm that "Taylor, the only military man present, does not argue a hawkish line throughout" the conferences.[103] Taylor later became a proponent of a limited, coercive bombing campaign against North Vietnam. His conception of Limited War was much more inclusive of nontraditional approaches to the use of force than was Ridgway's.[104] For example, in testimony before the Senate Foreign Relations Committee on February 17, 1966, Taylor would approvingly describe the American policy in Vietnam as follows:

> In summary then, our four point strategy consists of a complex but coherent package of measures designed to improve the effectiveness of our forces on the ground in South Vietnam, to exploit our air superiority by attacking military targets in North Vietnam, to stabilize the political, social, and economic systems in South Vietnam, and to seek an honorable negotiated settlement of the conflict.
>
> It is limited as to objective, as to geographical scope, as to weapons and forces employed, and as to targets attacked.[105]

Clearly, Maxwell Taylor did not continue to regard the use of force in an exclusively military context.[106]

That a different approach to war-fighting was in the air in the late 1950s and early 1960s is well illustrated by remarks in an oral history interview with former Army General Douglas V. Johnson. Johnson had been the Director, Plans and Policy Office, Joint Chiefs of Staff (1958–60) and, later, Director, Policy Review, Department of Defense (1960–64).[107] Johnson remarked that Taylor's idea was "to have forces that would allow the president to move where anything was required, from an MP (Military Policeman) to a nuclear weapon, so that in between there he had freedom to do something and countering guerrillas was one of things in there."[108]

The schemes for limiting the use of force that would become prevalent in the Kennedy Administration did not impress General Johnson. He credited the RAND Corporation with having first devised the excessively unrealistic aspects of flexible response that shaped policy in the Vietnam War: "The object of the thing was to avoid provoking the enemy into nuclear attack by keeping these wars on a small scale. You kick me in the shins, I'll kick you in the shins. . . . Well, it was a manner of making war which no military type has ever believed in. We had always thought from . . . Clausewitz on, that the way to fight a war was to get in and win it, end it, not this drawn out thing."[109]

The ideas took a turn for the worse at the Pentagon: "I saw the [study] when it came into DOD, but it seemed so ridiculous to me I didn't say anything about it, let it go along. By that time Nitze was gone and [William P.] Bundy was out of there, but McNaughton and some of those fellows . . . they loved this thing. And I suppose Mr. McNamara loved it although he never talked to me about it. But as you know, the present war has been conducted under that theory."[110] Thus, professional military skepticism of the limited war concept was quite high.

The Navy and Air Force

During the 1950s members of the army and navy, even though each made vigorous attempts to undermine the air force's near dominance of America's nuclear capabilities, also argued that the U.S. needed to acquire substantial limited war capabilities. As noted above, there were always ambiguities in the definition of limited war: for some it could be merely non-nuclear conventional war of the greatest magnitude; for others it could be conflict with serious politically imposed limitations. With all that said, the prestigious naval journal, *Naval Institute Proceedings*, contains articles that reveal distinct uneasiness with the New Look in the years 1956–58. These articles expressed the belief that limited war capabilities like those possessed by the navy were necessary to ensure the security of the nation.[111] In his article "Sea Power and Limited War," Commander Malcom Cagle argues that the navy's traditions are consistent with conducting limited wars:

> The U.S. Navy has traditionally been the champion of limited war. Naval leaders have long insisted that our country should not over concentrate on one weapon or prepare slowly for one kind of war. Especially, since the end of World War II, they have pleaded for a flexible military policy, for versatile, balanced forces capable of fighting any war, anywhere, any time.[112]

In assessing the kind of wars which were most likely to occur he stated:

> Limited war is the navy's forte, and, despite the Sputniks, limited war is still the most likely type of conflict that might occur in the years ahead.[113]

His recognition of the importance of limited wars did not keep him from criticizing the way the Korean War was conducted. Cagle wrote,

"The sentinel mistake of the Korean war, then, lay not in recognizing the need to win the war and in not having the fortitude to do so—all the while keeping it limited." He also argued that "the lesson of Korea, therefore, is to prepare for and win the limited wars of the future."[114] Cagle's thinking shows a marked resemblance to Trevor Dupuy's: both wanted to achieve traditional military victory in a limited war framework. Neither Cagle nor Dupuy addressed the difficult possibility that particular limitations accepted by the U.S. may make the attainment of decisive military victory impossible. Nevertheless, the author is broaching the possibility that future wars may come in many shapes and sizes.

Cagle's call for limited war capabilities in the face of the Mahanian philosophy that has dominated the U.S. navy since the turn of the century reflected the intellectual tensions within military thought over the proper balance between using force effectively and risking the escalation of hostilities. Recall that Alfred Thayer Mahan, the great American theorist of naval war power, applied Jominian principles to the use of naval force. Mahan once wrote, "War, once declared, must be waged offensively, aggressively. The enemy must not be fended off, but smitten down."[115] The heart and soul of naval warfare was having the capacity to defeat the enemy's fleet for the purpose of acquiring command of the sea. Wars, Mahan thought, were "won by the economic strangulation of the enemy from the sea."[116]

The need for clear command of the sea was a tenet of U.S. naval thinking in the 1950s and 1960s.[117] In 1954 the navy's director of strategic plans set forth its missions in a general war stating that "the navy must, by offensive operations, control the sea areas that the enemy wishes to use, denying him the use of these seas and permitting their use by our own naval forces, as avenues into enemy territory."[118] In 1963 the vice chief of naval operations, Admiral Claude Ricketts, argued in an article that the navy must have an "offensive naval strategy. Our Navy must be designed to carry the war to the enemy, both at sea and on land."[119] Even though the highest-ranking naval officials did not reject this analysis, many recognized, as did Commander Cagle, that the possibility of limited war had to be recognized and planned for. As the deputy chief of naval operations, Vice Admiral Robert P. Briscoe, noted in 1955 with respect to a new concept of amphibious warfare: "In the ten years since World War II our principal problem has not been all out atomic war. On the contrary, what we have been faced with daily is the peripheral type war, the limited war; the brush fire wherein atomic weapons have not been used and probably could not be."[120] The author then pointed out that the marines constituted America's frontline defense in such contingencies and that support for them and the navy was dwindling under the Eisenhower budget restrictions. All these statements demonstrate that many in the navy (and army) were struggling with this fundamental tension within the nature of force between the logic of military effectiveness and the logic of the political objective. There was clear skepticism about fighting with restrictions on the rules of engagement, but many soldiers also recognized, at least dimly, that military power had to be made to conform to political interests.

This recognition appears to have been less strongly felt within the air force which, on the other hand, had strongly supported Eisenhower administration's spending priorities under the New Look. Massive retaliation was consistent with the thinking of Guilio Douhet, the pre-World War II Italian theorist of air power. Beginning in 1956, however, even the air force was grudgingly arguing for its relevance in the conduct of limited wars. Its 1959 manual on basic doctrine explicitly recognized limited war as one of the possible types of conflict it might have to face.[121] However, Clodfelter demonstrates that the interest in Limited War was directed toward the problems associated with a non-nuclear conventional war of great proportions. "While John Kennedy's enchantment with guerrilla warfare," Clodfelter writes, "produced changes in army doctrine, it had no effect on air force policy. [General Curtis] LeMay guaranteed that his service would continue to emphasize strategic operations above all else and that theater air forces would perform tasks viewed as secondary."[122] In short, the air force did not really focus on the politico-military nature of limited wars. It is not even clear that there was a significant understanding within the air force of how limited a limited war might be. There was little recognition that in some "brushfire" wars tactical bombing would be more valuable than strategic efforts.

The Kennedy Administration

The election of John Kennedy to the presidency in 1960 brought change to the national security policies of the United States. Not all of them need to be discussed here, but the new president's interest in enhancing the limited war capabilities of the United States requires comment.[123] Using John Lewis Gaddis's terminology, the Kennedy administration moved away from the "asymmetrical" approach of Eisenhower and Dulles to a more "symmetrical" political-military strategy. It promised to meet communist aggression at its level of violence and in the threatened locations.[124] Gaddis also notes the explicit connection between the limited war writings of the 1950s and Kennedy's policy: "This symmetrical approach came to be known publicly, borrowing from Maxwell Taylor's book, *The Uncertain Trumpet*, as the strategy of "flexible response."[125]

That phrase accurately described Kennedy's desire to employ force in a flexible and controlled manner that would permit him more options. In a memo to the President dated June 26, 1961, Walt W. Rostow spelled out the logic of the Kennedy philosophy for confronting the Soviets and their proxies. It was, Rostow noted, to counter incremental, "nibbling" encroachments by America's opponents "in a thermonuclear age, that many men came to advocate, in the past ten years, a build-up of conventional forces. The rationale was to provide the U.S. with some usable means of force to substitute for the choice between surrender and nuclear war."[126] Similarly, Richard Smoke notes that the Kennedy Administration's political-military strategy reflected NSC-68's call for conventional forces to enhance deterrence across the spectrum of violence—a plea the Eisenhower Administration did not accept.[127]

The new administration's first budget message to the Congress on defense issues called for greater expenditures on conventional forces. President Kennedy regarded limited war as the major threat facing the United States: "The strength and deployment of our forces in combination with those of our allies should be sufficiently powerful and mobile to prevent the steady erosion of the Free World through limited wars; and it is this role that should constitute the primary mission of our overseas forces."[128]

He told the Congress that the defense posture of the United States must be "both flexible and determined." Its weapons and force structure would have to facilitate those ends:

> We must be able to make deliberate choices in weapons and strategy, shift the tempo of our production and alter the direction of our forces to meet rapidly changing conditions or objectives at very short notice

and under any circumstances. Our weapon systems must be usable in a manner permitting deliberation and discrimination as to timing, scope, and targets in response to civilian authority.[129]

This represented a substantial reversal from the All-or-Nothing aspects of the New Look. The emphasis on the development of conventional forces was also intended to reduce the reliance of the United States on nuclear weapons for deterrent and war-fighting purposes.

The President's emphasis on obtaining conventional and limited war capabilities also contained a set of policy goals that placed a high priority on the American development of counterinsurgency capabilities. The flames of this interest were fanned by Khrushchev's speech of January 6, 1961, which pledged Soviet support for "national wars of liberation." The Soviet leader's speech only increased the urgency of a problem that had been developing for some time: the French Indo-China War, the emergence of revolutionary fronts in other Latin American nations, and, finally, the French Algerian problem all contributed to the growing awareness of the phenomena now referred to as "low-intensity conflict."[130] Among the politicians of his day, Kennedy had been in the forefront of those who were cognizant of the special problems posed by insurgencies: i.e., the highly social and political nature of these struggles. He also knew that such wars needed to be approached with tactics that were not conventional in the manner of World War II and Korea.

Kennedy took a keen interest in bringing the armed services up to speed on counterinsurgency. In the first months of his term he inspected the equipment of American anti-guerrilla forces and their training manuals; in each instance he was dissatisfied. A special meeting of the Joint Chiefs of Staff was held so that the matter could be discussed.[131] He designated the green beret as a symbol of distinction for the army's special forces unit. In March 1961, a special interagency committee was established under Richard Bissell, Jr., of the CIA to study how the government should organize itself for the problem of fighting insurgencies. By June 1961 Kennedy had also recalled Maxwell Taylor to active duty as a special military assistant who "seemed to the president well qualified to represent his views to the military on the urgency of a more flexible posture."[132]

By late 1961 Bissell's study group had completed its report. Walt Rostow, the central force on this committee, was able to get the report's main features approved by the President; they were promulgated on

January 18, 1962, as NSAM (National Security Action Memorandum) 124.[133] As stated by NSAM 124, a "Special Group (Counter-Insurgency)" was established "to assure unity of effort and the use of all available resources with maximum effectiveness in preventing and resisting subversive insurgency and related forms of indirect aggression in friendly countries."[134]

The Special Group (C.I.) was instructed to "insure proper recognition throughout the U.S. government that subversive insurgency ('wars of liberation') is a major form of politico-military conflict *equal in importance to conventional warfare.*"[135] The Special Group would oversee the development "of broad lines of counter-insurgency policy" and ensure that the policy was being properly implemented by the relevant agencies within the government.[136] Maxwell Taylor was made chairman of the committee. If the relevant bureaucracies had not perceived the importance of this issue to the President, his brother, Robert Kennedy, the Attorney General, was also placed on the Special Group (C.I.).[137] President Kennedy also let it be known that advancement in the army would depend on sensitivity to the development of counterinsurgency programs: "Kennedy dropped a broad hint that future promotions of high ranking officers would depend upon their demonstration of experience in the counter-guerrilla or sublimited war field."[138]

Following this, special schools were established to teach civilian and military officials about insurgency and counterinsurgency. Programs of instruction were developed pursuant to NSAM 131 of March 13, 1962.[139] The various branches of the military, the CIA, and the Foreign Service Institute of the State Department developed courses to train the relevant personnel in these matters. The Foreign Service course, entitled the "National Interdepartmental Seminar," ran for six weeks, and was meant to train the highest level civilian officials. About this program begun in June 1962, Blaufarb says the following:

> Among the students enrolled for full-time participation were several ambassadors. Such administration notables as Robert F. Kennedy, General Maxwell Taylor, and Edward R. Murrow audited various lectures. Speakers included Walt W. Rostow, U. Alexis Johnson, Brigadier General Edward F. Lansdale, from the government and a number of highly qualified academics.[140]

At the end of the six-week course the students were taken to the White House where they met the President and Maxwell Taylor.

Within the military these training programs were given the highest priority as well. By July 1962, the Joint Chiefs had informed the NSC that nine special schools on insurgency had been created for officer training and that twenty-five courses (beyond the introductory level) had been established for enlisted men.[141] The rush to incorporate counterinsurgency into the army created an atmosphere in which this process was taken to absurd lengths; Blaufarb quotes an observer who witnessed some of the excesses:

> One civilian skeptic in a position to observe the military's compliance reported that "word went out from the Chief of Staff of the Army that every school in the Army would devote a minimum of 20 percent of its time to counterinsurgency. Well, this reached the Finance School and the Cooks' and Bakers' School, so they were talking about how to make typewriters explode . . . or how to make apple pies with hand grenades inside them.[142]

Admittedly this was an extreme case, but it does relate the intensity with which the President and his staff pushed for a recognition of the importance of limited war and counterinsurgency capabilities. Yet, as much as they did to bring new methods to the military, it is not clear that the methods or thinking of the services were greatly changed. Counterinsurgency was just added on as another task for all soldiers. Some Special Forces units were created for specialized tasks, but the basic army division was not restructured to meet this challenge. The division remained intensive in machinery and firepower suitable for war in Europe; no light divisions capable of off-road movement and pursuit on foot were created for this new mission.[143] The failure of the armed services to change was not wholly their fault. The civilians within the Kennedy administration did not recognize that the military was being asked to prepare to fight two different kinds of war. An organizational inability to square the circle should have been anticipated.

6 | Laos and the Never Again School

J ohn F. Kennedy became president at a time when tensions between the United States and the Soviet Union were being exacerbated by crises in Cuba, Berlin, and Indochina. In 1961 the most critical problem for the United States in Indochina lay not in Vietnam but Laos, a landlocked country surrounded by Thailand, North Vietnam, Cambodia, and South Vietnam. On his last full day in office President Eisenhower told the President-elect that Laos was, strategically speaking, the "key to the entire area of Southeast Asia."[1] The cause of the current Laos crisis lay in the increasing likelihood that Laos would emerge from its civil war under communist Pathet Lao domination.

The history of the civil war is complex: three major groups sought control of Laos. On the left the Pathet Lao was headed by Prince Souphanouvang; the centrist or "neutralist" factions were led by Souphanouvang's brother, the most prominent figure in Laotian politics, Prince Souvanna Phouma; on the right former army officer Phoumi Nosavan led the pro-American forces that desired the international alignment of Laos with the United States and Thailand. Alarmed by the growing influence of the communist Pathet Lao following elections in May 1958, the Eisenhower Administration stopped economic aid to Laos in August 1958. The anti-communist political forces used this crisis to topple Souvanna Phouma's parliamentary coalition with a no-confidence vote.[2] A new pro-American government was formed in August 1958 under Prime Minister Phoui Sananikone who removed the Pathet Lao representatives from the government. Phoui also appointed Souvanna Phouma ambassador to France thereby removing all the major neutralist and Pathet Lao factions from power. The new government attempted to force the assimilation of two Pathet Lao battalions into the Lao national army. One of the battalions rebelled with the assistance of North Vietnamese advisers. Claiming direct action by North Vietnam, the Laotian government asked for military help from the United States and the United Nations on September 4, 1959.[3]

Neither President Eisenhower nor the State Department pushed for military intervention. In fact, the Laotian claims of North Vietnamese involvement could not be supported. According to Charles A. Stevenson, the President worried that U.S. military action might drive the United States further apart from the Soviets at a time "when he was hoping to improve relations" with them.[4] Eisenhower was willing to consider the use of force if SEATO, the Southeast Asia Treaty Organization, required it, but "we would not do anything by ourselves."[5] An intelligence estimate dated September 18, 1958 observed of the Laos situation that "the Communist resumption of guerrilla warfare in Laos was primarily a reaction to a stronger anti-Communist posture by the Laotian Government and to recent US initiatives in support of Laos."[6] The assessment noted that China and the Soviet Union would, in general, wish to avoid openly committing combat forces to the struggle, but it also stated: "If, however, the Communists became convinced during the course of a series of actions and counteractions that the US intended to commit major US combat forces into Laos, we believe that the odds would be better than even that the Communists would directly intervene in strength with North Vietnamese and possibly Chinese military forces."[7] Of great interest is Stevenson's account of the reaction of U.S. military planners to the prospect of intervention: "Arguments against intervention proved decisive, even among the military. Laos was a landlocked country, with poor logistical facilities and often impenetrable weather. The navy could not be very effective from so far away. The air force was unwilling to get involved unless it could do strategic bombing. And the army was still dominated by the Never Again school, which strongly opposed getting involved again in a land war in Asia."[8]

In December 1959 General Phoumi Nosavan ousted the neutralist government under Phoui Sananikone and took control of the country. Phoumi's regime ran into immediate difficulties because it was not accepted by centrist leaders such as Souvanna Phouma. Corruption grew to alarming proportions, eroding the government's legitimacy at an alarming rate. An election, rigged by the CIA and the Lao government, was held in April 1960 when the right-wing factions led by Phoumi maintained their hold on the country.[9] Prince Somsanith, a political ally of General Phoumi's, became prime minister.

On the morning of August 9, 1960 a little known army captain named Kong Le seized the capital of Vientiane while Phoumi and his cabinet were visiting the King of Laos in the royal city of Luang Prabang. Kong Le wanted Laos to have no political alignment with the United States or the Soviet Union. He even wanted American economic assistance to be stopped due to its corrupting influence on local political leaders.[10] Kong Le asked Souvanna Phouma to assist in the formation of another government. Souvanna Phouma insisted that the National Assembly oust Prince Somsanith, which it did on August 13, 1960. Three days later Souvanna formed his government.

The Eisenhower administration did not cheer the reappearance of Souvanna Phouma. Even though the American ambassador to Vientiane, Winthrop Brown, strongly supported Souvanna Phouma as the best hope for the United States, the administration was deeply worried about Souvanna's willingness to negotiate with the Pathet Lao.[11] The administration's distrust of Souvanna increased in September 1960 when the prime minister began direct talks with the Pathet Lao. As David Hall notes, he also permitted the Soviet Union to establish an embassy in Laos. Hall writes, "The decisions precipitated another crisis in Washington. A deal was concluded with the new prime minister [Souvanna Phouma] whereby he would continue to receive American financial support but would agree to allow Phoumi to receive deliveries of United States military assistance. Souvanna was told that Phoumi promised to use this aid against Kong Le, and thus bring down the new government, but would only use it against the Pathet Lao."[12]

Souvanna Phouma and Souphanouvong, leader of the Pathet Lao, agreed to create a coalition government excluding Phoumi Nosavan. Phoumi then began to take steps to overthrow the new coalition, his forces moved on Vientiane in late November and early December. On

November 16, 1960 Souvanna Phouma, reacting to Phoumi's actions, moved against the West by denouncing America's failure to control Phoumi and by sending goodwill emissaries to Beijing and Moscow. The Soviets began to supply the neutralists in Vientiane with rice and oil from Hanoi on December 3, 1960. Phoumi's attack on Vientiane commenced on December 8, and Kong Le was forced to retreat from the city on December 16.

A destructive battle had given Phoumi possession of the capital. However, Kong Le and his forces were able to escape to central Laos where he then requested and received massive Soviet assistance via airlift from North Vietnam. Additionally, government forces loyal to Souvanna Phouma stationed near Luang Prabang refused to recognize the regime imposed on Laos by Phoumi's capture of Vientiane. Within a short time the United States, Britain, France, and Thailand officially recognized the new Phoumi government; others like India, the Soviet Union, China, and North Vietnam continued to regard Souvanna Phouma as the legitimate ruler of Laos. However, Phoumi's pursuit of Kong Le was a military failure that allowed the 10,000 soldiers under Kong Le and 15,000 Pathet Lao troops to grow stronger as supplies from North Vietnam and the Soviet Union were airdropped into Laos. On December 31, 1960 these two forces launched a combined assault on an all-weather airfield in the Plain of Jars held by forces of the Royal Lao Army. The attack was a success, and soon 45 tons of Soviet supplies were landing each day from North Vietnam.

The seriousness of the military situation and the announcement, contrived by the new government, that seven North Vietnamese battalions had entered Laos forced the Eisenhower administration to consider intervention. Eisenhower was reluctant. He is reported to have said, "I came into office because of Korea. I'm not going to fight another Korea. This place is even worse than Korea. So I won't approve the use of airplanes or anything until I'm convinced we'll be successful."[13]

By the time Eisenhower's term ended he appears to have taken the position that the United States should become militarily involved in Laos *only* if the U.S. were willing to reverse all communist advances in the Indochinese region. Stevenson supports the interpretation that Eisenhower opposed military intervention that would be indecisive. He describes the President's motivations: "Since President Eisenhower was reluctant to act unless he could be assured of victory [tactical air support], too, was ruled out."[14] During a briefing on January 2, 1961 he stated, "If we ever have to resort to force [in Laos], there's just one thing to do: clear up the problem completely."[15] The Joint Chiefs adopted a similar position, one which they would, for the most part, adhere to throughout the Laos crises of 1961–62:

> General Lemnitzer [the Chairman] was apparently for [intervention], at least under some circumstances. But General Decker, Chief of Staff of the Army, stated widespread army opposition to getting bogged down in another land war in Asia. [Chief of Naval Operations] Admiral [Arleigh] Burke, as in 1959, was ready to support intervention if necessary for Phoumi's forces to win. Air Force General White, apparently supported by some other chiefs, preferred a policy of air strikes, and against North Vietnam rather than in Laos. The military planners reasoned that North Vietnam was the source of the trouble because of its support for the Pathet Lao and wanted to strike at the source.[16]

The outgoing administration had backed away from intervention by the first week of January 1961, but did engage in a series of actions designed as a show of force including sending two aircraft carriers to Indochinese waters. This opposition to unilateral and nondecisive intervention was balanced by a strong feeling on the part of the President that Laos was of great strategic value to the United States. In a White House meeting of December 31, 1960 Eisenhower had told his staff "we cannot afford to stand by and allow Laos to fall to the Communists. The time may soon come when we should employ the Seventh Fleet, with its force of marines"[17] Given Eisenhower's position about intervention at Dienbienphu, this should probably be regarded as a preparatory step should action in Laos be required.[18]

Back in Laos, Phoumi's military actions were unsuccessful, and his political strength deteriorated. To make matters worse for Phoumi and the United States Souvanna Phouma established a provisional government at Kong Le's headquarters.[19] The situation in Laos became more difficult for the pro-Western forces during the early months of 1961 but would assume crisis proportion only after March 11, 1961 when neutralist and Pathet Lao forces captured the critical road junction at Sala Phou Khoun. In accomplishing this task they were able to sever the only road between Vientiane and Luang Prabang. Later in March these troops would begin moving south, while Pathet Lao units conducted attacks in other areas of the country—indicating their relative strength.

By this time, however, the new Kennedy administration would have to deal with the issues.[20]

The Kennedy Administration and Laos

It was immediately apparent that the Kennedy administration's policy would differ from its predecessor's. In his first press conference, on January 25, 1961, Kennedy indicated that he would not seek a pro-Western regime in Laos: "the United States is anxious that there be established in Laos a peaceful country—an independent country not dominated by either side."[21] On the same day that the Pathet Lao launched their offensive on Sala Phou Khoun, March 9, 1961, Khrushchev received a letter from Kennedy which made these points: "The President expressed his determination not to abandon Laos, even if it meant intervention by American forces. The United States was willing, however, to agree to measures to guarantee a truly neutral Laos, such as a revived [International Commission for Supervision and Control in Laos, the ICC]. But no agreements could be reached until the Soviet airlift stopped and a cease-fire had been achieved."[22]

According to Stevenson the most important American goal was to secure Thailand from attack through the Mekong Valley. At that time the movement of men and supplies from North Vietnam through Laos to South Vietnam was believed to be minimal, a problem that Washington thought South Vietnam could control.[23] The Soviets gave no immediate response to Kennedy's March 9 letter, so the United States government waited until later in the month when Soviet Foreign Minister Andrei Gromyko would be at the United Nations in New York City. It was hoped that Secretary of State Dean Rusk could obtain concessions from Gromyko when they met. After a five-hour discussion on March 18, 1961 Rusk emerged with no Soviet concessions. And why should there have been? U. Alexis Johnson, the U.S. ambassador to Thailand at this time, observes, "the Pathet Lao, who currently had the upper hand and held reasonable prospects of complete victory eventually, had no incentive to bargain. We had to provide one."[24] Kennedy decided that American threats would have to be made more credible; he called an NSC meeting for March 20, 1961 to discuss the matter with his highest advisers.

This meeting and another the next day were occasions on which Never Again objections to intervention were voiced. Walt Rostow argued for a small commitment of forces to Thailand—ready to move to Laos if necessary. The Joint Chiefs argued vociferously against this course of action. The Chiefs felt that a deployment of the kind envisaged by Rostow would trigger a North Vietnamese, or possibly Chinese, intervention. Because of that contingency, they wanted 60,000 troops to go in with unrestricted air cover—even if that meant using nuclear weapons against North Vietnam or China.[25] Stevenson summarizes the position of the military as follows:

> Although the Chiefs disagreed on the desirability of direct intervention, they shared a faith in the efficacy of shows of force. They also believed that if intervention became necessary, the military should not be restricted on its use of weapons or targets. If the Chinese or North Vietnamese were directly involved in the fighting, for example, the U.S. officers wanted to be able to strike directly at the source of the trouble. Even Army Chief of Staff, George H. Decker, who otherwise argued against intervention, wanted full freedom of action. He said: "If we commit troops, we should be prepared to go all the way so as not to get bogged down in an endless war."[26]

Later, General Decker explained that this was the position he adopted in the spring of 1961. Decker told Kennedy that the army was ready to go if so commanded, but he told the Commander-in-Chief, "Mr. President, if you do commit the army into Laos, I hope that you will see it through." The former Army Chief of Staff summarized this position as: "Don't get the Army in there and then get it bogged down," or "Use all the military means at your disposal to resolve this situation satisfactorily."[27] Unfortunately, Kennedy's options were restricted by the forces that were then in readiness. He had already learned that even a movement of 10,000 men to Southeast Asia would virtually eliminate the strategic reserve forces available to the United States.[28]

These two meetings produced a decision whereby the United States would make a limited show of force in the region. In the days that followed three aircraft carriers with 1,400 marines moved toward Laos, while 150 marine mechanics were sent to Thailand to service fourteen helicopters that had recently been given to the Royal Lao Army. Two thousand marines in Japan were put on alert, and covert actions in Laos were stepped up including reconnaissance flights over the region.[29] As the mobilization of forces was taking place, on March 23, 1961, President Kennedy read a prepared statement on Laos to a national television audience before taking questions from the press. Without mentioning the troop movements that were underway, he stated these objectives:

> First, we strongly and unreservedly support the goal of a neutral and independent Laos, tied to no outside power, threatening no one, and free from any domination. Our support for the present duly constituted government is aimed entirely and exclusively at that result. And if in the past there has been any possible ground for misunderstanding of our desire for a truly neutral Laos, there should be none now.
>
> Secondly, if there is to be a peaceful solution, there must be a cessation of the present armed attacks by externally supported Communists. If these attacks do not stop, those who support a truly neutral Laos will have to consider their response.

Later in his address Kennedy attempted to bolster the image of the United States as being willing to engage its armed forces in Laos:

> My fellow Americans, Laos is far away from America, but the world is small. Its two million people live in a country 3 times the size of Austria. The security of all Southeast Asia will be endangered if Laos loses its neutral independence. Its own safety runs with the safety of us all—in neutrality observed by all.
>
> I want to make it clear to the American people and to all of the world that all we want in Laos is peace, not war; a truly neutral government, not a cold war pawn; a settlement concluded at the conference table not the battlefield.[30]

A Soviet response to the speech and troop movements came quickly.

The day after the Kennedy news conference, Foreign Minister Gromyko requested and was granted an appointment to meet with the President on March 27. At that meeting Kennedy reiterated his desire for a neutralized Laos, and he stressed his willingness to stand firm on the issue. On April 1, 1961 the Soviet government, responding to a diplomatic note from Britain, "expressed a willingness to join with Britain in appealing for a cease-fire and implied that that appeal could precede the convening of an international conference."[31] The Soviets, however, stated that the cease-fire should go into effect only upon agreement by all parties of the details that would govern the talks.

As April passed, the position of Phoumi Nosavan's forces weakened. Khrushchev told the U.S. ambassador to the Soviet Union that Laos "will fall into our hands like a rotten apple."[32] From the Soviet perspective the worse thing that could happen would have been direct American intervention, but this was being seriously considered in the White House. On April 11, 1961 Kenneth Landon, a national security aide, wrote to MacGeorge Bundy that the "division of Laos could be brought about by limited military intervention from Thailand, Vietnam, the Philippines, and perhaps a showing of U.S. Marines in Thai and Vietnamese areas adjacent to the scene of conflict."[33] Landon felt that SEATO would not unanimously support such action, so bilateral agreements would have to be reached with the respective SEATO governments that were "ready to act."

Events in Laos were then overshadowed by the April 1961 Bay of Pigs fiasco. Nevertheless, Kennedy issued orders on April 18, 1961 for "civilian" American advisers in Laos to wear their military uniforms and advance into combat areas with the Royal Lao forces.[34] He did this to signal the Soviets that American resolve in Laos would not be diminished by the Cuban debacle. The United States was seeming to commit itself more deeply to the outcome in Laos. A series of meetings in the Soviet Union and China with Souvanna Phouma and Souphanouvong from April 16 to 22 prompted the release of a joint communiqué notifying the West that "at present real conditions exist to normalize the situation in Laos."[35] On April 24, 1961 the Soviet Union joined with the United Kingdom, as these nations were the co-chairs of the 1954 Geneva Conference that settled the French Indochina War, and agreed to reactivate the International Commission for Supervision and Control in Laos (ICC) and send it to Laos to supervise a cease-fire called for May 3, 1961. The British and Soviets also announced that invitations were being sent to thirteen nations for an international conference scheduled to meet in Geneva on May 12 for the purpose of neutralizing Laos politically.[36]

No word came from the neutralist and Pathet Lao leadership. This was especially troubling because their forces were engaged in an offensive that had the capture of Vientiane as its objective. On April 24 the city of Vang Vieng fell to the Pathet Lao thereby removing the last major defensive position available to the Royal forces north of Vientiane.[37] Ambassador Brown became so worried that he requested authority from Washington to send A-26s on bombing runs directly against Pathet Lao forces as circumstances warranted.[38] Consequently, the U.S. government had to wonder whether the Soviet call for a cease-fire and conference was merely a ruse designed to make the United States sit back and impotently watch as Laos was conquered. Finally, on May 2, 1961 North Vietnamese radio broadcast acceptance of the terms for the cease-fire, but in the meantime a contentious debate had taken place in Washington concerning intervention in Laos. The NSC meetings held on April 27 and 29 and May 1, 1961 saw the emergence of objections to American involvement, some of which were quite similar to those given during the Dienbienphu crisis.

The NSC and the 1961 Crisis

The NSC meeting of April 27, 1961 was convened so that the impending collapse of the U.S. backed forces in Laos could be discussed. According to Gibbons, Walt Rostow recommended that the administration deploy a limited number of troops to Thailand as a signal to the communist forces in Laos. Averell Harriman, who was to be the head of the American negotiating team at the upcoming Geneva talks concurred with Rostow's recommendation. Gibbons also states that: "The JCS again argued that if there was to be a show of force, there should be an adequate force available to undertake a military offensive, should one be required. This time, possibly in part because of the Bay of Pigs experience, the JCS proposed a force of 120- 140,000 men, with authority to use nuclear weapons if necessary."[39]

Arthur Schlesinger supports this recounting of the Joint Chiefs' recommendation:

> For all their differences, the military left a predominant impression that they did not want ground troops at all unless they could send at least 140,000 men equipped with tactical nuclear weapons. By now the Pentagon was developing what would become its standard line in Southeast Asia—unrelenting opposition to limited intervention except on the impossible condition that the President agree in advance to every further step they deemed sequential, including, on occasion, nuclear bombing of Hanoi and Peking.[40]

It is not clear how committed each of the Chiefs was to this argument; it seems that Lemnitzer (who was not in attendance on April 27) and Burke were more willing to intervene. Theodore Sorenson, a top-level

White House official in the Kennedy administration, has written that a majority of the Chiefs favored "landing American troops in Thailand, South Vietnam, and the government-held portions of the Laotian panhandle."[41] A failure to produce a cease-fire by these actions would have led, under the Chiefs' plan, to attacks on the Pathet Lao and the use of tactical nuclear weapons, if necessary. The entry of China or North Vietnam into the war would have been met with direct reprisals by air attack on the homelands of each nation. In any case, the thrust of their advice to Kennedy appears well established: limited intervention should be avoided.

The scholarly literature varies as to what transpired at the NSC meetings which began on April 27, 1961. From the outset of the first meeting, in Alexis Johnson's account, President Kennedy expressed concern that Vientiane was in immediate danger of falling into enemy hands. Then Johnson describes the presentation of military options given by Secretary McNamara and Admiral Burke in these words:

> Secretary McNamara and Admiral Burke presented the military alternative [to allowing communist control of Laos], SEATO Plan 5,[42] but it was hardly encouraging. It envisioned landing 11,000 American troops in the major cities of the Mekong Valley in the first week supplemented by 4,000 Thai soldiers and 2,000 Pakistani.[43] The JCS said this was not enough.[44] If the North Vietnamese or Chinese communists intervened, as well they might, the JCS estimated that they could put five soldiers in Laos for every one of ours. In this event the JCS thought we would have no alternative but to use nuclear weapons. Our strategic reserves were too low to permit a commitment of ground forces sufficient to do the job without nuclear support. A vivid image thus became fixed in the President's mind of a small band of beleaguered Americans stuck on the Vientiane airstrip while he contemplated resorting to nuclear war with China to rescue them.[45]

Johnson's account does not cite "140,000" as the number of troops that the JCS required as a precondition for entry into a ground war (as the Stevenson and Schlesinger versions do).[46] He later argues that the Joint Chiefs favored "Plan 5 as the best way to deal with the communists advance."[47] Whatever the disparities in the details of these various accounts, they share an underlying consistency. Gibbons, Johnson, Schlesinger, and Stevenson all confirm that the JCS, as a group, was opposed to a limited intervention in Laos. Later, Johnson did not disagree with an interviewer's summary of the Chiefs' position as "if you went in you had to go in prepared to go all the way."[48] These accounts reveal that other advisers (Rostow, Hilsman, and Harriman) put forward proposals that were more "political" and in keeping with tenets of flexible response.

Roger Hilsman, Director of the State Department's Bureau of Intelligence and Research and one of the administration's foremost proponents of counterinsurgency and Limited War strategies, has said much about the behavior of the Chiefs in his memoirs, *To Move a Nation*. He begins by discussing the various lessons taken from the Korean War: "Most students of international politics think of the Korean War as a success—an overt aggression was stopped and the Communists brought to discipline their ambitions by a limited use of force which confined the war and prevented its spiralling to engulf the whole world. But to many of the higher-ranking military, the Korean War was a frustrating humiliation."[49]

Hilsman continues by describing how the limitations on bombing above the Yalu was particularly frustrating because the U.S. Army was fought to a standstill. He asserts that by 1961 the attitude "that the United States should never again fight a limited war in Asia" had become so commonly held that its adherents were referred to as members of the " 'Never Again' Club" (p. 129). Not all members of the military subscribed to this point of view. Hilsman goes on to state an essential tenet of the Limited War school: "Everyone in Washington—civilian and military—dreaded the thought of getting bogged down in a niggling, harassing quagmire of a war in the jungles. But many among both civilians and military were also convinced that the alternatives—either a very big war or the abandonment of Asia—would be worse" (p. 129).

The advocates of the All-or-Nothing position would not accept the limited war option. Their view of the matter, Hilsman continues, "seemed to be that if force were to be used at all it should be used all-out—striking at the sources of enemy power (p. 129)." In other words, they believed that military power should be used to obtain decisive objectives. Hilsman then adds, "Not all of the Joint Chiefs fully ascribed to the 'Never Again' view, but it seemed to the White House that they were at least determined to build a record that would protect their position and put the blame entirely on the President no matter what happened (p. 129)". What the Never Again people wanted from Kennedy was a guarantee of no holds barred in the conduct of a war.

Later in the chapter Hilsman supports Schlesinger's description of events at the NSC meetings of late April 1961. Both authors stressed the inhibiting influence which the Bay of Pigs fiasco had on the JCS. The Bay of Pigs was considered a limited operation that did not have the necessary military power to succeed. The fact that the civilian leadership refused to permit previously planned air strikes to be carried out probably troubled the Chiefs as well. Although the Joint Chiefs did not favor the small deployment advocated by Rostow, their own positions varied somewhat as well. According to Stevenson, Vice President Johnson suggested that they write out their respective positions for consideration by the President and discussion at the next NSC meeting. Kennedy agreed to this, and the President then met with a delegation of congressional leaders about the Laos crisis. Stevenson tells us: "Admiral Burke [the acting JCS chairman while General Lemnitzer was in Laos at the time] addressed the group, arguing for a firm stand in Laos even at the risk of war. When the President asked others for their advice, only the Vice President supported Burke's statement. It was clear that Congress had no stomach for further military adventures."[50] It appears that the Congressmen were more disposed to intervening on behalf of Thailand and Vietnam.

On April 29, 1961 the NSC met once again. On this occasion they had before them the recommendations of the various military advisers on the NSC. The assortment of plans for action presented was so bewildering to Kennedy that he "ordered the men to reconcile their differences at least so as to present him with fewer options."[51]

Gibbons presents excerpts from the record of this meeting, and the image conveyed by the record is that the discussion lacked coherence.[52] McNamara seems to have argued that Thailand and Vietnam were more important places "to take a stand" (p. 27). He also argued that a defense of Laos would require direct attacks on North Vietnam. Admiral Burke was willing to intervene and a take a tough stand in Laos itself; he also stated, "We would have to throw enough in to win—perhaps the works." General Decker also felt that Southeast Asia was not a very desirable location to fight a war, but he believed that "we must hold as much as we can of Vietnam, Cambodia, and Laos" (p. 28). Later in the meeting Decker added, "we cannot win a conventional war in Southeast Asia; if we go in, we should go in to win, and that means bombing Hanoi, China, and maybe using nuclear weapons" (p. 28). The Army Chief of Staff believed that a deployment of troops to Thailand and Vietnam might be a able to persuade the Pathet Lao to agree to a cease-fire. Differing opinions by Chester Bowles, Dean Rusk, and Robert Kennedy were also expressed; the meeting ended inconclusively with the President waiting for a more unified set of military recommendations to be brought to him.

Two days later on May 1, 1961 the NSC met once again to consider the worsening situation in Laos. Gibbons describes the setting for the meeting and its outcome as follows: "The situation in Laos was more ominous, and the group decided that the U.S. had no choice but to threaten to take military action unless a cease-fire was arranged. Unlike the meeting on April 29, at which they were divided, the military agreed on the need to act" (p. 32).

Gibbons also quotes from a memo written to President Kennedy in which Bundy expresses great surprise at the reconciliation of the view of the military advisers. The note reads, "On Saturday [April 29] the Joint Chiefs of Staff divided 1–1 (Navy-Air vs. Army-Marine) on going into Laos; it's not at all clear why they are now unanimous"[53] (p. 32). We may know how this new consensus was formed. Charles Stevenson interviewed Paul Nitze, who served as Assistant Secretary of Defense for International Security Affairs from 1961 to 1963, and was told the agreement of the military advisers was brought about by Secretary McNamara on the evening of April 29 after the NSC meeting had taken place. Stevenson does not go into great detail about this meeting but does tell us: "Two hours after the [NSC] meeting adjourned at 8:00 p.m., the disagreeing officers met with McNamara and worked out a compromise formula. Immediate action was postponed. The Chiefs alerted CINCPAC (Commander-in-Chief, Pacific), however, to be ready to launch air strikes against North Vietnam and southern China and to be ready to deploy two 5,000-man combat brigades, one to northeast Thailand and the other to Da Nang, South Vietnam. They cautioned that no firm decision had been made for such action."[54]

It appears that McNamara was able to build this consensus by acceding to one of the most important demands of the Never Again advisers. The orders sent to CINCPAC requiring preparation for the bombing of North Vietnam and China satisfied their prerequisite condition that there be no geographical limitations on the use of that force deemed necessary to defeat the Pathet Lao, North Vietnamese, or Chinese. Planning for the use of nuclear weapons does not appear to have been authorized by McNamara.

In any case, by May 1961 Kennedy had become quite skeptical about sending ground forces into Laos. This increasing wariness probably stemmed from two factors. First, the reluctance of the Joint Chiefs, as a whole, to become involved must have diminished the President's enthusiasm for a test of wills in Laos. Schlesinger notes the opposition of the JCS "to limited intervention had a powerful effect."[55] Aside from the difficulty of introducing soldiers into combat and possible death, there were formidable problems, described by General Decker, related to logistics and disease in a jungle environment. Second, Kennedy met with Douglas MacArthur on April 28, 1961 who strongly advised the President against committing soldiers to a ground war in Southeast Asia. Fortunately, before any military measures had to be taken, the Pathet Lao, as mentioned above, on May 2, 1961 agreed to the cease-fire proposal made by the United Kingdom and the Soviet Union.

The Lull in the Action

A cease-fire was arranged in Laos and the Geneva talks began on May 12, 1961. At an NSC meeting one week before, a consensus was reached that "the chance for salvaging anything out of the cease- fire and coalition government was slim indeed."[56] In early June President Kennedy and Premier Khrushchev agreed in Vienna that the establishment of a neutral Laotian government would be in the interest of both nations. The negotiations dragged on into late 1961. By December 1961 a neutrality agreement had been reached by the members of the Geneva Conference, but its implementation awaited the "actual formation of a provisional coalition government for Laos that could initial the new accords."[57] General Phoumi wanted the defense and interior ministries to be under the control of individuals sympathetic to him. The stalemate continued and eventually forces under his control came under attack from the Pathet Lao in late February 1962; these forces were located in the town of Nam Tha near the Chinese border. As the situation in Laos grew worse, support for direct involvement was vanishing in the United States. On February 21, 1962 the President, Vice-

President, and several high-ranking Senators discussed Laos. Senate Majority Leader Mike Mansfield (D-Montana) felt that involvement in Laos would be "the worst possible move we could make." Senator Russell believed that the Laotians were not worth fighting for. The new majority whip of the Senate, Hubert Humphrey, concurred in these opinions.[58]

Also, the belief that the neutralization agreement would eliminate difficulties for the United States in Laos was questioned by Averell Harriman on February 20, 1962 in testimony given during a closed session of the Senate Foreign Relations Committee. Gibbons summarizes his testimony as follows: "Harriman described for the committee the agreement for the neutralization of Laos, but said, interestingly enough, that he had no confidence that North Vietnam would comply with those arrangements, including the provision that Laos would not be used for access to any other country (which was intended to apply specifically to the Ho Chi Minh Trail)."[59]

This pessimism with regard to the probable effects of the agreement was not the public position of the administration. The face presented to the world was much more optimistic concerning the outcome of the Geneva talks.

Despite the Pathet Lao's ability to achieve outright victory, the Pathet Lao, North Vietnamese, and Chinese saw the neutralization agreement as delivering distinct political advantages to them:

> Ultimately, the neutralization of Laos under Souvanna Phouma's leadership was sufficient improvement over prior events in Laos to gain Chinese and North Vietnamese support. International guarantees of Laotian neutrality would require the withdrawal of U.S. military personnel from Laos and remove that country from the protective orbit of SEATO. At the same time, the mechanisms envisioned for policing this neutrality would be inadequate to prevent discreet use of eastern Laos by North Vietnamese soldiers.[60]

For the United States—the agreement was a way to save face by having forged an agreement with its adversaries. Not all aspects of this arrangement were detrimental to American interests: even though the agreement would undoubtedly be violated, the anticipated de facto partition of Laos would provide a buffer zone for Thailand as the Royalist Lao forces occupied the area north of the Mekong River near Vientiane.[61]

The May 1962 Crisis

The military situation for Phoumi grew demonstrably worse in early May 1962. Pathet Lao attacks on Nam Tha increased at that time, and the news that another part of Phoumi's army situated in a nearby town had been defeated sent the troops in Nam Tha into a headlong retreat which did not stop until they had reached Thailand some several hundred miles to the south.[62] The United States was alarmed by the devastating success of the Pathet Lao's general offensive, and the State Department came to the conclusion that it could not cede Laos as a result of military conquest.[63]

The NSC met on May 10, 1962 to consider the new crisis in Laos. This meeting decided little of consequence. However, the broad outlines of the debate were drawn at this meeting. Similar to their recommendations a year earlier, Harriman and Hilsman proposed that the United States inform Britain, India, and the Soviet Union of our opposition to the recent developments in Laos, and they also argued for the deployment of American troops to signal American resolve in Southeast Asia. It was hoped that this move would also reassure Thailand and Phoumi Nosavan that American assistance would still be forthcoming. As had happened the previous year, the Joint Chiefs opposed intervention "unless they could use sufficient force to meet any reaction by the other side."[64] The Chiefs were willing, however, to send diplomatic protests and deploy the fleet to the area as a show of force. Kennedy agreed to these minimal steps, so a naval task force was dispatched to the South China Sea. Harriman and Hilsman were worried that the Pathet Lao and North Vietnamese would construe this action as a sign of weakness, so they were determined to repeat their argument for the deployment of U.S. troops to Thailand.[65]

On May 12, 1962 the NSC met, this time with McNamara and Lemnitzer in attendance. Having already been informed that Eisenhower favored a strong response in Laos, McNamara's announcement that he and Lemnitzer "supported the initial troop movements and most especially . . . the improvement of the communication and supply lines" prompted the President to agree to send 5,000 troops to Thailand, for movement into Laos if necessary.[66]

After Kennedy's decision on May 12 to send troops to Thailand, Gibbons tells us that "the debate over Laos continued . . . as deep cleavages developed between the 'all or nothing' view of the JCS, supported by others, including W. W. Rostow, and the Harriman-Hilsman preference for limited military action."[67] Roger Hilsman describes this division over policy in some detail:

> . . . . not all the officers in the Pentagon shared the "all-or-nothing" view. Neither did all the high officials in the State Department share this "political" view. Walt Rostow, head of the Policy Planning Council, for example, felt that serious consideration should be given to bombing North Vietnam. And some members of both the State Department and the Pentagon—the Secretary of State, for example—shifted their view. For the question was never simple, and there were legitimate and persuasive arguments on both sides. But although there were these layers of opinion—and shadings and shiftings—within each department and agency, the dominant view in the Pentagon was toward "all-or-nothing" and the dominant view in the State Department was toward the political, that is, to limit and tailor the force used so that it would carry a political signal.[68]

During a meeting held at the White House on May 13, 1962 the NSC considered what the American response would be to a continued effort—in the face of U.S. troop movement to Thailand—by the Pathet Lao to conquer Laos. Proponents of the all-or-nothing perspective argued for a plan to deploy U.S. and allied forces across the Laotian panhandle in order to stop the infiltration into Vietnam; if this action did not cause the rapid cessation of the infiltration, there were to be direct attacks on North Vietnam from the land, sea, and air.[69]

Hilsman and others argued for the "political view" in these meetings. The basic assumption of his thinking was: "the proposition that for international political reasons any use of force had to be tailored to our goal of a neutral Laos achieved through negotiations and a government of national union. If we were to have international support for our move, the intervention had to be to restore the cease fire and not encroach on the territory held by the Communists."[70]

In other words, he was advocating the use of *limited means* to attain a *limited objective*: a neutralized Laos; the use of force to achieve this objective was not easily reconciled with the all-or-nothing approach that had been advocated by others.

The limited war plan Hilsman envisaged was primarily static and defensive. He summarizes the "political" position as follows:

[The] "political" argument . . . was that for the United States the strategic objective was to *deny* the Mekong lowlands and the North-South
road to the Communists. . . . And if the Communists did not accept a
neutral Laos and a government of national union as a way out, we would
be holding the lowlands, denying them to the communist side. This
would put us in a sound international position politically, and militarily in a good position for defense, manning a line that we could hold at
the least possible cost.[71]

This approach would have allowed no chance for American military
power to decisively engage and defeat its opponent. This fact made the
"political" plan unacceptable to the Joint Chiefs and their sympathiz-
ers. Hilsman, in fact, captures the essential difference between the
"military" and "political" positions in these two sentences: "The 'military' approach started with grave doubts that Laos could be successfully neutralized through a government of national union and negotiations with the Communists. *But what the advocates of the 'military'
approach really objected to was any course of action that might lead them
to a limited war or defensive position—no matter how good it was.*"[72]
Fortunately events did not force the United States to make a choice
between these alternatives.[73]

The Aftermath of the Neutralization Agreement[74]

The defeat of Phoumi's forces and the deployment of the several thousand U.S. soldiers, announced at the White House on May 15, 1962
after a meeting with former president Eisenhower, quickened the pace
of events. Phoumi retreated from the tough stand he had been taking at
the bargaining table; the Pathet Lao halted their advance into southern
Laos when faced with the prospect of facing American forces. Within a
month, on June 11, 1962, Souvanna Phouma was able to assemble a
shaky coalition government between the left, right, and center factions.
In this government the important ministries of defense and interior
were to be held by the neutralists. On July 6, 1962 the new Laotian
government presented its credentials to the Geneva Conference, and on
July 23 the "Declaration on the Neutrality of Laos" was signed by the
foreign ministers of the fourteen member nations.[75] With that event
the Geneva Conference came to a close, but that was not the end of
political turmoil in Laos.

In the course of six months the Pathet Lao had resumed its attempt to conquer Laos. On June 6, 1963, Hall notes, "Souvanna for the first time publicly accused the Pathet Lao of relying on weapons and soldiers from North Vietnam. On [June 24, 1963] he terminated military budget funds for the Pathet Lao and then turned to the United States for additional military assistance."[76] Almost a year later, on May 2, 1964, Souvanna announced that he was forming a neutralist-rightist coalition to govern Laos in the face of a new and vigorous communist offensive. Soon thereafter President Johnson authorized the use of the United States Air Force stationed in Thailand to bomb Pathet Lao-North Vietnamese attacks on the armed forces of the new coalition government. The communist offensive was stopped by this direct application of American air power.[77] In December 1964, the United States commenced regular bombing of the Laotian panhandle with Operation Barrel Roll in an attempt to interrupt the flow of supplies along the Ho Chi Minh trails into South Vietnam.

Conclusions

This study of the Laos Crises reveals that Never Again and Limited War arguments vied for implementation within the Kennedy Administration. The path of coercive diplomacy that President Kennedy chose more closely resembled the "political" or "limited war" options that were presented to him. Not only did Kennedy have limited objectives, but he employed quite limited threats and use of force to achieve his objectives. With that having been said, there are some other conclusions that may be taken from this chapter.

Opinions of the various actors concerning the use of force did not necessarily correspond to the bureaucratic position of the person under consideration. Eisenhower stated that if force were used it should be used to clear the communists out of the region; his predisposition was not favorable to the static, defensive wars that Hilsman advocated to Kennedy. Kennedy does not appear to have shared Eisenhower's beliefs about the use of force; he was more willing to consider using force for the purpose of signaling and for limited engagements that were primarily defensive. Within the Joint Chiefs of Staff several positions were noticeable. The Chairman, General Lemnitzer (army), was not opposed to intervention as a matter of course, but he appears to have been quite cautious. Admiral Burke was the strongest advocate of intervention among the Chiefs, but as he has been quoted above he believed that the United States would have to be "willing to throw enough in to win—perhaps the works." What emerges from the available sources on the Laos debates is that General Decker, the Chief of Staff of the Army, had probably the most forceful personality in the group, and he opposed the idea of nondecisive intervention categorically. It was he who said, "if we go in, we should go in to win, and that means bombing Hanoi, China, and maybe using nuclear weapons." There is a noticeable similarity between Eisenhower and Decker on this issue.

Roger Hilsman was insightful in his diagnosis of the Never Again position when he observed "what the advocates of the military approach really objected to was any course of action that might lead them to a limited war or defensive position—no matter how good it was." Richard Betts supports Hilsman in his analysis:

> The Joint Chiefs, on the other hand, seemed to waver between timid opposition to any military intervention and a frightening proviso that they be given the option to use tactical nuclear weapons if United States forces were committed. Actually the military—especially Army Chief of Staff George Decker—wanted to avoid a show of force or a limited action which could end in disaster. They wanted either massive commitment sufficient to win or a complete avoidance of military entanglement.[78]

Within the Kennedy administration there were officials who like Hilsman and Harriman were sympathetic to the "political" perspective on the use of force. Thus, through the example of the Laos case, we are finally able to observe that the tension between the Never Again and Limited War Schools is essentially related to their respective philosophies of the use of force.

7 | Vietnam, 1964–65: The Debates Over the Use of Limited Force

After the crisis in Laos was temporarily alleviated with the signing of the Geneva Agreement in the summer of 1962, the attention of the American leadership turned more intently toward South Vietnam. The success of that nation's attempt to defeat an insurgency that was materially assisted and substantially controlled by North Vietnam became crucial to the Kennedy and Johnson administrations' determination to resist Communist aggression as promoted in "wars of national liberation." This chapter analyzes the events of 1964 through July 1965, which led the United States to launch an air campaign against North Vietnam and then to introduce combat ground forces into South Vietnam. The Vietnam case is of interest because the conception of using force never appeared in its classic form, as the Joint Chiefs did not argue for the "nothing" part of the "All-or-Nothing" proposition. In 1964 and 1965 various Chiefs of Staff slowly eliminated their differences and came to agree that actions approximating an "all" approach of aggressive combined arms warfare was necessary to prevent a North Vietnamese victory. Objections to the nondecisive use of force were not made with the vehemence seen during the Dienbienphu or Laos Crises. The task of this case study is to analyze the politico-military environment that existed in Washington and Vietnam and determine which factors were able to neutralize the formal advocacy powers of the JCS.

Background

The First Indochina War came to an end on July 20, 1954, when representatives from the French and Viet Minh high commands signed a truce agreement in Geneva that called for the partition of Vietnam into two nations—with a Demilitarized Zone centered on the 17th parallel separating North and South Vietnam. In the North Ho Chi Minh's Communist Party created a government that was seated in Hanoi. In the South it was not clear who would rule. Bao Dai, the Emperor of Vietnam, asked Ngo Dinh Diem, a prominent anti-colonialist Catholic, to form a government in the South.[1] Diem was beset, almost immediately, with problems of the greatest magnitude. No political institutions existed in South Vietnam. Consequently, civil insurrection and conspiracies against the government became commonplace. While Diem made progress in consolidating power, his government never attained the level of control of the population enjoyed by the Viet Minh in North Vietnam—despite the large sums doled out by the U.S. in economic and military assistance.

Ho had never abandoned his goal of a united Vietnam under communist rule. An underground network controlled by North Vietnam was left in place for the time when the armed struggle would be renewed. That decision came in the spring of 1959 when the Central Executive Committee of North Vietnam "authorized the resumption of armed struggle and took active measures to support it."[2] Within a short time it became apparent that the activity sponsored by North Vietnam was effective. Stanley Karnow points out that between 1959 and 1961 the number of South Vietnamese government officials who were assassinated "soared from twelve hundred to four thousand a year."[3] These facts should *not* be interpreted as implying that a critical aspect of the rebellion lay in the social problems that existed in South Vietnam. In terms of assessing the causes of the Second Indochinese war it is probably wisest to believe as William Duiker does that even though political discontent with the Diem regime "was widespread throughout the South, it is highly unlikely that the unrest would have achieved enough coherence and dynamic force to challenge the power of the Saigon regime without the organizational genius provided by the Party leadership in Hanoi."

"In that sense," Duiker adds, "the insurgency was a genuine revolt based in the South, but it was organized and directed from the North."[4]

The connection to the rebellion in the South was palpable. Douglas Pike has recently observed, "Only now do Hanoi historians corroborate the fact that there was deep [North Vietnamese Army] command and control in the South from the earliest days, as well as systematic logistic support during the war."[5]

During 1964 the deterioration of the political structures of South Vietnamese society was indicated by the fact that, as William Duiker notes, the insurgents were "spearheaded by an estimated thirty to forty-five main force battalions, supplemented by 35,000 guerrillas and 80,000 irregulars." Duiker goes on to estimate the Northern involvement in South Vietnam during 1964 this way:

> Although the precise figure is controversial, there was a clear rise in the movement of D.R.V. units into South Vietnam during the year, facilitated by the completion of the so-called Ho Chi Minh trail through southern Laos. Regular units of the People's Army of Vietnam (PAVN) began preparing to move to the South as early as April, and according to U.S. intelligence sources the first complete tactical unit left the North in October and arrived in the South two months later.[6]

Concomitant with this increased activity in the South was a rise in the casualty rate for the South Vietnamese army: it jumped from 1,000 casualties per month in January 1964 to 3,000 per month by December of that year. Clearly, by the end of 1964, the situation was rapidly worsening as South Vietnamese units were beginning to be destroyed as quickly as they could be constituted.[7] This violence and turmoil devastated the political scene in South Vietnam which evinced "a dizzying succession of revolving door governments."[8]

The previous year, 1963, had brought great changes to South Vietnam and the United States. The American embassy in Saigon had been lulled into a false optimism by what seemed to be a positive military trend in 1962. Soon the events of 1963 erased those hopes as the country started to unravel during that spring. The proximate cause of this change was a national uprising by the large Buddhist community in May 1963 in the city of Hue. The revolt became more intense in June 1963 with the famous immolation of the Buddhist monks. The Diem government was soon shaken to its core. In Washington a group of top officials—Harriman, Hilsman, and Forrestal—seized a fortuitous occasion to set the wheels in motion for a *coup d'état*; President

Kennedy had several months to withdraw American support for the disloyal South Vietnamese generals but chose not to do so. After a couple of months of precariously remaining in power, Diem was overthrown and murdered on November 1, 1963. Three weeks later President Kennedy was assassinated in Dallas. As 1963 came to a close both South Vietnam and the United States faced the future with new leadership.

1964: Setting the Stage for War

The political condition of South Vietnam after Diem's assassination resembled the circling descent of water in a whirlpool. South Vietnam experienced a series of coups causing great political instability. This is not to say that Diem's leadership was exemplary, but it was only after his death that the centrifugal forces that constituted Vietnamese politics became fully apparent. This descent into political self-destruction was the trigger that brought increased American involvement including the sustained bombing of the North and the introduction of American ground forces into South Vietnam. Upon taking office Lyndon Johnson was as determined to maintain the independence of South Vietnam as Kennedy had been. Four days after Kennedy's death, on November 26, 1963, Johnson approved NSAM 273, which "reaffirm[ed] the U.S. commitment to defeat the VC in South Vietnam."[9] Additionally, the document stated the administration's desire to withdraw 1,000 troops by the end of the year. The Mekong Delta region was to be the focal point for overt military, political, and economic efforts by the U.S. American support for the post-Diem regime was to be continued at the same fiscal levels. However, NSAM 273 also directed that covert actions in Laos and North Vietnam would be authorized. Despite these various forms of continued and new assistance, the situation in South Vietnam continued to deteriorate.

On March 11–16, 1964, Secretary McNamara again visited South Vietnam accompanied by General Taylor and Director John A. McCone of the Central Intelligence Agency. The report that McNamara delivered to the President upon his return formed the basis for the newest formulation of American policy, NSAM 288.[10] Issued on March 17, 1964, NSAM 288 was a lengthy document which reaffirmed the U.S. objective of maintaining an "independent, non-Communist South Vietnam," but its greater significance lay in its advocacy of closer American ties to the outcome in Vietnam, which entailed greater resolve on the part of the United States.[11] McNamara's memo reflected the fact that the South had weakened since November 1963, but its greater significance lay in the fact that it "involved an assumption by the United States of a greater part of the task, and an increased involvement by the United States in the internal affairs of South Vietnam, and for these reasons it carried with it an enlarged commitment of U.S. prestige to the success of our effort in that area."[12] Among other things NSAM 288 called for the United States to make its commitment to South Vietnam unequivocal and urged the full social and economic mobilization of South Vietnam with concomitant increases in the size of its ground forces.[13] The McNamara paper of March 16 was discussed at a meeting of the National Security Council the next day. General Taylor told the President that the Joint Chiefs "found the proposed program acceptable" but were not convinced that it would be "sufficient to save the situation in Vietnam." The Chiefs, he told those assembled, wanted to be prepared to react quickly against North Vietnam because such military action "might be necessary to make effective the program recommended by Secretary McNamara."[14] Apparently, the Chiefs of Staff were not convinced of the military efficacy of the plans being considered by the Administration. The final two recommendations were the most important in terms of pushing U.S. policy forward. They were summarized at the end of the memo in paragraphs 11 and 12 (of Section VII). They instructed the relevant United States government agencies:

> 11. To authorize continued high-level U.S. overflights of South Vietnam's borders and to authorize "hot pursuit" and South Vietnamese ground operations over the Laotian line for the purpose of border control. . . .
>
> 12. To prepare immediately to be in a position on 72 hours' notice to initiate the full range of Laotian and Cambodian "Border Control" actions (beyond those authorized in paragraph 11 above) and the "Retaliatory Actions" against North Vietnam, and to be in a position on 30 days' notice to initiate the program of "Graduated Military Pressure" against North Vietnam.[15]

In the body of the paper it was clear that the "border control" operations would include the "expansion of the patrols into Laos to include

U.S. advisers and re-supply by U.S. aircraft." "Retaliatory Actions"
would include "retaliatory bombing strikes and commando raids on a
tit-for-tat basis by the [South Vietnamese] against [North Vietnamese]
targets."[16] Immediately upon approval of NSAM 288 plans began to be
created for the implementation of paragraphs 11 and 12. On April 17,
1964, the Joint Chiefs of Staff approved OPLAN 37–64, whose target
list and logistical annexes were later employed in the campaign of escalation conducted against North Vietnam in 1965 and later.[17] Even
though the President had decided in favor of greater action in Indochina, NSAM 288 was undeniably directed toward assisting Saigon in
developing the military capabilities to effectively defend itself against
North Vietnam.

The Summer of 1964

The summer of 1964 was a period of decline for South Vietnam. The
first three days of June witnessed a conference in Honolulu that was
attended by all top officials from Washington and Saigon. Gibbons
writes that the "general consensus . . . was that attacks on the North or
on Laos were not required at that time (the JCS disagreed), and that
plans for future action would have to be more carefully planned." Honolulu is of particular interest here because it was the site of a major disagreement between the Chiefs of Staff of the respective services and
Maxwell Taylor, the Chairman of the Joint Chiefs of Staff. The other
Chiefs, General Curtis LeMay (USAF) being the most vociferous,
wanted to begin a direct air campaign against the North to destroy their
will and capabilities.[18] Taylor wanted a much more limited bombing
campaign, "a lesser attack," that would have the dual purpose of per-
suading the North from aiding the Viet Cong and the Pathet Lao and
of obtaining the North's cooperation in "calling off" the insurgents in
the South.[19] Taylor's approach had the flavor of forceful coercive diplomacy whereas that of the other Chiefs smacked of a traditional Jominian attack that would deliver punishing blows against an opponent with
the intent of effecting his abject capitulation.

A number of remarks in August and September 1964 indicate that a
political conception of using force was deeply rooted in the minds of
top-level members of the administration. Donald Mrozek writes, "In a
memo to the President on 13 August 1964, McGeorge Bundy implied

that Taylor's interest in various proposals stemmed from their likely political or psychological effects."[20] In an outgoing memo of August 13, 1964, drafted by William P. Bundy to CINCPAC and all high-ranking officials in the Saigon embassy, the following observation is made: "Basically solution in both South Vietnam and Laos will require combination military pressure and some form of communication under which Hanoi (and Peiping) eventually accept idea of getting out."[21]

And, finally, one finds the Special Assistant for Far Eastern Affairs, Michael V. Forrestal, writing to John McNaughton, Assistant Secretary of Defense for International Security Affairs, that the air strikes were not justified because of their military effectiveness but rather because they would convince Hanoi that the U.S. was slowly moving up the ladder of escalation.[22] Thus, a combination of military signals and negotiations would bring about the desired outcome for the United States.

The remainder of the summer was punctuated in the middle by events of great importance—the Tonkin Gulf Crisis. A detailed account of those actions is not required for this book, but a brief description is necessary. Since their approval in January 1964 the United States (under OPLAN 34-A) had sanctioned and supported South Vietnamese commando raids against the North Vietnamese coast. The United States had also conducted surveillance patrols by U.S. destroyers in international waters off the North Vietnamese coast since 1962; these operations received the code name "De Soto patrols." In early August 1964 an American De Soto patrol and a South Vietnamese 34-A raid were conducted in the same general area. On August 2, 1964, the destroyer *U.S.S. Maddox* was attacked by three North Vietnamese torpedo boats, which probably thought that the U.S. ship had been involved in the 34-A raid. The *Maddox* fired on the torpedo boats and drove them away with the help of aircraft from the *U.S.S. Ticonderoga*.

Not wanting its right to navigate in open seas to remain challenged, the Navy sent the *U.S.S. Turner Joy* and the *Maddox* on another patrol. What happened the next evening has remained a matter of debate for years. On August 4, 1964, the two destroyers reported that they had come under attack—later evidence questioned whether an attack had actually occurred or whether anxious personnel on the destroyers had imagined one by misreading their instruments. In any case, this incident immediately created the largest political implications. On August

5, 1964, President Johnson ordered reprisal raids against North Vietnam from the aircraft carriers *Constellation* and *Ticonderoga*.[23] The bombing strikes knocked out torpedo boat bases and oil storage facilities near the location of the attack on the destroyers. President Johnson seized the opportunity to obtain the Congressional authorization he desired. On August 7, 1964, both houses of Congress overwhelmingly passed the joint resolution which has come to be known as the Tonkin Gulf Resolution.[24]

Events during the summer of 1964 also provided evidence that North Vietnam was in the war for the long haul. On June 18, 1964, James B. Seaborn, a Canadian member of the International Control Commission (for the Geneva agreements), visited the North Vietnamese Premier, Pham Van Dong, in Hanoi. Seaborn made this trip at the behest of the United States and delivered a message that its intentions were limited and "essentially peaceful." However, the patience of the United States was not infinite. The American government knew how closely the North controlled the Viet Cong, and if it were forced to escalate the war in defense of South Vietnam—"the greatest devastation would of course result for the D.R.V. itself." During a second trip in August 1964, Seaborn issued the same warning, but the North Vietnamese expressed little interest in any outcome except the unconditional American withdrawal from South Vietnam.[25]

The Autumn of 1964

By early September 1964 the situation in Vietnam had deteriorated to the point that two members of the Joint Chiefs of Staff believed that the United States should take military action against North Vietnam even if the U.S. had to provoke an incident to enter the war: they were General Wallace M. Greene (Marines) and General John P. McConnell (Air Force). The new Chairman of the JCS, General Earle C. Wheeler, and the two remaining Chiefs, General Harold K. Johnson (Army) and Admiral David L. McDonald (Navy), agreed with Ambassador Taylor that responding as required to North Vietnamese actions was still the best policy.[26] Throughout September and October plans were being formulated for direct military American action in Southeast Asia. The *Pentagon Papers* observed a trend in America's Vietnam policy:

In their Southeast Asia policy discussions of August-October 1964, Administration officials had accepted the view that overt military pressures against North Vietnam probably would be required. Barring some critical developments, however, it was generally conceded that these should not begin until after the new year. Preparations for applying such pressures were made in earnest in November.[27]

The President approved NSAM 314 on September 10, 1964. In it the United States decided to resume a number of covert naval and air operations; there was also agreement that preparations should be made for responses against the DRV "in the event of any attack on U.S. units or any *special* DRV/VC action against SVN." The final point in NSAM 314 reflected the concern of American officials that political stability had to be achieved in South Vietnam before any serious military commitment could be made; part seven states that "the first order of business at present is to take actions which will help to strengthen the fabric of the Government of South Vietnam; to the extent that the situation permits, such action should precede larger decisions."[28] On October 14, 1964, Ambassador Taylor informed Washington that September and October had "seen little or no progress in the overall situation" (with one possible minor exception), and that the political strength of the government had, most probably, become weaker. Taylor added, "I feel sure that we must soon adopt new and drastic methods to reduce and eventually end such infiltration if we are ever to succeed in South Vietnam."[29] In the same cable he presented the alarming news that the rate of inflation of communist units into South Vietnam had increased dramatically.[30]

Within days the Joint Chiefs of Staff (on 21 October 1964) called for a greater effort to seal the borders of South Vietnam: "Application of the principle of isolating the guerrilla force from its reinforcement and support and then to fragment and defeat the forces has not been successful in Vietnam. . . . The principle must be applied by control of the national boundaries or by eliminating or cutting off the source of supply and direction."[31]

On October 27, 1964, the Joint Chiefs submitted another memo to the Secretary of Defense reiterating their position that "strong military actions are required now in order to prevent the collapse of the US position in Southeast Asia."[32] Appendix B focused on actions that should be taken outside of South Vietnam and was clearly concerned with cross-border infiltration of soldiers and materiel. Actions #3 suggested permitting South Vietnamese units "to pursue VC forces which cross into Cambodia" thereby preventing the use of "safe havens." Action #7 discussed "air strikes and armed route reconnaissance" in the Laotian panhandle.[33] These proposals were being evaluated when the Viet Cong attacked an American air base on November 1, 1964, at Bien Hoa killing four Americans and wounding 57. On the morning of November 3, 1964, the "NSC Working Group on SVN/SEA" was convened under William P. Bundy and given the task of examining and evaluating the options that were open to the United States in Southeast Asia.[34]

On November 1 Ambassador Taylor characterized the attack as a "deliberate act of escalation and a change of the ground rules under which [the VC] have operated up to now. It should be met promptly by an appropriate act of reprisal against DRV target, preferably an airfield."[35] The Joint Chiefs were not accepting of this argument: they told McNamara the same day that Taylor's "tit-for-tat" approach "was unduly restrictive and limited U.S. initiative." The Chiefs on November 4 offered a plan that eschewed joint U.S.-South Vietnamese actions and called for "a series of specific actions to be taken in the next 3 days which included air strikes, landing of U.S. forces, and evacuation of dependents."[36] They felt that the Taylor proposal was "unduly restrictive" and reactive in the sense that it handed over "to the DRV substantial initiatives with respect to the nature and timing of further U.S. actions."[37] The JCS believed that the Viet Cong had fundamentally altered their own rules of engagement, and the United States should not allow this act to go unpunished. Yet, no retaliatory action was taken after Bien Hoa: a central consideration was the effect that such actions might have on the upcoming presidential election. Nevertheless, the instability of the government in Saigon was of great concern to President Johnson and probably would have prevented a reprisal raid in and of itself.

On November 3, 1964, William Bundy set forth three options for the Working Group to consider—A, B, and C. The three options remained essentially the same when they appeared in a memo by John McNaughton at the end of November 1964.[38] Option A was to be an extension of the policy then in place; there would be "maximum assistance within South Vietnam, . . . [and] specific individual reprisal actions . . . against any recurrence of VC 'spectaculars' such as Bien Hoa."[39] Under Option A negotiations were to be avoided.

Option B was referred to as the "fast/full squeeze" by McNaughton, and it was the approach favored by the Joint Chiefs. It called for "a systematic program of military pressures against the north, with increasing pressure actions to be continued at a fairly rapid pace and without interruption until we achieve our present stated objectives."[40] These intense bombings and covert measures were to be combined with negotiations at some point, but the American position would be essentially uncompromising towards North Vietnam.

Finally, the third option, C, called for a steady, deliberate campaign of escalating pressures combined with "communications with Hanoi and/or Peiping." The military actions were to be taken "against infiltration targets, first in Laos and then in the DRV, and then against other targets in [North Vietnam]."[41] Option C also made provision, not mentioned in the McNaugton summary, for a possible "significant ground deployment to the northern part of South Vietnam, either in the form of a U.S. combat force or a SEATO-members force." These forces were to serve "as an additional bargaining counter" and as a deterrent to a possible North Vietnamese invasion of the South in response to the coercive bombing campaign.[42] With respect to negotiations the United States was to indicate "from the outset a willingness to negotiate in an affirmative sense, accepting the possibility that we might not achieve our full objectives."[43]

The Joint Chiefs desired a policy that would approximate an all out effort against the North—that is, Option B. Their hostility to the "tit-for-tat" element implicit in Option A was supported with a well-reasoned, Jominian argument:" 'Tit-for-tat' is considered unduly restrictive, inhibits US initiative, and implies an undesirable lack of flexibility both as to the nature and level of response. Adoption and announcement of a policy of a 'tit-for-tat' basis only would serve to pass to the DRV substantial initiatives with respect to the nature and timing of future actions."[44]

With regard to Option C, it received JCS criticism because it did not demonstrate to the opponent that the United States possessed the will to see the war through to the end.[45] Gibbons summarizes the JCS position as follows: "In general, the Joint Chiefs of Staff took the position that force had to be used, and used decisively, against North Vietnam and in Laos. They were leery of a land war, however, and advocated primary use of the Air Force and the Navy."[46]

They believed that the new policy should extend "to the full limit of what military actions can contribute toward national objectives."[47] By March 1965 the Army Chief of Staff, General Harold Johnson, would abandon any Army opposition to the use of American ground forces for a combat role. But it would still be the case that President Johnson and his civilian advisers would reject the military's plans for employing force: these plans being more traditional and conventional in that they focused on the military's desire to achieve substantial military objectives. A case in point was the military's desire to physically cut the Ho Chi Minh trails in South Vietnam and Laos.

It is no secret that the Joint Chiefs, with the exception of Maxwell Taylor, were never part of the esteemed inner circles of the high officials in the Kennedy and Johnson administrations; this might not have been so debilitating in all administrations, but in these two which relied to a great extent on an ad hoc advisory process the results were particularly unfortunate.[48] For example, the famous Tuesday lunches at which Johnson set forth much of his weekly agenda with respect to foreign policy and Vietnam always included the Secretary of State, the Secretary of Defense, and the National Security Adviser. It was not until the fall of 1967 that the Chairman of the Joint Chiefs was included as a regular member.[49] Even if the opinions of the military leaders were not greatly sought after, at least one member of the administration realized the importance of getting the Chiefs to approve of any military actions. On November 14, 1964, Presidential Assistant Jack Valenti wrote a memo to the President recommending "that before you make final decisions on the problems in Vietnam, you 'sign on' the Joint Chiefs in that decision. . . . " He continued: "If, for example, something should go wrong later and investigations begin in Congress, it would be beneficial to have the Chiefs definitely a part of the Presidential decisions so there can be no recriminations at these hearings, should they be held."

Valenti then pointed out how helpful Omar Bradley had been during the Korean War in countering Douglas MacArthur—a point that probably meant a great deal to Johnson who seems to have been greatly traumatized by the Yalu debacle. The memo continues by suggesting that General Wheeler might be invited to "one" of the "Bundy- McNamara-Rusk luncheons." He then wrote: "or you might include the entire Chiefs at one of the NSC meetings so they could have their views expounded to the Commander-in-Chief, face to face. That way, they will have been heard, they will have been part of the consensus, and our flanks will have been covered in the event of some kind of flap or investigation later."[50] It is doubtful that one could obtain a clearer impression of the manner in which the Joint Chiefs were regarded by this administration. Still, it is hard to imagine how a government could contemplate going to war and have such disregard for the opinions of its military leaders.

On December 1, 1964, President Johnson met with the "principals," Ambassador Taylor, present from Saigon, and Vice-President Humphrey to consider the policy recommendations that had been produced in the previous weeks of meetings. It was clear that powerful, sustained efforts would have to be made to strengthen the political institutions of South Vietnam. With respect to military options George Kahin observes that President Johnson's "long meeting with his top advisers on December 1 reduced the working group's three options to two: the Joint Chiefs' Option B was discarded. From then on, A and C were referred to respectively as "Phase I" and "Phase II" of a potentially two-stage program."[51] According to Gibbons, President Johnson "authorized the beginning of the first phase, to consist primarily of additional 34-A [maritime] raids, and armed reconnaissance operations in Laos (Barrel Roll) by which U.S. planes would conduct bombing raids in the corridor areas."[52] These actions were consistent with the alternatives available to the President under Option A. With respect to launching a Phase II (Option C) campaign against North Vietnam, Johnson "did not make any commitment at this point to expand the war through future operations against North Vietnam."[53] Burke and Greenstein write that Johnson left his senior advisers with "the impression that he had accepted their recommendations in general outline, but made it evident that because of the instability of the government of South Vietnam, he was not immediately authorizing new military steps."[54] In fact, the President did not agree to anything dramatically beyond NSAM 314 of September 10, 1964, "except to make more concrete the concept of possible future operations against North Vietnam."[55] The meeting made clear that Johnson saw some semblance of political stability as being the *sine qua non* for greater American involvement in the war.[56]

Wallace Thies observes that the operations approved at the December 1 meeting were carried out so that they "resulted in little, if any, new pressure on the DRV."[57] It is not surprising, therefore, that the government of South Vietnam did not evince greater stability during the final weeks of 1964. On December 20, 1964, a military coup directed by General Nguyen Khanh announced that an Armed Forces Council would run South Vietnam. This revolt undermined the perception of South Vietnam's political legitimacy in the United States. Then on December 24, 1964, the Viet Cong attacked an American officers' billet at the Brinks Hotel in Saigon killing two and injuring fifty-eight U.S. soldiers. Ambassador Taylor, CINCPAC, and the JCS urged swift retaliatory measures against the North. Johnson, Rusk, and McNamara opposed the reprisal attacks during a meeting on December 29. No military action was taken, much to Ambassador Taylor's consternation. The President reasoned that the "continuing political turmoil" and "general confusion in South Vietnam" were not conducive to the initiation of retaliatory bombing.[58] On December 30, President Johnson cabled Taylor outlining, among other things, his thoughts regarding the relative merits of using air and ground forces in the war. Later in the cable the president complained to the Ambassador:

> Every time I get a military recommendation, it seems to me that it calls for a large scale bombing. I have never felt that this war will be won from the air, and it seems to me that what is much more needed and would be more effective is a larger and stronger use of rangers and special forces and marines, or other appropriate military strength on the ground and on the scene. *I am ready to look with great favor on that kind of increased American effort,* directed at the guerrillas and aimed to stiffen the aggressiveness of Vietnamese military units up and down the line. Any recommendation that you or General Westmoreland take in this sense will have immediate attention from me, although I know that it may involve the acceptance of larger American sacrifices. *We have been building our strength to fight this kind of war since 1961, and I myself am ready to substantially increase the number of Americans in Vietnam if it is necessary to provide this kind of fighting force against the Viet Cong.*[59]

In a letter to Larry Berman, the author of *Planning a Tragedy*, McGeorge Bundy described Johnson's message as "an important cable. . . . [It] is an LBJ effort to get attention to well-designed ground action and it also shows clearly the temper of readiness to go further *inside South*

Vietnam that he shows steadily from here on for 3 years in spite of all contrary counsel. Along with other indications I take this to show that he was never swayed on this basic issue by Ball or anyone else."[60]

This is not to say that he had decided for direct intervention with regular U.S. ground forces. William Bundy tells us that in January 1965 Johnson's most trusted advisers "were convinced he had not made up his mind—and were concerned at that lack of decision."[61] It is evident from the documentary evidence that Johnson was really grappling with this problem. He was concerned that bombing would not stop the North's intrusion into South Vietnam and seemed to believe the war had to be won on the ground in the South. In the message to Taylor he appears to be saying that this war would have to be fought through counterinsurgency methods for which the United States had been preparing itself since Kennedy's inauguration—rather than with the strictly conventional means of a coercive bombing campaign. If the Vietnamese need advisers in order to develop the appropriate "fighting force" then he would approve such a request.

On December 31, 1964, Taylor cabled Washington again urging, with the concurrence of General Westmoreland, the initiation of Phase II concluding: "Without Phase II, we see slight chance of moving toward a successful conclusion." He argued that the sustained bombing campaign was the only real hope of promoting political stability in South Vietnam noting that the political free fall the country was experiencing exposed that nation to the danger that "panicked by what could be interpreted as abandonment, the leaders here would rush to compete with each other in making a deal with the National Liberation Front. This danger could be offset if at the time we were engaged in reprisal attacks or had initiated Phase II operations against [North Vietnam]."[62]

On January 6, 1965, Taylor responded to President Johnson's cable of December 30.[63] His assessment of political conditions in South Vietnam was decidedly grim. Taylor described the various historical and social factors that were impeding the development of stable political institutions. These factors were out of the control of the United States, and real progress could not be made "unless something new" were added "to make up for those things we cannot control." The new element which could counteract these centrifugal forces in the South was Phase II bombing: it was an "old recipe" but it was a highly flexible instrument that would allow the U.S. to bring its superior military power to bear against "the will of the chiefs of [North Vietnam]."

"As practical men," he continued, "they cannot wish to see the fruits of ten years of labor destroyed by slowly escalating air attacks." The Ambassador then took the occasion to make a case against the introduction of American ground forces:

> The Vietnamese have the manpower and the basic skills to win this war. What they lack is motivation. The entire advisory effort has been devoted to giving them both skill and motivation. If that effort has not succeeded there is less reason to think that U.S. combat forces would have the desired effect. In fact, there is good reason to believe that they would have the opposite effect by causing some Vietnamese to let the U.S. carry the burden while others, probably the majority, would actively turn against us. Thus intervention with ground combat forces would at best buy time and would lead to ever increasing commitments until, like the French, we would be occupying an essentially hostile foreign country.[64]

General Taylor has been *inaccurately* called a member of the Never Again School.[65] From the quote above (and other statements before and after this) Taylor's position exhibited considerable sensitivity to the political nature of the war in Vietnam; one does not see in his objection to the introduction of ground forces any blanket indictment of the concept of Limited War or the nondecisive use of force.[66] Taylor realized that the introduction of foreign troops might cause the disaffection of the South's population and give the appearance of a new round of imperialism.

The South's Decline Continues: Pleiku to Rolling Thunder

The political turmoil in Saigon showed no signs of abatement in December 1964. The details of the various plots and machinations is too intricate to describe here, but suffice it to say that the political instability as evidenced by the "purge" of December 20–21 or the considerable military defeat at Binh Gia did not undermine American support for the South Vietnamese government: Barrel Roll continued, and Maxwell Taylor was arguing in favor of going to Phase II within ten days. This is surprising given President Johnson's demand at the December 1, 1964, meeting that the political effectiveness of the

Saigon government would have to improve before further American measures could be taken on behalf of that government.

Taylor was not alone among high-level administration officials arguing that immediate escalation of some sort was necessary to save the situation in the South. On January 6, 1965, William P. Bundy wrote a memo to the Secretary of State in which he urged that the United States "consider some additional actions short of Phase II."[67] Due to the plummeting morale in the South, Bundy wrote "that the situation in Vietnam is now likely to come apart more rapidly than we had anticipated in November."[68] However, he attributed the low morale of the Saigon government not to their own incompetence and corruption but to the "widespread feeling that the U.S. is not ready for stronger action and indeed is possibly looking for a way out."[69] Bundy also described the damage to American credibility that would take place in Cambodia, Laos, and Thailand if South Vietnam were to fall: thus, he recommended commencing "reprisal action against the DRV" and "low-level reconnaissance of the DRV at once."

The most striking aspect of the memo was Bundy's observation: "We all think [starting these limited actions] would be a grave mistake in the absence of stronger action, and if taken in isolation would tremendously increase the pace of deterioration in Saigon."[70] The logic of the manner by which one should have sought to obtain a stable government in the South had thus been completely turned on its head. For the President, political stability, at least on December 1, was to be a precondition for escalation, but to his advisers escalation had become a way to reach the goal of strengthening the morale of South Vietnam. Finally, Bundy noted that introducing "limited US ground forces into the northern area of South Vietnam still has great appeal to many of us, concurrently with the first air attacks into the DRV." He believed that such an action "would have a real stiffening effect in Saigon, and a strong signal effect to Hanoi."[71]

On January 7 the President replied to Ambassador Taylor making the following points while once again accepting the notion of reprisals and declining to commit himself to the commencement of Phase II at that time:

> We concur in your judgment that large new American forces are not now desirable for security or for direct combat roles. . . .

We concur in your view that any action against the North should be designed *for political and psychological results.* We want to avoid destruction for its own sake and to minimize risk of rapid escalation.

We agree with your implicit assessment that strength and clarity of US commitment and determination are of major importance in political and even military balance in SVN.

We are not certain that any course of action now open to us can produce necessary turn-around in South Vietnam in coming months, but we are convinced that it is of high importance to try.

We are inclined to adopt a policy of prompt and clear reprisal, together with a readiness to start joint planning and execution on future military operations both within South Vietnam and against the North, but without present commitment as to the timing and scale of Phase II.[72]

It is interesting that the memo takes special note of Taylor's desire to attack the North for "political and psychological results." The President's desire to reject a fast and powerful escalation of the bombing clearly rebuffs the position of the JCS.

One week later, on January 14, 1965, a cable was sent to Taylor from the Secretary of State which, as Larry Berman describes it, instructed him that " 'immediately following the occurrence of a spectacular enemy action you would propose to us what reprisal action you considered desirable,' so that Phase II bombing could begin."[73] At the end of January John McNaughton wrote a memo to Secretary McNamara that "underscore[d] the importance of [Southeast Asia] for the US and then suggest[ed] that [the United States might] have to adopt Phase II as the only way to save the current situation."[74] This observation was supported by McGeorge Bundy who wrote to the President on January 27, 1965, that the morale in Saigon was deteriorating; the anti-communists were no longer willing to take risks to help the Americans. He added that he and McNamara "believe that the worst course of action is to continue in this essentially passive role which can only lead to eventual defeat."[75]

By the end of January it seems evident that President Johnson's advisers were looking for a provocation that could be used to initiate a campaign of retaliations which might then be made to dovetail with a campaign of coercive pressures against Hanoi.[76] Upon his return to Washington from Saigon on February 7, 1965, McGeorge Bundy delivered a lengthy memo to the President urging the initiation of a policy of "sustained reprisal":

> The prospect in Vietnam is grim. The energy and persistence of the Viet Cong are astonishing. . . . Yet the weary country does not want them to win. There are a host of things the Vietnamese need to do better and areas in which we need to help them. The place where we can help most is in the clarity and firmness of our commitment to what is in fact as well as rhetoric a common cause. There is one grave weakness in our posture in Vietnam which is within our own power to fix—and that is a widespread belief that we do not have the will and force and patience and determination to take the necessary action and stay the course. This is the overriding reason for our present recommendation of a policy of sustained reprisal. . . . One final word. At its very best, the struggle in Vietnam will be long.[77]

Bundy also noted in his Annex A that his focus in advocating the "sustained reprisals" was directed toward improving the situation in *South* Vietnam; the will of Hanoi was "an important but longer-range purpose." The new bombing campaign was to be directed at the minds of the South Vietnamese and the Viet Cong cadres.[78]

After an NSC meeting on February 8, 1965, President Johnson decided to move from a policy of reprisals to one of sustained bombing of the North which Johnson called "continuing action." The President cabled Saigon that "I have today decided that we will carry out our December plan for continuing action against North Vietnam with modifications up and down in tempo and scale in light of your recommendations as Bundy reports them, and our continuing review of the situation."[79]

Two days later, on February 10, 1965, the Viet Cong attacked a U.S. enlisted man's barracks in Qui Nhon leaving 23 men dead. The event led to an immediate reprisal against North Vietnam on February 11 with Flaming Dart II. At the NSC meeting on February 10, which discussed the Viet Cong attack, Secretary McNamara raised the point that the United States would "soon be facing the difficulty of taking Phase II actions even though there are no incidents created by the Viet Cong." McGeorge Bundy replied that "at an appropriate time we could publicly announce that we had turned a corner and changed our policy but that no mention should be made now of such a decision."[80]

Press reports of the first Rolling Thunder raid on March 2, 1965, stated directly that this bombing mission was "the first that was not in direct retaliation for Viet Cong guerrilla assaults on U.S. installations in South Vietnam."[81] It is worth noting that the administration's spokesmen indicated that there had been no change in policy after the first Rolling Thunder mission. There were probably several reasons for this: 1) a fear that the North might increase its guerrilla attacks on U.S. installations in the South; 2) Johnson's belief that a declared policy of escalation might provoke Chinese or Russian intervention; 3) the President's desire to keep up the appearance that his policies were a mere extension of his predecessors; 4) the fact that Johnson's domestic political agenda might have been damaged had it been clear that an Asian war was in the offing.[82]

Even though "sustained bombing" was approved there was disagreement as to what such a program should comprise. For example, McGeorge Bundy and Ambassador Taylor agreed on the level at which the bombing should be conducted. Taylor argued for "a measured, controlled sequence of actions against the DRV taken in reprisal for DRV-inspired actions in South Vietnam . . . carried out jointly with the GVN and . . . directed solely against DRV military targets and infiltration routes. . . ."[83] But they had different goals in mind for Rolling Thunder: "Whereas Bundy's main objective was to influence the course of the struggle in the *South* (providing a boost to GVN morale and cohesion, affording an opportunity for increased American influence upon and bargaining power with the GVN, and exerting a depressing effect upon VC cadres), Taylor's principal aim was 'to bring increasing pressure on the DRV to cease its intervention.' "[84]

Taylor's comments during this period indicate an effort on his part to signal America's intentions to Hanoi. In the *New York Times* (February 15, 1965) he is reported to have said that "our objective is limited—namely, to oblige Hanoi, to persuade Hanoi, to desist in its efforts to maintain an insurgency." During a CBS News interview he maintained, "The limited actions which we have taken have been deliberately planned, moderately sponsored, to suggest the possibility of other and bigger forms of reaction."[85] One clearly sees a coercive threat here aimed at the North Vietnamese by Taylor. The Ambassador wanted a higher level of military power used against the North than did in fact occur, but he did not support the program put forward by the JCS and

Admiral Sharp (CINCPAC). In a Congressional Research Service interview Bundy argued that the reprisals were too heavily dominated by military influences. He observed, "I'm not blaming anyone for that because it may have been quixotic to suppose that you conduct a military campaign *with an essentially political purpose. But, of course, that was what Vietnam was all about all the way.*"[86] Whether the military aspects of the bombing were too strong is debatable, but it cannot be denied that even after President Johnson made the decision there was considerable confusion in the government as to the nature of his policy. On February 16 McGeorge Bundy sent the President a memo plaintively seeking a clear statement of the new policy: "Precisely because this program represents a major operational change and because we have waited many months to put it into effect, there is a deep-seated need for assurance that the decision has in fact been taken. . . . Bob McNamara repeatedly stated that he simply has to know what the policy is so that he can make his military plans and give military orders."[87]

Bundy's perceptions (just stated) would have been of interest to Admiral Sharp (CINCPAC) who felt that bombing throughout the war was rendered ineffective by political restrictions on the use of force. Admiral Sharp objected to the reprisal program advocated by Bundy. Ambassador Taylor's interest in putting pressure on Hanoi was more consistent with the Admiral's position but even Taylor's concept of "graduated reprisals" did not convey the decisive power that Sharp wished to use.[88] On February 17, 1965, in a message to the Joint Chiefs of Staff he stated his concerns:

> While it may be politically desirable to speak publicly in terms of a "graduated reprisal" program, I would hope that we are thinking, and will act, in terms of a "graduated pressures" philosophy which has more of a connotation of steady, relentless movement toward our objective of convincing Hanoi and Peiping of the prohibitive cost [to] them of their program of subversion, insurgency, and aggression in SEAsia.[89]

The Joint Chiefs were asked by Secretary McNamara to prepare plans for a sustained bombing campaign against the North. The most important parameter for the bombing was the insistence that all targets be located south of the 19th parallel or about 100 miles north of the DMZ—not very far into the DRV. The JCS prepared plans for the "initial overt air strikes" of the sustained bombing. The plans set forth an eight-week concept for bombing four fixed targets per week in North Vietnam. Even though the Joint Chiefs' sent a plan forward for consideration, they harbored reservations about the course of action being taken by the President.[90]

President Johnson took time to consult with Dwight Eisenhower in mid-February 1965 on matters related to Southeast Asia. John McCone, the director of the CIA and the person responsible for briefing the former president about Vietnam, noted that in their conversations Eisenhower had expressed great alarm at John Kennedy's increased involvement in the region. With respect to greater American involvement, McCone notes, ". . . . Eisenhower felt that the situation could escalate very rapidly and was very much opposed to it unless we were determined to use our total resources to win."[91] Consistent with that belief the former president told Johnson on February 17, 1965, that "the U.S. has put its prestige onto the proposition of keeping SE Asia free. . . . We cannot let the Indo-Chinese peninsula go. He hoped it would not be necessary to use the *six to eight* divisions mentioned, but if it should be necessary then so be it."[92]

Eisenhower also urged Johnson to warn the Chinese privately through back channels of the dire consequences they would face in the event of their intervention in Vietnam. He believed the United States should not let the Chinese "get the idea that we will go just so far and no further in terms of the level of war we would conduct. That would be the beginning of the end, since they would know all they had to do was go further than we do." The meeting merits attention for two reasons. First, Eisenhower was being briefed in mid-February 1965 about the possibility of sending six to eight divisions into South Vietnam. Second, the former president stated a fundamental element of his approach to diplomacy: never reveal to an opponent one's unwillingness to defeat him by force of arms. Eisenhower certainly must have questioned Johnson's letting it be known that U.S. policy did not contemplate the Hanoi government's destruction under any scenario.

Unhappiness with Rolling Thunder

As demonstrated by his message of December 30, 1964, (mentioned above), President Johnson was uneasy about relying on bombing to change the direction of the war. His insecurities were not helped when

General Westmoreland sent a cable to Washington on February 25 in which he observed that "the pacification effort had virtually halted." The General, as the *Pentagon Papers* note, believed that in six months the Saigon government would be holding only "islands of strength around provincial and district capitals that were clogged with refugees and beset with 'end the war' groups asking for a negotiated settlement." If events continued along their present course a Viet Cong takeover was possible within a year.[93] To counteract this trend Westmoreland proposed "adding three Army helicopter companies, flying more close support and reconnaissance missions, opening a 'land line' from Pleiku in the highlands to the coast, and changing U.S. policy on the use of combat troops." Consequently, the President decided on March 2 to dispatch Army Chief of Staff General Harold Johnson and a team of assistants to Vietnam to assess the nature of the war.

Meanwhile, Rolling Thunder raids were supposed to be occurring with regularity but, in fact, no such pattern emerged. The initial strikes of March 2 and 3 were not followed by another strike until March 14. Wallace Thies writes, "The long delay between strikes, combined with British and French efforts to promote a negotiated settlement, was a source of constant irritation to Ambassador Taylor."[94] The Ambassador cabled a powerful critique of the bombing campaign to Washington on March 8. Taylor criticized the administration for being too willing to follow up on British and French diplomatic initiatives to stop the war; he felt that the "feverish diplomatic activities" were undercutting the image of resolve the United States wished to send to Hanoi. With regard to the nature of the bombing campaign he wrote, "I fear that to date Rolling Thunder in [Hanoi's] eyes has been merely a few isolated thunder claps."[95]

On the same day, Taylor sent another cable to Washington that was approved by General Westmoreland as well. This second message, in the words of the *Pentagon Papers*, argued "for a more dynamic schedule of strikes, a several week program relentlessly marching North to break the will of the DRV."[96] After consulting with Taylor and Westmoreland in Vietnam, General Johnson formulated proposals to increase the scope, tempo, and regularity of the Rolling Thunder bombings (points 5 and 6 of Johnson's 21-point plan).[97] The combination of Taylor's criticisms of the bombing and General Johnson's recommendations prompted the President to approve Rolling Thunder 7 of March

19–25, which was to give the impression of "regularity and determination."[98] Thies observes that after mid-March "much of the hesitation
that characterized the Administration's handling of the initial air strikes
was wearing off."[99] The missions were escalating in the direction
desired by Taylor; on April 3 and 4 this process culminated in attacks
(Rolling Thunder 9) against critical railway bridges 70 miles outside
Hanoi.

The air campaign "had thus graduated to the status of a regular and
continuing program. What now remained to be more carefully re-
examined . . . was the problem of target emphasis."[100] During this
period, however, the character of the bombings changed as the military
objective of interdiction became predominant. The attention of the
JCS, Westmoreland, and Taylor turned toward interrupting the 120
miles of rail lines that existed in North Vietnam below the 20th parallel.[101] Actions were also to be directed at the infiltration routes in
Laos.[102] However, the military was unable to obtain either the Secretary of Defense's or the President's approval for a multi-week bombing
proposal.[103]

Introducing Ground Forces

The commencement of Flaming Dart, the retaliatory bombings of
North Vietnam launched after the Pleiku attack, highlighted the vulnerability of U.S. air bases and pointed to the need for ground troops
to secure the perimeters around those bases. In a cable to CINCPAC on
February 22, 1965, General Westmoreland requested that two of the
three Battalion Landing Teams organic to the 9th MEB [Marine Expeditionary Brigade] be sent ashore at Da Nang with the third BLT to be
held offshore as a reserve.[104] Ambassador Taylor sent a cable to the State
Department on the same day reiterating his opposition to introducing
combat ground forces into South Vietnam.[105] The Joint Chiefs and
CINCPAC favored the deployment which President Johnson approved
on February 26, 1965. Consequently, 3,500 U.S. marines went ashore
at Da Nang on March 7–8, 1965.

It was also at this time that Lyndon Johnson complained to the Joint
Chiefs that he was not being given options other than bombing, which
was the reason he sent, as mentioned above, Army Chief of Staff
Harold K. Johnson to Vietnam to find some answers—or as only Lyn-

don Johnson could put it, "You get things bubbling, General."[106] General Johnson, who was in South Vietnam from March 5 to 14, 1965, delivered his report to the President the day after his return. Berman summarizes Johnson's report and the President's reaction this way:

> General Johnson's recommendations included proposals for increasing U.S. combat aid and logistical support, creation of an international force for an anti-infiltration role along the DMZ, and dispatching another army division to defend U.S. installations. The president approved more American military aid and combat support but took no action on logistical support nor on the international force along the DMZ.[107]

It seems that General Johnson made these recommendations despite his belief that the United States Army should not go into South Vietnam. David Halberstam notes that Johnson told two *New York Times* reporters that "he had no great desire to go to war in Vietnam. He knew too well what it would be, Korea all over again, only worse, an enemy using sanctuaries, the United States unable and unwilling to use its full power, all the old frustrations again."[108] Why did General Johnson go along with the escalation then? As he stated in an interview, the United States "had no alternative except to deploy forces if Vietnam were to remain a nation."[109] General Johnson appears to have believed that the President wanted to save the South at all costs. Consequently, the "nothing" of an "all-or-nothing" position dropped out as an option. There were only going to be various forms of intervention, so if we were going to get in we ought to do it right. For that reason, the Army Chief of Staff was most concerned with cutting the infiltration routes with an international ground force and instituting a more serious air campaign aimed at destroying the military and logistical capabilities of the North in the infiltration areas.[110]

According to General Goodpaster, Gen. Johnson "sent a shock wave through the administration" when he returned because he told the President that the war would require 500,000 men and would take five years to bring to a conclusion.[111] In an interview with Fred Greenstein, Goodpaster claimed that the 500,000 figure is contained in the still-classified sections of the full report.[112] In sum, Johnson was considering an all-arms concept for the war that would employ massive ground forces in conventional and nonconventional roles as well as direct and destructive missions for naval and air force aviation. It should not surprise us that General Bruce Palmer, Jr., has written of General Johnson that he often remarked "if the United States was not willing to go 'all the way,' that is, to include direct confrontation with the Soviet Union and China . . . then we had best not get in at all."[113]

The Joint Chiefs "put the first major recommendation for ground troop commitment on the docket" in JCSM-204–65 of March 20, 1965, only five days after General Johnson's report. In the memo the Chiefs noted that the military situation had been stable for a short time but had now begun to deteriorate again. American ground forces were needed in order to prevent imminent defeat. The Joint Chiefs were *not* in an operationally defensive frame of mind: "As they said, 'the requirement is not simply to withstand the Viet Cong, however, but to gain effective operational superiority and assume the offensive. To turn the tide of the war requires an objective of destroying the Viet Cong, not merely to keep pace with them, or slow down their rate of advance.' "[114] They argued that three divisions be sent to South Vietnam. Two would be American and one would be South Korean. This later came to be known as the "three division plan."

The call for ground forces continued—this time from Saigon. On March 26 Westmoreland told Washington that he wanted the equivalent of two divisions for use on the ground by June 1965—more if Rolling Thunder failed; the forces were to be deployed in the highlands and coastal enclaves.[115] The next day Ambassador Taylor cabled the State Department stating that if U.S. ground forces were to be used he favored that they be deployed in coastal enclaves and given the ability to react to threats with offensive mobility. At the end of March Taylor came to Washington for a series of meetings. In those meetings which ran from March 29 to April 2, Taylor opposed the "three division plan" of deployments to South Vietnam.

Apparently the Ambassador was able to head off the JCS and Westmoreland arguments for larger ground forces, but the President did agree to send in two more marine battalions (to Da Nang and Phu Bai). The President also approved a "slowly ascending tempo" in the Rolling Thunder strikes, and, of the greatest importance, he allowed "a change of mission for all Marine Battalions deployed to Vietnam to permit their more active use under conditions to be established by the Secretary of Defense in consultation with the Secretary of State."[116] These new actions were promulgated without any public notice in NSAM

328 on April 6, 1965.[117] Not all of the officials in the administration were sanguine about the halting steps being taken toward greater involvement. One official, CIA Director John McCone, wrote an important memo on April 2, 1965, criticizing the ineffective manner in which force was being used by the administration.

McCone was not one of the administration's "doves," in fact, he may have been the only civilian in the meetings of late November 1964 who supported Option B, the plan advocating the most intense bombing campaign against the North. As far as the civilians were concerned McCone was at the other end of the politico-military spectrum from George Ball. After the April 1, 1965, meeting McCone wrote a lengthy memo to the President's principal advisers concerning NSAM 328.[118] Early in the memo he challenged the efficacy of Rolling Thunder as it was being conducted, he noted that the bombing strikes "to date have not caused a change in the North Vietnamese policy of directing Viet Cong insurgency, infiltration cadres and supplying material. If anything, the strikes to date have hardened their attitude."[119] He criticized the limitation on the bombing doubting its ability to defeat the North Vietnamese: "Since the contemplated actions against the North are modest in scale, they will not impose unacceptable damage on it, nor will they threaten the DRV's vital interests. Hence, they will not present them with a situation with which they cannot live, though such actions will cause the DRV pain and inconvenience."[120]

He argued that the Soviet Union and China would be able to support the war with minimal risks to themselves. McCone then accurately predicted that the North would infiltrate more forces into the South—putting more intense pressure on the South. In turn, this would bring the United States eventually to the point where: "In effect, we will find ourselves mired down in combat in the jungle in a military effort that we cannot win, and from which we will have extreme difficulty in extracting ourselves."[121] The remainder of the memo argued that a change in the ground force mission required the intensification of Rolling Thunder:

> Therefore it is my judgment that if we are to change the mission of the ground forces, we must also change the ground rules of the strikes against North Vietnam. We must hit them harder, more frequently, and inflict greater damage. Instead of avoiding the MIGs, we must go in and take them out. A bridge here and there will not do the job. We must

strike their air fields, their petroleum resources, power stations and their
military compounds. This, in my opinion, must be done promptly with
minimum restraint.

If we are unwilling to take this action now, we must not take the
actions concerning the mission of our ground forces for the reasons I
mentioned above.[122]

Later in the month McCone reiterated these beliefs in a letter to the
President. He made it clear that he was not in favor of unrestricted
bombing, "I am not talking about bombing centers of population or
killing innocent people, though there will of course be some casualties.
I am proposing to 'tighten the tourniquet' on North Vietnam so as to
make the Communists pause to weigh the losses they are taking against
their prospect for gains."[123]

McCone's advice was ignored, and the escalation continued.[124] In
April 1965 the United States began Operation Steel Tiger, which called
for striking targets in the Laotian panhandle. An intragovernmental
controversy erupted in mid-April when General Westmoreland
attempted to sneak the two-battalion 173rd Airborne Brigade into
Vietnam in order to protect the Bien Hoa military installations. Westmoreland was opposed on this issue by Ambassador Taylor who wanted *no* more ground forces sent to SVN. Taylor was also disturbed by the
pace at which NSAM 328 was being made obsolescent by Washington's
increasing willingness to deploy ground forces to Vietnam; communications between Washington and its representative in Saigon had virtually broken down. In effect, the Ambassador demanded that the emerging American policy be made clear to him, so a set of meetings was
hastily arranged. The differences of opinion were then resolved at an
important conference in Honolulu on April 20, 1965.

The Honolulu Conference

The one-day Honolulu conference served to forge consensus among a
growingly fractious set of advisers. It also had the effect of bringing
Maxwell Taylor on board. The Ambassador abandoned his objections
to the President's decision to send substantial American ground forces
to Vietnam, and a hasty consensus for introducing ground forces was
created.[125] Taylor had come to realize that the President was no longer
indecisive on the matter of ground forces but that he had "crossed the

Rubicon."[126] It was decided that 33,500 more U.S. troops would be sent to Vietnam bringing the "American troop level to a total of 82,000, with the understanding that additional deployments would be considered later."[127] Concerning the bombing program, McNamara wrote this group recommendation: "With respect to strikes against the north, it was agreed that the present tempo is about right, that sufficient increasing pressure is provided by repetition and continuation. All of them envisioned a strike program continuing at least six months, perhaps a year or more, avoiding the Hanoi/Haiphong/Phuc Yen areas during that period."[128]

The United States and South Vietnam would attain their objectives if they could "break the will of the DRV/VC by denying them victory."[129] It was agreed that air strikes in the *South* would be given relative priority over those against North Vietnam. After Honolulu a consensus existed within the U.S. government to commit more ground forces to the conflict. The strategy of decisively compelling Hanoi to stop its actions in the South was now deemed less plausible: yet variants of such a concept were advocated by Taylor, Admiral Sharp, and the Joint Chiefs.[130] As a matter of course, the United States was moving toward a strategy of denial—the North, the U.S. government believed, would cease its efforts when it perceived that it could not succeed in the South.[131] This was to be a war of attrition fought primarily in the South with the eventual goal being a political settlement favorable to Saigon and American interests. President Johnson summarized the meeting's "consensus" as the conclusion "that a settlement in Vietnam would come as much or more from Communist failure in the South as from "pain" in North Vietnam.[132] Johnson notes, in his memoirs, that McNamara described the emergent strategy in these terms: "Their strategy for "victory" over time is to break the will of the [North Vietnamese and Viet Cong] by denying them victory. Ambassador Taylor put it in terms of a demonstration of Communist impotence, which will lead eventually to a political solution,"[133]

The increased presence of allied and U.S. ground forces would relieve pressure on the Army of South Vietnam (ARVN), *but* the President's intention remained that of helping the South Vietnamese achieve the stability needed to conduct the war by themselves. It was estimated that this strategy of denial might take one to two years.[134] Consistent with that goal after Honolulu a number of the units sent to

Vietnam shortly after the conference were logistical troops that assisted both the ARVN and the American forces.[135] The President did not set an upper level on troop commitments, nor did he rule out changes in the concept of fighting the war in the future.

Send More Troops

On May 11, 1965, the South Vietnamese countryside erupted as the Viet Cong launched a series of powerful attacks. Within the course of one month the South Vietnamese Army had seen its best mobile battalions chewed up.[136] The government collapsed and was replaced with a military junta. The situation looked especially grim to General Westmoreland, and it was at this point, in early June 1965, that he made his famous request for a total of 44 battalions—equivalent to about 180,000 total men—of which 34 were to be American. The other ten would come from other Asian allies, it was hoped; if these forces could not be procured then they would have to be American also. Westmoreland prediction's were not optimistic; the requested U.S. troops would be no panacea: "The VC are destroying battalions faster than they can be reconstituted and faster than they were planned to be organized under the buildup program. The [South Vietnamese] commanders do not believe they can survive without the active commitment of U.S. ground combat forces."[137]

Over the course of the next month and a half the United States took the most important steps toward embarking in a major ground war in Vietnam. On June 24 Westmoreland informed Admiral Sharp and the JCS that the 44 battalions would be able only to prevent the collapse of South Vietnam; he added that it was not clear that their presence would alter the behavior of North Vietnam with respect to its war aims. About a week later on July 2 the Joint Chiefs endorsed the idea of deploying "such additional forces at this time as are required to insure that the VC/DRV cannot win in SVN at their present level of commitment."[138] The Chiefs also advocated a much more severe bombing campaign against the North. Meanwhile, events did not stand still; American forces were gradually accumulating in South Vietnam: by July 12 the United States had 15 maneuver battalions in South Vietnam. And more were on the way.

From July 16 to 20 Secretary McNamara, accompanied by JCS Chairman Wheeler, visited General Westmoreland in Saigon. Upon returning to the United States McNamara urged that Washington greatly increase its activities on behalf of South Vietnam in accordance with a plan approved by the JCS.[139] In his recent book, *Four Stars*, Mark Perry argues that this concept for the war was produced by the Army Chief of Staff Harold K. Johnson. Perry writes that by April 1965 General Johnson "was not only the Army's leading tactician but one of its best known skeptics, an officer who believed that deploying troops should be the nation's last resort in a conflict and undertaken only if civilian leaders are willing to make 'an irrevocable commitment.' "[140] In the spring General Johnson convinced his JCS colleagues that the war could not be won without a full military mobilization, and in May 1965 that idea was formally endorsed by the JCS.[141] However he came to the conclusion, in his meeting with the President and others on July 21, 1965, McNamara recommended that the Reserves be called up to create a contingent force of 600,000 men ready for use by mid-1966.[142] With all the military might he hoped would be used, McNamara still observed at the end of the memo that it "is not obvious how we will be able to disengage our forces in Vietnam."[143]

After another round of meetings on July 22, President Johnson went to Camp David to think about these issues for the weekend. While there Johnson received information about the anticipated financial costs of the war under different scenarios. He also spoke with three of his most trusted political confidants: Clark Clifford, Supreme Court Justice Arthur Goldberg, and Robert McNamara. Both Clifford and Goldberg opposed mobilization of the nation for war.[144] By the time of the final meetings on July 27, 1965, Johnson had backed away from mobilizing the nation—if he had ever intended to do so in the first place.

The decision to fight the war without mobilization stunned much of the leadership of the military; this was not the kind of war they had anticipated or desired to fight.[145] According to David Halberstam the most important moment in the critical NSC meeting that afternoon came when Johnson polled those in attendance whether they concurred with his decision. It was critical that the Chairman of the Joint Chiefs sign on, and Halberstam writes, "Everyone in the room knew Wheeler objected, that the Chiefs wanted more, that they wanted a wartime footing and a call-up of the reserves; the thing they feared most was a partial war and a partial commitment. But Wheeler was boxed in; he had the choice of opposing and displeasing his Commander in Chief and being overruled, anyway, or going along. He went along."[146]

On July 27 President Johnson met with the NSC and then later with some of the high ranking Congressional leadership of both parties. In effect, he told these groups there were two plausible choices before him.[147] The first choice was "to go to Congress and ask for all the money and men we might need, calling up the reserves and asking for billions and billions in appropriations and even declaring a state of emergency." The second choice "would be to give the commanders the men and materials they say they need from existing forces to use money authority—to try not to bluff or brag or thunder"—while diplomatic options were tried. Johnson argued that full mobilization would be like throwing the gauntlet down in front of the Russians and Chinese, but of great importance as well for backing the more limited option was Johnson's fear of the Congressional and domestic opposition that might damage his Great Society programs.[148] Lyndon Johnson had decided to make a gradual, nontraumatic entry into the war, and this plan did not include a mobilization of the nation and the calling up of the Reserves. The President displayed a moderate tone in his news conference on July 28, 1965, when he told the nation, "I have asked the commanding general, General Westmoreland, what more he needs to meet this mounting aggression. He has told me. We will meet his needs."[149] Later the President stated: "I have concluded that it is not essential to order the Reserve units into service now. If that necessity should later be indicated, I will give the country due and adequate notice before taking such action, but only after full preparations."

And, when asked if sending these 100,000 men indicated "any change in the existing policy of relying on the South Vietnamese to carry out offensive operations," Johnson replied, "It does not imply any change in policy whatever. It does not imply any change of objective." President Johnson's honest fears of provoking the Soviets and the Chinese should be given due consideration; with that being said, the President's announcement to the nation on July 28 was certainly not a rousing call for all patriots to come to arms.

Thoughts on the Never Again School in Vietnam

One might argue that the mere fact the United States was engaged in a limited war in Southeast Asia indicates that Never Again concepts had been abandoned by the responsible officials. Such an inference is incorrect because a Jominian perspective on the use of force was still potent in the mid-1960s. The Joint Chiefs, excluding General Taylor, and John McCone clearly supported a military effort that would attempt to be decisive.[150] As we have seen in the previous cases, the institutional strength of this position has been formidable when held by members of the military—this was evident during the Dienbienphu and Laos crises. Their influence on questions of military intervention is especially potent when directed at civilian presidents: Eisenhower, who did not want to intervene in 1954, could probably have rolled over the Chiefs; a nonmilitary president has less latitude. Why were opponents of a gradual, limited involvement unable to block that course of action in 1965? A number of factors contributed to the weakness of the Never Again position in 1964–65.

First, the "nothing" component of the "All-or-Nothing" formula dropped out of the equation. Among those policy advisers in the Johnson administration who were truly credible none advocated walking away from South Vietnam. For the JCS and advisers like John McCone this left a course that recommended a total commitment to the outcome of defeating North Vietnam. Logically though, if Vietnam were worth a total commitment then it was certainly worth a limited involvement. And limited involvements were the kinds of wars the United States had been preparing for under the operational framework of "flexible response."

Second, the military seemed to believe that it would eventually get the support it needed to fight the war in accordance with military precepts. President Johnson's decision to support General Westmoreland's request on July 28, 1965, disappointed the military because it did not announce a call-up of the reserves or a mobilization of the nation for war. In fact, Johnson didn't really close the door on the military until after the Tet Offensive when he rejected Westmoreland's February 27, 1968, request for an additional 206,000 men. Until that time no upper limits had been spelled out. Speaking of the President's need to prevent an open break with Chiefs over the way the war was being conducted Herbert Schandler observes:

> President Johnson was aware of the possible political effects of such a military defection, and he temporized in order not to push his loyal military leaders to such a point. Although he never approved the strategy that the Joint Chiefs continued to recommend, he never completely ruled it out either. He allowed the military chiefs a gradual increase in their combat forces and held out the possibility of greater combat authority in the future. He was successful in pointing out the political limitations that prevented his meeting all of their requests, while never finally rejecting those requests.[151]

Perry argues that the Chiefs almost resigned *en masse* during the Stennis hearings in the summer of 1967 after McNamara testified before the Senate Armed Services Committee that the Johnson war policy was achieving its objectives in Indochina.[152] At that point the scales fell from the eyes of the JCS, and the best efforts of General Wheeler were required to persuade the other Chiefs that such a resignation would be mutinous. Whatever the timing, there appears to have been great dissatisfaction on the part of the Joint Chiefs of Staff with the way the war was being fought in 1967–1968. Former general Bruce Palmer, Jr., attributes the military's reticence to confront Johnson to a number of factors:

> As I understand it the Chiefs were very close to resigning en masse in the fall of '67 when they were turned down again on the question of mobilizing and really getting into the war. General Wheeler talked them out of it. I've changed my mind over the years, but at the time, I argued and the rationale was something like this: First, it would be taken as disloyal to the President—even as a mutiny. Second, there was this strong "can do" syndrome. The military guy is trained to carry out his mission. And third, there was a feeling that "all the president has got to do is accept our resignations and put someone else in there who will do what he wants."[153]

Third, the views of military advisers, the Joint Chiefs of Staff, were undercut within the Johnson administration because they were *not* deemed to possess unique qualifications for determining how the war should be fought. Part of this grew from the intellectual arrogance of McNamara and the civilian "whiz kids." But, more important, was the fact that the most respected military person in the administration, Maxwell Taylor, disagreed with the Joint Chiefs on a number of occasions. Taylor had self-servingly undercut the Chiefs for a number of years. He did so after the failed April 1961 Bay of Pigs invasion when he accepted the role of special military adviser to the President.[154] Taylor then served as, what might be called, a "super-chairman" of the Joint Chiefs whose military influence was considerable even after his posting to Vietnam as the American ambassador to Saigon. In effect, his voice greatly negated the authority of the Joint Chiefs. Later, as the situation on the ground became more important in the spring of 1965, General Westmoreland's willingness to go into Vietnam piecemeal also undercut the ability of the Chiefs to take a determined stand against entering into a nondecisive war in Asia. In fact, even Taylor's opinions became less valuable as Westmoreland's assessment of the situation in South Vietnam was accepted by the administration.

The System Worked?

If, as Leslie Gelb and Richard Betts contend in *The Irony of Vietnam*, the system worked, what then was the strategy that the Johnson Administration had in mind when it embarked on fighting a war in Indochina? However much one might wish to compare policies across administrations, the Truman administration's giving monetary assistance or Eisenhower's decision to increase the American advisory presence is not equivalent to the Westmoreland/Johnson 44 battalion decision of the summer of 1965 or the decision to begin Rolling Thunder. Eisenhower never wanted to send troops to Indochina, as Melanie Billings-Yun has demonstrated. He approved financial and military assistance, but this was still a low level of intervention. Are we to accept the proposition that President Johnson's performance as the Hamlet of limited war was identical to the manner in which Eisenhower would have conducted a war against Hanoi? No. In fact, we know enough about Eisenhower's approach to war-fighting to know that had he gone in he probably would have done so with a military effort that would have been decisive. "Strategy" is a difficult term to define, but one recent definition stands out. David Fraser writes:

the art of strategy is to determine the aim, which is or should be political: to derive from that aim a series of military objectives to be achieved:
to assess these objectives as to the military requirements they create, and
the preconditions which the achievement of each is likely to necessitate:
to measure available and potential resources against the requirements:
and to chart from this process a coherent pattern of priorities and a rational course of action."[155]

Given such a demanding, but plausible, criteria it is hardly likely that
anyone could give the decision-making process in Vietnam a passing
grade. No unified concept of action existed: for example, there was
never agreement on how bombing was supposed to assist in ending the
war. Consequently, there were numerous plans for the use of airpower,
but none of the participants supported their positions with any hard
data or hard reasoning that would suggest DRV capitulation if their
plan was followed. At least with the Joint Chiefs' conception of Rolling
Thunder one can understand how crushing destructive power could
bring an enemy to its knees—although in light of the bombing surveys
of World War II even this was by no means certain. But the bombing
scheme of "Phase II" as envisaged by Maxwell Taylor seems complete
fantasy in retrospect. How were limited demonstrations of bombing
supposed to stop a near victorious conqueror from finishing off the
enemy? This query is especially relevant given the historic bellicosity
and stamina of the Vietnamese in the face of foreign opposition.

Alexander George has identified two forms of coercive diplomacy.[156]
The first type he calls the "try-and-see approach" which is the "weak
variant" of coercive diplomacy; he writes: "When employing a try-and-
see approach, the coercing power may make a more or less specific
demand on the opponent to stop his encroachment or to pull back altogether; but it does not create a sense of urgency for his compliance with
the demand."[157] The strong variant is called the "tacit-ultimatum"
which places a specific demand on the opponent, warns of a time limit,
and delivers a credible threat of punishment. Johnson applied an
extremely weak variant of coercive diplomacy: no urgency was imparted to North Vietnam, a specific demand was not given, nor was the
conduct of the bombing in the spring of 1965 performed in a manner
that would instill fear of major escalation in the breast of the opponent.[158] Once ground troops were committed to the war, there was still
no sustained and coordinated military-diplomatic effort that could

have achieved the result of forcing North Vietnam to cease its support of the Viet Cong in the South. It is charitable to say that the United States used a proper strategy. The best that can be said is that the Johnson Administration stumbled into an attempt to use a weak version of the "try-and-see approach."

The adequacy of strategic thought in the Johnson Administration is captured well in a memo to the Secretary of State from James L. Greenfield who helped to oversee press relations at the State Department. He wrote this memo on February 16, 1965, when the Administration was making its transition from "tit-for-tat" reprisals to a campaign of coercive diplomacy. Greenfield told Rusk that he needed to answer press inquiries but that he did not have any guidance from his superiors. Some of the questions he listed were as follows: "What is our objective in bombing the North? Why do we think the Viet Cong will give up if we bomb the North? Under what circumstances will we continue to bomb the North?"[159] As it happened no one in the Administration had satisfactory answers to these questions: the connections between achieving real physical, military objectives and attaining American political goals were not delineated as they should have been. The unsupported notion that mere demonstrations of American military power would bring a rational enemy to terms seems to have been pervasive in the administration. Another area of critical disagreement concerned the way ground forces should be used in the South. Were they to concentrate on pacification, on "search and destroy," on blocking the trails from Laos and North Vietnam, or on defending coastal enclaves?

When a firm decision rule was reached, new circumstances would prompt the rule to be broken. The most important instance of this was President Johnson's decision at the December 1, 1964, meeting to require political stability in the South before any "Phase II" bombing would be allowed. This valid and important precondition for greater American involvement was broken in a little over two months. The fact is that the informal and personal decision-making style of President Johnson does not appear to have been well suited for making a thorough assessment of policy assumptions and expectations. Burke and Greenstein write, "The decision-making process of the Johnson presidency cried out for routinized, rigorous procedures for coming to grips with the complex problems of policy toward Vietnam."[160] For example, the Tuesday luncheons in which war strategy for the *week* was laid out did not include the Chairman of the Joint Chiefs until 1967: this is no way to devise strategy or operational plans in war.

In short, Gelb and Betts's book, *The Irony of Vietnam*, was a much-needed antidote to the various arguments that found the Vietnam involvement implausible on its own politico-military terms. However, the fact that a decision-making system exposes a President and his advisers to unfavorable forecasts and analyses of a situation does not suffice in satisfying Fraser's test stated above. There has to be a real sense of getting from A to Z in a concatenation of actions that are strategically interconnected both militarily and politically. The system need not always "win" in order for it to have *worked*, but defeat certainly makes claims of systemic sufficiency much harder to accept. Even victory does not assure that the verdict of history will pass positive judgment on the strategic choices of leaders. Because the conceptions of causal relationships between military actions and political goals were so nebulous in Vietnam it is unreasonable to argue that defeat in this case represented anything but strategic and operational confusion of the worst sort at the highest levels of the American government.

Morale and Limited War in Vietnam

The drastic decline of U.S. morale in Vietnam during the period of American withdrawal has been widely noted. What is less well known is that the Army noticed as early as 1964 that the indecision as to goals at the highest levels of the Administration translated quite directly into confusion for the foot soldier. In a study for the Army conducted by the Division of Psychiatry, Walter Reed Army Institute of Research, a number of problems were noticed. First, there was "a lack of common objectives between the government of the United States and the government of Viet Nam."[161] There was little sense of a "broadly conceived, common objective for the Viet Nam—United States effort." When asked what the U.S. objectives were, some answered, "I wish I knew." The report then states:

> For the most part, the answer has been given as a series of clichés or political metaphors. Most unfortunately, the same situation prevails in several different offices in Washington. . . . It is not possible to develop teamwork without both intermediate and long range objectives. It is not surprising that the research team found a prominent lack of effective

teamwork since, as such, long range and intermediate goals have not, as yet, been specified either by the government of the United States or the government of Viet Nam.[162]

Continuing along this line, the study points out, "Major US agencies have had difficulty developing valid operational doctrine. Since neither the intermediate nor long range objectives have been specified, it has not been possible to develop valid operational doctrine. As a consequence, US advisers often work in a vacuum without benefit of appropriate job definition. Very few, if any, advisers have any concrete notion about parameters of their job or just what the expectations should be."[163] After observing that the "American advisers are required to function without adequately defined goals," the Rioch report observes that "one gets a general impression that the military advisers suffer from a vague loneliness and uncertainty in the areas of their competence and defend against this loneliness and uncertainty by socializing with each other."[164]

This small study illustrates the point that morale problems associated with a lack of clear objectives were present, and had been detected by the U.S. Army in 1964, prior to America's placing ground combat troops into the South. It is plausible to conclude that the greater level of stress that accompanies ground combat would have made these feelings of frustration and purposeless more acute. As noted above in the chapter on the Korean War, war-fighting directed at military objectives whose fulfillment bring little sense of purpose or general accomplishment in the war may lead to demoralization. This is not intended to be a blanket criticism of limited wars as such: if one's political objectives require restraint on the use of force, so be it. However, the evidence presented here and about the Korean War suggest that the maintenance of effective morale requires that soldiers be given clearly defined objectives which, if accomplished, provide a sense of purpose for the operation in which they are engaged. Once again, we find support, in unexpected quarters, for the old-fashioned "principles of war" which were shunned at the strategic level by the Johnson Administration in favor of fighting a war of attrition with no clear military objectives.

The fact that the modern "principles of war" provide important directives for conducting combat operations becomes more clear in Admiral Ulysses S. Sharp's Vietnam War memoir, *Strategy for Defeat.* In one passage, Sharp reproduces a briefing Commander James B. Stockdale delivered to his pilots aboard the USS *Oriskany.*[165] In a talk to his command, Stockdale describes his view of war and personal behavior in combat that is the heart of the military dimension, if you will, of warfighting. Stockdale began by telling his pilots of a previous group that had flown under his direction on the USS *Ticonderoga.* These aviators were perplexed by the requirements of limited war. Stockdale summarized their concerns:

> Like most of you, they were well read, sensitive, sometimes skeptical—those educated in the American liberal tradition to think for themselves—those who are often our most productive citizens—and just as often our best soldiers. They realized that bombing heavily defended targets is serious business and no game—that it is logically impossible, in the violence of a fight, to commit oneself, as an individual, only in some proportion of his total drive and combative instinct. It has to be all or nothing; dog eat dog over the target. I think they were asking themselves, as you might—where do I as a person, a person of awareness, refinement and education, fit into this "limited war," "measured response" concept?[166]

Continuing, Stockdale perceptively noted the tension that exists between the needs of policy and the requirements for effectively engaging an enemy in combat:

> I want to level with you right now, so you can think it over here in mid-Pacific and not kid yourself into imagining "stark realizations" in the Gulf of Tonkin. Once you go "feet dry" over the beach, there can be nothing limited about your commitment. "Limited war" means to us that our target list has limits, our ordnance loadout has limits, our rules of engagement have limits, but that does *not* mean that there is anything "limited" about our personal obligations as fighting men to carry out assigned missions with all we've got. If you think it is possible for a man, in the heart of battle, to apply something less than total *personal* commitment—equated perhaps to your idea of the proportion of *national* potential being applied, you are wrong. It's contrary to human nature. So also is the idea I was alarmed to find suggested to me by a military friend in a letter recently: that the prisoner of war's Code of Conduct is some sort of "total war" document. You can't go half way on that, either. The Code of Conduct was not written for "total wars" or "limited wars," it was written for all wars, and let it be understood that it applies with the full force to this Air Wing—in *this* war.[167]

These words convey a most essential aspect of the All-or-Nothing perspective: that organized fighting or war, as a thing in itself, has a logic of its own that is consistent with certain aspects of human nature. The soldier is a strategic thinker who wishes to use combinations of offense and defense in a purposeful manner, either individually or as part of an organization, to mass his forces so as to achieve decisive victory against any opponent with surprise, maneuver, and the final crushing blow. A strategy of attrition in a limited war with precise, restrictive rules of engagement eliminates the heart and soul of this military logic.

8 | The "Lessons" of Vietnam for the Use of Force

$\bigvee$ ietnam and the "lessons" derived from it intensified the disagreements as to whether limitations on the use of force were appropriate.[1] This chapter will first look at four significant scholarly works that have taken up the issue: Andrew Krepinevich's *The Army Concept and Vietnam*, Robert Osgood's *Limited War Revisited*, Harry G. Summers, Jr.'s *On Strategy*, and Samuel P. Huntington's article, "Playing to Win." The last three express dissatisfaction with using force as a mere element of diplomatic bargaining. After this review, the development of the current U.S. Army operational doctrine, "AirLand Battle," will be traced from Vietnam until the release of the 1986 Army field manual on operations (FM 100–5).[2] It was this operational method for ground combat that proved so devastating in the Persian Gulf War against Saddam Hussein's forces. The doctrine represented a return to the traditional military recognition of the need for aggressive action.[3]

Most significantly, AirLand Battle focussed on the "operational" level of war, thereby connecting war's tactical and strategic aspects. It was the failure to link them that created the professional military's disenchantment with the army's approach to fighting North Vietnam. AirLand Battle requires that commanders connect the tactical clash of forces in battles as part of campaigns leading to the destruction of enemy resistance. Although not apparent at first, AirLand Battle attempts to forge an unbreakable conceptual chain between combat at the lowest level and strategic plans to end the war.

Put another way, the questions that have arisen during the Bosnian crisis of 1992–93 have been: "What is the endgame? How do we know when it's over?" Those who devised it seek to *indoctrinate* their soldiers with an analytical structure that requires the linkage of the tactical, the operational, and the strategic levels of war. Essentially, AirLand Battle will direct those trained within its conceptual framework to question the feasibility of military action that does not provide a significant possibility of using military engagements within campaigns to decisively impose one's will upon an enemy.

A Need to Fight Small Wars

The most important contribution to the post-Vietnam limited war position is Major Andrew F. Krepinevich, Jr.'s *The Army and Vietnam*.[4] Because of its thorough scholarship, Krepinevich's book is undoubtedly one of the more important books to discuss the Vietnam War. His argument is straightforward: Krepinevich believes that the way the U.S. Army prosecuted the war caused the American defeat. The army, he believes, used highly destructive conventional tactics and operations that were inappropriate to the situation. Krepinevich worries that this method of war-fighting still pervades the army's thinking about fighting small wars against insurgencies. At the heart of the army's approach to the use of force is what Krepinevich calls the "Army Concept" which "is the product of an organizational character that has evolved over time and that, because of [the army's] high regard for tradition, has become deeply imbedded in the service's psyche, or memory."[5] He continues his definition with this description:

> The Army Concept of war is, basically, the Army's perception of how wars *ought* to be waged and is reflected in the way the Army organizes and trains its troops for battle. The characteristics of the Army Concept are two: a focus on mid-intensity, or conventional, war and a reliance on high volumes of firepower to minimize casualties—in effect, the substitution of material costs at every available opportunity to avoid payment in blood.[6]

Krepinevich believes that the institutional focus on conventional wars

like the Civil War, World War I, World War II, and Korea in which
ground forces had to observe few restrictions, laid the cognitive groundwork for the "Army Concept."[7] The United States had never lost a large
conventional war before Vietnam, and for that reason, the strategic
influence of earlier but more political conflicts like the Revolutionary
War, the Indian Wars, and the Philippine insurrection at the turn of the
twentieth century has been minimal.[8] Consequently, the organizational and operational doctrines of the army, despite the best efforts of President Kennedy, were not altered to match the new strategic environment prior to Vietnam and, more surprisingly, have still not been corrected since the defeat that ended that war.[9]

One could argue that Krepinevich is writing merely about tactics
and is not addressing the tension between the Limited War and Never
Again perspectives. Although he does not explicitly plant the flag of
limited war he implies it. The "mid-intensity" approach to conflict that
the army supports, according to him, embodies those Jominian concepts of war that require decisive victory. That style of war-fighting
advocates escalation to a higher level of violence if victory cannot be
achieved with less power. Krepinevich writes: "In sum, it appears the
military wants a blank check to fail, and not lose popular support, or to
escalate the conflict if it becomes frustrated with the nuances of counterinsurgency warfare as in Vietnam."[10]

Clearly, Krepinevich does not look on this attitude with favor. He
wants the armed forces of the United States to be capable of understanding the "nuances" of counterinsurgency. At the same time Krepinevich believes that regular combat units must be able to deal effectively with insurgent enemies without escalation: "Unfortunately, as the
army ought to have learned in Vietnam, America's enemies are not
going to play to its military strong suits; rather, they will exploit its weak
points."[11]

Although the author does not call for a limited war capacity, he is
arguing that the United States must be able to restrain the means it
commits to waging war and fight essentially political struggles in the
future. For that reason, it is fair to characterize Krepinevich's work as
being part of a post-Vietnam Limited War School.[12]

Considerable controversy remains about the nature of the war
itself. That is, was it primarily an insurgency or a conventional conflict? Note that while guerrilla activity was widespread and deadly

after the Tet offensive, the Easter Offensive of 1972 and the final offensive drive of 1975 both had massive, conventional, noninsurgent components. One of Krepinevich's All-or-Nothing adversaries in the debate, former General Bruce Palmer, Jr., criticizes Krepinevich for seeming

> to believe that pacification, sometimes called "the other war," was separable from the so-called "big war," the battle of main forces, whereas, of course, they were always both integral parts of the same war. Moreover, he appears to overlook the fact that Hanoi, regardless of what the United States did, always had the option to escalate to a higher level of conflict (or de-escalate to a lower level). Hanoi was determined to subjugate the South no matter how long it took or what it cost.[13]

While Krepinevich may go a little far in one direction, Palmer and his allies certainly place insufficient emphasis on the insurgency. Future histories of Vietnam will probably move in the direction of a brief, article-length piece by James Ward that balanced its conventional and unconventional elements.[14] Ward argued in a special issue of *Military Review* dedicated to the Vietnam War that these two aspects of the war cannot be neatly separated: the individual effects and interaction of both parts of the war must be studied. This point has been taken even further in a brilliant essay by Rod Paschall who convincingly makes the case that the success of North Vietnam's 1975 offensive was due in large part to the flanking and rear area protection afforded the DRV forces by the insurgents that were located in the I and II Corps. Paschall's analysis directly contradicts writers like Harry G. Summers, Jr., who assert that insurgents in the South were of little military value after the Tet Offensive (1968).[15]

Krepinevich's focus is on the army, but more attention could profitably have been given to discussing the tactics of the Marine Corps in I Corps (the military zone furthest north and closest to the DMZ in South Vietnam). Krepinevich presents a brief account of how General Lewis W. Walt (USMC) introduced the counterinsurgency program that relied on CAPs, or Combined Action Platoons. One CAP came to consist of fifteen Marines and 34 "popular forces" that lived in a particular village or hamlet. The marines did not swoop down out of helicopters and assault the enemy. Rather, they lived with the villagers, used their roads, and "were engaged in continuous night patrols in the areas surrounding the village, stalking the VC, setting ambushes, disrupting the insurgents' plans and activities. The result was the VC's abandonment of the village." The CAPs also focused their attention on high population areas instead of activity in the highlands.[16] As a result, they were much more effective in defending the villagers from the Viet Cong and achieved these results "at a casualty rate lower than that found in units operating search-and-destroy missions."[17] Krepinevich consigns the history of the CAPs to about five pages whereas this counterinsurgent approach warrants a closer inspection that would support his argument. At the very least Walt's use of CAPs indicates that Americans approach war-fighting in ways that are not inevitably bound to an exclusively Jominian use of force.[18]

The Rebirth of Never Again—Post-Vietnam Style

More common than books like Krepinevich's, which take fighting insurgencies seriously, are those arguing that the United States should avoid conflicts that might require political limitations on the use of force. In the post-Vietnam period two reasons have usually been given for requiring the decisive use of military force: first, public support can be maintained only if progress is being made on the battlefield; second, the very nature of military force requires adherence to the Jominian principles of war if force is to be an effective tool of policy.[19] So it has been, that, in the wake of defeat in Indochina, intellectual support for fighting politically focused limited wars has eroded to minimal levels. Yet, not all re-examinations of the limited war position reject it completely. Robert Osgood, the author of one of the most important books arguing for a limited war capacity in the 1950s, sketches a position in *Limited War Revisited* that reflects hard-earned learning about waging war, but he still recognizes the possibility that limitations on the use of force may be necessary.[20]

In effect, Osgood believes that winning the Vietnam War was beyond American capabilities: even the most massive attacks on the North could not have diverted that state from its ultimate goal of conquering the South. He also argues that South Vietnam was so vulnerable to insurgency that any U.S. effort against this enemy would have been defeated (p. 37). Later on Osgood argues that the United States must continue to support its general grand strategy of containment of

Soviet power (pp. 100–102), but this leaves the United States with the problem of deciding when to use, or threaten the use of force. He writes that during the Cold War America's perceived national security needs "became more sweeping and generalized than United States' vital interests warranted" (p. 105) during the Cold War, and also believes that "the doctrine of limited war not only exaggerated the efficacy and underestimated the costs of armed force, but also exaggerated the U.S. security interest and the nature of the threat to them."

Although earlier in the book Osgood discusses how the United States should act if it decides to intervene, he provides no sweeping formula for success. Given the range of circumstances in which the United States may find itself, Osgood observes, "one can prudently generalize only to the extent of saying that henceforth U.S. interests . . . must not be assessed only in terms of a general commitment to stopping the expansion of communism or defeating Communist aggression" (p. 49). American economic interests must be considered along with the "prospect of a local Communist victory" and the effect such a victory might have on the larger balance of power. The experience of Vietnam "puts a greater justification on the advocates of intervention, but it does not exclude all large-scale intervention and certainly not a variety of smaller, more controllable interventions" (p. 49). Osgood remarks that rapid escalation to win the war will probably risk wider conflict, and graduated escalation is likely to involve the United States in a long, messy war. No easy answer to all cases is possible, but at least "these lessons serve as antidotes, if we need any, to the grand simplifications and ingenious stratagems of the Kennedy era" (p. 51).

Arguably, the most influential work in the post-Vietnam literature is Harry G. Summers, Jr.'s *On Strategy*, which first appeared in 1981.[21] This book embraces those opinions expressed inside and outside the military that blamed the U.S. defeat on the political limitations on force that were imposed by America's civilian leadership.[22] *On Strategy* is a multifaceted book, and its most forcefully argued points discuss the necessity for public opinion to be mobilized in support of American wars: declarations of war, he believes, are a necessity; the mobilization of reserve forces is also important in this respect. Simply stated, Summers' analysis contradicts Krepinevich's thesis. Summers believes that the flaw in American strategy was its excessive emphasis on fighting the *insurgents* when the fundamental problem of the war was defeating the

North Vietnamese invasion of the South. This American emphasis on counterinsurgency, Summers believes, caused the United States to err strategically by focusing its efforts on fighting a war against irregular forces that would have been better left to the South Vietnamese. *On Strategy* argues that the army in conjunction with South Vietnamese and Korean regular forces should have formed a *cordon* near the DMZ across South Vietnam and the Laotian panhandle all the way to Thailand. According to Krepinevich this was the heart of the El Paso plan which was drawn up by the MACV staff for Westmoreland in 1966.[23]

The book claims that the United States entered the war without a plan as to "how" it would achieve its military results. It assumed the default strategy of attrition and never isolated the battlefield in the South from the northern enemy. Consequently, the South Vietnamese developed no military capabilities of their own, and they were easily defeated when the North launched its final offensive in March 1975. Summers correctly argues that the North Vietnamese involvement was a critical strategic problem on the ground after 1964, but his contention that the "search and destroy" strategy represented an undue concern for pacification of the insurgency is bizarre. Krepinevich convincingly demonstrates that the army fought the European, mid-intensity war for which it was prepared—but in Southeast Asia. Few concessions to counterinsurgency methods were ever made before 1969. "Search and destroy" was the residual strategy that remained after the army was denied the resources and the political support to go into Laos and Cambodia to cut the Ho Chi Minh trails and deny its enemy sanctuaries. Being forced to deploy an insufficient number of troops throughout South Vietnam with no operational strategy, the army did the best thing it could do—it sought out the enemy in an attempt to attrit the VC and North Vietnamese. The army justly criticized Maxwell Taylor's enclave strategy because it would have concentrated U.S. forces in coastal bases with essentially defensive missions. The army was particularly wary of breaking its units into smaller components only to have them attacked by massed VC or North Vietnamese forces. Krepinevich argues that a pacification strategy in which the Americans controlled the populous coastal areas would have been successful, but such a plan, Summers believes, ignores the problem conventional, large-unit forces would have posed had they been free to mass in the highlands with little threat from American forces. It was such a concentration that prompted the Battle of the Ia Drang in November 1965.

Summers analysis contains a more interesting dimension which revolves around his reasons for advocating an All-or-Nothing approach to fighting limited wars. He presents two considerations for opposing Vietnam-type limited, military interventions. First, Summers discusses the consequences of the decision by the Johnson administration to not mobilize the nation to fight the war. The failure to do so denied the army the option of calling up its reserve forces, and the resultant manpower shortages negatively affected the way the United States was able to prosecute the war. Summers believes that the lack of sufficient manpower "led to [the] failure of the military leadership to push for strategic concepts aimed at halting North Vietnamese aggression and led to campaigns against the symptoms of aggression—the insurgency in the South—rather than against the aggressor itself."[24] On Strategy devotes much attention to the need for declarations of war and the mobilization of the American public when it is deemed necessary to enter a war.

The second reason Summers gives for not favoring the concept of limited war, as practiced in Vietnam, is its violation of time-honored tenets of sound military operation. Summers asserts that the U.S. Army altered the approach by which it intended to fight after the Korean War. He argues that "in the Korean war 'limited war' was defined in terms of limited objectives."[25] The point is that in Korea the United States did *not* limit the *means* it used, but did limit its objectives.[26] Historically, this is a dubious assertion. Were not the refusals to bomb Manchuria or use atomic weapons limitations on the means used to fight the war? Also, the political decisions in the summer of 1951 to accept the adversary's call for cease-fire negotiations and to halt the pursuit of the badly mauled communist forces suggests more limitations of means by the United States.

According to Summers, the negative doctrinal change came in the 1962 U.S. Army field manual, FM 100–5, which dropped the "concept of 'wars of limited objective' which we had adopted after the Korean war and introduced the concept of limited means."[27] How far did the 1962 manual take this idea of limiting the means used in war? I would argue that it advocated the concept but only on a superficial level. The field manual still contains a lengthy section that lists the principles of war, and it describes these principles as "fundamental truths governing the prosecution of war." In its definition of the principle of the "Objective," the manual states:

> Every military operation must be directed toward a clearly defined, decisive, and attainable objective. The ultimate military objective is the destruction of the enemy's armed forces and his will to fight.[28]

This does not sound like the doctrine of an army that has gone soft with respect to overwhelming its opponent with the application of decisive military power. Or consider this statement:

> Military objectives selected must be compatible with the limitations which national policies impose upon the area of conflict, weapons, participants, or other factors. The principle of primacy of national objectives is not in conflict with the sound military concepts expressed in the Principles of War.[29]

Once again we see the army trying to square this politico-military circle by claiming that decisive military actions are never inconsistent with political objectives. The incompatibility is indeed not necessary, but it is a distinct possibility.

In fact, the army's fundamental concept of war-fighting did not change much in the 1950s and 1960s even though a great deal of attention was given to irregular forms of warfare. As discussed in an earlier chapter, the army used the same term that civilian strategists used in this period, "limited war," but defined it differently. To the army "limited war" referred to a non-nuclear conventional conflict of tremendous destructiveness in which it would use force decisively to achieve its military objectives—Krepinevich's "mid-intensity" war. For the civilian writers, the term represented a flexible style of war-fighting in which objectives and means could be limited as one tacitly bargained with the enemy.

Interestingly, Summers does not condemn all limited wars. He regards Korea as having been a victory because the United States achieved its objective of maintaining the Republic of Korea's independence. Korea was the war that taught the United States that a policy of total war was not always realistic. Summers does not question the fact that *objectives* must often be limited, but he criticizes the fact that the 1954 field manual removed "victory" as a relevant concept in war-fighting.[30] He feels that the armed forces should be able to do whatever is necessary to achieve even limited objectives. Consequently, the reader may be justified in questioning the support for limited war offered in *On Strategy*, for it seems obvious that the limitation of objectives will often require the limitation of means—as was the case in Korea.

Summers' approach to war-fighting is essentially Jominian and not Clausewitzian.[31] There is considerable irony in this given the excellent use Summers makes of Clausewitz throughout the book. Later chapters in his book bear the names of various principles of war: objective, offensive, mass, economy of force, maneuver, unity of command, security and surprise. Each of these chapters seeks to describe how the failure to adhere to these principles contributed to failure in Vietnam.[32] *On Strategy* is Jominian in the sense that it accepts the idea that there are immutable and definite tenets for the sound conduct of war—dictated by the very nature of force itself. Clausewitz did not take such a position.[33] To violate these principles is to use one's military instrument inefficiently. The principles of the objective, mass, and the offensive focus on using military power in a crushing, decisive manner that retains the initiative in war.[34] It is fitting, therefore, that Summers regards the limitation of means in post-1962 army doctrine (if in fact that did occur) as a catastrophic error. Consequently, his recommendation for future uses of force is that the military high command must have a clear set of objectives and must be given the requisite resources and freedom from constraints to achieve them. Wars fought on the cheap, as Summers believes Vietnam was, should not be tolerated again by the leadership of the United States's armed forces.

Samuel P. Huntington, one of the nation's most distinguished academic students of the military, has contributed a major piece to the post-Vietnam literature. His article, entitled "Playing to Win," makes a Summers-like argument that the United States should use force only if it can "intervene rapidly, in an offensive mode, in a decisive manner, and so far as possible with overwhelming force, with a view to defeating enemy military forces in the shortest time possible."[35]

The path Huntington takes to this conclusion is not straightforward. He presents a two-pronged argument: the first is grounded in American social and institutional values; the second, which is stated only briefly, appears to advocate this course of action because it is *the only* appropriate manner in which force should be used. The heart of Huntington's first argument follows a long discussion of American military competence. He warns that Americans cannot be expected to fight wars in a way that is not suited to them: "American strategy, in short, must be appropriate to our history and institutions, both political and military. It must not only be responsive to national needs but also reflect our national strengths and weaknesses. It is the beginning of wisdom to recognize both" (p. 13).

Huntington then observes that America is "a big, lumbering, pluralistic, affluent, liberal, democratic, individualistic, materialistic if not hedonistic, and technologically supremely sophisticated society." It should not need to be pointed out that our politico-military strategy should draw on our strengths. He states that the United States has, in its most recent past, made the mistake of drawing away from these strengths:

> For three decades, we have generally pursued, with the best of intentions and the best strategic analysis, a strategy for the use of conventional force that deviates sharply from earlier strategic traditions. It has emphasized not how to use force to win, but, how to avoid or to limit the use of force. In the nuclear age, these latter are clearly critical objectives, but they cannot be the only ones. (p. 14)

The article then proceeds to list five "elements" an American grand strategy must contain in order to be successful. The first element is that the U.S. should act quickly and achieve decisive results rapidly in order to avoid conflicts of attrition; he writes: "public opinion will not support a prolonged 'slow bleed' of American blood" (p. 14). Second, the new American strategy must once again imbue its armed forces with the spirit of the offensive in fighting conventional wars. Huntington's reason for returning to the offensive spirit is grounded in his belief that war must end quickly: "If the United States is going to achieve its objectives in timely fashion, however, in either Europe or in the Third World, it must engage in prompt offensive action against the central enemy targets" (p. 14)[36]

The third element relates to American technological superiority. Huntington argues that the United States is the most technologically advanced nation in the world, and it should use this advantage in its approach to war-fighting. The United States, he adds, should *not* fight guerrillas on their level "by sending out small counter-insurgent teams to best the guerrillas at the type of war they know best" (p. 15). Fourth, the United States is a massive nation in terms of resources and population. We should fight in a manner that recognizes that truth. Our strategy should be to overwhelm our opponents, Huntington argues. He closes this section with the comment: "We can afford four services; we can afford four air forces. When the need exists, we should use all of them" (p. 15).

The fifth element of Huntington's proposed strategy is especially important because he provides no connection to American social, institutional, scientific, demographic or political characteristics as a justification for it. This final aspect of Huntington's approach represents his opinion of the proper way to use force:

> Finally, if American forces have to be used, they should be used to achieve military objectives. Military forces are not primarily instruments of communication to convey signals to an enemy; they are instruments of coercion to compel him to alter his behavior. Nor are they normally good instruments of political and social appeal, to win the hearts and minds of people. Military forces are designed to defeat opposing military forces; they are not very useful in the pursuit of other goals. . . . This may at times lead, as the critics allege, to a total disregard of strategic maneuver and deception and to a commitment to attack head-on where the enemy is strong, but it does rest on the correct understanding that the principal purpose of military forces is to crush other military forces. (pp. 15–16)[37]

This passage reflects a truly Jominian conception of war-fighting that emphasizes the decisive use of force and the rejection of flexibility as to the aims of war.

Later in the same paragraph Huntington even quotes Napoleon on the singular necessity of crushing the main body of the enemy's forces. Huntington admits that these five recommendations "are simply restatements of the traditional principles of war set forth in the manuals of all the services: the objective, offensive, mass, simplicity, economy of forces" (p. 16).[38] This is particularly true of his fifth recommendation in which Huntington sets forth the logic of the force as dictating the manner of its employment. Despite these assurances, one must feel discomfort at the ease with which Huntington separates military objectives and means from the political importance of the objectives being sought.

Post-Vietnam: The Emerging Army Doctrine

The U.S. Army's war-fighting doctrine has undergone pronounced change since Vietnam. This can be seen by examining the various editions of its *Operations* field manual (FM 100–5).[39] The army had to reconsider its force posture and military concepts because its military readiness was alarmingly low. The diminished popularity of the armed services led to budget cuts that undercut the Defense Department's preparations for two and a half wars—its readiness goal in the 1960s. Instead, the United States could prepare only for conflict in Europe with the Soviets and for a half-war contingency elsewhere—most probably in the Middle East. America was also reducing its world-wide commitments. This change from the expansive commitments of the Kennedy era was signalled by President Nixon at Guam on July 25, 1969, in remarks he made to reporters. This new strategic framework, which was later referred to as the "Nixon Doctrine," was stated in response to a journalist's question about the extent of the American commitment to other Asian states in the wake of Vietnam. Mr. Nixon first pledged that the U.S. would adhere to its treaty obligations. He then observed that the United States would expect other nations to assume the primary responsibility for defending themselves against most internal and external security threats.[40] Of course, the United States would not allow friendly states to be bullied by another major power—especially with nuclear weapons—but in most instances the United States would confine its involvement to providing material assistance with no direct intervention. Soon thereafter the Nixon Administration began to reconsider its readiness for a war in Europe.

The U.S. Army was in poor shape. Racial tensions, drug abuse, and problems with the draft had eroded its strength. Paul H. Herbert notes that the "Army's theoretically highest-priority unit, the Seventh Army in Europe, was probably at the lowest state of readiness in its history."[41] Vietnam had damaged the army in another way: tactics and operations developed there against a poor and technology-starved opponent would not necessarily be worthwhile against an enemy like the Warsaw Pact nations, which had an abundance of resources and technological capabilities. For example, as Herbert notes, the heavy use of helicopters to transport troops and supplies took place in an environment in "the relative absence of enemy air defense capability." Herbert goes on to summarize the military situation, "In short, a decade of war in Vietnam had rendered the U.S. Army an unlikely instrument with which to protect America's European interests (p. 6)."

The inadequacy of American preparedness in both doctrine and force structure became more apparent in the wake of the Yom Kippur War (October 6–24, 1973). Egypt and Syria attacked Israel during the religious observance of Yom Kippur, October 6, 1973. The fighting that took place between these mid-sized powers was characterized by tremendous lethality and the massive consumption of war materials. In a period lasting less than three weeks Egypt and Syria lost 2,000 tanks from an initial deployment of 4,500. These two nations also lost 500 of their 1,100 airplanes. Israel saw 800 of its 2,000 tanks destroyed, and 114 of its 550 airplanes met the same fate. The Egyptian and Syrian casualties were terrible: approximately 15,000 dead and wounded. The Israeli Defense Forces suffered 2,812 killed and 7,500 wounded.[42] To put these figures in perspective, Herbert notes that the total tank and artillery losses of both sides in the Yom Kippur War exceeded the inventory of the U.S. Army in Europe, in both categories (p. 30). The destructiveness that characterized the war was due in large measure to the introduction of precision guided munitions (PGMs) that comprised "smart bombs," anti-tank weapons, and surface-to-air missiles. The performance of these weapons prompted the United States Army to begin a weapons development and replacement program that in the 1980s became its largest in history.[43]

Doctrinally the army produced its first post-Vietnam FM 100–5 in July 1976. The Yom Kippur War, Herbert notes, had indicated to the Training and Doctrine Command (TRADOC) of the U.S. Army that "future conventional warfare would be significantly different, if not altogether revolutionary, from previous American war experiences" (pp. 30–31). General William E. DePuy, the head of TRADOC, determined that "a critical issue on future battlefields would be how best to protect U.S. forces from this lethality while maximizing the potential of the new weapons to inflict casualties on the enemy" (p. 31). The United States would have to be prepared to fight these sorts of intense conflicts in the Third World as well. Soviet military assistance and the wealth of some Third World states created an environment in which the United States might face well-equipped non-European forces in a conventional war. DePuy felt that future wars would be characterized by initial periods of the utmost ferocity that would subside either as the stores of costly precision weaponry were consumed or as negotiations commenced to control and end the wars (p. 31). Consequently, the United States would have to defeat its opponent quickly in order to achieve a favorable outcome before hostilities abated. DePuy believed that "U.S forces would have to concentrate on the battlefield against the enemy's main force and defeat it quickly" (p. 31). This would require an immense improvement in intelligence and communications capabilities so that precise estimates of the enemy's whereabouts could be made and passed along to the various general staffs.

So it was that in an environment in which the army was by no means assured of having superiority in numbers or firepower, it developed a doctrine that relied on such superiority. The 1976 manual appeared to back away from the American proclivity for the offensive, relying instead on an enhanced role for the defense without describing it as the decisive form of war: "Without actually going that far, the manual suggested that an active defense could exploit the lethality of modern weaponry to destroy a portion of the enemy's armed forces before the transition to an American offensive should occur."[44] The commander was to concentrate his forces quickly with the intention of exploiting enemy weaknesses. At the same time he would do his utmost to minimize the exposure of his forces to enemy fires. As Weigley observes of this doctrine, often called "active defense," it "envisioned ultimate American and NATO success in Civil War- or World War II-style battles achieving annihilation of the enemy through attrition, despite the unfavorable balance of resources."[45] Because the 1976 manual emphasized the concentration of firepower through movement, it contained the seeds for the operational approach that would follow in 1982 and which would be much more focused on maneuver that could allow concentration against the enemy's center of gravity.

On August 20, 1982, the army issued a new FM 100–5 which enunciated the doctrine called "AirLand Battle." The new manual was produced at TRADOC under the guidance of General Don Starry who had assisted in the writing of the 1976 FM 100–5. After taking command of the V Corps in Europe during March 1976 Starry soon came to realize that there were important deficiencies in Active Defense. It was the recognition of these problems that led to important developments in army thinking as the 1982 manual was being produced. In

1976 Starry was coming to realize that, as Herbert notes, "the doctrine did not address all the problem's a corps commander would face. . . . Although the doctrine was helpful for organizing battalions, brigades, and even divisions for the initial defensive battle, it did not help [him] deal with enemy follow-on echelons, which were of great concern at the corps level" (p. 97). Stated another way, the 1976 manual had paid great attention to the tactical considerations involved with repulsing the first wave of Soviet troops at the initial line of resistance, but it was inattentive to the longer-term battle in which enemy reinforcements would arrive on the battlefield and have to be defeated.

AirLand Battle was a breakthrough in the army's military thought because it formally recognized the need for specific planning at the "operational level" of war.[46] This level exists between the tactical and strategic and corresponds to the planning of military campaigns by corps commanders. The emphasis in AirLand Battle shifted from the destruction of enemy forces *per se* in 1976 to, as Herbert notes, "how the Army must conduct campaigns and battles to win" (p. 98). Additionally, the Clausewitzian notion of the "culminating point" of the offensive was introduced in the 1986 update of the FM 100–5. Clausewitz had observed that offensives, unless they decisively defeat the opponent, will eventually reach a point where they lose their forward momentum. The army recognized that its commanders would have to anticipate these culminating points and plan for a transition to the defensive so that the enemy's counterattack could be parried as the next offensive phase of operations was being conceived.[47] The concern with the Soviet second and third echelon forces also led to calls for "deep strikes" against the enemy rear with artillery, precision guided munitions, and air forces.[48]

All in all, AirLand Battle recognized the trend of modern warfare toward tremendous lethality and the need for combined arms action at lower levels in the military chain of command. At the same time the 1982 and 1986 manuals envisaged a more sophisticated army that, like a great chess master who plans his actions many moves in advance, would set forth an operational plan of maneuver and fires to disrupt and defeat the enemy's forces. While attrition could not be ignored in any plans for a major war, the AirLand Battle concept tried to leave behind the American tradition of relying merely on overwhelming firepower to defeat an opponent.[49] This new operational doctrine is more reliant on knowledge of the enemy (intelligence) and on rapid creation of plans to disrupt and defeat the opponent. The decisive advantages in this sort of war are to be gained by having smarter weapons, better intelligence, faster signals, and a more accurate grasp of the operational art of war than the opponent.

Army doctrine exploded with intellectual creativity after Vietnam. The 1986 FM 100–5 may be the most intellectually challenging manual ever produced by the army and represents a sophistication that is highly unusual in documents that attempt to reach such a wide audience. But what does AirLand Battle tell us about the problem of limited war? In short, the 1982 and 1986 manuals do not even mention the term *limited war*. The terms *limited, limitations,* and *limits* do not appear in their indexes. The 1986 FM 100–5 has a section on "High- and Mid-Intensity Conflict" (pp. 2–4) and a section on "Low-Intensity Conflict" (pp. 4–5). Clearly, AirLand Battle is envisaged as taking place in the "high-" or "mid-" intensity levels: mid-intensity usually meaning a conventional war without nuclear weapons. This leaves "low-intensity conflict" (or LIC) as the only arena in which limits on the use of force in a full-fledged war might be possible. This prospect is soon eliminated by the definition the army gives to LIC:

> This form of warfare falls below the level of high- and mid- intensity operations and will pit Army forces against irregular or unconventional forces, enemy special operations forces, and terrorists. LIC poses a threat to US interests at all times, not just in periods of active hostilities.[50]

"Low-intensity conflict" designates irregular forms of warfare in which special forces might be used. Nowhere in this definition do we see a place for limited wars against regular forces in the style of Korea or Vietnam, nor does one appear later. However, the manual does include the following description of some of the special features of low-intensity warfare:

> Fighting in the low end of the conflict spectrum requires special forces composition and task organization, rapid deployment, and *restraint* in the execution of military operation[s].[51]

This use of "restraint" appears to be the manual's only acknowledgment that the use of force may require limitations.

The problems that the modern army has in defining "low-intensity conflict" prompted Colonel Richard Swain to ponder whether LIC could properly be considered "war."[52] Swain quotes the Field Circular 100–20, *Low Intensity Conflict*, which says that "LIC involves the actual or contemplated use of military capabilities up to, but not including, combat between regular forces."[53] Any form of conflict that does not involve regular forces cannot be equivalent to the lengthy and massive wars the United States fought in Korea and Vietnam. In testimony before the Senate Armed Services Committee in January 1987, General Paul Gorman is quoted as saying, "US combatants would transform the intensity of any conflict. Any time a US infantryman dies in combat anywhere, we will be impelled to wage mid- or higher intensity warfare, to use ordnance in quality and quantity which almost surely will escape sensible definitions of 'low intensity,' "[54]

Steven Metz has observed that in low-intensity conflict the U.S. Army seeks "total, unambiguous victory."[55] The author then describes the numerous difficulties that accompany this All-or-Nothing approach: "A strategy that seeks total, unambiguous victory, however, is politically dangerous. It can breed public frustration with ambiguous outcomes and leave us able to deal only with relatively simple problems such as those in Panama and Grenada. Counterinsurgency is not simple."[56]

The desire for total victory should be abandoned in favor of more realistic objectives against insurgencies: "Put simply, as long as the United States believes total, unambiguous victory in counterinsurgency is possible and encourages our friends to think likewise, insurgencies will be controlled but not extinguished."[57]

Metz urges the army to change its Jominian ways and adopt a more realistic set of goals for these wars: The United States "should state explicitly that, in most insurgencies, we seek a negotiated compromise between the government and the insurgents rather than unambiguous victory by the government. The goal of the United States should be to make *both* belligerents recognize that absolute victory is unattainable— to serve as balancer and interlocutor."[58] If the American aim against insurgencies is total victory, this expectation is more strongly felt in conventional wars.

The army's concept of low-intensity conflict does not include limited wars fought between powerful, conventional forces. This relatively new term describes a specific category of conflict that includes a variety of irregular war-fighting from terrorism to guerrilla operations. This definition, however, is problematic because guerrillas can fight in larger units and use conventional tactics to defeat regular forces. For proof of this point one need only consider Neil Sheehan's riveting account of the Battle of Ap Bac (January 1963) in which Viet Cong forces defeated ARVN units in a conventional battle.[59]

The AirLand Battle concept was not designed with the political complexities of limited war in mind, for the 1986 FM 100–5 may be the most Jominian field manual in army history.[60] This new army doctrine calls for the decisive defeat of the opponent through rapid maneuver, concentration, and the application of firepower—all essential elements of the Napoleonic concept of warfare.[61] It is offensive even though its strategic objective was to *defend* Western Europe. AirLand Battle reflects the reality of the technological environment of modern conventional warfare, which as the Yom Kippur War revealed has become frighteningly fast-paced and which was seen once again, with devastating effect, in the American liberation of Kuwait. It also reflects a new vision of war that intends to destroy the mental composure of the enemy by directing rapid, decisive attacks at his center of gravity.

The army believes that it has prepared for fighting all low- and mid-intensity wars. Yet, the true limited wars, which may be constrained by domestic and international political factors, slip between these two classifications. This subject was approached by General Carl E. Vuono, the Chief of Staff of the United States Army during his 1990 Bernard Brodie lecture at the University of California at Los Angeles.[62] The remarks were later published in *Parameters*.[63] In that article, Vuono makes a coherent argument for the proposition that the new strategic environment facing the United States requires a strong conventional force capability. He states:

> The most important lessons of the postwar era can be summed up as follows. Since the advent of the nuclear age, the value of strategic nuclear forces has been limited to their passive ability to deter a Soviet attack. They are useful only when they are not used. It is equally apparent that the value of conventional forces has resided in our ability to employ them actively in a wide variety of peacetime tasks as well as in combat. They are useful when they are properly used. As we move into a new and uncertain future, neither theoreticians nor practitioners of national security can afford to ignore this fundamental difference. (p. 4)

President Eisenhower would have hotly disagreed with Vuono concerning the utility of nuclear weapons, but this is certainly a fair assessment of the period after the Soviet Union achieved nuclear parity with the United States. Vuono went on to note the increasing destructiveness of wars in the Third World—i.e., the Yom Kippur War and the Iran-Iraq War, and he argued, "Conflict in the developing world is not business as usual. It is a new and expanding challenge that we must be prepared to confront" (p. 6). The Army Chief of Staff then lists "insurgencies, guerrilla warfare, international terrorism, and the trafficking in illicit drugs" as kinds of conflict in which the United States may have to fight.

Vuono also observes that controlling land is essential if wars are to be won, and this requires an excellently equipped and trained army: "the United States must have conventional forces that can be tailored to respond to challenges across the operational spectrum ranging all the way from peacetime competition to major war" (p. 9). Vuono appears willing to fight in all sorts of wars even if they are protracted and politically difficult. He argues that "our conventional forces must be deployable—able to project substantial combat power rapidly wherever our interests are threatened" (p. 9).

Vuono leaves the door open for the possibility that American political interests might only require the restoration of the status quo and not the military defeat of the opponent. This opening is soon shut off, however, with the observation that American forces do not have an adequate sealift or airlift potential to support our commitments to far off regions of the world. He remarks, "But the solution to this dilemma does not lie in stripping our forces of their combat power; it would be folly to commit American forces to battle without giving them the wherewithal to fight and win" (p. 10). He advocates beginning a spending program to redress these transportation shortages. Additionally, Vuono wants to increase the destructiveness of American weapons and to have the funds necessary to continue realistic military training. These observations culminate in Vuono's statement that the army must be lethal if it is to perform effectively and do its duty when called: "For if we are committed to battle, we will go to win, and we will do what we must to achieve victory. In the midst of our discussions about the future of our conventional forces, we must never lose sight of this single, overriding requirement—to fight and win the wars of our nation" (p. 10).

A similar argument was made one year earlier in *Parameters* by Major Daniel P. Bolger.[64] In what must be described as a contentious article, Bolger divides the army into two camps—two Armies. The first is composed of planners for the "Big One" with the Soviet Union who focus on deterring the outbreak of war. The other contingent in the army comprises those who are warriors at heart.[65] He makes the following assessment of the essential purpose of an army:

> The most important thing about an expeditionary army, the idea that gives it purpose even under the nuclear umbrella, is its devotion to victory. These soldiers fight to win, and their triumphs are measurable things: civilian lives saved, friendly governments restored, terrorists killed, enemy forces defeated and ejected. There is no dalliance with deterrence or tripwires or escalatory firebreaks on the road to Ragnarok. Expeditions either succeed, as in the Dominican Republic or Grenada, or they fail, as in the aborted hostage rescue in Iran or the fruitless Marine efforts at the Beirut airport. But either way, soldiers know whether their work is worth it.[66]

Even though Bolger's style is a bit harsh, he makes excellent points. The logic of force does prod us in that direction: toward the exertion of total effort to compel an enemy to submit to one's will.[67] Bolger's "warrior ethos" is very much at the core of the new army and its aggressive mentality which comports with the needs of military decisiveness. The author argues consistently with his position, "That which does not contribute to success in battle must be ruthlessly excised. Warriorship is a way of life."[68]

In short, after Vietnam and the Yom Kippur War the U.S. Army revolutionized its methods. Respect for the Jominian principles of war and for Clausewitz's recognition of decisiveness in war-fighting formed the intellectual backbone of the tactical and operational changes that constitute AirLand Battle. However, the army has not come to terms with the issue of limited war: conflict that precludes the possibility of decisively defeating the opponent is not a real concern for AirLand Battle. Such contingencies, however, must be anticipated.[69] Andrew Krepinevich's "Army Concept" has been altered by the army's current operational approach so that the new army directs enormous amounts of conventional firepower, but it is now capable of doing so with maneuver, deception, deep strikes, and aggressive attacks. Defeat will come not only from the bloody erosion of attrition but also from attacking the overall coherence of the enemy's defense.[70] As one commentator has noted of AirLand Battle: "The concepts of initiative and agility signalled a return to the aggressive warrior spirit."[71]

The Navy, Marine Corps, and Air Force Seek Decisive Victory

The U.S. Navy, Marine Corps, and Air Force have also reaffirmed their faith in the decisive use of force. We shall briefly note, in the remainder of this chapter, some of the similar developments taking place in other branches of the armed forces to illustrate the existence of a conceptual trend. The Marine Corps appears to have come closest to the army in that its operational doctrine was changed signficantly, but the 1980s also saw intellectual ferment within the navy and air force. Harry Summers provides an important analysis that describes these developments in the other military branches.[72] Each adopted a more aggressive, force-projecting doctrine. Consider these remarks of September 10, 1989, made by then Chairman of the Joint Chiefs, Admiral William Crowe, now U.S. Ambassador to Great Britain. He was asked, "What is the principal change or shift that has occurred on your watch?" Crowe answered, "I would say that the principal difference is that we have reoriented our rules of engagement, we have assumed a more aggressive stance around the world, in light of the new technology" possessed by our adversaries .[73] He also noted that American ships have to be more vigilant today and "you have to be prepared to defend yourself even before the first shot is fired." Crowe was also well aware of the quick victories demanded by the American public:

> I face this problem all the time. You're talking about drugs in Colombia. But every time I face the problem of having to deploy in third region—Third World contingencies, instabilities, what the American public wants is for the U.S. military to dominate the situation, to do it quickly, to do it without the loss of life, to do it without any peripheral damage, and then not to interrupt what's going on in the United States or affect the quality of our own lives.[74]

Crowe's remarks reflected developments within the navy during the Reagan Administration. This new concept was called the "Maritime Strategy," and from it "flowed not only naval doctrines and tactics but the composition and organization of the fleet as well."[75] Secretary of the Navy John F. Lehman, Jr., wanted a "600-ship Navy" that would have comprised "fifteen carrier battle groups, four battleship surface action groups, one hundred attack submarines, an adequate number of ballistic missile submarines, and lift for the assault echelons of a Marine amphibious force, and a Marine amphibious brigade."[76] This would have been a massive undertaking, but it would have provided a wide array of operational opportunities. The "Maritime Strategy" was spelled out in articles published simultaneously by the Secretary of the Navy (John F. Lehman, Jr.), the Chief of Naval Operations (James D. Watkins), and the Marine Corps Commandant (P. X. Kelley) in a supplement to the January 1986 issue of *Proceedings*, the journal of the U.S. Naval Institute. These articles reintroduced an aggressive, offense-minded approach to the Navy's war-fighting attitude. Barnett and Barlow demonstrate how the offense-minded philosophy supporting the "maritime strategy" had been preferred by the navy for decades. Thus, the Reagan "maritime strategy" must be placed within the proper post-war context of continuous naval planning and refinement:

> it seems clear that the preferred strategy for the U.S. Navy since the time of the Second World war has been one that emphasizes deterrence, and if deterrence should fail, fighting far forward with the assistance of allies. Sea control has always been a central function, and during those periods of time when the navy was clearly preponderant or on the upswing it has emphasized both forward offensive operations to secure control of the seas and power-projection operations against enemy forces or territory.[77]

The basic idea was that the navy would gain control of the seas and then take the war to the Soviet homeland, making control of the sea lines of communication even more secure as enemy ships were pushed further away from the central Atlantic shipping channels. It should not be surprising that this theory of naval power, reflecting the navy's Mahanian traditions, would be at the core of the U.S. Navy's focus.

The Marine Corps, which was closely involved with the development of the Maritime Strategy, also adopted an aggressive doctrinal position as they modernized their doctrine. The Marines, like their army counterparts, saw the need for maneuver which they defined in *Warfighting*, their basic doctrinal analysis of war, as "a warfighting philosophy that seeks to shatter the enemy's cohesion through a series of rapid, violent, and unexpected actions which create a turbulent and rapidly deteriorating situation with which he cannot cope."[78] Contrasted with the attritional doctrines which had held sway in the U.S., the "object of maneuver warfare is not so much to destroy physically as it is to shatter the enemy's cohesion, organization, command, and psychological balance" (p. 29). Clearly, decisively defeating one's opponent is to be highly prized.

One might judge from this that *Warfighting* would be unbalanced and stereotypically Jominian. Such is not the case. In fact, the document is Clausewitzian in the best ways possible. The short volume places great emphasis on the primacy of the political elements in war and paraphrases Clausewitz in many places using apt historical examples (see especially pp. 19–20 in the chapter entitled "Theory of War"). The Marines' historical familiarity with a range of fighting scenarios has required that they be more amenable to the notion of a "spectrum of conflict" determined by the adversaries' "policy objectives, military means available, national will, and density of fighting forces or combat power on the battlefield" (p. 21). The Marine Corps' attempt to present a general military framework in this volume succeeded. It even avoids the rote listing of the Jominian principals of war. Lest it be thought that the marines have gone soft, for all the talk of the primacy of political objectives one finds passages like the following: "It is not enough simply to generate superior combat power. We can easily conceive of superior combat power dissipated over several unrelated efforts or concentrated on some indecisive object. To win, we must concentrate combat power toward a decisive aim" (p. 35).

In a paragraph that relies on Clausewitz and then makes practical military conclusions, one recognizes the familiar call for military decisiveness as being at the heart of war-fighting for the USMC:

> The aim of war is to achieve our will. The immediate requirement is to overcome our enemy's ability to resist us, which is a product of the physical means at his disposal and the strength of his will. We must either eliminate his physical ability to resist or, short of this, we must destroy his will to resist. In military terms, this means the defeat of the enemy's fighting forces, but always in a manner and to a degree consistent with the national policy objective. (p. 20)

Even though the manual acknowledges a great range of military and political objectives, that language is not present here. There is no talk of limited war or of deterrence. In this document the Marine Corps, as Harry Summers observes, closed the Vietnam loop.[79]

The air force has pursued a similar philosophy of war-fighting—one from which it had never really strayed. Mark Clodfelter, a professor of history at the Air Force Academy in Colorado Springs observes:

> The current edition of the Air Force Manual 1–1, Basic Doctrine, stress-es the perceived need for unbridled air power by quoting the Italian Air Marshall Giulio Douhet: 'The employment of land, sea, and air forces in time of war should be directed towards one single aim: VICTORY. . . . The commander[s] of the Army, Navy, and Air Force should be given the greatest freedom of action in their respective sphere.' [80]

Summers underscores this thinking by reproducing part of a prewar interview with Lieutenant-General Charles A. Horner, chief of the Cen-tral Command air forces during the Gulf War. Horner looked back at Vietnam and forward to his next war with these thoughts: "Many of us here who are in this position now were in Vietnam, and that war left a profound impact on our feelings about how our nation ought to conduct its business." He went on, "We will carry out any particular policy but as individuals we think that war is a very serious business and it should not be dragged out in an effort to achieve some political objective.[81]

Clodfelter argues that the "unspoken belief" of the air force hierar-chy "is that since Linebacker II [the December 19, 1972 air attacks on Hanoi-Haiphong] demonstrated bombing effectiveness, political lead-ers *must* realize that bombing can win limited wars if unhampered by political controls."[82] Of course, Clodfelter's air force leaders have missed the point here: the essence of limited war is the political control of force to achieve limited ends. What the military leader understands is that limiting the manner in which force is used often undermines its power to overthrow the opponent—this seems to be particularly true with air power. Because air power does not itself bring about control of the land on which the enemy lives, its contribution is necessarily indi-rect. The air force's manual that sets out basic doctrine takes the point of air decisiveness so far as to say that "as a critical element in the inter-dependent land-naval-aerospace team, aerospace power can be the deci-sive force in warfare."[83]

Kenneth P. Werrell, professor of history at Radford University in Radford, Virginia, notes that air power was certainly a major factor in the coalition victory in the Gulf War. Werrell compares the air force's effectiveness in Vietnam and the Persian Gulf War and offers many interesting insights. He notes, for example, that much of its inability to coerce North Vietnam was due to pronounced failures in its technology, tactics, and targeting.[84] He recognizes that the criticism of "gradualism" is justified, but "it conveniently overlooks the military's part of the responsibility for air power's ineffectiveness."[85] Werrell notes that in the twenty-five years from Rolling Thunder to Desert Storm the air force had oriented its technology, tactics, and targeting to conduct a conventional war.[86] That was a primary reason for American success in the Gulf War. At the end of the article, Werrell analyzes the "differences between [the] Vietnam and Gulf Air Wars" and presents lessons. His first and longest point focuses on the need for a "clear and limited purpose" as found in the Gulf War objective of liberating Kuwait:

> This clear purpose better mated political ends and military means than was the case in the Vietnam experience. Most important, these purposes could be achieved. In war, air power is primarily a military tool, not a political one. In addition, airmen have difficulty correctly gauging their weaponry's military, psychological, and political impact, since air power is a blunt, crude weapon. Seeing and using air power as a military, not a political, tool allowed decisionmakers to avoid the trap of hopes and promises.[87]

Werrel's claim that air power is primarily a military tool, not a political one is a bit off target. That proposition is true of all forms of military power: they have military purposes primarily. However, that truth does *not* negate the truth of another proposition, that military purposes are directed toward *political* ends, the *raison d'être* of war. Werrell's point might be stated more accurately as follows: *air power is more likely to assist in the attainment of political objectives when it is employed against the military and economic capacities of the enemy; vague objectives such as inducing psychological and political shock have limited success.* Fortunately, Desert Storm was not designed to re-create the psychological campaign of signalling to North Vietnam nor to be a morale boost for dispirited South Vietnam's ARVN forces; instead, it was directed at helping to defeat the enemy militarily which, in turn, destroyed Saddam's capacity to sustain resistance in the theater of war. Even though Werrell does not wholly accept air force explanations for the causes of failure in Vietnam, and he cites Clodfelter approvingly, his argument helps to support the "never again" perceptions that air power should be used against well-defined targets for well-defined purposes to a decisive effect.

These Developments Reconsidered

There can be little doubt that by the middle of the 1980s a definitive turn had been taken by the armed services of the United States. They had learned the "lessons" of Vietnam and were adapting so that the United States would not be caught in endless wars of attrition in which the issues at stake were not decided by military means. Consistent with much recent thought on the subject, Patrick Glynn of the American Enterprise Institute has recently noted of Vietnam "that the very hope that the war could be waged in such a limited fashion . . . owed much to the faulty Democratic memory of Korea and to limited war theory." He adds, "The existence of a model of limited war, with all its fallacies, clouded the real choice facing the president, which was in truth one between humiliating withdrawal and major escalation entailing large risks. The theory permitted Johnson to believe—or half-believe—that the self-restrained manner in which he was waging the war might work."[88]

The Johnson Administration, Glynn believes, was led astray, to some extent, by President Kennedy's successful use of graduated coercive diplomacy during the Cuban Missile Crisis of 1962. Ultimately, however, the Johnson Administration fell prey to its own "remarkable lack of strategic insight, an almost astonishing incomprehension of the logic of employing military force."[89] It was an analysis rejecting those prior perspectives that shaped the Reagan administration's general caution about using force—caution that was greatly reinforced by the disastrous Marine Corps peace-keeping mission in Lebanon. When George Bush assumed the Presidency from Ronald Reagan in January 1989 he commanded an American military that probably was the most sophisticated technologically, best equipped, best trained, best staffed, and most doctrinally aggressive in our history.

The development of AirLand Battle doctrine is an essential component of the American military's response to Vietnam—it is an intellectual symbol of an era. Harry Summers has observed that Army Chief of Staff Creighton Abrams, following the Vietnam War, successfully restructured the army so as to make it impossible for a future president to enter into a large-scale conflict without calling up the army's reserves, thereby mobilizing the nation for war.[90] In an analogous manner the adoption of AirLand Battle has forged an unseverable, conceptual link between the various levels of war in army doctrine:

> Operational art is the employment of military forces to attain strategic goals in a theater of war or theater of operations through the design, organization, and conduct of campaigns and major operations. A campaign is a series of joint actions designed to attain a strategic objective in a theater of war.[91]

The tactical level of analysis provides a similar framework:

> While operational art sets the objectives and pattern of military activities, tactics is the art by which corps and smaller unit commanders translate potential combat power into victorious battles and engagements. Engagements are small conflicts between opposed maneuver forces.[92]

The army's new concept of war-fighting will make it difficult for the army to enter the static wars of attrition and pacification that Krepinevich discussed earlier. Just as organizational restructuring can force the nation to mobilize its reserves in wartime, so too can doctrine channel the analysis of war down well-defined paths that inhabit the willingness and ability of officers to engage in static, limited war. As the 1986 manual describes the doctrine:

> AirLand Battle doctrine describes the Army's approach to generating and applying combat power at the operational and tactical levels. It is based on securing or retaining the initiative and exercising it aggressively to accomplish the mission. The object of all operations is to impose our will upon the enemy—to achieve our purposes. To do this we must throw the enemy off balance with a powerful blow from an unexpected direction, follow up rapidly to prevent his recovery and continue operations aggressively to achieve the higher commander's goals. The best results are obtained when powerful blows are struck against critical units or areas whose loss will degrade the coherence of enemy operations in depth, and thus most rapidly accomplish the mission. From the enemy's point of view, these operations must be rapid, unpredictable, violent,

and disorienting. The pace must be fast enough to prevent him from taking effective counteractions.[93]

AirLand Battle's aggressive approach to war-fighting produced its desired effect in the devastation of the Iraqi armed forces in the 1991 Gulf War. That victory was the result of "a campaign to rebuild the spirit and confidence of the U.S. military after Vietnam."[94] One writer noted: "For Norman Schwarzkopf and his lieutenants, this war lasted not six weeks but twenty years."[95] After the war the army re-examined AirLand Battle doctrine and issued a new FM 100–5 that continued the conceptual development that started with the 1976 operational manual.

The new version of *FM 100–5 Operations* was released on June 14, 1993, in Washington, D.C. Detailed analysis of the document will take some time, but, when compared to other manuals produced by the American armed services, it may be the most theoretically and strategically sophisticated document yet produced by the United States military. As a device for teaching the fundamentals of war, it is clearly written and analytically powerful. Although the term AirLand Battle does not seem to be used in the new manual, it clearly builds on the conceptual framework developed after Vietnam. One might think that a step had been taken away from decisive war-fighting, for the manual contains a chapter dealing with "Operations Other Than War."[96] Yet, in that section there is no attempt to sneak limited war philosophies into army doctrine through a back door. These activities, the "operations other than war," are given their own principles of operation the first of which is "Objective." It states: "Direct every military operation toward a clearly defined, decisive, and attainable objective" (p. 13–3). These activities "other than war" include the following: noncombatant evacuation operations, arms control, support to domestic civil authorities, humanitarian assistance and disaster relief, security assistance, nation assistance, support to counterdrug operations, combatting terrorism, peacekeeping operations, peace enforcement, show of force, support for insurgencies and counterinsurgencies, attacks, and raids (pp. 13–4 to 13–8).[97] The manual also examines "war termination and postconflict operations" stating that "successful combat operations are designed to bring an end to the war" (pp 3–11 to 3–12). Thus, the army is breaking new ground here, but the new manual's heart lies in what it has to say about fighting wars.

There the emphasis on the decisive use of force is continued without mistake. The manual notes regarding "Strategic Goals and the Use of Force" that the "objective of the military in war is victory over the opposing military force at the least cost to American soldiers" (p. 1–4). We are told that "the American people expect decisive victory and abhor unnecessary casualties. They prefer quick resolution of conflicts and reserve the right to reconsider their support should any of these conditions not be met"(p. 1–3). The Principles of War are presented again to stunning effect. With regard to the Objective the manual directs: "The ultimate military purpose of war is the destruction of the enemy's armed forces and will to fight" (p. 2–4).[98] Every military operation is to seek "a clearly defined, decisive, and attainable objective" (p. 2–4) The discussion of the principle of the offensive is even more illuminating. Military leaders are directed to "seize, retain, and exploit the initiative." We are informed: "Offensive action is the most effective and decisive way to attain a clearly defined common objective." What is more fascinating is the army's relegation of the defensive to secondary importance: "Commanders adopt the defensive only as a temporary expedient and must seek every opportunity to seize the initiative" (p. 2–4). Later one reads that "military forces defend only until they gain sufficient strength to attack" (p. 9–0).[99]

While a more complete analysis of the new FM 100–5 awaits the literature that will inevitably follow its release, clearly, the army's new operational field manual continues the conceptual development of an approach to war fighting that seeks decisive victory over the opposing military force, comprehends the fluid nature of offense and defense, recognizes the relationship between the different levels of warfare, emphasizes the use of combined arms doctrine, and realizes that using the initiative to disorient the enemy is one element, if not the critical one, in waging war victoriously.

9 | Reagan and Bush

The United States received a respite in the 1970s from the ongoing philosophical struggle over the way to use force. The turmoil of Watergate and of South Vietnam's final days focused the nation's attention on other issues. The Carter Administration did not confront the issue directly for two reasons. First, the trauma of defeat in Vietnam continued, as it had for President Ford, to undermine considerations of the protracted use of military force. In addition, the Carter Administration, by and large, did not have occasion to use military power. The most notable exception was the attempted hostage rescue mission into Iran made in April 24–25, 1980. The unusual circumstances prompting the attack and the focus on special operations rendered that military effort of little use as a guide for using force. Hostage taking and international terrorism became even greater problems during the Reagan Administration.

The Limited War / Never Again debate resurfaced, in a fashion, during the Reagan and Bush Administrations. The Reagan-Bush philosophy argued that force, when used, should overwhelm the opponent. Even with regard to coercive diplomacy the Reagan-Bush approach leaned in the direction of what might be called overpowering coercive threats. The years from 1981 to 1994 have contained considerable analytical ferment as the use of force has been reconsidered through the perspective of Beirut, Grenada, Panama, the Gulf War, Somalia, and possible intervention in the Balkans. Whether the hard line philosophy of the Reagan and Bush presidencies will be maintained as a new generation of leaders assumes control of American foreign policy is yet to be determined (see Epilogue).

Ronald Reagan and America's New Assertiveness: Central America, an Early Test

In order to understand the Reagan Administration's foreign policy one must first realize how deeply that policy depended on the personality and character of Ronald Reagan. To those around him and to much of the nation, Reagan exuded a self-confidence and optimism that had not graced the White House since John F. Kennedy's tenure there. It should be of little surprise that Reagan, a staunch anticommunist and political conservative, would not assume a passive position internationally vis-à-vis the Soviet Union or with respect to socialism as a political theory. With regard to the Soviets, Reagan developed a policy meant to place them on the strategic defensive in areas in which they had violated the territorial norms of the Cold War: Angola, Nicaragua, and Afghanistan.

A facet of this new approach was the increase in defense spending that permitted force modernization and the adoption of more offense-minded operational strategies by the U.S. armed forces. One original aspect of the program was President Reagan's determined effort to create a strategic defense in space. With regard to fighting socialist political ideas internationally the Administration's attack was most focused at the United Nations under the direction of Ambassador Jeane J. Kirkpatrick. Reagan's rejection in April 1982 of the Law of the Sea Treaty, which incorporated the principles of the New International Economic Order in its deep seabed mining provisions, indicated a willingness to brook international disapproval if capitalist economic rights were at stake. All of this indicated a more assertive attitude abroad by the United States. The Reagan administration, immediately upon taking office, faced a trouble spot in Central America, where the revolutionary Sandanista government of Nicaragua had recently come to power and where El Salvador was being torn apart by civil war.

A policy debate raged in Washington from the outset of the Reagan administration concerning the form that American opposition should take against the communist social and political movements in Central America and, more specifically, Nicaragua and El Salvador. The Central America debate provided the opportunity for the American military to influence policy in an area where protracted direct military involvement was a distinct possibility, as Petreaus notes: "In the debate over Central America, more than in the debate over any other post-Vietnam issue involving the potential use of U.S. troops, America's senior soldiers have been willing to make their views known in public, as well as in private."[1]

Later he notes that the military's advice had been relatively uniform: "Many of the senior military have feared a Central American Vietnam, and by making their views known in advance they have sought to shape the debate and preempt certain policies. Most important, the military have advised publicly against the commitment of U.S. combat units in the region except under certain conditions—conditions developed with an eye to avoiding another Vietnam."[2] A fear of involvement in another Vietnam was not the military's only concern. Many of the officers, especially those in Latin America, were wary of exacerbating fears of U.S. imperialism; according to Petraeus, they were also concerned lest military power be used to solve problems that were essentially political and social in nature. Alexander M. Haig, Jr, President Reagan's first Secretary of State, provides an insightful discussion of the Central America crisis. He begins by discussing the lessons he learned as a soldier in Korea and Vietnam. From Korea, Haig tells us, the most critical point to be remembered is that "only after a new President, Dwight D. Eisenhower, sent the enemy a message containing the veiled threat that nuclear weapons would be used on the battlefield" was an agreement reached.[3] In Haig's opinion only the American threat to devastate China forced the war's end.[4] Haig also wanted the American leadership to recognize the essential truth of Vietnam as he saw it:

> To start small, to show hesitation, was to Vietnamize the situation. . . . Such a policy, in my view, could only lead us into the old traps of committing ever larger resources to a small objective. If it is easier to escalate step by small step, it is easier for an adversary to respond to each step with a response that is strong enough to compel yet another escalation on our part. That is the lesson of Vietnam. If an objective is worth pursuing then it must be pursued with enough resources to force the issue early.[5]

Unfortunately for Haig, the other principal actors within the administration did not share his point of view. His most persistent opponent was Caspar Weinberger, the Secretary of Defense. We are told that Weinberger "genuinely feared the creation of another unmanageable tropical war into which American troops and American money would be poured with no result different from Vietnam."[6] The Secretary of Defense repeatedly revealed to Haig that Vietnam weighed heavily on his mind: "In the NSC and in private meetings with me over breakfast, Cap Weinberger insistently raised the specter of Vietnam and worried over the possibility that the President would be drawn into an 'involuntary escalation.' "[7]

According to Haig, the opposition of Weinberger and other civilians divided the debate into two camps. The first advocated the use of military and political aid as part of a low-key, local response to the problem (most probably through the use of proxies, one should add). The members of this group included Vice President George Bush, Secretary Weinberger, National Security Advisor Richard Allen, and the CIA Director William Casey. Haig writes that he was "virtually alone" in advocating that the United States bring its "overwhelming economic and political influence" to bear on the Soviets and Cubans. It appears that Haig and Thomas Enders, the assistant secretary of state for inter-American affairs, were trying to produce a policy that would "as a first step, seek to seal off the export of arms from Cuba to Central America."[8] As history indicates, those who wanted to localize the issue prevailed. Subsequently, a campaign of coercive diplomacy was directed at the Sandanista government.[9]

How did the nation's highest military advisers feel about the possibility of U.S. involvement in the Central American fray? It appears they generally shared a perspective that included four elements: 1) military training, arms, and logistical expertise should be provided to friendly governments in the region; 2) if American armed forces were employed, this should be accompanied by unequivocal public support; 3) U.S. forces, if placed in combat situations, would have to be allowed to pursue military victory (here we revisit the All-or-Nothing position); 4) despite having given a list of preconditions for the use of force, it was generally accepted that military power was an inappropriate tool for solving "political" problems like those in Central America. Force should be used only where it can be effective—and not against "political"

opponents. If at all possible, the U.S. government should avoid messy
entanglements with little hope for a military solution. Richard Halloran, a military correspondent for the *New York Times*, supports this
assessment in an article about JCS Chairman, General John Vessey, Jr.
(formerly of the Army): "The military advice of the Joint Chiefs of Staff
on immediate issues has been marked by restraint. General Vessey and
the Chiefs have urged the President to be wary of deploying American
forces to the Persian Gulf. They have proposed limiting the American
military presence in Central America to maneuvers. In 1983, they
advised against sending the Marines to Lebanon and were ahead of the
administration in urging that they be withdrawn."[10]

Halloran later quotes Vessey, who seems to be summing up the military's approach as first exhibited in Central America: "Don't send military forces off to do anything unless you know what it is clearly that
you want done." American soldiers must not be put at risk in ambiguous situations "for some phony sort of military and political objectives
that we don't understand."[11] Clearly, the "nothing" component of the
All-or-Nothing perspective was still operative and rendering powerful
advice as to whether U.S. armed forces should be engaged in wars. With
respect to Central America, General Paul Gorman, the Commander of
the United States' Southern Command in the mid-1980s, believed that
the best strategy for the United States was to increase military, economic, and political assistance to the region. William Taylor and David
Petraeus have observed: "Testimony by General Gorman in August
1984 before a House subcommittee seemed to indicate the military's
views had not changed. Gorman said he 'could foresee no circumstances when it would be useful' to commit U.S. troops to combat in
El Salvador."[12]

The *Washington Post* reported that a number of generals with "strong
views about the commitment of U.S. troops abroad" had been promoted to extremely influential positions within the Army. Wilson
wrote: "According to Pentagon colleagues, all four generals, based on
their Vietnam experience, are opposed to committing U.S. forces to the
region unless the American public supports it and commanders are
given a freer hand in waging war than they had in Vietnam." Wilson,
equating the incoming Army Chief of Staff, General John Wickham,
with his predecessor, E. C. Meyer, noted that both were believers "that
the United States must not repeat in Central America the Vietnam mis-

take of putting soldiers out at the end of a string' without the full support of the American people."[13] Wilson's article indicates that, for the Army, the two critical elements of any American decision to employ American forces into combat would be obtaining the widespread support of the public and the permission to employ their forces in a militarily effective manner.

The opposition of the American military to direct deployment of U.S. forces to Central America was almost solid. General Wallace H. Nutting's belief that the United States would have to learn to live with the Sandinistas the way it did with Castro was expressed in a *New York Times* interview.[14] Halloran noted, "Officers in Washington said General Nutting's opposition to invading Nicaragua reflected a view widely held among senior military officers and echoed recommendations made by the Joint Chiefs of Staff to the President and Secretary of Defense." Nutting's reluctance was based on his estimation that the political and military costs of a war with Nicaragua would exceed its potential benefits. JCS Chairman Vessey told an audience in New Orleans on May 13, 1983, there was no Pentagon support, either military or civilian, for "introducing U.S. combat forces to try to implement an American military solution to the problems of Central America"[15]

One of the more important articles on the reluctance of the military to become involved in Central America appeared in the *Wall Street Journal* on June 24, 1983,: Walter Mossberg focused on the Army's tacit preconditions for the use of force: the requirements for domestic political support and real operational latitude making them free from political constraint. Mossberg makes it clear that these requirements stem from the beliefs of Army officers about their Vietnam experience: "In Vietnam, they believe, U.S. troops were sent by politicians to fight a war for which the politicians hadn't won public support. Lacking that support, the politicians imposed limits on military tactics which, many officers believe, made the war unwinnable."[16] The article then paraphrases the remarks of the outgoing Army Chief of Staff, General Meyer, at a "farewell press breakfast." In his remarks Meyer emphasized the need for popular support and "consensus" within the United States as to the military effort.

General Meyer also discussed the need for clear political objectives and accurate assessments of the military feasibility of potential policies.

As reported by Mossberg, Meyer told the assembled members of the media: "Before the troops could be sent," he said, the military would want the president to make a "clear statement of what you want the forces to do. And then there would have to be a clear evaluation on the part of the military as to whether or not it's possible to do that with the military forces that you're permitted to employ."[17]

Meyer's point, obviously, is that professional soldiers want to be given clear objectives and the requisite military forces to accomplish them. Meyer deemed the willingness of the military chiefs to stand up to the civilians and argue against unworkable policies to be essential to the formulation of successful policies: "If it isn't possible," the general said, "then the military should stand up and say, 'We can't do that with the forces involved.' We didn't do that in Vietnam. We inched our way into it, and all of a sudden you were there . . . I was a bit confused as to why I was over there."[18]

Mossberg also notes that the military's "concerns about combat in El Salvador don't derive solely from Vietnam's lesson's about lack of public support and lack of operational leeway." He also conveys the conviction of General Meyer and many other soldiers that "guerrilla uprisings, no matter how anti-American or how dependent on Soviet assistance, spring largely from genuine economic and political grievances that can't be swept away by U.S. troops." The military instrument can't be a solution for all political problems; it cannot create political institutions where none exist. Mossberg argues that this is another important lesson that the military has drawn from Vietnam. Perhaps it is not as widely articulated as the Never Again lesson because it contradicts the position, deeply held by many members of the armed forces, that Vietnam was a war that could have been won.

Thus, we see that a number of reasons for not intervening in Central America were given by the administration's highest military advisers. Their two greater concerns were that public support for their actions would be lacking and that they would be fettered operationally by civilian controls. Also present, but given less emphasis, was the argument that the social and political problems in the region undermined the desirability of using force. It is difficult to determine what part the professional military's lack of enthusiasm for a Central American involvement had on the Administration's decision not to pursue direct military action by the U.S. Certainly, public opinion did not favor such a step. No doubt both were important constraints on American policy in the region.

Lebanon: 1982–84

The Joint Chiefs and Secretary Weinberger reacted with a similar reluctance to use military power when the option of introducing American forces into Lebanon was considered in 1982. The deployment of U.S. Marines to Beirut took place in August 1982 as part of an American effort to shore up the failing Lebanese government as Syrian and Palestinian forces were being evacuated from the capital city. All of these events stood against the backdrop of the Israeli invasion of Lebanon launched in June 1982, which had taken that nation's powerful army to the outskirts of Beirut.[19] It should be remembered that there were two deployments of marines to Beirut. The first lasted for a little over two weeks and came to an end on September 16, 1982, after Syrian and PLO forces were removed from Beirut. On September 14, 1982, Bashir Gemayel, the president-elect, was assassinated in a bombing of his political headquarters, and four days later a three-day-long massacre of 800 Palestinian refugees began. By the end of September 1982 the Reagan administration redeployed American forces (along with those from Britain, Italy, and France). This deployment, which would last sixteen months, saw the multinational force become embroiled in the internecine conflicts of Lebanon and eventually fall victim to the marine compound bombing.

A split developed in the administration between those who wanted a more active policy in Lebanon designed to maintain the government and those who believed that the problems in Lebanon were essentially "political" and not amenable to applications of force. In the first group could be counted Secretary of State Shultz, and National Security Advisers William Clark and his successor, Robert McFarlane.[20] The second group consisted primarily of Secretary Weinberger and the nation's top military advisers. The Shultz-McFarlane position argued that the United States needed "to get Vietnam behind us" and again assert its military power in those areas in which it considered its interests to be at stake.[21] Its advocates believed that the coercive power of military force was required to protect the Lebanese government which was pro-Western in its foreign policy. According to Hallenbeck, the deployment of 15,000 troops was considered and then abandoned after objections were made that the size of forces would tie the United States into Lebanon in a manner reminiscent of the Vietnam involvement.[22]

On the other side of the issue, Weinberger and the JCS saw the making of a quagmire—even with small numbers of troops: to these officials Beirut was a potentially unlimited commitment with no clear military objectives. According to Shultz, Secretary Weinberger protested adamantly, in retrospect seemingly correctly, about the lack of clarity in the mission: "It was too uncertain, [Weinberger] said, to put the [multinational force] in Beirut and then simply hope for the best. The mission needed to be defined. I [Shultz] said the mission was defined— help the Lebanese get control of and stabilize their situation—but it could be narrower, perhaps limited just to Beirut."[23]

Force was being advocated as part of a diplomatic show designed to make a political point. Richard Halloran writes concerning the Beirut involvement: "The Joint Chiefs of Staff vigorously opposed the deployment, asserting that the issues were political, not military. They contended that American troops might be forced to fire on Arabs, which would harm the standing of the United States in the Middle East."[24] His analysis continues with the thoughts of one officer: "Let's not get involved in something without public support." At that time, General Vessey, ever cautious when speaking in public, expressed the feeling of the Joint Chiefs: "I think one has to think through very carefully putting troops in any kind of operation where we're using them as a political lever." He went on to tell the interviewer: "I think it's fair to say that everyone in the military, and the Secretary of Defense, and everyone in the government urged caution and was concerned about what [we were] doing in Lebanon."[25]

Clearly, Vessey had reservations about "political" uses of force. The distrust of the policy felt by these advisers affected the military operations of the American forces. This opposition group ensured "that any deployment [would be] kept small, militarily non-committal, and ready to be withdrawn as soon as politically possible."[26] Mark Perry supports Halloran's interpretation of the JCS position. The Joint Chiefs were unanimously against the deployment but were brought to support the insertion of U.S. ground forces by Chairman John Vessey's argument that the President wanted the marines sent back in and the military had to obey his orders.[27]

President Reagan never resolved the debate within the administration. Consequently, the United States was seen to be claiming that it had important interests at stake in Lebanon, but it was unwilling to commit the military power to sustain our policy and political objectives. Shultz writes with some unhappiness, "I was, under this 'plan,' supposed to conduct diplomacy without strength, with no military backup."[28] Shultz's political objectives in this effort at pressure diplomacy were not limited to reflect the constraints being imposed on usable options by Weinberger et al. The American policy remained ambitious, but the coercive power of the Reagan administration was weak. This fact was surely not lost on our adversaries in Lebanon, for they were able to attack the Marine compound on Sunday, October 23, 1983, killing approximately 241 soldiers with impunity. After this attack, the marines were withdrawn from Lebanon—the last leaving the vicinity of the Beirut airport on February 27, 1984.

Grenada: Reagan's Lightning War

The American invasion of the Caribbean Island of Grenada began on the morning of October 25, 1983. In less than one week the island had been secured although the opposition was unexpectedly stiff. The crisis was precipitated on October 14, 1983, when the Marxist Grenadian Prime Minister, Maurice Bishop, was arrested by a rival Marxist faction led by General Austin. Under Bishop's leadership the government of Grenada had developed strong ties to Cuba, and it was feared by the United States government that an even less friendly government might come to power there. Of immediate concern was the well-being of some 1,000 American medical students on the island. Consideration of a military option began on October 17.

The situation worsened two days later on October 19, when Bishop and other prominent citizens were executed and a "shoot-on-sight" 24-hour curfew was imposed on the populace.[29] U.S. officials feared that the American students might be taken hostage either singly or en masse by the government or its agents; they were also concerned with the threat to political stability that would arise in the Caribbean were this regime to remain in power. Efforts to evacuate the students by plane and ship were blocked by the new government.[30] On the morning of Saturday, October 22, 1983, President Reagan made the decision to go

ahead with the rescue plan; the final "go ahead" order was given around
6:00 p.m. on Monday, October 24 with actual operations beginning
that night and in the early-morning darkness. By the end of Operation
Urgent Fury, the United States had deployed "some 6,000 troops (U.S.
Marines, Army Rangers, and elements of the U.S. Army 82nd Airborne
Division plus some token forces (about 500 troops) from the neigh-
boring Caribbean States to defeat approximately 600 Cuban combat
engineers and 1,000 largely useless members of the Grenadian Army.[31]
Grenada fits into the politico-military pattern established with Central
America and Lebanon in that Secretary Weinberger and the Joint
Chiefs of Staff were hesitant about using force in Grenada. Richard
Halloran comments as follows concerning the willingness of the Penta-
gon to give approval for this operation:

> Similarly [to Central America], the Joint Chiefs were reluctant to exe-
> cute the President's plan to invade Grenada. Said an administration offi-
> cial, "Jack Vessey was the last one to jump aboard on Grenada," refer-
> ring to General John W. Vessey, Jr., then Chairman of the Joint Chiefs
> of Staff. With their advice overridden by the President, the chiefs insist-
> ed that overwhelming American force be employed to ensure success
> quickly, before the American public could question the operation.[32]

According to George Shultz, Weinberger argued strenuously against the
invasion of Grenada: "Cap was continuing to say that there had to be
far greater preparation and a much larger force before an operation
could begin. I knew this was the counsel of no action at all."[33] Shultz
argued against this reluctance and pressed successfully for the intervention. He believes that the Joint Chiefs were strongly influence by memories of Indochina:

> The Joint Chiefs of Staff were reluctant, because of their Vietnam War
> experience, to attempt the Grenada operation. They and other officers
> of that generation had been colonels, commanding brigades and wings
> and serving in planning and operations in Vietnam and Washington.
> They had seen, from one perspective or another, the dark side of the
> Vietnam War: sound tactical and strategic decisions overturned for
> "political reasons"; restrictions on winning; the military, individually
> and collectively, trashed on the campuses, in the news, and in Congress.
> All this left a bitter taste for many years, and especially among the mili-
> tary professionals, who spent years rebuilding the pride, prestige, and

capabilities of their institutions. *The result was that the Joint Chiefs did not just resist mounting an operation; they could take forever to put one together.*[34]

Part of the Pentagon's reticence stemmed from prudent apprehension about the time-constrained planning for this mission. The military pressed for more time to gather intelligence and conduct planning.[35] Shultz observes that the persuasiveness of Langhorne Motley, assistant secretary of state, was critical to getting the Chiefs to move: "He convinced them that all the alternative means had been exhausted and that if we didn't go in quickly, we would have to do so eventually under much worse conditions."[36] The military's influence (and Weinberger's) on operations reflected an acute awareness of the problems experienced in Vietnam: first, overwhelming power was applied against the enemy forces on Grenada; second, the news media were not allowed near the battle zone for days until the worst combat was over. This was done to control the news being sent back to the United States, the maintenance of public support having been deemed absolutely essential.[37] As mentioned above, the Joint Chiefs' natural post- Vietnam reluctance to support the use of force was certainly justified to some extent in Grenada by the crisis-like tempo of events and inadequate planning. But the primary cause of their hesitation lay in their strong desire to run the mission their way, and they were allowed to do so. David Petraeus has written that the military executed the operation "without the level of civilian (not to mention press) oversight customary throughout the Vietnam period and much of its aftermath."[38] Once the green light was given, the military was able to exclude civilian control and media observation.

In the discussion of Grenada in his memoirs, Shultz concludes with comments on "The Use of Force." He writes of what he calls the argument that "Force should be used only as a last resort." Shultz notes that this argument, which I take to be a shorthand for the All-or-Nothing position, seems credible but is actually strategically unsound:

> The use of force, and the credible threat of the use of force, are legitimate instruments of national policy and should be viewed as such. Waiting to use force as a last resort would have meant possibly enduring hostage taking and having to use force then. The use of force should obviously not be taken lightly, but better to use force when you *should*

rather than when you *must*; *last* means *no other*, and by that time the level of force and the risk involved may have multiplied many times over.[39]

In this passage Shultz seems to focus on one facet of the All-or-Nothing perspective that misunderstands the significance of this critique of prior American military actions. The Never Again objections were not primarily about timing or about using force as a "last resort," even though Weinberger and Reagan have included it in their delineations of the argument. In Korea and Vietnam those who opposed the limited use of force realized there were no options but to use force, for both states would have been conquered immediately without American intervention. The last resort requirement is so operationally imprecise as to be of little value as a policy guide: it is hard to imagine an American president using force without first exhausting the possibilities for other remedies. The soul of the Never Again criticism has been that if force is going to be used it must be used decisively and overwhelmingly. In Grenada, the lack of time available to prepare the mission created dangers whose consequences bore themselves out in higher casualties. Nevertheless, Shultz correctly observed the military's discomfort concerning the advisability of Urgent Fury. Putting Grenada in perspective regarding the ongoing discussion over the use of force, he writes, "A Shultz-Weinberger 'debate' on the question of whether and when force was required and justified was now well known. The debate I knew would continue long after the Grenada operation."[40]

The Shultz-Weinberger Dispute

One year later, in 1984, these differences again boiled to the surface. Beginning in October of that year Secretary Shultz and Secretary Weinberger conducted a running national debate on the subject. Not often mentioned is the fact that Secretary Shultz began this exchange of ideas with an address before the Trilateral Commission on April 3, 1984, in Washington; his speech made a strong *realpolitik* argument in favor of the limited and flexible use of force to achieve limited political objectives. In effect, Shultz argued that the force should be used to augment diplomacy: he wanted the United States to be willing to exercise strong variants of coercive diplomacy when the occasion so demanded.

This did not mean, however, that Shultz was committing himself to a fully developed advocacy of limited war as was seen before Vietnam.

The Secretary of State began his speech by contrasting two elements of American thinking about foreign interventions: first, that the United States should "pay any price, bear any burden" and, second, that military force is of little relevance to solving the "complicated social, economic, and religious" problems of the world.[41] The Secretary observed, "Somewhere between these two poles lies the natural and sensible scope of American foreign policy." The modern world is filled with dangers, and "there is no safety in isolationism." Consequently, the United States had to develop an understanding that "power and diplomacy always go together."[42] He then stated, "Certainly power must always be guided by purpose, but the hard reality is that diplomacy not backed by strength is ineffectual." Shultz continued by making the point that Americans tend to think "power and diplomacy are two distinctive alternatives."[43] This is not the case, Shultz believed, for both are interconnected elements of politics. In essence, Shultz was making a Clausewitzian argument. He then criticized the Long Commission's report on the bombing of the marine barracks in Beirut because it urged that more work be done "to pursue what it spoke of as 'diplomatic alternatives,' as opposed to 'military options.'" This, the Secretary said, "reflected a fundamental misunderstanding—not only of our intensive diplomatic efforts throughout the period but of the relationship between power and diplomacy."

Accordingly, one fact had to be recognized: diplomacy rests on a foundation of power, force, and coercion. He would not dispute the idea that rational persuasion and moral argument can affect diplomatic outcomes, but they certainly cannot be relied on to do so at all times. Shultz stated that the "lesson" of events like the bombing of the marine compound were as follows: "power and diplomacy are not alternatives. They must go together, or we will accomplish very little in this world."[44]

The Secretary then described the varieties of challenges the United States would face in the years ahead, noting that due to their isolation from global politics, "Americans tended to believe that war and peace . . . were totally distinct phenomena." The nation was "either in a blissful state of peace or else . . . embarked on an all-out quest for total victory." The condition of the current East-West relationship, Shultz asserted, is far less confrontational than the "old cold war," but "neither is it a normal relationship of peace or comfortable co-existence." As for the 1980s he observed: "most likely we will never see a state of total peace. We face instead a spectrum of often ambiguous challenges to our interests." Shultz then tied the policy dilemma of the 1980s into the Vietnam War experience: "It is often said that the lesson of Vietnam is that the United States should not engage in military conflict without a clear and precise military mission, solid public backing, and enough resources to finish the job. This is undeniably true. But does it mean there are no situations where a discrete assertion of power is needed or appropriate for limited purposes? Unlikely."

Noting the vast majority of cases, he observed, where force is employed (e.g., peacekeeping, shows of force, or localized military action) there "will always be instances that fall short of an all-out national commitment on the scale of World War II." Shultz then warned his audience: "The need to avoid no-win situations cannot mean that we turn automatically away from hard-to-win situations that call for prudent involvement. These will always involve risks; we will not always have the luxury to choose the most advantageous circumstances. And our adversaries can be expected to play rough." He repeated Clausewitz's dictum that war is merely the continuation of policy by other means and credited the Soviets for their strategic adherence to this philosophy. The Secretary then observed that "we cannot respond to gray-area challenges without adapting power to political circumstances or on a psychologically satisfying, all-or-nothing basis."[45] In other words, military requirements may have to serve political objectives, for few situations will be as clear cut as Grenada.

This speech was extraordinary, for it appears to have been the first explicit criticism of the Never Again / All-or-Nothing philosophy by a Cabinet-level official since Vietnam. All the elements were there: the approving reference to Clausewitz, the acknowledgement that many politico-military scenarios are murky, and the willingness to subordinate military effectiveness to political objectives. Surprisingly, this speech received little public attention at the time. The *New York Times* story of April 4, 1984, focused on the parts of the speech that explicitly discussed terrorism; the article also mentioned Shultz's criticism of the War Powers Act. No mention, however, was given to the philosophy of the use of force spelled out in this address.

It is important to note that Shultz was not really addressing the limited war issue. Remember that the rationale for limited war, as arising out of Korea, most specifically, was devised to introduce limits on objectives and/or means to prevent unwanted military escalation. Shultz is addressing a different problem: he wants to convince others that force should be threatened or used to create pressure that would assist American diplomacy. Secretary Weinberger did not acknowledge a break between political uses of force outside of war to aid diplomatic efforts and more political uses of force within war. There is no indication Shultz would have tolerated a limited war strategy had the U.S. been involved in a war while he was secretary of state. Shultz's primary concern was establishing effective diplomacy.

More than six months would pass before another address by the Secretary of State prompted Secretary Weinberger's foray on to the field. Shultz's speech, delivered on October 25, 1984, before the congregation of the Park Avenue Synagogue in New York City, dealt explicitly with the course America should take in response to terrorism. The Secretary observed that the United States was well- prepared to deter major conventional war with the Soviets, but he added, "It is not self-evident that we are as well prepared and organized to deter and counter the 'gray area' of intermediate challenges that we are likely to face—the low-intensity conflict of which terrorism is a part."[46] Shultz went on to consider how he believed terrorism should be combated, but perhaps, his most important remark was a statement made in passing that decisions to use force "cannot be tied to opinion polls."[47] It has been reported that this speech sent Secretary Weinberger into a "slow burn" upon reading it; interestingly, only hinted at the powerful position taken by Shultz in April, but even in its diluted form, Shultz's proposal for using force was able to drive Weinberger to distraction.[48] At any rate, it was at this time that the Secretary of Defense began to draft his most important speech, "The Uses of Military Power," which he would deliver to the National Press Club in Washington on November 28, 1984.[49]

At the National Press Club Weinberger presented his list of "six major tests" that should be used to judge whether the United States should deploy its conventional military forces. In the spring of 1986 Weinberger would list these preconditions in the journal *Foreign Affairs*.[50] (1) The United States should use force only when its vital interests are at stake; (2) "should the United States decide to commit its forces to combat, we must commit them in sufficient numbers and with sufficient support to win. If we are unwilling to commit the forces or resources necessary to achieve our objectives, or if the objective is not important enough so that we must achieve it, we should not commit our forces"; (3) if the U.S. commits forces to combat, they must have clearly defined political and military objectives. If these objectives cannot be formulated then military power should not be used; (4) the relationship between objectives and means should be continually reassessed and adjusted as necessary; (5) "Before the United States commits combat forces abroad, the U.S. government should have some reasonable assurance of the support of the American people and their elected representatives in the Congress"; (6) American forces for combat should be used as a last resort "only after diplomatic, political, economic and other efforts have been made to protect our vital national interests."[51]

Clearly, Weinberger's second, third, and fifth points were the heart of the matter. The first point, that force should only be used when vital interests are at stake, is clearly an overinclusive prohibition: it leaves undefined what constitutes a vital interest; it suggests that all interests that are not vital per se cannot justify the use of force. Such a proposition simply does not comport with the conduct of American foreign policy: for example, can the claim be made that the American invasion of Panama rested on the encroachment of *vital* American interests? The fourth point, that means and ends should be re-examined and adjusted, is certainly true but doesn't tell us much. Finally, the sixth condition, that force be used as a last resort, contributes little to the discussion unless we fear that a president would fly off the handle and launch the bombers with little or no provocation. It also requires far too much: waiting until all other remedies have been tried may let the moment of greatest opportunity pass without action. A case in point might be American inaction by the Bush and Clinton Administrations over Bosnia. Waiting until Sarajevo is being swallowed whole by the Serbs may permit the proper inference that all other avenues have been tried, but it may now be too late to act effectively.

James McCartney's *Miami Herald* story, mentioned above, discussed the reaction to the speech within the government. He quoted one high-ranking State Department official as saying: "If you accepted Weinberger's rules, we never would have gone into Grenada. And we wouldn't do anything else either." The article repeated an admonition made by Secretary Shultz to the effect that "a policy filled with so many qualifications and conditions that they all could never be met would amount to a policy of paralysis." McCartney also provided the opinion of a former State Department official that "Weinberger's rules accurately reflect the post-Vietnam views of the nation's professional military—and top military men agree."[52]

Shultz delivers the next blow in the confrontation on December 9, 1984, at Yeshiva University in New York. In his speech, entitled "The Ethics of Power," Shultz observes that the United States must deal with those "gray areas that lie between all-out war and blissful harmony."[53] "The truth is, power and diplomacy must always go together, or we will accomplish very little in this world," he speculates Later in his remarks Shultz casts two barbs at Weinberger who is not referred to by name. First, with regard to having public support for military operations Shultz makes the point that "a president who has the courage to lead will *win* public support if he acts wisely and effectively." Second, the Secretary notes that while "the use of force must always be a last resort" it is inescapable that "a great power cannot free itself from the burden of choice." Shultz implies that too much caution could lead to another kind of foreign policy error: inaction. He believes that the costs of inactivity have been palpable throughout history and cites the European democracies' repeated yielding to Hitler in the 1930s as an example of an undesirable outcome that can result from the inability to act when the times require it.

The final public thrust in this exchange is in Secretary Weinberger's Spring 1986 *Foreign Affairs* article, already mentioned. Before he presents the aforementioned "six tests" from the National Press Club Speech, Weinberger gives a short history of the development of Limited War thinking; he also evaluates this approach to the use of force:

> According to theories developed in the 1950s and early 1960s, limited war was essentially a diplomatic instrument—a tool for bargaining with the enemy. As such it had to be centrally directed by the political leadership and applied with precise control. The gradual application of American conventional power, combined with the threat of incremental increases in the application of that power, would, according to the theorists, persuade America's opponents to accept a settlement while they avoided strategic defeat.[54]

In this passage Weinberger presents a much abbreviated description of the Limited War approach and then offers one of his major criticisms: "The fatal flaw of these theories of the 1950s was their neglect of the domestic political realities of American democracy."[55] He proceeds to make a strong argument that the lesson of Vietnam is that "never again should the imperative of public support be ignored."

Next, the article presents the six conditions (noted above) that Weinberger feels should be met before the United States employs its armed forces. Weinberger's analysis, however, has its flaw as well. The Limited War theorists like Osgood and Kissinger were too sophisticated to regard war as a mere bargaining tool. Rather, their primary concern was that of unwanted escalation of conflict. The point being that the United States did not have to be "Red" or "Dead." There was a middle course in which America would defend limited objectives with limited means instead of capitulating to Communist aggression by not opposing it. The Limited War theorists' underestimation of the costs of limited war and the need for public support were great, but their concern was not imagined. Weinberger confuses the problems associated with limited war with those attendant upon the use of coercive diplomacy, Shultz's primary concern. Nowhere does Shultz argue for McNamara-style gradual escalation. Rather, he merely makes the point that if American diplomacy is to be effective, the threat of force, or its use, may have to accompany such actions. The strength of Weinberger's position rests on the fear that coercive diplomacy may slide into war with ill-defined goals and inappropriate means being employed.

After his presentation of the "six tests" Weinberger briefly sets forth the essential elements for the correct use of force: "When using force, the necessity to win requires a clearly defined, achievable objective on which there is clear agreement." The Secretary of Defense then states:

> When we define a clear objective, we must commit the forces necessary to achieve it. Gradualism is inherently attractive to some, but [is] almost always a mistaken way to achieve a military success. It exaggerates the illusion of control, violates the strategic principle of concentration of force, and encourages underestimation of the domestic political costs entailed by any use of American military forces abroad.

Thus, Weinberger attacks "gradualism" on three fronts. The first is an interesting crisis management-like critique arguing that gradualism imputes excessive rationality and control to decisionmakers. The second is the claim that gradualism violates those timeless, Jominian principles of war-fighting *per se* which dictate that a crushing, decisive blow should be delivered against the opponent.[56] This observation is supported by a comment made shortly below in the text which reads: "If combat forces are required, they should be introduced rapidly and in the strength necessary to achieve our objective at the least possible cost." Third, gradualism, he believes, encourages the underestimation of the political costs of intervention. The reader should consider the passage just quoted and Weinberger's interesting assertion that gradualism is "a mistaken way to achieve a military success." Why does he use the term "military success"? Isn't the purpose of policy to achieve, as Clausewitz would have said, a *political* success? Weinberger's choice of words reveals the essential elements of his thinking about the nature of war, and it is not clear that the pieces are put together correctly.[57]

Former President Reagan explicitly endorsed the core of the Weinberger criteria in his memoirs. In discussing the deaths of the U.S. Marines in Beirut, Reagan describes that event as "the source of my greatest regret and my greatest sorrow as president."[58] It was that event which prompted his administration to adopt a set of principles about the "application of military force" which he recommends to future presidents. Reagan writes that the new policy "included these principles":

1. The United States should not commit its forces to military action overseas unless the cause is vital to our national interest.

2. If the decision is made to commit our forces to combat abroad, it must be done with the clear intent and support needed to *win*. It should not be a halfway or tentative commitment, and there must be clearly defined and realistic objectives.

3. Before we commit our troops to combat, there must be reasonable assurance that the cause we are fighting for and the actions we take will have the support of the American people and Congress. (We all felt that the Vietnam War had turned into such a tragedy because military action had been undertaken without sufficient assurances that the American people were behind it.)

4. Even after all these other tests are met, our troops should be committed to combat abroad *only* as a last resort, when no other choice is available.[59]

As we have seen throughout the post-Vietnam period the former president's remarks evince a concern that wars should be fought to a victorious conclusion. Force should be committed decisively—not halfheartedly. This belief was at the core of the Reagan Administration's conception of how to conduct foreign policy. In an interview, Admiral William Crowe, Chairman of the Joint Chiefs of Staff from 1985–1989, summarized a troubling aspect of the much-needed, post-Vietnam rediscovery of the use of force under President Reagan:

> [The "dangerous syndrome"] runs along these lines: When dealing with limited crises, our armed forces must be able to dominate the situation. After we decide to use force, we must rush in there, deal with the situation decisively and emphatically, lose no people, not take long doing it—two weeks to 30 days—destroy our targets completely, and not disrupt American life. Don't reach out through conscription. Don't upset the stock market. Don't cause undue ripples. Just withdraw and come home after victory.[60]

Admiral Crowe regarded the American protection of the Persian Gulf sea lanes during the later stages of the Iran-Iraq War as a successful use of limited force. That war, which began in 1980, threatened to interrupt the shipment of oil from Kuwait, one of the great oil producing nations in the world. In December 1986 the U.S. ambassador in Kuwait "reported that he had received a feeler from the Kuwaitis, very discreet and unofficial, but clearly a probe" inquiring whether it would be possible to "put part of the Kuwaiti tanker fleet under the American flag."[61] It was later discovered that a similar inquiry was directed toward the Soviet Union. The United States was deeply committed to keeping the sea lanes open in accord with the principle of freedom of the seas.[62] Secretary Weinberger favored reflagging primarily to thwart possible Soviet gains in the region. Crowe felt the reflagging represented the best way "to repair our Arab policy and to make some significant headway in an area where it was absolutely crucial for us to forge the strongest ties we could manage."[63] U.S. planning took place during the spring of 1987.

Hostility to neutral shipping escalated in the same period as demonstrated when two Exocet missiles from Iraqi aircraft hit the USS *Stark* on May 17, 1987, killing 37 of its crew. The next day saw the first mine attack against Gulf shipping.[64] On July 21–22, 1987, the first U.S.-

escorted convoy of reflagged Kuwaiti tankers began its trek up the Persian Gulf. Two days later, one of the ships being escorted, the SS *Bridgeton*, was hit by a mine near the opening of the Gulf. This event did not disrupt the reflagging operations although numerous tactical and operational changes were effected. On April 14, 1988, the USS *Samuel B. Roberts* was severely damaged by a mine. This attack prompted American attacks against Iranian oil platforms on April 18, 1988. A short series of Iranian naval attacks met with devastating results as half of the Iranian navy was destroyed in one day.[65]

The most tragic event in the reflagging and patrol mission of the U.S. Navy occurred on July 3, 1988, when the Ticonderoga-class guided-missile cruiser USS *Vincennes* shot down Iran Air Flight 655 over the Persian Gulf killing all 290 passengers and crew. These operations in the Gulf wound down after August 20, 1988, when a U.N.-sponsored cease-fire went into effect "setting the stage for the suspension in December of formal U.S. Navy convoys in the Gulf."[66] During the Gulf activities fifty-three Americans lost their lives: thirty-seven on the *Stark* and of the remaining sixteen only two were killed during battle.[67] The reduction of American forces in the Gulf proceeded during 1989 but had not yet been completed by the beginning of 1990. Ronald O'Rourke, who summarized the events in the Gulf for the Naval Institute's journal *Proceedings*, wrote that this small war in the Gulf "helped restore U.S. credibility with the Gulf- Arab states, whose faith in the United States was shaken by the revelation in November 1986 of U.S. arms sales to Iran."[68] This had been Crowe's goal from the outset.

This mission exposed U.S. naval forces to protracted hostile action, yet Crowe felt it was important that the U.S. stand firm in defending maritime passage in the Gulf. Certainly, Secretary Shultz supported this position. Of greater interest was Secretary Weinberger's support, for the Persian Gulf operation seemed to violate the tenets of his philosophy for using force. Weinberger supported the reflagging for three reasons: first, he feared the intrusion of Soviet power into the region; second, by failing to reflag the Kuwaiti tankers the Soviets would have an opportunity to fill the power vacuum created by American inaction; and, third, the United States had a great interest in maintaining free passage of the seas.[69] In fact, the Secretary of the Navy, James Webb, a Vietnam veteran and ardent proponent of the Never Again philosophy, challenged Weinberger's honesty in being willing to live up to the tenets of his own doctrine. Webb argued in a July 1986 memo to Weinberger that the administration's involvement in the Persian Gulf did not satisfy the rigorous criteria that Weinberger had set forth for the use of American armed forces. Webb's confrontational approach to this and other issues later led to his resignation from the administration.[70] But Webb had a point with which Weinberger did not agree. Weinberger saw the mission as being clearly defined even though had the war continued there would have been no clear point at which to terminate the mission: the sea lanes had to be kept open. In addition a naval mission has distinct advantages over land operations: ships are isolated by the water that surrounds them. Maritime operations are inherently more secure for a powerful navy that has minesweeping capabilities and air protection with which to isolate itself. A similar task would be much harder for any Army—especially in a jungle or in mountainous terrain. And, finally, reductions in one's military presence can be accomplished with less fanfare if discretion becomes the better part of valor.

For these reasons, the size of the commitment and the nature of the American assistance to Kuwaiti shipping (protecting the legal principle of freedom of navigation on the high seas) kept the U.S. action within the parameters of the Weinberger Doctrine. Secretary Shultz was able to use military power here to physically and symbolically support international legal principles. As such these low-level actions did not commit American forces to military efforts that would properly raise Never Again concerns: war was not imminent. Had war been started by Iran, it is unlikely that weak coercive pressures would have been applied against that regime. In fact, in selling the operation to Congress Admiral Crowe recalls the Administration's argument that the War Powers Resolution need not be invoked: it "maintained the Gulf was not a war zone in the accepted sense of the term; large-scale commercial shipping was going on, oil rigs were operating normally, commercial air traffic was continuing with only slight route modifications."[71]

The Reagan Doctrine, Covert Action, and the Use of Force

An important dimension of Reagan Administration foreign policy was the President's commitment to indigenous rebels in nations recently fallen to communist guerrilla movements.[72] Reagan's commitment is relevant because we must ask whether covert action, of this type and others, has become a substitute for the use of force. If so, is it because of Never Again reasoning related to the cost of direct intervention? Finally, does the assistance rendered to anticommunist insurgencies presage a new phase in modern warfare in which proxy armies re-emerge in international politics?

All governments must act much of the time in private. Diplomacy would be impossible without confidentiality, so there is nothing sinister in secrecy *per se*. However, covert activities involve a more precisely defined set of actions that according to Ray Cline, a former CIA and Department of State official and one of the most highly regarded analysts of the OSS and the CIA, "includes all kinds of political, paramilitary, or propaganda moves undertaken secretly to gain support for U.S. foreign policies overseas."[73] These operations can also be directed at the secret activities of unfriendly foreign states attempting to undermine governments friendly to the United States. Cline feels that the importance of covert action has been greatly overstated: "most CIA covert action is small-scale, neither violent or illegal, plainly authorized by NSC directives, and, on the whole, rather successful in energizing local political groups to build their own parliamentary parties, free labor unions, and independent opinion media."[74]

According to Cline, the CIA's reputation for toppling regimes via covert action grew out of two successful operations undertaken by the Eisenhower Administration in the 1950s: the removal of Mohammed Mossadegh from power in Iran in 1953, and the infliction of fatal damage to the government of Guatemalan President Arbenz Guzman in mid-1954. In each case, Cline argues, the governments in question were so weak that little effort was needed for their overthrow. Later CIA efforts like that directed against President Sukarno of Indonesia in 1958 ended in failure. Additionally, the CIA-directed Bay of Pigs operation was a thorough disaster.

A great danger inheres in covert operations that keeps them at the periphery of foreign policy. That danger is loss of secrecy. The need for secrecy in a truly covert operation requires that the mission size be kept to a minimum. While one can imagine James Bond scenarios in which one person redirects history with daring exploits, the truth is that great endeavors often require great numbers. As Cline observes, "The weak point in covert paramilitary action is that a single misfortune that reveals the CIA's connection makes it necessary for the United States either to abandon the cause completely or convert to a policy of overt military intervention."[75] When this abandonment occurs the "friendly elements" who assisted the U.S. are left for certain destruction. Thus, covert action should only be attempted on those rare occasions where there is a high likelihood of success.

Military operations large enough to topple a government will usually be too large to direct covertly.[76] Consequently, the Reagan Administration policy of supporting anticommunist guerrilla movements with arms and funds was more accurately a quasi-secret policy in which American involvement was not so well hidden but the extent of it was obscured. In the case of Afghanistan the American assistance was extensive and reached 65,000 tons of supplies annually in 1987.[77] Certainly, it was cheaper and less risky to use surrogates in these situations, but the "Reagan Doctrine" does not seem wholly unlike the "Nixon Doctrine" of July 1969. As noted in chapter 8, President Nixon stated at Guam that governments would be primarily responsible for their own security: the U.S. would no longer use its own troops to defend all threatened friendly regimes around the world. Reagan's active support of anticommunist insurgencies was a logical extension of that principle, taking it from a defensive to an offensive attitude.[78] Yet, Reagan's willingness to sponsor such military activities did not contradict his support of the Never Again philosophy. All-or-nothing proponents never argued against covert operations or supporting "contras" under suitable circumstances, what they objected to was the inefficient application of conventional military power involving American soldiers, sailors, and pilots.

Did the Reagan Doctrine's call for funding of insurgencies represent a change in the nature of international relations?[79] Are we witnessing a reversion to the use of mercenaries in war? The short response is no. The counterrevolutionary forces supported by the U.S. in Afghanistan, Angola, and Nicaragua were nationalistically, ethnically, and ideologically motivated. These were not soldiers who could be as happy fighting in far flung areas of the world as long as the price was right. They were committed to their respective causes: to their respective nations and ethnic groups. To think of these forces as mercenaries is not accurate and would be like saying that the insurgents in Algeria or Vietnam were soldiers of fortune. The support for anticommunist insurgencies revealed that totalitarian regimes of the left were susceptible to the same sorts of instability that Soviet efforts had exposed earlier in pro-Western regimes. The Reagan Doctrine did not usher in a new phase in the conduct of international relations: more properly, it should be regarded as an assertive neo-Wilsonian effort to advance democracy where feasible and where American interests called for action but direct military intervention was either unwise or unwarranted. Neither did it contradict the All-or-Nothing philosophy of the Administration that pertained to the use of U.S. forces in direct combat.

The Bush Administration

All that still remained of the Cold War era faded away with the rapid failure of the Moscow coup of August 1991. The disappearance of the Soviet Union and the decisive American-led military victory in the Persian Gulf War have given the United States a new preeminence in world politics. Even though the U.S. is now the world's only superpower, it is natural to overestimate the American capacity to act by itself in international crises. The efforts of France and Germany to create a binational military corps, about which the U.S. was not sanguine, indicated that rivalries and important disagreements with Europe over security issues will certainly arise in the future.[80] America's foreign policy leaders will need to practice their art with greater subtlety: this is especially true in matters that they present to the U.N. Security Council where U.S. proposals must be accepted by the four other permanent members and at least four nonpermanent members. The disappearance of Cold War hostility and Soviet vetoes in the Security Council has thrust that body into a more prominent position in the conduct of foreign affairs. This pattern was reinforced by President Bush's heavy reliance on the U.N. during the Gulf War and the Yugoslav crisis. Consequently, America's newly emerging obligation to persuade its Security Council counterparts to "bless" U.S. action is becoming a powerful constraint on American foreign policy.

"Lessons" from the Persian Gulf War will certainly shape American military doctrines and decisions concerning when and how to use force. This is especially true because the Gulf War was conducted in Vietnam's shadow. The All-or-Nothing lessons from Vietnam were of the utmost importance in shaping the nature of the American response to Iraq's conquest of Kuwait. On the other hand, there were other American preferences that limited U.S. political objectives. They included the desire to prevent the dissolution of Iraq into its constituent parts, the desire to preserve Iraq as a functioning political counterweight to Syria and Iran, and the need to fight a coalition war with demanding Arab and European allies. The Bush Administration desired the removal of Saddam Hussein from power but did not want to extend the U.N. war aims to obtain that goal. It was hoped that the pressures brought to bear on Iraq would prompt domestic forces in that country to remove the Iraqi dictator. Thus, the Gulf War can be characterized as one in which a mixture of ambitious political objectives (removal of Hussein) and ambitious military goals (the incapacitation of the Iraqi armed forces and their expulsion from Kuwait) were combined with geographical limitations on the use of ground forces. The war exhibited classic problems of limited wars in that political objectives like the removal of Saddam Hussein conflicted with the preservation of Iraq as a regional power. In a total war like World War II, in which the unconditional surrender of the enemy is desired, such problems do not arise—total victory covers a multitude of problems. In important ways the Gulf War was a limited war, but it also had elements of total war in that the complete military defeat of the enemy was expected; this was the legacy of Korea, Vietnam, and Beirut. In that sense it comported with the Never Again desire to decisively defeat the opponent in the field of battle. Unfortunately, when one does not intend to occupy the opponent's land, eliminate his government, and rule his people even complete military defeat of the enemy state may not bring about the defeat of the nation in arms—or lead to the expulsion of its leadership.

The Invasion of Panama: Operation Just Cause

Before we examine the war with Iraq, let us reconsider the Bush Administration's all-but-forgotten military action against Panama. On December 20, 1989, the United States launched Operation Just Cause, directed at the government of the Central American nation of Panama. This action was taken in response to increasingly strained relations with that country.[81] The American campaign led to the capture of Panama's dictator, General Manuel Antonio Noriega, who was then extradited to Miami on January 3, 1990, after his surrender to the Papal nuncio in Panama City.[82] Before Noriega was captured and taken to the United

States, a new Panamanian government headed by Guillermo Endara was put in place. Endara was sworn in as president one hour before the beginning of Operation Just Cause. The Panama invasion is significant because it exemplifies the assimilation of the post-Vietnam, All-or-Nothing approach into U.S. policy. President Bush, more willing to use force on a large scale than was President Reagan, employed massive and overwhelming levels of force in Panama. This action was designed to proceed with the greatest of speed toward the goal of decisive victory, and it did so.

Throughout the summer and fall of 1989 plans for an invasion of Panama were being prepared by the U.S. Southern Command located in Panama City. The task of drawing up these plans fell to General Frederick Woerner and then to his replacement, General Max Thurman, who assumed control of Southern Command on the 30th of September. General Woerner opposed a military move against Panama and was replaced with a commander who favored the Bush Administration's position.[83] Both Woerner's and Thurman's plans were predicated on using overpowering force to defeat the Panamanians, as Kevin Buckley explains:

> Thurman's plan was strategically the same as Woerner's, but there were a number of tactical differences. Thurman's plan was almost entirely military in nature, unlike Woerner's. Woerner's scenario called for extraordinary controls on U.S. firepower, especially in the densely packed wooden tenement neighborhood called El Chorillo that surrounded the Comandancia. Woerner was concerned about civilian casualties, and he devoted as much if not more effort to planning the aftermath as he did to planning the attack. He foresaw, for example, the potential for looting once the PDF, the only authority in Panama, had collapsed and included in his plan measures to prevent such disorder. Woerner also wanted to implement a quick and effective assumption of power by Endara, Ford, and Arias Calderon. In short, Woerner designed his attack plan to bring about the political aims of the administration, as he saw them. Thurman's plan diminished most if not all of the "civic action" and politically oriented elements in Woerner's plan.[84]

Buckley is clearly predisposed to Woerner's positions and minimizes the military differences between their two plans, but that does not alter the fact that "word spread throughout the Pentagon that a large-scale operation with virtually no chance of failure was being planned."[85] Eventually, an invasion force of 22,500 was placed under the direct command of Lieutenant- General Carl W. Stiner who commanded the 18th Airborne Corps in Fort Bragg, North Carolina.[86] Much of the invasion took place from American bases inside the Canal Zone.

The *Washington Post* reported that the "year-old military plan inherited by Thurman and [JCS Chairman Colin] Powell called for a much slower-paced assault against Panamanian targets over a period of days or weeks."[87] Thurman was credited with having drawn up more militarily decisive plans: " 'The old plan wasn't serious,' said a U.S. official familiar with the proposal. 'This plan was serious. It was a massive operation—getting all the Military Airlift Command resources in from all over the world.' "[88] According to *Newsweek* magazine: "Thurman lobbied Washington for an all-out assault." One government official was quoted as saying: "Thurman felt quite rightly that if you're going to go in, the safest way both to end the violence quickly and to protect the Americans down there would be to do it with massive force."[89] The impact of this style of warfare was not lost on the Panamanian military. Major Ivan Gaytan, a Panamanian military planner, admitted, "The whole infrastructure of our force was destroyed in the first hour."[90]

Operation Just Cause overwhelmed the enemy, thus serving to reinforce the "lesson" of Vietnam that force should be used decisively and massively. If these sources are accurate, even General Woerner's plan would have overwhelmed Panama rather quickly, but not with the speed of Just Cause. The Panama operation has not been the subject of a great deal of military attention because the Gulf War, which was such an enormous endeavor, has obscured our memories of the earlier operation. It will probably be seen as the inadvertent tune-up for the massive war in the Persian Gulf. Nevertheless, an article by Lieutenant-Colonel William C. Bennett (U.S. Army) usefully places Panama in the context of the postwar debate about the use of force.[91]

Bennett explicitly uses the methodology of Harry Summers' *On Strategy: The Vietnam War in Context* to analyze the success and failures of the Panama invasion. He assesses Operation Just Cause from the perspective of whether the various principles of war were satisfied in the planning and execution of the operation. Like Summers he erroneously attributes this Jominian concept (i.e., principle of war) to Clausewitz, but the larger point remains that "the author finds that the principles . . . still apply to current U.S. doctrine." Bennett notes that one of the errors in Vietnam was our failure to make use of the principles of war. That error has been corrected in the current FM 100–5, Army field manual on Operations, but, he argues, a post mortem needs to be done to learn from past mistakes. While the specifics of the article are not significant for our purposes, its mere existence tells us a great deal. The power of Vietnam as an example and writings like Summers's *On War* laid the conceptual ground work for the military campaign that was waged in Panama and would be conducted against Saddam Hussein in Iraq and Kuwait.

The Gulf War: Operation Desert Storm

The concept that force should always be applied decisively, the pre-eminent military lesson from the Vietnam War, had not yet been tested in a major conflict until Iraq was crushed by American and allied military power. The Persian Gulf War would prove to any still doubting that a new conception of using force held sway in American foreign policy. President Bush, Secretary of Defense Dick Cheney, Chairman of the Joint Chiefs of Staff Colin Powell, or General H. Norman Schwarzkopf were quoted to this effect on numerous occasions after the Iraqi invasion of Kuwait on 2 August 1990.[92]

Bob Woodward of the *Washington Post* supports this observation with this description of actions by Cheney:

> By now Cheney had come to realize what an impact the Vietnam War had on Bush. The President had internalized the lessons—send enough force to do the job and don't tie the hands of the commanders. In a September 12 speech in California, Cheney had said, "The President belongs to what I call the 'Don't screw around' school of military strategy."[93]

Woodward also describes how Cheney reassured Schwarzkopf that his forces would not be left hanging with a war to fight and no political support from the administration: "The administration was committed. The military commanders would not have their hands tied. The President, Cheney and Powell had to sign off on the plan, but once it was approved, it would for the most part be in Schwarzkopf's hands."[94]

It is worth noting how the distinguished military historian, John Keegan, analyzed the intellectual motivation of the two foremost strategists in this war:

Vietnam haunted everything that Powell and Schwarzkopf did. At root
of the United States' ordeal in Southeast Asia lay the policy of "incrementalism"—no more troops were sent at any one time than the situation seemed to warrant, reinforcement was authorized only under
pressure of crisis, and strategy was determined only in response to
events. . . .

For Powell and Schwarzkopf, the policy of incrementalism was
almost as much the enemy as Saddam. From the outset they insisted on
taking whole units to the Gulf and keeping them there, intact, until battle was joined. . . . They also insisted on having the resources their judgment told them a strategy of victory demanded. . . . Powell and
Schwarzkopf fought for victory and the extinction of the slur of Vietnam—a cause to them as important as the military reputation of the
United States itself.[95]

The decline of the Limited War position had continued without
abatement during the Bush Administration. Bush, Cheney, and Powell each expressed the desire to get past Vietnam. None of them
expressed any sympathy for the "McNamara model" that one author
describes as entailing "the forfeiture of the traditional objective of victory in armed combat, and the substitution of increments of pain-
infliction for direct political bargaining without disarming the
enemy."[96]

Over Thanksgiving, Bush made a trip to Saudi Arabia, during which
he ate a meal with some marines. As he was seated on the hood of a military vehicle he made the following remark: "I'll guarantee you there
ain't going to be any other Vietnams. People at home say, 'We don't
want any more Vietnams.' That's right. There won't be any. Anybody's
asked to fight—they're going to fight to win."[97]

Shortly thereafter the President addressed the issue again at a press
conference. Again he made a pointed reference to Vietnam and the
lessons it held for the war he might have to lead:

> In our country, I know that there are fears about another Vietnam. Let
> me assure you: should military action be required, this will not be anoth-
> er Vietnam; this will not be a protracted, drawn-out war. The forces
> arrayed are different, the opposition is different, the resupply of Sad-
> dam's military would be very different, the countries united against him
> in the United Nations are different, the topography of Kuwait is differ-
> ent and the motivation of our all-volunteer force is superb.

I want peace. I want peace, not war. But if there must be war, we will not permit our troops to have their hands tied behind their backs, and I pledge to you there will not be any murky ending. If one American soldier has to go to battle, that soldier will have enough force behind him to win, and then get out as soon as the U.N. objectives have been achieved.

I will never, ever agree to a halfway effort.[98]

Secretary of Defense Richard Cheney expressed similar sentiments to those of the President. In an interview on *Face the Nation* he told his questioners: "We do not believe in gradual escalation. We don't believe in sending in insufficient force. It seems to me we've got an obligation to make certain that there's no question about what the outcome would be should hostilities result."[99]

Given that these were the top civilians in the administration talking one wonders how tough the generals must have been. Eleanor Clift and Thomas DeFrank noted that Colin Powell thought that the sort of signalling which was central to the crisis management element in the Limited War approach to warfighting was actually inherently dangerous, that is, not conducive to safety:

In the hot regional conflicts of the post-cold-war world, a symbolic show of strength is more apt to be seen as a sign of weakness. In a recent off-the-record seminar with fellow officers, Powell summed up his approach. "If you finally have to commit military force, you've got to be as massive and decisive as possible. Decide your target, decide your objective and try to overwhelm it."[100]

Rudy Abramson and John Broder tied the JCS Chairman's ideas about the use of force to Vietnam: "Powell and many of his colleagues had come away from Vietnam convinced that a clear statement of mission is a prerequisite to any military action, that military power should not be applied incrementally, that firm public support is essential and that political authorities should not meddle in purely military decisions."[101] And, one should not forget General Powell's famous remark at a Pentagon briefing on January 23, 1991, after the bombing campaign had begun, concerning allied plans for defeating the Iraqi Army: "Our strategy to go after this army is very, very simple. First, we're going to cut it off, and then we're going to kill it."[102]

According to Woodward, General Norman Schwarzkopf, the head of Central Command, reiterated to Colin Powell in Saudi Arabia on

October 22, 1990, if the President wanted an offensive it would be necessary to send considerably more forces to Saudi Arabia.[103] This message was not new: Schwarzkopf sent a team to Washington to brief the
President on his plans for conducting the ground war. The meeting
with Bush took place on October 11, 1990, in Washington.
Schwarzkopf's chief of staff, Major-General Robert B. Johnston,
briefed President Bush on the prospects for an offensive operation at
that time. When the impatient request for a briefing was made of Central Command, Schwarzkopf is reported to have been furious because
"he had been as explicit as he could have been in spelling out the differences between the defense of Saudi Arabia and an offensive plan that
would push Saddam Hussein out of Kuwait."[104] Schwarzkopf had too
much to do, so he had Johnston fly west and brief the President and the
military leadership on an offensive plan based on the defensive force
that the President had authorized. This first-cut offered conventional
military thinking in the form of a direct assault on Kuwait with tremendous reliance on air power. But Schwarzkopf refused to offer a pie in the
sky briefing given the resources at his command. Johnston's briefing
was not well received at the Pentagon on October 10 or at the White
House the next day.[105] During the White House briefing former air
force general and current national security adviser, Brent Scowcroft,
was highly critical of these first impressions of a military attack. Scowcroft questioned the proposition that expelling Saddam from Kuwait
could be done with anything but ground forces; air power would not
suffice.[106] He was also curious why anyone would want to fight "force
on force"—i.e., a direct attack on the Iraqis in Kuwait. In response to
these challenges Johnston made it clear that a true offensive capacity
would require the transfer of VII Corps from Europe, which would
take several months.[107] This additional force, as Schwarzkopf noted in
his memoirs, was needed to "guarantee [a] successful outcome."[108]

The General goes on to note that dissatisfaction with his call for
greater troops prompted some in the White House to criticize him for
passivity. By mid-October it was clear what plan should be put in place:
"The textbook way to defeat [the Iraqi] force would have been to hold
it in place with frontal attack while sending an even bigger army to out-
flank it, envelop it, and crush it against the sea" (p. 362). This plan
would "require the largest maneuver of armor in the desert in U.S. military history—but it seemed the way to end a ground war decisively and

fast (p. 362)." Therefore, when Colin Powell met with Schwarzkopf in Saudi Arabia on October 22 he was given a hard sell for a western envelopment of the Iraqi Army. Schwarzkopf challenged the White House's predisposition for a direct invasion of Kuwait. He observed that Iraq was pouring troops into Kuwait thereby making an allied attack in that area vulnerable to stiff enemy opposition:

> "If we have to go on the offensive, I need more forces."
>
> "I'm not sure we can bring more troops without a clear mandate from Congress and the American public," he [Powell] countered. I nodded. Nobody wanted another Vietnam, and I understood Powell's determination to avoid political as well as military mistakes. Unless we were confident of public support, it would be better not to launch an offensive at all.
>
> In the course of that conversation, [Powell] made up his mind. "If we go to war," he promised, "we will not do it halfway. The United States military will give you whatever you need to do it right." (p. 367)

President Bush decided on October 30, 1990, "first, to set in motion the machinery for a mid-winter war against the Iraqi Army and, second, to win a United Nations mandate for that war."[109] In fact, with respect to abandoning the allies' defensive posture, Freedman and Karsh write: "On 30 October Bush met with Baker, Cheney, Quayle, Sununu, Scowcroft, and Powell to decide on whether to switch to the offensive option. For the first time he was briefed on the concept of holding Saddam's forces with an initial attack while they were being cut off by a flanking attack to the west. To achieve this, the planned forces need to be doubled."[110]

On November 14, 1990, Schwarzkopf revealed how Vietnam and its limitations on the use of force affected his thoughts on fighting Iraq. At a meeting of senior commanders he described his priorities for fighting the war: (1) to disable the Iraqi Army's command and control capabilities; (2) to gain and maintain air superiority; (3) to cut enemy lines of supply and destroy Saddam's chemical, biological, and nuclear capabilities; (4) "to destroy—not attack, not damage, not surround—I want you to *destroy* the Republican Guard. When you're done with them, I don't want them to be an effective fighting force anymore. I don't want them to exist as a military organization."[111] He directed certain remarks to those who had fought in Vietnam: "I emphasized that 'we're not going into this with one arm tied behind our backs. We're not gonna say we want to be as nice as we possibly can, and if they draw back across the border that's fine with us. That's bullshit. We are going to destroy the Republican Guard.' If we were ordered to go on the offensive, we would be free to use our full military strength and attack across the border into Iraq."[112]

Powell told the President that he did not "do marginal economic analysis looking for crossover points. I go in with enough to make sure . . . we're not operating at the margin." Powell wanted to "win decisively" as did Cheney. Cheney "wanted to get the build-up over with and not return regularly with requests for extra forces."[113] On October 31, 1990, Powell called Schwarzkopf informing him the President had approved his requests: in fact, Powell wanted more capacity for attack, so he also moved the Army's "Big Red One" 1st Infantry Division (Mechanized), based in Fort Riley, Kansas, to Saudi Arabia. Powell told Schwarzkopf that more air, naval, and marine forces should be brought to the Gulf.[114] Schwarzkopf did not disagree.

While these arguments for the decisive use of force have great validity, the Schwarzkopf-Powell recollection of history ignores the problem that political decisionmakers faced in Korea and Vietnam: namely, avoiding escalation to higher levels of military violence. Recently, William E. Simons has noted that those concerns were quite real for the Johnson Administration. Perhaps their perception of the threat from China was exaggerated, but it was not unreasonable. Simons writes the "Johnson administration was acutely concerned over a Chinese military reaction in the event of direct U.S. intervention in the Vietnam War." The administration considered North Vietnam to be its primary opponent, but it regarded the "PRC's role in the crisis as significant and potentially dominant."[115] Consequently, President Johnson "was being advised [in February 1965] to avoid a public posture that would tend to demand some reciprocal action on the part of the Chinese or Communists."[116] What the All-or-Nothing proponents did notice was the possibility of a prolonged campaign of coercive diplomacy sliding into limited war.

Congressional elections were held on November 6, 1990, and the result was a House and Senate similar in political makeup to the previous Congress. The President told the nation of his plans to build a force capable of substantial offensive operations against Iraq on November 8 at a White House news conference: "After consultation with King Fahd and our other allies, I have today directed the Secretary of Defense to increase the size of U.S. forces committed to Desert Shield to insure that the coalition has an adequate offensive military option should that be necessary to achieve our common goals."[117] Interestingly, this decision was reported primarily as being a key element of a campaign of coercive diplomacy.[118] If the pressure did not dislodge Saddam then the force would be used to defeat Iraq's army. News accounts were fully aware that the anti-Iraqi coalition in the Gulf would include at least 380,000 Americans by the early part of 1991.[119] VII Corps was moved from Europe, and the United Nations Security Council provided international support for military action against Iraq. This occurred most notably on November 29, 1990, when the Council passed Resolution 678 (1990) authorizing those member states cooperating with the legitimate government of Kuwait to use "all necessary means to uphold and implement resolution 660 (1990) and all subsequent resolutions and to restore international peace and security in the area."[120]

Consistent with Schwarzkopf's references to Vietnam made at the 14 November staff meeting were his observations made shortly after the passage of U.N. Security Council Resolution 678: "I think we have vastly superior fire power and technology, . . . and I can assure you that if we have to go to war, I am going to use every single thing that is available to me to bring as much destruction to the Iraqi forces as rapidly as I possibly can in the hopes of winning victory as quickly as possible."[121] Patrick E. Tyler of the *New York Times* analyzed the impact of Schwarzkopf's remarks in this way: "In recent weeks, General Schwarzkopf's statement has rippled through the United States military establishment as the quintessential expression of post-Vietnam military doctrine, one that implies taking enough forces to the battle to assure an overwhelming victory at the least cost—and one that implies a clear-cut military objective and political backing at home."[122] The story also contained this observation succinctly in a box: "No jungle, no sanctuary, no Ho Chi Minh Trail." Eric Schmitt, another reporter for the *Times* correctly noted the connection to another military disaster: the U.S. involvement in Lebanon from 1982 until 1984.[123] This theme was also expanded upon by Thomas Friedman of the *New York Times* who compared the U.S. involvement in the Gulf to Israel's invasion of Lebanon: "The Israelis invaded Lebanon to drive out the P.L.O., but they eventually concluded that this could [only] be done by going all the way to Beirut and decapitating the organization. Stopping short of that would simply have involved them in an endless war of attrition."[124]

The lessons of war-fighting from Vietnam were also evident in the slowness with which the Bush Administration responded to the plight of the Kurdish refugees after the rebellion against Saddam Hussein had been crushed. The fear of entering a "quagmire" kept the Administration disabled until the President became convinced that the humanitarian crisis facing the Kurds would have to be addressed.[125] Before he could assist the Kurds President Bush and his advisers had to overcome the constraints of the conceptual framework they had developed about the proper conduct of war—one that worked well until the tanks stopped before Baghdad. Edward Mortimer of the *Financial Times* captured the power of these ideas when he observed America's reluctance to assist the Kurds: "The real problem is not legal but political: that very 'Vietnam syndrome' which Mr. Bush claims to have conquered, but which evidently continues to haunt him. He does not want 'a police role in downtown Baghdad.' "[126] Anyone watching American television news should have been struck by the rapidity with which the word "quagmire" began to be used with respect to Kurdistan. "Quagmire" is a word forever linked to Vietnam, and its instantaneous linkage to the Kurds by the news media and members of the administration signalled how close the jungles of Indochina were to the hearts and minds in the West Wing of the White House.

One would be well advised to note the important differences between Vietnam and the Gulf War that permitted an All-or-Nothing application of force during the war. (1) Policymakers had no fear of military escalation by the opponent that would risk a wider, bloodier conflict. (2) The Gulf War was a purely conventional war, not one in which there was a substantial guerrilla component. (3) The Middle East is a desert, and Vietnam was a jungle in many areas. (4) The geopolitical context was favorable to the United States (i.e., the Soviet Union was disengaged and China had no great stake in the outcome). (5) Iraq's aggression was unambiguous whereas North Vietnam was able to cast its actions in the context of a "civil war." (6) President Bush and Secretary of State Baker were able to muster critical domestic and international support.[127]

The war itself was conducted pretty much as planned until the last hours of the ground offensive when it appears that American forces stopped too soon before trapping many of Saddam's forces near Basra. The air campaign was a devastating contrast with Rolling Thunder of the Vietnam era. As one observer wrote, "Saddam Hussein would do well to read President Bush's lips: No more Vietnams."[128]

The ground war began at 4 a.m. on February 24, 1991, and ended with a self-imposed cease-fire at 8 a.m., February 28, 1991, (both Riyadh times). During the course of the air and ground war between 70 and 115,000 Iraqi military were killed, 85% of Iraqi tanks were destroyed, 50% of Iraq's armored personnel carriers were eliminated, and 90% of its artillery was eliminated.[129] American casualties were as follows: 146 killed in action (244 allied troops K.I.A.), 159 troops dead outside combat. In summing up the results of the Gulf War Lawrence Freedman and Efraim Karsh, both members of the Department of War Studies, King's College, London, commented that "the most important feature of the Gulf War in military terms was its decisive, overwhelming character."[130] Freedman and Karsh also note the example of the Vietnam War "had an impact on coalition strategy in both the setting of objectives and the choice of strategy designed to achieve those objectives."[131]

Lieutenant-Colonel Thomas R. DuBois of the U.S. Air Force supported this assessment in an article that analyzed the Gulf War in terms of its consistency with the Weinberger Doctrine: "Unlike our involvement in Vietnam, this time there would be no doubt in the minds of our troops, politicians, media, populace, or enemy that should hostilities erupt, US armed forces were there to secure military victory."[132] "The war plan developed to support this force," DuBois observed, "had as its objective, swift, decisive, and unequivocal destruction of the enemy with minimum allied casualties. Absent were convoluted rules of engagement, safety zones, and ever-changing political restrictions placed upon warfighters."[133]

It may be that the "botched" ending of the war will lend even greater support to the All-or-Nothing approach to the use of force. This may arise from a feeling in the Pentagon that Desert Storm was "a case of unfinished business" that permitted Saddam to keep his grip on power.[134] Even though Saddam Hussein is still in power, it would not have been possible to dismantle his frightening atomic bomb building organization had the war not been fought.[135] Nevertheless, this decisive victory in the Gulf has supported the All-or-Nothing conception of using force. The Limited War concept retains little support in Washington. Quick, but limited, military strikes by air power are accepted, but the use of ground forces with operational restrictions will not be. With that in mind, reprisals for terrorist strikes, etc., are acceptable. Consequently, Secretary Shultz's position in favor of using forceful diplomacy can be tolerated as long as the possibility of protracted entanglements in messy conflicts is kept to a minimum. Once real war has begun the United States will seek decisive victory in the attainment of clearly defined political and military objectives.

Bush and Bosnia: The Pattern Continues

The Sarajevo Crisis of 1992 provides further insight into the various perspectives within the Bush Administration on using force.[139] In the spring of 1992 after Bosnia's declaration of independence, Serbian nationalist forces surrounded Sarajevo and enforced a blockade by closing its airport. Meanwhile, Sarajevo was being shelled heavily by the Serbs, and there was heavy loss of life and growing malnutrition. Finally, a commercial blockade of Serbia was imposed by the U.N. Security Council (Resolution 757 of May 30, 1992,). Peacekeeping forces were "authorized to reopen the airport in Sarajevo for delivery of aid to Bosnia and Herzegovina" by Security Council Resolution 761 passed on 29 June 1992"[137] On October 9, 1992, in Resolution 781 the Security Council banned military flights, except those by U.N. approved forces, over Bosnia. The Bush Administration was adamant about receiving U.N. authorization for any actions it would take in relieving the Sarajevo airport. This reinforced the somewhat exalted position the U.S. had given the United Nations as it sought legitimacy for the Persian Gulf War. As a crisis in Yugoslavia loomed, the U.S. was constrained not only by its self-inflicted deference to the evolving norm of seeking United Nations approval for the use of force, but also by the Never Again mentality that permeated the Bush Administration. Barton Gellman of the *Washington Post* made the following observation with regard to Bush's Balkan policy: "The road the Bush administration has traveled in the past three weeks from nonengagement to military commitment in the Balkans has left some senior military leaders with deep misgivings about the compromises made along the way."[138]

The United States had become more deeply committed to the situation in Bosnia-Herzegovina by agreeing to ferry supplies into the Sarajevo airport. On June 30, 1992, Secretary of Defense Cheney said that "U.S. forces would be limited to naval and air power and would take part in armed escort operations only if the current ceasefire breaks down. He added that the United States would get involved only 'under United Nations auspices' and with explicit authority from the U.N. Security Council."[139] The Bush Administration, however, was always skeptical of limited uses of military power, and Bosnia was particularly troubling. On May 9, 1993, Brent Scowcroft outlined the Joint Chiefs' objections to involvement in the Balkans: "if you're going to use military force, you need to be precise about what your objectives are, you need to understand that military force can accomplish those objectives at an acceptable cost; and after its done, you can get the force back out."[140] Scowcroft concurred with the Chiefs' reservations on Bosnia "because they were unable to answer those questions about the use of military force that were answered especially in the case of the Persian Gulf."[141]

According to Barton Gellman of the *Washington Post* many senior military officials believe this mission "is an attempt to strike a balance among political, diplomatic, humanitarian and military exigencies." These advisers feared that the political crisis might swallow up the self-imposed constraints if the cease-fire fell apart. The goal of American policy was unclear at that time: "Should force become necessary, senior defense policy officials and two-, three-, and four-star officers suggested in interviews this week that even those who would have responsibility for planning or executing the operation do not know exactly what they may be asked to do or which allies they could count on for a coalition."[142]

Discomfort with the Bush policy was noticed from other sources. Martin Sieff of the *Washington Times* reported that the "new U.S. policy of limited military engagement in the Yugoslav conflict marks an uneasy compromise between the views of champions of the 'new world order' and military leaders concerned about avoiding the mistakes of Lebanon."[143] Later in the article, Sieff provided more details of the inter-administration debate: "Mr. Cheney and Gen. Powell were concerned that deployment of U.S. troops on the ground in Yugoslavia would lead to heavy casualties, just as the commitment of U.S. Marines to an ambiguous peacekeeping role in Beirut in 1982 led to the deaths of 241 of them in a suicide truck-bomb attack."[144]

Secretary of State Baker also appears to have been affected by thoughts of Vietnam and Beirut. Baker's press conference of July 1, 1992, intended to describe an approaching presidential trip to Europe revealed this. He was asked whether involvement in Bosnia would set precedents for involvement in "many other areas like Moldova and other parts of the Soviet Union?" Baker did not really answer the question—probably because it was too broad, but he noted his concerns about Sarajevo with this awkward reply:

> "You've heard us say before that there is a quagmire potential here; that we cannot be the world's policeman. But you've also heard us say that we should not just sit back and not participate when the kind of humanitarian nightmare that we see going on there is continuing."[145]

Of course, "quagmire" says a great deal here as it did during the Kurdish crisis of 1991. It immediately brings to mind the calamity of Vietnam and warfare that is impossible to end. In an interview on August 4, 1992, President Bush expressed his worries about Yugoslavia in terms that are by now familiar: "Before I'd commit American forces to a battle, I want to know what's the beginning, what's the objective, how's the objective going to be achieved and what's the end."[146] The President noted that he was old enough to remember that ending a war is not a trivial matter as was the case in Vietnam and the Second World War. Bush made these remarks as a rejoinder to Democrat presidential candidate Governor Bill Clinton's urging of the U.N. Security Council on August 5, 1992, to state its willingness to use force in Bosnia. Three days later, the President referred to Vietnam in discussing the Bosnian crisis and stated, "I do not want to see the United States bogged down in any way into some guerrilla warfare. We've lived through that once already."[147] President Bush also suggested that military involvement of this kind would be a great misuse of the military both morally and as an effective policy instrument.

In 1989 Bernard Trainor, a former Marine Corps lieutenant general and military correspondent for the *New York Times* had observed that Colin Powell was Caspar Weinberger's military assistant in 1984 when the Secretary of Defense presented what came to be known as the "Weinberger Doctrine."[148] Trainor noted that Powell and other members of the JCS "were relatively junior officers in the Vietnam War, and share bitter memories that have influenced their thinking. They saw a highly capable American army unaccustomed to defeat, become corrupted by drugs, poor discipline and racial strife in a protracted war that seemed to have lost its purpose."[149] The military leadership supported force during the Reagan Administration when "the mission was clearly defined, judged an acceptable risk and could be achieved in a reasonable time"—that is, when the decisive attainment of well-defined objectives was desired by the civilian leadership. The Chiefs did not support the 1982 Lebanon mission, nor did they support plans for direct involvement in Nicaragua.[150] In an October 1992 op-ed article Powell stated "President Bush, more than any other recent President, understands the proper use of military force. In every instance, he has made sure that the objective was clear and that we knew what we were getting into."[151] The JCS Chairman went on to say that "decisive means and results are always to be preferred."

Similar points to Trainor's were made by Michael Gordon of the *New York Times* during the Bosnian crisis in August 1992. Gordon noted that the U.S. government seemed to be greatly affected by the memory of past failures in the use of limited force. He first pointed out that prominent figures like Margaret Thatcher and Bill Clinton had recently suggested "that there may be options the West could exercise that would help dampen the conflict, or at least help the Bosnians defend themselves if the fighting continues, while avoiding the long-term involvement that is feared by the Administration and the Pentagon in particular."[152] Military options in a limited campaign of this type might include "punitive air strikes, raids to seize the detention camps and the lifting of the arms embargo so that the poorly equipped Bosnians could better acquit themselves against the well-armed Serbs."[153] Gordon also stated that none of the parties engaged in the debate had called for the introduction of a "huge ground force to pacify the region."[154] He then proceeded to summarize the U.S. military perspective on Yugoslavia:

> From the Pentagon's vantage point, the Balkan war is not an inviting conflict. In Panama and again in the Persian Gulf, the Pentagon demonstrated that its vision of warfare is a short violent conflict in which the United States brings overwhelming force to bear and then quickly withdraws, leaving the local inhabitants to sort things out for themselves.

Anything short of that tends to be seen as a quagmire in which each small step deepens the military's involvement and raises the prospects of defeat.

It is a dichotomy born out of the military's bitter experience in Vietnam and Lebanon. And over the last weeks Pentagon officials have made clear that they see Balkan conflict as a potential Lebanon, where 241 [sic] American servicemen were killed in the truck bombing at the Marine headquarters in 1983. The plans that Western powers are developing for possible military intervention are shaped more by the desire to avoid becoming entangled in the region's blood feuds than to put an end to fighting."

Later Gordon observed that critics of the Bush Administration complain that it "and its Western allies have allowed themselves to become paralyzed by the All-or-Nothing school of military thinking and the possibility that limited measures may not succeed. Limited military objectives, they say, can be precisely defined."[155]

America's use of force will be restrained by precedents that Mr. Bush helped to establish. These include his obtaining U.N. approval for the use of force in the Persian Gulf, his expression of strong Never Again sentiments, and his concerns over domestic public opinion. In a final review of foreign policy before leaving office, President Bush assessed the Yugoslav situation for the assembled cadets at West Point on January 5, 1993. Of the crisis in Bosnia he said, "There are . . . important humanitarian and strategic interests at stake there, but up to now it's not been clear that the application of limited amounts of force by the United States and its traditional friends and allies would have had the desired effect, given the nature and the complexity of that situation."[156] The President then made the following generalization about when the use of force is justified:

> Using military force makes sense as a policy where the stakes warrant, where and when force can be effective, where no other policies are likely to prove effective, where its application can be limited in scope and time, and where the potential benefits justify the potential costs and sacrifice. . . .
>
> But in every case involving the use of force, it will be essential to have a clear and achievable mission, a realistic plan for accomplishing the mission, and criteria no less realistic for withdrawing U.S. forces once the mission is complete.[157]

Thus, while the military officers in the Pentagon may have been more adamant in their advocacy of the All-or-Nothing approach to using force there is no evidence to suggest that President Bush, NSC Adviser Brent Scowcroft, or Secretary Cheney disagreed substantially with that position. In the waning days of his administration, Bush seemed to adopt a position of "tit-for-tat" with respect to Saddam Hussein's violations of the Gulf War ceasefire.[158] This reflected the fact that Bush "simply did not feel that he had a mandate from the American people to engage in a huge attack on Iraq in the last week of his presidency."[159] Any appearance of inconsistency with Bush's approach to using military power should be placed within the proper political-military context. "Tit-for-tat" reprisals would have occurred when Iraq was in the grip of U.N. sanctions, weapons inspections, and a freeze on its overseas assets. In short, Bush had softened his stance toward Saddam very little, if at all.

10 | Conclusion

The rise and fall of America's Limited War School has been the central historical concern of this book. Limited war theory, as first formulated in the 1950s, prudently recognized the devastating potential of the undesired escalation of war. Unfortunately, the Limited War perspective relied on that truth and then neglected the long-understood principles describing the effective use of military power. Our leaders' "theories" of the nature of force, as modified by the "lessons" they have taken from the Korean, Vietnam, and Persian Gulf Wars, have influenced this nation's postwar use of military power. A pattern has emerged indicating that the All-or-Nothing approach to the use of force dominates the thinking of those political leaders who have recently directed American foreign policy. The "lessons" taken from significant historical events like the Korean and Vietnam Wars have become involved in a complex learning process in which individuals have altered their inclination toward the All-or-Nothing or Limited War perspective depending upon their interpretations of events. Both the All-or-Nothing and Limited War philosophies contain such significant elements of truth that each is often put forward, without the other, as a complete analysis of the relationship of political goals to the use of force. Such analyses thereby offer an incomplete understanding of this tension that forms part of the essential nature of war itself. This book has used Clausewitz's analysis as a first step in understanding this great debate over the use of force. The powerful tendency of war to reach for higher levels of violence, what I have called the "logic of force," is an enduring conceptual reality. It will not be subordinated to realist considerations of the structure of international power or to the organizational interests decisionmakers may have. The logic of force is not nearly as easily subordinated to policy objectives in limited war as Clausewitz's rationalist framework would lead us to believe. We must also remember that the logic of policy, the war's objective, is to subordinate all means including force to its own purposes whatever the means may require for their effective use.

The Alternative Explanations Considered

In chapter 1 a number of orthodox arguments were offered to explain the Never Again-Limited War tension. None are sufficient to explain the policy preferences and policy choices described above. Modern balance of power theory (or structural realism) was discussed first. Structural realism predicted that nuclear parity between the two superpowers would compel their competition in arenas of lesser violence. In a bipolar (or multipolar) nuclear world one would expect to see the dominance of the Limited War philosophy, which argues force must be brought under the tight reign of political considerations, even if that requires constraining the military destructiveness of one's armed forces. The All-or-Nothing philosophy of force no longer remained plausible in its absolute forms with the advent of atomic weapons and the enhanced destructiveness of modern conventional arsenals. For these reasons, the strict control of military activity by policy goals could not be avoided. To a considerable degree, the structural realist predictions were accurate, and they provide a useful starting place for considering the policy preferences of decisionmakers since the Korean War. However, structural theory fails to account for the persistence and the significant influence of the All-or-Nothing position. Nor does realist theory predict that this perspective would, on occasion, be able to prevent or shape the limited use of force when American interests have called for limited military intervention.

In addition, the bureaucratic politics model must be considered. As was true of structural realist theory, it can also be said that bureaucratic politics when interpreted as "where you sit determines where you stand" has some predictive power. One could assert, generally, that military figures tend to sympathize with the Never Again position and political figures subscribe to the Limited War philosophy. Upon closer examination this proposition does express a general tendency, but there have been major counter-examples to this pattern since the Korean War. For example, Generals Omar Bradley and J. Lawton Collins (who was the Army Chief of Staff in 1950–51) supported the limitations put in place during the Korean War—as did former Army Chief of Staff George Marshall. Also, one of the more prominent advocates of the Limited War concept was General Maxwell Taylor, the man who coined the term "flexible response."

On the civilian side there has also been a great mix of attitudes about the proper way to use force. Consider the tremendous differences that existed between Truman, Eisenhower, and Kennedy. Truman and Kennedy were amenable to placing limitations on the use of force if need be. Eisenhower, on the other hand, revealed in Korea, at Dienbienphu, and in the Jominian elements of his defense strategy, his deep misgivings about any nondecisive use of military power. Eisenhower had a keen awareness of the relationship of ends to means and possessed a soldier's direct awareness of that which is required to fight efficiently and defeat one's opponent. Eisenhower's conflicted statements about the need for fiscal restraint, and his recognition of the horrors of war when juxtaposed with his statements about the need to use force decisively, reflect the tension between the ends and means of war. Whether learned from the writings of Clausewitz directly or gathered intuitively from his experiences, Eisenhower had a nuanced appreciation of the use of force that mirrors the tension between the "political" and "military" elements of war. But, Eisenhower leaned toward the All-or-Nothing side in his analysis.

By and large, officials in the Reagan Administration were much more sympathetic to the All-or-Nothing perspective than members of preceding administrations had been. President Reagan never addressed the issue in a sustained manner as did Secretaries Shultz and Weinberger. However, we do know that a recurring theme in Ronald Reagan's campaigns for the Presidency was his condemnation of military involvements in which American soldiers would not be permitted to "win." Reagan expressed this belief with great eloquence before the Vietnam Memorial on Veteran's Day in 1988. In a moving speech he told the assembled audience: "Perhaps at this late date we can all agree that we've learned one lesson: that young Americans must never again be sent to die unless we are prepared to win."[1] President Reagan was committed to this maxim. When events turned sour after the Marine stockade in Beirut was destroyed by a car bomb, the American forces were withdrawn. And in the Persian Gulf, while U.S. forces were certainly "in harm's way" when they tried to protect Gulf shipping, they were never exposed to long-term casualties as ground forces would have been. President Reagan's "philosophy of force," if we can invent such a term, resembled Eisenhower's more than any other president's. Reagan, like Eisenhower, was never avid to use force.

George Bush, on the other hand, made use of military power much more freely than Reagan. This is interesting because Reagan was constantly derided, especially in Europe, as a "cowboy" when, in fact, "preppy" George Bush was much more aggressive as Commander-in-Chief. Although both adhered to the tenets of the All-or-Nothing approach to the use of force, Reagan shied away from it while willing to assert U.S. power; Bush was an aggressive internationalist in his willingness to assert American interests. The Clinton Administration appears to hew to a line similar to that espoused by Secretary Shultz. There is a willingness to couple the use of force and the threats of its use to diplomatic efforts, but President Clinton and Secretary of State Christopher are clearly not advocates of a Limited War position. With that being recognized, the Clinton-Aspen position does not seem to entail a willingness to place limits on the use of violence in a mid- or high-intensity conventional war.

Also of relevance in evaluating the bureaucratic politics model is the inconsistency of the opinions expressed by individuals who held the same bureaucratic role. The most striking comparison comes from examining the positions of two Secretaries of Defense: McNamara and Weinberger. McNamara, while representing the more hard-line faction within the Kennedy Administration, conceived of the use of force in a way that horrified Weinberger. Reagan's first Secretary of Defense took the lesson from Vietnam that force must be used with overwhelming power and concentration to undermine the opponent's material and psychological equilibrium. Weinberger was also aware that domestic political factors would come into play in a long struggle of attrition. McNamara, on the other hand, was a figure of his times and as such was willing to use force in a more "political" manner in order to achieve the state's political objectives. A less pronounced dichotomy may be taking shape between Secretaries Cheney and Aspin with Cheney accepting the hard line All-or-Nothing position while Aspin's position resembles that of former Secretary of State Shultz who argued for a greater willingness to use force and threats of its use as part of American diplomacy and its "war" against international terrorism. The variance in these four cases reveals the weakness of the bureaucratic politics model as a predictor of the positions individuals take in bureaucratic roles.

Next, the "national attribute" argument positing the existence of an American tendency to fight wars à l'outrance must be considered. Specific versions of this argument differ: Huntington attributes this kind of behavior to the influence of liberalism; Russell Weigley and John Shy argue that circumstances unique to America's historical development have created a collective sense among the American people that wars should be fought to decisively defeat one's opponent. It is hard to deny this as a general proposition. However, universal arguments of this kind do not explain counter-examples and changes in American policy that reveal little uniformity in the American approach to using force. Therefore, this argument fails for the following reasons. First, chapter 2 gave examples in which the United States used force in ways in which a total, crushing victory over the opponent was not sought (i.e., the Quasi-War with France, the War of 1812, the Mexican-American War).[2] Second, a number of early American leaders infused aspects of realism into their foreign policy approaches. When one considers the foreign policy preferences of George Washington, Alexander Hamilton, John Adams, and John Quincy Adams one concludes that they were sober statesmen well aware that foreign policy's means and ends must be aligned. Their example presents a difficult anomaly for the claims of "national attribute" arguments: Americans clearly need not shun all considerations of realpolitik to be true to their liberal ideals. Third, the period following World War II, in which we see the rise of Limited War thinking and "flexible response," is another anomaly that neither Shy nor Weigley handle well. Shy admits that flexible response "explicitly repudiates what were taken to be traditional American ideas about the All-or-Nothing use of force." He soon thereafter links flexible response to the All-or-Nothing position with the following dubious assertion: "The doctrine of flexible response, while stating that force should be carefully proportioned to the military strength of the threatening force, implies that *all* unfriendly force endangers American security and so deserves forceful confrontation; it explicitly rejects the inherently passive posture of merely threatening to retaliate."[3] Implicit in this is the incorrect notion that "flexible response" abandoned the idea of deterrence. A major component of the argument in support of "flexible response" was the idea that the build-up of conventional forces to counter lower levels of aggression would enhance the American capacity to *credibly* deter hostile actions by an opponent.[4]

In sum, it must be said that the "national attribute" arguments, while claiming too much, do alert us to the propensity of America's use of arms to be guided by an All-or-Nothing philosophy. Clausewitz's theory of a dual nature of war provides a more universal way to think about this. The great problem of keeping the means used in war proportionate to the ends is not solely American: for example, Bismarck had great difficulties with the Prussian military during the wars with Austria and France. The United States has had a unique historical experience in which the major wars that it fought were total wars; learning from them supported a Jominian tradition for the use of force. But, when faced with the need to engage in limited wars in Korea and Vietnam, the United States was able to overcome its "immutable" heritage and wage limited war even in the face of its liberal values and Jominian military traditions.

Finally, the analysis offered by the "cult of the offensive" critics like Jack Snyder incorrectly diagnoses the reason military organizations prefer offensive strategies that seek decisive victory. There are two marked difficulties with the "cult of the offensive" perspective. First, Scott Sagan has noted that states may legitimately use offensive doctrines as part of a strategy to support a weak ally in a balance of power system. Sagan writes, "By focusing on the organizational interests of the professional military, the 'cult of the offensive' theory has overlooked the more fundamental causes of the World War I offensive doctrines: the political objectives and alliance commitments of the great powers."[5] Second, the "cult of the offensive" writings seem to ignore the fact that there are different "levels of war" at which one must operate. They are most commonly listed in increasing scale as the tactical, operational, strategic, and grand strategic. Whereas "tactical" refers to the smallest movements of troops, "operational" often describes military action at the size of a corps, "strategic" refers to the activities in a theater of operations, and the "grand strategic" takes place at the level where the political, military, economic, and psychological elements of warfare meet at the highest level. Clearly, a nation may devise a war policy that is defensive at the strategic level but is offensive at the tactical or operational levels. This point goes to the observation made by Sagan above, the "cult of the offensive" analysis seems focused on the offense/defense balance at the tactical and operational levels of war. A sense of the relationship between the levels appears to be absent.

A recent analysis of the offense-defense relationship that carries forward the subtlety of Clausewitz's thought appeared, quite interestingly, in the U.S. Marine Corps manual *Warfighting, FMFM-1* (March 1989). In contrast with the "cult of the offensive" argument, the marines demonstrate a solid understanding of the relationship between offense and defense in warfighting. The Marine Corps, under the direction of its Commandant General A. M. Gray, drafted a 77-page manual on warfare that adroitly mixes complex Clausewitzian ideas into a document intended for mass circulation to its soldiers.[6] The end of the section on "Offense and Defense" offers this accurate analysis: "We conclude that there exists no clear division between offense and defense. Our theory of war should not attempt to impose one artificially. The offense and defense exist simultaneously as necessary components of each other, the transition from one to the other is fluid and continuous."[7]

An interesting functional difference between these two states of war was set forth. The offense, it was argued, "contributes *striking power*" and "generally has as its aim some positive gain; it is through the offense that we seek to impose some design on the enemy."[8] On the other hand, the defense "contributes *resisting power*, the ability to preserve and protect oneself. Thus, the defense generally has a negative aim, that of resisting the enemy's will."[9] It is by the offensive that one imposes one's will on the enemy. While both parties to a war may begin with offensive plans, soon the weaker party will be forced on to the defensive. Using basic concepts that the "cult of the offensive" literature ignores, the inseparability of offense and defense is described:

> While opposing forms, the offense and defense are not mutually exclusive. In fact, they cannot exist separately. For example, the defense cannot be purely passive resistance. An effective defense must assume an

offensive character, striking at the enemy at the moment of his greatest vulnerability. It is "not a simple shield, but a shield made up of well-directed blows."[10] The truly decisive element of the defense is the counterattack. Thus, the offense is an integral component of the concept of the defense.

Similarly the defense is an essential component of the offense.[11] The offense cannot sustain itself indefinitely. At some times and places, it becomes necessary to halt the offense to replenish, and the defense automatically takes over. Furthermore, the requirement to concentrate forces at the focus of effort for the offense often necessitates assuming the defensive elsewhere. Therefore, out of necessity we must include defensive considerations as part of our concept of the offense.[12]

Clausewitz's idea of the "culminating point" of the attack is then discussed: it is that moment when the energy of the attack can no longer be sustained and one's forces assume the defensive. It is also at this point that an attacking army is most susceptible to a counterattack from the defending force. The manual concludes this section, as stated above, by observing that the offense and defense cannot be wholly separated conceptually.[13]

The offensive is a natural and essential aspect of *any* military's warfighting capabilities. It is perfectly reasonable that military organizations would plan to wage offensive war; otherwise, they would find it extremely difficult to compel an opponent's submission except perhaps through an effective, passive war of attrition. Compulsion possesses an inherent offensive component.[14] Therefore, the "cult of the offensive" writings, while demonstrating how reliance on the attack can be excessive, nevertheless are prejudiced against offensive military action. The All-or-Nothing approach to the use of force did not arise merely out of parochial organizational interests or from the cognitive errors of decisionmakers; rather it reflects a clear recognition of the true nature of war-fighting.

The Argument Revisited

The tension between the political and military elements of war will not disappear with the passage of time. During the last several centuries, states have accumulated a seemingly inexorable amount of administrative, political, technological, and destructive power. This aggrandizement of institutional power has combined with a vast expansion of the scope of the state's regulatory authority to make possible the astounding destructiveness of modern war. Of course, the scientific and technological revolutions of the last 400 years have been, when harnessed by the state's war machine, an integral part of this development.

This aggrandizement of power by the state became most visible during the French Revolution when all aspects of society were mobilized for complete exertion in war against the Republic's enemies.[15] The societal energy that was channeled by the Napoleonic state into the pursuit of total war, caused war to approach that ideal form of absolute exertion recognized by Clausewitz. The American Civil War, the First World War, and the Second World War drove the point home with greater finality. Yet, nothing has made this evolutionary process more apparent than the advent of nuclear weaponry. With that invention it became altogether possible for war of total devastation, with little political purpose, to be waged within the course of a few hours. These factors, which have increased the state's capacity to marshal resources for war thereby adding to its destructiveness, have contributed to the recurring tension between war's military and political elements.

The power of some states to easily annihilate their opponents, lies side by side with their need to limit warfare in order to suit its larger political purposes. One might expect that it would not be a difficult matter for a state to control its conduct of war, but such is not the case. I have argued that force has a logic peculiar to itself that, left unchecked, will direct those using military power to do so efficiently, decisively, and with overwhelming exertion. This logic is the essence of the Jominian "principles of war" which have been at the heart of American Army doctrine for at least a half century. The Clausewitzian dictum that "war is merely the continuation of policy by other means," implying as it does that military activity must be kept subordinate to political objectives, accords more closely with Realist premises than does the "logic of the instrument." That is to say, the inner logic of force is a conceptual phenomenon not deducible from the nature of the international environment. This observation has been supported by the fact that American foreign policy since Korea has seen great objections develop to even the limited use of force—though structural theory seems to require that the Limited War philosophy should predominate in an era of nuclear weapons and expansive state power. At the same time it must be remembered that Clausewitzian dictum (and Realist premises) reflect a "logic of the ends" which powerfully dictates the conceptual subordination of the use of the means to one's political objectives.

Since the Korean War, and particularly after Vietnam, animosity toward the Limited War position has been building. Within the army, willingness to become involved in limited wars probably saw its high water mark when Maxwell Taylor was Chief of Staff of the Army in the late 1950s. Before his tenure a number of high-ranking officers like Omar Bradley and J. Lawton Collins supported the Limited War policy in Korea. Although I have cast doubt on General Ridgway's willingness to engage in genuine limited wars, it seems clear that Maxwell Taylor was a Limited War advocate. With the experience of two bitter limited wars behind it, the army seems to have virtually no high-ranking officers who would today endorse the Limited War position. David Petraeus, an army officer and Princeton Ph.D. in political science, observing the military's reaction to Vietnam writes: "In short, Vietnam reinforced and gave dramatic new impetus to views that many officers already held, rather than generating the development of completely new ones. The military are more cautious than before, rather than newly cautious. The factors which the military have said should be present before force is used are more explicitly stated and detailed, but not completely new."[16] Those views "already held" were the Jominian concepts of war-fighting that had become the heart of the U.S. Army's operational field manual, the FM 100–5.

Petraeus argues that Vietnam profoundly influenced the thinking of current military officers—making them excessively conservative with respect to the use of force. He notes that there are those in the military who "have argued that the lessons of Vietnam are not lessons at all, but rather 'truisms' long honored by prudent military leaders."[17] Petraeus attempts to refute this position by presenting the case that Vietnam was critical to this intellectual development within the military:

> There is one major problem with such contentions, however. During the pre-Vietnam (post-World War II) period, senior military leaders frequently did not honor what Vessey, Meyer, and others have termed truisms regarding the use of force. Such truisms were never widely shared, as deeply institutionalized, or as explicitly applied as they have been since the final days of America's involvement in Vietnam. Even

during the heyday of the post-Korea never again club there was never the
kind of universal conscription to lessons on the use of force as has characterized the period since 1973. The military super-hawks of the 1950s
and 1960s have no counterparts in the contemporary landscape. It is,
moreover, hard to imagine either General Vessey or General Meyer, for
example, acquiescing in military commitments as their 1960s predecessors did. Vietnam made a difference with the military.[18]

He overstates his case slightly, for there were MacArthurs, Clarks, and
Deckers in the 1950s and 1960s. American military thinking before
Korea, particularly army thinking, was more flexible on this point than
it is today.[19] It seems that the operational concepts now guiding mili-
tary thought are strongly linked to those truisms, the "principles of
war," which have had a strong historical presence in the United States
Army. Petraeus is clearly correct in noting the tremendous impact of
Vietnam on the military.

Why should Vietnam have been so critical in shaping perceptions? I
have argued that two conceptually distinct and analytical paths of the
use of force lie in tension with each other and have, on occasion, pulled
American foreign policy in their respective directions over the past thir-
ty-five years. The "lessons" from events like Korea and Vietnam were
bound to affect the credibility of these two "concepts" relative to each
other. For members of the military the Korean and Vietnam experiences have strongly reinforced the idea that the failure to use one's military power decisively and overwhelmingly will inevitably lead to the
ineffective use of military power. Vietnam has had the effect of undermining much of the intellectual foundation of the Limited War position even among civilians. This may change if more people expand on
the lead taken by George Shultz and argue that the United States should
adopt a more politically attuned approach to the use of force once war
has begun; this would go beyond Shultz's narrower argument calling for
a tighter linkage of force and diplomacy. For the present, however, it
seems that military and civilian actors will be strongly influenced by the
principle underlying President Reagan's maxim that "young Americans
must never again be sent to die unless we are willing to win."

Consequently, we should not be surprised to learn, as was pointed
out in the chapters on Korea and Vietnam, that the morale of soldiers
suffers in limited wars in which military objectives are not clear and

force is not decisive. Clausewitz would *not* have been persuaded by such protestations, because war is a political act above all else. For that reason, the soldier's goal must be the political goal. Yet, this affinity between the soldier and the desire to decisively defeat an opponent is more than just "macho" behavior, the promotion of organizational self-interest, the fear of losing domestic political support, or the manifestation of skewed perceptions of reality. Even Clausewitz, the great advocate of policy's primacy, admitted this point. He defended the usefulness of the concept of the "absolute form of war" despite the long list of factors that limit war in practice (e.g., friction, emotion, uncertainty). War is changed by many factors "in which strictly logical reasoning plays no part at all" and "war can be a matter of degree":

> Theory must concede all this; but it has the duty to give priority to the absolute form of war and to make that form a general point of reference, so that he who wants to learn from theory becomes accustomed to keeping that point in view constantly, to measuring all his hopes and fears by it, and to approximating it *when he can* or *when he must.*
>
> A principle that underlies our thoughts and actions will undoubtedly lend them a certain tone and character, though the immediate causes of our action may have different origins, just as the tone a painter gives to his canvas is determined by the color of the underpainting.[20]

For the soldier, the ideal form of war must constantly be kept in mind because he may be forced to reach for it "when he can or when he must." Clausewitz should not be interpreted here as undermining the predominance of the political objective in guiding war policy; rather, he is stressing the omnipresence of the influence of the "absolute form of war" as a conceptual and motivational focal point. In fact it might be said that Clausewitz's dictum on the nature of war is too rationalistic. Recall his analysis of the diverse forms of war; speaking of the unusual nature of a war of limited objectives, he writes: "the less intense the motives, the less will the military element's natural tendency to violence coincide with political directives. As a result, war will be driven further from its natural course, the political object will be more and more at variance with the aim of ideal war, and the conflict will seem increasingly *political* in character."[21]

Here "ideal war" is war in its absolute, logical extension of violence. Clausewitz is saying that in limited wars, the political will gain ascendancy over the military. His argument must rest on the rational frame-work he uses: in limited wars, he seems to be saying, the political objective must dominate because that is the defining characteristic of such conflicts. However, as this book has demonstrated, even being in an age of Limited War yields no respite from the conceptual jugger-naut presented by force's logical tendency to reach for that greater level of violence needed to dominate the enemy. Clausewitz's linkage of Limited War in the style of the eighteenth century to a more rational analysis by its participants neglects the truth that all war contains that logical element which impels combatants to greater levels of often unwanted violence.

Assessing the Limited War School

Since the summer of 1992, with the onset of the Bosnian crisis, the prob-lem surrounding limited wars has become a much discussed subject. Many policy analysts have been dissatisfied with the argument that the U.S. must react as if it were in a total war or it should not respond to Ser-bian aggression. On August 13, 1992, Jim Hoagland of the *Washington Post* argued that Yugoslavia was not like Iraq and that "there would be no quick, decisive military result." He then went on to evaluate America's policy options: "But neither is Yugoslavia necessarily a new Vietnam or Lebanon. It is not an inevitable quagmire so complex that America's mil-itary and political leaders will automatically repeat the mistakes they made in the 1960s, as if they had learned nothing. The choices in 1992 do not have to be for America to do everything or to do nothing."[22]

Leslie Gelb, a foreign-policy editorial page writer for the *New York Times*, argued on the August 11, 1992, *McNeil-Lehrer Newshour* that the United States needed to find a "middle path" between doing noth-ing and all-out war. He suggested, in language reminiscent of the 1964–1965 bombing debates over Vietnam, that the U.S. put "a strate-gic squeeze on the Serbians."[23] Thus, there is a current resurgence of concern over the limitation of policy options that the All-or-Nothing philosophy requires. We have seen this desire surface in policy, as the Clinton Administration has argued for a policy that "levels the battle-field" in Bosnia.

The strength of the Limited War approach is that it reflects the truth of Clausewitz's maxim that war is an instrument of policy. Logically, the use of force should be calibrated to the politico-military context. One desires that policy not be undermined by a lack of suitable military options. The ability to employ limited force has four benefits. First, it permits a nation to pursue a policy of coercive diplomacy in which the threat of beginning or escalating the use of force is employed to modify another state's behavior. Second, limited options can also enhance the potential for deterrence. The perception that a potential defender will not respond for fear of unwanted escalation will certainly not deter aggression, and the threat of a total Armageddon-like reaction to an opponent's advance may not be credible. Consequently, a range of less violent responses provides the decisionmaker with the ability to respond to and deter a variety of threats. Third, and related to the previous advantage, is limited war's important objective of reducing escalatory pressures that might cause the unwanted increase of violence in war. Fourth, one's political objectives may not require, or even desire, the total defeat of the enemy's military forces. Not all disputes between states demand the decisive defeat of an opponent. What may be sought by the use of force is for the other party to refrain from some action in which it is currently engaged. The decisive defeat of the opponent may embitter relations between the states during the ensuing peace and thus work against the state's long-term political interests.

Consequently, a range of less violent responses provides the decisionmaker with the ability to respond to and deter a variety of threats. Still, it must be recognized that a weakness of the Limited War philosophy lies in its willingness to sacrifice the critical operational needs of the military. Understandably, the political leadership may feel that certain limitations on force will lead to a negotiated settlement; however, in some circumstances and with some opponents, using less power than one possesses may be perceived as weakness rather than strength. In other circumstances, the limitations placed on the use of force result in the ineffective application of military power: force may lack the coercive power and capacity for shock needed to bring the parties to meaningful negotiations.

Assessing the Never Again School

The rise of the Never Again School in American strategic thinking had a profound significance for those studying and conducting American foreign policy. The existence of this school also tells us, as this book has argued, a great deal about the nature of war itself. This All-or-Nothing perspective certainly reflects a deep reaction by the military to the defeat the U.S. suffered in Vietnam and to the agonies of Korea and Beirut, but it also reflects deeper truths about the intrinsic characteristics of military power. The essential insights of using force have been handed down to new soldiers by way of the Jominian "principles of war" that are prominent in modern field manuals like the army's FM 100–5. In his book *Neither Liberty Nor Safety*, General Nathan F. Twining (USAF), the retired Chairman of the JCS from 1957–1960, passionately criticized the concept of limited war as applied in Korea and contemplated in the 1950s and 1960s.[24] In a chapter entitled "Principles of War," Twining was most concerned (p. 200) with the "Objective." He described how battles define campaigns and campaigns should be directed toward obtaining the objective of the war. He indirectly noted one of the problems with "cost-effectiveness theories" that consider limitations on the use of force: these theories "become largely academic once military forces are joined in combat (p. 198)." "The opposing forces," Twining observes, "use what they have and attempt to devise strategy and tactics to best meet the objectives of the specific battle, campaign and war in which they are involved." In sum, efforts to limit force are working against the natural tendency of war to escalate to higher levels of violence as each side seeks to compel the enemy's submission.

The principle of the Objective "means simply that the American government should determine specifically purposeful goals for its military forces" (p. 200) Twining's point is one often repeated by All-or-Nothing proponents: there should be a clearly reasoned concatenation of planned military actions that will lead, with some reasonable chance of success, to the attainment of one's political objectives. Because limited war tends to become a war of attrition fought in static positions it often violates this principle: for example, the "government seemed to lose focus, or objective . . . when it failed to attack China at the time of its entry into the Korean War" (p. 200). Twining argues for the "persuasive continuity" of the principles of war in opposition to the skepticism of some "social scientists and natural scientists" and proceeds to give extended presentations and definitions of the principles (p. 217). Two definitions are particularly worthy of mention as examples of the seriousness with which the ideas behind the principles are expounded and for their content:

> *The Selection and Definition of the Aim*
> 8. *Definition.* "In the conduct of war as a whole and in every operation of war, it is essential to decide on and clearly to define the aim. When once the aim has been decided on, all effort must be continually directed toward its attainment so long as it is attainable, and every plan or action, must be tested by its bearing on this end.
> [Points 9–12 omitted.]
> *Offensive Action*
> 12. *Definition.* Offensive action is the necessary forerunner of victory; it may be delayed, but until the offensive is taken victory is impossible.
> 13. Offensive action is the only way to gain and retain the initiative, and with it liberty or action. It tends to force a defensive attitude on the enemy, to raise the morale of our own forces and to lower that of the enemy (p. 222–23).

Lest anyone think this assessment of the offensive is esoteric consider this famous and important passage from Clausewitz in which he discusses the "character of the strategic defensive":

> We have already stated what the defense is—simply the more effective form of war: a means to win victory that enables one to take the offensive after superiority has been gained; that is, to proceed to the active object of the war.
>
> Even when the only point of the war is to maintain the *status quo*, the fact remains that merely parrying a blow goes against the essential nature of war, which certainly does not consist merely in enduring. Once the defender has gained an important advantage, he must strike back, or he will court destruction. Prudence bids him strike while the iron is hot. . . . For the moment we shall simply say that this transition to the counterattack must be accepted as a tendency inherent in the defense—indeed, as one of its essential features. . . .
>
> A sudden powerful transition to the offensive—the flashing sword of vengeance—is the greatest moment for the defense.[25]

Thus, offense and defense are two sides of the same coin, and the purpose of the defense is not merely to "parry blows" but also to produce the "flashing sword of vengeance" which will take the offensive to the enemy. It is a strength of the Never Again argument that it does not allow the offensive to be cast aside as a threatening element of war that should be avoided.

Vietnam has produced particularly strong memories among civilian and military leaders in the United States. In many cases, the "lessons" taken support the All-or-Nothing position. For example, Mark Clodfelter reproduces part of a letter written in July 1969 by General William W. Momyer, the commander of the 7th Air Force (Vietnam), to Air Force Chief of Staff General John McConnell upon the announcement of the Chief's retirement. In the letter Momyer expressed profound dissatisfaction with the way the war was being fought from a military perspective, a view shared by McConnell:

> It has been a privilege to serve as a member of your team. My regret is we didn't win the war. We had the force, skill, and intelligence, but our civilian betters wouldn't turn us loose. Surely our Air Force has lived up to all expectations within the restraints that have been place upon it. If there is one lesson to come out of this war, it must be a reaffirmation of the axiom—don't get in a fight unless you are prepared to do whatever is necessary to win. This axiom is as old as military forces, and I suppose a military man will always be in the dilemma of supporting policy even though he knows it surely restricts the capacity of military forces to produce the desired effect. One has no alternative but to support the policy and take the knocks that inevitably follow when military forces don't produce the desired effects within the constraints of policy.[26]

The Never Again approach is most clearly attuned to the need to use force with a clear strategy and with a decisive intent. As stated above, however, the use of force in such a manner may undermine one's political objectives, which may be quite limited.

Ambassador Jeane J. Kirkpatrick, the permanent representative of the United States to the United Nations from 1981–1985, recalled in an interview, the moment in her political career when the odd ramifications of this philosophy became apparent to her.[27] During the Carter Administration, Fidel Castro, in what came to be known as the Mariel boatlift, sent approximately 100,000 Cubans to the U.S. in hundreds of boats and ships that were allowed to pick up refugees and take them to Florida. In that large population of ordinary Cubans seeking relief from repression was a group of several thousand incorrigibly criminal men who were soon put in prisons. President Reagan was outraged by Cuba's duplicity, and so there was talk of finding ways to inject these criminals back into the Cuban island. One suggestion was that they could be released out of the gates at Guantanamo one evening. Another was that the navy conduct a landing on some part of Cuba about which Cuban authorities would be forewarned. The navy was asked to draw up a plan for such a contingency, and Caspar Weinberger, the Secretary of Defense, later delivered a briefing on their projected needs to the National Security Council. According to Kirkpatrick, the navy seemed to want a force that would have been more appropriate for the great Pacific Ocean naval battles of the Second World War. In what was a skillful attempt to kill any operation of this kind, the navy used its bureaucratic position as planner for naval operations to make the requirements for action so stringent that the proposal was torpedoed.

The use of military power is a far more complex endeavor than today's widespread and, by now, threadbare use of Clausewitz's maxim reveals. This is especially true in limited wars because military power does not bring about a Carthaginian peace in which all issues are settled on the victor's terms. The strategic credibility of the Limited War School, which soared in the 1950s and 1960s, has declined precipitously since Vietnam and the Gulf War. An approach favoring the decisive use of force has become today's "common wisdom."

Over the last forty-five years America has learned a great deal about the practical problems of waging limited war. The Never Again objections to placing limits on force have channeled strategic thinking down a different path: political leaders now realize that military action must be directed by a strategy that realistically assesses the means needed to attain one's political objectives. Calculations of this kind represent the core of strategic thought, but Limited War thinking had glossed over the hard truths essential to the effective use of military power in its desire to check communist advances by inflicting heavy attrition on the enemy.[28] On the other hand, waiting for the perfect conditions to manifest themselves before permitting force to be used has real costs as well. Jim Hoagland of the *Washington Post* noted in 1992 that "events abroad and the [political] campaign at home have begun to raise hard questions about an absolutist position that, as one senior American diplomat puts it, 'suggests that America's political and military leaders lack the judgment to distinguish between the Boxer Rebellion and Vietnam' while spending $290 billion a year on defense."[29] This observation that the All-or-Nothing criteria may inhibit valid uses of force must be contemplated. Involvement in limited war is fraught with dangers for any state, especially one like the United States in which maintaining popular support for waging war cannot be ignored.

Unquestionably, exhortations to use force in a limited manner *should* be subjected to rigorous and skeptical examination. The prudent statesman must never forget, however, that fighting in a manner true to the tenets of the All-or-Nothing philosophy may unleash forces that can lead to dangerous, undesired escalation in an age when weapons, both nuclear and conventional, possess the most awesome destructive power. Limited wars will not disappear, and the problems associated with matching force and political objectives will continue to distress political leaders who must continue to face the tension between the logic of force and the requirements of policy.

Epilogue: Clinton's First Year

Soon after assuming office, President Clinton confronted the problems posed by limited war. As one would have suspected, the disappearance of the Cold War's superpower rivalry did sweep away the tension between the military and political elements of war. However, concerns of military escalation stemming from the U.S-Soviet struggle ceased to dominate strategic thought. Low-level peacekeeping and nation-building missions like those presented in Bosnia and Somalia threatened long-term involvement in *political* struggles more characteristic of civil war and social disintegration than the conventional warfare for which the United States had prepared itself militarily. This observation is not meant as a criticism of American military planning. Even in a world in which low-intensity conflicts proliferate they do not, in general, threaten vital American interests. Consequently, preparation for conventional warfare and the maintenance of America's nuclear deterrent will continue to demand the most substantial portion of defense spending.

The political nature of these police actions has made them susceptible to the criticism that American forces will be drawn into Vietnam-style quagmires. The analogy to Vietnam is clearly overdrawn because neither the Serbs in Bosnia nor the warlords in Somalia possess the military power of a Ho or the protection of an international patron like the Soviet Union or China. Rather, Bosnia and Somalia have the potential for becoming lengthy low-intensity conflicts. The Clinton Administration has not presented the nation with a cogent outline of an American interest in either of these wars. This would clearly be a difficult task for any president because the threat of Soviet advances around the world could easily support an expansive definition of the national interest. With that threat diminished, calculations supporting intervention in distant lands had to satisfy a higher level of proof. The administration's difficulty in presenting a politically convincing framework for analysis left it unprotected when the winds of political opposition began to blow. The world's new political murkiness was not clarified when President Clinton and his aides failed to present the nation with a unified philosophy for the use of military power.

Somalia

Somalia's horrors began in January 1991 when heavy fighting started between rebel forces of the United Somali Congress and soldiers under Somalia's President Mohammed Siad Barre. On January 28, 1991 Siad Barre fled the capital, Mogadishu, but the fighting continued. Living conditions in the country deteriorated as the country's habitability declined and famine spread: the lack of political control in Somalia made the distribution of relief supplies by the United Nations difficult. On August 12, 1992, one of the warlords, General Mohammed Farrah Aidid, agreed to allow 500 U.N. troops into Somalia to protect relief convoys. Two days later the United States began an airlift of supplies to Somalia. Still there was extensive interference with the supply planes and ships. On November 24, 1992, a U.N. relief ship carrying 10,000 tons of supplies was shelled while trying to enter a Somali harbor. The vessel returned to sea without delivering its cargo.

By November 30, 1992, U.N. Secretary General Boutros-Boutros Ghali had recommended that the United Nations use force to restore peace and livable conditions in Somalia. On December 3, 1992, the Security Council unanimously passed Resolution 794 (1992) which stated that "the magnitude of the human tragedy caused by the conflict in Somalia, further exacerbated by the obstacles being created to the distribution of humanitarian assistance *constitutes a threat to international peace and security.*" Having recognized this threat, the Security Council stated that "action under Chapter VII of the Charter of the United Nations should be taken in order to establish a secure environment for humanitarian relief operations in Somalia as soon as possible."[1] The resolution then indicated that the Security Council "acting under Chapter VII of the Charter of the United Nations, *authorizes* the Secretary-General and Member States . . . to use all necessary means to establish as soon as possible a secure environment for humanitarian relief operations in Somalia."[2]

On December 4, 1992, President Bush announced that U.S. forces would be sent to Somalia. He addressed the nation on television stating: "I understand the United States cannot right the world's wrongs." The President then added, "But we also know that some crises in the world cannot be resolved without American involvement, that American action is often necessary as a catalyst for broader involvement of the community of nations." The President observed that the mission had two parts: 1) to "create a secure environment in the hardest-hit parts of Somalia so that food can move from ships overland to the people in the countryside now devastated by starvation;" and once the secure environment was created 2) to hand back the security mission to the regular U.N. peacekeeping force. U.S. forces landed on December 9, 1992, when the first contingent of U.S. Marines came ashore in assault copters and hovercraft.[3] The administration planned to land U.S. Marines for deployment into Mogadishu by mid-December 1992. In the first five months of the operation the United States deployed almost 26,000 troops to Somalia. One might wonder how this limited intervention fits within the pattern set by the Reagan and Bush administrations that force should be used only when there are clear objectives that can be accomplished efficiently.[4] The most straightforward answer is that the size of the mission and the threat to U.S. forces was too modest to arouse vehement Never Again objections to presidential action. The Pentagon was concerned that the warring clans would merely disappear until the Americans had gone and then plunge the nation into war once an opportunity presented itself:

> The problem is not that military officials fear a Vietnam-style morass. Pentagon officials are confident that the Marine and Army troops can make short work of any organized opposition by Somali clans.
>
> Rather, Pentagon officials said, the concern is that the armed bands may reemerge as the American force tries to withdraw and a less powerful United Nations force moves in.[5]

Events following the U.S. troop reduction in May 1993 proved such assessments correct. Before that reduction, the size of the American force left no doubt that if the native factions decided to attack American forces, those opponents would be overwhelmed and defeated. Michael Gordon of the *New York Times*, writing of the briefing delivered by JCS Chairman Powell and Secretary of Defense Cheney on December 4, 1992, noted that Powell had "outlined the Pentagon plan for decisive military action."[6] Powell told the press that American forces "would not only defend themselves but would launch pre-emptive attacks if necessary.[7] The resolution permitted all U.N. members to "use all necessary means" to establish the "secure environment." Clearly, the United States had no intentions of allowing itself to be involved in a distant African nation lacking the authority to use any necessary level of force required for the defense of its forces.

Soon thereafter a dispute arose with the U.N. Secretary-General as to what the mission would be. Resolution 794 had authorized that "secure environment for humanitarian relief operations in Somalia" be provided for as soon as possible. After the passage of the December 3 resolution Boutros-Boutros Ghali wrote to President Bush seeking clarification as to his interpretation of "secure environment." According to the *Economist*, the Secretary-General "hoped it meant removing the land mines, left behind by the civil war, that are causing hideous casualties in the north. But, above all, he thought it meant disarming the gunmen who, over the past year, have run Somalia as their fief, using the starving as their pawns."[8] Such a mission, which would have entailed pacifying the countryside, was firmly rejected by the United States. In the December 4 press conference, Secretary of Defense Cheney said, "We are not in the business of rounding up every AK-47 in the country."[9] Cheney then noted that the Somalia action was a clearly defined "humanitarian operation."

Lest anyone believe that American armed forces were becoming engaged in an ill-defined U.N. police action, General Powell stated that U.S. forces would be used "in a rather decisive way so there will be no question in the mind of any of the faction leaders in Somalia that we have the ability to impose a stable situation, if it came to that, without their cooperation." He observed that the U.S. had "put in a large enough force that we could dominate the entire country and not just find ourselves trapped in a port or in a single city. And, essentially, we wanted to seize the initiative away from those who might not wish to see the humanitarian effort proceed."[10]

In the end, the activities of the American forces were not so clear cut as was initially planned, for "it was not long before United States troops found themselves doing more than simply securing the delivery of food relief—patrolling the streets at night, disarming some of the factions and shepherding a political reconciliation among the 15 rival factions."[11] The participation of Americans in such activities should not obscure the fact that Never Again objections prior to the American involvement were essentially satisfied. The U.S. was to have a limited mission, and it was authorized to defeat any opposition that threatened the American forces. In short, Somalia was not a conceptual problem for the post-Vietnam All-or-Nothing model. Finally, after the American presence was reduced and U.N. control was achieved the nature of the mission appears to have become murkier, possibly in keeping with Boutros Ghali's more ambitious policy goals.

U.S. Marine Corps Lieutenant-General Robert Johnston handed over command of the relief operation in Somalia to the United Nations on May 4, 1993.[12] By the time of the change of command, food was reaching every town although there were small areas in the country where food and supplies could not be taken. The United Nations was expected to command a total of 28,000—4,000 of whom would be American troops left behind as key elements in the new operation under United Nations commanding officer, Lieutenant-General Cevik Bir of Turkey.[13] Surprisingly, some American troops were being placed under the command of a foreign officer even though the U.S. "has for decades refused to allow its troops to be commanded by an officer from another country."[14] There was one minor exception to this policy in Western New Guinea in 1962 when an American military unit was placed under direct United Nations control.[15] When the U.N. assumed control of the Somalia operation in May 1993 only the 2,700-man logistical contingent was placed under the international organization's command. The 1,300 soldiers in the American "Quick Reaction Force" remained under the control of U.S. officers.

Interestingly, a September 1993 analysis by Keith B. Richburg in the *Washington Post* argues that when the Somali mission was under U.S. control General Aidid and his compatriots, were kept in check by aggressive U.S. patrolling. Richburg notes, "During the U.S.-led operation, Aidid occasionally tried to pose a military challenge—and each time, the warlord and his militia were slapped down hard."[16] A senior U.S. marine officer added: "They knew what kind of a response they would get from us. And it wouldn't be proportional." The United Nations, on the other hand, when met with resistance virtually disappeared from the streets the Americans had been vigorously patrolling: "Today the 13,000 U.N. troops in Mogadishu stay largely confined behind the high walls and barbed wire of their fortified compound, leaving Somali gunmen in control of entire neighborhoods."[17] The result is that on the streets of Mogadishu, "where visible presence counts, foreign troops have been noticeably absent." Richburg lamented the abandonment of the checkpoints in favor of patrols conducted "from the safety of the skies." There were several high-visibility aerial assaults led by American helicopter gunships, but such efforts do not pacify a restive population.

By the summer of 1993, the Somalia effort began to have the look of another "political" war slowly turning into a military quagmire. On June 5 Somalis reputed to serve Aidid ambushed U.N. soldiers guarding a food distribution center in Mogadishu, killing 24 Pakistanis. One week later the United States and U.N. forces began retaliatory raids against Aidid's strongholds. A resolution was passed in the U.N. Security Council calling for the capture and punishment of those responsible for killing the Pakistani soldiers; it was presumed that Aidid was ultimately responsible for the attacks. These events in June marked a change in the nature of the military involvement in Somalia. Robert Burns of the *Washington Times* wrote, "The violence rode an upward escalator, and U.S. forces never were able to get off."[18] During the summer a number of aerial attacks were made by American forces against positions held by Aidid's clan. More than the increase in violence, the new military actions marked a shift from a successful humanitarian mission to one in which the military pacification of Aidid's political organization became paramount.[19]

The Administration gave the impression on August 27, 1993, that it was willing to accept the low-level violence in Somalia almost indefinitely when Secretary of Defense Les Aspin delivered a major policy address to the Center for Strategic and International Studies, a Washington-based policy research organization. That week the Administration had sent 400 U.S. Rangers and an elite counter-terrorist unit to

Somalia as part of an effort to seize General Aidid.[20] The Secretary noted that there would be no easy solution in Somalia and then stated that the U.S goal there was "to restore order in south Mogadishu and to rebuild the country's shattered economy and political structure."[21] The six goals that would lead to the completion of the mission were: 1) reach the 28,000 man ceiling on troops set by the U.N.; 2) establish police forces in the large cities and town that can control the population; 3) get the warlords to give up their heavy weaponry; 4) develop a unified U.N. plan linking its political, military, and economic actions; 5) get other African nations to form a "core" group of nations that would speed the economic and political recovery in Somalia; 6) reinvigorate the national reconciliation process that had attempted to rebuild the political structures of the nation (the U.N. and the Organization of African Unity would have this responsibility).[22] Aspin noted that American withdrawal would be possible: "When the three conditions are met—south Mogadishu, heavy weapons, and police forces in the major population centers—then I believe that the U.S. quick-reaction forces can come back." Not surprisingly, these amazingly unrealistic objectives which focused on "rebuilding" Somalia, appeared open ended and poorly defined. Even though Aspin did not advocate limiting the use of force to avoid escalation or to "signal" an opponent of one's violent intentions, this concept of using force for "nation building" was a departure from the clear-cut operations that the Never Again School recommends. His was not a classic Limited War argument, but it certainly rejected, to a large extent, the common wisdom that military operations should have clearly defined objectives that will bring about the desired political results.

The actual turmoil within Somalia became more apparent as anti-United Nations resistance increased and Western casualties started to rise. For example, four Americans were killed on August 8, 1993, when they set off a land mine. Another three died on September 25, 1993, when their Blackhawk helicopter was shot down by a rocket propelled grenade, bringing the total of Americans killed in Somalia to fifteen.[23] These developments aroused greater Congressional opposition to the Somalia mission. Congressional approval had never been sought by either Presidents Bush or Clinton for U.S. involvement in what was reputed to be a humanitarian mission. On September 28, 1993, the House of Representatives passed a resolution (406–26) "demanding that the Administration put limits on its mission or face the probability of a cut-off of funds." This non-binding resolution which had already passed the Senate called on President Clinton to seek Congressional authorization by November 15 for the continued deployment of troops. Senator Robert C. Byrd (D-W.VA) led the opposition to the Clinton policy arguing, "Without a legitimate purpose, we will be drawn further into this quagmire, with a very real prospect for the continued loss of American lives."[24]

By the end of September the Administration's support for the Somalia operation appeared to be fading. The confident statement of long-term commitment expressed by Secretary Aspin one month earlier was crumbling by September 20, 1993, when Secretary of State Christopher requested of the U.N. that American combat forces in Somalia only be used "for emergency operations and not routine patrols" that could be performed by forces from other nations.[25] The letter that one U.N. official described as a "bombshell" also informed the Secretary General that the U.S. wanted to move its troops "over the horizon" (U.N. official's term) and out of harm's way. Also, Mr. Boutros-Ghali was informed that the U.S. might be compelled to withdraw its combat forces if domestic political support for the operation continued to erode. Administration sources told the New York *Times* that U.N. officials reacted too strongly to these warnings, one of which was delivered to the Secretary General by President Clinton on September 27, 1993, on the occasion of his visit for the president's annual address to the General Assembly. Administration claims of U.N. overreaction appear unjustified: these U.N. officials certainly realized that the new conditions for the use of American personnel signalled a significant shift in American support for the Somali operation.

Any hopes by the Clinton Administration that a slow withdrawal from Somalia could be achieved with minimal political costs vanished in early October when elite U.S. forces were battered in an intense fire-fight with Somali forces of General Aidid. On October 3, 1993, U.S. Army Rangers were pinned down in Mogadishu as they attempted to strike at and capture Aidid's staff. Unfortunately, the intelligence assessment had underestimated the number of Aidid's forces in the area, leaving the U.S. Rangers in deep trouble when one of their helicopters was shot down.[26] The command and control weaknesses of the U.N. forces became apparent as it took four hours for Pakistani and Malay armored vehicles to reach the Americans who had been pinned down by Somali gunfire and rocket attacks. Thomas Friedman observed that the anti-American and U.N. attack exposed the "33-country United Nations peacekeeping unit in Somalia as a tower of Babel, and driving home to Americans the real weighty role they would have to play if Somalia is to succeed."[27]

In the days that immediately followed this debacle, a U.N. spokesman, Major David Stockwell of the U.S. Army, made a number of extraordinary observations regarding the Somali Operation:

> meanwhile in Mogadishu, the Army major who is the chief spokesman for the U.N. mission in Somalia said U.S. forces have switched from peacekeeping to a "fugitive hunt" for Somali warlords—a job they are not trained for.
>
> "We have this fugitive hunt—this is not a military operation," said Major David Stockwell. "So the military winds up taking casualties and looking inept. If there is a problem, maybe it is with the mission."[28]

This statement was unusual in that an American officer working in Somalia as a spokesman with the U.N. publicly discussed the strategic weaknesses of the U.S. mission. Newspapers reported on October 7 that twice in September Secretary of Defense Aspin had rejected Colin Powell's requests for tanks and armored vehicles to support the Americans in Somalia. Aspin was apparently most concerned that such a request would rouse Congressional desires that it authorize the Somali mission.

As a result, there were was insufficient striking power on the ground available to the American command when the Rangers were pinned down on October 3. Major Stockwell then noted, "If U.S. forces had armor, they could have reacted more quickly, since they have common communications, training and tactics."[29] Stockwell's comment pointed to a little noticed weakness of U.N. operations: the fact that not all militaries have similar equipment, doctrine, communications skills, and competence. An underlying assumption of the rush to U.N. action and placing Americans under U.N. control appeared to be that military personnel and units are fungible. It was thought that no problem would ensue if soliders from Country A were placed under the command of officers from Country B within a U.N. command structure. As Stockwell's comments above make clear: armies are not interchangeable parts like a car's spark plugs. Each military organization has its methods of performance, and they may *not* fit together efficiently with those of other countries. The "peace enforcement" concept which envisages a real United Nations command structure seems to ignore these important operational problems.

There is another, more serious question that accompanies using American forces in peacekeeping operations: will the use of combat forces in these missions degrade their comabt efficiency? Representative Ike Skelton (D-Missouri), chairman, House Armed Services Subcommittee on Military Forces and Personnel, has worried aloud on C-SPAN, noting that peacekeeping requires patience and moderation in the use of force, whereas combat requires the disabling and decisive use of military power. Skelton has wondered whether the nature of peacekeeping will dull that razor's edge sharpness that soldiers need to perform at their peak military efficiency. If, as the chairman suspects, peacekeeping significantly degrades performace, then American participation in U.N. operations may have to be curtailed.

With that being said, the Administration was criticized for its decision to not send tanks to Somalia as requested by Powell. Eighteen American soldiers were killed, 75 others were wounded, and one was captured on October 3.[30] The fighting was fierce:

> The 100 elite U.S. infantrymen, who tried to beard a Somali warlord in his den, suffered 70 percent casualties—a figure compared by sickened officers yesterday to a 1965 massacre in Vietnam's Ia Drang Valley. So badly pinned down were the Americans in Mogadishu that they could not evacuate their wounded, Ranger commander, Lt. Col. Danny McKnight, for nine hours.[31]

In an October 5 Congressional session the Secretaries of Defense and State appealed for more time to develop a plan and timetable for withdrawing U.S. forces. The members of Congress were confused by the White House's mixed signals. On the one hand, the Administration seemed to be placating Capitol Hill by advocating a definite, rapid withdrawal. On the other, a small contingent of reinforcements ("600 troops with specialized weapons—including tanks, armored vehicles and special operations helicopters") was being sent to Somalia.[32] This meager reaction was apparently criticized within the Pentagon where many senior military officers "saw it as a half measure that would not make any significant difference on Mogadishu's urban battlefield."[33] Political hostility from Congress and the nation, as a whole, indicated quite clearly that maintaining an American presence in Somalia was probably no longer feasible. Ending the American presence in Somalia without incurring debilitating damage to American prestige became the foremost goal of President Clinton's Somalia policy.

On Thursday, October 8, 1993, President Clinton addressed the nation on television. He revealed that 1,700 soldiers would be sent to Mogadishu, 3,600 Marines to ships offshore, and 100 armored vehicles.[34] The aircraft carrier *Abraham Lincoln* would support the mission from the Indian Ocean. Simultaneously, the President promised that all American forces would be out of Somalia by March 31, 1993-less than six months away. The *New York Times* reported that there had been a strong reaction in the Pentagon to the recently disastrous turn of events in Somalia. Clinton's doubling of the force "was designed to address what the military viewed as basic flaws in the existing arrangement: its lack of adequate power, its vaguely defined mission and its tangled chain of command."[35] From now until the end of the mission the military wanted the Somali effort "to be unambiguously directed and unambiguously powerful." The deployment of the *Abraham Lincoln* and its battle group was intended to convey the seriousness with which the United States considered Somalia's threat to American forces. Whatever the military and operational details, by October 10 key Clinton national security advisers "agreed on one clear message: As far as the U.S. action was concerned, Somalia was all over but the leaving."[36] While this point was not communicated effectively to the nation that day, it was clear that the United States had little desire to remain engaged in Somalia.

The new phase in America's Somalia policy marked by the president's remarks of October 8 also reflected a growing disenchantment with the United Nations. Elaine Sciolino of the *New York Times* reported: "After embracing the United Nations as the global peacemaker of the future, President Clinton has broken sharply with it over Somalia, signaling the Administration's intense displeasure with Secretary General Boutros Boutros-Ghali and complicating United States participation in peacekeeping operations elsewhere."[37] The Administration's animosity toward the United Nations arose out of months of frustration which eventually led to the conclusion: "the United Nations is not up to the job." It was also reported that Administration was turning away from its venture in multilateralism whereby it had been willing to place U.S. forces under foreign command: "Now, the Administration has returned to one of its guiding principles of post-World-War-II foreign policy: if American soldiers are put in harm's way, they take orders solely from American commanders."[38]

This new thinking about the U.N. marked a departure from President Clinton's warm feelings for the United Nations. In April 1992, candidate Clinton had endorsed Boutros-Ghali's "proposal for creating an international standing army from perhaps a score of countries whose troops would be ready to risk their lives for making peace."[39] On that occasion, Clinton expressed his willingness to allow an international military unit of this kind to participate in missions including "standing guard at the borders of countries threatened by aggression, preventing mass violence against civilian populations, providing humanitarian relief and combatting terrorism."[40] Madeleine Albright, the American representative to the United Nations in New York, had promoted this new element of international politics embodied in the multinational military cooperation with the United Nations in Somalia. In the spring of 1993 she described it as "assertive multilateralism."

Assertive multilateralism represented the hopes that President Clinton seemed to have concerning the evolution of international relations between states. The Security Council and the Secretary General would present diverse perspectives thereby ensuring that military forces would be used to truly promote multilateral interests. This was consistent with Clinton's reluctance to use U.S. troops as the world's police force and his wish to concentrate on domestic policy while the U.N. did the policing. The United States would still be contributing the bulk of the forces needed to accomplish these various missions. Now, however, it would not be clearly in command of the operations. In Somalia a parallel command and control structure developed under the United Nations leading to operational confusion. Slowly, the Clinton Administration came to realize that the costs of not leading could be high. It reasserted control over American forces and began to pursue a diplomatic policy that essentially cut the United Nations out of the serious diplomacy in Somalia: the U.S. wanted out, and the feelings of United Nations bureaucrats would not be getting in the way.

The Administration did this by commencing a multifaceted effort to extricate itself from Somalia. Beginning his second term in the post, American envoy to Somalia, Robert B. Oakley, arrived in Mogadishu on October 10 and met with leaders in Aidid's clan. Simultaneously, Admiral Jonathan Howe of the U.N. command told reporters that United Nations forces would continue to pursue warlord Aidid as required by the June 1993 Security Council resolution calling for the apprehension of all those involved in planning the ambush of the Pakistani peacekeepers. On another front, the United Nations Secretary General announced that he and African, Arab, and Muslim leaders would meet the following week in Somalia to discuss the construction of a regional political process to prevent Somalia's return to chaos once the American forces were withdrawn—which would occur on March 31, 1994, at the latest. Secretary of State Christopher agreed that the African leaders would play a central role in the Administration's diplomatic efforts to solve what he referred to as "an African problem."[41] By October 14, 1993, the new American strategy was "to prod the Somali factions with various sticks and carrots into a minimum level of political reconciliation that will allow the United States to withdraw without seeing an immediate collapse into chaos." The United States would shed its old role as "sheriff" and engage "in the sort of murky politics and gray compromises it believes are necessary to stabilize the country."[42]

As the Somalia controversy was swirling around the Administration, another trouble spot was brewing: Haiti. In July 1993 the U.N. had lifted an oil embargo of Haiti in return for a settlement in which the elected President of Haiti, Father Jean-Bertrand Aristide, would be returned to power.[43] As part of this U.N. settlement a 1,600-man international force was supposed to enter Haiti and separate the military from the police officers; 600 members of that force were to be Americans. Operationally the military mission of the Americans posed the potential of being more dangerous than the street fighting of Mogadishu. The U.N. forces had arrived to monitor the Haitian military and provide training for the police. The forces were not sent to Haiti to perform policy or combat functions. This force, unlike the one in Somalia, had "no mandate to disarm criminals or intervene in violence. Only selected members of the force were to be equipped with sidearms."[44] The *New York Times* reported that "in case of trouble, the foreign police and soldiers had been instructed to 'run the other way.' "[45]

The situation in Haiti became threatening on October 11, 1993, when the *U.S.S. Harlan County* with 174 Americans and 25 Canadians aboard anchored in Port-au-Prince Harbor. The vessel was prepared to send ashore its contingent bound for the United Nations force, but armed demonstrators apparently under the control of the Haitian military rioted in the port, threatened American diplomats including the U.S. chargé d'affaires Vicki Huddleston, and blocked the arrival of the U.N. forces. The protesters kicked reporters yelling, "We are going to make this another Somalia!"[46] The Americans and Canadians did not go ashore where their meager arms would have left them virtually unprotected. American officials said that the *Harlan County* would remain off-shore until the Haitian military had secured the port.[47] Steven A. Holmes of the *New York Times* made the following observation with respect to the change in resistance evinced by the Haitians: "State Department officials have stressed for some time that while gunmen have often intimidated Haitians, they have not threatened diplomats or human rights monitors in Haiti. Thus today's threats against Vicki Huddleston . . . represents an ominous development, they said."[48]

In response to this defiance by the Haitian military, the United States led the way for the reimposition of trade sanctions against Haiti. The United Nations Security Council voted unanimously on October 17, 1993, to impose an oil and arms embargo against Haiti that would go into effect at 11:59 p.m. on October 18. On October 17, the President issued orders sending six warships to Haitian waters to enforce the embargo. Six hundred marines were flown from Camp Lejeune, North Carolina, to the Guantanamo naval base in Cuba in case Americans in Haiti needed protection on short notice.[49] At this point negotiations between various Haitian factions, the U.S., and the United Nations went into high gear.

Only the passage of time will reveal how the Haitian crisis will be resolved. In the meantime, however, the distraction generated by the American policy in Haiti exacerbated the sense of uncertainty surrounding the Administration's actions in Somalia. Turning the nation's attention back to Africa, President Clinton announced on October 19, 1993, that 750 Army Rangers would leave Somalia immediately, thus "effectively ending the American role in the search for the clan leader who international officials have said is responsible for the deaths of scores of United Nations peacekeepers."[50] This withdrawal left 6,300

American soldiers on the ground in Somalia with about one-third being used by the U.N. operations. Another 12,342 were then stationed off-shore. The President also described American diplomacy in Somalia as "engaging in a political process to see how we can resolve our mission in Somalia."[51] On the same day Major General Thomas H. Montgomery, the American commander in Somalia, said the U.S. role would be "to protect peacekeeping operations and food deliveries" should fighting resume. The mission to capture Aidid had essentially ended. The *New York Times* observed:

> As sketched by senior United States and United Nations military officials, including the general, the operation is notably narrower than two weeks ago, when Pentagon officials suggested that the armored forces being dispatched to Somalia would provide for a more regular American military presence in the Mogadishu area.

Montgomery defined his mission regarding the American soldiers: "Will they go out in the streets and patrol the city? No. That is not a U.S. mission. My mission is to protect the force."[52] The United States had clearly moved to a casualty-limiting strategy for the remainder of the Somalia mission.

The Administrations policy in Somalia met with powerful opposition in the United States Senate. Finally, at 1:15 a.m. on Friday, October 15, 1993, the Administration gained support for its gradual withdrawal from Somalia. Senator Byrd, one of the most influential Senate Democrats, criticized the Administration for allowing a "migration of responsibility" in Somalia from the United States to the United Nations. Byrd's remarks were mild compared to those of other Senators—even some in the Democrat Party. For example, Senator Bill Bradley (D-N.J.) described the Administration's course of action in Somalia as: "A series of ad hoc decisions, divorced from any overall strategy, led our troops into an ill-defined, poorly planned and open-ended mission." Mr. Clinton's pledge to remove all American forces in Somalia by March 31, 1994, was too late for many in the Senate. It took the considerable negotiating skills of Senator George Mitchell of Maine, the Democrat leader, and Senator Robert Dole of Kansas, the Republican leader, to fashion a compromise salvaging the White House position, but Senator Byrd had clearly made his point. Representative Robert Torricelli (D-N.J.) commented that owing to the policy disaster in Somalia "it probably will be impossible to win Congressional support for a peacekeeping role in Bosnia, where American participation is critical."[53] The United States was leaving Somalia as fast as possible. In fact, the capitulation was so complete and rapid that General Aidid even returned the captured American helicopter pilot, Chief Warrant Officer Michael Durant, to United States forces on October 14, 1993, without further political demands: why kick "the world's *only* superpower" when it's down?[54]

With the Somalia experience behind it, the Senate then turned its attention to its oversight of Bosnia and Haiti. On the evening of October 20 Senator Robert Dole accepted a compromise softening his prior advocacy for a binding resolution that would have required Congressional approval before U.S. troops could be sent to Bosnia or Haiti. Instead of requiring White House compliance before acting, the Senate leadership "made clear their desire for advance approval of military operations by Congress and for detailed reports in cases where prior authorization is not possible, along with an improvement in what many lawmakers regard as inadequate consultation."[55] The Senate approved a Bosnia resolution (99–1) that "simply urged the President to seek Congressional approval."[56] Later in the week, the Senate defeated a tougher resolution than Dole's original proposal. This later bill, sponsored by Senator Jesse Helms (R-N.C.) would have required Congressional authorization before American forces could be placed in Haiti. It was defeated 81–19. The Administration, arguing against the Congressional mandates, claimed that such a bill would present an unconstitutional intrusion into the president's powers to conduct foreign policy. There is a constitutionally sophisticated counter-argument to the President's position, as former Stanford law school dean and noted constitutional scholar, John Hart Ely, wrote in the *New York Times*:

> The Constitution gives the President no general right to make foreign policy. Quite the contrary. It makes sense for one person to negotiate for the country, and the President is the obvious choice. But virtually every substantive constitutional power touching on foreign affairs is vested in Congress. Specifically, the power to declare war is placed unequivocally in the legislative process.[57]

According to Ely, Dole's original proposal to limit the President's authority to send troops to Haiti was clearly constitutional.[58] The position Senator Dole seemed to be taking, and the stronger variant endorsed by Senator Helms, are reminiscent of long-discarded Republican concerns, most memorably espoused by Senator Robert A. Taft (R-Ohio), for safeguarding the Constitution's separation of powers and protecting Congressional control in the face of claims for greater authority by the executive. Robert Taft (1889–1953), son of President William Howard Taft, served in the U.S. Senate from 1939 until his death when he was majority leader.

The policy crises in Somalia and Haiti exposed such glaring weaknesses in the post-Cold War ascendance of the United Nations and in multilateralism, more generally, that a future decision to send American troops to Bosnia as part of a United Nations peacekeeping or peace enforcement effort would necessarily face greatly increased Congressional and popular resistance. It is to the Bosnia crisis that we now turn.

Clinton and Bosnia

The Bush Administration dealt with the Bosnia-Herzegovina crisis, as described in chapter 9, by staying as far away from it as possible. Presidential candidate Bill Clinton, on August 5, 1992, took issue with that policy when he told an audience in East St. Louis, Illinois, that the Bush Administration had not done enough to stop the violence in Yugoslavia and that the United States might have to use force. "I would begin with air power against the Serbs," he said.[59] A few months later, President-elect Clinton suggested at a news conference on December 11, 1992, that the U.S. "turn up the heat a little" in Yugoslavia by more strictly enforcing the U.N. Security Council approved "no-fly zone."[60] President Clinton incorporated an interventionist theme within his inaugural address delivered on January 20, 1993: "When our vital interests are challenged, or the will and conscience of the international community is defied, we will act—with peaceful diplomacy whenever possible, with force when necessary."[61]

After the new administration's initial policy review, on February 10, 1993, Secretary of State Warren Christopher presented a six-point initiative that promised an active American role in the negotiating process.[62] Secretary Christopher listed the six points the United States would pursue as part of its new Balkan policy: (1) the U.S. would actively engage itself in the Vance-Owen negotiations. (2) the President would indicate to the various parties "that the only way to end this conflict is through negotiation." (3) the President would tighten sanctions to prevent the Serbs from winning the war. (4) the President would "tak[e] steps to reduce the suffering and bloodshed" in the region. (5) the President would signal to all involved that America "is prepared to do its share to help implement and enforce an agreement that is acceptable to all parties." (6) the President will continue to consult with our allies on these matters.[63]

Christopher's announcement was taken to be a strong endorsement for the Vance-Owen plan. Named for Cyrus Vance, former U.S. Secretary of State and U.N. negotiator, and Lord David Owen, the representative of the European Community, this plan to end the fighting called for the creation of ten autonomous provinces in Bosnia under a weak central government designed to provide protection for ethnic minorities.[64] In his remarks Secretary Christopher indicated, but did not pledge, that the United States would be willing to employ ground forces as peacekeepers in Yugoslavia if (and only if) a settlement were reached.[65] Unfortunately, there was little in these plans that instilled fear in the heart of the Serbians, so the conquest and annexation of Bosnia continued. Nor was there evidence of European willingness to engage in real fighting for the sake of the Bosnians. During April 1993 the crisis became acute as the Serbs shelled Sarajevo.

It was widely known that General Colin Powell "forcefully questioned even the most limited intervention to protect the Muslims, reflecting the concern that such steps would involve the United States in a quagmire without stopping the fighting."[66] There appears to have been no discontinuity between Powell's perspective on using military power in the Bush Administration and his position as an adviser to President Clinton. Secretary of Defense Les Aspin is reported to have "made it clear" in policy debates that the United States should be willing to use force "in a wider variety of shapes and sizes" than the Bush advisers would have done; the *Wall Street Journal* stated Aspin believed the "end of the Cold War standoff with the Soviet Union gives the U.S. more flexibility to use military force in an incremental fashion in regional trouble spots such as Iraq without fear of being sucked into long-term quagmires."[67]

There was much that was reasonable in this perception. The end of the Cold War had not banished the fear of nuclear warfare in all circumstances: thus, the problem of escalation might still exist. However, liberation from the deadly struggle with the Soviets could free the United States to experiment with the limited strikes against weak, isolated opponents whose resistance to American interests might previously have been supported by the Soviet bloc.

In early April 1993, the *New York Times* reported that Aspin "continues to believe that air strikes should be considered and is sympathetic to the notion of lifting the arms embargo on the Muslims."[68] The article noted "Mr. Aspin has yet to press hard for using limited military force." The position ascribed to Aspin is noteworthy because it is roughly the policy adopted by the Administration in late April 1993. Additionally, the new Secretary of Defense is reported to have assessed the effectiveness of air power differently than did Colin Powell who felt that air strikes "alone would not be decisive in halting the Serbian forces." Aspin argued that the Serbian forces "may be overrated and that air attacks might be effective in deterring Serbian attacks, Administration officials said."[69] All of these positions were put forward at a time when the Administration repeatedly stated its opposition to the introduction of ground combat forces; a position from which it has not wavered. This reluctance to place American soldiers in Bosnia was matched at home by a clear lack of popular support for this type of military action.[70] Powell argued that using ground forces would not be simple after manpower constraints were considered:

> Putting a division into Bosnia would require a so-called rotational base of three divisions; that, in turn, would prevent Clinton from [reducing] the Army as much as he aims to. . . .
> At a meeting on Tuesday, April 20th, Clinton ruled out using United States ground forces in a peacemaking role. . . . A possible Catch-22 loomed: America wouldn't help with a peacemaking initiative, but there might not be any peace to keep unless it was imposed by force.[71]

Christopher did not explicitly define his philosophy of employing force, but Vietnam appears to have made him appropriately cautious. On April 27, 1993, Christopher told a Senate Appropriations subcommittee that he was "quite prepared to see the United States use force, not only [in Yugoslavia] but any place around the world." "But," he added, "it has to meet some pretty severe tests."[72] The Secretary "laid out four strict tests for the use of force: the goal must be stated clearly to the American people, there must be a strong likelihood of success, there must be an 'exit strategy' and the action must win sustained public support" Elaine Sciolino of the *New York Times* noted that "Mr. Christopher offered the diplomatic equivalent of the cautious military doctrine enunciated by Gen. Colin L. Powell . . . asking a question that has become the Christopher mantra: what is the endgame?"[73]

The Secretary's remarks echo important elements of Caspar Weinberger's conditions for using force, revealing just how widespread the Never Again perspective had become in both Republican and Democrat parties. Even Secretary Aspin's willingness to flirt with a minimal form of graduated coercive diplomacy should not be taken as anything like an endorsement of an old-fashioned Limited War position. His caution and worry about entering a quagmire were real and well-informed with Vietnam experiences in the McNamara Pentagon.[74]

President Clinton did not explicitly address the issue, but he had made statements on occasion that reflect some Never Again principles. For example, on April 23, 1993, at a White House press conference when discussing the possible use of air power against the Serbs he stated: "I do believe that on the airstrike issue, the pronouncements that General Powell has made generally about military action apply there. If you take action . . . we must have a clearly defined objective that can be met, we must be able to understand it, and its limitations must be clear."[75]

On Saturday, May 1, 1993, President Clinton decided he would "commit airpower to help bring an end to the fighting in the Balkans."[76] Clinton's position focused on two, and possibly three, elements. First, the United States would seek an end to the U.N. Security Council's arms embargo, which now prevented the Bosnians from acquiring adequate weaponry. Second, the U.S. would allow its fighter-bombers to attack Serb positions in Bosnia if they continued to attack Muslim cities. The third option was to create "safe havens" for Bosnian Muslims to be protected by U.N. peacekeepers.[77] Warren Christopher "also specifically ruled out using American ground troops."[78] The Administration then consulted with its European allies on this proposal, called "lift and strike," in which the arms embargo would be *lifted* and the U.S. would *strike* with air power.

On May 2 Thomas L. Friedman of the *New York Times* provided an illuminating interpretation of the White House's thinking. He characterized the Clinton plan as reflecting a "least cost" approach that would minimize the possibility of derailing his domestic policy agenda while providing pressure on the Serbs to negotiate with respect to Bosnia. Speaking of President Clinton and his staff, he observed:

> They are looking for that perfectly calibrated policy that will be just enough to tilt the balance of power in Bosnia toward a settlement, just enough to convince historians that when genocide stalked Europe for the second time this century they didn't avert their eyes—but not so much as to be stuck in a quagmire. Clinton aides say that only by such a nuanced strategy can they hope to have Bosnia and the budget, Sarajevo and national service.
>
> That is the underlying logic of the policy course decided at the White House yesterday. While the details were not spelled out, Mr. Christopher said the President had decided in principle to commit a limited amount of American military power to try to end the fighting in the Balkans.[79]

Between May 2 and 9 more details of the Clinton strategy were given to the press. A more military rationale was presented: "lift and strike" was seen as a relatively cheap way to "level the battlefield."[80] According to Ann Devroy and Barton Gellman of the *Washington Post*, the Clinton Administration had few hopes at the beginning of May for bringing about a cessation of the war. Instead, the United States hoped to equalize the strength of the two opponents. The strategy was that the warring Bosnian Serbs and Muslims eventually would make peace if more equally armed. That would require putting weapons in the hands of the badly outgunned Bosnian Muslim militias:

> Meanwhile, the United States—ideally along with its European allies— would launch air strikes on Bosnian Serb military targets, protecting the militias (as well as the Serb-surrounded refugee enclaves of eastern Bosnia) until they can fight effectively on their own. The air strikes then would stop.[81]

There would be no attempt to decisively defeat the Serbs militarily or to shatter their psychological equilibrium. Rather, it was hoped that supplies of arms and military training in combination with limited air strikes would bring about a stalemate in the fighting. When the stalemate on the ground was reached, a negotiated settlement would follow as the Serbs realized victory was no longer possible. President Clinton told reporters the emerging policy would have " 'a beginning, a middle, and an end' to the U.S. military role, an unspoken reference to ongoing U.S. fears of an endless, Vietnam-style quagmire, and Clinton's campaign promise not to allow one."[82] Yet such peace talks, backed by insufficient military power as these would have been,[83] seemed most likely to draw the U.S. into the "quagmire" that the President and his advisers so greatly feared.[84] The determination of the Serbs to oppose world opinion and an international embargo contradicted the American assumption that they could be persuaded to cease their aggression, or harder still, give up their plunder at a price the West was willing to pay.

On May 7, 1993, Secretary of State Christopher returned to Washington after spending six days in Europe talking to other heads of state about the Balkan war. The European leaders rejected the Clinton proposal. Europe was most concerned with the American unwillingness to deploy ground forces in Yugoslavia to assist in the humanitarian efforts. The U.S. decision against ground forces made "differences over policy inevitable" with the European states.[85] The Europeans correctly recognized that a failure to commit ground troops signified minimal American resolve to follow through in resisting Bosnia aggression.[86] Had President Clinton said that ground forces would be deployed to Bosnia prior to a settlement, his strategy of lifting the arms embargo might have succeeded. American soldiers would then have been placed at risk, as the European soldiers would be, from the new arms soon to flow into Bosnia. As it was, these proposals had the potential to stir up a hornet's nest of Serbian aggression in the short term before the arms arrived, and a greater level of violence and destruction in the long run, after arms finally reached the Bosnians.

Clinton's quasi-commitment and weak advocacy of his program gained little respect within NATO, and his retreat from the issue as a whole on May 17–18 brought denials by Christopher that there was a rift within the alliance.[87] However, a leadership gap within the West was quickly perceived, prompting the moribund Russian government to attempt to thrust itself back on the world diplomatic stage.[88] Thus,

the Clinton Administration's lack of success in attaining European support for its Bosnia initiative did throw "the NATO alliance into its most
serious crisis since the end of the Cold War."[89] Ironically, the Bosnia crisis hit many of NATO's weakest points, although it occurred outside
the NATO boundaries, and without an attack on any NATO member.
Also, Germany, the major European power, was hamstrung by its weakened financial condition, which had resulted from reunification and by
the memories of the atrocities it had perpetrated in the Balkans some
50 years before. Even with all these problems, assertive American leadership and a commitment of ground troops might have succeeded in
gaining the Continent's support; Europe wanted to be led.

During the summer of 1993 negotiations about Bosnia continued to
drag on, and no solution seemed forthcoming. At the end of September a settlement of some sort appeared to be in the making. Although
inequitable, it would have preserved at least something of Bosnia. This
possibility prompted journalists to note that the President was firmly
committed to sending a force of 25,000 soldiers and marines to
Yugoslavia as part of a peacekeeping force. Observers like R. W. Apple,
Jr. of the *New York Times* thought it was debatable whether Clinton
would follow through. Apple noted on September 19 that many analysts felt there would be substantial costs to the United States if the
United States did not fulfill its obligation:

> United States diplomats and their foreign colleagues argue that a failure
> by Mr. Clinton to follow through on his pledges would not only con-
> stitute a violation of moral obligation but badly damage American cred-
> ibility abroad. For that reason if no other, they say, Mr. Clinton will
> summon the will to send American troops, however risky he and others
> may consider such a step.[90]

That the United States would send troops to Bosnia became much less
clear after the President's speech and later remarks at the United
Nations on September 27, 1993. The president, while dutifully affirm-
ing American international leadership and its support for peacekeeping,
placed substantial restrictions on American involvement in low-intensity conflicts recalling Never Again tenets. The President informed the
General Assembly: "The United Nations simply cannot become
engaged in every one of the world's conflicts. If the American people are
to say yes to U.N. peacekeeping, the United Nations must know when

to say no."[91] He then complained that the American portion of peace-keeping expenses should be lowered from 30.4% to 25%. These, however, were not his most important observations concerning the U.N. and the use of force. With regard to Bosnia he gave a long list of pre-conditions that would have to be met before American forces would be sent to Yugoslavia; he made these remarks at a press conference later that day:

> I would want a clear understanding what the command and control was. I would want the NATO commander in charge of the operation. I would want a clear timetable for the first review and ultimately the right to terminate American involvement. I would want a clear political strat-egy along with a military strategy. After all, there will be more than sol-diers involved in this. And I would want a clear expression of support from the United States Congress. Now, there are 20 other operational things I would want, but those are the big policy issues.[92]

Clinton posed four questions that would need to be asked of each peacekeeping operation: *1) Is there a real threat to international peace? 2) Does the proposed mission have clear objectives? 3) Can an exit point be identified for those who will be asked to participate? 4) How much will the U.N. mission cost?*[93]

These new questions and conditions presented by the President echoed Secretary Weinberger's concerns about the effective use of mili-tary power. As noted above, Secretary Christopher voiced similar con-cerns in the Administration's first year. The contrast between the Clin-ton Administration's political-military philosophy and the two preced-ing administrations should be considered. A competent observer should have known that Reagan and Bush were concerned with main-taining public support for military operations, but one also sensed that they tended toward the All-or-Nothing position from a deep commit-ment that wars should be fought decisively. This argument was made from a moral as well as practical standpoint. If push came to shove, one sensed that they would use force—and then use it overwhelmingly. On the other hand, one must wonder what motivates President Clinton's apparent acceptance of Never Again requirements for using force. The administration's tentative actions regarding Bosnia, Somalia, and Haiti suggest that it is not comfortable with the idea of using force.

Notes

1 | The Logic of Force, the Dilemma of Policy

1. Jay M. Shafritz, *Words on War: Military Quotations from Ancient Times to the Present* (New York: Prentice Hall, 1990), p. 425.

2. Patrick E. Tyler, "Vietnam and Gulf Zone: Real Military Contrasts," *New York Times*, December 1, 1990, p. 8.

3. Jim Hoagland, "August Guns: How Sarajevo Will Reshape U.S. Strategy," *Washington Post*, August 9, 1992, sec. C, p. 1.

4. Ibid.

5. Ibid. American participation in various wars around the world was a necessary condition for any United Nations efforts to settle those conflicts: "Desert Storm proved that European military forces cannot fight a modern war beyond their own territory without the logistical and intelligence infrastructure that only the United States can provide. Not only will the Europeans not go, they could not get there on their own if they tried." Jim Hoagland, "With Whose Army?" *Washington Post*, August 13, 1992, sec. A, p. 25.

6. Hoagland, "August Guns," sec. C4, p. 2. A political cartoon (by Oliphant) appeared on the second page of the Hoagland article. It showed a soldier dressed in 1990s battle garb walking down a road as two other soldiers approached. The first was dressed as a soldier from the First World War, the second as a Second World War soldier. The 1990s infantryman asks the other two: "Pardon me—which way to the quagmire?" The other two, without turning around, point their thumbs over their shoulders to their rear where stands a sign pointing in the same direction with the following names: "Bosnia-Herzegovina, Serbia, Croatia, Slovenia."

7. Harry G. Summers, Jr., *On Strategy: A Critical Analysis of the Vietnam War* (Washington, D.C.: GPO, 1981).

8. Harry G. Summers, Jr., "Can Force Solve the Problem?" *Washington Times*, August 14, 1992, sec. F, p. 1.

9. Harry G. Summers, Jr., "An Overwhelming Argument on Force," *The Washington Times*, January 28, 1993, sec. G, p. 4; my emphasis. By "this" Summers is referring to the military's preference for decisive military action.

10. Summers, "An Overwhelming Argument on Force," sec. G, p. 4.

11. The Limited War School bears intellectual similarities to the policy of "flexible response" adopted by the Kennedy administration.

12. The word "decisive" is often seen in a military context, but its full implications are rarely considered. When used as an adverb to describe a way to fight a war, "decisively" implies that force will *decide* the issue at hand: the enemy will be defeated and unable to resist. The decisive use of force does not envisage protracted negotiations to end a war, for in that situation force is *not* deciding the issue. An important doctoral thesis has examined the never again approach in U.S. foreign policy. See David Petraeus, "The American Military and the Lessons of Vietnam: A Study of Military Influence and the Use of Force in the Post-Vietnam Era," Ph. D. dissertation, Princeton University, 1987.

13. The use of ideas, beliefs, or cognitive factors as explanations in international relations theory has not been uncommon in the last decade. For examples of work of this kind see Robert A. Packenham, *Liberal America and the Third World* (Princeton: Princeton University Press, 1973); John Odell, *U.S. International Monetary Policy: Markets, Power, and Ideas as Sources of Change* (Princeton: Princeton University Press, 1982); John Gerard Ruggie, "International Regimes, Transactions, and Change: Embedded Liberalism in the Postwar Economic Order," in Stephen D. Krasner, ed., *International Regimes* (Ithaca, NY: Cornell University Press, 1983), pp. 195–231. An interesting edited volume argues for the importance of "public ideas" as an explanatory variable for government policy-making; see Robert B. Reich, ed., *The Power of Public Ideas* (Cambridge, MA: Ballinger, 1988). A classic history that notes the different approaches to implementing the concept of containment, see John Lewis Gaddis, *Strategies of Containment: A Critical Appraisal of Postwar American National Security Policy* (Oxford: Oxford University Press, 1982). A recent book that uses "ideas and values" as independent variables in explaining the foreign aid policies of Western industrial democracies is David H. Lumsdaine, *Moral Vision in International Politics: The Foreign Aid Regime, 1949–1989* (Princeton: Princeton University Press, 1992).

14. Even in total war one usually witnesses the implementation of some

political limitations on the use of force. For example, in World War II poison gases were not used.

15. Peter Paret, "Clausewitz," in Peter Paret, ed., *Makers of Modern Strategy from Machiavelli to the Nuclear Age*, (Princeton: Princeton University Press, 1986), pp. 198–199, p. 200.

See the excellent commentary on the same subject in Michael Howard, *Clausewitz* (Oxford: Oxford University Press, 1983), chapters 2–4.

16. Paret, "Clausewitz," p. 198, bottom.

17. Michael Howard, *Clausewitz* (Oxford: Oxford University Press, 1983), p. 34.

18. Carl von Clausewitz, *On War*, trans. and ed. Michael Howard and Peter Paret (Princeton: Princeton University Press, 1978), bk. I, ch. 1, pp. 75–77. Clausewitz states: "The thesis, then, must be repeated: war is an act of force, and there is no logical limit to the application of that force." *On War*, bk. I, ch. 1, p. 77. Subsequent references will be found in parentheses in the text.

19. The terms "logic of the instrument" and "logic of force" are mine not Clausewitz's.

20. Paret, "Clausewitz," p. 199 and note 14.

21. Michael I. Handel, "Introduction," in Michael I. Handel, ed., *Clausewitz and Modern Strategy*, (London: Frank Cass, 1986), p. 5. This group of studies first appeared in a special issue on Clausewitz and Modern Strategy of *The Journal of Strategic Studies*, Vol. 9, no. 2 and 3.

22. Garry Wills, "Critical Inquiry (Kritik) in Clausewitz," in W.J.T. Mitchell, ed., *The Politics of Interpretation*, (Chicago: University of Chicago Press, 1982), p. 160.

23. For a recent debate on the nature of the offensive in war (which will be discussed in this study's conclusion) see: Jack Snyder, "Civil-Military Relations and the Cult of the Offensive, 1914 and 1984," *International Security* 9 (Summer 1984): 108–146; Jack Snyder, *The Ideology of the Offensive: Military Decision Making and the Disasters of 1914* (Ithaca, NY: Cornell University Press, 1984); Stephen Van Evera, "The Cult of the Offensive and the Origins of the First World War," *International Security* 9 (Summer 1984): 58–107.

24. William G. Eckhardt, " 'We the People' Go to War: The Legal Significance of the Weinberger Doctrine," *Small Wars and Insurgencies* 1 (August 1990): p. 134.

25. Eckhardt, p. 142, fn. 5.

26. Michael Geyer, "German Strategy in the Age of Machine Warfare, 1914–1945," in *Makers of Modern Strategy*, p. 546.

27. Ibid., p. 550.

28. Martin van Creveld, *The Transformation of War* (New York: Free Press, 1991), p. 142.

29. Azar Gat, *The Origins of Military Thought from the Enlightenment to Clausewitz* (Oxford: Clarendon Press, 1989), p. 221.

30. *On War*, Book VIII, ch. 6B, p. 606.

31. This point is supported by examining the headings of some of the sections in book 1, chapter 1. Section 3 is called "The Maximum Use of Force;" Section 4 is "The Aim is to Disarm the Enemy," and Section 5 is "The Maximum Exertion of Strength." However, a change occurs with Section 6, "Modifications in Practice." This new emphasis is continued in the rest of the chapter in which these "modifications" are described in greater detail.

32. Handel, "Introduction," p. 5.

33. *On War*, bk. I, ch. 1, p. 87.

34. Clausewitz, *On War*, Bk. I, ch. 1, p. 88; my emphasis. He also observes that when the "motives for war" are "more powerful and absolute" then war will "approach its abstract concept" and the "military aims and political objects of war will coincide." (pp. 87–88)

35. Peter Paret, "Military Power," chap. in *Understanding War: Essays on Clausewitz and the History of Military Power* (Princeton: Princeton University Press, 1992), p. 19.

36. See *On War*, bk. I, ch. 1, sec. 6, "Modifications in Practise." In this section Clausewitz provides a forceful warning against thinking of war in the abstract apart from its political environment.
Bernard Brodie suggests that Clausewitz could not have imagined the degree to which military imperatives would dominate political interests in World War I. See Bernard Brodie, *Strategy in the Missile Age* (Princeton: Princeton University Press, 1959), pp. 67–69.

37. Gat, *Origins of Military Thought*, p. 106.

38. Ibid., p. 123.

39. For a brief summary see C. Kenneth Allard, *Command, Control and the Common Defense* (New Haven: Yale University Press, 1990), pp. 48–49.

40. John Shy, "Jomini," in *Makers of Modern Strategy*, pp. 145–46. The emphasis appears in the Shy article, but the footnote does not indicate whether it was placed there by Shy or Jomini. Also, it should be noted from the dates given by Shy in fn. 6 that Jomini expressed these thoughts some twenty to thirty years before the publication of Clausewitz's *On War*. Another classic work on Jomini is Michael Howard's "Jomini and the Classical Tradition in Military Thought." See Michael Howard, *Studies in War and Peace* (New York: The Viking Press, 1970), pp. 21–36.

41. John I. Alger, *The Quest for Victory: The History of the Principles of War* (Westport, CT: Greenwood Press, 1982), pp. 19–27; the quote appears on

p. 23. The modern versions of the principles of war with their most tightly focused codifications appear to owe much to the British soldier J. F. C. "Boney" Fuller, whose First World War expressions of the principles were incorporated into the 1920 British *Field Service Regulations—Operations.* See Alger, *Quest for Victory*, pp. 122–123.

42. Shy, "Jomini," p. 184.

43. Shy, "Jomini," p. 179.

44. Geoffrey Till, *Maritime Strategy and the Nuclear Age* (New York: St. Martin's Press, 1982), p. 30.

45. The reader should not conclude that the American, postwar focus of this study indicates that the subject matter is a problem peculiar to the United States. The escalatory pressure that inheres between the war's political and military elements during limited wars has been seen in a number of wars like the Crimean War, the Franco-Prussian War, and, most interestingly, the Boer War (October 1899–May 1902). Regarding the Boer War, R. Ernest Dupuy and Trevor N. Dupuy note that the British had to escalate the conflict into one of great savagery to subdue the Boers. The British were unable to control the guerrilla tactics of the mounted Boers with the extension of fixed outposts into hostile territory. So, "Kitchener then copied the Spanish procedure in Cuba. The country was swept by flying columns of mounted infantry; the farms on which the Boer raiders depended for sustenance were burned and some 120,000 Boer women and children were herded into concentration camps, in which an estimated 20,000 of them died of disease and neglect. Under these harsh measures, all resistance collapsed." They also add that the British Empire required "2 years and 8 months to subdue a foe whose man-power potential was 83,000 males of fighting age, and which never had in the field at one time more than approximately 40,000 men. British forces engaged in the beginning totaled not more than 25,000, but before it was ended some 500,000 men were in South Africa. . . ." A situation in some ways reminiscent of America's in Vietnam.

See R. Ernest Dupuy and Trevor N. Dupuy, *The Encyclopedia of Military History from 3500 B.C. to the Present* (New York: Harper, 1986), p. 855. For an interesting survey of Britain's colonial wars of the nineteenth century one can read Byron Farwell, *Queen Victoria's Little Wars* (New York: Norton, 1972).

46. General Mark Clark (USA, retired), *From the Danube to the Yalu* (New York: Harper, 1954), p. 328.

47. It should be noted that my use of the term Never Again School does not refer so much to the persons as to the set of ideas which they advocated.

48. Morris Janowitz, *The Professional Soldier: A Social and Political Portrait,* (New York: The Free Press, 1961), pp. 264–321. In fact, Janowitz credits

Lieutenant-General James M. Gavin as being one of the first writers to recognize this strategic dichotomy in U.S. policy. Gavin refers to the two schools as "conservative" and "liberal." See Janowitz, p. 265 and note 9 on p. 279. See also James M. Gavin, *War and Peace in the Space Age*, (New York: Harper, 1958), pp. 248ff.

49. Joseph Kraft, *Profiles in Power*, (New York: The New American Library, 1966), chapter 14, "The Never Again Club," pp. 139–146.

50. Richard Betts, *Soldiers, Statesmen, and Cold War Crises*, (Cambridge: Harvard University Press, 1977), pp. 167–170, p. 266, note 9.

51. Before the Korean War a limited war philosophy was being developed within the government which culminated in the writing of NSC 68, a critical national security memo written during the Truman administration. Those Americans most relevant to the pre-Korean movement toward a limited war posture were George Kennan and Paul Nitze. In fact, Basil Liddell Hart, a British writer, had argued during World War II (before Hiroshima) that future wars would have to be kept limited if humanity were to survive. This subject is discussed in some detail in chapter 2.

52. Robert E. Osgood, *Limited War: The Challenge to American Strategy*, (Chicago: University of Chicago Press, 1957), p. 13.

53. Maxwell D. Taylor, *The Uncertain Trumpet* (New York: Harper, 1959).

54. Harry G. Summers, *On Strategy: A Critical Analysis of the Vietnam War*, (Washington, D.C.: GPO, 1981). Stephen Peter Rosen, "Vietnam and the American Theory of Limited War," *International Security* 7 (Fall 1982): 83–113.

55. The means used were not "total" in anything like the sense employed during the World Wars, but authorization was given to use all necessary means to achieve the political objective of recapturing the islands. Of course, one has to recognize that the British most certainly excluded the use of nuclear or chemical weapons.

56. Kenneth Waltz, *A Theory of International Relations* (Reading, MA: Addison Wesley, 1979).

57. Stephen D. Krasner, *Defending the National Interest: Raw Materials Investments and U.S. Foreign Policy* (Princeton: Princeton University Press, 1978), pp. 40–42. Krasner notes that deriving predictions about the behavior of hegemonic nations like the United States is particularly difficult. He writes, "A logical deductive approach to the problem of the national interest is not of much use when dealing with a hegemonic or imperial state whose territorial and political integrity is completely secure. *Even if* a realist theory suggests that such a state will be expansionary, it does not indicate the forms such thrusts will take. Will a hegemonic state move to military conquest, or will it

be satisfied with informal control?" My emphasis; *Defending the National Interest*, p. 41. Arnold Wolfers made a similar point when he discussed the vast differences that can arise between states in the way they define their "milieu goals." See Arnold Wolfers, *Discord and Collaboration: Essays on International Politics* (Baltimore: Johns Hopkins University Press, 1962), chapter 5.

58. Waltz took the "avoid high-intensity war" assumption of the structural position to its logical extreme when he argued that America's Rapid Deployment Force should not be designed to fight wars but rather to seize territory and deter enemy attacks (à la Schelling's throwing the steering wheel out of the car when playing Chicken). See Kenneth N. Waltz, "A Strategy for the Rapid Deployment Force," *International Security* 5 (Spring 1981): 49–73. Thomas Schelling, an economist and strategic thinker at Harvard, wrote extensively on limited war in the 1960s; see chapter 5.

59. See Graham Allison's Model III in *The Essence of Decision: Explaining the Cuban Missile Crisis* (Boston: Little, Brown, 1971). For other descriptions of the bureaucratic politics approach see Morton H. Halperin, *Bureaucratic Politics and Foreign Policy*, (Washington, D.C.: Brookings, 1974); I. M. Destler, *Presidents, Bureaucrats, and Foreign Policy: The Politics of Organizational Reform* (Princeton: Princeton University Press, 1972).

For an excellent description of bureaucratic politics arguments, see Robert Jervis, *Perception and Misperception in International Politics* (Princeton: Princeton University Press, 1976), pp. 24–25. The first chapter of this book provides an important summary of the "levels of analysis" problem.

60. This seems to be the prediction that is most fair to the bureaucratic politics perspective. However, it is not always simple to generate predictions from the bureaucratic politics model. For more on this see Jervis, *Perception and Misperception*, pp. 26–28.

61. Russell F. Weigley, *The American Way of War: A History of United States Military Strategy and Policy* (Bloomington, Indiana: University of Indiana Press, 1973), p. xxi. Weigley, to his credit, makes his argument with little hedging. Elements of his approach seem to rely on historical learning as a constraint on future behavior; other aspects of the argument seem to make the somewhat structural argument that the American approach to war-fighting is a result of material abundance.

62. Caleb Carr, "Should War Be Left to the Generals?" review of *Sheridan: The Life and Wars of General Phil Sheridan* by Roy Morris, Jr., and *A Battle from the Start: The Life of Nathan Bedford Forrest* by Brian Steel Wills, *New York Times Book Review*, July 5, 1992, p. 1.

63. John Shy, *A People Numerous and Armed: Reflections on the Military Struggle for American Independence* (New York: Oxford University Press, 1976), ch. 10. (This chapter is a reprint of an article by Shy in the February

1971 issue of the *Journal of Interdisciplinary History*.) Shy emphasizes the importance of learning from past events in shaping present historical choices.

64. Samuel P. Huntington, *The Soldier and the State: The Theory and Politics of Civil-Military Relations* (Cambridge: Harvard University Press, 1957), pp. 151–153. He discusses the importance of American political "ideals" on its foreign policy in "American Ideals versus American Institutions," *Political Science Quarterly* 97 (Spring 1982): 1–37. In the book on which the article is based, Huntington ties American values to its conduct of wars. See Samuel P. Huntington, *American Politics: The Promise of Disharmony* (Cambridge: Harvard University Press, 1981), p. 242. In support of his position he cites Seymour Martin Lipset, "The Banality of Revolt," *Saturday Review* 58 (July 18, 1970): 26. For an account of the influence of liberalism on Continental politics see Michael Howard, *War and the Liberal Conscience* (New Brunswick, N.J.: Rutgers University Press, 1978).

65. For the principal works written from this perspective see Snyder, *The Ideology of the Offensive*; Snyder, "Civil-Military Relations and the Cult of the Offensive, 1914 and 1984," and Van Evera, "The Cult of the Offensive and the Origins of the First World War." One should also see Barry R. Posen, *The Sources of Military Doctrine: France, Britain, and Germany between the World Wars* (Ithaca, NY: Cornell University Press, 1984).

66. Snyder, *Ideology of the Offensive*, p. 24.

67. Yuen Foon Khong, *Analysis at War: Korea, Munich, Dien Bien Phu, and the Vietnam Decisions of 1965*, (Princeton: Princeton University Press, 1992). On attitude change see Deborah Welch Larson, *Origins of Containment: A Psychological Explanation* (Princeton: Princeton University Press, 1985), chapter 1.

68. The Jominian principles, I have noted, correlate strongly with the "military element" in the "dual nature of war."

69. During the Korean War President Truman painfully learned the truth of this observation. After the disaster near the Yalu and the subsequent problems with General MacArthur, Truman imposed much tighter controls on his military commanders in Korea. It was no longer tolerable to defer judgments to the commander in the field when such great political consequences could follow from a mistaken military action. Alexander George has observed: "Indeed, the Korean War taught not only Truman but all succeeding administrations as well that the president's responsibility does not stop with establishing the political objectives to be pursued in a conflict; he must also *maintain firm control over the level of costs and risks that are acceptable* in pursuing those objectives. To exert control over costs and risks requires that the president be willing to control military strategy and tactics." See Alexander L. George, "The Development of Doctrine and Strategy," in Alexander L.

George, David K. Hall, William E. Simons, eds., *The Limits of Coercive Diplomacy: Laos, Cuba, and Vietnam* (Boston: Little, Brown, 1971), p. 4.

70. See, for example, John Keegan, *The Mask of Command* (New York: Viking Press, 1987), pp. 2–6.

2 | Patterns in America's Use of Force Before the Korean War

1. Seyom Brown, *The Faces of Power: Constancy and Change in United States Foreign Policy from Truman to Johnson* (New York: Columbia University Press, 1968), p. 8; see also the section in NSC 68 ("United States Objectives and Programs for National Security") entitled "II. Fundamental Design of the United States," *FRUS* (1950), 1: 238; for Eisenhower's NSC 162/2 on this point, see *FRUS* (1952–54), 2: 578 (in particular the section: "Basic Problems of National Security Policy").

2. Weigley, *The American Way of War*, passim.

3. Reginald C. Stuart, *War and American Thought: From the Revolution to the Monroe Doctrine* (Kent, Ohio: Kent State University Press, 1982).

4. See, Alexander DeConde, *The Quasi-War: The Politics and Diplomacy of the Undeclared War with France, 1797–1801* (New York: Charles Scribners, 1966); also, Edward P. Nash, *The Forgotten Wars: The U.S. Navy in the Quasi-War with France and the Barbary Wars, 1798–1805* (South Brunswick, NJ: A.S. Barnes, 1968).

5. DeConde, *The Quasi-War*, p. 332.

6. Ibid., p. 126.

7. Stuart, *War and American Thought*, chapter 6.

8. Donald R. Hickey, *The War of 1812: A Forgotten War* (Urbana, IL: University of Illinois Press, 1989), pp. 46-47.

9. Hickey, *The War of 1812*, p. 45.

10. Thomas A. Bailey, *The American Pageant: A History of the Republic*, 3rd. ed. (Boston: D. C. Heath, 1966), p. 211.

11. Hickey, *The War of 1812*, pp. 294–295. However, the defeat of Jackson might have prompted the British to reject ratification of the Treaty.

12. Hickey, *The War of 1812*, p. 296.

13. Weigley, *The American Way of War*, p. 76.

14. Ibid., pp. 71–72. Note that Scott also limited the means at his disposal.

15. John S. D. Eisenhower, *So Far from God: The U.S. War with Mexico, 1846–1848* (New York: Random House, 1989), p. xxi.

16. Weigley, *The American Way of War*, p. 76.

17. Ibid., chapter 7.

18. Bailey, *A Diplomatic History*, p. 481; John Dobson, *Reticent Expan-*

sionism: The Foreign Policy of William McKinley (Pittsburgh, PA: Duquesne Univ. Press, 1988), chap. 8.

19. Theodore Roosevelt's "Corollary" to the Monroe Doctrine called for American intervention in the region to prevent European intervention in the Western Hemisphere; the Europeans were usually exercised over matters related to the repayment of debt.

20. Hugh Thomas, *Cuba: The Pursuit of Freedom* (New York: Harper, 1971), p. 648.

21. Michael Howard, "The Classical Strategists," in his *Studies in War and Peace* (New York: Viking Press, 1971), p. 157.

22. Such conclusions were supported by the strategic bombing surveys conducted by the United States during and after the war although these analyses did provide evidence undermining the "decisive" nature of strategic bombing. See Harry Borowski, *A Hollow Threat: Strategic Containment before Korea* (Westport, CT: Greenwood Press, 1982), p. 20. Borowski cites *The United States Strategic Bombing Survey Over-all Report, European War* (Washington, D.C.: Government Printing Office, 1945), p. 107; and *USSBS, Pacific War* (Washington, D.C.: GPO, 1946), p. 28.

23. Howard, "The Classical Strategists," p. 157–158. In particular see the quotes from Blackett and Vannevar Bush. See Freedman's discussion of the "Spatz Report" of October 23, 1945 which outlined the great limitations on the usefulness of atomic weapons. Lawrence Freedman, *The Evolution of Nuclear Strategy* (New York: St. Martin's, 1981), pp. 50–51 and fn. 6, p. 406.

24. David Alan Rosenberg, "American Atomic Strategy and the Hydrogen Bomb Decision," *The Journal of American History* 66 (June 1979): 63–64. See also Rosenberg's fn. 6.

25. "American Atomic Strategy," pp. 63–64, 67.

26. Freedman, *The Evolution of Nuclear Strategy*, p. 54.

27. Rosenberg, "American Atomic Strategy," p. 68 and his fn. 27.

28. Rosenberg, "American Atomic Strategy," p. 69.

29. NSC-30, "United States Policy on Atomic Warfare," *Foreign Relations of the United States* (1948), 1: 624–28. (Hereafter abbreviated as *FRUS.*)

30. NSC-30, *FRUS* (1948), 1: 628.

31. Rosenberg, "American Atomic Strategy," p. 71.

32. In comparison, the United States spent $81.6 billion in 1945 (or 38.5 percent of GNP). In FY 1950 only $13.1 billion (or 5.1 percent of GNP) was spent, a reduction from the budget request of $1.3 billion. See John Lewis Gaddis, "Appendix: National Security Expenditures as a percentage of Total Government Expenditures and Gross National Product: 1945–1980," in *Strategies of Containment: A Critical Appraisal of Postwar American National Security Policy* (Oxford: Oxford University Press, 1982), p. 359.

33. Steven L. Rearden, *The Evolution of American Strategic Doctrine: Paul H. Nitze and the Soviet Challenge* (Boulder, Colorado: Westview Press, 1984), p. 11.

34. John Lewis Gaddis, *The Long Peace: Inquiries into the History of the Cold War* (New York: Oxford University Press, 1987), pp. 110–111. Freedman (1981) supports Gaddis's interpretation (1987) of these events; see Freedman, *The Evolution of Nuclear Strategy*, p. 53. He also has an interesting quote from Secretary of Defense Forrestal to the effect that virtually all major political leaders on both sides of the Atlantic expected and desired that atomic weapons be used in the event of war with the Soviet Union (pp. 52–53).

35. Brian Bond, *Liddell Hart: A Study of His Military Thought* (New Brunswick, N.J.: Rutgers University Press, 1977), p. 166. The epilogue to Hart's book was written in the autumn of 1945.

36. Freedman, *The Evolution of Nuclear Strategy*, p. 97. One should note that Hoffman Nickerson urged states to adopt policies of limited war before World War II in *Can We Limit War?* (New York: Frederick A. Stokes, 1933). Nickerson felt that disarmament efforts would be futile and that the future of Western civilization depended upon the self-restraint of warring nations.

37. Brian Bond, *Liddell Hart*, p. 5.

38. Freedman, *The Evolution of Nuclear Strategy*, pp. 98–99.

39. B. H. Liddell Hart, *The Revolution in Warfare* (London: Faber and Faber, 1946), p. 76. Subsequent page references to Hart's work will be cited in the text.

40. Jacob Viner, "The Implications of the Atomic Bomb for International Relations," *Proceedings of the American Philosophical Society*, 40, 1 (January 29, 1946): 53. The address was presented on November 16, 1945.

41. Viner, p. 54.

42. Viner, p. 54. My emphasis; and "standard" I take to mean what today is called "conventional."

43. Bernard Brodie, *The Atomic Bomb and American Security* (Yale University, Memorandum No. 18, November 1, 1945), p. 12. Viner does not refer to this piece by Brodie in the published version of his address *supra*.

44. Bernard Brodie, "The Implications for Military Policy," in Brodie, ed., *The Absolute Weapon: Atomic Power and World Order* (New York: Harcourt Brace, 1946), p. 76. In this chapter Brodie cites Viner's address described above. Brodie had been a student of Viner's, and they maintained a close intellectual collaboration. Thus, it would probably be unwise to assert that one of the two men indisputably discovered these ideas before the other.

45. Bernard Brodie, *War and Politics* (New York: Macmillan, 1973), p. 378.

46. George F. Kennan, *Memoirs: 1925–1950* (Boston: Pantheon, 1977), p. 308. Subsequent page references to Hart's work will be cited in the text.

47. One might disagree with Kennan's characterization of the Spanish-American War (1898) as part of the pattern of total war he discusses. The United States limited its war efforts geographically by not attacking Spain: the fighting was concentrated in Cuba and the Philippines. It has been noted that President McKinley maintained strict civilian control of the military and "devised an appropriate strategy that effectively utilized force to further his political objectives." [Allan R. Millett and Peter Maslowski, *For the Common Defense: A Military History of the United States of America* (New York: Free Press, 1984), p. 269.] Millett and Maslowski also note, "He pursued a peripheral strategy, directing attacks against Spain's colonies, hoping that many small victories, even if far from the enemy homeland, would have a cumulative effect." [Millett and Maslowski, p. 269.] Although I would differ with Kennan on this point, it is a close call. On the other side of the argument, Admiral Dewey's naval strategy appears to have incorporated a Mahanian commitment to obtain command of the high seas by engaging the opposing fleet in battle.

48. Kennan, *Memoirs: 1925–1950*, p. 312. Not all writers believed that the limited war solution was viable. Edward Mead Earle wrote that future prospects for peace could be sustained only by diplomatic negotiations and through the United Nations. See Edward Mead Earle, "The Influence of Air Power, *The Yale Review*, 35 (March 1946): 577–93.

49. Rosenberg, "American Atomic Strategy," p. 72.

50. "Evaluation of Effect on Soviet War Effort Resulting from Strategic Air Offensive," May 11, 1949. The text is included in Thomas H. Etzold and John Lewis Gaddis, eds., *Containment: Documents on American Policy and Strategy, 1945–50* (New York: Columbia University Press, 1978), p. 362; for comparison of Harmon to "Harrow" see Rosenberg, p. 72.

51. Etzold and Gaddis, *Containment*, p. 362; later Liddell Hart supported this military pessimism. See Basil Liddell Hart, "The Defence of the West," chap. in *Defence of the West* (New York: Morrow, 1950), pp. 102–17.

52. David Alan Rosenberg, "The Origins of Overkill: Nuclear Weapons and American Strategy, 1945-1960," *International Security* 7 (Spring 1983): 16. According to Rosenberg, *passim*, the Strategic Air Command did not take this more tactical responsibility very seriously.

53. I have relied here on Jerald A. Combs, "The Compromise That Never Was: George Kennan, Paul Nitze, and the Issue of Conventional Deterrence in Europe, 1949–1952," *Diplomatic History* 15 (Summer 1991): 366–371. The quote is on page 371.

54. NSC 68, *FRUS* (1950), 1: 268; cited in Combs, p. 373.

55. See Paul H. Nitze, *From Hiroshima to Glasnost: At the Center of Deci-*

sion, A Memoir (New York: Grove Weidenfeld, 1989); and Walter A. McDougall, *The Heavens and the Earth: A Political History of the Space Age* (New York: Basic Books, 1985).

56. *FRUS* (1950), 1: 141–2.

57. Paul Y. Hammond, "NSC 68: Prologue to Rearmament," in Warner R. Schilling, Paul Y. Hammond, Glenn H. Snyder, eds., *Strategy, Politics, and Defense Budgets* (New York: Columbia University Press, 1962), p. 294.

58. Rearden, *Evolution of American Strategic Doctrine*, p. 18.

59. Hammond, "NSC-68," p. 294–5.

60. Hammond, "NSC-68," p. 296.

61. For the letter see *FRUS* (1950), 1: 234–235; for the full text of NSC 68 before it was amended, see *FRUS* (1950), 1: 235–292.

62. Minutes, Policy Planning Staff meeting of October 11, 1949, *FRUS* (1949), 1: 399. The minutes were prepared by Harry H. Schwartz of the Policy Planning Staff. The quotes in this paragraph are taken from p. 402.

63. Ibid.

64. NSC 68, *FRUS* (1950), 1: 252.

65. Ibid.

66. Ibid., p. 253.

67. Ibid., pp. 287–289. For NSC 20/4, see "Note by the Executive Secretary on U.S. Objectives with Respect to the USSR to Counter Soviet Threats to U.S. Security," November 23, 1948, *FRUS* (1948), 1: 662–69. chapters 2–4 in Gaddis's *Strategies of Containment* provide a detailed accounting of the differences between Kennan's and Nitze's approaches to containment.

68. NSC 68, *FRUS* (1950), 1: 287–288.

69. NSC 68, *FRUS* (1950), 1: 273.

70. Preventive war was passed over because it would probably not disarm the Soviets and because "a surprise attack upon the Soviet Union, despite the provocativeness of recent Soviet behavior, would be repugnant to many Americans. Although the American people would probably rally in support of the war effort, the shock of responsibility for a surprise attack would be morally corrosive. Many would doubt that it was a 'just war' and that all reasonable possibilities for a peaceful settlement had been explored in good faith." See NSC 68, *FRUS* (1950), 1: 281.

Although preventive war was formally rejected, informal contingency planning continued within the U.S. government. The Air War College conducted a study in 1953–1954 called Project Control. The strategy it proposed called for "a highly aggressive strategy that would have forced the Soviets both to disarm and to abandon their empire in Eastern Europe; a rejection of these demands would have led to a discriminate counterforce attack and perhaps ultimately to full-scale war." See Mark Trachtenberg, "A 'Wasting Asset':

American Strategy and the Shifting Nuclear Balance, 1949–54," *International Security* 13 (Winter 1988–89): 42, fn. 154. Trachtenberg cites an unpublished manuscript by Tami Biddle Davis, "Handling the Soviet Threat: Arguments for Preventive War and Compellance in the Early Cold War Period," draft manuscript presented at conference of the Society for Historians of American Foreign Relations, Washington, D.C., June 9–11, 1988.

71. NSC 68, *FRUS* (1950), 1: 290.

72. NSC 68, *FRUS* (1950), 1: 266–267. On pp. 265–266 the study informs the reader that although the United States had the capacity to "deliver a serious blow against the Soviet Union" it would not be sufficient to cause the Soviets "to sue for terms or prevent Soviet forces from occupying Western Europe." Such a blow, as was capable of being delivered at that time, might tip the balance in favor of the United States in a war of long duration.

73. Rearden, p. 15; NSC 20/4, *FRUS* (1948), 1: 668.

74. Melvyn P. Leffler, *A Preponderance of Power: National Security, the Truman Administration, and the Cold War* (Stanford: Stanford University Press, 1992), p. 356. The passage in quotes appears at *FRUS* (1950), 1: 241—which Leffler cites. However, the last word of quote should be "step" (which is in brackets) not "task" which appears in the book. There is no difference in the meaning.

75. Nitze, *From Hiroshima to Glasnost*, p. 96.

76. Hammond, "NSC-68," p. 311.

77. Ibid., p. 312.

78. Ibid..

79. Richard Smoke, *National Security and the Nuclear Dilemma: An Introduction to the American Experience* (New York: Random House, 1987), p. 61.

80. Gaddis, *The Long Peace*, p. 114.

81. Hammond, "NSC-68," p. 320.

82. Gaddis, *The Long Peace*, p. 114.

83. Lawrence Freedman, "The First Two Generations of Nuclear Strategists," in Peter Paret, ed., *Makers of Modern Strategy* (Princeton: Princeton University Press, 1986), p. 738. NSC 68 makes the following recommendation: "it appears to be imperative to increase as rapidly as possible our general air, ground, and sea strength and that of our allies to a point where we are militarily not so heavily dependent on atomic weapons." See NSC 68, *FRUS* (1950), 1: 267.

84. Smoke, *National Security and the Nuclear Dilemma*, p. 61; emphasis in original.

85. NSC 68, *FRUS* (1950), 1: 244.

86. Ibid.

87. Ibid., pp. 277–78.

88. Ibid.p. 264.

89. Trachtenberg, "Wasting Asset," p. 6. (Subsequent page references will be cited in the text.)

90. Nitze, *From Hiroshima to Glasnost*, p. 97.

91. Trachtenberg, "Wasting Asset," p. 12, fn. 24.

92. NSC 68, *FRUS* (1950), 1: 266, 4.

93. Leffler, *A Preponderance of Power*, p. 356. Later Leffler observed that NSC 68 did not lead to a great debate within the Administration: "It could not do so because it introduced no new programs. . . . In fact, it simply reaffirmed the geopolitical and ideological basis of U.S. foreign policy. Its major point was that Soviet atomic capabilities greatly intensified the Soviet threat by enhancing the Kremlin's penchant for risk-taking. In response, the United States had to enlarge its military capabilities if it were to fulfill its own objectives. But Nitze did not make the case for any particular level of spending." Ibid., p. 359.

94. NSC 68, *FRUS* (1950), 1: 291.

95. Leffler, *A Preponderance of Power*, pp. 359–360. He writes with great accuracy of limited war's treatment within the document: "Although the stress on limited war was an absolutely critical part of NSC 68, it was so buried in the long, rambling, and repetitive paper that it did not receive the attention it deserved. Ever since autumn 1945, U.S. military officials had wanted to know where, when, how, and in what circumstances the United States would employ force. . . . Yet in mid-1950, clear answers were still not forthcoming." Ibid. p. 360.

96. Dean Acheson, *Present at the Creation* (New York: Norton, 1969), p. 374.

97. Acheson, *Present at the Creation*, p. 376.

98. Freedman, *The Evolution of Nuclear Strategy*, p. 75.

99. Acheson, *Present at the Creation*, p. 377.

100. Freedman, *The Evolution of Nuclear Strategy*, p. 75 (fn. 13, p. 408); Testimony of Secretary of State Acheson, Hearings of the Senate Foreign Relations and Armed Services Committees, *Assignment of Ground Forces of the United States in the European Area*, February 1951, p. 79.

3 | Korea: The Struggle to Wage Limited War

1. See Acheson, *Present at the Creation*, p. 405.

2. Despite these difficulties popular support for the war was high as evidenced by the results of a Gallup poll conducted from August 20–25, 1950 which indicated that 65% of those asked thought the United States had *not* made a mistake by entering the Korean War. See Dr. George Gallup, *The*

Gallup Poll: Public Opinion, 1935–1971, vol. 2: 1949–58 (New York: Random House, 1972), p. 938.

3. NSC 81/1, *FRUS* (1950) 7: 712–21; for an important discussion of the document by one of the participants see Omar N. Bradley and Clay Blair, *A General's Life*, (New York: Simon and Schuster, 1983), pp. 559–564.

4. "Acting Secretary of State to the United Nations Mission at the United Nations," September 26, 1950, *FRUS* (1950) 7: 781, par. 1.

5. NSC 81/1, *FRUS* (1950) 7: 713–14, sec. 7–9 and p. 716, sec. 15–7. MacArthur's orders, in part, paraphrased NSC 81/1. See *FRUS* (1950) 7: 781, par. 2.

6. Roger Dingman, "Atomic Diplomacy During the Korean War," *International Security* 13 (Winter 1988/89): 55. One should also study the book-length academic examination of the Korean War and the limitations placed on the use of force, see Rosemary Foot, *The Wrong War: American Policy and the Dimensions of the Korean Conflict, 1950–1953* (Ithaca, NY: Cornell University Press, 1985).

7. Dingman, "Atomic Diplomacy," pp. 55–60. The B-29 movement was reported in the July 11 edition of the *New York Times*.

8. Dingman, "Atomic Diplomacy," pp. 63–64. The story appeared in the August 1, 1950 edition.

9. Dingman, "Atomic Diplomacy," p. 65.

10. Foot, *The Wrong War*, p. 16.

11. *FRUS* (1950) 7: 852, fn. 1.

12. David Rees, *Korea: The Limited War* (New York: St. Martin's Press: 1964), p. 107; K. M. Panikkar, *In Two Chinas* (London: Allen and Unwin, 1955), pp. 110–111; Clay Blair, *The Forgotten War: America in Korea, 1950–1953* (New York: Times Books, 1987), p. 336.

13. *FRUS* (1950) 7: 826, fn. 1.

14. *FRUS* (1950) 7: 904.

15. In a Gallup poll conducted from September 17 to 22, 64% of those surveyed believed that the "United States should continue the fight in [North Korean] territory until they have surrendered." See Gallup, p. 943.

16. James F. Schnabel and Robert J. Watson, *The Joint Chiefs of Staff and National Policy: The Korean War*, vol 3. parts I and II (Wilmington, Delaware,: Michael Glazer, 1979), p. 295, fn. 15.

17. Clay Blair, *The Forgotten War*, pp. 386, 388.

18. "List of Points Prepared by the Secretary of State for Discussion with the Secretary of Defense and the Joint Chiefs of Staff," *FRUS* (1950) 7: 1204, pt. 6. For a description of the conversation, see "Memorandum of Conversation, by the Ambassador at Large (Jessup)," *FRUS* (1950) 7: 1204–8.

19. *FRUS* (1950) 7: 1237.

20. *FRUS* (1950) 7: 1242.

21. *FRUS* (1950) 7: 1243.

22. *FRUS* (1950) 7: 1264.

23. *FRUS* (1950) 7: 1278.

24. Foot, *The Wrong War*, pp. 117–118.

25. Schnabel and Watson, *JCS History*, p. 386.

26. Foot, *The Wrong War*, pp. 114–115.

27. Michael Schaller, *Douglas MacArthur: The Far Eastern General* (Oxford: Oxford Univ. Press, 1989), p. 225. Both Foot and Schaller cite Records of the Army Staff, G3 091 Korea TS, 5 July 1951, box 38 A, RG 319, National Archives. John Lewis Gaddis disputes the assertion that MacArthur formally requested the use of atomic weapons. He writes, "The accounts of Schnabel and James suggest that MacArthur, in the document cited by Foot, was simply responding to inquiries from the Joint Chiefs of Staff as to how such weapons *might* be used." See John Lewis Gaddis, *The Long Peace*, p. 116, footnote.

28. *FRUS* (1950) 7: 1631. The message from the JCS to MacArthur of December 29, 1950 may be found on p. 1625.

29. Foot, *The Wrong War*, pp. 121–122. Jessup was an adviser to Secretary Acheson and held the title of Ambassador-at-Large.

30. Foot, *The Wrong War*, pp. 118, 119; Schnabel, *Policy and Direction*, pp. 328–9. NSC 101 may be found in *FRUS* (1950) 7: 71–72.

31. Schnabel and Watson, *JCS History*, pp. 403, 406.

32. Blair, *The Forgotten War*, p. 618.

33. Another gloomy MacArthur cable was sent to Washington on January 10, 1951; in this cable he told Washington, in effect, that the political limitations on his use of force were so onerous that the United States should consider evacuating its forces from the Korean peninsula. See *FRUS* (1951) 7: 55–56. Blair has an excellent account of the discrepancy between MacArthur and Ridgway, see Blair, *The Forgotten War*, pp. 620–630.

34. Rosemary Foot, *The Wrong War*, p. 115; the quote is from NSC 100 (a report to the NSC by Symington), "Recommended Policies And Actions in Light of the Grave World Situation," *FRUS* (1951) 1: 9; Symington also advised withdrawal from Korea in the November 28, 1950 NSC meeting which followed the Chinese attack (see *FRUS* (1950) 7: 1247).

35. NSC 100, *FRUS* (1951) 1: 7.

36. Oral history interview with Stuart Symington, Oral History #374, pp. 69–70, conducted May 1981, available at the Truman Presidential Library.

37. Foot, *The Wrong War*, pp. 115–16.

38. *FRUS* (1951) 1: 33n.

39. Schnabel and Watson, *JCS History*, p. 437; Schnabel, *Policy and Direction*, pp. 326–27.

40. Schnabel, *Policy and Direction*, p. 327.

41. See Memorandum by Lucius Battle, January 19, 1951, *FRUS* (1951) 7: 102–5; for the quote see top of p. 104.

42. Schnabel, *Policy and Direction*, p. 330.

43. Schnabel and Watson, *JCS History*, p. 440.

44. Schnabel and Watson, *JCS History*, p. 450.

45. Foot, *The Wrong War*, pp. 147–48. For the full text of NSC 48/5 see *FRUS* (1951), 6 (Asia and the Pacific): 33–63; for those parts pertaining only to Korea, see *FRUS* (1951) 7: 439–42.

46. Schnabel, *Policy and Direction: The First Year* (Washington, D.C.: GPO, 1972), p. 393.

47. Blair summarizes the military activities that would be used in response to these two contingencies. They resemble the actions advocated by MacArthur in December 30, 1950 cable to Washington, *supra*. Blair, *The Forgotten War*, p. 906.

48. For an excellent discussion of NSC 48/5, see Blair, *The Forgotten War*, pp. 905–908; Ridgway's orders of May 31 are described on pp. 908–910. The Ridgway orders can be found in *FRUS* (1951) 7: 487–493. Blair writes (p. 908): "Generally, the JCS imposed tighter reins on Ridgway, for example, denying his earlier requests for authority to launch instant retaliatory attacks on Red China in event of a disastrous reverse or a Soviet attack and to withdraw Eighth Army from Korea for the defense of Japan at his discretion." For the relevant text see *FRUS* (1951) 7: 490–491.

49. Gaddis, *Strategies of Containment*, p. 122; Foot, *The Wrong War*, p. 148.

50. Schnabel, *Policy and Direction*, p. 393.

51. The limited war policy set forth in NSC 48/5 was confirmed with President Truman's signing of NSC 118/2 on December 20, 1951. Rosemary Foot writes of this document, "NSC 118/2 was therefore a reaffirmation of America's limited war policy, since it rejected courses of action designed to achieve its maximum objectives in Korea." (Foot, p. 169) In another passage Foot notes that NSC 118/2 was "a major restatement of NSC 48/5 of May 1951" but one that discussed at length "action to be taken if armistice talks failed." (p. 158) Despite plans for all sorts of contingencies NSC 118/2 "came out against a policy of attempting to achieve a military victory in Korea, and in favor of using political means to work for a unified and independent Korea." (p. 159)

The *JCS History* confirms this opinion by stating that "the Senior Staff concluded that US national interests would be best served by a course of limited war." In the event the negotiations failed NSC 118/2 allowed for an intensification of the war within Korea as long as these measures "did not result in disproportionate losses." It also allowed for defensive attacks on Chinese air bases "whenever the scale of enemy activity threatens to jeopardize the security of the United States forces in Korea." See Schnabel and Watson, *JCS History*, p. 639. For NSC 118/2 see *FRUS* (1951) 7: 1382–99. Increased military pressure was to be applied *within* Korea, but American interests, as the annex to NSC 118/2 concluded, would be best served by continuing the course of limited war (see *FRUS* (1951) 7: 1393–1395, especially sec. 29).

52. Smoke, *National Security and the Nuclear Dilemma*, pp. 77–78.

53. Michael H. Hunt, "Beijing and the Korean Crisis," *Political Science Quarterly* 107 (Fall 1992): p. 460.

54. Hunt, "Beijing and the Korean Crisis," p. 463. The first major Chinese crossing of the Yalu occurred on October 19, 1950. Hunt, p. 463.

55. Thomas J. Christensen, "Threats, Assurances, and the Last Chance for Peace: The Lessons of Mao's Korean War Telegrams," *International Security* 17 (Summer 1992): 139. Christensen continues with this point about the analyses that suggest MacArthur's actions, not the decision to unify Korea, provoked China's wrath: "So even if MacArthur had adopted the most conciliatory of reassurance strategies—never engaging Chinese troops north of Pyongyang and Wonsan in Late October, maintaining the largest of the various proposed buffer areas, and forging the November 24 offensive—Mao still planned to attack American troops in force.

56. See Schnabel, *Policy and Direction*, chap. 20, pp. 365–77; Schnabel and Watson, *JCS History*, chap. 10, pp. 505–546; Rees, chap. 11 & 12, pp. 196–229; and Blair, *The Forgotten War*, pp. 758–797 passim.

57. *Public Papers: Truman*, 1951: p. 223; this format will be used for citations from the Public Papers of the President series published by the Government Printing Office.

58. *Public Papers: Truman*, 1951: p. 226.

59. U.S. Senate Committees on Armed Services and Foreign Relations, *Military Situation in the Far East* (Hereafter *Military Situation*; Washington, D.C.: GPO, 1951), 82nd Congress, 1st session, 1951, p. 39. The transcript of the hearings has been completely declassified and is available at the Legislative Branch of the National Archives in Washington, D.C.; (Hereafter *Declassified Hearings*). Microfilm copies are available.

60. *Military Situation*, p. 40.

61. *Military Situation*, p. 67.

62. *Military Situation*, p. 45.

63. *Military Situation*, p. 324.

64. *Military Situation*, p. 365; my emphasis.

65. *Military Situation*, p. 365.

66. *Military Situation*, p. 610.

67. *FRUS* (1951) 7: 174–175.

68. *Military Situation,* p. 732.

69. *Military Situation,* p. 730.

70. Trachtenberg, "Wasting Asset," p. 27.

71. *Hamlet,* III, ii, 13. "It out-herods Herod."

72. Foot, *Wrong War,* p. 136.

73. *Military Situation,* p. 366.

74. *Military Situation,* p. 937.

75. *Declassified Hearings,* p. 2324. This seems consistent with Bradley's more "Clausewitzian" outlook: if the method of attrition did not work another approach to fighting the war would be found.

76. *Declassified Hearings,* p. 2445.

77. *Military Situation,* p. 899

78. Schnabel and Watson, *JCS History,* p. 558.

79. Blair, *The Forgotten War,* pp. 685–712.

80. Callum MacDonald, *Korea, The War Before Vietnam* (Houndmills, Basingstoke, UK: Macmillan, 1986), p. 218.

81. Dingman, "Atomic Diplomacy," pp. 72.

82. Dingman, "Atomic Diplomacy," p. 73.

83. Dingman, "Atomic Diplomacy," p. 75. Dingman adds (p. 76): "While the nuclear weapons remained on Guam, the bombers logged training flight time to prepare for using them. Early in June, in a departure from previous practice that the enemy might interpret as a prelude to expanding fighting, reconnaissance aircraft overflew airfields in Manchuria and Shantung to obtain target data." For more on the domestic political intricacies of this action in relation to the dismissal of General MacArthur see pp. 76–78.

84. Dingman, "Atomic Diplomacy," p. 76. The actual order appears in *FRUS* (1951) 7: 386–387. These orders were consistent with NSC 48/5 which was signed on May 17, 1951.

85. Dingman, "Atomic Diplomacy," p. 79. Keeping the war from flaring up again was part of bringing the war to an "acceptable conclusion."

86. MacDonald, *Korea,* pp. 218–219; Blair, *The Forgotten War,* pp. 897–902.

87. Maurice Matloff, *American Military History* (Washington, D.C.: GPO, 1969), p. 566. For a more detailed discussion of NSC 118/2 see fn. 51, this chapter, *supra.*

88. Matloff, *American Military History,* p. 567.

89. MacDonald, *Korea,* p. 234. The intensity of these raids was a mere continuation of the trends that became evident during the Second World War.

90. MacDonald, *Korea,* p. 235.

91. Stephen E. Ambrose, *Eisenhower: Soldier, General of the Army, Presi-*

dent-Elect, 1890–1952, vol. 1 (New York: Touchstone/ Simon and Schuster, 1983), p. 569.

92. Stephen E. Ambrose, *Eisenhower: The President*, vol. 2 (New York: Touchstone/ Simon & Schuster, 1984), p. 31.

93. McGeorge Bundy, *Danger and Survival: Choices about the Bomb in the First Fifty Years* (New York: Random House, 1988), pp. 240–241. Bundy presents evidence "from a Chinese friend of high professional standing" who "had heard from three separate individuals that they been told by Zhou Enlai himself that Stalin's death was what made the armistice possible." Of course, it is possible that Zhou Enlai may have had his own personal or political reasons for shifting the blame for the war's extension on to Stalin.

94. See, the editorial note, *FRUS* (1952–54), 15: 824; a summary of Zhou's remarks from March 30, 1953 is presented. The summarized remarks do not appear in quotation marks because they are a paraphrase.

95. *FRUS* (1952–54) 15: 824.

96. It should be noted that these events of April 1953 took place against a backdrop of the heaviest Chinese offensives since the spring of 1951.

97. For NSC 118/2 see *FRUS* (1951) 7: 1382–1387. Rosemary Foot comments on NSC 118/2 in *The Wrong War*, pp. 158–159. NSC 118/2 still argued for a policy quite similar to that of NSC 48/5, but it focused more on possible courses of action in the event the armistice talks failed. It is interesting to note that 118/2 called for intensifying the war effort in Korea, but it still recognized limits. Air attacks against China itself were still placed within the context of defense against Chinese air activity of such a scale as to seriously jeopardize the UN forces (pp. 1385–1386). It should be noted that Foot sees greater differences between 48/5 and 118/2 than this analysis presents. I see the sharp break coming between the policies of Truman and Eisenhower.

98. NSC 147, *FRUS* (1952–54), 15: 839–840.

99. NSC 147, *FRUS* (1952–54), 15: 840. The use of the word "current" indicates that policymakers saw themselves as still being involved in a war in which distinct and substantial limitations on the use of force were still in place.

100. NSC 147, *FRUS* (1952–54), 15: 840. It must be noted A, B, and C would not have extended the war from Korea, and the objectives remained limited: for A, maintain the war at its present level; for B, make the war of attrition much more costly; for C, move to the "waist" of Korea while inflicting maximum casualties. Options D, E, and F would have extended the war to China in various ways. Here, the final option, "F," called for MacArthur's solution to the war: eradicate the communist presence from the Korean peninsula.

101. *FRUS* (1952–54), 15: 845, sec. 21.

102. The appendices may be found at the Eisenhower Presidential Library,

White House Office: Office of the Special Assistant for National Security Affairs (OSANSA): Records 1952–1961, NSC Series, Policy Paper Subseries, Box 2, folder NSC 118/2, Appendices A and B to "Future Courses of Action in Connection with the Situation in Korea," March 28, 1953. For more information on the various documents in circulation at the time NSC 147 was formulated see *FRUS* (1952–54), 15, pp. 838–839, fns. 1–9.

103. Appendix "B," note 102, *supra*, 4c, pp. 6–7.

104. Appendix "B," sec. 17, p. 14.

105. Appendix "B," sec. 17b, p. 14.

106. Appendix "B," sec. 24, p. 17.

107. Schnabel and Watson, *JCS History*, p. 958.

108. *FRUS* (1952–54), 15: 1014.

109. *FRUS* (1952–54), 15: 1016.

110. Schnabel and Watson, *JCS History*, p. 959; for the text of the memo see *FRUS* (1952–54), 15, pp. 1059–64. This included Bradley and Collins: two of the strongest advocates of the Truman administration's limited war policy. Their reversal seems to indicate a perception that the cost of the war, with little potential for termination, had become unbearable for the United States. The war would have to be stopped or its prestige and position as a great power might be undermined.

The JCS also listed a number of important potential risks which had to be faced if the war were widened so as to defeat the Chinese and North Koreans. These included the possibility of a war with the Soviets in Asia or the possibility of another world war. See Schnabel and Watson, *JCS History*, pp. 959–60.

111. *FRUS* (1952–54), 15: 1061.

112. *FRUS* (1952–54), 15: 1061, 4b.

113. *FRUS* (1952–54), 15: 1061, 4c.

114. *FRUS* (1952–54), 15: 1062, par. 8; in an appendix entitled "Major Implementing Actions" the first item listed was "[o]btain from the President authority to employ atomic weapons" (p. 1063).

115. NSC meeting, May 20, 1953, *FRUS* (1952–54), 15: 1065. Those who disagree with the importance I place on this meeting *may* be supported by the fact that these questions were decided in the absence of Secretary of State Dulles. However, the implementation of this decision would have taken something like nine months; therefore, the fact that Dulles was absent certainly did not preclude future discussions with the President on this matter.

116. *FRUS* (1952–54), 15: 1066. "Fell" is in the text.

117. *FRUS* (1952–54), 15: 1066.

118. *FRUS* (1952–54), 15: 1067.

119. *FRUS* (1952–54), 15, pp. 1067–1068; my emphasis.

120. Schnabel and Watson, *JCS History*, vol. 1, p. vi.

121. Robert J. Watson, *History of the Joint Chiefs of Staff: The Joint Chiefs of Staff and National Policy, 1953–1954*, vol. 5. (Washington, D.C.: JCS Historical Division, 1986), p. 228.

122. Betts, *Nuclear Blackmail*, p. 42.

123. The figure of 9–12 months is also used explicitly in a memo to the Secretary of Defense (Wilson) on November 27, 1953. See *FRUS* (1952–54), 15: 1627, 2a.

124. Betts, *Nuclear Blackmail*, pp.. 41, 42.

125. In *Mandate for Change*, p. 181, Eisenhower's writing seems to imply that the first use of escalatory threats occurred before February 22, 1953 when General Clark wrote a letter to the Chinese making an offer for the exchange of sick and wounded prisoners. He says notice was discreetly given that the United States "intended to move decisively without inhibition in our use of weapons, and would no longer be responsible for containing the war to Korea." This dating of the initial threats is earlier than that of the late May 1953 efforts by Secretary Dulles, Ambassador Bohlen and General Clark. See Dwight D. Eisenhower, *Mandate for Change, 1953–1956* (Garden City, NY: Doubleday, 1963). Betts considers this less well known effort to threaten the Chinese, see Betts, *Nuclear Blackmail*, p. 44; for the text of Clark's letter see *FRUS* (1952–54, 15, pp. 788–9.

126. Memorandum of Conversation, by the Secretary of State, May 21, 1953, *FRUS* (1952–54), 15: 1068.

127. Memorandum of Conversation, by the Secretary of State, 22 May 1953, *FRUS* (1952–54), 15: 1071.

128. *FRUS* (1952–54), 15: 1096.

129. Dingman, "Atomic Diplomacy," pp. 86–87, 85.

130. Dwight D. Eisenhower Library, oral history interview with Andrew J. Goodpaster, Jr., April 10, 1982, OH# 477, p. 3.

131. Rosemary J. Foot, "Nuclear Coercion and the Ending of the Nuclear Conflict," *International Security* 13 (Winter 1988–89): 99 (92–112). Foot's lengthier study of the armistice talks expresses skepticism that atomic diplomacy forced the settlement. She sees a much more complex set of circumstances preventing the termination of the conflict. Of great importance was the "tendency to ignore Communist hints" which "arose out of a lack of familiarity with the art of negotiation, the mediators' insecurities about their skills for the task, and a deep distrust of their opponents." Clearly, Foot considers decision-making, bargaining, and misperception as critical factors in the long delay in ending the war. Rosemary Foot, *A Substitute for Victory: The Politics of Peacemaking at the Korean Armistice Talks* (Ithaca, NY: Cornell University Press, 1990), p. 215.

132. Foot, "Ending the Korean Conflict," p. 101. She writes: "What evidence is there to indicate that the threats were perceived as such by the communist side, or that the results were reflected in Chinese concessions at the truce talks? The evidence so far is inconclusive."

133. Foot, "Ending the Korean Conflict," p. 98. For the NSC study see NSC 140/1, Attachment, Report of the Special Evaluation Subcommittee of the National Security Council, May 18, 1953, *FRUS* (1952–54), 2: 333. This report will be referred to again in chapter 5.

134. Sherman Adams, *Firsthand Report: Inside the Eisenhower Administration* (New York: Harper, 1961), pp. 48–9.

135. Foot, *The Wrong War*, p. 214; for Dulles's remarks at Bermuda on December 7, 1953 see *FRUS* (1952–54), 5: 1711–1713.

136. Martin Gilbert, *Winston S. Churchill: 'Never Despair,' 1945–65*, vol. 8 (Boston: Houghton Mifflin, 1988), pp. 917–918.

137. Martin Gilbert, *Churchill*, p. 928.2

138. See The Joint Chiefs of Staff to the Commander in Chief, Far East (Clark), May 22, 1953, *FRUS* (1952–54), 15:1082–1086.

139. Clark, *From the Danube to the Yalu*, p. 267.

140. Rees, *Korea: The Limited War*, p. 417.

141. Rees, *Korea: The Limited War*, p. 436.

142. Dept. of State, *American Foreign Policy: Basic Documents, 1950–1955* (Washington, D.C.: GPO, 1957), p. 2662.

143. Indochina was then becoming a major worry for U.S. policymakers.

144. Foot, *The Wrong War*, pp. 214–5. Also of note, on May 12, 1953 President Eisenhower appointed "an entirely new group of generals and admirals to fill the positions of Joint Chiefs of Staff." General Collins was to be replaced by General Ridgway on August 15; Admiral Carney would replace Admiral Fechteler on August 15; General Twining would replace General Vandenberg as Chief of Staff of the Air Force on June 30; the new Chairman would be Admiral Arthur Radford, replacing Omar Bradley effective on June 30, 1953.

145. NSC 170/1, "U.S. Objectives and Courses of Action in Korea," *FRUS* (1952–54, 15, pp. 1622–1623.

146. Foot, *The Wrong War*, pp. 215. In a memo from the JCS to the Secretary of Defense on November 27, 1953, the Chiefs indicated that the best response to a sudden attack in Korea would rely most heavily on the "large scale" use of atomic weapons against China, Manchuria, and North Korea; see *FRUS* (1952–54), 15: 1627. They stated that the policy recommendations made before the May 20 NSC meeting were "no longer applicable to the situation in Korea."

Secretary Dulles strongly opposed the new JCS proposal because it advocated the use of atomic weapons in a manner that was not focused and limited to the local problem in Korea and would, therefore, be likely to bring the Soviet Union into the war. The issues were brought before the NSC on December 3, 1953 (Ibid., pp. 1636–45) and January 8, 1954 (Ibid., pp. 1704–10). Eventually, a position similar to State's was adopted: nuclear arms would be used, but a general war was not approved—this still allowed for the use of atomic weapons against military targets outside Korea that were supporting the communist operations on the peninsula; see JCS memo to the Secretary of Defense, December 18, 1953, *FRUS* (1952–54), 15: 1674–5. For a discussion of this debate see Robert J. Watson, *The Joint Chiefs of Staff and National Policy, 1953–1954*, pp. 228–229.

147. *FRUS* (1952–54), 15: 1709; my emphasis.

148. *FRUS* (1952–54), 15: 1709.

149. On this topic see Edward C. Keefer, "President Dwight D. Eisenhower and the End of the Korean War," *Diplomatic History* 10 (Summer 1986): 267–289; John Wilson Lewis and Xue Litai, *China Builds the Bomb* (Stanford: Stanford University Press, 1988), pp. 11–19; Jonathan D. Pollack, "A Chinese Achievement," book review of Lewis and Litai, *Science* 24 (23 September 1988): 1691–1692; McGeorge Bundy, *Danger and Survival*, pp. 238–245.

150. See Alexander L. George and Richard Smoke, *Deterrence in American Foreign Policy: Theory and Practice* (New York: Columbia University Press, 1974), pp. 238–240. A comparison of this interpretation with Dingman's is of interest, "Atomic Diplomacy," pp. 85–86.

151. Trachtenberg, "Wasting Asset," p. 28.

152. NSC 114/2, "United States Programs for National Security," October 12, 1951, *FRUS* (1951) 1: 187.

153. Memorandum by the Policy Planning Staff, "Briefing Memorandum on NSC 114/2," October 16, 1951, *FRUS* (1951) 1: 225.

154. NSC 140/1 (May 18, 1953), Attachment: Report of the Special Evaluation Subcommittee of the National Security Council, undated, *FRUS* (1952–54), 2: 333.

155. Trachtenberg, "Wasting Asset," p. 33.

156. For example, the U.S. estimated in 1955 that even under the improbable situation that only 5 percent of Soviet aircraft survived an American attack, that "75 weapons could be lifted against the United States." These would have been weapons ranging in size from 60 kilotons to 1 megaton.

See David Allan Rosenberg, "A Smoking Radiating Ruin at the End of Two Hours," p. 32. In a reprint of Defense Department Weapons System Evaluation Group (WESG) report of February 1955, WSEG 12, "Evaluation of an Atomic Offensive in Support of the Joint Strategic Capabilities Plan."

157. Trachtenberg, "Wasting Asset," p. 37 and note 136.

158. Trachtenberg, "Wasting Asset," p. 45.

159. Trachtenberg, "Wasting Asset," p. 37.

160. Brodie, *War and Politics*, p. 106.

161. Brodie, *War and Politics*, p. 63.

162. Osgood, *Limited War*, p. 178.

163. Maxwell Taylor, *Swords and Plowshares* (New York: Norton, 1972), p. 171.

164. Even President Truman's final comprehensive policy review for national security policy did not contain any recommendation for the use of atomic weapons. See "NSC 135/3, "Reappraisal of United States Objectives and Strategy for National Security," September 25, 1952. *FRUS* (1952–54), 2: 142–156; and NSC 141, "Reexamination of United States Programs for National Security," *FRUS* (1952–54), 2: 209–222.

165. Gaddis, *Strategies of Containment*, pp. 119–20.

166. William V. O'Brien, *The Conduct of Just and Limited War* (New York: Praeger, 1981), p. 257.

167. Osgood, *Limited War*, p. 189; quoted in Petraeus, dissertation, p. 42. *Limited War* was written prior to the Vietnam War.

168. Betts, *Soldiers, Statesmen, and Cold War Crises*, p. 20.

169. Roger Hilsman, *To Move A Nation: The Politics of Foreign Policy in the Administration of John F. Kennedy* (Garden City, N.Y.: Doubleday, 1967), p. 128–129.

170. MacDonald, *Korea*, p. 224. It is clear that Maxwell Taylor's name should have been added to Ridgway's.

171. Matthew B. Ridgway, *Soldier: The Memoirs of Matthew B. Ridgway* (New York: Harper), pp. 275–279. Ridgway's actions during the Dienbienphu crisis will be discussed in the next chapter.

172. *The New York Times*, February 11, 1953, "Van Fleet Leaves amid Controversy," p. 2.

173. *The New York Times*, February 15, 1953, p. 1.

174. In the May 11 article (p. 132), he said of the devastating U.N. counter-attacks to the massive Chinese spring offensives of 1951, "Though we could readily have followed up our successes and defeated the enemy, that was not the intention of Washington." The second article contained information about the collapse of the center of the Chinese main line of resistance after their attack in the fall of 1952 at White Horse Mountain (p. 164–169).

175. U.S. Congress, Senate, Subcommittee of the Senate Judiciary Committee to investigate the Administration of the Internal Security Act, *Interlocking Subversion in Government Departments*, 83rd Congress, 2nd session (Washington: GPO, 1954–55), pp. 2028, 2029; my emphasis. The name of

the counsel was Alva C. Carpenter. (These hearings will be cited hereafter as *Interlocking Subversion*; they are also referred to as the Jenner Subcommittee Hearings.)

176. General Almond began to testify on November 23, 1954.

177. *Interlocking Subversion*, pp. 2047–2048; see *U.S. News and World Report* interview, February 13, 1953, pp. 40–49. Almond told the interviewer (p. 45), "Throughout my service as an officer, I have followed the Clausewitzian theory that the main objective of a nation's army in battle is the hostile army."

178. *Interlocking Subversion*, p. 2073.

179. General Mark Clark (USA, Ret.), *From the Danube to the Yalu* (New York: Harper, 1954), p. 328.

180. MacDonald, *Korea*, p. 201.

181. Anthony Kellet, *Combat Motivation: The Behavior of Soldiers in Battle* (Kluwer: Nijhoff Pub., 1982), p. 251.

182. Kellet, p. 252; Kellet quotes Herbert Fairlie Wood, *Strange Battleground: The Operations in Korea and Their Effects on the Defence Policy of Canada* (Ottawa: Queen's Printer, 1966), p. 181.

183. MacDonald, *Korea*, p. 224; see also fn. 145 on p. 225.

184. Wood, *Strange Battleground*, p. 260.

185. Wood, *Strange Battleground*, p. 260.

186. Captain James A. Thomas, "Limited War: Theory and Practice," *Military Review*, 53 (February 1973): 80; Thomas cites Walter Hermes, *Truce Tent and Fighting Front* (Washington, D.C.: GPO, 1966), p. 509.

4. | The Dienbienphu Crisis

1. Every effort has been made to make the following account consistent with the only book-length history of the Eisenhower Administration's deliberations over Dienbienphu. See Melanie Billings-Yun, *Decision against War: Eisenhower and Dien Bien Phu, 1954* (New York: Columbia University Press, 1988). Hereafter referred to as *Decision against War*. For a quick guide to the Vietnam war as a whole see George C. Herring, *America's Longest War: The United States and Vietnam, 1950–1975*, 2nd ed. (New York: Knopf, 1986). Hereafter referred to as *Longest War*.

2. Philip B. Davidson, *Vietnam at War: The History, 1946–1975* (Navato, CA: Presidio Press, 1988), pp. 165–7. Davidson served in Vietnam as General Westmoreland's highest-ranking officer in charge of intelligence, J-2.

3. Davidson, *Vietnam at War*, pp. 203–204.

4. Ronald H. Spector, *Advice and Support: The Early Years of the United States Army in Vietnam, 1941–1960* (Washington: GPO, 1985), p. 189; Herring, *Longest War*, p. 30.

5. For an important account of the diplomatic and international influence on events see George C. Herring and Richard H. Immerman, "Eisenhower, Dulles, and Dienbienphu: 'The Day We Didn't Go to War' Revisited," *The Journal of American History* 71 (Sep 1984): 343–363. For an account of the Army's opposition to intervention see Ronald H. Spector, *Advice and Support: The Early Years of the United States Army in Vietnam, 1941–60* (Washington: GPO, 1985), chapter 11, pp. 191–214.

6. NSC 162/2, October 30, 1953, *FRUS* (1952–54), 2: 584, sec. 13b.

7. Spector, *Advice and Support,* p. 194.

8. NSC 5405 (*previously numbered NSC 177*), January 16, 1954, "United States Objectives and Courses of Action with Respect to Southeast Asia," *FRUS* (1952–54), 13: 971–976; see also *The Pentagon Papers* (Gravel ed.), 1: 434–43. NSC 5405 also confirmed the Truman administration's assessment, in NSC 124/2, with respect to Indochina's strategic value. See NSC 124/2, June 25, 1952, *FRUS* (1952–54), 12: 125–34; also in *The Pentagon Papers* (Gravel ed.), 1: 384–90.

9. NSC 5405, *FRUS* (1952–54), 13: 971, sec. 1a.

10. Spector, *Advice and Support,* p. 196.

11. NSC 5405, *FRUS* (1952–54), 13: 973–976.

12. Discussion at 179th meeting of the NSC, January 8, 1954, *FRUS* (1952–54), 13: 948.

13. Discussion at 179th meeting of the NSC, January 8, 1954, *FRUS* (1952–54), 13: 949.

14. Discussion at 179th meeting of the NSC, January 8, 1954, *FRUS* (1952–54), 13: 951.

15. Later, Admiral Radford told the group "that the French situation at [Dienbienphu] was serious because the Vietminh had succeeded in moving up heavy anti-aircraft support." Discussion at 179th meeting of the NSC, January 8, 1954, *FRUS* (1952–54), 13: 952.

16. Discussion at 179th meeting of the NSC, January 8, 1954, *FRUS* (1952–54), 13: 952. According to the minutes the only member of the JCS present for this part of the NSC meeting was the chairman, Admiral Radford.

17. Discussion at 179th meeting of the NSC, January 8, 1954, *FRUS* (1952–54), 13: 953.

18. Billings-Yun, *Decision against War,* p. 76.

19. Billings-Yun, *Decision against War,* p. 77.

20. William Conrad Gibbons, *The U.S. Government and the Vietnam War: Executive and Legislative Roles* (Princeton: Princeton University Press, 1986), pt. 1, p. 155; Gibbons is quoting William Arthur Radford, *From Pearl Harbor to Vietnam* (Stanford, CA: Hoover Institution Press, 1980), p. 383. Gibbons

has produced a study (now with three volumes; at least one more is expected) for the Senate Foreign Relations Committee. He has been affiliated with the Congressional Research Service of the Library of Congress.

21. Spector, *Advice and Support*, p. 195.

22. *The Pentagon Papers* (Gravel ed.), 1: 89; Anderson's words are in single quotes, those of the *Papers* constitute the remainder.

23. *The Pentagon Papers* (Gravel ed.), 1: 89. Just as there was a difference of opinion over intervention between the political actors, there was also disagreement between members of the military—even between members of the same service. Vice Admiral Davis seems to be combatting two ideas: (1) that ground forces could be excluded from the war once the U.S. engaged in fighting and (2) that it was possible to fight a war with less than a large and sufficient devotion of resources and effort to its prosecution.

24. The best account of the capture of Dienbienphu is still Bernard Fall's *Hell in a Very Small Place* (Philadelphia: Lippincott, 1967); his book *Street Without Joy* (New York: Schocken, 1972) covers the whole of the First Indochina War. According to Philip Davidson, General Giap, the Vietminh commander, had 49,000 combat soldiers and 10,000 to 15,000 logistical support personnel at Dienbienphu on March 13, 1953. The French had 10,800 men in the valley, but only 7,000 of them were combat soldiers. Davidson, *Vietnam at War*, pp. 223–224.

25. Fall, *Street Without Joy*, p. 315. Subsequent page references are cited in the text.

26. Radford, *From Pearl Harbor to Vietnam*, p. 391.

27. Spector, *Advice and Support*, p. 191; and, Billings-Yun, *Decision against War*, p. 31.

28. For the minutes of the conversations see *FRUS* (1952–54), 13: 1137–40.

29. *FRUS* (1952–54), 13: 1139.

30. *FRUS* (1952–54), 13: 1139–40.

31. *FRUS* (1952–54), 13: 1140.

32. Memo Conversation, Ridgway, March 22, 1954, Matthew B. Ridgway Papers, Box 30, US Army History Institute, Carlisle Barracks, PA.

33. Ibid., my emphasis.

34. "Memorandum by the Director," March 23, 1954, *FRUS* (1952–54), 13: 1144–5.

35. Memorandum for the President's Special Committee on Indochina, March 29, 1954, *The Pentagon Papers* (Gravel ed.), 1: 456, sec. 6 & 7.

36. *The Pentagon Papers* (Gravel ed.), 1: 458, sec. 15.

37. Memorandum of Conversation, by the Secretary of State, *FRUS* (1952–54), 13: 1150. The next day President Eisenhower would spell out

these necessary preconditions at an NSC meeting. The meeting of March 24 was a private one between Dulles and Eisenhower.

38. Memorandum by the Secretary of State to the President, March 23, 1954, *FRUS* (1952–54), 13: 1141.

39. Billings-Yun, *Decision against War*, p. 51.

40. Billings-Yun, *Decision against War*, p. 50.

41. Richard H. Immerman, "Between the Unattainable and the Unacceptable: Eisenhower and Dienbienphu," in *Reevaluating Eisenhower: American Foreign Policy in the 1950s*, ed. Richard A. Melanson and David Mayers (Urbana, IL: University of Illinois Press, 1987), p. 131.

42. NSC Meeting, 25 March 1954, *FRUS* (1952–54), 13: 1163–68.

43. Minutes of NSC meeting, 25 March 1954, *FRUS* (1952–54), 13: 1165. See the description of NSC 5405 above.

44. Minutes of NSC meeting, 25 March 1954, *FRUS* (1952–54), 13: 1166.

45. Gibbons gives the following historical description of the term "Associated States:" "On March 8, 1949, the French government took a step designed to placate the Vietnamese while preserving French control. By the Elysée Agreement between President Vincent Auriol and Emperor Bao Dai, it was decided that Vietnam, along with Laos and Cambodia, was to become an Associated State in the French Union." Gibbons, pt. 1, p. 50.

46. Minutes of NSC meeting, 25 March 1954, *FRUS* (1952–54), 13: 1167.

47. Minutes of NSC meeting, 25 March 1954, *FRUS* (1952–54), 13: 1167–68.

48. *The Joint Chiefs of Staff and the War in Vietnam: History of the Indochina Incident, 1940–1954* (Washington, D.C.: Historical Division of the Joint Secretariat, printed Wilmington, DE: Michael Glazier, 1982), p. 377; hereafter referred to as *The JCS History*. The *FRUS* version was prepared by S. Everett Gleason, the *JCS History* uses the "Gerhart 'Account.' " Air Force Major General John K. Gerhart was the JCS Special Assistant (or representative) for National Security Affairs. Gerhart was the JCS representative to the National Security Council Planning Board.

49. *JCS History*, p. 377.

50. *JCS History*, p. 377.

51. NSC 5405, *FRUS* (1952–54), 13: 974, sec. 23. France and the Associated States were encouraged to "produce a working relationship based on equal sovereignty within the general framework of the French Union."

52. Billings-Yun, *Decision against War*, p. 54. She does note this meeting did have one significant result: the creation of the Southeast Asia Treaty Organization (SEATO). SEATO's advantage for the U.S. would be the existence of

another relevant international organization besides the U.N. Security Council to work with—thus avoiding pro-Vietnamese vetos. Also, it would be a regional organization in which the French would not be able to block American action in the region. Remember, regional security organizations are permitted under the U.N. Charter.

Spector, *Advice and Support*, p. 229, informs us that on "9 September [1954] representatives of Britain, France the United States, New Zealand, Australia, Pakistan, the Philippines, and Thailand signed the Southeast Asia Collective Defense Treaty, which established a loose regional defense organization."

53. This paper by the NSC Planning Board was discussed by the NSC on April 6, 1954. The report can be found in *The Pentagon Papers* (Gravel ed.), 1: 462–471. For more information see Gibbons, pt. 1, p. 197, fn. 56.

54. *JCS History*, p. 378. From his address to the Overseas Press Club on March 29, 1954.

55. Gibbons, pt. 1, p. 176; see pp. 176–81 for a fascinating account of the ground work laid for the delivery of this speech.

56. Gibbons, pt. 1, p. 178.

57. Editorial Note, *FRUS* (1952–54), 13: 1181; Richard Nixon, *R.N.: The Memoirs of Richard Nixon* (New York: Gossett and Dunlap, 1978), p. 151.

58. Billings-Yun, *Decision against War*, p. 64.

59. Billings-Yun, *Decision against War*, pp. 67–68.

60. Billings-Yun, *Decision against War*, p. 74.

61. Billings-Yun, *Decision against War*, p. 79.

62. Gibbons, pt. 1, p. 203.

63. Gibbons, pt. 1, p. 203; I should point out that Gibbons does not present opinion in Congress as being monolithic with regard to this issue.

64. Memorandum for the File of the Secretary of State, April 5, 1954, *FRUS* (1952–54), 13: 1224.

65. Memorandum for the File of the Secretary of State, April 5, 1954, *FRUS* (1952–54), 13: 1224.

66. Memorandum for the File of the Secretary of State, April 5, 1954, *FRUS* (1952–54), 13: 1225.

67. Minutes of NSC meeting, April 6, 1954, *FRUS* (1952–54), 13: 1254.

68. Gallup, p. 1146, 1170, and 1243.

69. Memorandum by the Joint Chiefs of Staff to the Secretary of Defense (Wilson), *FRUS* (1952–54), 13: 1198.

70. Memorandum by the Chief of Staff, U.S. Army, April 2, 1954, *FRUS* (1952–54), 13: 1220.

71. Memorandum by the Chief of Staff, U.S. Army, April 2, 1954, *FRUS* (1952–54), 13: 1220; my emphasis.

72. Billings-Yun, *Decision against War*, p. 56.

73. Memorandum by the Chief of Naval Operations, April 2, 1954, *FRUS* (1952–54), 13: 1222.

74. Memorandum by the Commandant of the United States Marine Corps (Shepherd), April 2, 1954, *FRUS* (1952–54), 13: 1223.

75. Billings-Yun, *Decision against War:*, pp. 71–72.

76. Memorandum by the Chief of Staff, U.S. Air Force, April 2, 1954, *FRUS* (1952–54), 13: 1222.

77. Herring and Immerman, p. 349 and fn. 16. They do not cite any particular JCS memo.

78. James M. Gavin, "The Easy Chair—A Communication on Vietnam from Gen. James M. Gavin," *Harper's*, Feb. 1966. Gavin's remarks to this effect also appear in Spector, *Advice and Support*, p. 208. It was believed that the introduction of American troops into the region would be a *causus belli* as far as the PRC was concerned. Consequently, Ridgway and Gavin did not feel that military action in Indochina would be decisive, and there was no point in wasting one's military assets in nondecisive engagements. Dienbienphu and Indochina were analogous to the type of mess that the U.S. had dug itself into in Korea.

79. From available information it appears that the contemplated strikes under Vulture would use conventional not nuclear bombs.

80. Billings-Yun, *Decision against War*, p. 120.

81. The Ambassador in France to the State Department, April 5, 1954, *FRUS* (1952–54), 13: 1237.

82. The Ambassador in France to the State Department, April 5, 1954, *FRUS* (1952–54), 13: 1237.

83. *The Pentagon Papers* (Gravel ed.), 1: 456, sec. 8. In a set of minutes agreed to by Ély and Radford the U.S. agreed to push its military planners for the occasion "when and if our governments decided to oppose enemy air intervention over Indo-China if it took place."

84. Memorandum of Presidential Telephone Conversation, April 5, 1954, *FRUS* (1952–54), 13: 1241–1242.

85. Memorandum of Presidential Telephone Conversation, April 5, 1954, *FRUS* (1952–54), 13: 1242; or *The Pentagon Papers* (Gravel ed.), 1: 476.

86. *JCS History*, p. 382.

87. *FRUS* (1952–54), 13: 1240.

88. *FRUS* (1952–54), 13: 1308 and fn. 3.

89. *The Pentagon Papers* (Gravel ed.), 1: 102. Eden also expressed the fear that "united action" might lead to Chinese intervention once the tide of war began to recede from the Vietminh.

90. *FRUS* (1952–54), 13: 1312.

91. Secretary of State to the President, April 13, 1954, *FRUS* (1952–54), 13: 1322–1323.

92. Merchant was the Assistant Secretary of State for European Affairs. See Memorandum of Conversation by the Special Adviser to the U.S. Delegation (Merchant), April 27, 1954, *FRUS* (1952–54), 16: 1411.

93. *FRUS* (1952–54), 13: 1335.

94. *FRUS* (1952–54), 13: 1361 and fn. 1; Dulles was in Paris from April 21 to 24.

95. Herring and Immerman, p. 358.

96. *The Pentagon Papers*, I, 477; these words are Dulles's paraphrase of the discussion.

97. *FRUS* (1952–54), 13: 1269–70.

98. A copy was sent to the Secretary of the Army on April 24, 1954. Carlisle Barracks, Box 30, U.S. Army History Institute, Carlisle Barracks, PA.

99. Ridgway memo to Secretary of the Army, pt. 6; also in 6 April version at *FRUS* (1952–54), 13: 1269.

100. *FRUS* (1952–1954), 13: 1269.

101. *FRUS* (1952–1954), 13: 1270.

102. Spector, *Advice and Support*, p. 209.

103. Billings-Yun, *Decision against War*, p. 154.

104. Minutes of NSC meeting, April 29, 1954, *FRUS* (1952–54), 13: 1435.

105. Minutes of NSC meeting, April 29, 1954, *FRUS* (1952–54), 13: 1440.

106. Minutes of NSC meeting, April 29, 1954, *FRUS* (1952–54), 13: 1441–1442; my emphasis. The troop estimates given by the President resemble those presented by the NSC Planning Board to the NSC on April 6, 1954 (as requested by the NSC on March 25, 1954). Gibbons summarizes its estimates as follows: "if the U.S. intervened after French withdrawal, 605,000 ground forces would be required, of which 330,000 would be indigenous and 275,000 (seven divisions and support personnel) would be U.S. or allied forces. . . . This latter figure (275,000) is quite close to the number of U.S. forces that, during the Kennedy administration, Secretary of Defense Robert S. McNamara first estimated would be needed to win the war." Of course, Eisenhower's response to this estimate and what it entailed was quite the opposite of President Johnson's. See Gibbons, pt. 1, p. 198, fn. 56.

107. Eisenhower, *Mandate for Change*, pp. 354–355.

108. *FRUS* (1952–54), 13: 1449. Also in *Mandate for Change*, pp. 354–355.

109. Eisenhower, *Mandate for Change*, p. 354; or see the Editorial Note, *FRUS* (1952–54), 13: 1448–1449.

110. Also, keep in mind some of the statements made by Eisenhower regarding military options if truce talks failed in Korea.

111. Memorandum Prepared in the Department of State, May 11, 1954, *FRUS* (1952–54), 13: 1533.

112. *FRUS* (1952–54), 13: 1534.

113. The Sec. of State to the Embassy in France, May 11, 1954, *FRUS* (1952–54), 13: 1534–1535. This cable was written by the Secretary and approved by the President (see fn. 1).

114. Spector, *Advice and Support*, p. 213.

115. Spector, *Advice and Support*, p. 213.

116. *The Pentagon Papers* (Gravel ed.), 1: 508–509.

117. *FRUS* (1952–54), 13: 1590–2.

118. Lt. General John W. O'Daniel assumed command of the U.S. Military Assistance Advisory Group (or MAAG) in Hanoi on March 31, 1954. Soon thereafter O'Daniel lost confidence in the French commander, Lt. Gen. Henri Navarre. As Dienbienphu was succumbing to the Vietminh, O'Daniel and his staff, believing that the game was not yet lost, created a war-plan for the French. Code named Redland, and based on General Van Fleet's plans in Greece during its post-World War II civil war, it was a three-phase operation that was to be completed in two-years. Redland appears to have ignored the revolutionary aspects of the war and focused excessively on conventional military tactics and strategy. Nevertheless, it demonstrates that the U.S. MAAG had no intention of fighting a passive, defensive war against the Vietminh. Spector, *Advice and Support*, p. 222.

119. *The Pentagon Papers* (Gravel ed.), 1: 127.

120. *The Pentagon Papers* (Gravel ed.), 1: 511; emphasis in original.

121. *The Pentagon Papers* (Gravel ed.), 1: 509–10; also in *FRUS* (1952–54), 12: 514–6.

122. *The Pentagon Papers* (Gravel ed.), 1: 509–19.

123. John Foster Dulles memorandum, memorandum of conversation with Eisenhower, May 25, 1954, White House Memorandum series, "Meetings with the President 1954 (3)," Dulles Papers, Seeley G. Mudd Library, Princeton University.

124. Herring, *Longest War*, pp. 38–39.

125. Spector, *Advice and Support*, p. 214.

126. Herring and Immerman, p. 363.

127. Billings-Yun, *Decision against War*, p. 159.

128. Billings-Yun, *Decision against War*, p. 160.

129. Hagerty Diary, April 26, 1954, *FRUS* (1952–54), 16: 1411.

130. See James M. Gavin, *Crisis Now* (New York: Random House, 1968), pp. 46–47. Gavin, Ridgway's G-3 in 1954, explicitly links the Korean War experience with planning in this crisis.

5. | The Ascendance of Limited War Theory in the 1950s and 1960s

1. Freedman, *The Evolution of Nuclear Strategy*, pp. 77–78.

2. NSC 162/2, sec. 39.b.1. in *FRUS* (1952–54) 2: 593. This section states, "In the event of hostilities, the United States will consider nuclear weapons to be as available for use as other munitions." NSC 162/2 was signed on October 30, 1953.

3. Freedman, *Evolution of Nuclear Strategy*, pp. 77–78.

4. David Alan Rosenberg, "A Smoking Radiating Ruin at the End of Two Hours": Documents on American Plans for Nuclear War with the Soviet Union," *International Security* 6 (Winter 1981/82): 14.

5. 8 May 1950, *FRUS* (1950) 1: 311.

6. 28 April 1953, *FRUS* (1952–54) 2: 307.

7. NSC 162/2, *FRUS* (1952–54) 2: 588. In *Strategies of Containment* John Lewis Gaddis discusses the relationship of political grand strategy to economic policy. I concur with Gaddis's assessment of Eisenhower's fiscal conservatism and its effect on the New Look but place greater emphasis on the military philosophy underlying Ike's grand strategy.

8. John Foster Dulles, "Policy for Security and Peace," *Foreign Affairs* 32 (April 1954): 358.

9. Dulles, "Policy for Security and Peace," p. 359.

10. NSC 162/2, *FRUS* (1952–54) 2: 581.

11. John Lewis Gaddis, "The Unexpected John Foster Dulles: Nuclear Weapons, Communism, and the Russians" in *John Foster Dulles and the Diplomacy of the Cold War* (Princeton: Princeton University Press, 1990), p. 58.

12. Gaddis, "The Unexpected John Foster Dulles," p. 58.

13. Gaddis, "The Unexpected John Foster Dulles," p. 52.

14. NSC 162/2, *FRUS* (1952–54) 2: 590–591, sec. 32.b.

15. NSC 162/2, *FRUS* (1952–54) 2: 581, sec. 6c. This important section reads in part: "increasing Soviet atomic capability may tend to diminish the deterrent effect of U.S. atomic power against peripheral Soviet aggression."

16. NSC 162/2, *FRUS* (1952–54) 2: 595, sec. 43.a, b.

17. Gaddis, *Strategies of Containment*, p. 157–8.

18. Samuel P. Huntington, *The Common Defense: Strategic Programs in National Politics* (New York: Columbia University Press), p. 105.

19. George and Smoke, p. 30; Freedman (*Evolution of Nuclear Strategy*, p. 113, n. 9) tells us that Liddell Hart coined the term in a letter to the London *Times* on August 29, 1955.

20. Huntington, *The Common Defense*, p. 105.

21. Gaddis, *Strategies of Containment*, pp. 147–148.

22. George and Smoke, p. 563.

23. Freedman, *Evolution of Nuclear Strategy*, p. 89.

24. Freedman, *Evolution of Nuclear Strategy*, p. 90.

25. Maxwell Taylor wrote that it was difficult to argue persuasively for Limited War capabilities and doctrine during the Eisenhower administration. "Limited war," Taylor says of these members of the executive branch, "suggested Korea, a thought which was repulsive to officials and public alike." See Maxwell Taylor, *Swords and Plowshares* (New York: Norton, 1972), p. 171.

26. Trachtenberg, "Wasting Asset," p. 37.

27. Gaddis, *Strategies of Containment*, p. 135.

28. Gaddis, *Strategies of Containment*, p. 135.

29. Richard H. Immerman, "Confessions of an Eisenhower Revisionist: An Agonizing Reappraisl," *Diplomatic History* (Summer 1990), p. 325.

30. Gaddis, *Strategies of Containment*, p. 135.

31. Richard H. Immerman, "Confessions of an Eisenhower Revisionist: An Agonizing Reappraisal," *Diplomatic History* (Summer 1990): 326, n. 26.

32. Immerman, "Confessions of an Eisenhower Revisionist," p. 328.

33. H.W. Brands writes that "[a] deterrent, nuclear or otherwise, must be believable to be effective." See H. W. Brands, "The Age of Vulnerability: Eisenhower and the National Security State," *American Historical Review* 94 (October 1989): 972.

34. Privately, Dulles appeared to have a much more subtle grasp of Sino-Soviet differences for example. See Gaddis's description of the briefing he delivered to Eisenhower and Churchill at the December 1953 Bermuda Conference. Gaddis, "The Unexpected John Foster Dulles," pp. 61–62.

35. George G. Kistiakowsky, *A Scientist at the White House: The Private Diary of President Eisenhower's Special Assistant for Science and Technology* (Cambridge: Harvard University Press, 1976), p. 400.

36. Marc Trachtenberg, "Strategic Thought in America, 1952–1966," *Political Science Quarterly* 104 (Summer 1989): 329. This is an abridged version of the article; the full-length version see Marc Trachtenberg, "Strategic Thought in America, 1952–1966," chap. in *History and Strategy* (Princeton: Princeton University Press, 1991), pp. 3–46.

37. Trachtenberg, "Strategic Thought in America," p. 329 and fn. 78.

38. Trachtenberg, "Strategic Thought in America," p. 330.

39. Trachtenberg, "Strategic Thought in America," in *History and Strategy*, p. 41 , fn. 88.

40. Freedman, *Evolution of Nuclear Strategy*, p. 93.

41. For an excellent bibliography of works from this period on Limited War, see Morton H. Halperin, *Limited War in the Nuclear Age* (New York: John Wiley, 1963), pp. 133–184.

42. "Atomic Weapons and the Korean War," Editorial, *Bulletin of Atomic Scientists* 6 (July 1950): 194, 217. The quote appears on p. 217.

43. William W. Kaufmann, ed., *Military Policy and National Security* (Princeton: Princeton University Press, 1956). "The Requirements of Deterrence" was actually written in 1954. This chapter was circulated as Memorandum Number Seven at the Center of International Studies (at Princeton University) on November 15, 1954.

44. Kaufmann, *Military Policy and National Security*, "The Requirements of Deterrence," p. 29.

45. Kaufmann, *Military Policy and National Security*, "Limited War," p. 135.

46. It should also be noted that Bernard Brodie wrote one of the earliest pieces in the post-Korea Limited War School. See Bernard Brodie, "Unlimited Weapons and Limited War," *The Reporter* 11 (18 Nov. 1954): 16–21. In the article he stated (p. 19), "if total war is to be averted, we must be ready to fight limited wars with limited objectives—if for no other reason than that limited objectives are always better than unlimited disaster." Later in the article Brodie added: "limited war does not necessarily mean war without victory."

47. Robert Endicott Osgood, *Limited War: The Challenge to American Strategy* (Chicago: University of Chicago Press, 1957).

48. "War is the mere continuation of politics but by other means." See Osgood, *Limited War*, p. 21.

49. Henry A. Kissinger, *Nuclear Weapons and Foreign Policy* (New York: Harper, 1957).

50. In fairness to the Eisenhower administration we should remember its emphasis in NSC 162/2 on diplomatic, psychological, and economic courses of action as well.

51. Kissinger, *Nuclear Weapons*, ch. 6, sec. 3.

52. Kissinger, *Nuclear Weapons*, ch. 6, sec. 3: 125.

53. "Escalation" was first used in its present strategic context by Wayland Young a proponent of nuclear disarmament in *Strategy for Survival: First Steps in Nuclear Disarmament* (London: Penguin Books, 1959); for this fact see Lawrence Freedman, "On the Tiger's Back: The Development of the Concept of Escalation," chap. in Roman Kolkowicz, ed. *The Logic of Nuclear Terror* (Boston: Allen & Unwin, 1987): 115.

54. Henry A. Kissinger, "Limited War: Nuclear or Conventional?—A Reappraisal," *Daedalus* 89 (Fall 1960): 800–817. Not all analysts came to this conclusion. Bernard Brodie argued in the spring of 1963 (see *The Reporter*, "What Price Conventional Capabilities in Europe?" May 23, 1963) that it was possible to control escalation in a major war using tactical nuclear weapons.

55. Maxwell D. Taylor, *The Uncertain Trumpet* (New York: Harper & Row, 1959), pp. 6–7. Taylor provides a powerful and emotional defense of the limitation of ends and means exhibited by U.N. policy in the Korean War (see pp. 14–15).

56. Taylor, *The Uncertain Trumpet*: 151.

57. Taylor, *The Uncertain Trumpet*, pp. 145–146. For confirmation of Maxwell Taylor's advocacy of the Limited War position see Rosenberg, "Origins of Overkill," passim. Michael Carver writes that Taylor's policy "would mean that the United States, and it was to be hoped that the West as a whole would have the capability to employ whatever means was appropriate to the threat, from diplomatic, political, or economic action, through clandestine or "special" forces, to full-scale conventional campaigns anywhere in the world." Michael Carver, "Conventional Warfare in the Nuclear Age," in Peter Paret, ed., *Makers of Modern Strategy from Machiavelli to the Nuclear Age* (Princeton: Princeton University Press, 1986): 787.

58. See Thomas C. Schelling, "Bargaining, Communication and Limited War," *Journal of Conflict Resolution* 1 (1957): 19–36; *Nuclear Weapons and Limited War* (Rand P-1620: Feb. 20, 1959); and *The Strategy of Conflict* (Cambridge: Harvard University Press, 1960); *Arms and Influence* (New Haven: Yale University Press, 1966), the book was apparently finished by November 1965.

59. Smoke, *National Security and the Nuclear Dilemma*, p. 80.

60. Herman Kahn, *On Escalation: Metaphors and Scenarios* (New York: Praeger, 1965). Also, *On Thermonuclear War* (Princeton: Princeton University Press, 1960).

61. Freedman, *Evolution of Nuclear Strategy*, p. 216.

62. Freedman, "On The Tiger's Back," p. 5.

63. Freedman, *Evolution of Nuclear Strategy*, p. 217.

64. Although I will not discuss them in the text, it should be noted that the service journals associated with the Army published important articles related to the debate over Limited War capabilities; see *Combat Forces Journal* from 1953–6. Of particular importance are Hanson W. Baldwin, "Strategy of Restraint or Chaos Unlimited," *Combat Forces Journal* 4 (January 1954): 10–13; Rear Admiral John D. Hayes, "Peripheral Strategy . . . Littoral Tactics . . . Limited War," *Combat Forces Journal* 5 (September 1954): 36–9; Anonymous authors, "Mission for the Army: The Winning of World War III," *Combat Forces Journal* 5 (February 1955): 16–20; General Maxwell D. Taylor, "The Changing Army," *Combat Forces Journal* 6 (October 1955): 10; Hanson W. Baldwin, "Landpower as an Element of National Power," *Combat Forces Journal* 6 (January 1956): 16–21.

The journal *Military Review* also contains articles on the massive retaliation-limited war debate. See "Readiness for the Little War—Optimum Integrated Strategy," *Military Review* 37 (April 1957): 14–26; "Readiness for the Little War—A Strategic Security Force," *Military Review* 37 (May 1957): 14–21; George Fielding Eliot, "Less-Than-Total Solutions," *Military Review* 37 (October 1957): 3–10 [see, especially, the paragraph by Maxwell Taylor following Eliot's article]; Raymond L. Garthoff, "Soviet Views on Limited War," *Military Review* 37 (January 1958): 50–60; General Willard G. Wyman, "The United States Army: Its Doctrine and Influence on U.S. Military Strategy," *Military Review* 37 (March 1958): 3–13.

65. A. J. Bacevich, *The Pentomic Era: The US Army Between Korea and Vietnam* (Washington, D.C.: National Defense University Press, 1986), p. 27. At the time of this writing, Bacevich was a colonel in the U.S. Army.

66. Bacevich, *Pentomic Era*, p. 28.

67. Bacevich, *Pentomic Era*, p. 29.

68. Apparently, Admiral Carney, the Chief of Naval Operations, also signed off on the Ridgway paper. *FRUS* (1952–54) 2: 639. The text of NSC 5410/1 appears on pp. 644–646. Approved by the President on 29 March 1954.

69. *FRUS* (1952–54) 2: 640.

70. Eisenhower's reasoning appears to contradict what the theory of structural realism would predict in this situation. That is, the mutual nuclear capabilities of the United States and the Soviet Union should have made the President more receptive to the argument in favor of Limited War capabilities. In 1953 Eisenhower was well informed about the amount of damage the Soviet Union could inflict upon the United States. NSC 140/1 (May 1953) stated that an optimal placement of nuclear bombs on the United States by the Soviets would be able to produce a maximum of 9 million casualties in 1953 and 12.5 million in 1955; half of these would be deaths. In 1953 one-third of U.S. industrial production would have been affected, two-thirds in 1955. See NSC 140/1, Attachment, Report of the Special Evaluation Subcommittee of the National Security Council, May 18, 1953, *FRUS* (1952–54) 2: 333.

71. *FRUS* (1952–54), 2: 640–641.

72. Bacevich, *Pentomic Era*, pp. 37–38; my emphasis. It is interesting to note that Ridgway saw this debate as relating to considerations about preventive war.

73. *FRUS* (1952–54) 2: 804.

74. *FRUS* (1952–54) 2: 805–806.

75. Bacevich, *Pentomic Era*, p. 41.

76. Ridgway, *Soldier*, p. 324. Dated June 27, 1955.

77. Bacevich, *Pentomic Era*, p. 51.

78. For a description of this restructuring, see Bacevich, chapter 5.

79. Bacevich, *Pentomic Era*, pp. 109–110.

80. For the command and control problems see Bacevich, *Pentomic Era*, pp. 132–136.

81. Bacevich, *Pentomic Era*, pp. 141–142.

82. Consider the following quotes which demonstrate that Ridgway associated total war with nuclear war; they appear in *The Korean War* (Garden City: Doubleday, 1967):

"Before Korea, all our military planning envisioned a war that would involve the world, and in which the defense of a distant and indefensible peninsula would be folly. But Korea taught us that all warfare from this time forth must be limited. It could no longer be a question of *whether* to fight a limited war, but of *how* to avoid fighting any other kind. Unlimited war, now that many nations own thermonuclear weapons or the skill to build them, is no longer possible, for it would mean mutual annihilation." (pp. vi- vii)

"A limited war is not merely a small war that has not yet grown to full size. It is a war in which the objectives are specifically limited in the light of our national interest and our current capabilities. A war that is 'open-ended' . . . is a war that may escalate itself indefinitely, as wars will, with one success requiring still another to insure the first one. An insistence on going all-out to win a war may have a fine masculine ring, and a call to "defend freedom" may have a messianic sound that stirs our blood. But the ending of an all-out war in these times is beyond imagining. It may mean the turning back of civilization by several thousand years, with no one left capable of signaling the victory." (p. 245)

83. Taylor, *The Uncertain Trumpet*, pp. 14–15.

84. Harry G. Summers, *On Strategy: The Vietnam War in Context* (Washington, D.C.: GPO, 1981), p. 65; Summers cites U.S. Cong., Senate Committee on Foreign Relations, *Vietnam Hearings*, "To Amend Further the Foreign Assistance Act of 1961 as Amended," 89th Cong., 2nd sess. (Washington, D.C.: GPO, 1966), p. 440, 460.

85. Taylor, *Swords and Plowshares*, p. 163. Note Taylor's use of the word "conclusion" not "victory."

86. Matthew B. Ridgway, *Soldier*, p. 277. "Again" is clearly a reference to the Korean War. This thesis's interpretation of Ridgway's behavior at Dienbienphu is supported by Trachtenberg, "A 'Wasting Asset," p. 42, fn. 154. Trachtenberg also has interesting assessments of the behavior of the other members of the Joint Chiefs of Staff.

87. Ridgway, *Soldier*, pp. 323–332. David Petraeus asserts that Ridgway's assistant, General James M. Gavin, was not truly disposed to fighting limited wars, as he stated in the late 1950s. He writes: "Despite Gavin's apparent argument for fighting limited wars, he opposed American military involvement in Vietnam (both in 1954 and in the early 1960s—the latter while in retirement)

and Laos—leaving some question as to just what kind of limited war he felt the United States should fight (p. 53)." It seems that Ridgway is implicated in this observation as well, for he professed support for Limited War capabilities but never seemed to find one worth fighting.

88. The 1954 manual did not have a definition of limited war *per se*; the version of the FM 100–5 released in 1962 contains a definition that will be discussed below.

89. Department of the Army Field Manual 100–5, *Field Service Regulations: Operations* (Washington, D.C.: GPO, Sept. 1954), Ch. 1, sec. 2: 4. Hereafter, FM 100–5.

90. FM 100–5 (1954), Ch. 1, sec. 4, p. 5; my emphasis.

91. FM 100–5 (1954), Ch. 1, sec. 8., p. 7.

92. FM 110–5 (1954): 25; emphasis in original.

93. FM 100–5 (1954), sec. 70, p. 25; emphasis in original.

94. FM 100–5 (1954), sec. 72, p. 26; emphasis in original.

95. FM 100–5 (1962), sec. 9, p. 5.

96. FM 100–5 (1962), sec. 9. p. 5.

97. This interpretation is supported by the field manual's definition of total war, sec. 10.

98. Colonel T. N. Dupuy, "War without Victory," *Military Review*, 35 (March 1956): 28–32. At the time Colonel Dupuy was a professor of military science and tactics at Harvard University. Subsequent page references to the work are cited in the text.

99. Ridgway, *Soldier*, p. 295; my emphasis.

100. Matthew B. Ridgway, "The Soldier and National Policy," p. 2; delivered February 14, 1955, Council on Foreign Relations (New York), John J. McCloy presiding. The digest of this meeting is available from the Council's archives.

101. Bacevich, *Pentomic Era*, p. 63.

102. According to Harry Summers, Decker was "one of the few senior officers who resisted President John F. Kennedy's pressure to turn the military into a counterinsurgency force." See Harry G. Summers, Jr., *Vietnam War Almanac* (New York, Facts on File, 1985), p. 136. Summers's characterization of Kennedy's plan for the Army is too extreme: Kennedy did not wish to convert the Army into a force intended to exclusively fight counterinsurgencies; rather, he wanted to develop genuine and effective capabilities of this kind.

103. David A. Welch and James G. Blight, "An Introduction to ExComm Transcripts," *International Security* 12 (Winter 1987/88): 24.

104. Maxwell Taylor's tenure as Chief of Staff of the Army (1955–59) had much in common with Ridgway's in that they both battled for expanded funding of conventional forces and both became personae non grata within the

Eisenhower administration. The differences between Ridgway and Taylor concerning their conceptions of limited war were not particularly visible at that time. The claim that Taylor was a genuine advocate of all forms of limited warfare including counterinsurgency warfare has been challenged recently. See Andrew F. Krepinevich, Jr., *The Army and Vietnam* (Baltimore: Johns Hopkins Press, 1986). Krepinevich argues that Taylor was interested only in beefing up mid-intensity forces (i.e., conventional) and was not greatly concerned with lower intensity conflict. While it may be true that Taylor's focus was on mid-intensity conflict, Krepinevich's revisionism is too sweeping in its criticism of Taylor.

105. Taylor testimony, *Vietnam Hearings*, p. 438.

106. The variety of opinion within the Army can also be seen at the level of colonels within the service. My examination of the thesis papers written by students (colonels or lieutenant colonels) of the Army War College at Carlisle Barracks in the 1950s revealed a heightened awareness and receptivity to the civilian school of Limited War thinkers. However, there were some students who were bitterly opposed to involvement in limited wars, and their papers reflect this attitude. [Note: only some of the theses discussed the issue of Limited War.]

107. Oral history interview of Douglas V. Johnson, by William W. Moss for the John F. Kennedy Library, 13 July 1970 in Alexandria, VA.

108. Johnson oral history, p. 12.

109. Johnson oral history, p. 13.

110. Johnson oral history, p. 13.

111. See Dr. James B. Atkinson and Colonel Donovan: Yeuell, Jr., "Must We Have World War III?," *Naval Institute Proceedings* 82 (July 1956), p. 711–721; Commander Malcolm W. Cagle, "Errors of the Korean War," *Naval Institute Proceedings* 84 (March 1958): 31–36; Commander Malcolm W. Cagle, "Sea Power and Limited War," *Naval Institute Proceedings* 84 (July 1958): 23–7.

112. Cagle, "Sea Power and Limited War," p. 23. This was the lead article in that months issue.

113. Cagle, "Sea Power and Limited War," p. 25.

114. Cagle, "Errors of the Korean War," p. 35.

115. Quoted in John Gooch, "Maritime Command: Mahan and Corbett," in *Seapower and Strategy*, ed. Colin S. Gray and Roger W. Barnett (Annapolis, MD: Naval Institute Press, 1989), p. 34.

116. Gooch, "Mahan and Corbett," p. 34.

117. See Roger W. Barnett and Jeffrey G. Barlow, "The Maritime Strategy of the U.S. Navy: Reading Excerpts," in *Seapower and Strategy*, ed. Colin S. Gray and Roger W. Barnett (Annapolis, MD, p. Naval Institute Press, 1989), pp. 330–333.

118. Barnett and Barlow, "Maritime Strategy," p. 331.

119. Barnett and Barlow, "Maritime Strategy," p. 333.

120. Barnett and Barlow, "Maritime Strategy," pp. 331–332.

121. Air Force Manual 1–2 *United States Air Force: Basic Doctrine* (Washington, D.C.: 1959), p. 1.

122. Clodfelter, *The Limits of Air Power*, p. 34.

123. For an excellent overview of Kennedy's defense policies see John Lewis Gaddis, *Strategies of Containment*, chapter 7.

124. Gaddis, *Strategies of Containment*, p. 214. The term "asymmetry" was used in an important memo on basic national security policy from Walt Rostow to Kennedy (see: 214, fn. 39).

125. Gaddis, *Strategies of Containment*, p. 214.

126. Papers of President Kennedy, National Security Files, Countries, General, box 130, folder: 6/1/61-6/26/61, memorandum to the President from Walt W. Rostow, June 26, 1961. John F. Kennedy Presidential Library.

127. Smoke, *National Security and the Nuclear Dilemma*, pp. 61–2.

128. 28 March 1961, "Special Message to Congress on the Defense Budget," *Public Papers: Kennedy, 1961*, pp. 231–232.

129. *Public Papers: Kennedy, 1961*, p. 232.

130. The best book on the development of counter-insurgency doctrines to the war in Vietnam is Douglas Blaufarb, *The Counterinsurgency Era: U.S. Doctrine and Performance, 1950 to the Present* (New York: Free Press, 1977).

131. Blaufarb, *Counterinsurgency Era*, pp. 55–56.

132. Blaufarb, *Counterinsurgency Era*, p. 57.

133. Blaufarb, *Counterinsurgency Era*, p. 67. NSAM 124 was not the report of the Bissell group.

134. NSAM 124, *The Pentagon Papers* (Gravel ed.), 2: 660.

135. NSAM 124, *The Pentagon Papers* (Gravel ed.), 2: 660.

136. Subject to the President's approval.

137. The other members were: the deputy under secretary of state for political affairs, U. Alexis Johnson; the deputy secretary of defense, Roswell Gilpatrick; the Chairman of the Joint Chiefs of Staff, General Lyman L. Lemnitzer; the director of the CIA, John McCone; the special assistant to the president for national security affairs, McGeorge Bundy; the administrator of the Agency for International Development, Fowler Hamilton; and the director of the United States Information Agency, Edward R. Murrow. This was not an assemblage of insignificant persons within the government.

138. Summers, *On Strategy*, p. 46; he cites Lloyd Norman and John B. Spore, "Big Push in Guerrilla Warfare," *Army* (March 1962): 33.

139. *The Pentagon Papers* (Gravel ed.), 2: 667–669.

140. Blaufarb, *Counterinsurgency Era*, p. 72.

141. Blaufarb, *Counterinsurgency Era*, pp. 70–71.

142. Blaufarb, *Counterinsurgency Era*, p. 71; he cites Robert Amory, recorded interview by Joseph E. O'Connor, February 9, 1966, p. 9, John F. Kennedy Library Oral History Program.

143. Blaufarb, *Counterinsurgency Era*, pp. 79–82; also Krepinevich, *The Army and Vietnam*, passim.

6. | Laos and the Never Again School

1. Summers, *Vietnam War Almanac*, p. 226. There is some confusion over what Eisenhower told Kennedy. Greenstein and Immerman have described the meeting "as a fascinating episode in which Eisenhower, on the last day of his presidency, met with his Democratic successor and several of his own and John F. Kennedy's advisers in a Rashomonesque meeting from which the participants emerged with diametrically opposed interpretations of what Eisenhower had said." See Fred I Greenstein and Richard H. Immerman, "What Did Eisenhower Tell Kennedy about Indochina? The Politics of Misperception," *The Journal of American History*, 79 (September 1992): 569.

By the end of his administration, Eisenhower was willing to consider military intervention to preserve Laos, but Kennedy and other participants at the meeting may have misinterpreted Eisenhower's willingness to take the option seriously to be a true commitment to save that country. Greenstein and Immerman, "What did Eisenhower Tell Kennedy?" pp. 577–578. Kennedy's aide-memoire of the meeting indicates that he felt Eisenhower had expressed a willingness to intervene in Laos if it invoked the protection of SEATO.

2. David K. Hall, "The Laos Neutralization Agreement, 1962," in Alexander L. George, Philip J. Farley, and Alexander Dallin, eds., *U.S.-Soviet Security Cooperation: Achievements, Failures, Lessons* (New York: Oxford University Press, 1988), p. 437.

3. Hall, "The Laos Agreement," p. 438.

4. Charles A. Stevenson, *The End of Nowhere: American Policy Toward Laos Since 1954* (Boston: Beacon Press, 1972), pp. 80–83.

5. *FRUS* (1958–1960), 16: 620.

6. *FRUS* (1958–1960), 16: 624.

7. *FRUS* (1958–1960), 16: 626.

8. Stevenson, *End of Nowhere*, p. 82. Stevenson cites a "Confidential Source" for this information. This appears to be the first time that a "Never Again" argument was used to oppose direct military involvement in Laos by U.S. forces.

9. Timothy N. Castle, *At War in the Shadow of Vietnam: U.S. Military Aid to the Royal Lao Government, 1945–1975* (New York: Columbia University

Press, 1993), p. 19. Castle states that covert military aid to Laos began in December 1955 when the Department of State "placed the management of American military assistance to Laos under the control of a thinly disguised, but politically defensible, military aid organization called the Programs Evaluation Office (PEO). This decision set the precedent for nearly two decades of covert U.S. military aid to the Royal Lao government." Castle, p. 16.

10. Castle, p. 21.

11. Stevenson, *End of Nowhere*, p. 104.

12. David K. Hall, "The Laos Crisis, 1960–1," in Alexander L. George, David K. Hall, and William R. Simons, eds. *The Limits of Coercive Diplomacy: Laos, Cuba, Vietnam* (Boston: Little, Brown, and Co., 1971), pp. 39–40. Material in the next two paragraphs is based on information from Hall, p. 438 .

13. Stevenson, *End of Nowhere*, p. 124. Stevenson cites "Confidential Sources."

14. Stevenson, *End of Nowhere*, p. 125.

15. See Dwight D. Eisenhower, *The White House Years: Waging Peace, 1956–61* (Garden City, N.Y.: 1965), p. 611. Eisenhower also states that he did not want to become engaged in a situation that was "costly in both blood and treasure, without achieving objectives."

16. Stevenson, *End of Nowhere*, p. 125; he cites interviews with Admiral Burke, General Decker, and Assistant Secretary of Defense John Irwin.

17. *FRUS* (1958–1969): 1025.

18. In the December 31, 1960 White House session, Livingston T. Merchant, the Under Secretary of State for Political Affairs, pointed out that SEATO action was unlikely at that time as "the Thais, the Filipinos, and the Pakistanis will probably stand by us in the SEATO Council; but the British and French will not support us in backing [the current government] to the hilt at this moment. *FRUS* (1958–1960), 16: 1027.

19. Hall, "The Laos Agreement," p. 438.

20. Stevenson, *End of Nowhere*, p. 141.

21. Hall, "The Laos Crisis," in *The Limits of Coercive*, p. 52.

22. Stevenson, *End of Nowhere*, p. 140.

23. Stevenson, *End of Nowhere*, p. 136.

24. U. Alexis Johnson with Jef Olivarius McAllister, *The Right Hand of Power* (Englewood Cliffs, NJ: Prentice Hall, 1984), p. 304.

Johnson also writes (p. 304): "The Joint Chiefs, still smarting from the frustrations of the Korean War, had no taste for a drawn out struggle for limited political objectives in a remote Asian country with difficult terrain."

25. Gibbons, *The U.S. Government and the Vietnam War*, pt. 2, p. 20.

26. Stevenson, *End of Nowhere*, pp. 136–137.

27. Oral history interview with General George H. Decker, September 18, 1968, p. 4. Interviewer: Larry J. Hackman. John F. Kennedy Presidential Library.

28. Stevenson, *End of Nowhere*, p. 135; he cites the February 22, 1961 issue of the *New York Times*.

29. Stevenson, *End of Nowhere*, p. 146; Gibbons, pt. 2, p. 21.

30. *Public Papers: Kennedy, 1961*, p. 241. The precise details of the troop movements were available to the public in newspapers the next day. For example, see *The New York Herald-Tribune*, March 24, 1961. The amount of information printed concerning military activities related to Laos must have been noted by the Soviets—reinforcing their impression of American resolve.

31. Stevenson, *End of Nowhere*, p. 148.

32. Alexis Johnson, *Right Hand of Power*, p. 322.

33. Memo of Kenneth P. Landon to MacGeorge Bundy, April 11, 1961, Papers of President Kennedy, National Security Files, Countries, Laos, General, box 130, folder: 4/11/61 to 4/16/61, JFK Library.

34. Hall, "The Laos Crisis," p. 67. The Bay of Pigs Operation began on April 15, 1961.

35. Stevenson, *End of Nowhere*, p. 149.

36. Hall, "The Laos Crisis," p. 67.

37. Stevenson, *End of Nowhere*, p. 150.

38. Alexis Johnson, *Right Hand of Power*, p. 322.

39. Gibbons, pt. 2, p. 26. It should be remembered that Rostow had made a similar recommendation on March 21, 1961, *supra*. The estimate of the number of troops required had increased from the 60,000 deemed necessary at the March 20–21 NSC meetings.

40. Arthur M. Schlesinger, Jr., *A Thousand Days: John F. Kennedy in the White House* (Boston: Houghton Mifflin, 1965), p. 338. Schlesinger also makes another observation (p. 338) that merits consideration. He remarks that the JCS planning was almost incoherent in that a number of options were thrown at the President without important contingencies being adequately contemplated; Schlesinger writes: "The President was appalled at the sketchy nature of American military planning for Laos—the lack of detail and unanswered questions." The fact that this crisis took place in the immediate aftermath of the Bay of Pigs probably highlighted any weaknesses the plans may have had.

41. Theodore C. Sorenson, *Kennedy* (New York: Harper, 1965), p. 645. Sorenson's account seems impressionistic concerning the dating of events. Gibbons is usually quite precise about dates, and he places this conversation on April 27, 1961. I will do so as well, even though Sorenson seems to say that it took place on May 1, 1961.

42. The best description of SEATO Plan 5 is in Gibbons (pt. 2, p. 22): " 'Plan 5/60' (usually referred to as SEATO Plan 5, . . . was a contingency plan for the deployment of a major SEATO force to Laos and Vietnam which would seek to defend Southeast Asia from a position on the Mekong River) under which U.S. Marines would be augmented by the Mobile Commonwealth Brigade consisting of troops from Britain, New Zealand, and Australia."

Stevenson, *End of Nowhere*, p. 176; describes SEATO Plan 5 as a military plan that "called for spearheads across the Mekong to hold major towns in Laos. It required 25,000 troops initially, but with a projected ceiling of 40,000." Stevenson does not give the total number of Americans that would have been involved under this plan—these figures may include Thai, Lao, and other allied forces. It appears that the French and British were extremely reluctant to commit any ground troops.

43. Note that Alexis Johnson does not make mention of the Mobile Commonwealth Brigade as Gibbons did.

44. It is not clear at this point in the narrative whether Admiral Burke is speaking for the other Chiefs or they are entering the discussion individually.

45. Alexis Johnson, *Right Hand of Power* p. 323. Note that Johnson *does not mention* the limited troop deployment proposed by Rostow. Both Gibbons (pt. 2, p. 26) and Stevenson, *End of Nowhere*, p. 151, include Rostow's proposal in their accounts of the April 27 meeting.

46. Stevenson, *End of Nowhere*, p. 151, also states that the JCS argued for 140,000 troops. In his endnote 60, p. 151, he writes, "The Chiefs of Staff were not really worried about war with China. Their plans in case of Chinese intervention, however, were quite frightening. These called for seizure of Hainan Island, which was defended by three Chinese divisions, deployment of 250,000 U.S. troops to South Vietnam, followed by operations across North Vietnam into Laos to block Chinese intrusions. If these U.S. forces were in danger of being overrun, the Chiefs expected to use nuclear weapons. (Confidential Source)"

47. Alexis Johnson, *Right Hand of Power*, p. 323. Because the details of the various contingency plans are not available it is not clear whether the JCS were backing SEATO Plan 5 or a more potent variant of it. From the available accounts it appears that the JCS were arguing for a much more intensive plan of military action.

48. Oral history interview of U. Alexis Johnson, interviewed by William Brubeck, 1964, p. 9. John F. Kennedy Library. Permission granted.

49. Hilsman, *To Move a Nation*, p. 128.

50. Stevenson, *End of Nowhere*, p. 151–152; Admiral Burke was the military adviser most willing to enter the fight in Laos. For a list of the members of Congress in attendance see Gibbons, pt. 2, p. 29 and fn. 79.

51. Stevenson, *End of Nowhere*, p. 152; the new plans were to be made ready for the next NSC meeting.

52. Gibbons, pt. 2, pp. 27–8. Subsequent page references are cited in the text.

53. The Bundy note may be found in the "Kennedy Library, POF Country File, Laos."

54. Stevenson, *End of Nowhere*, p. 152. Stevenson cites an interview with Paul Nitze.

55. Schlesinger, *A Thousand Days*, p. 338.

56. *The Pentagon Papers* (Gravel ed.), 2: 9.

57. Hall, "The Laos Agreement," p. 439.

58. Gibbons, pt. 2, p. 113.

59. Gibbons, pt. 2, p. 113. Gibbons cites U.S. Congress, Senate, Committee on Foreign Relations, unpublished executive session transcript, February 20, 1962.

60. Hall, "The Laos Agreement," p. 451.

61. Hall, in *Limits of Coercive Diplomacy*, p. 74. Hall adds, "Both Washington and Hanoi were willing to settle for the half of Laos which was felt to be most vital to its immediate national interest."

62. Gibbons, pt. 2, p. 115. It should be noted that the abandonment of Nam Tha occurred on May 6, 1962 as a result of *no* communist attack.

63. Stevenson, *End of Nowhere*, p. 175.

64. Stevenson, *End of Nowhere*, p. 175; Stevenson cites an interview with General Decker.

65. Roger Hilsman reports that on May 10, 1962 those who were in agreement with him "were all braced for a battle between the 'Never Again' view that either all out force should be used in Asia or none at all versus the politically tailored recommendations that had been laid before the President. For even though many officers in the Pentagon did not share the 'Never Again' view, it was clearly dominant at the very top." See Hilsman, *To Move a Nation*, p. 143.

66. Hilsman, *To Move a Nation*, pp. 145–146; Stevenson, *End of Nowhere*, p. 177, claims that 3,000 troops were sent to Thailand. This figure is use by Castle, p. 46.

67. Gibbons, pt. 2, p. 117. The inclusion of Rostow in the Never Again category seems incorrect given his advocacy of the limited use of ground forces in Thailand and Laos, *supra*.

68. Hilsman, *To Move a Nation*, p. 163. This passage is probably the source for Gibbons's inclusion of Rostow with the Never Again group. Once again, I believe Hilsman is incorrect in placing Rostow in this group.

69. Hilsman, *To Move a Nation*, p. 147.

70. Hilsman, p. 147.

71. Hilsman, p. 149.

72. Hilsman, p. 149; my emphasis. Notice how Hilsman places "political" and "military" in quotes. He does this because there was no strict correlation of members of the "military" group to military personnel involved in the process, the same holds true of "political" perspective.

73. Gibbons at pt. 2, p. 117 writes that, "according to Hilsman," the limited response group was able to get the President to sign NSAM 157 (May 29, 1962, *The Pentagon Papers*, Gravel ed., 2: 672–673) which directed the appropriate officials to develop contingency plans "for military action in Laos, under which Thai forces, with U.S. assistance, would seek to take and hold a province on the Mekong River in the western part of Laos, while Thai, Vietnamese, or U.S. forces would recapture and hold the "panhandle" in the southern part of Laos."

74. The following section of this chapter was written with the help of material from: Hall, "The Laos Agreement," pp. 457–61; Stevenson, *End of Nowhere*, pp. 177–179.

75. The American forces remained in Thailand until December 1962. Johnson, *The Right Hand of Power*, p. 326.

76. Hall, "The Laos Neutralization Agreement," p. 460.

77. Hall, "The Laos Agreement," p. 460.

78. Richard K. Betts, *Soldiers, Statesmen, and Cold War Crises*, pp. 37–38.

7. | Vietnam 1964–65: The Debates Over the Use of Limited Force

1. In this chapter the following abbreviations may appear: "DRV" stands for the Democratic Republic of Vietnam (North Vietnam); "GVN" stands for the Government of Vietnam (South Vietnam).

2. Herring, *Longest War*, p. 67.

3. Stanley Karnow, *Vietnam: A History* (New York: Viking Press, 1983), p. 238.

4. William J. Duiker, *The Communist Road to Power in Vietnam* (Boulder, Co.: Westview Press, 1981), p. 198.

5. Douglas Pike, *PAVN: People's Army of Vietnam* (Navato, CA: Presidio Press, 1986), p. 47.

6. Duiker, *Communist Road to Power*, p. 228. It should be noted that the Tonkin Gulf Crisis occurred in August 1964; Rolling Thunder began in February 1965.

7. Given this information it is not surprising that cutting the Ho Chi Minh trails remained one of the most contentious issues within the U.S. government throughout the war. The problem of fighting the insurgency while

leaving a critical source of supplies open was contrary to the general practice of counterinsurgency, which attempts to isolate the insurgent from his resources and sanctuaries. Debates over the Laos problem were repeated during the war.

For a recent treatment that will provide some examples see Norman B. Hannah, *The Key to Failure: Laos and Vietnam* (Lanham, MD: Madison Books, 1987). Also of interest are: W. W. Rostow, *The Diffusion of Power* (New York: Macmillan, 1972), pp. 286–288, 513; William C. Westmoreland, *A Soldier Reports* (Garden City, NY: Doubleday, 1976), p. 148.

8. Burke, John P. and Fred I. Greenstein, *How Presidents Test Reality: Decisions on Vietnam, 1954 and 1965* (New York: Russell Sage Foundation, 1989), p. 119.

9. *The Pentagon Papers* (Gravel ed.), 2: 223; and Gibbons, pt. 2, pp. 209–11.

10. For the text of McNamara's memo to the President which became NSAM 288 see "Memorandum from the Secretary of Defense (McNamara) to the President," March 16, 1964, *FRUS* (1964–68), vol 1.

The Pentagon Papers (Gravel ed.), 3: 499–510.

11. The quote may be found in the precursor document to NSAM 288, McNamara's March 16, 1964 letter to the president, *The Pentagon Papers* (Gravel ed.), 3: 499.

12. *The Pentagon Papers* (Gravel ed.), 3: 50.

13. Herring, *Longest War*, p. 116.

14. Summary Record of the 524th Meeting of the National Security Council, Washington, March 17, 1964, *FRUS* (1964–68), 1: 171.

15. *FRUS* (1964–68), 1: 159; *The Pentagon Papers* (Gravel ed.), 3: 509–10. Graduated military pressure would go "beyond reacting on a tit-for-tat basis. It would include air attacks against military and possibly industrial targets." *FRUS* (1964–68), 1: 159, (pt. 3).

16. *FRUS* (1964–68), 1: 159.

17. Letter of June 22, 1989 from Dr. William E. Simons of the RAND Corporation, Washington, D.C.; p. 3. OPLAN 37–64, as described in the *Pentagon Papers*, 3: 287–288, was never put into effect although components of this program found their way into later plans.

For an excellent summary of American military planning for a land defense of South Vietnam see Alexander S. Cochran, Jr., "American Planning for Ground Combat in Vietnam, 1952–1965," *Parameters* 14 (Summer 1984): 63–69.

18. *The Pentagon Papers* (Gravel ed.), 3: 172.

19. *The Pentagon Papers* (Gravel ed.), 3: 179.

20. Donald J. Mrozek, *Air Power and the Ground War in Vietnam* (Wash-

ington, D.C.: Pergammon-Brassey's, 1989), p. 182. Mrozek correctly notes that even though Taylor favored a coercive approach he was also aware that force would be ineffective if it did not inflict some pain.

21. Presidential Studies Archive, University of California at Davis, Institute for Governmental Affairs, Chronological File, Box One, File 10: August 9–14, 1964, Memo from Depts. of State/Defense to Saigon, "III. Essential Elements of U.S. Policy," see pt. III.C.

22. Mrozek, *Air Power and the Ground War in Vietnam*, p. 64 (and fn. 32 for his citation).

23. Gibbons, pt. 2, pp. 285–297.

24. For the text of the resolution see Gibbons, pt. 2, pp. 302–303. Gibbons also has an interesting discussion of Johnson's response to the torpedo boat attacks and the doctrine of coercive diplomacy. See Gibbons, pt. 2, p. 342 and fn. 147. Gibbons analysis of the Tonkin Gulf literature is extensive. See also John Galloway, *The Gulf of Tonkin Resolution* (Rutherford, NJ: Fairleigh Dickinson University Press, 1970).

25. According to Wallace J. Thies Pham Van Dong was angered by the American position and threatened widening the war to all of Southeast Asia; he also pointed out that the DRV had powerful socialist allies. Near the end of the talk with Seaborn the Premier appears to have expressed some interest in negotiations with the United States. See Thies, *When Governments Collide: Coercion and Diplomacy in the Vietnam Conflict, 1964–68* (Berkeley, CA: University of California Press, 1980), pp. 47–48. Thies relies on Seaborn's summary of the discussion.

26. Gibbons, pt. 2, p. 352. Gibbons cites "Johnson Library, NSF Country File, Vietnam, JCS Memorandum CM-124-64, 9 September 1964." Gibbons notes, as well, that "The Chiefs also agreed that the war was not being won and that U.S. forces would have to be used in order to win." Maxwell Taylor left the Joint Chiefs of Staff and became the American ambassador to South Vietnam in July 1964.

27. *The Pentagon Papers* (Gravel ed.), 3: 206–7. One would not have to be cynical to notice that these dates might also support the conclusion the government was waiting for the passage of the 1964 election to seriously begin preparations.

28. For NSAM 314 see *FRUS* (1964–68), 1: 758–61, pts. 4 & 7; *The Pentagon Papers* (Gravel ed.), 3: 565–6.

29. *The Pentagon Papers* (Gravel ed.), 3: 583–584. Not reproduced in *FRUS.*

30. *The Pentagon Papers* (Gravel ed.), 3: 207–208.

31. *The Pentagon Papers* (Gravel ed.), 3: 208.

32. "Memorandum from the Joint Chiefs of Staff to the Secretary of

Defense (McNamara)," JCSM-902- 64, 27 October 1964, *FRUS* (1964–68), 1: 847–857.

33. *FRUS* (1964–68), 1: 854–855.

34. This working group of second level officials was composed of William P. Bundy (Chair; State Dept.), Marshall Green (State), Michael Forrestal (State), Robert Johnson (State), John McNaugton (Defense), Vice Admiral Lloyd Mustin (JCS), and Harold Ford (CIA). The working group was to report to the "Principals Group" of NSC members that comprised Dean Rusk, Robert McNamara, John McCone, General Wheeler, George Ball, and McGeorge Bundy.

35. "Telegram from the Embassy in Vietnam to the Department of State," November 1, 1964, *FRUS* (1964–68), 1: 873.

36. *FRUS* (1964–68), 1: 875, fn. 3. These recommendations formed the nucleus of the JCS memo to the group on November 4, 1964.

37. For the analysts discussion of the JCS response to Taylor on November 4, 1964 see *The Pentagon Papers* (Gravel ed.), 3: 210. Some parts of the November 4 JCS reply appear to have been used again in JCSM 955–64, November 14, 1964, *The Pentagon Papers* (Gravel ed.), 3: 628: see *infra*.

38. *The Pentagon Papers* (Gravel ed.), 3: 656–66. See *FRUS* (1964–68), 1: 897–898. The revised McNaughton draft was dated November 21, 1964.

39. *The Pentagon Papers* (Gravel ed.), 3: 659.

40. *The Pentagon Papers* (Gravel ed.), 3: 659.

41. *The Pentagon Papers* (Gravel ed.), 3: 659.

42. *The Pentagon Papers* (Gravel ed.), 3: 224. Walt Rostow wrote memos to Sec. McNamara dated November 16, 1964 (*FRUS* [1964–68], 1: 906–7; or, *The Pentagon Papers* [Gravel ed.], 3: 632–633) and to Dean Rusk on 23 November 1964 (*The Pentagon Papers* [Gravel ed.], 3: 645–647) that urged a U.S. ground force commitment for South Vietnam and, possibly, in the Laos Corridor. In the November 23 memo Rostow called for "the introduction into the Pacific Theater of massive forces to deal with any escalatory response, including any forces aimed at China as well as North Viet Nam, should the Chinese Communists enter the game." Interestingly, the memo of November 16 deemed the introduction of ground forces to be an essential element in the bargaining strategy: "The withdrawal of the ground forces could be a critically important part of our diplomatic bargaining position. Ground forces can sit during a conference more easily than we can maintain a series of mounting naval pressures." I must thank William E. Simons for pointing out the ground force aspect of Option C and the Rostow memos.

43. *The Pentagon Papers* (Gravel ed.), 3: 659–60. The three options appear as well in Gibbons, pt. 2, pp. 367–368. From the minutes of a meeting of the "principals" on November 24, 1964, the *Pentagon Papers* analyst was able to

place the positions advocated by the participants in the debate. George Ball favored "A" (a position rejected out of hand by the William Bundy Working Group); General Wheeler "clearly favored a B;" John McCone (CIA) "may have supported" B as well "although this was not clear." Various forms of "C" were favored by McNamara, McNaughton, Rusk, and the two Bundys. *The Pentagon Papers*, 3: 239. Maxwell Taylor argued for a combination of "A" and "C," *ibid.*, p. 243.

44. JCSM 955–64, November 14, 1964, *The Pentagon Papers* (Gravel ed.), 3: 628. See also JCSM-967–64, 18 November 1964, *The Pentagon Papers* (Gravel ed.), 3: 639–40.

45. *The Pentagon Papers* (Gravel ed.), 3: 233. It is claimed that these observations come from a JCS document dated November 17, 1964.

46. Gibbons, pt. 2, p. 369.

47. *The Pentagon Papers* (Gravel ed.), 3: 233.

48. Michael W. Davidson, "Senior Officers and Vietnam Policymaking," *Parameters* 16 (Spring 1986): 55–62.

49. Gibbons, pt. 3, fn. 73 on pp. 155–156. The most important work on this subject is by Henry F. Gaff, *The Tuesday Cabinet* (Englewood Cliffs, N.J.: Prentice-Hall, 1970).

50. Presidential Studies Archive, University of California at Davis, Institute for Governmental Affairs, Box 1, File 12: October 12–December 31, 1964, Memo to the President from Jack Valenti, November 14, 1964. Jack Valenti served as Special Assistant to the President from November 23, 1963 until May 1966.

51. George Kahin, *Intervention: How America Became Involved in Vietnam* (New York: Knopf, 1986), p. 252.

52. Gibbons, pt. 2, p. 375. The first Barrel Roll operation was conducted on December 14, 1964; see *The Pentagon Papers* (Gravel ed.), 3: 92. Gibbons also notes that no NSAM (National Security Action Memorandum was issued from the meeting of December 1.), Gibbons, pt. 2, p. 375.

53. *The Pentagon Papers* (Gravel ed.), 3: 251. Another NSAM was not issued after these meetings. In fact little action beyond NSAM 314 (September 9, 1964) was agreed upon.

54. Burke and Greenstein, p. 122.

55. *The Pentagon Papers* (Gravel ed.), 3: 251.

56. Gibbons, pt. 2, p. 376.

57. Thies, *When Governments Collide*, p. 65.

58. "Telegram from the President to the Ambassador in Vietnam (Taylor)," December 30, 1964, *FRUS* (1964–68), 1: 1057.

59. "Telegram from the President to the Ambassador in Vietnam (Taylor)," December 30, 1964, *FRUS* (1964–68), 1: 1058–1059; my emphasis. It

is unlikely that Taylor read Johnson's December 30, 1964 cable before sending his Phase II cable the next day. For original copy, see White House to Ambassador Saigon, December 30, 1964, LBJ library, Papers of Lyndon Johnson, National Security File, National Security Council History, Deployment of Forces to Vietnam, Box 40, tab 1.

60. Larry Berman, *Planning a Tragedy: The Americanization of the War in Vietnam* (New York: Norton, 1982), p. 34. Kahin cites an interview with McGeorge Bundy in which Bundy presents a different case for the importance of this cable. Bundy paraphrased Johnson's meaning as "I'm unwilling to agree to a program of bombing the North to save the South, because that won't work; but I'm prepared to be helpful by permitting use of US ground forces now already available on the scene in Vietnam if you wish to use them in combat to strengthen ARVN." Kahin, *Intervention,* p. 261.

61. William P. Bundy manuscript, Box 1 of Bundy Papers, Lyndon Johnson Library, chapter 20, p. 27.

62. "Telegram from the Embassy in Vietnam to the Department of State," December 31, 1964, *FRUS* (1964–68), 1: 1062–1063. Even though this cable appears to have been sent after President Johnson's of the previous day, it was not a response to that cable.

63. For large blocks of the text see Gibbons, pt. 2, pp. 387–389. The text of the cable may be found in Saigon to Washington (Message #2052–8), January 6, 1965, LBJ Library, Papers of Lyndon Johnson, National Security File, National Security Council History, Deployment of Forces to Vietnam, Box 40, tab 3.

Another major event also occurred during the week in which these Johnson-Taylor exchanges took place. From December 26 to January 2, 1965, the Viet Cong mauled two ARVN battalions at the battle of Binh Gia. Herbert Schandler notes, "This was the first time that enemy forces had chosen to remain on the battlefield and meet government forces in sustained combat." See Herbert Y. Schandler, *The Unmaking of a President: Lyndon Johnson and Vietnam* (Princeton: Princeton University Press, 1977), p. 11.

64. Gibbons, pt. 2, p. 388.

65. Kraft, *Profiles in Power,* pp. 145–146.

66. Compare this with the statement by the Joint Chiefs of Staff at the Honolulu Conference. See JCSM-461–64, June 2, 1964, *The Pentagon Papers* (Gravel ed.), 3: 172.

67. *The Pentagon Papers* (Gravel ed.), 3: 15; the text appears on pp. 684–686.

68. *The Pentagon Papers* (Gravel ed.), 3: 685.

69. *The Pentagon Papers* (Gravel ed.), 3: 684.

70. *The Pentagon Papers* (Gravel ed.), 3: 686.

71. Note the word "signal" here to convey the role such actions would have in a process of tacit bargaining. *Ibid.*, p. 686, pt. 7e.

72. Berman, *Planning a Tragedy*, p. 37; my emphasis. These remarks are contained in the first draft of the cable.

73. Berman, *Planning a Tragedy*, p. 37.

74. *The Pentagon Papers*, 3: 15.

75. Presidential Studies Archive, University of California at Davis, Institute for Governmental Affairs, Box One, file 15: Jan. 15, 1965 to Jan. 30, 1965, Memo for the President from McGeorge Bundy (Re: Basic Policy in Vietnam), January 27, 1965. This is a manipulative McGeorge Bundy memo to Johnson in which he puts forth his alternative, lists another one that is implausible, states his preference, and then urges more study to give an even-handed appearance to the note.

76. Burke and Greenstein (pp. 132–133) recount an interview with Douglas Dillon, Secretary of the Treasury under Johnson. From 1957 to 1961 he had been under secretary of state for economic affairs in the Eisenhower Administration. In the NSC meeting of February 6, 1965 Johnson polled those in attendance as to whether the U.S. should attack North Vietnam in response to Pleiku. Dillon answered: "I agree Mr. President, with what is proposed but only on the understanding that we are prepared to go full out, including the mining of Haiphong." Dillon continued, "I made my statement knowing full well that both McNamara and Ball . . . were in favor of using force to the minimum extent possible, and I wanted to make it clear that I felt we should not attack Vietnam at all unless we were prepared to go all the way. I was the only person to make such a reservation, but I am sure that, if asked, McCone and Wheeler would have been in full agreement with me."

Dillon also noted in a letter to Fred Greenstein that his "views of the use of force were based on the views expressed by President Eisenhower while I was in the State Department."

77. Berman, *Planning a Tragedy*, p. 43. This Bundy cable is also described in *The Pentagon Papers*, 3: 308–315.

78. *The Pentagon Papers* (Gravel ed.), 3: 689. This document (#250) is Appendix A of the Bundy report.

Part II.6. contains this summary of Bundy's purpose which clearly does not include the decisive military use of force: "This reprisal policy should begin at a low level. Its level of force and pressure should be increased only gradually— and as indicated above it should be decreased if VC terror visibly decreases. The object would not be to 'win' an air war against Hanoi, but rather to influence the course of the struggle in the South." (p. 688)

79. Gibbons, pt. 3, p. 67.

80. Gibbons, pt. 3, p. 78.

81. Burke and Greenstein, p. 158.

82. William E. Simons, draft paper, pp. 77–81. Simons lists all but one of these possible motivations for the lack of change in the declaratory policy of the United States.

83. *The Pentagon Papers* (Gravel ed.), 3: 315.

84. *The Pentagon Papers* (Gravel ed.), 3: 315. Taylor's focus on altering the will and preferences of the DRV leadership can be seen in his February 12, 1965 reply to Washington in which he lists the primary objective of the "graduated reprisals" as being the "will of the Hanoi leaders." See Gibbons, pt. 3, pp. 67–68. The reader should recall that Taylor, in his December 31, 1964 cable to Washington, was much more interested in bombing's potential for shoring up political stability in the South.

85. Both quotes are cited by William E. Simons, "The Vietnam Intervention, 1964–1965," in Alexander L. George, David K. Hall, and William R. Simons, eds., *The Limits of Coercive Diplomacy* (Boston: Little, Brown and Co., 1971), pp. 145–146.

86. Gibbons, pt. 3, pp. 59–60. The interview with McGeorge Bundy took place on January 8, 1979; my emphasis.

87. Gibbons, pt. 3, p. 105. Bundy closes with the following paragraph: "Thus it seems essential to McNamara—and to me too—that there be an absolutely firm and clear internal decision of the U.S. Government and that this decision be known and understood by enough people to permit its orderly execution."

88. CINCPAC had operational control of the bombing in Southeast Asia. Even after the United States landed considerable ground forces the bombing missions were still controlled by CINCPAC not Westmoreland (COMUS-MACV).

89. *The Pentagon Papers* (Gravel ed.), 3: 318.

90. *The Pentagon Papers* (Gravel ed.), 3: 320. General Bruce Palmer notes that there was a division among the services concerning the possibility that bombing would be successful. He claims that the Army and Navy (this must not include CINCPAC) were skeptical; the Air Force and the Marines were more supportive of the proposed air campaign. See Bruce Palmer, Jr., *The 25-Year War: America's Military Role in Vietnam* (New York: Touchstone/ Simon & Schuster, 1984), pp. 34–35.

91. Burke and Greenstein, p. 155.

92. Papers of Lyndon Baines Johnson, Meeting Notes File, Box 1, meeting with General Eisenhower and Others on February 17, 1965, p. 13. My emphasis; copy heavily sanitized.

93. *The Pentagon Papers* (Gravel ed.), 3: 337.

94. Thies, *When Governments Collide*, p. 84.

95. *The Pentagon Papers* (Gravel ed.), 3: 335.

96. *The Pentagon Papers* (Gravel ed.), 3: 335.

97. *The Pentagon Papers* (Gravel ed.), 3: 338.

98. *The Pentagon Papers* (Gravel ed.), 3: 339, pt. 6. See the top of the page for the changes that were to be made in the Rolling Thunder strikes.

99. Theis, *When Governments Collide*, p. 87.

100. *The Pentagon Papers*, 3: 340 (Gravel ed.).

101. Thies, *When governments Collide*, pp. 88–90; Thies cites Simons, "Vietnam Intervention, 1964–1965," pp. 190–191. See also, *The Pentagon Papers* (Gravel ed.), 3: 340–5.

102. *The Pentagon Papers* (Gravel ed.), 3: 342–344. There was genuine disagreement within the services over the bombing. General McConnel (Air Force) wanted to conduct a 28-day strike against the original 94 targets that the Joint Chiefs had discussed previously. He withdrew this proposal when it became clear that the other Chiefs favored a plan put forward by CINCPAC to attack the LOCs (lines of communication).

103. Gibbons, pt. 3, pp. 178–179.

104. *The Pentagon Papers* (Gravel ed.), 3: 418.

105. *The Pentagon Papers*, 3: 419. The opinion expressed on this date is consistent with those sent to Washington in the January 6, 1965 cable.

106. David Halberstam, *The Best and the Brightest* (New York: Random House, 1972), pp. 564; for quote see Berman, *Planning a Tragedy*, p. 54 (he cites Westmoreland, *A Soldier Reports*, p. 124).

107. Berman, *Planning a Tragedy*, p. 54. Berman does not mention the augmentation of Rolling Thunder that flowed from Johnson's report. It should also be noted that General Johnson urged that an international force deployed to cut the Ho Chi Minh trails on the ground. This proposal was not accepted by President Johnson, but the incident does reveal some of the persistence with which the military argued that this was an essential element of winning the war.

108. Halberstam, *The Best and the Brightest*, p. 490.

109. Gibbons, pt. 3, p. 169.

110. Gibbons, pt. 3, pp. 169–173, describes General Johnson's differences with Westmoreland over the manner in which the war should be conducted in the South. Johnson wanted to cut the trails in Laos and decisively defeat the Viet Cong with small units in the South. Westmoreland's idea of search and destroy sweeps was not appealing to him. Johnson's concept is more similar to the tactical approach adopted by the U.S. Marine Corps in Vietnam.

111. Gibbons, pt. 3, p. 166.

112. Burke and Greenstein, p. 161.

113. Palmer, *The 25-Year War*, p. 28.

114. *The Pentagon Papers* (Gravel ed.), 3: 468–469.

115. *The Pentagon Papers* (Gravel ed.), 3: 407.

116. The quotations come from NSAM 328, April 6, 1965, *The Pentagon Papers* (Gravel ed.), 3: 702–703.

117. Halberstam describes the administration's actions: "There was one other important thing the President and his aides decided on April 1: although they were changing the nature of the American commitment and the mission of the marines, there was to be no announcement of it. Quite the reverse; everyone was to minimize any change, to say that the policy had not changed. The President had enough problems with his domestic programs without being hit from the other side about going to war. . . . James Reston of the *Times* was later to write that Lyndon Johnson escalated the war by stealth; he could not have been more right." Halberstam, *The Best and the Brightest*, pp. 569–570.

118. Excerpts are from Berman, *Planning a Tragedy*, pp. 58–59.

119. Berman, *Planning a Tragedy*, p. 58.

120. Berman, *Planning a Tragedy*, p. 58.

121. Berman, *Planning a Tragedy*, p. 59.

122. Berman, *Planning a Tragedy*, p. 59.

123. Berman, *Planning a Tragedy*, p. 59.

124. McCone was replaced as Director of Central Intelligence on April 23, 1965 by Admiral William F. Raborn.

125. In attendance at the conference were Secretary McNamara, General Westmoreland, General Wheeler, William P. Bundy, John McNaughton, Admiral Sharp, and Ambassador Taylor.

126. Maxwell D. Taylor, *Swords into Plowshares* (New York: Norton, 1972), pp. 342–343.

127. Leslie H. Gelb and Richard K. Betts, *The Irony of Vietnam: The System Worked* (Washington, D.C.: Brookings, 1979), p. 123. These new forces were to be placed in brigade-sized defensive enclaves—a strategy advocated by Maxwell Taylor. The "enclave strategy" was offered in opposition to the more offensive and free-wheeling plan for operations put forth by Westmoreland and the Joint Chief Staffs.

128. *The Pentagon Papers* (Gravel ed.), 3: 358. An interesting observation is made in the minutes that Ambassador Taylor argued that the perimeter just mentioned should remain inviolate because "it is important not to 'kill the patient' by destroying the North Vietnamese assets inside the 'Hanoi donut.' "

129. *The Pentagon Papers* (Gravel ed.), 3: 359.

130. Admiral Sharp was later vehement in arguing that the political restrictions imposed on the bombing undermined its effectiveness. See Ulysses G.

Sharp, *Strategy for Defeat* (San Rafael, CA: Presidio Press, 1978), chapter 8. Even though Taylor was on the other side of the divide from Sharp and the Chiefs in that he accepted the coercive-political framework for warfighting, he, at least, had practical experiences (e.g., Korea) of the difficulties involved in using military power to compel behavior by one's opponent.

131. *The Pentagon Papers* (Gravel ed.), 4: 293. The *Pentagon Papers'* analysis of the definition of victory prevalent among U.S. policy makers states: "the definition of 'win,' i.e., succeed in demonstrating to the VC that they cannot 'win,' indicates the assumption upon which the conduct of the war was to rest—that the VC would be convinced in some meaningful sense that they were not going to win and that they would then rationally choose less violent methods of seeking their goals. But the extent to which this definition would set limits of involvement or affect strategy was not clear."

132. Lyndon Baines Johnson, *The Vantage Point: Perspectives of the Presidency, 1963–1969* (New York: Holt, 1971), p. 141.

133. Johnson, *Vantage Point*, p. 141.

134. *The Pentagon Papers* (Gravel ed.), 3: 358, par. 1.

135. I am indebted to William E. Simons' letter, *supra*, p. 262, fn. 18.

136. Karnow, *Vietnam*, pp. 421–422.

137. *The Pentagon Papers*, 4: 609. Westmoreland to CINCPAC, June 13, 1965. The original in the *Pentagon Papers* is ungrammatical.

138. *The Pentagon Papers* (Gravel ed.), 3: 416.

139. Kahin, *Intervention*, pp. 354–356.

140. Mark Perry, *Four Stars: The Inside Story of the Forty-year Battle between the Joint Chiefs of Staff and America's Civilian Leaders* (Boston: Houghton-Mifflin, 1989), p. 151. Chapter 5 argues that the Joint Chiefs held to an "all" position about entering war in Vietnam. The most vociferous in this regard was Harold Johnson. Perry is a Washington based reporter who writes for *The Nation* specializing on military and intelligence issues.

141. Perry, *Four Stars*, p. 152. He cites an interview with Edward C. Meyer who was later Army Chief from 1979 to 1983. This is also supported by the Fred Greenstein interview with General Goodpaster, *supra*.

142. Gibbons, pt. 3, p. 400.

143. On the July 20 memo see Kahin, *Intervention*, pp. 362–365. McNamara's earlier July 1 memo, the precursor of the one presented three weeks later, proposed actions included mining DRV harbors, bombing key bridges, bombing rail yards, and, finally, destroying the war-making capacity of North Vietnam. For the Bundys' position see Kahin, *Intervention*, pp. 358–360.

144. Kahin, *Intervention*, pp. 390–391.

145. Perry, *Four Stars*, pp. 155–156. He discusses the reactions of Generals Wheeler, Johnson, and Kinnard. Also, see Halberstam, *Best and Brightest*,

pp. 596, 599–600; and, Chester L. Cooper, oral history interview (Ac 74–200), LBJ Library, pp. 17–18.

146. Halberstam, *The Best and the Brightest,* pp. 599–600.

147. He actually mentioned three other options as well, but they were not in serious contention. See July 27, 1965, NSC Meeting, Joint Leadership meeting, Papers of Lyndon Baines Johnson, Meeting Notes File, Box 1.

148. For example, Johnson was clearly worried about House minority leader Gerald Ford's reaction to calling up the reserves. In the July 22 meeting, Johnson stated, "Gerald Ford has demanded the President testify before Congress and tell why we are compelled to call up the reserves. Indications are that he will oppose calling up the reserves." Kahin, *Intervention,* p. 386.

On Johnson's reasons for not mobilizing see Halberstam, *Best and Brightest,* pp. 593–594.

149. *The Pentagon Papers* (Gravel ed.), 3: 476–477; and for the quotes below.

150. Consider the repeated attempts of various military advisers and Walt Rostow to argue for cutting the Ho Chi Minh trails as a necessary condition for defeating the Viet Cong. Their insistence on an initially devastating air campaign against the North is of the same piece.

151. Schandler, *Unmaking of a President,* p. 59. Schandler's remarks are completely consistent with the position advocated by Jack Valenti in November 1964.

152. Perry, *Four Stars,* pp. 160–6.

153. Kim Willenson, *The Bad War: An Oral History of the Vietnam War* (New York: New American Library, 1987), p. 90.

Morris Janowitz argues that the "token resignation" of the soldiers involved, "particularly the Chief of Staff of the ground forces," should have occurred. This, however, did not take place because the military bureaucracy had "become 'overprofessionalized'—more prepared to follow orders than to exercise professional skill and judgment." See Morris Janowitz, "Towards a Redefinition of Military Strategy in International Relations," *World Politics* 26 (July 1974): 494–495, fn. 44.

154. Taylor, for example, was the unsurpassed "political" general who never challenged the Kennedys' incompetent handling of the Bay of Pigs and their scapegoating of the JCS. Maxwell Taylor's report of June 13, 1961 on the Bay of Pigs, despite the admission that the JCS had not seen the real plan of the Operation until April 15, managed to place most of the blame on the JCS. Mark Perry writes, "It was a startling and, considering what history says of the JCS's actual doubts, an almost unbelievable conclusion." Perry, *Four Stars,* pp. 114–115.

Taylor's cynical performance stands in sharp contrast to the principled position of Chief of Naval Operations Arleigh Burke who, whether correctly or incorrectly, urged Kennedy to use American naval air and sea assets to neutralize Castro's military and thereby aroused the President's ire. Kennedy refused, saying that he did not "want the United States involved in this." To which Burke replied, "Hell, Mr. President, but we *are* involved!"

See E. B. Potter, *Admiral Arleigh Burke* (New York: Random House, 1990), pp. 437–438.

155. David Fraser, *Alanbrooke* (London: William Collins Sons, 1982), p. 215. See also Leslie H. Gelb and Richard K. Betts, *The Irony of Vietnam: The Systen Worked.* Washington, D.C.: Brookings, 1979).

156. Alexander L. George, "The Development of Doctrine and Strategy," in *The Limits of Coercive Diplomacy*, pp. 1–35.

157. George, "The Development of Doctrine and Strategy," p. 27.

158. Simons, "The Vietnam Intervention," p. 197.

159. Presidential Studies Archive, University of California at Davis, Institute for Governmental Affairs, Box 1, File 17: February 15–18, 1965, Memo to Dean Rusk from James L. Greenfield, 16 February 1965.

160. Burke and Greenstein, p. 278.

161. Rioch Report of Psychiatric stress on American troops, April 1964, Papers of James C. Thomson, Jr., Southeast Asia: Vietnam (1963–1964), box 24, folder: 1964, John F. Kennedy Presidential Library, p. 5.

Dr. David McK. Rioch, director of the Neuropsychiatry Division of the Walter Reed Army Institute of Research spent 19 days in Vietnam complementing the four months of investigation compiled by other staff members (p. 1).

162. Rioch Report, p. 4.

163. Rioch Report, p. 4.

164. Rioch Report, pp. 4–5.

165. Sharp was the Commander-in-Chief (Pacific) from 1964–8 and controlled the aerial bombing campaign against North Vietnam. Stockdale was shot down over North Vietnam and received the Congressional Medal of Honor for his heroic behavior in captivity. He later became a senior fellow at the Hoover Institute and vice-presidential candidate in 1992 on the ticket with H. Ross Perot of Texas.

166. Sharp, *Strategy for Defeat*, p. 97.

167. Sharp, *Strategy for Defeat*, p. 98.

8. | The "Lessons" of Vietnam for the Use of Force

1. For two articles that attempt to summarize the growing Vietnam literature see George C. Herring, "American Strategy in Vietnam: The Postwar Debate,"

Military Affairs 46 (April 1982): 57–63; and, Robert A. Divine, "Vietnam Reconsidered," *Diplomatic History* 12 (Winter 1988): 79–93. The following edited volumes contain excellent articles that analyze the U.S. political and military policies during the war: Peter Braestrup, ed., *Vietnam as History: Ten Years after the Paris Peace Accords* (Washington, D.C.: University Press of America, 1984); Richard A. Hunt and Richard H. Schultz, Jr., eds., *Lessons from an Unconventional War: Reassessing U.S. Strategies for Future Conflicts* (New York: Pergamon Press, 1982); George K. Osborn, Asa A. Clark, IV, Daniel J. Kaufman, and Douglas E. Lute, eds., *Democracy, Strategy, and Vietnam: Implications for American Policymaking* (Lexington, MA: Lexington Books, 1987).

2. AirLand Battle was actually first promulgated in 1982.

3. The first post-Vietnam Army field manual on operations was written under the direction of General William E. DePuy who had commanded the 1st Infantry Division (the "Big Red One") in Vietnam. DePuy's 1976 manual FM 100–5 marked a significant step toward the development of the Airland Battle. Harry Summers writes its approach to training was *revolutionary* because it stated that "the need for battle overrides every aspect of unit missions." The manual also directed: "The commander's first concern must be to order all the activities of his unit to meet his primary obligation . . . produce a unit ready to fight and win now." Harry G. Summers, *On Strategy II: A Critical Analysis of the Gulf War* (New York: Dell, 1992), p. 143; words in quotes are found in the 1976 FM 100–5.

4. Andrew F. Krepinevich, Jr., *The Army and Vietnam* (Baltimore: Johns Hopkins University Press, 1986). Krepinevich is a lieutenant colonel in the U.S. Army.

An article based on the book will also be cited; see Krepinevich, "Past as Prologue: Counterinsurgency and the U.S. Army's Vietnam Experience in Force Structure and Doctrine," in George K. Osborn et al., eds., *Democracy, Strategy, and Vietnam* (Lexington, MA: D.C. Heath and Co., 1987), pp. 269–83. [The article will be referred to as simply "Past as Prologue."]

5. Krepinevich, *The Army and Vietnam*, pp. 4–5.

6. Krepinevich, *The Army and Vietnam*, p. 5; emphasis in original. His observation about the focus on conventional war is consistent with my observations in chapter 5 about the Jominian elements that were present in the Army's "limited war" approach in the 1950s and early 1960s.

7. Members of the Never Again School would clearly not accept the idea that Korea permitted the relatively unfettered use of the armed services. In fact, it has been shown in previous chapters that Army and Marine generals from that war would not have shared Krepinevich's assessment.

8. Krepinevich, *The Army and Vietnam*, p. 5. One might also consider Kre-

pinevich's analysis here as presenting a counter-argument to the notion of a universal "American way" of fighting wars.

9. According to Krepinevich the Kennedy effort failed because he appointed men to oversee his counterinsurgency team "who were either novices in the art of insurgency warfare (as in the case of his brother Robert . . .) or men who approached this unconventional topic in a conventional manner (such as Generals Maxwell Taylor and Lyman Lemnitzer)." See Krepinevich, "Past as Prologue," p. 273. Krepinevich's placement of Maxwell Taylor in this rogue's gallery of advocates of the "Army Concept" can be challenged. While Taylor may not have been swept off his feet with counterinsurgency doctrine, he clearly saw the political dimensions of the war in Vietnam.

10. Krepinevich, "Past as Prologue," p. 276.

11. Krepinevich, *The Army and Vietnam*, p. 275.

12. For another piece in this evolving literature, Eliot Cohen has written an article arguing that the United States should have the capacity militarily, institutionally, and politically to fight "small wars." Eliot Cohen, "Constraints on America's Conduct of Small Wars," *International Security* 9 (Fall 1984): 151–181. At the begining of the article he provides his defination of a small war.

13. Bruce Palmer, Jr., review of *The Army and Vietnam*, by Andrew Krepinevich, *Parameters* 16 (Autumn 1986): 84.

14. James R Ward, "Vietnam: Insurgency or War," *Military Review* 69 (January 1989): 14–23. Ward's article is the first published work I have seen that convincingly strikes a balance between the two sides to this debate.

15. Rod Paschall, "Low-Intensity Conflict Doctrine: Who Needs It?" *Parameters* 15 (Autumn 1985): 39, 33–45. At the time that the article appeared in *Parameters* Paschall was the Director of the U.S. Army Military History Institute, Carlisle Barracks, PA. He had served in Laos, Cambodia, and Vietnam.

Interestingly, toward the end of the article Paschall makes a point of which Krepinevich would probably not approve (p. 43). He urges that if the U.S. engages in future low-intensity wars it cannot allow its enemy to maintain sanctuaries in which they are free from harm by the counterinsurgent ground forces. This point is more conventional-minded and shows how difficult it is to separate doctrinal aspects of conventional and irregular warfare. Paschall wishes the sanctuaries to be spoiled by forces at the mid-intensity level—certainly a move away from the heavy emphasis on political factors one sees in Krepinevich.

16. Krepinevich, *The Army and Vietnam*, p. 173. For a detailed discussion of CAPs see Michael E. Peterson, *The Combined Action Platoons: The U.S. Marines' Other War in Vietnam* (New York: Praeger, 1989). Peterson's first three chapters give an excellent account of Marine Corps ideas about fighting guerrillas, the beginnings in Vietnam, and the development of CAPs. The

author makes one observation that is worth noting here (p. 18): "The Army's doctrine contained a dangerous conceptual pitfall in that it overlooked a vital distinction between two types of guerrilla warfare: partisan and insurgent." Partisans, he explains, operate as auxiliaries to the "external, regular forces of another nation." The insurgent, however, is an "extension of a political movement within the country, and is potentially capable of being independent of external support." While the two are not mutually exclusive, the partisan is clearly a more conventional foe—less tied to the political and social context than is the insurgent.

17. Krepinevich, *The Army and Vietnam*, p. 174.

18. *Deadly Paradigms*, by Michael Shafer, presents an even harsher assessment of American political, military, and institutional abilities to devise a feasible strategy for defeating insurgencies which he feels are analytically *sui generis*. Thus, the comfortable maxims of 1960s counterinsurgency doctrine must be disposed of and replaced by a more acute understanding of the elements of revolutionary warfare that are peculiar to each nation's social, political, and economic milieu. Throughout the postwar period, he argues, "American policy makers misunderstood past insurgency situations, prescribed inappropriate solutions to them, and overestimated the United States' role in the process." See D. Michael Shafer, *Deadly Paradigms: The Failure of U.S. Counterinsurgency Policy* (Princeton: Princeton University Press, 1988), p. 276.

19. Second thoughts about "gradualism" certainly did not wait for the end of the war. In his memoirs, entitled *Swords and Plowshares* (1972), Maxwell Taylor recanted the strategy of "gradualism" which called for "the piecemeal employment of military forces at slowly mounting levels of intensity." A little later he adds: "While this carefully controlled violence may have had some justification at the start, it ended by defeating its own purposes. Designed to limit the dangers of expanded war, it ended by assuring a prolonged war which carried with it dangers of expansion. The restrained use of air power suggested to the enemy a lack of decisiveness." Taylor also notes that while "gradualism" undermined the coercive efforts of the United States against Hanoi, "it also violated the military principles of surprise and mass as means to gain prompt success with minimum loss."

As critical as Taylor is of the Limited War concept he does not abandon it altogether. The former Army chief of staff urges that political leaders approach war-fighting with a greater awareness of military realities: i.e., the Jominian principles cannot be denied (p. 430). Yet, Taylor recognizes that wars of this kind will never be easily fought due to the tension between escalation and the ineffective use of force. He regards limited war as preferable to the " do-nothing option which offers the prospect of a progressive attrition of our interests"

(p. 404). Maxwell D. Taylor, *Swords and Plowshares* (New York: Norton, 1972), pp. 403–404.

20. Robert E. Osgood, *Limited War Revisited* (Boulder, CO: Westview Press, 1979). Subsequent page references are cited in the text.

21. Harry G. Summers, Jr., *On Strategy: The Vietnam War in Context* (Washington, D.C.: Government Printing Office, 1981). Harry Summers wrote *On Strategy* while in attendance at the Army War College (Carlisle Barracks, Pa.); he later retired from the Army as a colonel. He fought in the Korean and Vietnam Wars. For an accurate description of the impact of *On Strategy* see Harry G. Summers, Jr., *On Strategy II: A Critical Analysis of the Gulf War* (New York: Dell Publishing, 1992), pp. 131–133.

22. An earlier article written primarily by General Fred C. Weyand with the assistance of Harry Summers observed: "Although it might sound paradoxical to civilians, the most 'humane' way to fight a war is by the violent and overwhelming use of military force. Attempts to use force sparingly, to hold back, to gradually put pressure on the enemy, serves only to prolong the war and to ultimately increase casualties and suffering." See General Fred C. Weyand and Lt. Col. Harry G. Summers, Jr., "Vietnam Myths and Military Realities," *Armor* (September–October 1976), p. 35.

A 1982 article made a substantial contribution to the analysis of limited war strategies and the Vietnam War. See Stephen Peter Rosen, "Vietnam and the American Theory of Limited War," *International Security* 7 (Fall 1982): 83-113. Rosen, a Harvard-trained, military intellectual and academic working in the Office of the Secretary of Defense, wrote what Harry Summers has called "his landmark article on the Vietnam War." Summers, *On Strategy II*, p. 48. (Interestingly, even though Rosen's article appeared one year after Summers' *On War* he does not refer to it in his article). I have analyzed Summers' work in greater detail for three reasons: 1) it preceded Rosen's; 2) it has had an almost immeasurable impact on recent strategic thinking in the U.S. military; and 3) as a book it presents a much more developed theory of the problems encountered in Vietnam: in other words, if the Rosen article is a "landmark" then *On Strategy* is Gibraltar.

Rosen makes these interesting observations: **One)** "A reconsideration of limited war strategy in light of what we can learn from historical experience leads to a new strategy to supplement the old. Limited wars are not only political wars...but *strange* wars. The general problem of limited war is not only the *diplomatic* one of how to signal our resolve to our enemy, but the *military* one of how to adapt, quickly and successfully, to the peculiar and unfamiliar *battlefield* conditions in which our armed forces are fighting. Diplomatic success will depend on military success since resolve cannot survive repeated failure on the battlefield." (p. 83) **Two)** "This state of affairs came to a head with the Tet offensive. To sum up the state of affairs before the communists launched their attack we can say that: 1) there was no generally agreed upon comprehensible military strategy for winning the war, and no clear definition of the amount of resources to be devoted to the war; 2) there was a limited war theory of signalling, but it had been a complete failure; and 3) as a result of the limited war attitude and other causes, decisionmaking had become centralized in Washington." (p. 101) **Three)** "Civil military relations must be improved. The civilian leadership in the Pentagon for the most part does not trust the military to wage war properly and the military has vivid and painful memories of the Vietnam War. It hates the sound of the term 'limited war.'" (p. 112)

23. Krepinevich, *The Army and Vietnam*, p. 262. Krepinevich argues that one of the reasons this plan was shelved in the spring of 1965 was its enormous logistical requirements: 18,000 engineers would have been required. I believe that Summers and his allies in this debate would reply that had President Johnson permitted the military's request for another 200,000 troops in the spring of 1968, this would have provided the necessary forces to carry out the blocking operation. These increases would have required calling up the reserves in the United States.

24. Summers, *On Strategy*, p. 15.

25. Summers, *On Strategy*, p. 41. He notes that this concept was embodied in the 1954 FM 100–5 (Army field manual on operations) that recognized the existence of wars of "limited objective." Summers thinks this was a positive step, but he also argues that the same field manual's observation that "victory" was no longer required in warfare was a grave error. This is much the same argument made by Trevor Dupuy that was discussed in chapter 5.

26. Summers, *On Strategy*, p. 41. He writes: "the U.S. strategy in Korea was not so much one of limiting the means as it was one of tailoring the political ends so that they could be accomplished within the military means that our political leaders were willing to expend.

27. Summers, *On Strategy*, p. 42. He means "wars of limited means." This change was probably intended to make the Army's concept of limited war more similar to that espoused by the civilian strategic community.

28. Department of the Army Field Manual FM 100–5, *Field Service Regulations: Operations* (Washington, D.C.: USGPO, February 19, 1962), p. 46.

29. FM 100–5 (1962), p. 8.

30. Summers, *On Strategy*, p. 41. Summers correctly observes that attaining one's "limited objectives" may signal a genuine victory. But the 1954 manual had to fight MacArthur's usage of the term which tended to equate "victory" with the total defeat of one's opponent.

31. Alger discusses why the "principles of war" are not Clausewitzian—as some have claimed. See Alger, *The Quest for Victory*, pp. 28–31.

32. His book, *On Strategy II: A Critical Analysis of the Gulf War,* take the same approach.

33. Such steadfast adherence to principles as Summers presents was alien to Clausewitz's understanding of war. Clausewitz's sense of the limitations of "principles" becomes apparent in this definition (which Alger quotes, p. 31): "*Principle* is also a law for action, but not in its *formal, definitive meaning;* it represents only the spirit and the sense of the law; in cases where the diversity of the real world cannot be contained within the rigid forms of law, the application of principle allows for a greater latitude of judgment. Cases to which principle cannot be applied must be settled by judgment; principle thus becomes essentially a support, or lodestar, to the man responsible for the action." Clausewitz, *On War,* p. 151.

34. Apparently, using Summers' methodology of analyzing war through the Jominian principles is useful for military practitioners. See a Summers-like analysis of the U.S. invasion of Panama: Lt. Col. William C. Bennett, "Just Cause and the Principles of War," *Military Review* 71 (March 1991): 2–13.

35. Samuel P. Huntington, "Playing to Win," *The National Interest* (Spring 1986): 16; the article was originally presented as one of two lectures given in honor of Admiral Chester W. Nimitz in the spring of 1985. See Samuel P. Huntington, "The Elements of American Strategy" in *American Military Strategy* (Berkeley, CA: Institute of International Studies, 1986), pp. 3–17. Subsequent page references are cited in the text.

36. He does not address the potential problem that arises if one has limited "objectives." Namely, military needs may require that a greater violence be employed than political circumstances will permit.

37. Note the words "primarily" and "normally" are used to blunt the severity of the argument but don't really fit into the spirit of the passage. It should be noted that Huntington recognizes the existence of an All-or-Nothing school in the article but does not consider himself to be part of it. His criticisms of the All-or-Nothing position are undercut by the statement quoted here.

38. He adds: "They can almost be summed up in the familiar phrase about 'getting thar fustest with the mostest.' They do represent a shift back to more traditional ways of thinking about strategy and the use of military force compared to those that have dominated strategic thinking in recent years."

39. FM 100–5s for 1954 and 1962 were discussed in chapter 5. On December 31, 1973 the U.S. military contingent in Vietnam was reduced by law to 50. Summers, *Vietnam War Almanac,* p. 58.

40. *The Public Papers of the Presidents: Nixon,* 1969: p. 549. See also Gaddis, *Strategies of Containment,* p. 298, and 298–306.

41. Paul H. Herbert, *Deciding What Has to Be Done: General William E.*

Depuy and the 1976 Edition of FM 100–5, Operations (Leavenworth Papers No. 16) (Fort Leavenworth, Kansas: Combat Studies Institute, 1988), p. 5. This Leavenworth Paper is the most detailed source available concerning the vociferous doctrinal debates that took place within the Army before the promulgation of this FM 100–5. For a few pages of enjoyable reading on this topic see U.S. News and World Report, *Triumph Without Victory*, pp. 158–164. The book's notice of the Hungarian-born U.S. Army officer, Wass de Czege, underscores the importance of individuals in the developing ideas. Subsequent page references will be cited in the text.

42. Russell Weigley, *History of the United States Army*, 1984 ed., p. 584.

43. Weigley, *History of the United States Army*, 1984 ed., p. 585.

44. Weigley, *History of the United States Army*, 1984 ed., p. 578.

45. Weigley, *History of the United States Army*, 1984 ed., p. 579.

46. The "operational level" had long been discussed in the Soviet and German armies.

47. George M. Hall, Colonel, "Culminating Points," *Military Review* 69 (July 1989): 79–86. For Clausewitz on culminating points see *On War*, pp. 566–573.

48. Clyde J. Sincere, Captain, "Target Acquisition for the Deep Battle," *Military Review* 69 (August 1989): 23–28; Schreyach, Jon C., Colonel, "Fire Support for Deep Operations," *Military Review* 69 (August 1989): 29–37.

49. There may be a bit of wishful thinking in the way these manuals attempt to substitute superior maneuver, communications, and intelligence (which NATO could develop) for superior numbers and firepower (which the Soviets always had in Europe). This sanguine estimation of maneuver by the Army was paralleled by the development of such ideas in the late 1970s and early 1980s by a military reform movement in civilian circles. Although members of the civilian group claim some degree of credit for the development of AirLand Battle it is not clear that General Starry needed their advice to assess the doctrinal needs of his service.

For some readings on the overestimation of maneuver in relation to firepower see John Terraine's *The Smoke and the Fire*, and *The White Heat*. In both books Terraine criticizes the analysis of World War I set forth by Basil Liddell Hart. For a criticism of the "military reform movement's" excessive reliance on maneuver, see Robert L. Goldich, "The Strategic Importance of Mass," *The National Interest* (Winter 1986/7): 66–74.

50. U.S. Department of the Army Field Manual (FM) 100–5, *Operations* (Washington, D.C.: Government Printing Office [GPO], May 1986), p. 4.

51. FM 100–5 (1986), p. 4; my emphasis.

52. Swain, Richard M., Colonel, "Square Pegs from Round Holes: Low-

Intensity Conflict in Army Doctrine," *Military Review* 69 (December 1987): 2–15. See, especially, pp. 7–10.

53. Swain, "Square Pegs," p. 8; U.S. Department of the Army, TRADOC Field Circular 100–20, *Low Intensity Conflict* (Fort Monroe, VA: Headquarters, July 16, 1986).

54. Swain, "Square Pegs," p. 9.

55. Steven Metz, "Victory and Compromise," *Military Review* 72 (April 1992): 48.

56. Steven Metz, "Victory and Compromise," p. 48.

57. Metz, "Victory and Compromise," p. 50.

58. Metz, "Victory and Compromise," p. 48.

59. Neil Sheehan, *A Bright Shining Lie: John Paul Vann and America in Vietnam* (New York: Random House, 1988), pp. 203–265.

60. The 1976, 1982, and 1986 manuals all present versions of the principles of war. The 1986 FM 100–5 states of the principles: In the years following their introduction in 1921, "the original principles of war adopted by our Army have been slightly revised, but they have essentially stood the tests of analysis, experimentation, and practice." FM 100–5 (1986), Appendix A, p. 173.

61. For a valiant attempt to fit AirLand Battle into the LIC context see Steven Metz, "AirLand Battle and Counterinsurgency," *Military Review* 70 (January 1990): 32–41.

The June 1991 issue of *Military Review* is devoted to LIC. See Steven Metz, "U.S. Strategy and the Changing LIC Threat," *Military Review* 71 (June 1991): 22–29. In a later issue see William H. Burgess III, "Toward a More Complete Doctrine: Special Operations Forces in AirLand Battle Future," *Military Review* 71 (February 1991): 30–37.

62. Bernard Brodie, as discussed in chapter 2, was one of the earliest postwar strategic thinkers to recognize the difficulties that would characterize the use of force in the nuclear era. He taught in the History Department at UCLA.

63. General Carl E. Vuono, Bernard Brodie Lecture, June 1, 1990, Center for International and Strategic Affairs, University of California at Los Angeles. See Carl Vuono, "The Strategic Value of Conventional Forces," *Parameters* 20 (September 1990): 2–10. Subsequent page references are cited in the text.

64. Major Daniel P. Bolger, "Two Armies," *Parameters* 19 (September 1989): 24–34.

65. My favorite line in the article is: "Warriors need not be rocket scientists, but they must be both smart and clever." Bolger, "Two Armies," p. 33.

66. Bolger, "Two Armies," p. 32.

67. The editors of *Parameters* placed a disclaimer with the article and invited comments from readers (p. 25).

68. Bolger, "Two Armies," p. 33.

69. For some first steps in this direction see, Lt. Col. Andrew J. Bacevich, "The Army in the 1990s," *Military Review* 69 (July 1989): 87–95, esp. 92; Capt. Russel G. Allen, "A New Army for the 1990s," *Parameters* 70 (July 1990): 76–83.

70. FM 100–5 (1982), p. 8–1.

71. Allard, *Command, Control, and the Common Defense,* p. 178.

72. See *On Strategy II,* chapters 5 and 6.

73. "John McLaughlin's One on One," September 10, 1989, interview with Admiral William Crowe, p. 14.

74. "John McLaughlin's One on One," September 10, 1989, p. 5. This point supports Harry Summers' belief on the critical need for a president to seek Congressional legitimation before using force in a situation of war.

75. Summers, *On Strategy II,* p. 84.

76. Summers, *On Strategy II,* p. 84.

77. Barnett and Barlow, "Maritime Strategy," p. 347.

78. Summers, *On Strategy II,* p. 91. For this quote see, U.S. Marine Corps, *Warfighting,* FMFM-1 (Washington, D.C.: Department of the Navy, HQ U.S. Marine Corps, March 6, 1989), p. 59 Subsequent page references are cited in the text.

79. Summers, *On Strategy II,* p. 91. The other Marine Corps document of great importance in this process was: U.S. Marine Corps, *Campaigning,* FMFM 1–1, (Washington, D.C.: Department of the Navy, HQ U.S. Marine Corps, 1990).

One of the best expositions of the relationship between offense and defense may possibly be in *Warfighting,* pp. 24–27.

80. Clodfelter, *The Limits of Air Power,* p. 208. Douhet's great work, *Command of the Air,* was published in 1921.

81. Summers, *On Strategy II,* p. 112. From Michael R. Gordon, "Generals Favor 'No Holds Barred' by U.S. if Iraq Attacks the Saudis," *New York Times,* 25 August 1990, p. 1.

82. Clodfelter, *The Limits of Air Power,* p. 208. Clodfelter is very critical of the misinterpretation of the effects of Linebacker that afflicts the Air Force and now overestimates the decisive impact that strategic bombing can have in wars. Linebacker I & II were both Nixon Administration bombing campaigns against North Vietnam. Linebacker I started on May 10, 1972 and ended on October 23, 1972. Linebacker II ran from December 18 to 29, 1972.

83. AFM 1–1, *Basic Aerospace Doctrine of the United States Air Force* (Washington, D.C.: Department of the Air Force, March 16, 1984), 1–3. One might recall that the Air Force Chief of Staff, General Michael J. Dugan, was fired by Secretary of Defense Cheney in September 1990 for telling reporters

who accompanied him on a trip to the Middle East that air power would decide the outcome of the war.

84. Kenneth P. Werrell, "Air War Victorious: The Gulf War vs. Vietnam," *Parameters* 22 (Summer 1992): p. 43.

This point is supported by Clodfelter, *Limits of Air Power*, pp. 32–33. Clodfelter brings our attention to two RAND reports written in 1957 and another 1957 report for the Pacifica Air Forces (PACAF) Headquarters that pointed to the inadequacy of U.S. air power capabilities for the purpose of fighting limited wars.

85. Werrell, "Air War Victorious," p. 43. He writes, "Perhaps most telling, the air proponents speak with disgust of the gradualism that permitted the North Vietnamese to build up their defenses, disperse their resources, and adjust to the air assault. Gradualism also allowed the North to exploit the bombing in terms of politics and propaganda, to focus on civilian casualties and damage, and to stir up public pressure both within the United States and abroad against the bombing of North Vietnam specifically and against the war in general. These, along with the ambitious goal of breaking the enemy's will, were indeed factors in Rolling Thunder's failure."

86. Summers lays out the history of greater Army-Air Force cooperation that developed in the 1980s with respect to increased tactical air support for ground forces. The turning point in this relationship occurred in April 1983 when General Edward C. Meyer, Chief of Staff of the Army, and General Charles A. Gabriel, Chief of Staff of the Air Force, signed a memorandum of understanding that "committed the Army and Air Force to cooperate in 'joint tactical training and field exercises based on AirLand Battle doctrine.' " Another memorandum was signed on May 22, 1984 taking the air-land combat team to greater levels of cooperation. Summers, *On Strategy II*, p. 148.

87. Werrell, "Air War Victorious," p. 49.

88. Patrick Glynn, *Closing Pandora's Box: Arms Races, Arms Control, and the History of the Cold War* (New York: Basic Books, 1992), p. 221.

89. Glynn, *Closing Pandora's Box*, p. 222.

90. Summers, *On Strategy II*, p. 73.

91. FM 100–5 (1986), p. 10.

92. FM 100–5 (1986), p. 10.

93. FM 100–5 (1986), p. 14.

94. Barton Gellman, "Revisiting the Gulf War: Book Depicts a Raging, Imperial Schwarzkopf," *Washington Post*, July 25, 1993, sec. A, p. 20.

95. Gellman, "Revisiting the Gulf War," sec. A, p. 20. The writer quoted by Gelman is Rick Atkinson from his forthcoming *Crusade: The Untold Story of the Persian Gulf War* published by Houghton Mifflin.

96. U.S. Dept. of the Army, *Field Manual 100–5: Operations* (Washing-

ton, D.C.: Dept. of the Army, 14 June 1993), chapter 13 (pp. 13–0 to 13–8). (Subsequent page references are cited in the text.)

97. Some clarification may be necessary for some of these terms. "Nation assistance" refers to efforts to buttress "a host nation's efforts to promote development, ideally through the use of host nation resources." Curiously, "peace enforcement is included here. That term "implies the use of force or its threat to coerce hostile factions to cease and desist from violent actions." Peace enforcement would be conducted under the auspices of the U.N. However one labels such actions they seem to be warlike and not clearly appropriate in a section of the manual focused on operations other than war.

98. The use of "military purpose" supports this book's argument that the military element of war can push the state in a different direction than does its political element.

99. Interestingly, apologetic reasons are given for using the defense: "Though the outcome of decisive combat derives from offensive operations, it is often necessary, even advisable, to defend. Commanders choose to defend when they need to buy time, to hold a piece of key terrain, to facilitate other operations, to preoccupy the enemy in one area so friendly forces can attack him in another, or to erode enemy resources at a rapid rate while reinforcing friendly operations." FM 100–5 (1993), p. 9–0.

9. | Reagan and Bush

1. Petraeus, dissertation, p. 210.

2. Petraeus, dissertation, p. 210.

3. Alexander M. Haig, Jr., *Caveat: Realism, Reagan, and Foreign Policy* (New York: Macmillan, 1984), p. 119.

4. The reader should remember the discussion of this topic from chapter 3. There I noted that the reasons for China's decision to terminate the war in the Spring-Summer 1953 are not clearly understood. What does seem certain is that Eisenhower was willing to use nuclear weapons to end the war.

5. Haig, *Caveat*, p. 125. Haig's approach to coercive diplomacy bears a strong resemblance to the "military" approach to the use of force—get in quickly, use mass and concentration of effort to apply one's power decisively. As mentioned previously, Haig is not very specific about his policy recommendations, but he does describe Lyndon Johnson's seizure of the Dominican Republic in 1965 with approval.

6. Haig, *Caveat*, pp. 127–128. This remark is curious. If Haig was not advocating the use of force, why was Weinberger afraid of going to war?

7. Haig, *Caveat*, p. 128.

8. Haig, *Caveat*, p. 130.

9. For a well-researched treatment of the subject that disagrees with the Reagan policy objectives see Kenneth Roberts, "Bullying and Bargaining: The United States, Nicaragua, and Conflict Resolution in Central America," *International Security*, 15 (Fall 1990): 67–102.

Nor is it clear that Haig's analysis was correct. Involving the Soviets and the Cubans in a major confrontation would not have addressed the regional social and political problems that became part of the discussions of the Contadora process. See George P. Shultz, *Turmoil and Triumph: My Years as Secretary of State* (New York: Scribner's, 1993), pp. 401–404.

10. Richard Halloran, "A Commanding Voice in the Military," *New York Times*, July 15, 1984, p. 18. The deployment to the Persian Gulf mentioned here is related to the threat to shipping during the Iran-Iraq War.

11. Halloran, "A Commanding Voice," p. 52.

12. William J. Taylor, Jr., and David H. Petraeus, "The Legacy of Vietnam for the U.S. Military," in George K. Osborn et al., eds., *Democracy, Strategy, and Vietnam* (Lexington, MA: Lexington Books, 1987), p. 260. William Taylor, Jr., was, at the time of the book's publication, the operating officer and director of the Center for Strategic and International Studies (CSIS) then, but not now, affiliated with Georgetown University. Taylor was also a retired Army colonel.

13. George C. Wilson, "Top U.S. Brass Wary on Central America," *Washington Post*, June 24, 1983, sec. A, p. 20. Wilson was a columnist for the *Washington Post* specializing in military affairs. The "top brass" were Gen. John A. Wickham, Jr. (Chief of Staff), Gen. Paul F. Gorman (US Southern Command, Panama), Gen. Wallace F. Nutting (US Readiness Command, Tampa), and Lt. Gen. Robert L. Schweitzer (Inter-American Defense Board, Fort McNair).

14. Richard Halloran, "General Opposes Nicaragua Attack," *New York Times*, June 30, 1985, sec. A, p. 3.

15. "Pentagon is Opposed to Use of Troops in Central America," *New York Times*, June 5, 1983, p. 5.

16. Walter Mossberg, "The Army Resists a Salvadoran Vietnam," *Wall Street Journal*, 24 June 1983, p. 22.

17. Mossberg, "The Army Resists," p. 22.

18. Mossberg, "The Army Resists," p. 22. Drew Middleton also writes that the Chiefs want "the military viewpoint to be presented to the President more firmly than, many feel, it was done by the Joint Chiefs of Staff at critical phases of the Vietnam engagement." See Drew Middleton, "Vietnam and the Military Mind," *New York Times Magazine*, January 10, 1982, p. 91.

19. For the most thorough accounts of this event see Petraeus, dissertation, pp. 173–98; Ralph A. Hallenbeck, "Force and Diplomacy: Examining

America's Strategy in Lebanon," Diss. Pennsylvania State University 1986; Eric Hammel, *The Root: The Marines in Beirut, August 1982—February 1984* (New York: Harcourt, Brace, and Jovanovich, 1985). Hammel lists the rules of engagements for the U.S. Marines (Appendix I, p. 427). They were as follows: 1) When on post, mobile or on foot patrol, keep loaded magazine in weapon, bolt closed, weapon on safe, no round in chamber; 2) Do not chamber a round unless told to do so by a commissioned officer unless you must act in immediate self-defense where deadly force is authorized; 3) Keep ammo for crew served weapons readily available, but not loaded. Weapon is on safe; 4) Call local forces to assist in self-defense effort. Notify headquarters; 5) Use only minimum degree of force to accomplish the mission; 6) Stop the use of force when it is no longer needed to accomplish the mission; 7) If you receive effective hostile fire, direct your fire at the source. If possible use friendly snipers; 8) Respect civilian property; do not attack it unless absolutely necessary to protect friendly forces; 9) Protect innocent civilians from harm; 10) Respect and protect recognized medical agencies such as Red Cross, Red Crescent, etc.

20. Haig's resignation was announced on June 25, 1982, but, at Reagan's request, he directed the Lebanon policy until George Shultz could properly assume office. *Haig agreed to the brief first deployment* of American (and other national forces) to Beirut. Haig's policymaking role ended on July 5, 1982 when the President finally accepted his resignation. The next day President Reagan announced that he would allow U.S. troops to assist in escorting PLO fighters from their positions in the Port of Beirut. After that, weeks were consumed in petty negotiations over the manner in which the PLO would leave Lebanon. In *Caveat*, Haig does not outline a position on the second Marine deployment.

21. Petraeus, dissertation, p. 177.

22. Petraeus, p. 178, fn. 100.

23. Shultz, *Turmoil and Triumph*, p. 108.

24. Richard Halloran, *To Arm a Nation* (New York: MacMillan, 1986), p. 29.

25. Halloran, *To Arm a Nation*, p. 29.

26. Petraeus, dissertation, pp. 179–80; Petraeus cites Hallenbeck, p. 108.

27. Perry, *Four Stars*, p. 309. Reports to Washington noted that the Beirut airport was militarily indefensible: "it was 'a mini Dien Bien Phu' surrounded by high mountains" where unfriendly Moslems would be able to perfectly target their artillery on the Marines."

28. Shultz, *Turmoil and Triumph*, p. 108.

29. Shultz, *Turmoil and Triumph*, p. 325.

30. Shultz, *Turmoil and Triumph*, p. 326.

31. Dupuy and Dupuy, *The Encyclopedia of Military History*, p. 1395. Resistance lasted sixty hours. U.S. casualties: 18 killed, 83 wounded.

32. Halloran, *To Arm a Nation*, p. 29.

33. Shultz, *Turmoil and Triumph*, p. 330.

34. Shultz, *Turmoil and Triumph*, p. 343; my emphasis.

35. Petraeus, dissertation, p. 199.

36. Shultz, *Turmoil and Triumph*, p. 343.

37. For more on National Security Council and Grenada see Constantine C. Menges, *Inside the National Security Council: The True Story of the Making and Unmaking of Reagan's Foreign Policy* (New York: Simon & Schuster, 1988), chap. 2.

38. Petraeus, dissertation, p. 208. Or, to use another term—there was to be no "micro-management" of this military action.

39. Shultz, *Turmoil and Triumph*, p. 345.

40. Shultz, *Turmoil and Triumph*, p. 341. Former two-term Chairman of the Joint Chiefs of Staff (1985–1989), Admiral William J. Crowe, Jr., observed that the Shultz-Weinberger rivalry had followed the two men from the Bechtel Corporation where they had both worked to government service. He observed of their many disagreements: "Often it seemed that the subject was less important than prevailing in the argument. Their contention was one of the most serious problems within the Reagan Administration." William J. Crowe, Jr., with David Chanoff *The Line of Fire: From Washington to the Gulf, the Politics and Battles of the New Military* (New York: Simon & Schuster, 1993), p. 127.

41. George Shultz, address before the Trilateral Commission on April 3, 1984, *Department of State Bulletin*, May 1984, p. 12.

42. Shultz, Trilateral address, p. 13.

43. His use of "power" seems to be synonymous with "force" in this passage.

44. Shultz, Trilateral address, p. 13.

45. Shultz, Trilateral address, p. 13. For a discussion of this topic in his memoirs see Shultz, *Turmoil and Triumph*, pp. 643–651. See especially his reference to one of William Safire's columns, "Only the Fun Wars," *New York Times*, December 3, 1984, sec. A, p. 23. Safire had endorsed the Shultz position claiming that his opponents in the debate like Weinberger wanted to fight only the fun wars. Safire sent a copy of the column to Shultz on which Henry Kissinger had written: "Bill—one of your best. We must never be in the position where our only options are waging total war or accepting total defeat." Shultz, *Turmoil and Triumph*, p. 651.

46. George Shultz, address to Park Avenue synagogue, October 25, 1984, *Department of State Bulletin*, December 1984, p. 15.

47. Shultz, Address to synagogue, p. 16.

48. For an excellent account of this debate within the Reagan administration see James McCartney, "Pentagon Puts Brakes on U.S. Attack Projects," *Miami Herald*, April 12, 1984, sec. A, p. 1 & 14.

49. Reprinted in the January 1985 issue of *Defense*, a Department of Defense publication.

50. Caspar W. Weinberger, "U.S. Defense Strategy," *Foreign Affairs* 64 (Spring 1986): 684.

51. Weinberger, "U.S. Defense Strategy," pp. 686–687.

52. McCartney, "Pentagon Puts Brakes on U.S. Attack Projects," *Miami Herald*, April 12, 1984, sec. A, p.14.

53. Secretary George Shultz, address at Yeshiva University, December 9, 1984, *Department of State Bulletin*, February 1985 issue, p. 2.

54. Weinberger, "U.S. Defense Strategy," p. 684.

55. Weinberger, "U.S. Defense Strategy," pp. 684–685.

56. Weinberger does not cite Jomini.

57. Weinberger continues this section of the article with a direct criticism of the peacekeeping mission in Lebanon. He is clearly taking aim at Secretary Shultz's endorsement of such politico-military operations. One might add another criticism of "gradualism": when it does not succeed quickly it serves to *increase* the level of commitment that one has in the crisis. This can lead to a logic in which money wasted seems to create value in an ill-considered project under consideration. Instead of cutting one's losses, the participant stays in hoping for some positive return. Gamblers often think in this irrational manner.

58. Ronald Reagan, *Ronald Reagan: An American Life* (New York: Simon & Schuster, 1990), p. 466.

59. Reagan, *Ronald Reagan*, p. 466.

60. William J. Crowe, Jr. "What I've Learned," *Washingtonian* 25 (November 1989): p. 109.

61. Crowe, *Line of Fire*, pp. 174–175.

62. Crowe, *Line of Fire*, p. 180.

63. Crowe, *Line of Fire*, p. 181.

64. Ronald O'Rourke, "The Tanker War," *Proceedings* 114 (May 1988): p. 30.

65. Crowe, *Line of Fire*, p. 202.

66. Ronald O'Rourke, "Gulf Ops," *Proceedings* 115 (May 1989): 42.

67. Ronald O'Rourke, "Gulf Ops," p. 50 (see footnotes).

68. O'Rourke, "Gulf Ops," p. 50.

69. Crowe, *Line of Fire*, pp. 177, 180.

70. Jim McGee, "Navy Chief Challenged Gulf Buildup," *The Miami Herald*, September 6, 1987, sec. A, pp. 1 & 18.

71. Crowe, *Line of Fire*, p. 185.

72. For a book-length treatment of this subject see Mark P. Lagon, " 'Crusade for Freedom': International and Ideological Sources of the Reagan Doctrine" (Ph.D. dissertation, Georgetown University, 1991), pp. 217–388.

73. Ray S. Cline, *The CIA under Reagan, Bush, and Casey* (Washington, D.C.: Acropolis Books, 1981), p. 15.

74. Cline, *CIA*, p. 152.

75. Cline, *CIA*, p. 206.

76. Lagon, dissertation, p. 348: "Covert aid programs were largely impractical given press coverage of operations and what George Shultz called in an interview the phenomenon of 'covert' aid programs that everybody (the press and the Congress) knows about, but which the administration will not openly acknowledge."

77. This occurred two years after the March 1985 signing of National Security Decision Directive 166, which made the U.S. goal in Afghanistan the defeat of the Soviet forces. See Steve Coll, "Anatomy of a Victory: CIA's Covert Afghan War," *Washington Post*, July 19, 1992, sec. A, p. 24.

78. It should not be forgotten that the Ford Administration wanted to provide aide to UNITA, the Angolan insurgency directed by Jonas Savimbi. The Portuguese colonial regime had been expelled from Angola in 1975 by a pro-Soviet Marxist insurgency. The Clark Amendment was passed by Congress in the post-Vietnam haze to prohibit any president from becoming involved in the Angolan War and aiding the UNITA insurgency. The Clark Amendment was finally repealed after a strong effort by Capitol Hill conservatives in 1985. See Lagon, dissertation, pp. 274–279.

79. The term first appeared in a *Time* magazine essay by Charles Krauthammer on April 1, 1985 after Reagan began to specifically describe this new policy in speeches following his second inauguration. See Lagon, dissertation, p. 382.

80. Frederick Kempe, "U.S., Bonn Clash over Pact with France," *Wall Street Journal*, May 27, 1992, sec. A, p. 9.

81. For the text of President Bush's statement to the nation see "Text of President Bush's Address," *Washington Post*, December 21, 1989, sec. A, p. 38.

82. Noriega was convicted as a narcotics trafficker over two years later by a federal jury in Miami, Florida.

83. Kevin Buckley, *Panama: The Whole Story* (New York: Simon & Schuster, 1991), pp. 188–191. of Panama.

84. Buckley, *Panama*, pp. 222–223. This assessment was supported by *Time* magazine which observed: "Unlike his predecessor, General Frederick Woerner, Thurman saw Noriega as primarily a military rather than a political problem." See Ed Magnuson, "Sowing Dragon's Teeth," *Time*, January 1, 1990, p. 24.

85. Buckley, *Panama*, p. 223.

86. Ann Devroy and Patrick E. Tyler, "U.S. Forces Crush Panamanian Military; Noriega in Hiding as Fighting Continues," *Washington Post*, December 21, 1990, sec. A, p. 33.

87. Molly Moore and Rick Atkinson, "Despite Problems, Invasion Seen as Military Success," *Washington Post*, December 29, 1989, sec. A, p. 22.

88. Moore and Atkinson, sec. A, p. 22.

89. Russell Watson, "Bush's Big Gamble in Panama," *Newsweek*, January 1, 1990, p. 21. There were many reporters who worked on this story. Watson was the person cited as the writer (p. 22 bottom).

90. Ed Magnuson, "Passing the Manhood Test," *Time*, January 8, 1990, p. 43.

91. Lt. Col. William C. Bennett, "Just Cause and the Principles of War," *Military Review*, March 1991, pp. 3–13.

92. On August 2, 1990 the U.N. Security Council passed resolution 660 "condemning the invasion and demanding that Iraq immediately and unconditionally withdraw its forces to the positions they had occupied the previous day." See "United Nations Security Council Resolutions Relating to the Situation between Iraq and Kuwait," United Nations Department of Public Information, December 1991 (DPI/1104/Rev. 3), p. 2.

93. Bob Woodward, *The Commanders* (New York: Simon & Schuster, 1991), pp. 306–307.

94. Woodward, *The Commanders*, p. 347.

95. John Keegan, "The Lessons of the Gulf War," *Los Angeles Times Magazine*, April 7, 1991, p. 21.

96. Wendell John Coats, Jr., "The Malingering McNamara Model for the Use of U.S. Military Force," *Strategic Review* 17 (Fall 1989): 19.

97. *The McLaughlin Group*, November 23, 1990 (Washington: Oliver Productions). This televised segment first appeared on the NBC Nightly News.

98. "Excerpts from President's News Conference on Crisis in Gulf," *New York Times*, December 1, 1990, p. 6, columns 1 & 2.

99. *Face the Nation*, November 19, 1990 (Washington: CBS News).

100. Eleanor Clift and Thomas DeFrank, "Bush's General: Maximum Force—The GOP Eyes Powell as a 'Black Eisenhower,' " *Newsweek*, September 3, 1990, p. 36.

101. Rudy Abramson and John Broder, "Four-Star Power," *Los Angeles Times Magazine*, April 7, 1992, p. 60.

102. "Excerpts from Briefing at Pentagon by Cheney and Powell," *New York Times*, January 24, 1991, sec. A, p. 11.

103. Woodward, *The Commanders*, p. 310.

104. U.S. News & World Report, *Triumph without Victory: The Unre-*

ported History of the Persian Gulf War (New York: Random House, 1992), p. 156.

105. U.S. News & World Report, *Triumph without Victory*, p. 157.

106. U.S. News & World Report, *Triumph without Victory*, p. 166.

107. Lawrence Freedman and Efraim Karsh, *The Gulf Conflict, 1990–1991: Diplomacy and War in the New World Order* (Princeton: Princeton University Press, 1993), p. 205.

108. H. Norman Schwarzkopf, *It Doesn't Take a Hero* (New York: Bantam Books, 1992), pp. 359–361. Subsequent page references are cited in the text. The quotation is taken from the bottom of page 359.

109. Thomas L. Friedman and Patrick E. Tyler, "From the First, U.S. Resolve to Fight," *New York*

110. Freedman and Karsh, *The Gulf Conflict, 1990–1991*, pp. 206–207.

111. Schwarzkopf, *It Doesn't Take a Hero*, p. 381. As was later discovered, the Republican Guard was not destroyed during the conflict.

112. Schwarzkopf, *It Doesn't Take a Hero*, pp. 381–382. Also of significant interest is the "Draft Proposed Strategic Directive to Combined Commander" which Schwarzkopf drafted around November 18. This directive was modeled on the order given to Dwight Eisenhower in February 1944 concerning his mission for the invasion of France, and it gave in five paragraphs a statement of war aims that is the embodiment of decisive war-fighting. The section entitled "Operational Guidance" is of greatest interest: "The objectives of your offensive campaign will be to destroy Iraqi nuclear, biological, and chemical production facilities and weapons of mass destruction; occupy southeast Iraq until combined strategic objectives are met; destroy or neutralize the Republican Guard Forces Command; destroy, neutralize or disconnect the Iraqi national command authority; safeguard, to the extent practicable, foreign nationals being detained in Iraq and Kuwait; and degrade or disrupt Iraqi strategic air defenses." Schwarzkopf sent the message to Powell because the British government "wanted a clear definition of the coalition's strategic and political war aims." Curiously, this request for a specific war directive similar to the one given Eisenhower (and to Sherman by Grant) *was never answered* by Powell or Cheney. Ibid., pp. 386–387.

113. Freedman and Karsh, *The Gulf Conflict, 1990–1991*, pp. 207–208. According to another source the exact quote from Powell was: "I don't believe in doing war on the basis of macroeconomic, [sic: microeconomic] marginal-analysis models. I'm more of the mind-set of a New York Street bully: 'Here's my bat, here's my gun, here's my knife, I'm wearing armor. I'm going to kick your ass.' " See U.S. News & World Report, *Triumph without Victory*, p. 172.

114. U.S. News & World Report, *Triumph without Victory*, pp. 170–171.

115. William E. Simons, "U.S. Coercive Pressure on North Vietnam,

Early 1965," in Alexander L. George and William E. Simons, eds., *The Limits of Coercive Diplomacy*, 2nd ed. (Boulder, CO: Westview Press, 1994), p. 140.

116. Simons, *The Limits of Coercive Diplomacy*, 2nd ed., p. 151. On the same page, Simons notes, "The possibility of Chinese intervention had drawn greater attention with the recent discovery of Chinese MIGs based at the DRV's Phuc Yen airfield." In the same paragraph he adds: "Officials who believed the Chinese would probably respond to U.S. attacks against MIGs by operating them from bases in the southern PRC warned the president that he would then be under strong pressure to authorize attacks on those bases as well—and perhaps on Chinese nuclear production facilities. They warned further of the increasing threat of a Chinese introduction of ground combat forces, a contingency noted by intelligence estimates as increasingly likely as damage to North Vietnam became more severe." *Ibid.*, p. 151.

117. "Excerpts from Bush's Remarks on His Order to Enlarge U.S. Gulf Force," *New York Times*, November 9, 1990, sec. A, p. 1. "Desert Shield" and "Desert Storm" were operation names used by the U.S. in the Gulf. Desert Storm began on the night of January 16–17, 1991 with the commencement of allied air operations against Iraq.

118. R.W. Apple, Jr., "Message to Iraq: The Will and the Way," *New York Times*, November 9, 1990, sec. A, p. 1. Apple's lead paragraph states: "President Bush sought today to send an unmistakable message to President Saddam Hussein of Iraq that the United States had the will to go to war, that it would soon have the means to go to war, and that a war, if it came, would inevitably inflict terrible damage on Iraq."

119. Michael R. Gordon, "Bush Sends New Units to Gulf to Provide 'Offensive' Option; U.S. Force Could Reach 380,000," *New York Times*, sec. A, p. 1.

120. For the text of the U.N. resolutions see *U.S. News & World Report*, "Triumph without Victory," pp. 429–430.

121. Patrick E. Tyler, "Vietnam and Gulf Zone: Real Military Contrasts," *New York Times*, December 1, 1990, p. 8.

122. Tyler, "Vietnam and Gulf Zone," p. 8.

123. Eric Schmitt, "How to Fight Iraq: Four Scenarios, All Are Disputed," *New York Times*, November 19, 1990, sec. A, p. 12.

124. Thomas L. Friedman, "The Nightmare Haunting Washington is Set in Beirut, Not Vietnam," *New York Times*, October 7, 1990, sec. 4, p. 1.

125. George J. Church, "Mission of Mercy," *Time*, 29 April 1991, p. 40.

126. Edward Mortimer, " 'Safe Haven' Is Not Enough," *Financial Times*, April 10, 1991, p. 13.

127. Of great importance in these diplomatic efforts were John R. Bolton,

assistant secretary of state for international organization affairs, and Thomas Pickering, the U.S. ambassador to the United Nations in New York.

128. Colonel W.H. Parks, "Rules of Engagement: No More Vietnams," *Proceedings* 117 (March 1991): 28.

129. Douglas Waller and John Barry, "The Day We Stopped the War," *Newsweek*, January 20, 1992, p. 18.

130. Lawrence Freedman and Efraim Karsh, "How Kuwait Was Won: Strategy in the Gulf War," *International Security* 16 (Fall 1991): p. 5.

131. Freedman and Karsh, "How Kuwait Was Won," p. 16. I disagree with the authors' judgment (p. 39) that "Bush may have felt that his strategy represented a sharp break with that adopted in Vietnam, the real difference lay in the political military context, which was altogether simpler in the Gulf." It is true that the political milieu facing Johnson was more difficult in Vietnam due to Soviet and Chinese protection of North Vietnam and President Johnson's fear of unwanted escalation. This point about context does not undermine the thesis that a different philosophy for using military power had become accepted— as Woodward has shown (*The Commanders*, p. 310). When Schwarzkopf spoke of the need for the VII Corps if an offensive operation were to be launched against Iraq, his reasoning, and Colin Powell's as well, relied on 15 years of Army analysis about how best to conduct wars and offensive operations on the basis of "lessons" learned from Vietnam. Had they not been given VII Corps it is altogether possible that Bush would have faced resignations from high-level military commanders. Had the political military context threatened the possibility of escalation against a major power, as Vietnam did, it is difficult to imagine an administration with Bush, Cheney, Powell, and Schwarzkopf pursuing a weak and unclear variant of coercive diplomacy. Rather, it is most likely that the "all" or "nothing" variants would have been followed. "All" is something akin to what did happen in the Gulf, but it certainly would have been more difficult to achieve the international support necessary to pursue this option. Alternatively, a "nothing" approach would have begged off war with Iraq because the conditions for waging war properly were not auspicious. It was not merely the structure of the international power configuration that had changed since Korea and Vietnam; the American conception of using force had changed and Bush's approach was a break with Limited War thinking.

132. Thomas R. DuBois, "The Weinberger Doctrine and the Liberation of Kuwait," *Parameters* 21 (Winter 1991–92): 28.

133. DuBois, "The Weinberger Doctrine and the Liberation of Kuwait," p. 28.

134. Waller and Barry, "The Day We Stopped the War," p. 18.

135. On Iraqi atomic capabilities see Gary Mulhollin, "Building Saddam Hussein's Bomb," *New York Times Magazine*, pp. 30–36; Paul Lewis, "U.N.

Experts Now Say Baghdad Was Far from Making an A-Bomb before Gulf War," *New York Times*, May 20, 1992, sec. A, p. 6. On another round of the U.N.-Iraq "cat and mouse" game over the inspections see Paul Lewis, "U.N. Aide Tells Iraq It Risks Attack for Truce Defiance," *New York Times*, July 18, 1992, p. 3.

After Iraq had formally accepted the provisions of U.N. Security Council resolution 687 of April 3, 1991, which called for the elimination of Iraq's weapons of mass destruction and ballistic missiles with a range of more than 150 kilometers, the Secretary General Javier Perez de Cuellar called for the establishment of the United Nations Special Commission (UNSCOM) to see that the terms of 687 were satisfied. The commission was established and has issued a report on its activities in destroying Iraqi weapons capabilities. See "United Nations Focus: United Nations Special Commission (UNSCOM)" (New York: United Nations Department of Public Information in Cooperation with UNSCOM; DPI/1239, April 1992). As to the presence of a nuclear weapons program, UNSCOM reached this conclusion: "the IAEA/UNSCOM inspections have uncovered three clandestine uranium enrichment programmes or activities: electromagnetic, centrifuge, and chemical isotope separation as well as laboratory-scale plutonium separation. The sixth nuclear inspection led to the conclusive evidence of a nuclear weapons development programme, aimed at an implosion-type nuclear weapon possibly linked to a surface missile project" (p. 2). The following action was taken: "In the nuclear field, the Special Commission is assisting IAEA in removal of weapons-usable material from Iraq and in the disposal of all other relevant items and facilities covered by paragraph 12 of resolution 687, by destruction, removal or rendering harmless, as appropriate. The fresh uranium fuel of Iraq's nuclear reactors has already been removed from Iraq and arrangements are being made for the removal and reprocessing of irradiated fuel" (p. 3).

For greater details on the Iraqi program see United Nations Security Council, "Report on the Eleventh IAEA On-Site Inspection in Iraq under Security Council Resolution 687 (1991)," (UN Document: S/23947), May 22, 1992.

Also, on North Korean potential for building atomic weapons see Sheryl WuDunn, "North Korean Site Has A-Bomb Hints," *New York Times*, May 17, 1992, sec. A, p. 1. She writes: "Robert M. Gates, Director of Central Intelligence, told Congress this year that North Korea could be a few months to a few years away from producing its first bomb."

136. For background to the dissolution of Yugoslavia as a state and to the eruption of the Serbian aggression against the newly independent state of Bosnia see Aleksa Djilas, "The Nation That Wasn't," *The New Republic*, September 21, 1992, pp. 25–31. Also of some help is "A Whirlwind of

Hatreds: How the Balkans Broke Up," *New York Times*, February 14, 1993, sec. 4, p. 5.

137. "Text of U.N. Resolution Allowing the Dispatch of Troops," *New York Times*, p. A10. Resolution 757 was adopted by the Security Council in a vote of 13–0–2 with China and Zimbabwe abstaining; Resolution 761 was adopted unanimously.

138. Barton Gellman, "Military Uneasy at Balkan Commitment: Limited Use of Force May Be Inadequate to Accomplish Mission," *Washington Post*, July 2, 1992, sec. A, p. 1.

139. Barton Gellman, "U.S. Is Prepared to Commit Combat Forces," *The Washington Post*, July 1, 1992, sec. A, p. 28.

140. "This Week with David Brinkley," ABC News, May 9, 1993, p. 6.

141. "Brinkley," May 9, 1993, p. 6. Scowcroft criticized the Clinton administration's "lift and strike" proposal (see discussion below) for Bosnia because of the signal the limited American involvement gave the Serbs: "You remember a lot of people, in the buildup to the Persian Gulf, [said], 'Well, let's just use air power. Air power will do it.' And we said, 'Uh-Uh. We will use whatever is required.' Right now, we're specifically saying, 'No troops on the ground.' That tells Milosevic right away what he has to anticipate."

142. Gellman, "Military Uneasy," sec. A, p. 1. Also, for a powerful critique of Bush policy errors on Bosnia, see Patrick Glynn, "Balking: Clinton's Bosnia Crisis," *New Republic*, November 23, 1992, pp. 20ff.

143. Martin Sieff, "Baker, Cheney Clash on New Bush Policy," *Washington Times*, July 2, 1992, sec. A, p. 1 & 9.

144. Sieff, "Baker, Cheney Clash," sec. A, p. 9.

145. Press briefing by Secretary of State James A. Baker, III, on the President's Trip to Europe, The White House, July 1, 1992, p. 6.

146. Jessica Lee, "Bush Defends Gulf War Decisions," *USA Today*, August 5, 1992, sec. A, p. 2. His remarks about Vietnam appeared in TV news clips but were not mentioned in the *USA Today* article.

147. R. W. Apple, Jr., "Bush Says Any U.S. Action Must Come through the U.N." *New York Times*, August 8, 1992, p. 4.

148. See previous chapter for a detailed description of Weinberger's principles for the use of force.

149. Bernard E. Trainor, "Vietnam Experience Has Made the Joint Chiefs Cautious about Using Military Force," *New York Times*, August 17, 1989, sec. A, p. 13.

150. Trainor, "Vietnam Experience," sec. A, p. 13.

151. Colin L. Powell, "Why Generals Get Nervous," *New York Times*, October 8, 1992, sec. A, p. 35.

152. Michael R. Gordon, "Limits of U.S. Role: White House is Seeking to

Minimize Any Use of Military in Balkan Conflict," *New York Times*, August 11, 1992, sec. A, p. 6.

153. Gordon, "Limits of U.S. Role," sec. A, p. 6. A draft U.N. Security Council resolution being circulated on the day Gordon's article appeared merely called upon "all states to report to the Secretary General on measures they are taking in coordination with the United Nations to carry out this resolution, and invites the Secretary General to keep under continuous review any further measures that may be necessary to insure unimpeded delivery of humanitarian supplies." That the resolution would only support the delivery of humanitarian aid was considered to be of little value to the Bosnians who were also in need of military equipment. See "Text of the U.N.'s Draft Resolution on the Balkan Crisis," *New York Times*, August 11, 1992, sec. A, p. 6.

154. For example, former U.S. ambassador to the U.N. Jeane J. Kirkpatrick told *USA Today*: "I have felt that it was time for a limited commitment, air and naval power, for some time. . . . I don't think there should be any commitment of ground forces. See Jeane Kirkpatrick, "Is the U.N. Stretched Too Thin?" (Washington, D.C., August 1992), *USA Today*, August 11, 1992, sec. A. p. 11. That night on the *McNeil-Lehrer Newshour* she described Serbia as a violent, lawless state that should be deprived of its military sanctuary through air power. The former U.N. Ambassador opposed the use of ground forces in Yugoslavia. Rather she felt the U.S. air forces could be used in "limited focused military moves that can stop the Serbian military offensive." See *McNeil-Lehrer Newshour*, Educational Broadcasting Corporation, August 11, 1992.

155. Gordon, "Limits of U.S. Role," sec. A, p. 6.

156. "Bush's Talk to Cadets: When 'Force Makes Sense,' " *New York Times*, January 6, 1993, sec. A, p. 6.

157. *Ibid.*, Bush address at West Point.

158. See Michael R. Gordon, "Hitting Hussein with a Stick, with a Sledgehammer in Reserve," *New York Times*, January 14, 1993, sec. A, p. 8; Thomas L. Friedman, "Limiting the Response," *New York Times*, January 19, 1993, sec. A, p. 1.

159. Friedman, "Limiting the Response," sec. A, p. 4.

10. | Conclusions

1. Michael York, "Reagans Pay Emotional Visit to Vietnam Veterans Memorial," *Washington Post*, November 12, 1988, sec. A, p. 14.

2. Remember from chapter 2 that Russell Weigley notes how Scott's advance on Mexico City resembled the limited wars of eighteenth-century

Europe more than it did the Napoleonic clashes of the Civil War. See Weigley, *American Way of War*, pp. 75–76.

3. For both quotes see Shy, *A People Numerous and Armed*, pp. 250–251.

4. Weigley is correct in asserting that the military wanted to fight a decisive war against North Vietnam (see *American Way of War*, p. 466); however, the war as it was actually fought did not conform to their desires. Civilian control prevented anything like a decisive effort by the United States from being waged. Weigley's inclusion of Maxwell Taylor as just another tradition-bound member of the military is not consistent with my analysis of Talyor's understanding of "flexible response" and his disagreements with Eisenhower's defense policies.

5. Scott D. Sagan, "1914 Revisited: Allies, Offense, and Instability," *International Security* (Fall 1986): p. 153.

6. General Gray wanted to produce a "keystone" document that would provide the fundamental concepts of warfighting to marines in a sophisticated yet comprehensive manner. For a brief account of the history surrounding the manual see John E. Greenwood, "FMFM 1: The Line of Departure," *Proceedings* 116 (May 1990): 155.

7. USMC, *Warfighting, FMFM 1*, p. 27.

8. USMC, *Warfighting, FMFM 1*, p. 24.

9. USMC, *Warfighting, FMFM 1*, p. 24.

10. Here *FMFM 1* cites Clausewitz, *On War*, p. 357.

11. The manual contains this footnote: "Clausewitz argued (p. 524) that while the offense is an integral component of the concept of defense, the offense is conceptually complete in itself. The introduction of the defense into the concept of the offense is a necessary evil and not an integral component."

12. USMC, *Warfighting, FMFM 1*, pp. 25–26.

13. USMC, *Warfighting, FMFM 1*, p. 26.

14. It should be remembered that not all compulsion is the *direct* result of military action. It can also occur by forcing the enemy to relinquish his offensive aims by inflicting unacceptable costs on him which may arise from a variety of sources—not all military. These non-violent avenues of coercion have an offensive component in that they seek the opponent's change of behavior by altering the status quo in manner hostile to the enemy's interests.

15. On August 23, 1793 the Convention decreed a mass levy of all Frenchmen. François Furet writes, "The inspiring rhetoric of the Convention's decree on 23 August was less a prescription for an uncoordinated call to arms than a vision of a militarized commonwealth with every lever and pulley working in perfect mechanical articulation." The decree creating the *levée en masse* read: "From this moment on, until the enemies have been chased from the territory of the Republic, all Frenchmen are in permanent requisition for the service

of the armies. The young men will go to combat; married men will forge weapons and transport food; women will make tents and uniforms and will serve in the hospitals; children will make bandages from old linen; old men will present themselves at public places to excite the courage of the warriors, to preach hatred of kings and the unity of the Republic." See François Furet, *Citizen: A Chronicle of the French Revolution* (New York: Knopf, 1989), p. 762.

16. Petraeus, dissertation, p. 259.

17. Petraeus, dissertation, p. 262.

18. Petraeus, dissertation, pp. 262–263.

19. Eisenhower is also an interesting example of this balance.

20. Clausewitz, *On War*, pp. 580–581 (Book 8, Chapter 2); emphasis in original. Here Clausewitz once again makes brilliant use of an analogy to make his point more comprehensible.

21. *On War*, Bk. I, ch. 1, sec. 25, p. 88.

22. Jim Hoagland, "With Whose Army?" *Washington Post*, August 13, 1992, sec. A, p. 25.

23. "McNeil-Lehrer Newshour," August 11, 1992, Educational Broadcasting System.

24. Nathan F. Twining, *Neither Liberty nor Safety: A Hard Look at U.S. Military Policy and Strategy* (New York: Holt, 1966), chapter on "Limited War," pp. 102–120. Subsequent page references are cited in the text.

25. *On War*, Bk. VI, ch. 5, p. 370.

26. Clodfelter, *Limits of Air Power*, p. 145.

27. Conversation with Jeane J. Kirkpatrick, August 13, 1992, American Enterprise Institute, Washington, D.C.

28. For an excellent statement of the nature of strategy see David Fraser, p. 309.

29. Hoagland, "August Guns," sec. C, p. 2.

Epilogue

1. See Security Council Resolution 794 (1992); paragraph 7 (my emphasis).

2. See Security Council Resolution 794 (1992), paragraph 10 (emphasis in original).

3. Michael Wines, "Bush Declares Goal in Somalia Is to 'Save Thousands.' "*New York Times*, December 5, 1991, p. 1. On December 4, President Bush noted this limitation on the American operation: "Our mission has a limited objective, to open the supply routes, to get the food moving, and to prepare the way for U.N. peacekeeping force to keep it moving. This operation is not open-ended. We will not stay one day longer than is absolutely necessary." "Clinton's Words on Somalia: 'The Responsibilities of American Leadership,'

"*New York Times*, October 8, 1993, sec. A, p. 15; Jane Perlez, "U.S. Forces Arrive in Somalia on Mission to Aid the Starving," *New York Times*, December 9, 1992, sec A, p. 1.

4. Donatella Lorch, "As U.N. Prepares for Somalia Command, Rebuilding Is Most Urgent Task," *New York Times*, May 12, 1993, sec. 1, p. 16.

5. Michael R. Gordon, "U.N. Backs a Somalia Force As Bush Vows a Swift Exit; Pentagon Sees Longer Stay," *New York Times*, December 4, 1992, sec. A, p. 14.

6. Michael R. Gordon, "U.S. Is Sending Large Force As Warning to Somali Clans," *New York Times*, December 5, 1992, p. 5.

7. Gordon, "U.S. Sending Large Force," p. 5.

8. "Somalia: The Right to Bear Arms," *The Economist*, December 19, 1992, p. 42.

9. John Lancaster, "Powell Says Mission Duration is Flexible," *Washington Post*, December 5, 1992, sec. A, p. 17.

10. Gordon, "U.S. Sending Large Force," p. 5.

11. Diana Jean Schemo, "Declare Victory, Hand Off, Slip Out, Cross Fingers," *New York Times*, May 2, 1993, sec. 1, p. 4.

12. "U.S. General Hands over Relief Operation in Somalia to U.N.," *New York Times*, May 5, 1993, sec. A, p. 5. Johnston was commander of the 1st Marine Expeditionary force from Camp Pendleton, CA. He served as General Norman H. Schwarzkopf's chief of staff during the Persian Gulf War.

13. Lorch, "As U.N. Prepares for Somalia Command," p. 16.

14. Eric Schmitt, "Most U.S. Troops will Leave Somalia by April in U.N. Plan," *New York Times*, February 13, 1993, p. 4. The 5,000 Americans left in Somalia were "specialists in logistics, communications and intelligence, to be sure, not front-line combat soldiers, but they will be in a risky setting all the same." R. W. Apple, "U.N. and the Pentagon: Quietly, U.S. retreats from the Principle That No One Else Commands Its Troops," *New York Times*, February 14, 1992, sec. 1, p. 18. Apple notes that the remainder of Americans in Somalia will be the first American troops to serve directly under United Nations command. This was the first occasion such authority over Americans has been granted since the end of World War II.

15. Steven A. Holmes, "Clinton May Let U.S. Troops Serve under U.N. Chiefs," *New York Times*, September 18, 1993, sec. A, p. 1. The article cites a study, "The Evolution of U.N. Peacekeeping," by William Durch, as its source.

16. Keith B. Richburg, "American Casualties in Somalia: A Policy Time Bomb Explodes," *Washington Post*, August 21, sec. A, p. 1

17. Richburg, "American Casualties," sec. A, p. 1.

18. Robert Burns, "There Were Hints Months Ago Somalia Might Bog Down U.S.," *Washington Times*, October 10, 1993, sec, A, p. 6.

19. It could be argued the Clinton Administration actually acceded to an expansion of the U.N. mission well before the reprisals for the June 5 attack. On March 26, 1993, the Security Council passed Resolution 814 which appears to have moved from the more limited, relief-oriented language in Resolution 794 of December 3, 1992. For example, Resolution 794 speaks of establishing a secure environment for humanitarian relief operations in Somalia: it is filled with language emphasizing that purpose. Resolution 814's section A appears to this reader to present a much more expansive set of goals designed to reconstruct Somali civil society — not just deliver humanitarian relief.

20. Eric Schmitt, "U.S. Forces to Stay in Somalia to End Warlord Violence," *New York Times*, August 28, 1993, p. 1.

21. Schmitt, "U.S. Forces to Stay in Somalia to End Warlord Violence," p. 4.

22. Schmitt, "U.S. Forces to Stay in Somalia to End Warlord Violence," p. 4.

23. Reid G. Miller, "3 GI's Die in Somalia," *Washington Times*, 26 September 1993, sec. A, p. 1; Clifford Krauss, "House Vote Urges Clinton to Limit Role in Somali Conflict," *New York Times*, September 29, 1993, sec. A, p. 1 & 10.

24. Eric Schmitt, "U.S. Vows to Stay in Somalia Force Despite an Attack," *New York Times*, September 26, 1993, sec. 1, p. 22.

25. Elaine Sciolino, "U.S. Asks U.N. Not to Use American Troops on Patrol," *New York Times*, September 29, 1993, sec. A, p. 10.

26. For an excellent account of the October 3rd battle see Michael R. Gordon and Thomas L. Friedman, "Disastrous U.S. Raid in Somalia Nearly Succeeded, Review Finds," *New York Times*, October 25, 1993, sec. A, p. 1.

27. Thomas L. Friedman, "U.S. Pays Dearly for An Education in Somalia," *New York Times*, October 10, 1993, sec. 4, p. 3.

28. Bill Gertz, "Aspin under Fire for Saying No to Earlier Arms Requests," *Washington Times*, October 7, 1993, sec. A, p. 1.

29. Gertz, "Aspin under Fire," sec. A, p. 1.

30. Thomas L. Friedman, "Clinton Reviews Policy in Somalia As Unease Grows – Seeking a Balance," *New York Times*, October 6, 1993, sec. A, p. 1.

31. Barton Gellman, "U.S. Lacked Strong Plan to Aid Besieged Troops," *Washington Post*, October 6, 1993, sec. A, p. 1.

32. Ann Devroy, "New Deployment Raises Confusion on U.S. Goals," *Washington Post*, October 6, 1993, sec. A, p. 1.3

33. Devroy, "New Deployment Raises Confusion," sec. A, p. 16.

34. Douglas Jehl, "Clinton Doubling U.S. Force in Somalia, Vowing Troops Will Come Home in Six Months," *New York Times*, October 8, 1993, sec. A, p. 1; John H. Cushman, Jr., "How Powerful U.S. Units Will Work," *New York Times*, October 8, 1993, sec. A, p. 14.

35. Cushman, "How Powerful U.S. Units Will Work," sec. A, p. 14.

36. Ann Devroy and R. Jeffrey Smith, "Clinton Reexamines a Foreign Policy Under Siege," *Washington Post*, October 17, 1993, sec. A, p. 1.

37. Elaine Sciolino, "The U.N.'s Glow is Gone," *New York Times*, October 9, 1993, sec. A, p. 1.

38. Sciolino, "The U.N.'s Glow is Gone," sec. A, p. 1.

39. Sciolino, "The U.N.'s Glow is Gone," sec. A, p. 1.

40. Sciolino, "The U.N.'s Glow Is Gone," sec. A, p. 1.

41. Stephen Engelberg, "U.S. Envoy Meets Clan Leaders' Kin in Somali Capital," *New York Times*, October 11, 1993, sec. A, p. 1.

42. Thomas L. Friedman, "Somalia's Buzzwords: 'Constructive Ambiguity,' " *New York Times*, October 15, 1993, sec. A, p. 1.

43. Aristide was overthrown by the military and fled into exile on September 31, 1991. Howard W. French, "Diplomats Flee Port to Escape Protesters," *New York Times*, October 12, 1993, sec. A, p. 1 & 12.

44. French, Diplomats Flee Port to Escape Protesters," sec. A, p. 1.

45. French, Diplomats Flee Port to Escape Protesters," sec. A, p. 1.

46. French, "Diplomats Flee," sec. A, p. 1.

47. The vessel was soon removed from the vicinity of Haiti.

48. Steven A. Holmes, "U.S. Delaying Dispatch of Troops to Haiti," *New York Times*, October 12, 1993, sec. A, p. 12.

49. Douglas Farah, "U.S. Ships Set for Embargo," *Washington Post*, October 17, 1993, sec. A, p. 1.

50. Gwen Ifill, "750 Rangers Will Leave Somalia, President Says," *New York Times*, October 20, 1993, sec. A, p. 14. Of the 18 Americans killed in Somalia on October 3, 16 were U.S. Army Rangers. Elements of the elite counter-terrorist unit, Delta Force, were also used to track down General Aidid. Both uses seeming to be a misuse of these soldiers when considered in light of their small numbers and highly specialized training.

51. Ifill, "750 Rangers Will Leave Somalia, President Says," sec. A, p. 14.

52. Douglas Jehl, "U.S. Shifts Troops to Defensive Role in Somalia Mission," *New York Times*, October 20, 1993, sec. A, p. 14.

53. Clifford Krauss, "Despite Its Victory in Senate Vote, White House Pays for Somalia Policy," *New York Times*, October 16, 1993, p. 6.

54. Ferdinand Protzman, "Freed Pilot Elated to Leave Somalia," *New York Times*, October 16, 1993, p. 6.

55. Helen Dewar, "Senators Approve Troop Compromise," *Washington Post*, October 21, 1993, sec. A, p. 1.

56. Dewar, "Senators Approve Troops Compromise," sec. A, p. 1.

57. John Hart Ely, "Clinton, Congress and War," *New York Times*, October 23, 1993, p. 23. To begin a deeper examination of the issue see his *War and Responsibility* (Princeton: Princeton Univ. Press, 1993).

58. For a description of Dole's proposal in greater detail see Bill Gertz, "Dole Seeks Law to Tie Clinton's Hands in Haiti," *Washington Times*, October 7, 1993, sec. A, p. 1 & 20.

59. Warren Strobel, "U.S. Had, But Lost the Chance to Lead," *Washington Times*, May 9, 1993, sec. A, p. 9 (see box insert).

60. Strobel, sec. A, p. 9.

61. Strobel, sec. A, p. 9.

62. Elaine Sciolino, "U.S. Faces a Delicate Task in Intervening in Negotiations on Bosnia," *New York Times*, February 12, 1993, sec. A, p. 10.

63. "Christopher's Remarks on Balkans," *New York Times*, February 11, 1993, sec. A, p. 12.

64. The Secretary of State said, "The President decided the United States will actively engage in the Vance-Owen negotiations and bring the full weight of American diplomacy to bear." Elaine Sciolino, "U.S. Backs Bosnian Peace Plan, Dropping Threats to Use Force," *New York Times*, Feburary 11, 1993, sec. A, p. 1.

The Vance-Owen plan was eventually declared dead by Lord Owen on June 17, 1993 in Geneva. He told the Bosnian Muslims "to recognize that [they] could not win back much of the land lost to Serbs and Croats and to 'look very seriously' at a plan to carve up the country into three distinct enclaves." Paul Lewis, "Balkan Negotiator, in Shift, Backs Plan Dividing Bosnia," *New York Times*, June 18, 1993, sec. A, p. 8.

65. John Darnton, "Europeans Welcome U.S. Role in Bosnia, Especially Its Arms," *New York Times*, February 12, 1993, sec. A, p. 10.

66. Michael Kelly, "Clinton Said to Consider Troops to Bosnia," *New York Times*, February 10, 1993, sec. A, p. 6.

67. Gerald F. Seib, "Saddam Hussein Seen Trying to Boost Posture of Iraq in Dealing with Clinton Administration," *Wall Street Journal*, January 12, 1992, sec. A, p. 16.

68. Michael R. Gordon, "Limited U.S. Force Held Still an Option in Bosnia," *New York Times*, April 9, 1993, sec. A, p. 7.

69. Michael R. Gordon, "12 in State Department Ask Military Move Against the Serbs," *New York Times*, April 23, 1993, sec. A, p. 12. Worthy of consideration on fleshing out the new Department of Defense position is William Safire, "The case for 'Compellance,' " *New York Times*, April 19,

1993, sec. A, p. 19. Safire wrote, " Needed also is strategic coercion: 'compel-lance' is the word now being heard in the Pentagon. It means the use of air power to persuade by punishment."

70. John Newhouse, "No Exit, No Entrance," *The New Yorker*, June 28, 1993, p. 46. Political approval for a military operation in Bosnia "was judged to be close to zero" by the Clinton Administration.]

71. Newhouse, "No Exit, No Entrance," p. 47.

72. Elaine Sciolino, "Christopher Explains Conditions for Use of U.S. Force in Bosnia," *New York Times*, April 28, 1993, sec. A, p. 1.

73. Sciolino, "Christopher Explains," sec. A, p. 1.

74. *This Week with David Brinkley*, ABC News, March 7, 1993.

75. "Excerpts from Clinton News Conference: 'The U.S. Should Lead' on Bosnia?" *New York Times*, April 24, 1993, p. 7. The Chairman of the Joint Chiefs of Staff, General John M. Shalikashvili, then the highest ranking military officer in NATO, told the Senate Armed Service Committee on April 20, 1993 that "while limited air strikes might be effective in reducing the Serbian shelling of Muslim towns and cities in Bosnia, it is unlikely that they would bring the Serbs to the bargaining table." Michael R. Gordon, "NATO General is Reticent about Air Strikes in Bosnia," *New York Times*, April 21, 1993, sec. A, p. 10. Shalikashvili was particularly critical of U.N. Security Council restrictions on military flights over Bosnia designed to enforce the embargo: "he would like to have had the authority to attack airfields if they were used to launch aircraft in violation of the ban. But that option was foreclosed by the United States allies on the Security Council, who are reticent about confronting the Serbs with force."

On August 11, 1993 President Clinton nominated Shalikashvili to succeed Colin Powell as JCS Chairman. Soon thereafter Harry Summers noted that "Shali," a Vietnam veteran like Powell, understands that "using military force as a signalling device rather than for war-fighting was one of the major miscalculations of the academic limited war theorists and their 'whiz kid' disciples in the Pentagon during the Vietnam War." Harry Summers, "Soldiers, Leaders and a Road Well Traveled," *Washington Times*, August 19, 1993, sec. G, p. 1.

76. Thomas L. Friedman, "Bosnia Air Strikes Backed by Clinton, His Officials Say," *New York Times*, May 2, 1993, sec. 1, p. 1.

77. Friedman, "Bosnian Air Strikes Backed by Clinton," sec. 1, p. 1.

78. Friedman, "Bosnian Air Strikes Backed by Clinton," sec. 1, p. 1.

79. Thomas L. Friedman, "Any War in Bosnia Would Carry a Domestic Price," *New York Times*, May 2, 1993, sec. 4, p. 1.

80. Ann Devroy and Barton Gellman, "Levelling the Battlefield: U.S.

Seeks Now to Equalize Bosnia Factions," *Washington Post,* May 9, 1993, sec. A, p. 1.

81. Devroy and Gellman, "Levelling the Battlefield," sec. A, p. 1.

82. Devroy and Gellman, "Levelling the Battlefield," sec. A, p. 1.

83. The lack military leverage lay in the fact that Serbia itself was never threatened. If there was no threat to the security of the aggressor state, how could one reasonably expect to force their compliance with international norms?

84. See comments of Paul Wolfowitz, undersecretary of defense for policy under Bush, in Devroy and Gellman, "Levelling the Battlefield," sec. A, p. 27.

85. Roger Cohen, "Europeans Reject U.S. Plan to Aid Bosnia and Halt Serbs," *New York Times,* May 11, 1993, sec. A, p. 1.

86. This had been clearly communicated to the Clinton Administration before Christopher's early May trip to Europe. See Craig R. Whitney, "A View from the Fence," *New York Times,* April 28, 1993 sec. A, p. 11.

Concerning the lack of commitment by the U.S., Michael Kramer of *Time* wrote of "lift and strike": "the President seems bent on adopting a feelgood strategy—a limited action designed, above everything, to ensure a swift exit, a policy that defines success as merely having done *something* without regard to the ultimate result." Michael Kramer, "Clinton's Feelgood Strategy," *Time,* May 17, 1993, p. 36.

87. Richard C. Gross, "Christopher: Force Not an Option Now in Bosnia," *Washington Times,* May 19, 1993, sec. A, p. 1. My general impression is that some Europeans, particularly the Germans, felt greatly abused by the administration. "Lift and strike" and Warren Christopher's limp diplomacy appeared to the more cynical-minded to be a proposal designed for rejection. It was, according to this view, a policy designed for American political constituencies expecting U.S. action in Bosnia but constructed in such manner as to meet with objections from Europe. Difficulties that were quite solvable were then treated as insurmountable as the President abandoned his policy less than ten days after it was taken to Europe by the Secretary of State.

88. Steven Erlanger, "Moscow Stepping In," *New York Times,* May 20, 1993, sec. A, p. 12. Part of this new assertiveness may have been signaled at the U.N. Security Council when the Russians cast their first veto there since February 1984 (over Lebanon). See Frank J. Prial, "Russia Dusts Off an Old Tactic at U.N.: the Veto," *New York Times,* May 12, 1993, sec. A, p. 10.

89. Craig R. Whitney, "NATO's Leadership Gap," *New York Times,* May 29 1993, p. 4.

90. R.W. Apple, Jr., " The Moment of Truth," *New York Times*, September 19, 1993, sec. 1, p. 1.

91. "Clinton's Words: U.N. Cannot Become Engaged in Every World Conflict," *New York Times*, September 28, 1993, sec. A, p. 16.

92. Thomas L. Friedman, "Clinton, at U.N., Lists Stiff Terms for Sending U.S. Force to Bosnia," *New York Times*, September 28, 1993, sec. A, p. 1 & 16.

93. Friedman, "Clinton at U.N.," sec. A, p. 16

Bibliography

Abenheim, Donald. *Reforging the Iron Cross: The Search for Tradition in the West German Armed Forces.* Princeton: Princeton University Press, 1988.

Abrahamson, Rudy and John Broder. "Four-Star Power." *Los Angeles Times Magazine,* April 7, 1991, pp. 18–62.

Acheson, Dean. *Present at the Creation.* New York: W. W. Norton, 1969.

Adams, Sherman. *Firsthand Report: Inside the Eisenhower Administration.* New York: Harper, 1961.

Alger, John I. *The Quest for Victory: The History of the Principles of War.* Westport, CT: Greenwood Press, 1982.

Allard, C. Kenneth. *Command, Control, and the Command Defense.* New Haven: Yale University Press, 1990.

Allen, Russell G. "A New Army for the 1990s." *Parameters* 70 (July 1990): 76–83.

Allison, Graham. *The Essence of Decision: Explaining the Cuban Missile Crisis.* Boston: Little, Brown, and Company, 1971.

Apple, R. W., Jr. "Message to Iraq: The Will and the Way." *New York Times,* November 9, 1990, sec. A, pp. 1 & 13.

———. "Bush Says Any U.S. Action Must Come Through U.N." *New York Times,* August 8, 1992, p. 4.

———. "U.N. and the Pentagon: Quietly, U.S. Retreats from the Principle That No One Else Commands Its Troops." *New York Times,* February 14, 1993, sec. 1, p. 18.

———. "The Moment of Truth." *New York Times,* September 19, 1993, sec. 1, p. 1.

Atkinson, James B. and Donovan P. Yeuell, Jr. "Must We Have World War III?" *Naval Institute Proceedings* 82 (July 1956): 711–21.

"Atomic Weapons and the Korean War." Editorial. *Bulletin of Atomic Scientists* 6 (July 1950): 194, 217.

"A Whirlwind of Hatreds: How the Balkans Broke Up." *New York Times*, February 14, 1993, sec. 4, p. 5.

Bacevich, A.J. *The Pentomic Era: The US Army between Korea and Vietnam.* Washington, D.C.: National Defense University Press, 1986.

Bailey, Thomas A. *A Diplomatic History of the American People.* 6th ed. New York: Appleton-Century- Crofts, 1958.

————. *The American Pageant: A History of the Republic.* 3rd ed. Boston: D.C. Heath, 1966.

Baldwin, Hanson W. "Strategy of Restraint or Chaos Unlimited." *Combat Forces Journal* 4 (January 1954): 10–13.

————. "Landpower as an Element of National Power." *Combat Forces Journal* 6 (January 1956): 16–21.

Barnett, Roger W. and Jeffrey G. Barlow. "The Maritime Strategy of the U.S. Navy: Reading Excerpts." In Colin S. Gray and Roger W. Barnett, eds. *Seapower and Strategy*, pp. 324–49. Annapolis, MD: Naval Institute Press, 1989.

Bennett, William C. "Just Cause and the Principles of War." *Military Review* 71 (March 1991): 2–13.

Berman, Larry. *Planning a Tragedy: The Americanization of the War in Vietnam.* New York: Norton, 1982.

Betts, Richard. *Soldiers, Statesmen, and Cold War Crises.* Cambridge: Harvard University Press, 1977.

————. *Nuclear Blackmail and Nuclear Balance.* Washington, D.C.: Brookings, 1987.

Billings-Yun, Melanie. *The Decision Against War: Eisenhower and Dien Bien Phu, 1954.* New York: Columbia University Press, 1988.

Blair, Clay. *The Forgotten War: America in Korea, 1950–1953.* New York: Times Books, 1987.

Blaufarb, Douglas. *The Counterinsurgency Era: U.S. Doctrine and Performance, 1950 to the Present.* New York: Free Press, 1977.

Bolger, Daniel P. "Two Armies." *Parameters* 19 (September 1989): 24–34.

Bond, Brian. *Liddell Hart: A Study of His Military Thought.* New Brunswick, N.J.: Rutgers University Press, 1977.

Borowski, Harry. *A Hollow Threat: Strategic Containment Before Korea.* Westport, CT: Greenwood Press, 1982.

Bradley, Omar N. and Clay Blair. *A General's Life.* New York: Simon and Schuster, 1983.

Braestrup, Peter, ed. *Vietnam as History: Ten Years after the Paris Peace Accords.* Washington, D.C.: University Press of America, 1984.

Brands, H. W. "The Age of Vulnerability: Eisenhower and the National Security State." *American Historical Review* 94 (October 1989): 963–989.

Brodie, Bernard. "The Atomic Bomb and American Security." New Haven, CT: Yale University, Memorandum No. 18, November 1945.

———. "Implications for Military Policy." In Bernard Brodie, ed. *The Absolute Weapon: Atomic Power and World Order.* New York: Harcourt Brace, 1946, pp. 70–107.

———. "Unlimited Weapons and Limited War." *The Reporter* (Nov. 11, 18, 1954): 16–21.

———. *Strategy in the Missile Age.* Princeton: Princeton University Press, May 1959.

———. "What Price Conventional Capabilities in Europe?" *The Reporter* (May 23, 1963).

———. *War and Politics.* New York: Macmillan, 1973.

Brown, Seyom. *The Faces of Power: Constancy and Change in United States Foreign Policy from Truman to Johnson.* New York: Columbia University Press, 1968.

Brown, Seyom. *The Faces of Power: United States Foreign Policy from Truman to Clinton.* New York: Columbia University Press, 1994 (an extensive revision to the above).

Buckley, Kevin. *Panama: The Whole Story.* New York: Simon and Schuster, 1991.

Bundy, McGeorge. *Danger and Survival: Choices About the Bomb in the First Fifty Years.* New York: Random House, 1988.

Burgess, William H., III. "Toward a More Complete Doctrine: Special Operations Forces in AirLand Battle Future." *Military Review* 71 (March 1992): 30–37.

Burke, John P. and Fred I. Greenstein (in collaboration with Larry Burke and Richard H. Immerman). *How Presidents Test Reality: Decisions on Vietnam, 1954 and 1965.* New York: Russell Sage Foundation, 1989.

Burns, Robert. "There Were Hints Months Ago Somalia Might Bog Down U.S.." *Washington Times,* October 10, 1993, sec, A, p. 6.

"Bush's Talk to Cadets: When 'Force Makes Sense.' " *New York Times,* January 6, 1993, sec. A, p. 6.

Buzzanco, Bob. "The American Military's Rationale against the Vietnam War." *Political Science Quarterly* 101 (4): 559–576.

Cagle, Malcolm W. "Errors of the Korean War." *Naval Institute Proceedings* 84 (March 1958): 31–36.

————. "Sea Power and Limited War." *Naval Institute Proceedings* 84 (July 1958): 23–27.

Carr, Caleb. "Should War Be Left to the Generals?" Review of *Sheridan: The Life and Wars of General Phil Sheridan* by Roy Morris, Jr., and *A Battle from the Start: The Life of Nathan Bedford Forrest* by Brian Steel Wills. *New York Times Book Review*, July 5, 1992, p. 1 (section 7).

Carver, Michael. "Conventional Warfare in the Nuclear Age." In Peter Paret, ed. *Makers of Modern Strategy from Machiavelli to the Nuclear Age*, pp. 779–814. Princeton: Princeton University Press, 1986.

Christensen, Thomas J. "Threats, Assurances, and the Last Chance for Peace: The Lessons of Mao's Korea War Telegrams." *International Security* 17 (Summer 1992): 122–154.

"Christopher's Remarks on Balkans." *New York Times*, February 11, 1993, sec. A, p. 12.

Church, George J. "Mission of Mercy." *Time*, April 29, 1991, p. 40.

Clark, Mark (General, USA, retired). *From the Danube to the Yalu*. New York: Harper & Row, 1954.

Clark, Wesley K. "Gradualism and American Military Strategy." *Military Review* 60 (Sept. 1975): 3–13.

Clausewitz, Carl von. *On War*. Michael Howard and Peter Paret, trans. and ed.. Princeton: Princeton University Press, 1978.

Clift, Eleanor and Thomas DeFrank. "Bush's General: Maximum Force — The GOP Eyes Powell as a 'Black Eisenhower.' " *Newsweek*, September 3, 1990, pp. 36ff.

"Clinton's Words: U.N. Cannot Become Engaged in Every World Conflict." *New York Times*, September 28, 1993, sec. A, p. 16.

"Clinton's Words on Somalia: 'The Responsibilities of American Leadership.' " *New York Times*, October 8, 1993, sec. A, p. 15.

Coats, John Wendell, Jr. "The Malingering McNamara Model for the Use of U.S. Military Force." Strategic Review 17 (Fall 1989): 18–30.

Clodfelter, Mark. *The Limits of Air Power: The American Bombing of North Vietnam*. New York: Free Press, 1991.

Cochran, Alexander S., Jr. "American Planning for Ground Combat in Vietnam, 1952–1965." *Parameters* 14 (Summer 1984): 63–69.

Cohen, Elliot A. "Constraints on America's Conduct of Small Wars." *International Security* 9 (Fall 1984): 151–81.

Cohen, Roger. "Europeans Reject U.S. Plan to Aid Bosnia and Halt Serbs." *New York Times*, May 11, 1993, sec. A, pp. 1 & 8.

Coll, Steve. "Anatomy of a Victory: CIA's Covert Afghan War." *Washington Post*, July 19, 1992, sec. A, pp. 1 & 24.

————. "In CIA's Covert Afghan War, Where to Draw the Line Was Key." *Washington Post*, July 20, 1992, sec. A, p. 1 & 12.

Combs, Jerald. "The Compromise That Never Was: George Kennan, Paul Nitze, and the Issue of Conventional Deterrence in Europe, 1949–1952." *Diplomatic History* 15 (Summer 1991): 361–386.

Crowe, William J., Jr. "What I've Learned." *Washingtonian* 25 (November 1989): 105–113.

Crowe, William J., Jr. with David Chanoff. *The Line of Fire: From Washington to the Gulf, the Politics and Battles of the New Military.* New York: Simon and Schuster, 1993.

Cushman, John H., Jr. "How Powerful U.S. Units Will Work." *New York Times*, October 8, 1993, sec. A, p. 14.

Darnton, John. "Europeans Welcome U.S. Role in Bosnia, Especially Its Arms." *New York Times*, February 12, 1993, sec. A, p. 10.

Davidson, Philip B. *Vietnam at War: The History, 1946–1975.* Navato, CA: Presidio Press, 1988.

DeConde, Alexander. *The Quasi-War: The Politics and Diplomacy of the Undeclared War with France, 1797–1801.* New York: Scribner's, 1966.

Deibel, Terry L. "Why Reagan is Strong." *Foreign Policy* 62 (Spring 1986): 108–125.

Destler, I. M. *Presidents, Bureaucrats, and Foreign Policy: The Politics of Organizational Reform.* Princeton: Princeton University Press, 1972.

Devroy, Ann. "New Deployment Raises Confusion on U.S. Goals." *Washington Post*, October 6, 1993, sec. A, p. 1.

Devroy, Ann and Barton Gellman. "Leveling the Battlefield: U.S. Seeks Now to Equalize Bosnia Factions." *Washington Post*, May 9, 1993, sec. A, pp. 1 & 27.

Devroy, Ann and R. Jeffrey Smith. "Clinton Reexamines a Foreign Policy Under Siege." *Washington Post*, October 17, 1993, sec. A, p. 1.

Devroy, Ann and Patrick E. Tyler. "U.S. Forces Crush Panamanian Military; Noriega in Hiding as Fighting Continues." *Washington Post*, December 21, 1989, sec. A, pp. 1 & 33.

Dewar, Helen. "Senators Approve Troop Compromise." *Washington Post*, October 21, 1993, sec. A, p. 1.

Dingman, Roger. "Atomic Diplomacy during the Korean War." *International Security* 13 (Winter 1988/89): 50–91.

Divine, Robert A. "Vietnam Reconsidered." *Diplomatic History* 12 (Winter 1988): 79–93.

Djilas, Aleksa. "The Nation That Wasn't." *The New Republic*, September 21, 1992, pp. 25–31.

Dobson, John. *Reticent Expansionism: The Foreign Policy of William McKinley.* Pittsburgh: Duquesne University Press, 1988), chap. 8.

Dubois, Robert R. "The Weinberger Doctrine and the Liberation of Kuwait." *Parameters* 21 (Winter 1991–92): 24–38.

Duiker, William J. *The Communist Road to Power in Vietnam.* Boulder, CO: Westview Press, 1981.

Dulles, John Foster. "Policy for Security and Peace." *Foreign Affairs* 32 (April 1954): 353–64.

Dupuy, R. Ernest and Trevor N. Dupuy. *The Encyclopedia of Military History from 3500 B.C. to the Present.* New York: Harper, 1986.

Dupuy, Trevor N. "War Without Victory." *Military Review* 35 (March 1956): 28–32.

Earle, Edward Mead. "The Influence of Air Power." *The Yale Review* 35 (March 1946): 577–93.

Eckhardt, William G. " 'We the People' Go to War: The Legal Significance of the Weinberger Doctrine." *Small Wars and Insurgencies* 1 (August 1990): 131–145.

Eisenhower, Dwight D. *Mandate for Change, 1953–1956.* Garden City, NY: Doubleday, 1963.

———. *The White House Years: Waging Peace, 1956–61.* Garden City, N.Y.: Doubleday, 1965.

Eisenhower, John S. D. *So Far from God: The U.S. War with Mexico, 1846–1848.* New York: Random House, 1989.

Elliot, George Fielding. "Less-Than-Total Solutions." *Military Review* 37 (May 1957): 14–21.

Ely, John Hart. *War and Responsibility.* Princeton: Princeton Univ. Press, 1993.

———. "Clinton, Congress and War," *New York Times,* October 23, 1993, p. 23.

Engelberg, Stephen. "U.S. Envoy Meets Clan Leaders' Kin in Somali Capital." *New York Times,* October 11, 1993, sec. A, p. 1.

English, John A. *A Perspective on Infantry.* New York: Praeger, 1981.

Etzold, Thomas H. "The End of the Beginning . . . NATO's Adoption of Nuclear Strategy." In Olav Riste, ed. *Western Security: The Formative Years, European and Atlantic Defence, 1947–1953,* pp. 285–314. New York: Columbia University Press, 1985.

Etzold, Thomas H. and John Lewis Gaddis, eds. *Containment: Documents on American Foreign Policy and Strategy, 1945–50.* New York: Columbia University Press, 1978.

"Excerpts from Briefing at Pentagon by Cheney and Powell." *New York Times,* January 24, 1991, sec. A, p. 11.

"Excerpts from Bush's Remarks on His Order to Enlarge U.S. Gulf Force." *New York Times*, November 9, 1990, sec. A, p. 12.

"Excerpts from Clinton News Conference: 'The U.S. Should Lead' on Bosnia?" *New York Times*, April 24, 1993, p. 7.

"Excerpts from President's News Conference on Crisis in Gulf." *New York Times*, December 1, 1990, p. 6, columns 1 & 2.

Face the Nation. November 19, 1991. Washington, D.C.: CBS News.

Fall, Bernard. *Street Without Joy.* New York: Schocken, 1972; first published 1965.

———. *Hell in a Very Small Place.* Philadelphia, Pennsylvania: Lippincott, 1967.

Farah, Douglas. "U.S. Ships Set for Embargo." *Washington Post*, October 17, 1993, sec. A, p. 1.

Farwell, Byron. *Queen Victoria's Little Wars.* New York: Norton, 1972.

Foot, Rosemary. *The Wrong War: American Policy and the Dimensions of the Korean Conflict, 1950–1953.* Ithaca, NY: Cornell University Press, 1985.

———. "Nuclear Coercion and the Ending of the Korean Conflict." *International Security* 13 (Winter 1988/89): 92–112.

———. *A Substitute for Victory: The Politics of Peacemaking at the Korean Armistice Talks.* Ithaca: Cornell University Press, 1990).

Foreign Relations of the United States. Washington, D.C.: Government Printing Office, annual. (Abbreviated as *FRUS* with year, volume, and pages.)

Fraser, David. *Alanbrooke.* London: William Collins Sons, 1982.

Freedman, Lawrence. *The Evolution of Nuclear Strategy.* New York: St. Martin's, 1981.

———. "On the Tiger's Back: The Development of the Concept of Escalation." In Roman Kolkowicz, ed. *The Logic of Nuclear Terror.* Boston: Allen & Unwin, 1987.

———. "The First Two Generations of Nuclear Strategists." In Peter Paret, ed. *Makers of Modern Strategy from Machiavelli to the Nuclear Age*, pp. 735–78. Princeton: Princeton University Press, 1986.

Freedman, Lawrence and Efraim Karsh. "How Kuwait Was Won: Strategy in the Gulf War." *International Security* 16 (Fall 1991): 5–41.

———. *The Gulf Conflict, 1990–1991: Diplomacy and War in the New World Order.* Princeton: Princeton University Press, 1993.

French, Howard W. "Diplomats Flee Port to Escape Protesters." *New York Times*, October 12, 1993, sec. A, p. 1 & 12.

Friedman, Thomas L. "The Nightmare Haunting Washington Is Set in Beirut, Not Vietnam." *New York Times*, October 7, 1990, sec. 4, p. 1.

———. "Limiting the Response," *New York Times*, January 19, 1993, sec. A, p. 1.

————. "Bosnia Air Strikes Backed by Clinton, His Officials Say," *New York Times*, May 2, 1993, sec. 1, p. 1.

————. "Any War in Bosnia Would Carry a Domestic Price," *New York Times*, May 2, 1993, sec. 4, p. 1.

————. "Clinton, at U.N., Lists Stiff Terms for Sending U.S. Force to Bosnia." *New York Times*, September 28, 1993, sec. A, p. 1.

————. "U.S. Pays Dearly for An Education in Somalia." *New York Times*, October 10, 1993, sec. 4, p. 3.

————. "Somalia's Buzzwords: 'Constructive Ambiguity.' " *New York Times*, October 15, 1993, sec. A, p. 1.

Friedman, Thomas L. and Patrick E. Tyler. "From the First, U.S. Resolved to Fight." *New York Times*, March 3, 1991, p. 1.

FRUS. *See Foreign Relations of the United States.*

Furet, François. *Citizens: A Chronicle of the French Revolution.* New York: Knopf, 1989.

Gacek, Christopher M. "No Talks Once the Ground War Starts." *New York Times*, February 11, 1992, sec. A, p. 15.

Gaddis, John Lewis. *Strategies of Containment: A Critical Appraisal of Postwar American National Security Policy.* Oxford: Oxford University Press, 1982.

————. *The Long Peace: Inquiries Into the History of the Cold War.* New York: Oxford University Press, 1987.

————. "The Unexpected John Foster Dulles: Nuclear Weapons, Communism, and the Russians." In Richard H. Immerman, ed. *John Foster Dulles and the Diplomacy of the Cold War*, pp. 47–78. Princeton: Princeton University Press, 1990.

Gallie, W.B. *Philosophers of Peace and War: Kant, Clausewitz, Marx, Engels, and Tolstoy.* London: Cambridge University Press, 1978.

Galloway, John. *The Gulf of Tonkin Resolution.* Rutherford, NJ: Fairleigh Dickinson University Press, 1970.

Gallup, George. *The Gallup Poll: Public Opinion, 1935–1971.* New York: Random House, 1972.

Garthoff, Raymond L. "Soviet Views on Limited War." *Military Review* 37 (January 1958): 50–60.

Gat, Azar. *The Origins of Military Thought from the Enlightenment to Clausewitz.* Oxford: Clarendon Press, 1989.

Gavin, James M. *War and Peace in the Space Age.* New York: Harper, 1958.

————. "The Easy Chair—A Communication on Vietnam from Gen. James M. Gavin." *Harper's*, February 1966.

————. *Crisis Now.* New York: Random House, 1968.

Gelb, Leslie H. and Richard K. Betts. *The Irony of Vietnam: The System Worked.* Washington, D.C.: Brookings, 1979.

Gellman, Barton. "U.S. Is Prepared to Commit Combat Forces." *The Washington Post*, July 1, 1992, sec. A, p. 28.

———. "Military Uneasy at Balkan Commitment: Limited Use of Force May Be Inadequate to Accomplish Mission," *Washington Post*, July 2, 1992, sec. A, pp. 1 & 34.

———. "Revisiting the Gulf War: Book Depicts a Raging, Imperial Schwarzkopf." *Washington Post*, July 25, 1993, sec. A, pp. 1 & 20.

———. "U.S. Lacked Strong Plan to Aid Besieged Troops." *Washington Post*, October 6, 1993, sec. A, p. 1.

Gellman, Barton and John Lancaster. "U.S. May Drop a 2-War Preparedness: Aspin Envisions Smaller, High-Tech Military to Win, Hold, Win." *Washington Post*, June 17, 1993, sec. A, pp. 1, 16 & 17.

George, Alexander L. "Quantitative and Qualitative Approaches to Content Analysis." In Ithiel De Sola Pool, ed. *Trends in Content Analysis*, pp. 7–32. Urbana:University of Illinois Press, 1959.

———. "The Development of Doctrine and Strategy." In Alexander L. George, David K. Hall, and William E. Simons, eds. *The Limits of Coercive Diplomacy: Laos, Cuba, Vietnam.* Boston: Little, Brown, 1971, pp. 1–35.

———. "Case Studies and Theory Development: The Method of Structured, Focused Comparison." In Paul Gordon Lauren, ed. *Diplomacy: New Approaches in History, Theory, and Policy.* New York: The Free Press, 1979, pp. 43–68.

———. "Case Studies and Theory Development." Unpublished manuscript, 1982.

George, Alexander L. and Timothy J. McKeown. "Case Studies and Theories of Organizational Decision Making." In *Advances in Information Processing in Organizations*, volume 2. JAI Press Inc., 1985, pp. 21–58.

George, Alexander L. and Richard Smoke. *Deterrence in American Foreign Policy: Theory and Practice.* New York: Columbia University Press, 1974.

Gertz, Bill. "Aspin under Fire for Saying No to Earlier Arms Requests." *Washington Times*, October 7, 1993, sec. A, p. 1.

———. "Dole Seeks Law to Tie Clinton's Hands in Haiti." *Washington Times*, October 18, 1983, sec. A, p. 1 & 20.

Geyer, Michael. "German Strategy in the Age of Machine Warfare, 1914–1945." In *Makers of Modern Strategy from Machiavelli to the Nuclear Age*, ed. Peter Paret, pp. 527–598. Princeton: Princeton University Press, 1986.

Gibbons, William Conrad. *The U.S. Government and the Vietnam War: Executive and Legislative Roles.* Pts. 1, 2 and 3. Princeton: Princeton University Press, 1986.

Gigot, Paul A. "Foreign-Policy President Finally Acts on Yugoslavia." *Wall Street Journal*, August 7, 1992, sec. A, p. 12.

Gilbert, Martin. *Winston S. Churchill: "Never Despair," 1945–65*. Vol. VIII. Boston: Houghton Mifflin, 1988).

Glynn, Patrick. *Closing Pandora's Box: Arms Races, Arms Control, and the History of the Cold War*. New York: Basic Books, 1992.

Goldich, Robert L. "The Strategic Importance of Mass," *The National Interest* (Winter 1986/7): 66–74.

Goldstein, Judith. "The Political Economy of Trade: Institutions of Protection." *American Political Science Review* 80 (March 1986): 161–84.

———. "Ideas, Institutions, and American Trade Policy." *International Organization* 42 (Winter 1988): 179–217.

———. "The Impact of Ideas on Trade Policy: The Origins of U.S. Agricultural and Manufacturing Policies." *International Organization* 43 (Winter 1989): 31–72.

Gooch, John. "Maritime Command: Mahan and Corbett." In Colin S. Gray and Roger W. Barnett, eds. *Seapower and Strategy*, pp. 27–46. Annapolis, MD: Naval Institute Press, 1989.

Goodwin, Doris Kearns. *Lyndon Johnson and the American Dream*. New York: Harper, 1976.

Gordon, Michael R. "Generals Favor 'No Holds Barred' by U.S. If Iraq Attacks the Saudis." *New York Times*, August 25, 1990, p. 1.

———. "Bush Sends New Units to Gulf to Provide Offensive Option; U.S. Force Could Reach 380,000." *New York Times*, November 9, 1990, sec. A, pp. 1 & 12.

———. "Limits of U.S. Role: White House Is Seeking to Minimize Any Use of Military in Balkan Conflict." *New York Times*, August 11, 1992, sec. A, p. 6.

———. "U.N. Backs a Somalia Force As Bush Vows a Swift Exit; Pentagon Sees Longer Stay." *New York Times*, December 4, 1992, sec. A, pp. 1 & 14.

———. "U.S. Is Sending Large Force as Warning to Somali Clans." *New York Times*, December 5, 1992, p. 5.

———. "Hitting Hussein with a Stick, with a Sledgehammer in Reserve." *New York Times*, January 14, 1993, sec. A, p. 8.

———. "Limited U.S. Force Held Still an Option in Bosnia," *New York Times*, April 9, 1993, sec. A, p. 7.

———. "NATO General Is Reticent About Air Strikes in Bosnia," *New York Times*, April 21, 1993, sec. A, p. 10.

———. "12 in State Department Ask Military Move Against the Serbs," *New York Times*, April 23, 1993, sec. A, p. 12.

———. "Cuts Force Review of War Strategies." *New York Times*, May 30, 1993, sec. 1, p. 16.

Gordon, Michael R. and Thomas L. Friedman. "Disastrous U.S. Raid in Somalia Nearly Succeeded, Review Finds," *New York Times*, October 25, 1993, sec. A, p. 1.

Greenstein, Fred I. and Richard H. Immerman. "What Did Eisenhower Tell Kennedy about Indochina? The Politics of Misperception." *The Journal of American History* 79 (September 1992): 568–587.

Greenwood, John E. "FMFM 1: The Line of Departure." *Proceedings* 116 (May 1990): 155–156.

Gross, Richard C. "Christopher: Force Not an Option Now in Bosnia," *Washington Times*, May 19, 1993, sec. A, p. 1.

Haig, Alexander M. *Caveat: Realism, Reagan, and Foreign Policy*. New York: Macmillan, 1984.

Halberstam, David. *The Best and the Brightest*. New York: Random House, 1972.

Hall, David K. "The Laos Crisis, 1960–1." In Alexander L. George, David K. Hall, and William E. Simons, eds. *The Limits of Coercive Diplomacy: Laos, Cuba, Vietnam*. Boston: Little, Brown, 1971, pp. 36–85.

———. "The Laos Neutralization Agreement, 1962. In Alexander L. George, Philip J. Farley, and Alexander Dallin, eds. *U.S.-Soviet Security Cooperation: Achievements, Failures, Lessons*. New York: Oxford University Press, 1988, pp. 435–65.

Hall, George M. "Culminating Points." *Military Review* 69 (July 1989): 79–86.

Hallenbeck, Ralph A. "Force and Diplomacy: Examining America's Strategy in Lebanon." Ph.D. dissertation, Pennsylvania State University, 1986.

Halloran, Richard. "A Commanding Voice in the Military." *New York Times*, July 15, 1984, p. 18.

———. "U.S. Will Not Drift into A Latin War, Weinberger Says." *New York Times*, November 29, 1984, sec. A, p. 1.

———. "General Opposes Nicaragua Attack." *New York Times*, June 30, 1985, sec. A, p. 3.

———. *To Arm a Nation*. New York: Macmillan, 1986.

Halperin, Morton H. *Limited War in the Nuclear Age*. New York: Wiley, 1963.

———. *Bureaucratic Politics and Foreign Policy*. Washington, D.C.: Brookings, 1974.

Hammel, Eric. *The Root: The Marines in Beirut, August 1982–February 1984*. New York: Harcourt, 1985.

Hammond, Paul Y. "NSC-68: Prologue to Rearmament." In Warner R.

Schilling, Paul Y. Hammond, and Glenn H. Snyder, eds. *Strategy, Politics, and Defense Budgets*, pp. 267–378. New York: Columbia University Press, 1962.

—. "Super Carriers and B-36 Bombers: Appropriations, Strategy, and Politics." In Harold Stein, ed. *American Civil-Military Relations*, pp. 465–567. Birmingham, AL: University of Alabama Press, 1963.

Handel, Michael I. "Clausewitz in the Age of Technology." In Michael I. Handel, ed. *Clausewitz and Modern Strategy*, pp. 51–95. London: Frank Cass, 1986.

Hanks, Robert J. "The Gulf War and U.S. Staying Power." *Strategic Review* 15 (Fall 1987): 36–43.

Hannah, Norman B. *The Key to Failure: Laos and Vietnam*. Lanham, MD: Madison Books, 1987.

Harden, Blaine. "Can the West Stop the Rape of Bosnia? Should It? *Washington Post*, July 24, 1992, sec. A, p. 30.

Hayes, John D. "Peripheral Strategy . . . Littoral Tactics . . . Limited War." *Combat Forces Journal* 5 (September 1954): 36–9.

Herbert, Paul H. *Deciding What Has to Be Done: General William E. Dupuy and the 1976 Edition of FM 100–5, Operations (Leavenworth Papers No. 16)*. Fort Leavenworth, Kansas: Combat Studies Institute, 1988.

Hermes, Walter. *Truce Tent and Fighting Front*. Washington, D.C.: GPO, 1966.

Herring, George C. *America's Longest War: The United States and Vietnam, 1950–1975*. 2nd ed. New York: Knopf, 1986; 1st ed., 1979.

—. "American Strategy in Vietnam: The Postwar Debate." *Military Affairs* 46 (April 1982): 57–63.

Herring, George C. and Richard H. Immerman. "Eisenhower, Dulles, and Dienbienphu: 'The Day We Didn't Go to War' Revisited." *The Journal of American History* 71 (Sept. 1984): 343–63.

Hickey, Donald R. *The War of 1812: A Forgotten Conflict*. Urbana, IL: University of Illinois Press, 1989.

Hilsman, Roger. *To Move a Nation: The Politics of Foreign Policy in the Administration of John F. Kennedy*. Garden City, NY: Doubleday, 1967.

Hoagland, Jim. "August Guns: How Sarajevo Will Reshape U.S. Strategy." *Washington Post*, August 9, 1992, sec. C, pp. 1 & 2.

—. "With Whose Army?" *Washington Post*, August 13, 1992, sec. A, p. 25.

Holmes, Steven A. "Clinton May Let U.S. Troops Serve under U.N. Chiefs." *New York Times*, 18 August 1993, sec. A, p. 1.

—. "U.S. Delaying Dispatch of Troops to Haiti." *New York Times*, October 12, 1993, sec. A, p. 12.

Horne, Alistair. *The Price of Glory*. New York: Penguin, 1964.

Howard, Michael. "Jomini and the Classical Tradition in Military Thought." In his *Studies in War and Peace*. New York: The Viking Press, 1970, pp. 21–36.

———. "The Classical Strategists." In his *Studies in War and Peace*. New York: Viking Press, 1971, pp. 154–83.

———. *War and the Liberal Conscience*. New Brunswick, N.J.: Rutgers University Press, 1978.

———. *Clausewitz*. Oxford: Oxford University Press, 1983.

———. "Brodie, Wohlstetter and American Nuclear Strategy." *Survival* 34 (Summer 1992): 107–116.

Hunt, Michael H. "Beijing and the Korean Crisis." *Political Science Quarterly* 107 (Fall 1992): 453–478.

Hunt, Richard A. and Richard H. Schultz, eds. *Lessons from an Unconventional War: Reassessing U.S. Strategies for Future Conflicts*. New York: Pergamon, 1982.

Huntington, Samuel P. *The Soldier and the State: The Theory and Politics of Civil-Military Relations*. Cambridge: Harvard University Press, 1957.

———. *The Common Defense: Strategic Programs in National Politics*. New York: Columbia University Press, 1963.

———. *American Politics: The Promise of Disharmony*. Cambridge: Harvard University Press, 1981.

———. "American Ideals Versus American Institutions." *Political Science Quarterly* 97 (Spring 1982): 1–37.

———. "Playing to Win." *The National Interest* (Spring 1986): 8–16.

———. "The Elements of American Strategy." In *American Military Strategy*. Berkeley, CA: Institute of International Studies, 1986, pp. 3–17.

Ifill, Gwen. "750 Rangers Will Leave Somalia, President Says." *New York Times*, October 20, 1993, sec. A, p. 14.

Immerman, Richard H. "Confessions of an Eisenhower Revisionist: An Agonizing Reappraisal." *Diplomatic History* (Summer 1990): 319–342.

———. "Between the Unattainable and the Unacceptable: Eisenhower and Dienbienphu." In *Reevaluating Eisenhower: American Foreign Policy in the 1950s*, ed. Richard A. Melanson and David Mayers, pp. 120–154. Urbana, IL: University of Illinois Press, 1987.

Janowitz, Morris. *The Professional Soldier: A Social and Political Portrait*. New York: The Free Press, 1961.

———. "Towards a Redefinition of Military Strategy in International Relations." *World Politics* 26 (July 1974): 473–508.

Jehl, Douglas. "Clinton Doubling U.S. Force in Somalia, Vowing Troops Will Come Home in Six Months." *New York Times*, October 8, 1993, sec. A, p. 1.

———. "U.S. Shifts Troops to Defensive Role in Somalia Mission." *New York Times*, October 20, 1993, sec. A, p. 1.

Jervis, Robert. *Perception and Misperception in International Politics*. Princeton: Princeton University Press, 1976.

———. *The Meaning of the Nuclear Revolution*. Ithaca, NY: Cornell University Press, 1989.

John McLaughlin's One on One. Television interview with the Chairman of the Joint Chiefs of Staff, Admiral William Crowe. September 10, 1989.

Johnson, James Turner. "Just War Thinking and Its Contemporary Application: The Moral Significance of the Weinberger Doctrine." *Small Wars and Insurgencies* 1 (August 1990): 146–170.

Johnson, U. Alexis with Jef Olivarius McAllister. *The Right Hand of Power*. Englewood Cliffs, NJ: Prentice Hall, 1984.

Joint Chiefs of Staff; Historical Division of the Joint Secretariat. *The Joint Chiefs of Staff and the War in Vietnam: History of the Indochina Incident, 1940–1954*. Wilmington, DE: Michael Glazier, 1982.

Jomini, Henri. *The Art of War: A New Edition with Appendices and Maps*. G.H. Mendell and W.P. Craighill, trans. Philadelphia: Lippincott, 1862. Rpt. Westport, CT: Greenwood Press, 1971.

Kahin, George. *Intervention: How America Became Involved in Vietnam*. New York: Knopf, 1986.

Kahn, Herman. *On Thermonuclear War*. Princeton: Princeton University Press, 1960.

———. *On Escalation: Metaphors and Scenarios*. New York: Praeger, 1965.

Karnow, Stanley. *Vietnam: A History*. New York: Viking Press, 1983.

Kaufmann, William W., ed. *Military Policy and National Security*. Princeton: Princeton University Press, 1956.

Kearns see Goodwin.

Keefer, Edward C. "President Dwight D. Eisenhower and the End of the Korean War." *Diplomatic History* 10 (Summer 1986): 267–89.

Keegan, John. *The Mask of Command*. New York: Viking Press, 1987.

———. "The Lessons of the Gulf War." *Los Angeles Times Magazine*, April 7, 1991, pp. 21 & 62.

Kellet, Anthony. *Combat Motivation: The Behavior of Soldiers in Battle*. Kluwer, The Netherlands: Nijhoff, 1982.

Kelly, Michael. "Clinton Said to Consider Troops to Bosnia." *New York Times*, February 10, 1993, sec. A, p. 6.

Kempe, Frederick. "U.S., Bonn Clash over Pact with France," *Wall Street Journal*, 27 May 1992, sec. A, p. 9.

Kennan, George F. *Memoirs, Vol. I: 1925–1950*. Boston: Little Brown, 1967.

Khong, Yuen Foon. *Analysis at War: Korea, Munich, Dien Bien Phu, and the Vietnam Decisions of 1965.* Princeton: Princeton University Press, 1992.

Kirkpatrick, Jeane J. "The Use of Force in the Law of Nations." Review of *On the Law of Nations* by Daniel Patrick Moynihan. In *Yale Journal of International Law* 16 (1991): 583–598.

———. "Is the U.N. Being Stretched Too Thin?" Interview by Lee Michael Katz (Washington, D.C., August 1992). *USA Today,* August 11, 1992, sec. A, p. 11.

Kissinger, Henry A. *Nuclear Weapons and Foreign Policy.* New York: Harper, 1957.

———. "Limited War: Nuclear or Conventional? A Reappraisal." *Daedalus* 89 (Fall 1960): 800–17.

Kistiakowsky, George B. *A Scientist at the White House: The Private Diary of President Eisenhower's Special Assistant for Science and Technology.* Cambridge: Harvard University Press, 1976.

Kraft, Joseph. *Profiles in Power.* New York: The New American Library, 1966.

Kramer, Michael. "Clinton's Feelgood Strategy." *Time,* May 17, 1993, p. 36.

Krasner, Stephen D. *Defending the National Interest: Raw Materials Investments and U.S. Foreign Policy.* Princeton: Princeton University Press, 1978.

Krauss, Clifford. "House Vote Urges Clinton to Limit Role in Somali Conflict." *New York Times,* September 29, 1993, sec. A, p. 1 & 10.

———. "Despite Its Victory in Senate Vote, White House Pays for Somalia Policy." *New York Times,* October 16, 1993, p. 6.

Krepinevich, Andrew F., Jr. *The Army and Vietnam.* Baltimore: Johns Hopkins University Press, 1986.

———. "Past as Prologue: Counterinsurgency and the U.S. Army's Vietnam Experience in Force Structure and the Doctrine." In George K. Osborn, Asa A. Clark, IV, Daniel J. Kaufman, and Douglas E. Lute, eds. *Democracy, Strategy, and Vietnam: Implications for American Policymaking.* Lexington, MA: Lexington Books, 1987, pp. 269–83.

Lagon, Mark P. "Crusade for Freedom: International and Ideological Sources of the Reagan Doctrine." Ph.D. dissertation, Georgetown University, 1989.

Lancaster, John. "Powell Says Mission Duration Is Flexible." *Washington Post,* December 5, 1992, sec. A, p. 17.

Larson, Deborah Welch. *Origins of Containment: A Psychological Explanation.* Princeton: Princeton University Press, 1985.

Lee, Jessica. "Bush Defends Gulf War Decisions." *USA Today,* August 5, 1992, sec. A, p. 2.

Leffler, Melvyn P. *A Preponderance of Power: National Security, the Truman*

Administration, and the Cold War. Stanford: Stanford University Press, 1992.

Lewis, John Wilson and Xue Litai. *China Builds the Bomb.* Stanford: Stanford University Press, 1988.

Lewis, Paul. "U.N. Experts Now Say Baghdad Was Far From Making an A-Bomb before Gulf War." *New York Times,* May 20, 1992, sec. A, p. 6.

———. "U.N. Aide Tells Iraq It Risks Attack for Truce Defiance." *New York Times,* July 18, 1988, p. 3.

———. "U.N. Is Developing Control Center to Coordinate Growing Peace-keeping Role," *New York Times,* March 28, 1993, sec. 1, p. 10.

———. "U.N. Is Authorizing Allied Air Strikes against the Serbs." *New York Times,* June 5, 1993, p. 1 & 6.

———. "Balkan Negotiator, in Shift, Backs Plan Dividing Bosnia." *New York Times,* June 18, 1993, sec. A, p. 8.

Liddell Hart, B. H. *The Revolution in Warfare.* London: Faber & Faber, 1946.

———. "The Defence of Western Europe." Chap. in *Defence of the West.* New York: Morrow, 1950.

Lipset, Seymour Martin. "The Banality of Revolt." *Saturday Review* 58 (July 18, 1970): 23–6, 34.

Lorch, Donatella. "As U.N. Prepares for Somalia Command, Rebuilding Is Most Urgent Task." *New York Times,* May 2, 1993, sec. 1, p. 16.

Lumsdaine, David H. *Moral Vision in International Politics: The Foreign Aid Regime, 1949–1989.* (Princeton: Princeton University Press, 1992).

Lupfer, Timothy L. *The Dynamics of Doctrine: The Changes in German Tactical Doctrine During the First World War.* Publication of the Combat Studies Institute, U.S. Army Command and General Staff College. Alice M. McCart, ed. Leavenworth Papers, no. 4. Fort Leavenworth, KS: Combat Studies Institute, July 1981.

McCartney, James. "Pentagon Puts Brakes on U.S. Attack Projects." *Miami Herald,* April 12, 1984, sec. A, pp. 1 & 14.

MacDonald, Callum. *Korea, The War Before Vietnam.* Houndmills, Basingstoke: Macmillan, 1986.

MacDougall, Walter A. *The Heavens and the Earth: A Political History of the Space Age.* New York: Basic Books, 1985.

McGee, Jim. "Navy Chief Challenged Gulf Buildup." *The Miami Herald,* September 6, 1987, sec. A, pp. 1 & 18.

The MacLaughlin Group. TV news commentary program. November 23, 1990. Washington, D.C.: Oliver Productions.

"The McNeil-Lehrer Newshour." TV news and discussion program. August 11, 1992. Washington, D.C.: Educational Broadcasting Corp.

Magnuson, Ed. "Sowing Dragon's Teeth." *Time,* January 1, 1990, pp. 24ff.

————. "Passing the Manhood Test: Operation Just Cause Was a Triumph for American Soldiers." *Time*, January 8, 1990, p. 43.

March, James G. and Johan P. Olsen. Introductory chapter from *Ambiguity and Choice in Organizations* (1971). In Grusky and Miller, eds. *The Sociology of Organizations*. 2nd ed. New York: Free Press, 1981.

March, James G. and Roger Weissinger-Baylon. *Ambiguity and Command: Organizational Perspectives on Military Decision Making*. Marshfield, MA: Pitman, 1986.

Marthinsen, Charles E. "The Historical Significance of the Weinberger Doctrine." *Small Wars and Insurgencies* 1 (August 1990): 118–130.

Matloff, Maurice. *American Military History*. Washington, D.C.: GPO, 1969.

Menges, Constantine C. *Inside the National Security Council: The True Story of the Making and Unmaking of Reagan's Foreign Policy*. New York: Simon & Schuster, 1988.

Metz, Steven. "AirLand Battle and Counterinsurgency." *Military Review* 70 (January 1990): 32–41.

————. "U.S. Strategy and the Changing LIC Threat." *Military Review* 71 (June 1991): 22–29.

————. "Victory and Compromise in Counterinsurgency." *Military Review* 72 (April 1992): 47–53.

Middleton, Drew. "Vietnam and the Military Mind." *New York Times Magazine*, January 10, 1982, p. 91.

Milhollin, Gary. "Building Saddam Hussein's Bomb." *New York Times Magazine*, March 8, 1992, pp. 30–36.

Miller, Reid G. "3 GI's Die in Somalia." *Washington Times*, 26 September 1993, sec. A, p. 1.

Millett, Allen R. *Semper Fidelis: The History of the United States Marine Corps*. Revised and expanded ed. New York: Free Press, 1991.

Millett, Allen R. and Peter Maslowski. *For the Common Defense: A Military History of the United States of America*. New York: Free Press, 1984.

"Mission for the Army: The Winning of World War III." *Combat Forces Journal* 5 (February 1955): 16- 20.

Moore, Molly and Rick Atkinson. "Despite Problems, Invasion Seen as a Military Success." *Washington Post*, December 29, 1989, sec. A, pp. 1 & 22.

Mossberg, Walter. "The Army Resists a Salvadoran Vietnam." *New York Times*, June 24, 1983, p. 22.

Mortimer, Edward. " 'Safe Haven' Is Not Enough." *Financial Times*, April 10, 1991, p. 13.

Mueller, John E. *War, Presidents, and Public Opinion*. New York: Wiley, 1973.

Nash, Edward P., Jr. *The Forgotten Wars: The U.S. Navy in the Quasi-War with*

France and the Barbary Wars, 1798–1805. South Brunswick, NJ: A.S. Barnes, 1968.

Newland, Samuel J. and Douglas V. Johnson. "The Military and Operational Significance of the Weinberger Doctrine." *Small Wars and Insurgencies* 1 (August 1990): 171–191.

Nickerson, Hoffman. *Can We Limit War?* New York: Frederick A. Stokes, 1933.

Nisbett, Richard E. and Lee Ross. *Human Inference: Strategies and Shortcomings in Social Judgment.* Englewood Cliffs, NJ: Prentice-Hall, 1980.

Nitze, Paul H. with Ann M. Smith and Steven L. Rearden. *From Hiroshima to Glasnost: At the Center of Decision, A Memoir.* New York: Grove Weidenfeld, 1989.

Nixon, Richard. *R.N.: The Memoirs of Richard Nixon.* New York: Grossett and Dunlap, 1978.

Norman, Lloyd and John B. Spore. "Big Push in Guerrilla Warfare." *Army* 12 (March 1962): 28–37.

NSC. *A prefix in official US government document numbers for "National Security Council."*

O'Brian, William V. *The Conduct of Just and Limited War.* New York: Praeger, 1981.

Odell, John. *U.S International Monetary Policy: Markets, Power, and Ideas as a Source of Change.* Princeton: Princeton University Press, 1982.

Osborn, George K., et al., eds. *Democracy, Strategy, and Vietnam: Implications for American Policymaking.* Lexington, MA: Lexington Books, 1987.

Osgood, Robert E. *Limited War: The Challenge to American Strategy.* Chicago: University of Chicago Press, 1957.

———. *Limited War Revisited.* Boulder, CO: Westview Press, 1979.

Packenham, Robert A. *Liberal America and the Third World.* Princeton: Princeton University Press, 1973.

Palmer, Bruce, Jr. Review of *The Army and Vietnam* by Andrew F. Krepinevich, Jr. *Parameters* 16 (August 1986): 83–85.

Panikkar, K.M. *In Two Chinas.* London: Allen and Unwin, 1955.

Paret, Peter. *Clausewitz and the State.* New York: Oxford University Press, 1976.

———. "Clausewitz." In Peter Paret, ed. *Makers of Modern Strategy from Machiavelli to the Nuclear Age*, pp. 186–213. Princeton: Princeton University Press, 1986.

———. "Military Power." Chap. in *Understanding War: Essays on Clausewitz and the History of Military Power.* Princeton: Princeton University Press, 1992.

Parks, W. H. "Rules of Engagement: No More Vietnams." *Proceedings* 117 (March 1991): 27–28.

Paschall, Rod. "Low-Intensity Conflict Doctrine: Who Needs It?" *Parameters* 15 (Autumn 1985): 33–45.

"Pentagon Is Opposed to Use of Troops in Central America." *New York Times*, June 5, 1983, p. 5.

Perlez, Jane. "U.S. Forces Arrive in Somalia on Mission to Aid the Starving." New York Times December 9, 1992, sec. a, p. 1

Perry, Mark. *Four Stars: The Inside Story of the Forty-year Battle Between the Joint Chiefs of Staff and America's Civilian Leaders.* Boston: Houghton-Mifflin, 1989.

Peterson, Michael E. *The Combined Action Platoons: The U.S. Marines' Other War in Vietnam.* New York: Praeger, 1989.

Petraeus, David Howell. "The American Military and the Lessons of Vietnam: A Study of Military Influence and the Use of Force in the Post-Vietnam Era." Ph.D. dissertation, Princeton University, 1987.

Pike, Douglas. "The Other Side," *The Wilson Quarterly* 7 (Summer 1983): 114–124.

———. *PAVN: People's Army of Vietnam.* Navato, CA: Presidio Press, 1986.

Pollack, Jonathan. "A Chinese Achievement." *Science* (September 24, 1988): 1691–2.

Posen, Barry R. *The Sources of Military Doctrine: France, Germany, and Britain Between the World Wars.* Ithaca: Cornell University Press, 1984.

Potter, E. B. *Admiral Arleigh Burke: A Biography.* New York: Random House, 1990.

Powell, Colin L. "Why Generals Get Nervous." *New York Times*, October 8, 1992, sec. A, p. 35.

Prados, John. *The Sky Would Fall: Operation Vulture, the U.S. Bombing Mission in Indochina, 1954.* New York: Dial Press, 1983.

Prial, Frank J. "Russia Dusts off an Old Tactic at U.N.: The Veto." *New York Times*, May 12, 1993, sec. A, p. 10.

Protzman, Ferdinand. "Freed Pilot Elated to Leave Somalia." *New York Times*, October 16, 1993, p. 6.

Public Papers of the Presidents. Washington, D.C.: GPO. (name of president, year, and pages.)

Radford, Arthur William. Edited posthumously by Stephen Jurika. *From Pearl Harbor to Vietnam.* Stanford, CA: Hoover Institution Press, 1980.

Reagan, Ronald W. *Ronald Reagan: An American Life.* New York: Simon & Schuster, 1990.

Rearden, Steven L. *The Evolution of American Strategic Doctrine: Paul H. Nitze and the Soviet Challenge.* Boulder, CO: Westview Press, 1984.

Rees, David. *Korea: The Limited War*. New York: St. Martin's Press, 1964.

Reich, Robert B. *The Power of Public Ideas*. Cambridge, MA: Ballinger, 1988.

Reynolds, Charles. *The Politics of War: A Study of the Rationality of Violence in Inter-State Relations*. New York: St. Martin's Press, 1989.

Ridgway, Matthew B. *Soldier: The Memoirs of Matthew B. Ridgway*. New York: Harper & Row, 1956.

———. *The Korean War*. Garden City, NJ: Doubleday 1967.

Roberts, Kenneth. "Bullying and Bargaining: The United States, Nicaragua, and Conflict Resolution in Central America." *International Security*, 15 (Fall 1990): 67–102.

Rosen, Stephen Peter. "Vietnam and the American Theory of Limited War." *International Security* 7 (Fall 1982): 83–113.

Rosenberg, David Alan. "American Atomic Strategy and the Hydrogen Bomb Decision." *The Journal of American History* 66 (June 1979): 62–87.

———. " 'A Smoking Radiating Ruin at the End of Two Hours:' Documents on American Plans for Nuclear War with the Soviet Union, 1954–1955." *International Security* 6 (Winter 1981/1982): 3–38.

———. "The Origins of Overkill: Nuclear Weapons and American Strategy, 1945–1960." *International Security* 7 (Spring 1983): 3–71.

Rostow, W. W. *The Diffusion of Power*. New York: Macmillan, 1972.

Ruggie, John Gerard. "International Regimes, Transactions, and Change: Embedded Liberalism in the Postwar Economic Order." In Stephen D. Krasner, ed. *International Regimes*. Ithaca, NY: Cornell University Press, 1983.

Sabrosky, Alan Ned. "Applying Military Force: The Future Significance of the Weinberger Doctrine." *Small Wars and Insurgencies* 1 (August 1990): 191–201.

Safire, William. "Only the 'Fun' Wars." *New York Times*, December 3, 1984, sec. A, p. 23.

Sagan, Scott D. "1914 Revisited." *International Security* 11 (Fall 1986): 151–175.

Schaller, Michael. *Douglas MacArthur: The Far Eastern General*. Oxford: Oxford University Press, 1989.

Schandler, Herbert Y. *The Unmaking of a President: Lyndon Johnson and Vietnam*. Princeton: Princeton University Press, 1977.

Schelling, Thomas C. "Bargaining, Communication and Limited War." *Journal of Conflict Resolution* 1 (March 1957): 19–36.

———. *Nuclear Weapons and Limited War* (Rand P-1620: Feb. 20, 1959).

———. *The Strategy of Conflict*. Cambridge: Harvard University Press, 1960.

———. *Arms and Influence*. New Haven: Yale University Press, 1965.

Schemo, Diana Jean. "Declare Victory, Hand Off, Slip Out, Cross Fingers." *New York Times*, sec. 4, pp. 1 & 4.

Schlesinger, Arthur M., Jr. *A Thousand Days: John F. Kennedy in the White House*. Boston: Houghton Mifflin, 1965.

Schmitt, Eric. "How to Fight Iraq: Four Scenarios, All Are Disputed." *New York Times*, November 19, 1990, sec. A, p. 12.

———. "Most U.S. Troops Will Leave Somalia by April in U.N. Plan." *New York Times*, February 13, 1993, pp. 1 & 4.

———. "U.S. Forces to Stay in Somalia to End Warlord Violence." *New York Times*, August 28, 1993, p. 1.

———. "U.S. Vows to Stay in Somalia Force Despite an Attack." *New York Times*, September 26, 1993, sec. 1, p. 22.

Schnabel, James F. *Policy and Direction: The First Year*. Washington, D.C.: GPO, 1972.

Schnabel, James F. and Robert J. Watson. *The Joint Chiefs of Staff and National Policy: The Korean War*, vol 3, parts I and II. Wilmington, DE: Michael Glazier, 1979.

Schreyach, Jon C. "Fire Support for Deep Operations." *Military Review* 69 (August 1989): 29–37.

Schwarzkopf, H. Norman with Peter Petre. *It Doesn't Take a Hero*. New York: Bantam Books, 1992.

Sciolino, Elaine. "U.S. Backs Bosnian Peace Plan, Dropping Threats to Use Force." *New York Times*, February 11, 1993, sec. A, p. 1.

———. "U.S. Faces a Delicate Task in Intervening in Negotiations on Bosnia." *New York Times*, February 12, 1993, sec. A, p. 10.

———. "Christopher Explains Conditions for Use of U.S. Force in Bosnia," *New York Times*, April 28, 1993, sec. A, p. 1.

———. "U.S. Asks U.N. Not to Use American Troops on Patrol." *New York Times*, 29 September 1993, sec. A, p. 10.

———. "The U.N.'s Glow is Gone." *New York Times*, October 9, 1993, sec. A, p. 1.

Seib, Gerald F. "Saddam Hussein Seen Trying to Boost Posture of Iraq in Dealing with Clinton Administration," *Wall Street Journal*, January 12, 1992, sec. A, p. 16.

Shafer, D. Michael. *Deadly Paradigms: The Failure of U.S. Counterinsurgency Policy*. Princeton: Princeton University Press, 1988.

Sharp, Ulysses G. *Strategy for Defeat*. San Rafael, CA: Presidio Press, 1978.

Sheehan, Neil. *A Bright Shining Lie: John Paul Vann and America in Vietnam*. New York: Random House, 1988.

Shultz, George. Address to the Trilateral Commission, April 3, 1984. *Department of State Bulletin*: May 1984.

————. Address to New York synagogue, October 25, 1984. *Department of State Bulletin*, December 1984.

————. Address to Yeshiva University, December 9, 1984. *Department of State Bulletin*, February 1985.

————. *Turmoil and Triumph: My Years as Secretary of State*. New York: Scribners, 1993.

Shy, John. *A People Numerous and Armed: Reflections on the Military Struggle for American Independence*. New York: Oxford University Press, 1976.

————. "Jomini." In Peter Paret, ed. *Makers of Modern Strategy from Machiavelli to the Nuclear Age*, pp. 143–85. Princeton University Press, 1986.

Sieff, Martin. "Baker, Cheney Clash on New Bush Policy." *Washington Times*, July 2, 1992, sec. A, pp. 1 & 9.

Simons, William E. "The Vietnam Intervention, 1964–1965." In Alexander L. George, David K. Hall, and William E. Simons, eds. *The Limits of Coercive Diplomacy: Laos, Cuba, Vietnam*. Boston: Little, Brown, & Co., 1971, pp. 144–210.

Sincere, Clyde J. "Target Acquisition for the Deep Battle." *Military Review* 69 (August 1989): 23–28.

Smoke, Richard. *National Security and the Nuclear Dilemma*. 2nd ed. New York: Random House, 1987.

Snyder, Jack. "Civil-Military Relations and the Cult of the Offensive, 1914 and 1984." *International Security* 9 (Summer 1984): 108–146.

————. *The Ideology of the Offensive: Military Decision Making and the Disasters of 1914*. Ithaca, NY: Cornell University Press, 1984.

"Somalia: The Right to Bear Arms." *The Economist*, December 19, 1992, pp. 41–42.

Sorenson, Theodore C. *Kennedy*. New York: Harper, 1965.

Spector, Ronald H. *Advice and Support: The Early Years of the United States Army in Vietnam, 1941–1960*. Washington, D.C.: 1985.

Stevenson, Charles A. *The End of Nowhere: American Policy Toward Laos Since 1954*. Boston: Beacon Press, 1972.

Strobel, Warren. "U.S. Had, But Lost the Chance to Lead." *Washington Times*, sec. A, p. 9 (see box insert).

Stuart, Reginald C. *War and American Thought: From the Revolution to the Monroe Doctrine*. Kent, Ohio: Kent State University Press, 1982.

Summers, Harry G. *On Strategy: A Critical Analysis of the Vietnam War*. Washington, D.C.: GPO, 1981.

————. *Vietnam War Almanac*. New York: Facts on File, 1985.

————. *Korean War Almanac*. New York: Facts on File, 1990.

————. *On Strategy II: A Critical Analysis of the Gulf War*. New York: Dell, 1992.

———. "Military Doctrine: Blueprint for Force Planning." *Strategic Review* 20 (Spring 1992): 9–22.

———. "Can Force Solve the Problem?" *Washington Times*, August 14, 1992, sec. F, p. 1.

———. "An Overwhelming Argument on Force." *Washington Times*, January 28, 1993, sec. G, p. 4.

Swain, Richard M. "Square Pegs from Round Holes: Low-Intensity Conflict in Army Doctrine." *Military Review* 69 (December 1987): 2–15.

Taylor, Maxwell D. "The Changing Army." *Combat Forces Journal* 6 (October 1955): 10.

———. *The Uncertain Trumpet.* New York: Harper, 1959.

———. *Swords and Plowshares.* New York: Norton, 1972.

Taylor, William J., Jr., and David H. Petraeus. "The Legacy of Vietnam." In George K. Osborn et al., eds. *Democracy, Strategy, and Vietnam.* Lexington, MA: Lexington Books, 1987, pp. 249–68.

Terraine, John. *The Smoke and the Fire.* London: Sidgwick & Jackson, 1982.

———. *White Heat: The New Warfare, 1914–18.* London: Sidgwick & Jackson, 1982.

"Text of President Bush's Address." *Washington Post*, December 21, 1989, sec. A, p. 38.

"Text of the U.N.'s Draft Resolution on the Balkan Crisis." *New York Times*, August 11, 1992, sec. A, p. 6.

"Text of U.N. Resolution Allowing the Dispatch of Troops," *New York Times*, June 30, 1992, sec. A, p. 10.

Thies, Wallace J. *When Governments Collide: Coercion and Diplomacy in the Vietnam Conflict, 1964- 1968.* Berkeley: University of California Press, 1980.

This Week with David Brinkley, ABC News, March 7, 1993.

Thomas, Hugh. *Cuba: The Pursuit of Freedom.* New York: Harper, 1971.

Thomas, James A. "Limited War: Theory and Practice." *Military Review* 53 (February 1973): 75–82.

Till, Geoffrey. *Maritime Strategy and the Nuclear Age.* New York: St. Martin's Press, 1982.

Trachtenberg, Mark. "A 'Wasting Asset': American Strategy and the Shifting Nuclear Balance, 1949–54." *International Security* 13 (Winter 1988–9): 5–49.

———. "Strategic Thought in America, 1952–1966." *Political Science Quarterly* 104 (Summer 1989): 301–334.

Trainor, Bernard E. "Vietnam Experience Has Made the Joint Chiefs Cautious about Using Force." *New York Times*, August 17, 1989, sec. A, p. 13.

Twining, David T. "The Weinberger Doctrine and the Use of Force in the Contemporary Era." *Small Wars and Insurgencies* 1 (August 1990): 97–117.

Twining, Nathan F. *Neither Liberty nor Safety: A Hard Look at U.S. Military Policy and Strategy.* New York: Holt, 1966.

Tyler, Patrick E. "Vietnam and Gulf Zone: Real Military Contrasts." *New York Times*, December 1, 1990, p. 8.

"U.N. Resolution on Protecting Safe Areas." *New York Times*, June 5, 1993, p. 6.

U.S. Congress. Senate. Committees on Armed Services and Foreign Relations. *Military Situation in the Far East.* 82nd Cong., 1st sess. Washington, D.C.: GPO, 1951.

U.S. Congress. Senate. Subcommittee of the Senate Judiciary Committee to investigate the Administration of the Internal Security Act. *Interlocking Subversion in Government Departments.* 83rd Cong., 2nd sess. Washington, D.C.: GPO, 1954–5. (Also known as the Jenner Sub- committee Hearings.)

U.S. Congress. Senate. Committee on Foreign Relations. To Amend Further the Foreign Assistance Act of 1961 as Amended. *Vietnam Hearings.* 89th Cong., 2nd sess. Washington, D.C.: GPO, 1966.

U.S. Congress. Senate. Subcommittee on Buildings and Grounds. *The Pentagon Papers (The Senator Gravel Edition).* 4 vols. Boston: Beacon Press, 1971.

U.S. Dept. of the Air Force. *Air Force Manual 1–2: United States Air Force: Basic Doctrine.* Washington, D.C.: GPO, 1959.

———. *Basic Aerospace Doctrine of the United States Air Force.* Washington, D.C.: Department of the Air Force, 16 March 1984.

U.S. Dept. of the Army. *Field Manual 100–5: Field Service Regulations: Operations.* Washington, D.C.: GPO, Sept. 1954, Feb. 1962.

———. *Field Manual 100–5: Operations.* Washington, D.C.: GPO, 19 February 1962.

———. *Field Manual 100–5: Operations.* Washington, D.C.: Headquarters, Dept. of the Army, August 20, 1982.

———. *Field Manual 100–5: Operations.* Washington, D.C.: Headquarters, Dept. of the Army, May 5, 1986.

———. *Low-Intensity Conflict,* TRADOC Field Circular 100–20. Fort Monroe, VA: Headquarters, 16 July 1986.

———. *Field Manual 100–5: Operations.* Washington, D.C.: Headquarters, Dept. of the Army, June 14, 1993.

U.S. Dept. of State. *American Foreign Policy: Basic Documents, 1950–1955.* Washington, D.C.: GPO, 1957.

"U.S. General Hands over Relief Operation in Somalia to U.N." *New York Times*, May 5, 1993, sec. A, p. 5.

U.S. Marine Corps. *Warfighting*, FMFM 1. Washington, D.C.: U.S. Department of the Navy, Headquarters United States Marine Corps, March 6, 1989.

U.S. Marine Corps. *Campaigning*, FMFM 1–1. Washington, D.C.: U.S. Department of the Navy, Headquarters United States Marine Corps, January 1990.

U.S. News and World Report Staff. *Triumph without Victory: The Unreported History of the Persian Gulf War* (New York: Times Books, 1992)

The United States Strategic Bombing Survey Over-all Report, European War. Washington, D.C.: Government Printing Office, 1945.

The United States Strategic Bombing Survey, Pacific War. Washington, D.C.: Government Printing Office, 1946.

Van Creveld, Martin. *The Transformation of War*. New York: Free Press, 1991.

———. "The Persian Gulf Crisis of 1990–1991 and the Future of Morally Constrained War." *Parameters* 22 (Summer 1992): 21–40.

Van Evera, Stephen. "The Cult of the Offensive and the Origins of the First World War." *International Security* 9 (Summer 1984): 58–107.

Van Fleet, James. "The Truth about Korea." *Life*, May 11 & 18,1953.

Viner, Jacob. "The Implications of the Atomic Bomb for International Relations." *Proceedings of the American Philosophical Society* 40 (January 1946): 53–58.

Vuono, Carl. "The Strategic Value of Conventional Forces." *Parameters* 20 (September 1990): 2–10.

Waller, Douglas and John Barry. "The Day the War Stopped." *Newsweek*, January 25, 1992, pp. 16–25.

Waltz, Kenneth. *A Theory of International Relations*. Reading, MA: Addison Wesley, 1979.

———. "A Strategy for the Rapid Deployment Force." *International Security* 5 (Spring 1981): 49–73.

Ward, James R. "Vietnam: Insurgency or War." *Military Review* 69 (January 1989): 14–23.

Watson, Robert J. *History of the Joint Chiefs of Staff: The Joint Chiefs of Staff and National Policy, 1953–1954*. Vol. 5. Washington, D.C.: JCS Historical Division, 1986.

Watson, Russell. "Bush's Big Gamble in Panama." *Newsweek*, 1 January 1990, pp. 12–22.

Welch, David A. and James G. Blight. "An Introduction to ExComm Transcripts." *International Security* 12 (Winter 1987/88): 5–29.

Weigley, Russell F. *The American Way of War: A History of United States Military Strategy and Policy.* Bloomington, IN: University of Indiana Press, 1973.

——. *History of the United States Army.* Enlarged ed. Bloomington, Indiana: Indiana University Press, 1984. Original ed. 1967.

Weinberger, Caspar. "U.S. Defense Strategy." *Foreign Affairs* 64 (Spring 1986): 675–97.

Werrell, Kenneth P. "Air War Victorious: The Gulf War vs. Vietnam." *Parameters* 22 (Summer 1992): 41–54.

Westmoreland, William C. *A Soldier Reports.* Garden City, NY: Doubleday, 1976.

Weyand, Fred C. and Harry G. Summers, Jr. "Vietnam Myths and Military Realities." *Armor* (September-October 1976): 30–36.

Whitney, Craig R. "A View from the Fence," *New York Times,* April 28, 1993, sec. A, p. 11.

——. "NATO's Leadership Gap," *New York Times,* May 29, 1993, p. 4.

Willenson, Kim. *The Bad War: An Oral History of the Vietnam War.* New York: New American Library, 1987.

Willoughby, Charles Andrew. *Maneuver in War.* Harrisburg, PA: The Military Service Publishing Co., 1939.

Williams, Daniel. "U.S. Decides to Use Force on Serbs in Bosnia War." *Washington Post,* May 2, 1993, sec. A, pp. 1 & 36.

Wills, Garry. "Critical Inquiry (Kritik) in Clausewitz." In *The Politics of Interpretation,* ed. W.J.T. Mitchell (Chicago: University of Chicago Press, 1982), pp. 159–180.

Wilson, George C. "Top U.S. Brass Wary on Central America." *Washington Post,* June 24, 1983, sec. A, p. 20.

Wilson, James Q. *Bureaucracy: What Government Agencies Do and Why They Do It.* New York: Basic Books, 1989.

Wines, Michael. "Bush Declares Goal in Somalia Is to 'Save Thousands.' " *New York Times,* 5 December 1992, p. 1.

Wolfers, Arnold. *Discord and Collaboration: Essays on International Politics.* Baltimore: Johns Hopkins University Press, 1962.

Wood, Herbert Fairlie. *Strange Battleground: The Operations in Korea and Their Effects on the Defense Policy of Canada.* Ottawa: Queen's Printer, 1966.

Woodward, Bob. *The Commanders.* New York: Simon & Schuster, 1991.

——. "The Secretary of Analysis," *The Washington Post Magazine,* February 21, 1993, p. 9.

"World Cop?" Editorial. *Economist,* 19 December 1992, pp. 13–14.

WuDunn, Sheryl. "North Korean Site Has A-Bomb Hints." *New York Times*, May 17, 1992, p. 1.

Wyman, Willard G. "The United States Army: Its Doctrine and Influence on U.S. Military Strategy." *Military Review* 37 (March 1959): 3–13.

York, Michael. "Reagans Pay Emotional Visit to Vietnam Veterans Memorial." *Washington Post*, November 12, 1988, sec. A, p. 14.

Young, Wayland. *Strategy for Survival: First Steps in Nuclear Disarmament*. London: Penguin, 1959.

Zakaria, Fareed. "The Reagan Strategy of Containment." *Political Science Quarterly* 105 (Fall 1990): 373–395.

Zakheim, Dov S. "A New Name for Winning: Losing." *New York Times*, 19 June 1993, p. 21.

Index